**Letts study aids**

# Revise Home Economics

A complete revision course for O level and CSE

**Ann Nield** Certificate in Education (Home Economics)

Head of Home Economics, Meridian School, Royston, Herts

**Zoë Hesmondhalgh** BA, Certificate in Education (Home Economics), MSc

Lecturer in Home Economics, Polytechnic of the South Bank

**Charles Letts & Co Ltd**
London, Edinburgh & New York

First published 1984
by Charles Letts & Co Ltd
Diary House, Borough Road, London SE1 1DW

Reprinted 1985

Editor: Gwen Lowman
Design: Anne Davison & Ben Sands
Illustrations: Chartwell Illustrators, David Lock

ISBN 0 85097 603 0

Printed by Charles Letts (Scotland) Limited

# Preface

The aim of this book is to present a concise and comprehensive coverage of the core content of twenty-nine CSE, SCE and GCE syllabuses offered by twenty-one Examination Boards. The text is based on an analysis of the 1984 syllabuses.

Home Economics is a very wide subject area and syllabuses differ widely in their title and content. This book is unique in that it endeavours in one volume to cover most aspects of Home Economics.

We have divided the core material into fourteen main chapters each of which is further sub-divided. The analysis table on pages 2 and 3 should be consulted to check which topics are part of the examination syllabus which you have been following.

Section I, the introduction to the book, gives advice on its use, an analysis table which summarises the contents of the twenty-nine syllabuses and a detailed contents list.

Section II contains summaries and explanations of core material which is presented in lists, charts and diagrams to aid easy learning and revision.

Section III contains the test yourself units with answers, which should play a very useful role in your revision programme.

Section IV advises on preparations for both the practical and theory examinations. It gives hints on how to approach your answers, a selection of examination questions together with guidance on how to answer some of them. We wish to thank the following Boards for granting us permission to use questions from past papers, but we would add that the Boards accept no responsibility whatsoever for the accuracy or method of working in the answers given: AEB, ALSEB, Cambridge, EAEB, EMREB, London, Oxford, SEREB, SWEB, WJEC, YREB. (Their full addresses can be found on p. viii.)

We are indebted to the following people for their helpful comments, criticisms and advice: Mrs Kathy Ward, Mrs Eleanor Jones and Miss Alice Bertram.

Our thanks go also to Pat Rowlinson, Karen Sparrock and Kim Bevis of the staff of Charles Letts and to Gwen Lowman who has ably edited the material for the book.

Finally we must thank our husbands and families for their patience and encouragement and our pupils and examination candidates who have provided experiences which have been invaluable to us as we have written this book.

Ann Nield
Zoë Hesmondhalgh
1984

## Acknowledgements

The authors and publishers are grateful to the following for permission to reproduce photographs (page numbers refer to this book):

Mary Evans Picture Library for Fig. 2.1, p. 1; Derek Widdicombe for Figs. 2.2, p. 2, 2.3, p.5, 2.7, 2.8, p. 11, 14.9, p. 177; World Health Organization: M. Jacot for Figs. 3.1, p. 18; J. Marquis for Fig. 3.2, p. 18; WHO/FAO for Fig. 3.3, p. 195; Dr. R. F. A. Dean for Fig. 3.4, p. 19; WHO for Fig. 10.3 p. 138; Flour Advisory Board for Figs. 4.3, 4.4, p. 26; 7.9, 7.10, p. 99; Van den Berghs for Figs. 4.8, p. 30, 4.23, p. 51; National Dairy Council for Fig. 4.14, p. 41; Home & Freezer Digest for Fig. 5.7, p. 71; Science Photo Library: Mr. J. Forsdyke for Fig. 7.11, p. 101; Dr. Tony Brain for Fig. 8.6, p. 114; Rentokil for Figs. 13.2a, 13.2b, p. 161, 13.3a, 13.3b, p. 162.

The authors and publishers are grateful to the Controller of Her Majesty's Stationery Office for permission to reproduce a specimen P45 form (Crown copyright) in Fig. 11.1 on p. 141.

# Contents

# Part I

# Introduction and guide to using this book

This Revision Course has been designed for students taking a range of O-level and CSE examinations in the area of Home Economics. In addition to the CSE and O-level Boards who call their examination Home Economics others use the following titles:

Food and Nutrition    Homecraft    Cook Host(ess)
Nutrition and Cookery    Homemaking

It is essential to know the exact title of the examination that you will be sitting. Some boards offer more than one title, especially O-level Boards, so if you are in any doubt about this ask your teacher. Your teacher will also indicate the depth of study required for your examination.

### Using the analysis table of examination syllabuses

The analysis tables are on pages 2 to 3. These tables show which elements of the core material are included in the syllabus for the examination you are sitting. Details of how to find out which sections you need to know for your examination are beneath the table on page viii.

### How to revise using this book

This book is not intended to replace good teaching or standard textbooks. It is intended to enable students to build on existing knowledge and to fill in gaps where they have missed areas of study. Most importantly the core material summarizes the information on a particular topic and helps the student to answer questions, which builds up confidence. Many pages are in list or tabular form to help the student to learn from them. Information needs to be thoroughly learnt so that it can be immediately recalled in the examination room. This book helps in this process by organizing the material in logical sequences.

(a) In good time write to the examination board (list of addresses on pages viii and ix) to obtain a copy of the **examination syllabus** for the year when you are sitting it and a selection of past **examination papers**. The board usually makes a charge for providing these. Alternatively, consult the syllabus and papers held in the school or college library.

(b) Start your revision early. Cramming often causes confusion. Draw up a calendar to show you how many topics it will be necessary to revise each week. Leave the last two weeks for general revision of all topics. In this way it is possible to cut out last minute panic. If you have left it rather late do not give up. Organize the time which you have left. Read the core material in each section then test yourself using the self-test unit. If you find the questions difficult refer again to the core material.

(c) Read carefully the section on answering examination questions and examination technique – Section IV. Section IV also contains some questions which you can work through.

# Table of analysis of examination syllabuses

• Major subject in examination papers
(•) Minor subject in examination papers

| | AEB Nutrition & Cookery | Cambridge Home Economics Food Studies | Cambridge Home Economics Home and Community | Cambridge Food and Nutrition | Cambridge Home Economics | N Ireland Home Economics | S Ireland Home Economics | JMB Home Economics Syllabus A | London Food and Nutrition | Oxford Home Economics | Oxford Food and Nutrition |
|---|---|---|---|---|---|---|---|---|---|---|---|
| Level | O | AO Syllabus A 8265 | AO Syllabus (Part) 8270 | O 6060 | O 6070 | O (Part) | O Part | O Food | O 180 | O 6889 | O 6890 |
| Theory Papers | 1 | 1 | 1 | 1 | 1 | 1 | | 1 | 1 | 1 | 1 |
| No. Hours | 2 | 2½ | 2½ | 2¼ | 2 | 3 | | 2½ | 2½ | 2¼ | 2¼ |
| Practical Paper | 1 | 1 | — | 1 | 1 | Either A or B | | 1 | 1 | 1 | 1* |
| No. Hours | 2½ | 2½ | — | 2¼ | 2½ | A Cookery 2 / B Needle-work 2½ | | 2½ | 2½ | 2½ | 2½ |
| Planning Time | 2 | 2½ | — | 1½ | 1½ | A 1¼ / B 1 | | 1½ | 2 | 1½ | 1½ |
| Other Assessments | | | Project Work | | | — | | | | Teacher Assessed Practicals | Teacher Assessed Practicals (*Alternati to Practica to Practical Paper 2 hrs) |
| **2 Family and community** | | | | | | | | | | | |
| 2.1.1 Working wives and mothers | | | • | (•) | (•) | (•) | | (•) | | • | (•) |
| 2.1.2 Relationships in the family | | | • | (•) | (•) | (•) | | (•) | | • | (•) |
| 2.1.3 The elderly | | | • | (•) | (•) | (•) | | (•) | | • | (•) |
| 2.1.4 Work and leisure | | | • | (•) | (•) | (•) | | (•) | | • | |
| 2.1.5 Unemployment | | | • | | (•) | | | | | • | |
| 2.2 The community | | | • | (•) | (•) | (•) | | (•) | | • | (•) |
| 2.2.1 Social Services | | | • | | (•) | (•) | | | | • | |
| 2.2.2 The National Health Service | | | • | | (•) | (•) | | | | • | |
| 2.2.3 Social Security and Welfare benefits available from the state | | | • | | (•) | | | | | • | |
| 2.2.4 Community ties | | | • | | (•) | | | | | | |
| **3 Nutrition** | | | | | | | | | | | |
| 3.1 Classification of nutrients, sources and functions | • | | | • | • | • | • | • | • | • | • |
| 3.2 Recommended daily allowances of food and nutrients | • | | | • | • | • | • | • | • | • | • |
| 3.2.1 Malnutrition | • | | | • | • | • | • | • | • | • | • |
| 3.3 The body's need for energy | • | | | • | • | • | • | • | • | • | • |
| 3.4 Digestion | • | | | • | • | • | • | • | • | • | • |
| **4 Commodities** | | | | | | | | | | | |
| 4.1 Ingredients used in family meals | • | | | • | • | • | • | • | • | • | • |
| 4.2 Additives to convenience foods | • | | | • | | | | | | | |
| **5 Meal planning and special dietary needs** | | | | | | | | | | | |
| 5.1 Meal planning | • | | | • | • | • | • | • | • | • | • |
| 5.2 Meal patterns | • | | | • | • | • | • | • | • | • | • |
| 5.3 Portions per person | • | | | • | • | • | • | • | • | • | • |
| 5.4 Different dietary needs and meals for special occasions | • | | | • | • | • | • | • | • | • | • |
| 5.5 The presentation of food | • | | | • | • | • | • | • | • | • | • |
| 5.6 Economy in the preparation of family meals | • | | | • | • | • | • | • | • | • | • |
| **6 Cookers and cooking** | | | | | | | | | | | |
| 6.1 Reasons for cooking food | • | | | • | • | • | • | • | • | • | • |
| 6.2 Methods of cooking – heat transference | • | | | • | • | • | • | • | • | • | • |
| e.g. browning of foods | • | | | • | | | | • | | | • |
| 6.3 Portable electrical appliances | • | | | • | • | • | • | • | • | • | • |
| 6.4 Cooking with microwaves | • | | | • | | | | | | | • |
| **7 Basic mixtures** | | | | | | | | | | | |
| 7.1 Basic recipes and methods | • | | | • | • | • | • | • | • | • | • |
| 7.2 Raising agents | • | | | • | | | • | • | • | • | • |
| 7.3 The storage of baked starch mixtures | • | | | • | • | • | • | • | • | • | • |
| 7.4 Preparation of baking tins | • | | | • | • | • | • | • | • | • | • |
| 7.5 Soups | | | | | | | | | | | |
| **8 Food storage and preservation** | | | | | | | | | | | |
| 8.1 General points on the storage of foods | • | | | • | • | • | • | • | • | • | • |
| 8.2 The refrigerator | • | | | • | • | • | • | • | • | • | |
| 8.3 Domestic preservation | | | | • | | • | • | • | • | | • |
| 8.4 Commercial preservation of foods | | | | • | | | | | | | |
| 8.5 The effect of processing on foods | | | | • | | | | • | | | • |
| 8.6 Food contamination | • | | | • | • | • | • | • | | • | • |
| 8.7 Left-over foods | • | | | • | • | • | • | • | | | • |
| **9 Pollution and conservation** | | | | | | | | | | | |
| 9.1 Sources and removal of household waste | | | | | • | | • | | | • | |
| 9.2 Conservation of energy in the home | • | | | • | • | • | • | • | | • | |
| 9.3 Conservation of human effort | | | | | • | | | | | • | |
| **10 Health and safety** | | | | | | | | | | | |
| 10.1 Safety in the home | (•) | (•) | • | • | • | • | • | • | • | • | • |
| 10.2 Making the home safe | (•) | (•) | • | • | • | • | • | • | • | • | • |
| 10.3 First aid | • | • | • | • | • | • | • | • | • | • | • |
| 10.4 The emergency services | (•) | (•) | (•) | • | • | • | • | • | (•) | • | • |
| 10.5 Action needed for some major and minor injuries | • | • | • | • | • | • | • | • | • | • | • |
| 10.6 Home nursing | (•) | (•) | (•) | (•) | • | • | • | (•) | (•) | • | (•) |
| 10.7 Good grooming and personal hygiene | (•) | (•) | (•) | (•) | • | • | • | • | (•) | • | (•) |
| **11 Money management** | | | | | | | | | | | |
| 11.1 Income | | | | (•) | | • | • | (•) | (•) | • | |
| 11.1.1 Pay | | | | (•) | | • | • | | (•) | • | |
| 11.1.2 Bank accounts | | | | (•) | | • | • | | (•) | • | |
| 11.2 Expenditure | | | | (•) | (•) | • | • | (•) | (•) | • | |
| 11.2.1 Accounting for your money | | | | (•) | (•) | • | • | (•) | (•) | • | (•) |
| 11.2.2 Savings | | | | (•) | | • | • | (•) | (•) | • | |
| 11.2.3 Credit | | | | | | • | • | (•) | (•) | • | |
| **12 Consumer studies** | | | | | | | | | | | |
| 12.1 Shopping | • | • | • | • | • | • | • | • | • | • | • |
| 12.2 Consumer information | (•) | (•) | • | • | • | • | | • | • | • | • |
| 12.3 Labels | (•) | (•) | • | • | • | • | | • | • | • | • |
| 12.4 Advertising | (•) | (•) | (•) | (•) | • | • | (•) | • | | • | (•) |
| 12.5 Organizations which aim to protect the consumer | | | (•) | (•) | • | • | | • | | • | (•) |
| 12.6 The consumer and the law | | | (•) | (•) | • | • | | | | • | (•) |
| **13 Home management** | | | | | | | | | | | |
| 13.1 Cleaning the dwelling | (•) | (•) | (•) | (•) | • | • | (•) | (•) | (•) | • | (•) |
| 13.2 Household pests | (•) | (•) | (•) | (•) | • | • | | • | • | • | (•) |
| 13.3 Home maintenance | (•) | (•) | (•) | | • | • | (•) | (•) | (•) | • | (•) |
| 13.4 Materials used in household equipment | • | • | (•) | • | • | • | | • | • | • | • |
| 13.5 Appliance design | • | • | (•) | • | • | • | | • | • | • | • |
| 13.6 Planning rooms | (•) | (•) | (•) | (•) | • | • | (•) | (•) | (•) | • | (•) |
| 13.7 Furniture | | | | | • | (•) | | • | • | • | |
| 13.8 Soft furnishings | | | | | | | | | | • | |

| Food and Nutrition | **Oxford Alt** Home and Community | **SEB** Food and Nutrition | **SUJB** Food and Nutrition | **WJEC** Home Economics | **ALSEB** Home Economics | **EAEB North** Home Economics | **EAEB South** Food and Nutrition | **EAEB South** Home Economics | **EMREB** Homecraft | **LREB** Home Economics | **MREB** Home Economics | **NREB** Home Economics | **NWREB** Home Economics | **SEREB** Homemaking | **SEREB** Cook and Hostess | **SREB** Food and Nutrition | **SREB** Home Economics | **SWEB** Home Economics | **WJEC** Home Economics | **WMEB** Home Economics | **YHREB** Housecraft Model |
|---|---|---|---|---|---|---|---|---|---|---|---|---|---|---|---|---|---|---|---|---|---|
| A | OA | O | O | O | CSE | CSE | CSE | CSE | CSE | CSE | CSE | CSE | CSE | CSE | CSE | CSE | CSE | CSE | CSE | CSE | CSE |
| 90 | 8889 (Part) | | | | | | | | | | | | | | | | | | | | |
| | 3 | 1 | 1 | 1 | 1 | 1 | 1 | 1 | 1 | 1 | 1 | 1 | 1 | 1 | 1 | 1 | 1 | 1 | 1 | 2 | 1 |
| /2 | 2½ | 2 | 2½ | 2½ | 2 | 1¾ | 2 | 1¾ | 1¾ | 1¾ | 3 | 1½ | 2 | 1½ | 1½ | 2 | 2 | 1¾ | 1½ | ¾+¼ | 2 |
| | — | 1 | 1 | 1 | Teacher | 1 | 2 | 1 | 6 hrs of | Syllabus | 1 | 1 | 1 | Continous | Continuous | 1 | 3×2 | 1 | 1 | Alt. 1: 2 | 1 |
| /2 | — | 1½ | 1½ | 2 | Assessed | 2½ | 1¼ & 1½ | 1½ | assign-ments plus 3hrs planning | A 2 B 2×1¼ | 2 | 2½ | 2½ | Assessment | Assessment — | 2 | Assignments | 1¾ | 2½ | Alt. .2: 2 | 1½+ 10 min |
| /2 | — | Practical Marked Internally | 2 | 1½ | | 1½ | 1 | 2 | | A 1½ B 2×1½ | 1¼ | 1½ | 2 | | | 2 | | 1¾ | 1¾ | Alt. 1: 1½ Alt. 2: 2 | 1¾+½ |
| rse k | Project partly Teacher Assessed | | | | | Course Work | Course Work | 10% Teacher Assessment | | | | Teacher Assessment may be Special Study | | Written Course Work | Written Course Work | | | | | Course Work | |
| | • | (•) | (•) | (•) | • | • | (•) | | • | • | • | • | (•) | • | (•) | | • | • | • | • | • |
| | • | (•) | (•) | (•) | • | • | (•) | | • | • | • | • | (•) | • | (•) | | • | • | • | • | • |
| | • | (•) | (•) | (•) | • | • | (•) | | • | • | • | • | (•) | • | (•) | | • | • | • | • | • |
| | • | (•) | (•) | (•) | • | • | (•) | | • | • | (•) | • | (•) | • | | | • | • | • | • | • |
| | • | | | (•) | • | • | | | • | • | (•) | • | | • | | | • | (•) | • | • | (•) |
| | • | (•) | (•) | | • | • | | | • | • | • | • | | • | | | • | • | • | • | • |
| | • | | | | • | • | | | • | • | • | • | | • | | | • | • | • | • | • |
| | • | | | | (•) | • | | | • | • | • | • | | • | | | • | • | (•) | • | • |
| | • | | | | • | • | | | • | • | • | • | | • | | | • | • | (•) | • | • |
| | • | | | | • | • | | | • | • | • | • | | • | | | • | • | (•) | • | • |
| | | | | | | | | | | | | | | | | | | | | | |
| | | • | • | • | • | • | • | • | • | • | • | • | • | • | • | • | • | • | • | • | • |
| | | • | • | • | | • | • | • | • | • | • | • | • | • | • | • | • | • | • | • | • |
| | | • | • | • | • | • | • | • | • | • | • | • | • | • | • | • | • | • | • | • | • |
| | | • | • | • | • | • | • | • | | • | • | • | • | • | • | • | • | • | • | • | • |
| | | | • | | | | | | | | • | | • | | | • | | | | | |
| | | | | | | | | | | | | | | | | | | | | | |
| | | • | • | • | • | • | • | • | • | • | • | • | • | • | • | • | • | • | • | • | • |
| | | | | • | | | | | | • | | | | | | | | | | | • |
| | | | | | | | | | | | | | | | | | | | | | |
| | | • | • | • | • | • | • | • | • | • | • | • | • | • | • | • | • | • | • | • | • |
| | | | • | • | • | • | • | • | • | • | • | • | • | • | • | • | • | • | • | • | • |
| | | • | • | • | • | • | • | • | • | • | • | • | • | • | • | • | • | • | • | • | • |
| | | • | • | • | • | • | • | • | • | • | • | • | • | • | • | • | • | • | • | • | • |
| | | • | • | • | • | • | • | • | • | • | • | • | • | • | • | • | • | • | • | • | • |
| | | • | • | • | • | • | • | • | • | • | • | • | • | • | • | • | • | • | • | • | • |
| | | | | | | | | | | | | | | | | | | | | | |
| | | • | • | • | • | • | • | • | • | • | • | • | • | • | • | • | • | • | • | • | • |
| | | • | • | • | • | • | • | • | • | • | • | • | • | • | • | • | • | • | • | • | • |
| | | | | • | | | | | | • | | | | | | | | | | | • |
| | | • | • | • | • | • | • | • | • | • | • | • | • | • | • | • | • | • | • | • | • |
| | | | • | | | | | • | | • | • | | • | • | • | • | | | | • | • |
| | | | | | | | | | | | | | | | | | | | | | |
| | | • | • | • | • | • | • | • | • | • | • | • | • | • | • | • | • | • | • | • | • |
| | | | • | • | • | • | • | • | • | • | • | | • | | • | • | | | • | | • |
| | | • | • | • | • | • | • | • | • | • | • | • | • | • | • | • | • | • | • | • | • |
| | | • | • | • | • | • | • | • | • | • | • | • | • | • | • | • | • | • | • | • | • |
| | | | | | | | | | | | | | | | | | | | | | |
| | | • | • | • | • | • | • | • | • | • | • | • | • | | • | • | • | | • | • | • |
| | | • | • | • | • | • | • | • | • | • | • | • | • | • | • | • | • | | • | • | • |
| | | | • | • | • | • | • | • | • | • | • | • | • | | • | • | • | | | • | • |
| | | | | • | | • | • | | • | • | | | | | | | | | • | | |
| | | | | • | | • | • | • | • | • | • | | • | | | • | | | | | • |
| | | • | • | • | • | • | • | • | • | • | • | • | • | • | • | • | • | | • | • | • |
| | | • | • | • | • | • | • | • | • | • | • | • | • | • | • | • | • | | • | • | • |
| | | | | | | | | | | | | | | | | | | | | | |
| | | | | • | | • | • | • | • | • | • | • | | • | | | | | | | • |
| | | • | • | • | • | • | • | • | • | • | • | • | • | • | • | • | • | | • | • | • |
| | | • | • | | | | | | | | | • | | | • | | | | | • | • |
| | | | | | | | | | | | | | | | | | | | | | |
| | • | • | • | • | • | • | • | | • | • | • | • | • | • | • | • | • | • | • | • | • |
| • | • | • | • | • | • | • | (•) | | • | • | • | • | • | • | (•) | • | • | • | • | • | • |
| • | • | • | • | • | • | • | • | | • | • | • | • | • | • | • | • | • | • | • | • | • |
| •) | • | • | (•) | • | (•) | • | • | | • | • | • | • | (•) | • | (•) | (•) | • | • | • | • | • |
| • | • | • | • | • | • | • | • | | • | • | • | • | • | • | • | • | • | • | • | • | • |
| | (•) | (•) | | • | (•) | • | (•) | | • | • | • | • | • | • | (•) | (•) | • | • | • | • | • |
| | (•) | (•) | | • | • | • | (•) | | • | • | • | • | • | • | (•) | (•) | • | • | • | • | • |
| | | | | | | | | | | | | | | | | | | | | | |
| | • | | | • | • | • | | | • | • | • | • | • | • | | | • | • | • | • | • |
| | • | | | • | • | • | | | • | • | • | • | • | • | | | • | • | • | • | • |
| | • | | | • | • | • | | | • | • | • | • | • | • | | | • | • | • | • | • |
| | • | (•) | | • | • | • | • | | • | • | • | • | • | • | (•) | | • | • | • | • | • |
| •) | • | (•) | (•) | • | • | • | • | | • | • | • | • | • | • | (•) | | • | • | • | • | • |
| | • | | | • | • | • | (•) | | • | • | • | • | • | • | | | • | • | • | • | • |
| | • | (•) | (•) | • | • | • | (•) | | • | • | • | • | • | • | (•) | (•) | • | • | • | • | • |
| | | | | | | | | | | | | | | | | | | | | | |
| • | • | • | • | • | • | • | • | | • | • | • | • | • | • | • | • | • | • | • | • | • |
| •) | (•) | • | (•) | • | • | • | • | | • | • | • | • | • | • | • | (•) | • | • | • | • | • |
| •) | (•) | • | • | • | • | • | • | | • | • | • | • | • | • | • | (•) | • | • | • | • | • |
| •) | (•) | • | (•) | • | • | • | • | | • | • | • | • | • | • | • | (•) | • | • | • | • | • |
| | (•) | • | (•) | • | • | • | • | | • | • | • | • | • | • | • | (•) | • | • | • | • | • |
| | (•) | • | (•) | • | • | • | • | | • | • | • | • | • | • | • | (•) | • | • | • | • | • |
| | | | | | | | | | | | | | | | | | | | | | |
| | (•) | • | (•) | • | • | • | (•) | | • | • | • | • | • | • | | • | • | • | • | • | • |
| | (•) | • | (•) | • | • | • | (•) | | • | • | • | • | • | • | | • | • | • | • | • | • |
| | (•) | • | (•) | • | • | • | • | | • | • | • | • | • | • | (•) | (•) | (•) | • | • | • | (•) |
| • | • | • | • | • | • | • | • | | • | • | • | • | • | • | • | • | • | • | • | • | • |
| • | • | • | • | • | • | • | • | | • | • | • | • | • | • | • | • | • | • | • | • | • |
| | | (•) | (•) | • | • | • | • | | • | • | • | • | • | • | (•) | (•) | (•) | • | • | • | (•) |
| | | | | (•) | • | • | (•) | | • | • | • | • | • | • | | | | • | • | • | (•) |
| | | | | (•) | • | • | | | • | • | • | • | • | • | | | | • | • | • | (•) |

## Table of analysis of examination syllabuses *continued*

- Major subject in examination papers
- (•) Minor subject in examination papers

| | AEB Nutrition & Cookery | Cambridge Home Economics Food Studies | Cambridge Home Economics Home and Community | Cambridge Food and Nutrition | Cambridge Home Economics | N Ireland Home Economics | S Ireland Home Economics | JMB Home Economics Syllabus A | London Food and Nutrition | Oxford Home Economics | Oxford Food and ... |
|---|---|---|---|---|---|---|---|---|---|---|---|
| Level | O | AO Syllabus A 8265 | AO Syllabus (Part) 8270 | O 6060 | O 6070 | O (Part) | O Part | O Food | O 180 | O 6889 | O 6890 |
| Theory Papers | 1 | 1 | 1 | 1 | 1 | 1 | | 1 | 1 | 1 | 1 |
| No. Hours | 2 | 2½ | 2½ | 2¼ | 2 | 3 | | 2½ | 2½ | 2¼ | 2¼ |
| Practical Paper | 1 | 1 | — | 1 | 1 | Either A or B | | 1 | 1 | 1 | 1* |
| No. Hours | 2½ | 2½ | — | 2¼ | 2½ | A Cookery 2 B Needle-work 2½ | | 2½ | 2½ | 2½ | 2½ |
| Planning Time | 2 | 2½ | — | 1½ | 1½ | A 1¼ B 1 | | 1½ | 2 | 1½ | 1½ |
| Other Assessments | | | Project Work | | | — | | | | Teacher Assessed Practicals | Teacher Assessed Practicals (*Alternati to Practica Paper 2 h |
| 13.9 Floors and floor coverings | (•) | (•) | (•) | (•) | • | • | (•) | (•) | (•) | • | (•) |
| 13.10 Interior decoration and colour schemes | | | | | | • | (•) | (•) | | • | |
| 13.11 Equipment for entertaining | • | (•) | (•) | | • | • | • | • | • | • | (•) |
| **14 Housing** | | | | | | | | | | | |
| 14.1 Choice of a home | | | | | | • | | | | • | |
| 14.2 The structure of a house | | | | | | • | | | | | |
| 14.3 Services to the home | | | | | | • | • | • | | • | |
| 14.4 Water heating | | | | | | • | • | • | | • | |
| 14.5 Heating the home | | | | | | • | • | • | | | |
| 14.6 Ventilation | | | | | | • | • | • | | | |
| 14.7 Lighting | | | | | | • | • | • | | | |
| **15 Textiles** | | | | | | | | | | | |
| 15.1 Choice of textiles | | | | | | • | • | • | | | |
| 15.2 Classification of fibres and textiles | | | | | | • | • | • | | | |
| 15.3 Other materials used in the house and elsewhere | | | | | | • | • | • | | | |
| 15.4 Textile terms | | | | | | • | • | • | | | |
| 15.5 The family wash | | | | | | • | • | • | | • | |
| 15.6 Irons and ironing | | | | | | • | | • | | • | |
| 15.7 Textile labelling | | | | | | • | • | • | | • | |
| 15.8 The hardness of water | | | | | | • | • | | | | |
| 15.9 Classification of detergents | | | | | | • | • | • | | • | |
| 15.10 Other products for textile care | | | | | | • | • | • | | • | |
| 15.11 Stain removal | | | | | | • | • | • | | • | |
| 15.12 Household textiles | | | | | | • | | • | | • | |

*How to find out which sections you need to know for your examination*

**(a) Look for the examination board and title of the examination at the top of the page** e.g. AEB Nutrition and Cookery.

**(b) Look down the column.** Everywhere a dot appears it means that that element is included in the examination. If you own your own copy of the book it may be helpful to colour in the sections which are included. If you wish to learn the whole syllabus it will be necessary to learn all the sections which you have coloured. (The list will only provide a guide because examination syllabuses change from time to time. Check the list you have made with an up-to-date syllabus.)

The information under the board and title also tells you how many papers must be taken, whether there is a practical or a project, and the length of examination time allocated.

## EXAMINATION BOARDS

### GCE Boards

*AEB*  Associated Examining Board
Wellington House, Aldershot, Hampshire GU11 1BQ

*Cambridge*  University of Cambridge Local Examinations Syndicate
Syndicate Buildings, 17 Harvey Road, Cambridge CB1 2EU

*JMB*  Joint Matriculation Board, Manchester M15 6EU

*London*  University Entrance and School Examinations Council
University of London, 66–72 Gower Street, London WC1 6EE

*Oxford*  Oxford Local Examinations
Delegacy of Local Examinations, Ewert Place, Summertown, Oxford OX2 7BX

*O and C*  Oxford and Cambridge Schools Examination Board
10 Trumpington Street, Cambridge; Elsfield Way, Oxford

*SUJB*  Southern Universities' Joint Board for School Examinations
Cotham Road, Bristol BS6 6DD

*WJEC*  Welsh Joint Education Committee, 245 Western Avenue, Cardiff CF5 2YX

### SCE Board

*SEB*  Scottish Examination Board
Ironmills Road, Dalkeith, Midlothian EH22 1BR

| Food and Nutrition | **Oxford Alt** Home and Community | **SEB** Food and Nutrition | **SUJB** Food and Nutrition | **WJEC** Home Economics | **ALSEB** Home Economics | **EAEB North** Home Economics | **EAEB South** Food and Nutrition | **EAEB South** Home Economics | **EMREB** Homecraft | **LREB** Home Economics | **MREB** Home Economics | **NREB** Home Economics | **NWREB** Home Economics | **SEREB** Homemaking | **SEREB** Cook and Hostess | **SREB** Food and Nutrition | **SREB** Home Economics | **SWEB** Home Economics | **WJEC** Home Economics | **WMEB** Home Economics | **YHREB** Housecraft Model |
|---|---|---|---|---|---|---|---|---|---|---|---|---|---|---|---|---|---|---|---|---|---|
| A | OA | O | O | O | CSE | CSE | CSE | CSE | CSE | CSE | CSE | CSE | CSE | CSE | CSE | CSE | CSE | CSE | CSE | CSE | CSE |
| 90 | 8889 (Part) | | | | | | | | | | | | | | | | | | | | |
| | 3 | 1 | 1 | 1 | 1 | 1 | 1 | 1 | 1 | 1 | 1 | 1 | 1 | 1 | 1 | 1 | 1 | 1 | 1 | 2 | 1 |
| ½ | 2½ | 2 | 2½ | 2½ | 2 | 1¾ | 2 | 1¾ | 1¾ | 1¾ | 3 | 1½ | 2 | 1½ | 1½ | 2 | 2 | 1¾ | 1½ | ¾+¼ | 2 |
| 1 | --- | 1 | 1 | 1 | Teacher Assessed | 1 | 2 | 1 | 6 hrs of assignments plus 3hrs planning | Syllabus | 1 | 1 | 1 | Continuous Assessment | Continuous Assessment | 1 | 3×2 | 1 | 1 | Alt. 1: 2 | 1 |
| ½ | — | 1½ | 1½ | 2 | | 2½ | 1¼ & 1½ | 1½ | | A 2 B 2×1¼ | 2 | 2½ | 2½ | | — | 2 | Assignments | 1¾ | 2½ | Alt .2: 2 | 1½+ 10 min |
| ½ | — | Practical Marked | 2 | 1½ | | 1½ | 1 | 2 | | A 1½ B 2×1½ | 1¼ | 1½ | 2 | | | 2 | | 1¾ | 1¾ | Alt. 1: 1½ Alt. 2: 2 | 1¾+½ |
| urse rk | Project partly Teacher Assessed | Internally | | | | Course Work | Course Work | 10% Teacher Assessment | | | | Teacher Assessment may be Special Study | | Written Course Work | Written Course Work | | | | | Course Work | |
| | (•) | • | (•) | • | • | • | • | | • | • | • | • | • | • | (•) | (•) | (•) | • | • | • | • |
| | | (•) | | • | • | • | | | • | • | • | • | • | • | | | | • | • | • | (•) |
| | | • | (•) | • | • | • | • | | • | • | • | • | • | • | • | (•) | (•) | • | • | • | • |
| | | | | | | | | | | | | | | | | | | | | | |
| | | | | • | • | • | | • | • | • | • | • | • | • | | | • | | • | • | |
| | | | | | | | | | | | | | | | | | | | | | |
| | | | | | • | • | | • | | • | • | • | | • | | | | | | • | |
| | | | | • | • | • | | • | • | | • | • | | • | | | | | | | |
| | | • | | • | | • | | • | • | | • | • | | • | | | • | | | • | |
| | | • | | • | | • | | • | • | | • | • | | • | | | | | • | • | |
| | | • | | • | • | • | | • | • | | • | | | • | | | • | | • | • | |
| | | | | | | | | | | | | | | | | | | | | | |
| | | | | | | | | • | | | | | | • | | | • | | | | |
| | | | | | | • | | | • | | • | • | • | • | | | | • | | • | • |
| | | | | | • | | | • | | | | | | | | | | • | | • | |
| | | | | | | | | | | | | • | | • | | | • | • | | • | • |
| | | • | | | • | • | | • | • | • | | • | • | • | | | | • | • | • | • |
| | | • | | | • | • | | • | • | • | • | • | | • | | | • | • | • | • | • |
| | | | | | • | • | | • | • | | | • | • | • | | | • | • | • | • | • |
| | | | | | | • | | • | | | • | • | | • | | | • | • | | • | • |
| | | • | | | • | • | | • | • | | • | • | | • | | | | | • | • | |
| | | | | | • | • | | • | • | | • | • | | • | | | • | • | • | • | • |
| | | • | | | • | • | | • | • | | • | • | • | • | | | • | • | • | • | • |
| | | | | | • | • | | • | | | | • | | • | | | • | • | • | • | • |

**CSE Boards**

*ALSEB* Associated Lancashire Schools Examining Board
77 Whitworth Street, Manchester M1 6HA

*EAEB* East Anglian Examinations Board
The Lindens, Lexden Road, Colchester, Essex CO3 3RL

*EMREB* East Midland Regional Examinations Board
Robins Wood House, Robins Wood Road, Apsley, Nottingham NG8 3NH

*LREB* London Regional Examinations Board
Lyon House, 104 Wandsworth High Street, London SW18 4LF

*NREB* North Regional Examinations Board
Wheatfield Road, Westerhope, Newcastle upon Tyne NE5 5JZ

*NWREB* North West Regional Examinations Board
Orbit House, Albert Street, Eccles, Manchester M30 0WL

*SREB* Southern Regional Examinations Board, 53 London Road, Southampton SO9 4YL

*SEREB* South East Regional Examinations Board
Beloe House, 2/4 Mount Ephraim Road,
Royal Tunbridge Wells, Kent TN1 1EU

*SWEB* South Western Examinations Board
23–29 Marsh Street, Bristol BS1 4BP

*WJEC* Welsh Joint Education Committee
245 Western Avenue, Cardiff CF5 2YX

*WMEB* West Midlands Examinations Board
Norfolk House, Smallbrook Queensway, Birmingham B5 4NJ

*WY&LREB** West Yorkshire & Lindsey Regional Examining Board
Scarsdale House, 136 Derbyshire Lane, Sheffield S8 8SE

*YREB** Yorkshire Regional Examinations Board
31–33 Springfield Avenue, Harrogate, North Yorkshire HG1 2HW

*Yorkshire and Humberside Regional Examinations Board, at the *YREB* address, now embraces *WY & LREB* and *YREB*

# Part II Core Units, chapters 2–15

# 2 Family and community

## 2.1 The family

The family is a group of people related either by blood or by marriage. These relations often form very meaningful social groups in which we feel comfortable and safe. The close bonds which we make usually last until they are broken by death or sometimes geographical distance. Members of a family are called **kin**.

### The nuclear family

The nuclear family is the social group in which most people live at some time. It is composed of mother, father and children – the nearest kin.

**Fig. 2.1** Queen Victoria and her family in 1900

### The extended family

This includes the rest of the **kinsfolk** – grandparents, uncles, aunts, cousins and more distant relatives. Examples of families which live in **extended family groups** rather than in nuclear family units are to be found in working communities such as farms, among many immigrant groups, or where 'granny units' have been built on to houses by families, so that parents can be looked after but still retain some independence.

The family is an important social group, whatever form it takes, and it fulfils many functions for its members.

### The functions of the family

1 It provides shelter.    2 It provides food.
3 It provides comfort and security.    4 It reproduces the species.
5 It may provide an economic unit. e.g. a farm where everyone works together.
6 Socialisation. This is the process where members learn about the way to behave in line with the family's expectations. Different families will have different views on what is appropriate and acceptable. Behaviour which is acceptable in one family may be quite unacceptable in another.
7 Recreation and leisure. The family may well provide a focus for this. Members may, for instance, collectively watch TV, go for holidays or play in the park.
8 Status. The family often sets the level of a person's place in the community. Royal children, for instance, have **ascribed status** in that they are born with it. Some families gain status by achievement; this is called **achieved status**. All families provide a social style which the children become part of at birth or adoption.

## 2.1.1 Working wives and mothers

Many women now work outside the home; there are many reasons why this is so.

### Economic reasons

1 To supplement the family income
2 To provide the family with its only income, e.g. single parents or where one parent is unemployed    3 To save for special items e.g. a car

### Social and psychological reasons

1 To provide friends and company    2 To prevent loneliness
3 To gain status (standing); being a housewife sadly often lacks status in our society
4 To make use of a training   5 To continue with a career
6 Because looking after a home and children seems unfulfilling work
The children of working mothers can be cared for in a number of ways as outlined below.

### Care of children while mothers work

**Day nurseries** may be private or run by the local authority. Local authority nurseries usually only take children in need, e.g. children of single parent families and there are relatively few places available. Private nurseries also tend to be too few in number; they may be expensive and are not evenly distributed geographically.

**Fig. 2.2** A nursery class in Huddersfield, W. Yorkshire

**Child minders** should be registered by the local authority who will have checked the premises and talked to the person in charge. Some minders may work in relatively poor premises, e.g. flats, and have several children to look after. It is a good scheme if you can find a good minder who is relatively cheap.

**Relatives** e.g. granny taking care of a child often works very well as the person is already part of the family. It can, however, cause friction if child-minding practices differ.

**Au pairs or mother's helps** are often suitable only if the wife works part-time. It is not usually wise to leave them in sole charge of small children for long periods of time. They often live in, and may therefore need accommodation in the house.

**Neighbours** are not usually available to be more than short-term or emergency carers.

**Nursery classes** are run by some schools for children from 3-5 years. They often take children for half-days only for up to five days a week and do not open during school holidays. They are not available everywhere.

**Crèches** are provided at some places of employment for employees' children. They are usually open during all working hours and are mostly available free or at a nominal charge.

**Playgroups** are usually voluntary organizations and are registered with the local authority. Play leaders do not need to be qualified in child care. They are usually unsuitable for working mothers as they mostly operate for only about three hours per day.

**Baby-sitters** are very useful to release parents for **short periods** of time. They are not suitable as full-time child minders. Some parents join baby-sitting circles where they take it in turn to mind each other's children. Friends, relatives or neighbours will often baby-sit, especially if there is an emergency. Teenagers are often prepared to baby-sit to earn extra pocket money.

The following points are important when choosing a baby-sitter.
1 It is better if the child knows (and likes) the baby-sitter.
2 The baby-sitter must be responsible and capable of acting sensibly in a crisis.

**3** They must be old enough. The law requires that children under 12 should never be left alone. They need to be older than 12, preferably 16+.

**4** It is helpful if they know the child's house so that they can find things.

**5** Ideally they need to be prepared continually to develop their relationship with the child, e.g. by reading stories or playing with them before they go to bed.

**Care of a child inside or outside the home** needs to be considered weighing up the advantages and disadvantages of both methods as outlined below.

*Advantages of care inside the home*

**1** Children often prefer to remain in their own home, especially insecure children.

**2** It saves having to get the child ready to go out first thing in the morning and having to collect them last thing at night.

**3** The child is more likely to get individual attention at home.

**4** There are no problems if the child is sick.

**5** Often the minder is also prepared to undertake other household tasks such as washing and ironing the child's clothes.

*Advantages of care outside the home*

**1** This method of care is often not dependent on one person, e.g. nurseries, so it is likely to be very reliable.

**2** It saves such expenses as lighting and heating if the child is cared for outside the home.

**3** Children can benefit from going to places where they are with other children. This aids socialisation.

**4** This type of care encourages independence.

## 2.1.2 Relationships in the family

The relationships within the family are very important and their nature creates the atmosphere found in the home. Each member of the family plays a series of different **rôles** e.g. a woman's rôle may be as a wife at one time and as a mother on another occasion. Most of us slip easily between differing rôles and other family members use verbal and non-verbal clues to tell us which rôle they want us to play.

**Status** is also an important concept in the family. Members hold different status positions and this will affect the way they treat one another and the expectations they have of each other. Fathers sometimes have greater status than mothers. The archetypal Victorian family is always seen as one in which father was boss–someone of high status in relation to the other family members. This is known as a **patriarchal** family. In other communities the mother is most important–this is a **matriarchal** family.

Families are not isolated social groups, they fit within the context of wider society; so external factors such as a person's occupation or earning power usually affect the way in which they behave at home. Research suggests that non-working mothers often have less status in their families than working mothers. Certain groups have generally less status in our society than others, e.g. the elderly, the handicapped, children, women who do not work outside the home.

The **ages** and **capacities** of different family members also affect relationships. Homes which have grandparents living in them, or have handicapped children have different relationship patterns from those which do not. Relationships are never static; the patterns, problems and benefits are continually changing throughout a person's life.

**Dual-career families**

With two working parents families can have relationship difficulties as well as practical ones. Below is a list of the kind of problems such families can have.

**1** It is usually necessary for both partners to share housework and child-care duties.

**2** The wife will feel that she should share in the decision-making processes in the home, particularly on how to spend the money. This can also occur where the wife is not working.

**3** The wife's work may be forced into second place if the husband considers it to be secondary to work in the home. **4** It is sometimes difficult to find child-minding facilities.

**Table 2.1** Technological developments which help both parents to work

| *Labour and time-saving equipment* | *Care of and comfort in the home* | *Shopping and entertainment* |
| --- | --- | --- |
| Wide range of equipment e.g. washing machines, dishwashers can be left working while people are out. The expanding use of microchip technology will increase this trend. Modern polishes, cleaners etc; reduce the amount of time spent on cleaning, e.g. anti-tarnish metal polishes, aerosol polishes. | Homes and furniture are now designed for easy care e.g. kitchen surfaces, easy-care textiles. Central heating has replaced open fires in many homes, reducing dirt and work. | Convenience and 'fast' foods have reduced meal preparation and cooking times. Freezers make bulk buying a possibility. TV and videos keep family members happy whilst household tasks are completed. Extended shopping hours make shopping easier. Shopping over the 'phone with a credit card is now possible and cable TV will make it possible to complete most shopping from an armchair. |

**Social developments**

Other social changes have been instrumental in enabling women to work outside the home.

   1 Increasing acceptance and availability of birth control
   2 Statutory changes such as maternity provisions which enable women in employment to take maternity leave with pay
   3 Changed attitudes which make it acceptable for mothers to work
   4 The fact that many husbands are now prepared to share housework and certain child-care duties
   5 Variable hours, flexitime and crêche facilities are offered by some employers to encourage women to work.
   6 Increasing understanding of the value of training and education for women, which enables them to continue with trades and professions throughout their married lives
   7 Smaller families which are geographically more isolated mean that women need to work for company and friends.
   8 The desire for home ownership and the rising cost of houses have meant that two salaries are often necessary to meet mortgage costs.

### 2.1.3   The elderly

An ever-increasing proportion of the British population is made up of people over 60 years owing to improvements in medicine. Britain is said to have an **old age structure**. This is very different from many Third World countries where the bulk of the population is made up of children. These countries are said to have a **young age structure**. Having so many elderly people in the population has some disadvantages, both for society and for families.

**Problems of the elderly** and those they create are numerous. The main ones are considered below.

   1 They can be incapacitated and need full-time care. Old age and disability may often be related.
   2 They make heavy use of the health and welfare services.
   3 They may need special accommodation and food.
   4 They are often poor as they have only their pensions to live on. In times of high inflation their savings fall in real value and may not be enough.
   5 Poverty may mean that they live in unsatisfactory accommodation with inadequate food and heating. In the winter elderly people can suffer from hypothermia and die of cold.
   6 They are often lonely. A major difficulty for many is transport to keep in contact with friends and the 'outside world'.
   7 The members of society who support those who do not work through their taxes are the **working population**. This small section of society has an increasingly large load to bear as the number of pensioners increases.

What is old age? When do you become old? Many people are active and have few problems right up until the very end of their lives. Facilities and help for those elderly people with problems are not always good.

### 2.1.4   Work and leisure

Work is the central interest in life for most people. They may not necessarily enjoy what they do, but it affects their whole way of life influencing such things as the amount of free time which is available, the friends they make and their spendable income.

   Occupation (the actual job done) is often used to 'place' a person in society. It defines their status. When people meet each other for the first time they often ask each other what work they do. It provides a series of clues about the life-style and expectations of a person.

*Definitions*

**Work** is usually something which is:
   1 Instrumental i.e. done to supply wants and needs, e.g. to earn money to supply them. Usually money is earned so it is something for which we are paid.
   2 Obligatory i.e. it is something which we are obliged to do. Even if we enjoy our work, there is an element of compulsion.
   3 Located in a certain area. Most work is located in a particular area or room, e.g. a factory. In industrialized societies we often have to leave our homes to go to work, so work and home life become totally split.

**Leisure** activities are those which we choose to do. There is no element of compulsion and usually no 'payment' or 'reward' except personal pleasure. Sometimes leisure activities are described as 'expressive'.

   Activities which fall into neither category, such as washing-up or having a bath, are sometimes described as **non-work** activities.

| Benefits of work | Benefits of leisure |
|---|---|
| Earn an income or goods in kind (e.g. a tied cottage) | Relaxation from tiring work |
| Make friends | Self-improvement, e.g. learning new skills |
| Occupy time | To divert the mind from the psychological stress of work |
| To use trade or professional training, i.e. a vocational calling such as nursing | Make friends |
| Develop and advance knowledge, e.g. research scientist | |
| Fulfil ambitions | |
| Because society needs people to work | |

Most people work for a combination of different motives. However, work is usually satisfying on some occasions and not on others.

**Mechanisation** is the use of machines to do work.

**Automation** is the use of automatic equipment to guide the work of machines, e.g. the car industry uses 'robots' to help make cars. Men are superfluous except as technicians.

### Leisure patterns

Leisure patterns are affected by occupation and there is a strong relationship between the two. The patterns may be:

 **1** Contrasting, where there is a strong division between work and leisure. Work activities do not carry over into leisure time. An example of this would be coal-mining where dangerous, taxing and heavy work is typically replaced in leisure time by relaxing in pubs and clubs.
 **2** Similar, where there is little division between work and leisure; pursuits are not rigidly divided. It occurs when people find their work very satisfying and therefore leisure time is occupied with related activities, e.g. a teacher reading.
 **3** Neutral, where workers do not seem to need to escape the boredom or danger of work; neither are they sufficiently interested in it to want to continue it into their leisure time.

**Occupation influences** leisure by determining:
 **1** The money available.
 **2** The time available.
 **3** The geographical location in which the person lives.
 **4** The political, cultural, economic and social attitudes.
 **5** The needs for leisure experiences, e.g. tiring or dangerous work.

**Fig. 2.3** A youth hostel scene at Holmbury St Mary

**Leisure needs of teenagers**

| *Reasons for need* | *Controlled by* | *Facilities provided by* |
|---|---|---|
| **1** Social–company, friends<br>**2** Physical–desire for something taxing or energetic<br>**3** Educational–to learn new skills<br>**4** Personal–psychological reasons e.g. to gain satisfaction. | Money available<br>Time available<br>Social and cultural background<br>Family experience<br>Amenities available | Youth clubs, Sea Cadets, Outward Bound, Boy Scouts, Girl Guides, Red Cross, St. John's Ambulance, Youth Hostel Association, Duke of Edinburgh Award Scheme<br>Special interest clubs e.g. athletics, swimming, judo<br>Libraries and museums<br>Discos, clubs, cinemas, theatres |

### 2.1.5  Unemployment

Unemployment can have serious consequences for families and individuals. Listed below are some of the main problems which it can cause.

**Economic**

1 Reduction in living standards
2 Failure to meet existing bills such as mortgage repayments or HP payments

**Effects on the family**

1 Can prevent children from staying on at school or college
2 Luxuries like holidays are cut out
3 It may mean that the other parent will have to look for work or work longer hours to support the family
4 The unemployed person may feel depressed or worthless as a result of loss of status. This can cause resentment or unhappiness in the home.
5 Applying for unemployment benefit and looking for work can be very demoralising.
6 The unemployed person has a lot of enforced leisure time.
7 Turning to petty crime for some income

The difficulties listed above are not only problems for the unemployed person but can cause distress to family and friends as well.

### 2.2  The community

**Local democracy**

**Overall control and planning** of life and activities is held by Parliament and central government, but most activities are organized at local and regional level by county, metropolitan, district or parish councils. The flow diagram and table below show how this works and the particular services for which each of these councils is responsible. These councils are made up of ratepayers who are elected as councillors on to these bodies

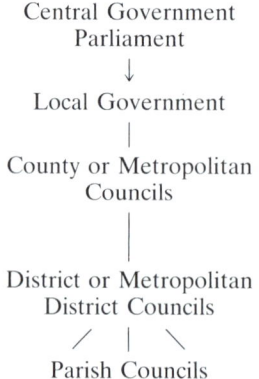

**Fig. 2.4** How local government is organized

In areas of dense population and large towns control is at present organized, until 1986, into metropolitan counties i.e. Greater Manchester, Merseyside, South Yorkshire, Tyneside, West Midlands.

**Table 2.2** Local Government responsibilities

| Amenities and service activities | County and Metropolitan Councils | District and Metropolitan District Councils | Parish Councils |
|---|---|---|---|
| Planning | √ | √ | involved |
| Parks/Gardens | √ | √ | √ |
| Allotments | √ | √ | √ |
| Transport/Roads | √ | | |
| Street lighting | √ | | |
| Refuse | | √ | |
| Street cleaning | | √ | |
| Cemeteries | | √ | |
| Sporting facilities | | √ | √ |
| Education | √ | | |
| Housing | √ | √ | √ |
| Maternity/Child Welfare | √ | | |
| Registrar | √ | | |
| Libraries | √ | | |
| Museums/Art Galleries | √ | √ | √ |
| Transport services | √ | √ | |
| Fire Service | √ | | |
| Police | √ | | |
| Probationary Service | √ | | |
| Traffic control | √ | | |
| Parking | √ | √ | √ |
| Weights and Measures | √ | | |
| Inspecting shops etc. | | √ | |
| Food and Drugs | √ | | |

## 2.2.1 Social services

Social and welfare services may be **statutory** or **voluntary**. Voluntary organizations and self-help groups fill in the gaps which statutory (state run) services are unable to fill.

**The rôle of voluntary organizations**

1 They complement, extend and supplement existing services.
2 They provide a pool of expert knowledge, e.g. the NSPCC (National Society for the Prevention of Cruelty to Children) provides expert information on all matters about children. If the government needs advice, it can always consult them.
3 They offer specialized services, e.g. St. John's Ambulance Brigade.
4 As they are not public bodies, they can quickly change their approach to cope with new needs and circumstances.
5 They provide support services for professional workers.
6 Many of them, e.g. Dr Barnardos, are registered charities and are not a drain on public funds.
7 They press the government for necessary reforms of the law in areas with which they are concerned.
8 They inform the public about the needs of special groups; for instance, the Royal Institute for the Deaf regularly brings the needs of the deaf to public notice.
9 They often provide the public with free advice; for instance, Age Concern will advise families on problems with elderly relatives.

**Self-help groups**

These fulfil the same role as voluntary organizations but are usually informal rather than formally constituted groups. They tend to arise and disappear as people feel a need for them. They provide mutual support for people with common problems and tend to be non-bureaucratic.

**Concerns and activities of some voluntary organizations**

**Age Concern**
Provides information and advice about the elderly
Is a centre for research
Discovers elderly people with problems and tries to help on a local level by providing clubs, day-centres, people to visit, holidays, transport, lunch-clubs, meals-on-wheels, advice on welfare rights
Produces publications and guides
Makes representations to the government on behalf of the elderly

**Gingerbread**

Provides help to one-parent families

Is a network of self-help groups where people offer each other support and help

Campaigns for social reform

Arranges social activities

Produces publications

**The Samaritans**

Provides a confidential life-line to people in distress–open 24 hours a day

Voluntary workers who work under the direction of a trained professional worker

They provide a counselling service rather than an advice service

Their most essential quality is the ability to listen; in this way, they can often help people to help themselves.

**Shelter**

Offers help and advice to families with any kind of housing problem

Produces research documents and publications

Represents the needs of the homeless to the government

Provides the public with information

**The National Marriage Guidance Council**

Co-ordinates the work of all the local Marriage Guidance Councils

Personnel are professionally trained

The counsellors aim to help those with marital or family difficulties to clarify their own problems

**NSPCC**–National Society for the Prevention of Cruelty to Children

Founded to look after children's needs

Will investigate reports of cruelty or neglect from the public and holds a register of children at risk

Offers advice and help to parents

Has a fund to provide for children in need

Organizes play-groups

Produces information and publications

Represents children to the government

**Salvation Army**

Founded to spread the Gospel

Provides homes for children and the aged, nurseries, hostels for working men, centres for alcoholics and drug addicts, hospitals, dispensaries, clinics, maternity homes for unmarried mothers, etc.

**Statutory Services**

The following Table 2.3 shows some of the main services provided by public funds.

**Table 2.3** Services provided for the community from public funds

| Children | Handicapped | The Elderly |
|---|---|---|
| Public day nurseries | Practical assistance at home e.g. home-helps, installation of lifts, property modifications | All services listed for the handicapped if necessary |
| Supervision of private nurseries | | Warden-controlled accommodation |
| Nursery classes (some areas) | | Residential homes |
| Take children into care where necessary | Provision of specialist equipment e.g. wheelchairs; telephones | Travel concessions |
| Supervise adoption and fostering | Leisure equipment e.g. radios | |
| Play-groups (some areas) | Assistance with travelling | |
| Preventative services related to the welfare of children generally | Holidays for the person or the family | |
| | Meals e.g. Meals-on-wheels | |
| | Recreation outside the home e.g. lunch clubs | |
| | Day centres for social contact etc; | |
| | All these facilities are designed to increase the person's independence | |

## 2.2.2   The National Health Services

These are available to everyone in need at whatever age. The diagram Fig. 2.5 shows how the Health Services are organized and controlled. Detailed below are some of the services.

**General practitioners** selected by anyone over 16 years. GP's will treat people on their list and anyone else holding a NHS card whose own doctor is unavailable. Apart from accidents and emergencies, all patients who go to hospital are referred there by doctors. Doctors give out immediate health-care such as dealing with minor ailments and general ante-natal and post-natal care.

**Community midwives** (Certified midwives) are supplied by the Area Health Authority to care

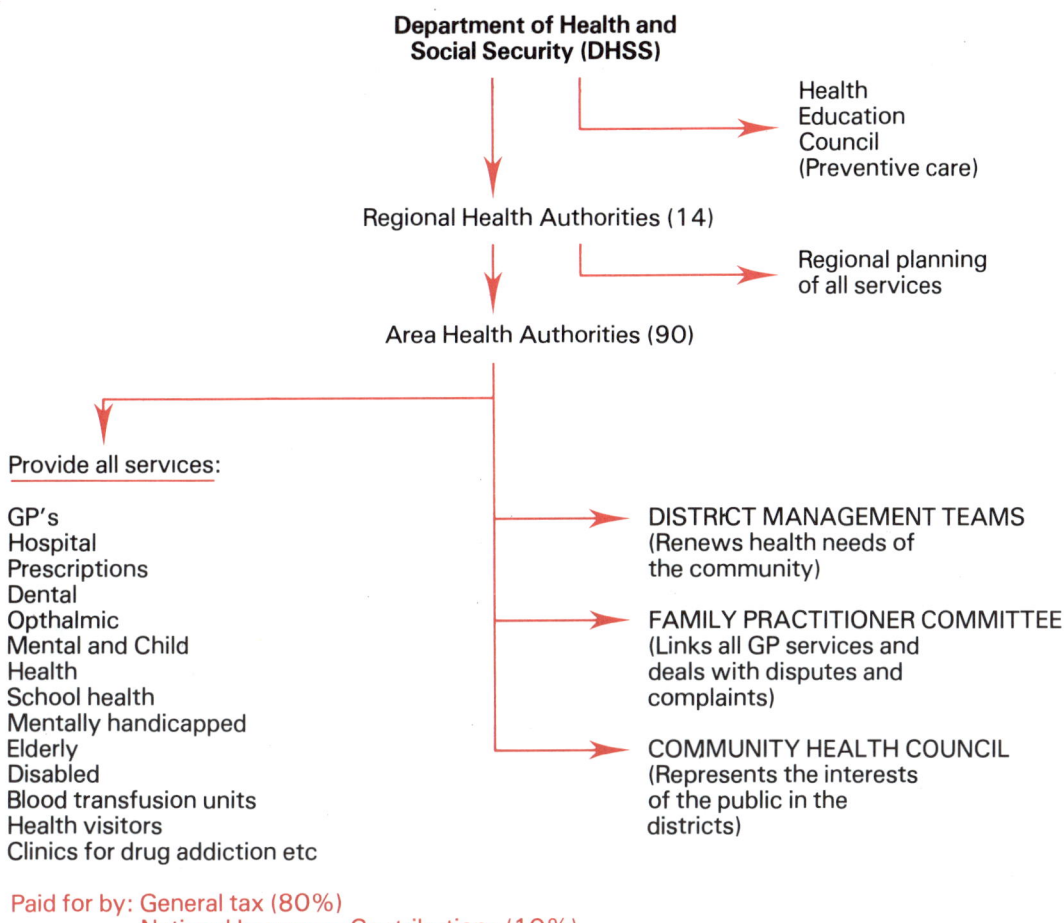

**Department of Health and
Social Security (DHSS)**

Health
Education
Council
(Preventive care)

Regional Health Authorities (14)

Regional planning
of all services

Area Health Authorities (90)

Provide all services:

GP's
Hospital
Prescriptions
Dental
Opthalmic
Mental and Child
Health
School health
Mentally handicapped
Elderly
Disabled
Blood transfusion units
Health visitors
Clinics for drug addiction etc

DISTRICT MANAGEMENT TEAMS
(Renews health needs of
the community)

FAMILY PRACTITIONER COMMITTEE
(Links all GP services and
deals with disputes and
complaints)

COMMUNITY HEALTH COUNCIL
(Represents the interests
of the public in the
districts)

Paid for by: General tax (80%)
National Insurance Contributions (10%)
Dental, opthalmic and prescription fees

**Fig. 2.5** Health services, their organization, control and finance

for women during childbirth and for 28 days thereafter. In many areas this service is run in co-operation with local hospitals and GP's. Midwives are also involved with ante-natal care.

**Health visitors** are employed by the Area Health Authority and give advice to expectant and nursing mothers, parents of young children, the sick and the elderly. They may work from health centres, maternity and child welfare clinics, or be attached to GP's. Some health visitors specialize in one particular aspect such as geriatrics.

**Family planning services** give advice on contraception and supply contraceptive substances and appliances. They also provide vasectomy services which are free of charge and are available to anyone.

**School medical care** provides periodic medicals, eye and hearing tests. Vaccinations are organized for German measles etc.

**Community or District Nurses** supply nursing services to elderly, sick or injured people in their own homes. Many of these nurses work from health centres or are attached to GP's.

**Social workers** are qualified personnel who supervise the social services for children, e.g. controlling day-nurseries and ensuring the welfare of families and young people. They also care for the elderly and those with special needs such as handicapped people. Their rôle is partly advisory but they can also ensure more practical help for their clients by helping them to claim any benefits or allowances to which they are entitled.

**Health centres** are usually staffed by co-ordinated teams of people such as doctors, nurses, midwives, health visitors, dentists and social workers. They provide all-round primary care within one unit; this is very advantageous for their clients as they only need to visit one place to get everything. Moreover, it means that communication between the professionals is easy and this liaison benefits the clients.

### 2.2.3   Social security and welfare benefits available from the State

The following diagram Fig. 2.6 shows some of the benefits and services available to different groups and members of society. Many benefits are dependent upon the payment of national insurance contributions.

**Benefits for children**

**Child benefit** or family allowance is payable to all people with children. It is a weekly tax-free cash benefit. Where a child lives with both his parents, the claim should be made by the mother. The basic sum may be increased for certain one-parent families. The benefit is payable up to the age of 18 if the child is in full-time education.
Dental treatment, glasses and prescriptions are free to children. In certain cases, school dinners, milk and uniforms are also provided.

**Benefits for women/mothers**

**Maternity grant,** a sum of £25 is payable to all women who are pregnant.
**Maternity allowance** is a weekly sum paid for up to 18 weeks. It is only available for working women who have already paid sufficient national insurance contributions.
Free dental treatment and prescriptions are available to pregnant women and mothers of babies of 12 months or less.

**Benefits for people with low incomes**

Benefits are often referred to by their initials e.g. FIS.

**Free** prescriptions, dental treatment, glasses, milk and vitamins, school dinners, milk and school clothing.

**Family income supplement (FIS)** is available for families with at least one child where the head of the family is in full-time work but is on a low income. Being able to claim this means that certain other means-tested benefits are also available, e.g milk and vitamins for expectant mothers.

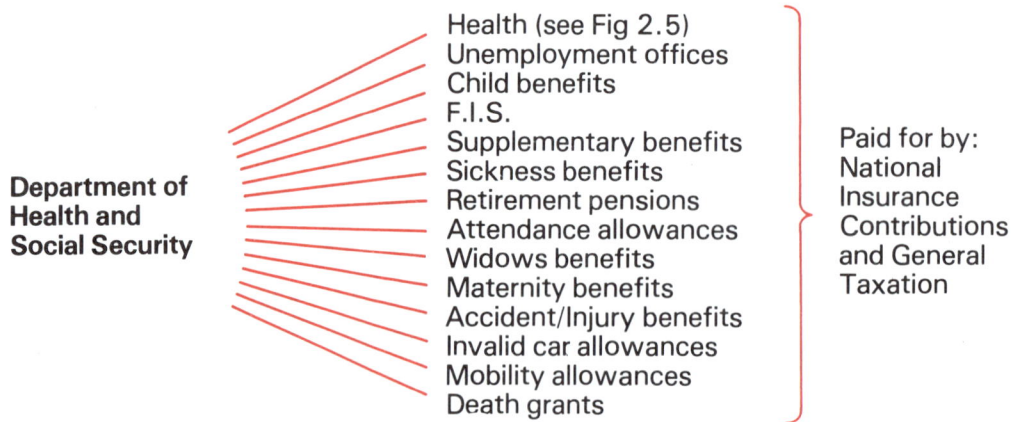

**Fig. 2.6** Social security/welfare benefits available and how they are paid for

**Supplementary benefit** is payable to anyone aged 16 or over who has left school and is not in full-time work. It is paid when the claimant's resources fall short of their needs. It is a means-tested benefit.

**Unemployment benefit**

This is paid (for 10 months only) to those registered as unemployed who have paid sufficient national insurance contributions of the appropriate class.

**Prescription charges**

A person continuously on medication e.g. a diabetic does not pay for prescriptions.

### 2.2.4 Community ties

The concept of community is very **difficult to define**. There are many different definitions, each of which seems appropriate in a particular context. There are, however, certain elements which are common to most definitions:

**A geographical area or neighbourhood** may be something well defined like a village or something more vague like a particular group of streets in a big city.

**A common 'spirit' or set of values** The people in the area possess certain attitudes, beliefs and values which are common. This leads to a collective view to which most people will subscribe. These values may be reinforced by particular hardships or disadvantages from which the community suffers. Fishing villages (Fig. 2.7) are well known for their community spirit. The dangerous and arduous work of mining helps to foster and develop fellow-feeling amongst villagers. In villages of this kind most people have similar life-styles, incomes and expectations.

Some communities are made up of people many of whom are related to each other. Communities with kinship ties of this sort usually have a very strong community spirit. Family ties serve to reinforce community feeling.

The term 'community' may also be used to describe religious institutions such as monasteries.

The following circumstances tend to weaken community ties:

1 Areas where many people have newly arrived or are immigrants from other countries.
2 In areas of high-rise housing (Fig. 2.8) it is more difficult for neighbours to get to know one another.
3 The geographical area of the community is large.
4 Areas where there are no facilities in which members can meet together for a common purpose e.g. churches, libraries, sports facilities, parks, swimming baths, health centres.

Town planning can either help or hinder the growth of community ties. Planning which helps to give individuality to urban areas and enables people to meet one another is more likely to engender community spirit.

Fig. 2.7 A fishing community, Staithes, North Yorkshire

**Fig. 2.8** High-rise flats

# 3 Nutrition

## 3.1 Classification of nutrients, sources, functions

### 3.1.1. Food and nutrients

**Nutrition** is the study of foods, the nutrients they contain and the ways in which these are used by the body. **A food** is anything which when eaten or drunk provides the body with nutrients needed to sustain life.

**Nutrients** are needed to provide the body with:
  1 Energy.     2 Material for growth, repair and renewal of body tissues.
  3 Substances which control body processes and keep us healthy.
Most nutrients have more than one rôle to play in body metabolism.
There are **six groups** of nutrients. These are:

  1 Carbohydrates (sugars, starches, cellulose/fibre)
  2 Lipids (fats and oils)     3 Proteins     4 Vitamins     5 Mineral elements
  6 Water (not a nutrient in the sense of groups **1** to **5** but essential to life)

**Cooking** can affect and change nutrients.

**Digestion** breaks down large food molecules into smaller nutrient molecules which can be absorbed into the blood stream.

### 3.1.2 Carbohydrates

**Carbohydrates** are produced in green plants by **photosynthesis**. They are made up of the elements **carbon, hydrogen** and **oxygen**.

**Plants** use the sun's energy to *change* water and carbon dioxide into glucose and oxygen.

$$6CO_2 + 6H_2O \xrightarrow[\text{sun's light energy}]{\text{green plants use the}} C_6H_{12}O_6 + 6O_2$$
$$\begin{pmatrix}\text{carbon}\\\text{dioxide}\end{pmatrix} \quad \text{(water)} \qquad\qquad\qquad \text{(glucose)} \quad \text{(oxygen)}$$

The plants then change glucose into more complex carbohydrates such as maltose, sucrose, starch and cellulose.

**Table 3.1** Types of carbohydrates

|  | Monosaccharides | Disaccharides | Polysaccharides |
|---|---|---|---|
| **Examples** | Simple sugars e.g. glucose, fructose. | Double sugars (2 simple sugar units) e.g. sucrose, maltose, lactose. | Complex sugars (long chains of simple sugar units). e.g. starch, glycogen, cellulose, pectin, dextrin. |
| **Functions in the body** | Energy production 16kJ/g (3.75kcal/g) | Energy production 16kJ/g (3.75kcal/g) | **Starch** } Energy production **Glycogen** } 16kJ/g (3.75kcal/g) **Cellulose** (fibre)–indigestible. Absorbs water and bulks up the contents of colon. This aids peristalsis and the egestion of faeces. **Pectin**–no direct food value but is the setting agent in jam. |
| **Digestion** | No digestion needed Simple sugars absorbed rapidly | **Small intestine** Enzyme *maltase* maltose to glucose Enzyme *sucrase* sucrose to glucose Enzyme *lactase* lactose to glucose and galactose | **In mouth** Enzyme *salivary amylase* cooked starch to maltose and dextrin **In duodenum** Enzyme *pancreatic amylase* starch to maltose **In small intestine** Enzyme *maltase* maltose to glucose |

All simple sugar molecules are absorbed into the blood capillaries of the **villi** of the small intestine. Excess sugar is stored as *glycogen* in muscle cells and in the liver. This can be quickly converted back to glucose. Any further excess is stored as body fat.

| | | |
|---|---|---|
| **Effect of cooking** | **Dry Heat**–sugars melt. Further heating evaporates water to form caramel and eventually carbon.<br><br>**Moist Heat**–sugars dissolve. Further heating evaporates water to form caramel and eventually carbon. | **Dry Heat**–starches lose water and form dextrin.<br><br>**Moist Heat**–starch grains absorb water and swell– gelatinization.<br>Cellulose is softened, its bulk is reduced and it is easier to eat. |

## 3.1.3   Lipids (Fats and Oils)

Fats are solids at room temperature, oils are liquid. They are made up of the elements **carbon**, **hydrogen** and **oxygen** and are composed of 1 unit of *glycerol* + 3 fatty acid units.

### Types of fats

**Saturated fats** have fatty acids which contain their full complement of hydrogen atoms

$$\cdots \text{C}-\text{C}-\text{C}-\text{C}-\text{C} \cdots$$

e.g. butter, lard, suet and most margarines.

**Monounsaturated fats** or oils contain less than their full complement of hydrogen atoms

$$\cdots \text{C}-\text{C}-\text{C}-\text{C}=\text{C} \cdots$$

e.g. olive oil, peanut oil, blended vegetable oils.

**Polyunsaturated** fats and oils have fatty acids with more than one double bond and so contain even fewer hydrogen atoms

$$\cdots \text{C}=\text{C}-\text{C}-\text{C}=\text{C} \cdots$$

e.g. sunflower seed oil, corn oil, safflower oil, fish oils and margarines labelled polyunsaturated.

**NB** Most fats have a mixture of the different types of fatty acid. Unsaturated fatty acids may be made saturated by the addition of hydrogen ions–hydrogenation.

**Essential fatty acids (EFA)** cannot be made by the body so they must be included in the diet. They are needed for the building of cell membranes. They are found in some seed oils–sunflower, soya, safflower, maize, in the oils of fatty fish and in dark green vegetables. A deficiency is unlikely. EFA are **linoleic acid**, **linolenic** and **arachidonic acid**. The last two can be made from linoleic acid.

### Functions of Fats

1 They are the most concentrated source of energy–38kJ/g (9kcal/g).
2 Fats are frequently a source of the fat soluble vitamins A, D, E and K.
3 Fats make food more palatable; give it more flavour e.g. butter on bread, knob of butter on boiled potatoes.
4 Lubricate food making it easier to digest
5 They have a high satiety value–their presence in the stomach slows down digestion to give a full feeling for longer.
6 Fats form a fuel reserve under the skin as an insulating adipose layer.
7 Fats form a protective layer around some organs e.g. the kidneys.

### Digestion of Fats

No digestion takes place until the fat reaches the duodenum.

**In the duodenum** bile salts from the liver emulsify fats (it breaks them down into tiny droplets) providing a larger surface area for enzyme action. Pancreatic lipase, steapsin, splits the fats into fatty acids and glycerol.

**In the small intestine** synthesis of glycerol and fatty acids occurs into fat droplets and these are absorbed into the lacteals of the villi.

Fats in excess of those needed for energy production form adipose tissue under the skin and layers of protective fat around organs.

### Effect of cooking on Fats

1 Melt when heated
2 At 100°C any water in the fat or oil is given off and can be seen as bubbles and steam.

**3** Each fat and oil has a different temperature at which decomposition starts if it is overheated. When this smoking point is reached some fatty acids are released and some of the glycerol is changed to a substance called *acrolein* which has an acrid, choking effect and is indigestible.
**4** Oils usually have a higher smoking point than solid fats.

### 3.1.4   Proteins

Proteins are derived from both plant and animal sources. They are made up of the elements *carbon, hydrogen, oxygen, nitrogen* and *sulphur*. They are our only source of nitrogen essential to the building of living tissue. The basic units of which proteins are made are **amino acids**.

#### Types of Proteins

**Proteins of high biological value (HBV)** contain the *essential amino acids*. **Ten** essential amino acids are needed by **children** and **eight** of them by **adults**.

HBV proteins contain these in the right number and proportions needed by the body. They are found in meat, fish, eggs, milk, cheese and soya.

**Proteins of low biological value (LBV) lack one** or more of the **10** essential amino acids or contain most of them but in the wrong proportions for our needs. A mixture of LBV proteins complement each other to increase the value of the foods to the body.

LBV proteins are found in good supply in green peas, beans, pulses, dried peas and beans, cereals, nuts and gelatine.

#### Functions of Proteins

**1** The building of new tissues and the replacement of worn or damaged tissues
**2** The production of body fluids such as blood cells, enzymes, hormones
**3** The production of anti-bodies
**4** If the body has an energy need which cannot be met by the carbohydrates and fats, proteins can be deaminised in the liver and used to produce energy–17kJ/g (4kcal)
**5** Carbohydrates and fats are sometimes called protein sparers because their presence means that protein can be used for building.

#### Digestion of Proteins

No digestion takes place until the food reaches the stomach.

**In the stomach** pepsin changes proteins to peptides in the presence of HCl.

**In the duodenum** trypsin from the pancreatic juices changes proteins to peptides.

**In the small intestine** erepsin changes peptides to amino acids.
Amino acids are absorbed into the blood capillaries of the villi of the small intestine. Proteins are not stored in the body.
Amino acids in excess of the body's needs are deaminated in the liver to give two parts:
**(a)** nitrogen-containing part which becomes urea and is excreted by kidneys,
**(b)** the remaining network of carbon, hydrogen and oxygen which is oxidised to produce energy.
A mixture of HBV and LBV proteins should be eaten every day.

#### Effect of cooking on Proteins

**1** Proteins coagulate when heated.
**2** Overcooking will denature protein and make it difficult to digest.
**3** Partial coagulation of milk proteins forms the skin on boiled milk and the scum left in the milk pan.
**4** Egg white sets at approximately 60°C just before the egg yolk.
**5** The muscle protein of meat, *myoglobin,* changes from a red to a brown colour.
**6** The meat proteins, *myosin* and *actin,* coagulate and shrink.
**7** Moist heat converts insoluble collagen, the connective tissue in meat, to soluble gelatine.
**8** Fish proteins coagulate at approximately 60°C. Collagen is converted into gelatine.
**9** The gluten in flour, after being stretched by raising agents, sets to give structure to baked goods such as bread and cakes.

**NB** HBV proteins are sometimes called 'complete' proteins and LBV proteins are called 'incomplete'.

Carbohydrates, fats and proteins are described as **macronutrients** because we need them in fairly large quantities.
Vitamins and mineral elements are called **micronutrients** because only small amounts are needed.

### 3.1.5  Vitamins

Vitamins are required by the body in small amounts and are found in small quantities in food. They play an important part in the building and functioning of our bodies. Lack of a particular vitamin in our diet can result in a deficiency disease (section 3.2.1). Vitamins are either fat soluble (A,D,E,K) or water soluble (C and B complex).

**Table 3.2** Vitamins – their functions and sources

| Vitamin | Functions | Good sources |
| --- | --- | --- |
| **Vitamin A** (Retinol) | The maintenance of *moist surface tissues* (epithelial), e.g. tissue at the front of the eyes, lining respiratory passages and digestive tract. Helps to regulate growth. Needed for the manufacture of visual purple in the retina and as such concerned with the perception of light in dim light. Sometimes called the anti-infective vitamin. | The body converts carotene (orange/yellow pigment) in fruit and vegetables to retinol (2 parts carotene makes 1 part retinol). Egg yolk, margarine, butter, liver, oily fish, fish liver oils Vegetable sources–carrots, green vegetables and tomatoes |
| **Vitamin D** | Concerned with *absorption of calcium* and *phosphorus* in the small intestine and with the laying down of these two elements in bones and teeth. | Our most important source is the action of *ultra-violet light* on the adipose tissue below the skin. Margarine, summer butter, egg yolk, oily fish, fish liver oils |
| **Vitamin E** | Not considered to be of great importance in man. | Most foods. Cereal products, meat and animal fats |
| **Vitamin K** | Helps in the clotting of blood. | Made by the bacteria in the intestines. Cabbage, spinach |
| **Vitamin C** (Ascorbic acid) | Needed for the formation of *connective tissue* collagen and of *intercellular cement*. Therefore has important part to play in the processes of growth and repair. Helps in the absorption of iron from eggs and plant foods therefore is linked to energy production. The body can store vitamin C for up to 6 months but this store is rapidly depleted when intake of the vitamin is low and when the body is physically or mentally stressed. | Blackcurrants, oranges, limes, lemons, grapefruit, strawberries, canned tomatoes, cabbage, brussels, cauliflower and peppers A daily intake is important. |
| **Vitamin B complex** | $B_1$ *Thiamin* for the release of energy from carbohydrates. It is necessary for *growth* in children. | Wholewheat and its products including breakfast cereals, yeast, pork, bacon, potatoes, milk |
| | $B_2$ *Riboflavin* for the *release of energy* from food especially amino-acids and fats. | Yeast, liver, milk, cheese, eggs, beef |
| | *Nicotinic acid* for the *release of energy* from food, and therefore growth. Healthy skin, tongue, digestive and nervous systems. | Yeast, liver, meat and meat products, white fish, cereal products including breakfast cereals, some fruits and vegetables–e.g. peas, beans, dried fruit |
| | $B_{12}$ *Cobalmin* is needed for the formation of red blood cells and for amino acid metabolism. | Milk, liver |

**The effect of cooking on Vitamins**

1 Vitamin A, both retinol and carotene are unaffected by most cooking processes. A little vitamin A may be lost in the oil when frying because it is fat soluble.

2 The B vitamins are all soluble in water and are destroyed by heat.

3 Vitamin C oxidises in the air, is soluble in water and is destroyed by heat–most is lost at temperatures below 100°C.

4 Vitamin D is unaffected by heat but as it is fat soluble a little may be lost when frying.

### 3.1.6  Inorganic food – mineral elements, water

**Mineral elements**

The body contains several inorganic elements called minerals. Of these, some are needed in larger quantities whilst others are needed in minute quantities and are called **trace elements**.

Mineral elements are to be found widely distributed in foods and with the exception of iron and calcium a deficiency is unlikely.

**Iron** is needed for the formation of haemoglobin in the red blood cells. The red pigment haemoglobin carries $O_2$ from the lungs to body cells for the oxidation of sugars to produce energy.

*Sources*

Liver, kidneys, corned beef, egg yolk, apricots, flour and other cereals, potatoes, green vegetables and cocoa.
Vitamin C helps absorption of iron from eggs and plant foods.

**Calcium** together with phosphorus and vitamin D are important in the formation of bones and teeth, for the normal clotting of the blood and for the normal functioning of muscles.

*Sources*

Milk, cheese, fortified bread and flour, green vegetables, fish whose bones are eaten e.g sardines, salmon, herrings, kippers.

**Phosphorus** in conjunction with calcium and vitamin D is important in the formation of bones and teeth. Phosphorus is needed in the production and utilization of energy and helps to regulate the acid balance of the body.

*Sources*

Most foods but particularly liver, kidney, eggs, meat, fish, cheese, milk and oats.

**Iodine** is needed for the production of thyroxine in the thyroid gland – the hormone that controls the metabolic rate.

*Sources*

Sea fish, water, iodized salt, vegetables grown on soil rich in iodine, such as by the sea.

**Fluoride** is needed for the formation of hard tooth enamel.

*Sources*

Water, tea, toothpaste, tablets, fluoride painted on teeth.
In some places fluoride is added to the water 1 part fluoride per million parts water. Excessive amounts can cause brown mottling of the teeth.

**Sodium** is present in all the fluids of the body and maintains the concentration of these fluids. The concentration of these should remain constant. More is needed in hot climates or working conditions when the body perspires more. Muscle cramp can result from lack of salt.

*Sources*

Table salt, bacon, kippers, cheese, margarine, butter, bread, salt tablets.

**Chlorine** is needed for the production of HCl in the stomach.

*Sources*

Table salt, bacon, kippers, cheese, margarine, butter, bread, salt tablets.

**NB** Iodine and fluorine are trace elements as are copper, manganese, cobalt, nickel, zinc and chromium.

### The effect of cooking on Mineral Elements

1 Foods cooked in soft water lose some of their calcium.
2 Foods cooked in hard water gain some calcium.
3 Heating milk may reduce the amount of calcium available.
4 Cooking cereals may make more calcium available.
5 Iron is lost when meat juices are discarded.
6 Salt may be lost when foods are boiled but this is mostly compensated for by the salt added during cooking.

### Water

Approximately 65% of the body's weight is water. Water is continually lost by way of the skin, lungs and kidneys and must be replaced. It is needed in the manufacture of all body fluids.

1 All metabolic processes take place in solution.
2 Water helps the processes of digestion, absorption and assimilation.
3 Water is needed for the efficient removal of solid waste from the bowel and liquid waste from the kidneys.

**4** Water helps to control body temperature.      **5** Water lubricates joints and membranes.

**Daily requirements** of water are approximately 2½ litres (4-5 pts).
  **1** Approximately 1½ litres (2-3 pints) comes from drinks.
  **2** The remainder comes from the food we eat. Fruit can be up to 90% water and foods such as bread 39% water.

### 3.1.7   Roughage or dietary fibre (see Section 3.4)

Liquid waste is excreted by way of the kidneys. Solid waste is egested as faeces by way of the bowel.

**Dietary fibre**

Dietary fibre consists of the undigested and unavailable carbohydrates such as cellulose. In the large intestine, dietary fibre absorbs water and bulks up the waste material making it soft and more easily pushed along the intestine by peristalsis.

**Lack of fibre** results in hard pelleted stools and constipation. The intestine walls cannot grip small hard faeces. If waste products are kept in the intestines for too long they can have a toxic effect. In addition to causing constipation, doctors now believe that there is a close link between a diet low in fibre and diseases such as appendicitis, diverticulitis, cancer of the bowel and colon, diabetes and gall stones.
  It is estimated that we need about 30g of fibre daily.

**Table 3.3** Sources of dietary fibre

| Food | Grams of fibre/ average portion | Food | Grams of fibre/ average portion |
|---|---|---|---|
| All Bran | 11.5g | Wholewheat macaroni | 5.5g |
| Stew dried apricots | 10g | Banana | 3.5g |
| Baked apple | 4.5g | Peanuts (28g) | 2.5g |
| Baked beans | 16.5g | Frozen peas | 9g |
| Red kidney beans | 7g | Jacket potato (200g) | 5g |
| Bran | 3g | Stewed prunes | 8.5g |
| Wholemeal bread (2 slices) | 6g | Raspberries | ·8.5g |
| White bread (2 slices) | 2g | Sweetcorn | 5.5g |
| Brussels sprouts | 3g | Weetabix (2) | 4.5g |
| Cabbage | 3g | Cooked carrots | 3.5g |

## 3.2   Recommended daily allowances of food and nutrients

If we eat a **variety** of foods we are unlikely to develop deficiency diseases. In the UK there is a wide variety of foodstuffs readily available and many foods such as breakfast cereals, margarine and other convenience foods are fortified with vitamins and minerals.
  The table below includes protein (a nutrient we eat in too great a quantity) and the nutrients which are likely to be in short supply in the diets of some people in the UK and other western countries.

**Table 3.4** Recommended daily allowances

| | | Protein g. | Iron mg. | Calcium mg. | Vitamin C mg. | Vitamin D µg. |
|---|---|---|---|---|---|---|
| Child | 0–1 | 30 | 6 | 600 | 15 | 10 |
| Child | 3–4 yrs | 40 | 8 | 500 | 20 | 10 |
| Child | 7–9 yrs | 53 | 10 | 500 | 20 | 2.5 |
| Boy | 9–11 yrs | 63 | 13 | 700 | 25 | 2.5 |
| Girl | 9–11 yrs | 58 | 13 | 500 | 25 | 2.5 |
| Boy | 15–18 yrs | 75 | 15 | 600 | 30 | 2.5 |
| Girl | 15–18 yrs | 58 | 15 | 600 | 30 | 2.5 |
| Man | 18–55 yrs | 75 | 10 | 500 | 30 | 2.5 |
| Woman | 18–55 yrs | 55 | 12 | 500 | 30 | 2.5 |
| Men | 65–75 yrs | 59 | 10 | 500 | 30 | 2.5 |
| Women | 55–75 yrs | 51 | 10 | 500 | 30 | 2.5 |
| In Pregnancy | | 60 | 15 | 1200 | 60 | 10 |
| Lactation | | 68 | 15 | 1200 | 60 | 10 |

Vegans may lack vitamin $B_{12}$ because it is found in animal products. More is needed during pregnancy and lactation.

Protein foods from animal sources are expensive to produce. In UK **we have more than enough** protein in our diets. The daily excess is used for energy, expensive energy. Because protein cannot be stored in the body it should be included in every meal.

### 3.2.1 Malnutrition

Malnutrition is the result of poor feeding. This can result in poor health because one or more nutrients may be missing from the diet, or because the diet includes too much of one or more nutrients. The table 3.5 shows some of the results of malnutrition.

**Table 3.5** Some of results of malnutrition

| Condition | Cause and effect | Dietary action |
|---|---|---|
| **Dental caries** | Bacteria in plaque on the teeth feed on sugar to produce acids which attack the tooth enamel and cause decay.(See Fig. 10.3) Most acid is formed in the first 10 minutes after eating. | **During pregnancy**–mother to have a diet rich in vitamin D, calcium, phosphorus and fluoride because milk teeth are laid down before birth. **Infants**–vitamin D drops, no sucrose or sugary drinks. **Childhood**–avoid sucrose and sugary foods, limited amount of sweets, cleaning teeth at least twice a day. Fluoride from water, seafish, toothpaste and tablets, or teeth painted with fluoride compound by the dentist. |
| **Obesity** | Being overweight is caused by too high an intake of high energy giving foods–those rich in fat and sucrose, combined with a lack of physical activity (see Section 3.3). There is a danger of high blood pressure, heart disease, respiratory illness, varicose veins, piles and with very high intakes of refined sugar present the risk of diabetes. | Reduction of fat and sucrose in the diet. Avoid cakes, pastries, biscuits, sweets, sweet drinks, cream and fried foods. Increase cereals, fruits and vegetables. |
| **Coronary heart disease** | This is the blockage of blood vessels supplying the heart muscles so the heart cannot function correctly. Two of the risk factors are thought to be obesity and a diet high in saturated fats. | Reduce the intake of sugar, fats (especially saturated fats), alcohol and salt. |
| **Intestinal ills** | Constipation, appendicitis, cancer, diverticulitis, gall stones, piles. All are more common when the diet is high in refined foods. | A high fibre diet is needed to reduce the risk of suffering from any of these complaints. Dietary fibre adds bulk to the colon, it retains more water and so aids peristaltic action in the removal of solid waste. Regular egestion of this waste keeps the intestines healthy. |

**Fig. 3.1** Obesity–a problem in the Western world

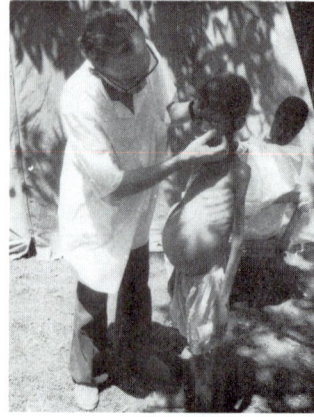

**Fig. 3.2** A young boy being checked for signs of xeropthalmia

**Fig. 3.3** Schoolchildren with the typical swollen necks of goitre

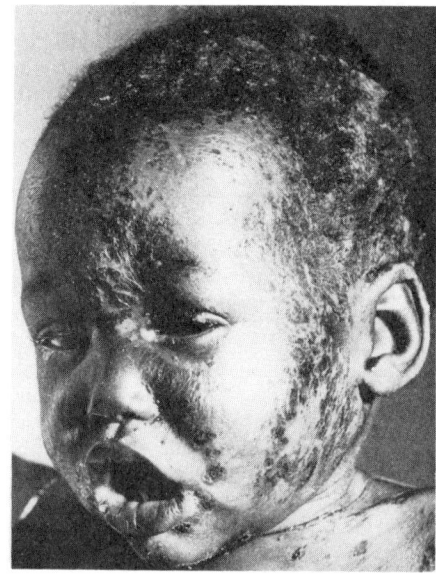

**Fig. 3.4** A young Ugandan boy suffering the effects of severe kwashiorkor

| Condition | Cause and effect | Dietary action |
|---|---|---|
| **Anaemia** | **Shortage of iron** The red blood cells are of the right size and number but they lack haemoglobin. Low haemoglobin = less $O_2$ from lungs = less energy produced. The results are tiredness and the body works less efficiently. | Eat more liver, kidney and other meats, corned beef, eggs, cocoa, cereals and dark green vegetables (+ vitamin C). |
| | **Shortage of vitamin $B_{12}$** The red blood cells are larger but fewer. They may be full of haemoglobin but their scarcity reduces $O_2$ reaching the cells. | Include more milk and liver in the diet. Vegans have specially fortified foods or $B_{12}$ tablets. |
| **Rickets and Osteomalacia** | **Rickets** is caused by lack of vitamin D which is needed for the absorption of calcium and the healthy formation of bones and teeth. There is poor bone development–short, soft, deformed. Rickets is found in Asian and African communities due to their skins inability to absorb sufficient sunlight to make Vitamin D. **Osteomalacia** is the adult version of rickets. The calcium content of bones gets less and they become brittle. | Increased exposure to sunlight. Inclusion of more vitamin D–more milk, eggs and the use of fortified margarine. |
| **Scurvy** | This is caused by a lack of vitamin C. Uncommon today. Wounds do not heal, teeth loosen and fall out, gums bleed and blood capillaries break down. Today a mild deficiency of vitamin C is likely to show itself as tiredness and infections such as colds can seem harder to shake off. | The body can store up to 6 months supply of vitamin C. If this is not replenished signs of scurvy could appear. Stress and poor diet will reduce the vitamin C store. The diet should include citrus fruit, blackcurrants, cabbage, brussels sprouts and cauliflower. Vitamin C tablets could be used. |
| **Beri-beri** | This is a disease of a rice-eating country caused by lack of vitamin $B_1$. The thiamin is removed with the bran and germ as the rice is polished. The nervous system is affected and heart muscle can be swollen. Muscular weakness and breathlessness result. | A diet which includes whole grains, liver, eggs, yeast, pork and green vegetables. |
| **Pellagra** | Caused by a lack of nicotinic acid. A disease which results from a diet mainly of maize. Sore, cracked skin, diarrhoea and nervous depression result. Partial paralysis can occur. | A diet which includes liver, legumes, yeast extract, milk and meat. |

| Condition | Cause and effect | Dietary action |
|---|---|---|
| **Xerophthalmia and Night blindness** | Xerophthalmia is associated with lack of vitamin A, poverty and dirt. Eyes become dry, grey and opaque. Infection leads to ulceration and blindness, (Keratomalacia). Lack of vitamin A means visual purple cannot be made so the retina of the eye does not adjust to dim light. | Social and dietary improvements are needed. Vitamin A from dairy foods, oily fish, margarine. Carotene from fruits and vegetables, apricots, tomatoes. Increase the amount of vitamin A in the diet. |
| **Goitre** | Lack of iodine means that less thyroxine is made in the thyroid gland so metabolism slows down and the front of the neck swells as the thyroid gland enlarges (see Fig. 3.3). | Include in the diet fish and vegetables from iodine rich soil. Use iodized salt. The doctor may prescribe tablets to remove the deficiency. |
| **Anorexia nervosa** | Loss of weight and appetite. The energy needs of the body are not supplied and it works less efficiently. Metabolic processes break down. Death can be final result (see Section 3.3). | Medical care is essential. Increase food intake to get the weight back to normal. The underlying cause for wishing not to eat must be dealt with. |
| **Kwashiorkor** | This is due to famine conditions. Affects mainly children 2-3 years old. A protein energy deficiency leads to poor growth, distended stomach, swellings due to water retention, diarrhoea and infections. Skin and hair are in a very poor condition (see Fig. 3.4). | More nutritionally balanced food. |
| **Marasmas** | Another protein energy malnutrition found amongst infants in their first year, where there is famine. Wasting of muscles, no body fat, pot belly, very emaciated appearance. | More nutritionally balanced food. |
| **Starvation** | These last two conditions of undernourishment can be improved if food becomes available but if there is no food sufferers eventually starve to death. | |

### 3.3   The body's need for energy

#### Why we need energy

The body's primary nutritional need is for energy to sustain life. Energy is produced in body cells by the oxidation of compounds containing carbon (simple sugar, fats).

#### Energy is needed
1 For growth and all metabolic processes    2 To maintain body temperature
3 For the transmission of nerve impulses
4 For muscular movement

#### The energy value of food

Foods are a mixture of nutrients. Energy values will vary with the differing compositions of food.

**Fats provide** the body with more than twice as much energy as the same weight of carbohydrate or protein.

**Protein** in excess of the body's need for growth and repair will be used to supply energy if there is insufficient carbohydrate or fat to meet energy needs.

$$1g \text{ of simple sugar} \longrightarrow \text{approx } 16kJ \ (3.75kcal)$$
(+ that from starches & double sugars)
$$1g \text{ protein} \longrightarrow \text{approx } 17kJ \ (4kcal)$$
$$1g \text{ fat} \longrightarrow \text{approx } 38kJ \ (9kcal)$$

Alcohol also provides energy at the rate of 29kJ/g (7kcal).

#### Units of energy

The energy value of food is found by burning carefully measured quantities of the food being tested in a **calorimeter**. The heat energy produced is measured.
*Kilojoule* (kJ) and *Kilocalorie* (kcal or Cal)

1 calorie will raise the temperature of 1g water through 1°C
1 kilocalorie will raise the temperature of 1000g water through 1°C
1 kilocalorie = 4.2kJ (kilojoules are metric units of energy measurement)

**How much energy do we need?**

**The amount of energy needed is affected by:** age, sex, height, body surface area, work done and state of health (illness can make energy needs higher or lower).

**Basal metabolic rate (BMR) or resting metabolism** is the energy required, when warm and resting, for the basic metabolic processes of life—heart beat, blood circulation, respiration, digestion, growth and tissue repair. It accounts for at least half of an individual's daily requirement.

### 3.3.1   Energy for work

The energy needed depends upon an individual's everyday activities, work done and recreational activities.

1 Everyday activities—washing, dressing, walking up and down stairs, walking.
2 Recreational activities—any game or sport, swimming.
3 Sedentary work—not very active e.g. office work, drivers.
4 Moderately active work—postmen, farm workers, plumbers, light engineering.
5 Very active work—builders, steelworkers, miners.

**Total metabolism**

Energy for basal metabolism + energy for work = total number kJ needed daily.

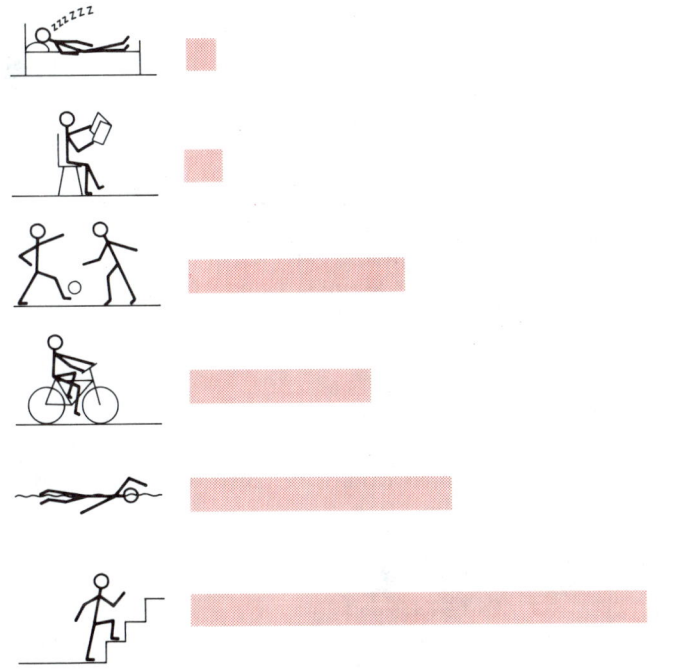

1cm on the bar graph represents 100 Kilocalories per hour.

**Fig 3.5** The daily energy needs for certain activities

|  |  | kJ | Cal |
|---|---|---|---|
| Child | 0–1 yr | 3 300 | 800 |
| Child | 3–4 yrs | 6 700 | 1 600 |
| Child | 7–9 yrs | 8 800 | 2 100 |
| Boy | 9–11 yrs | 10 500 | 2 500 |
| Girl | 9–11 yrs | 9 600 | 2 300 |
| Boy | 15–18 yrs | 12 600 | 3 000 |
| Girl | 15–18 yrs | 9 600 | 2 300 |
| Men | 18–65 yrs | 12 600 | 3 000 |
| Women | 18–55 yrs | 9 200 | 2 200 |
| Men | 65–75 yrs | 9 800 | 2 350 |
| Women | 55–75 yrs | 8 600 | 2 050 |
| Pregnancy |  | 10 000 | 2 400 |
| Lactation |  | 11 300 | 2 700 |

**Table 3.6** The daily energy needs for certain individuals

### 3.3.2   Other nutrients involved in the production of energy

**Iron**

Iron is needed for the production of haemoglobin in the red blood cells which carries oxygen from the lungs to body cells for the production of energy.

**Vitamin C**

This helps with the absorption of iron from eggs, cereals and green vegetables.

**Vitamin B complex**

These vitamins act as co-enzymes in the release of energy from foods.

**Phosphates**

Phosphates are involved in the storage and release of energy by muscle cells.

**Iodine**

Iodine is needed for the production of thyroxine by the thyroid gland which controls basal metabolic rate which in turn affects the amount of energy needed.

**Fuel reserves**

**Glucose** in excess of immediate energy needs is converted to **glycogen** and stored in the liver and muscle cells.

**Glycogen** which cannot be stored as such is converted to **fat** by the liver and stored as **subcutaneous fat**. Excess protein and fat also add to this store under the skin.

### 3.3.3   Energy balance

**Obesity**

If more energy units are consumed than are used, the excess will be stored as fat. An individual who is **20% overweight** is obese.

**Obesity can result** in earlier death, heart disease, toxaemia in pregnancy, varicose veins, high blood pressure, respiratory problems, diabetes and complications during surgical operations.

**Weight can be lost** by eating less and by increasing strenuous physical activities. A woman can expect to lose weight on a diet of 4200kJ (1000Cal) per day; a man on an intake of 6300kJ (1500Cal) per day.

**Weight loss**

If the energy value of food eaten is less than energy expended weight will be lost. The body must have energy to maintain the processes essential to life. If and when all fuel reserves are used up and if there is insufficient energy intake, the body will work less efficiently and the ultimate result will be death.

**Anorexia nervosa**

This is a complex condition where there is a dramatic weight loss and lack of desire to eat. The underlying cause, some emotional stress or strain, obsession about size and weight and perhaps a fear of growing up, will make a girl or boy diet drastically. Medical care and supervision is essential. When weight loss has ceased and weight is regained there may be some permanent damage to the body.

### 3.4   Digestion

Digestion breaks down larger nutrient molecules which cannot be absorbed, into smaller molecules which can be absorbed into the blood stream.

Double sugars
Complex sugars (starches) $\Big]$ → Simple sugars e.g. glucose
Lipids (fats & oils)          → Fatty acids and glycerol
Proteins                      → Amino acids

### 3.4.1   The digestive system

The **alimentary tract** is a continuous tube from the mouth to the anus. Different parts are adapted to deal with specific nutrients. The sight, smell and taste of food stimulates the production of **digestive enzymes**.

**Enzymes** are biological catalysts. They speed up chemical reactions.

1 Some work best in acid conditions others in alkaline.
2 Each enzyme has a specific function.

**Movement of food** through the tract is aided by lubricating **mucus** and by **peristalsis**, the regular contractions and relaxation of the gut which pushes food along.

Table 3.7 The main physical and chemical changes that take place during digestion

| Part of the alimentary tract | Physical changes | Chemical changes |
|---|---|---|
| **Mouth** | Mastication–teeth bite, tear and grind food. Tongue pushes food around the mouth and down to the oesophagus. Mucin moistens the food. | No change to proteins  No change to fats  Saliva is alkaline  *Salivary amylase* changes *cooked starch to maltose* |

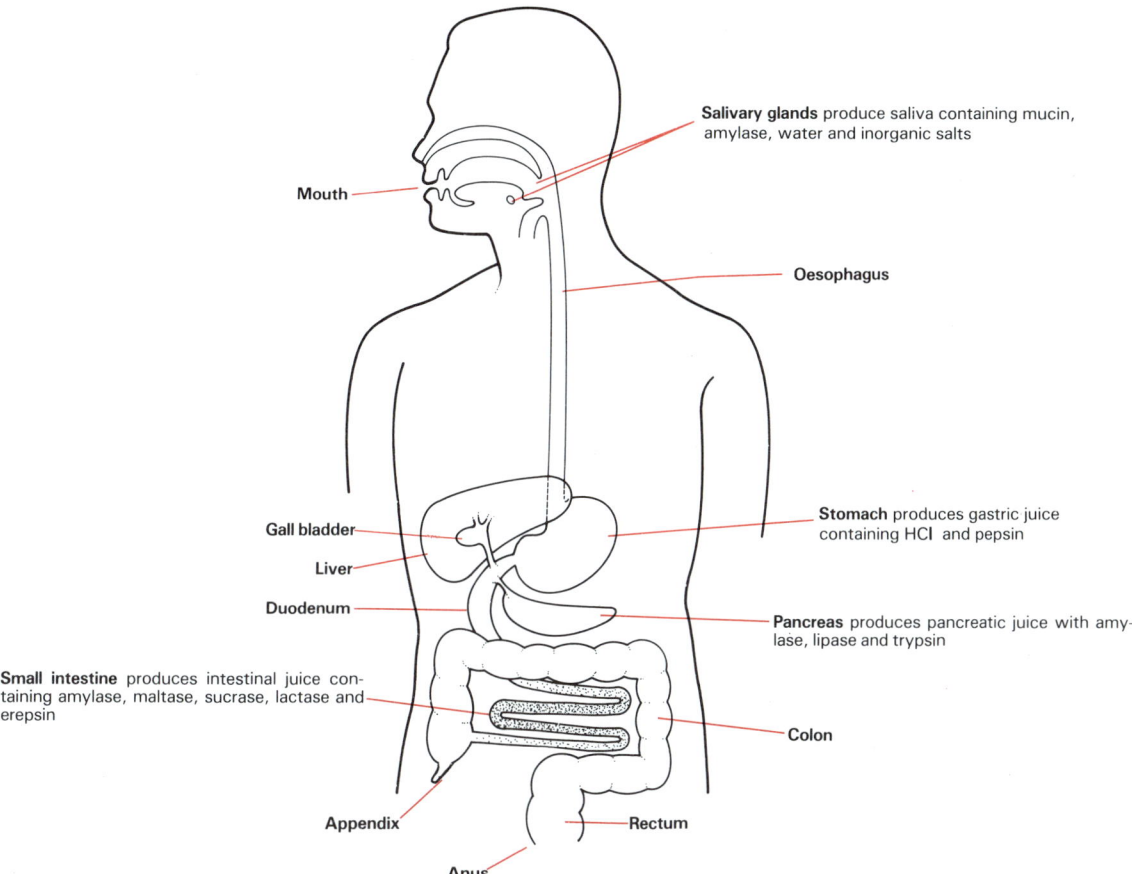

**Fig. 3.6** The digestive system

| Part of the alimentary tract | Physical changes | Chemical changes |
|---|---|---|
| **Oesophagus** | Peristalsis moves the food down to the stomach. | None |
| **Stomach** | The food is mixed with gastric juices by the muscular action of the stomach.<br>Food stays for 4-5 hours.<br>Food is broken down to form a semi-liquid mixture—chyme. | Gastric juice contains *HCl* and *pepsin*.<br>*Rennin* is only produced in the stomach of a baby. Its production ceases between the ages of six and nine months.<br>*HCl* destroys bacteria and stops the action of salivary amylase.<br>*Pepsin* changes *proteins* to *peptones* (smaller chains of amino acids).<br>No change to starch or sugar<br>No change to fats<br>The presence of fats can delay the action of pepsin because the enzyme cannot reach the proteins easily. |
| **Duodenum** | *Bile salts emulsify fats* to produce a larger surface area for the action of *lipase.* | Alkaline salt in bile neutralises the acid from the stomach.<br>*Lipase* from the pancreas splits *fats* to *fatty acids and glycerol.*<br>*Trypsin* from the pancreas breaks down *proteins* to *peptones.*<br>*Amylase* from the pancreas breaks down *starch* to *maltose.* |
| **Small intestine** | Absorption of simple sugars, amino acids, vitamins and minerals into blood capillaries of the villi.<br>Absorption of fatty droplets into the lacteals of the villi. | Enzymes from the intestinal juice act as follows:<br>*Erepsin* breaks down *peptones* to *amino acids.*<br>*Lipase* continues to split *fats* to *fatty acid and glycerol*<br>*Maltase* changes *maltose* to *glucose*<br>*Invertase* (sucrase) changes *sucrose* to *glucose*<br>*Lactase* changes *lactose* to *glucose and galactose* |

**Absorption**

The small intestine has its surface increased by thousands of finger-like projections called **villi**. Each villus has a single celled wall through which nutrients can pass. The nutrients **absorbed into the blood capillaries** are taken to the **liver** and then to all parts of the body. The **lacteals** are linked to the lymphatic system which carries fatty acids and glycerol around the body until they pass into the blood as insoluble fat, which is then made soluble in the liver. Fat soluble vitamins are absorbed with the fatty acids and glycerol.

**In the colon** water is absorbed from the contents of the colon and food residues become more solid. If too much water is absorbed back into the blood the stools become hard and constipation results. The presence of dietary fibre reduces the water absorbed. It retains the water and bulks up the contents of the colon stimulating peristalsis and a more efficient egestion of the faeces.

**Vitamin K** is synthesised by the bacteria found in the bowel.

**NB** There is a common misconception that fats are difficult to digest. The digestive system of a healthy person has no trouble digesting fats. Because they are not digested until they reach the duodenum their presence can *slow down* digestion in the stomach so the 'full, satisfied feel' is felt for longer.

# 4   Commodities

## 4.1   Ingredients used in family meals

### 4.1.1   Cereals

Cereals are the seeds or grains of cultivated grasses and are used to produce a wide variety of foods. They provide a wide range of nutrients and many cereal foods are also fortified.

**Cereals and their products**

**Wheat**  Flour, bread, semolina, pasta, breakfast cereals, e.g. Puffed Wheat

**Maize**  Cornflour, custard powder, blancmange powder, cornflakes, corn on the cob

**Rice**  Brown rice, polished rice, long grain and short grain rice, ground rice, rice flour, rice flakes, Rice Krispies

**Oats**  Rolled oats, coarse, medium and fine oatmeal

**Barley**  Pearl barley, barley flour, barley water, brewing

**Rye**  Rye bread, crispbreads, rye flour

**Structure and nutritional value**

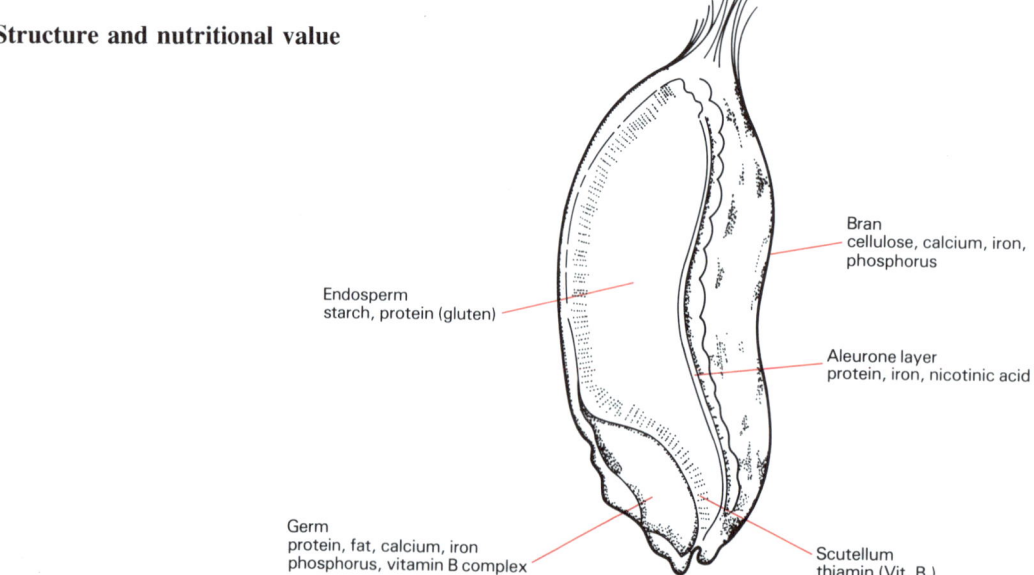

**Fig. 4.1**  A longitudinal section of a whole wheat grain

The diagram shown in Fig. 4.1 represents a whole wheat grain and is typical of all cereals. When the **bran** and **germ** are removed during milling, the **nutrients** they contain **are** also **lost**.

When we are advised to 'Eat more cereals' it is because they are a better source of energy than refined sugar and fats. They provide more micro-nutrients and dietary fibre, particularly if the **whole grain** is processed in the product.

**Wheat**

**The milling process** and its products

**1 Cleaning** to remove small stones, dust and chaff.

**2 Blending** Different grain varieties are blended to produce flours of different strengths.

**3 Grinding** Grains are crushed between grooved rollers to release the endosperm. Wholewheat flour is thus produced.

**4 Sieving** to remove the bran and germ.

**5 Grinding** The endosperm, now called **semolina**, is further crushed to produce a fine powder called flour.

**6 Fortification** Calcium carbonate, iron, thiamin and nicotinic acid are **added** to the flour **to replace** the nutrients lost with the germ and bran.

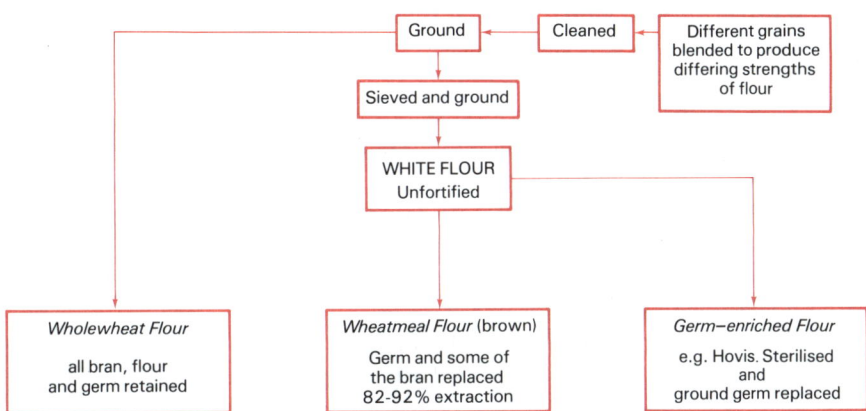

**Fig. 4.2** Types of flour and how they are produced

**Types of flour**

**1** Stone ground–100% of the grain is crushed between two round mill stones

**2** Soft Flour–from wheat, mostly grown in this country, with a low gluten content.

**3** High ratio–A very soft, fine, white flour used in packet cake mixes, but not widely available in this country.

**4** Medium strength household–Flour made from a mixture of strong and weak wheats

**(a)** plain white flour

**(b)** self-raising flour which has a raising agent added

**5** Strong Flour–made from hard wheat with a high gluten content. This wheat is mostly grown in Canada.

**Table 4.1** Flours sold for domestic use

| Type of flour | Use |
| --- | --- |
| Strong Plain Flour | Bread, other yeast mixtures, batters, flaky pastry, rough puff pastry, choux pastry |
| Plain White Flour (medium strength) | Cakes, short pastries, biscuits, scones, sauces |
| *Soft Wheat Sponge Flour (SR) | Whisked sponges, creamed cake mixtures |
| Self-raising Flour (medium strength) | Plain cake mixtures, scones |
| Wholewheat Plain | Scones, cakes, bread, short pastries, biscuits |
| Wheatmeal Plain (Brown) | Scones, cakes, bread, short pastries, biscuits |
| Wholemeal or Wheatmeal (SR) | Scones, cakes |
| *Granary Flour | Granary bread, pastry, scones |

*These two flours have just appeared in some supermarkets. They are produced by one of the well known manufacturers.

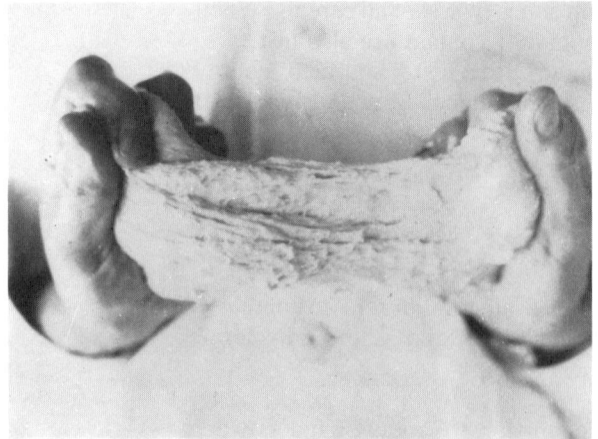

**Fig. 4.3** Dough low in gluten

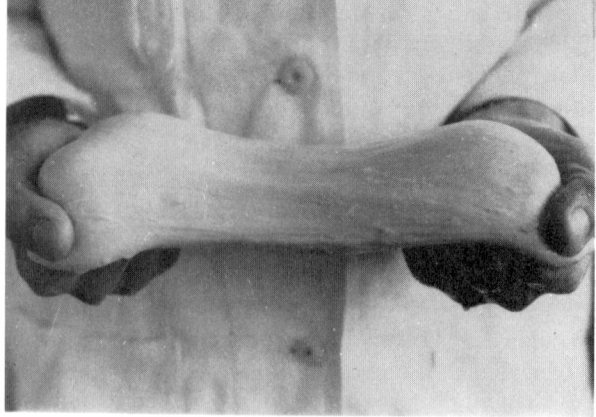

**Fig. 4.4** Dough high in gluten

**The action of gluten** When wheat flour is worked with water the proteins, **gliadin** and **glutenin** form an elastic substance called **gluten**. Gluten traps bubbles of gas (air, carbon dioxide and water vapour) in the mixture. Heat causes these gases to expand, become lighter and rise so stretching the gluten. This, being protein, sets in the heat of the oven. It is the gluten which gives structure to bread and other baked starched mixtures (see Figs. 4.3 and 4.4).

**Softening white flour using cornflour** Cornflour contains no gluten. If added to white flour it reduces the proportion of gluten in the flour making it softer and suitable for cakes and biscuits. This gives a lighter result with a finer crumb structure.

**Extracting and comparing the amounts of gluten in different flours**
1 Take 50g of (a) Strong flour, (b) Soft flour and (c) Wholewheat flour
2 Mix each to a stiff dough with cold water
3 Soak each ball of dough in cold water for 15 minutes
4 Place each ball in a small piece of muslin and knead under a running cold tap until all the milky fluid has been removed
5 Place on a greased baking sheet, comparing the three balls for weight and elasticity
6 Bake for 20 minutes at 250°C

**Pasta**

Pasta is made from the middlings (**semolina**) of hard wheat. The semolina is made into a **paste** with water or sometimes with egg. The paste is then **moulded** or **extruded** to produce assorted shapes. Pasta is cooked to accompany dishes made with meat, milk, cheese, tomatoes.

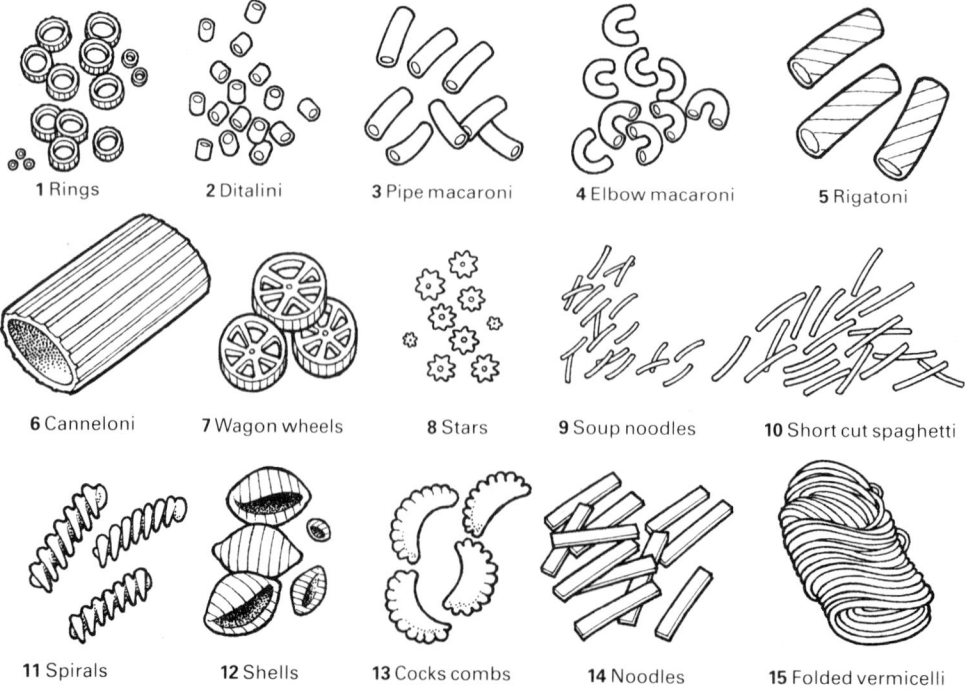

**1** Rings    **2** Ditalini    **3** Pipe macaroni    **4** Elbow macaroni    **5** Rigatoni

**6** Canneloni    **7** Wagon wheels    **8** Stars    **9** Soup noodles    **10** Short cut spaghetti

**11** Spirals    **12** Shells    **13** Cocks combs    **14** Noodles    **15** Folded vermicelli

**Fig. 4.5** Different types of pasta

**How to cook pasta**
 1 Boil a large saucepan of water
 2 Add salt and then the pasta (allow 50g per person)
 3 Stir in one tablespoon of oil–prevents strands sticking together
 4 Cook for the time stated on the packet with the lid off and take care because the pan contents quickly bubble up and boil over. When cooked, pasta should be firm with a centre which is neither hard nor mushy.
 5 Drain
 6 Melt a little butter in the pan
 7 Return the pasta to the pan and shake with a little pepper or nutmeg
**NB** Pasta has the nutritional value of the endosperm plus any nutrients that are added during manufacture. When cooked it has a high percentage of water. Pasta made from wholewheat is now available.

**Maize**

Maize is eaten as a vegetable (corn on the cob) or made into corn meal. Processing maize produces **cornflour** and **cornflakes**.

**Nutritional value of cornflour**
 1 Made from the crushed endosperm of the maize grain
 2 Approximately 100% starch
 3 No gluten

**Uses of cornflour**
 1 To soften white flour
 2 In the making of sauces when it is the thickening agent
 3 To produce a clear glaze to use on a fruit flan

**Gelatinization of starch** occurs when starch granules **absorb water** and swell when heated resulting in a **thickening** effect on the liquid.
 Starch granules have been confused with the cellulose walls of the cells of the plant in which they are found, e.g. starch granules within potato cells. The starch granules themselves do not have a cellulose covering so they cannot burst.
 1 Cornflour gelatinizes more readily than wheatflour
 2 The presence of sugar slows down gelatinization
 3 Overheating can cause the gelatinization of starch to convert to dextrose which makes the sauce go runny

**Rice, oats, barley, wheat and rye**

**Table 4.2** A comparison of the nutritonal value of rice, oats, barley, wheat and rye

|  | *Brown rice* | *Polished rice* | *Oats* | *Barley* | *Rye* | *Whole wheat* |
|---|---|---|---|---|---|---|
| **Fibre** | √ | Very little | √ | √ | √ | √ |
| **Starch** | √ | √ | √ | √ | √ | √ |
| **Protein** | √ | Very little | √ | Very little No gluten | √ | √ |
| **Fat** | √ | Very little | √ | Very little | Very little | √ |
| **Calcium** | √ | Very little | √ | Very little | Very little | √ |
| **Iron** | √ | Very little | √ | Very little | Very little | √ |
| **B vitamins** | √ | Most lost in polishing | √ | Very little | Very little | √ |

**Notes on nutritional value**

 1 The presence of phytic acid in the fibre of grains can inhibit the absorption of calcium and iron by the body.
 2 In countries where polished rice is the main staple food the deficiency disease Beri beri, due to lack of Vitamin $B_1$, occurs.
 3 In a few places the polished rice may be fortified. Polished rice supplies the least micronutrients of all the cereals.

**Cooking rice**

 **1 Savoury rice using long grain rice**
 **(a)** Allow up to 50g (2oz) rice per person
 **(b)** Pick over rice to remove bits other than rice grain
 **(c)** Wash in several bowls of cold water to remove starch
 **(d)** Rinse until water is clear

*Method I*

600ml (1pt) water to 200g (8oz) rice + 5ml salt

Put the water and rice into a saucepan. Add salt and bring to the boil. Stir.

Cover the pan tightly with a lid.

Simmer for 15 minutes to allow the water to be absorbed.

Spoon rice into a hot serving dish.

Separate grains with a fork.

*Method II*

Add the rice to large pan of boiling, salted water. Bring back to the boil.

Boil rapidly, uncovered, for 12 minutes. The rice should now be tender.

Drain, Rinse with hot water. Drain.

Serve as for method I.

**NB** Brown rice takes longer to cook, approximately 40 minutes

**2  Short or round grain rice used for desserts**

To serve four people use:

**(a)** 50g (2oz) round grain rice;
**(b)** 2 level tablespoons caster sugar;
**(c)** 600ml (1pt) milk;
**(d)** 5ml vanilla essence;
**(e)** a little grated nutmeg.

*Method I*

Put rice, sugar and milk into a heavy based pan. Cook over a low heat until simmering point is reached. Cover and simmer for 30 minutes. Add essence.

Place in hot serving dishes and sprinkle with a little nutmeg.

Can also be served cold.

*Method II*

Put all the ingredients into a buttered ovenproof dish (capacity 900ml/1½pt).

Bake at 150°C/300°F/mark 2 for two hours. Stir after 30 minutes.

### Breakfast cereals

These cereals are quick and easy to prepare and serve. There is a wide variety to choose from. Allow 30g-50g per person.

They are low in fat and contain many other nutrients. Many are fortified with micro-nutrients which were present in the whole grain but were removed in the processing of the cereal. Serving with milk improves their food value. Sprinkling with sugar is not necessary and those already coated with sugar are not the best nutritional buy. The greater use of bran has provided a range of cereal products with a high fibre content.

### Starchy foods which are not cereals

**Arrowroot** is a fine starch powder obtained from the underground stem (rhizome) of the West Indian **maranta** plant. It **gelatinizes** and **thickens** with heat and moisture.

It is used to make a glaze for flans (1 heaped 5ml spoon to 125ml fruit juice), for making fruit sauces to serve with puddings, arrowroot biscuits, and also as a medicine to calm the stomach and reduce vomiting.

**Sago** comes from the pith of the **sago palm.** The pith is pulped, strained, dried, and sieved to produce grains of starch which are roasted and graded large, medium or small.

It is used to make a milk pudding.

**Tapioca** is made from the underground stem of the tropical **cassava** plant. The rhizomes are washed, pulped and boiled down to a thick fluid. The poisonous part of the juice is washed out and the residue dried and roasted.

It is used to make milk puddings.

### The storage of cereals

1  Store cereals in a dry place. Dampness will cause moulds to develop.

2  Use containers with tightly fitting lids. Wash these frequently.

3  Flour is best stored in its bag in the container.

4  Plain flour can be stored up to 6 months.

5  SR flour can be stored for about 3 months.

6  Wholewheat flour and whole cereal flour can be stored for up to 2 months. These contain fat which can become rancid because of the oxidation of the fat they contain.

7  Use store items in rotation.

## 4.1.2  Fats and oils

### Their place in the diet

1  Doctors recommend that (a) we obtain not more than 30 to 35% of our energy from fats.

(b) we should increase the amount of polyunsaturated fats in our diet and eat less saturated animal fats. Hence the advice 'Eat **Less** Fat'.

**2** Fat is needed for the growth of body cells, especially those fats which contain the essential fatty acid **linoleic acid**.

**3** Some fats contain the fat-soluble vitamins A, D and E.

**4** Too much fat in the diet can cause obesity, a risk factor where heart disease is concerned.

**5** It has been demonstrated that the more **cholesterol** in the blood the greater the risk of heart disease. A diet rich in saturated fats will increase the natural blood cholesterol levels. Polyunsaturated fats help to reduce the level of cholesterol in the blood.

**6** Fats **lubricate** food and make it easier to eat. Fats make food more palatable.

**7** Fats have a high **satiety value.** Their presence in the stomach slows down digestion to give a full feeling for longer.

## Butter

**Manufacture** It takes the cream from 10 litres (20 pints) of milk to make 500g (1lb) of butter. The milk undergoes laboratory checks before the cream is separated from the milk.

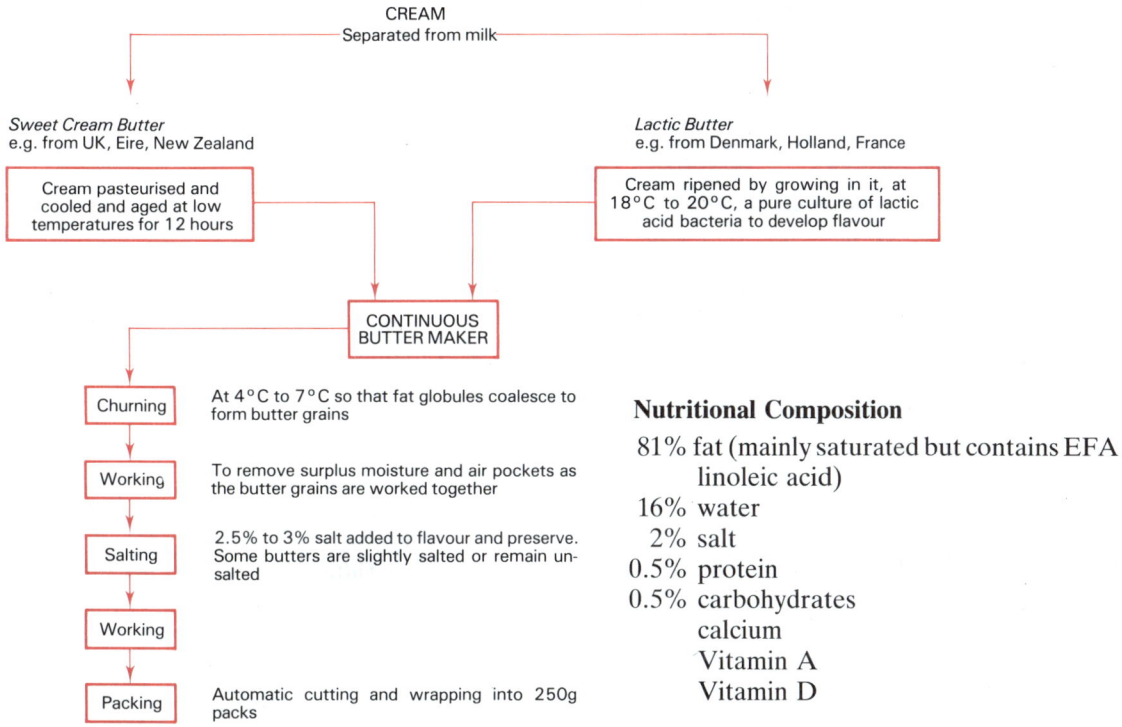

**Fig. 4.6** Flow diagram to show how butter is made

## Lard

**1** This is prepared by melting pig's fat. It is almost 100% fat.

**2** It contains mainly saturated fatty acids.

**3** Lard is a good shortening agent with an acceptable white colour and bland flavour.

**4** Lard has poor creaming properties.

## Dripping

**1** Dripping is the fat collected from meat when it is cooked.

**2** Meat fat can be rendered to extract the dripping which is then strained and cooled.

**3** Dripping is high in saturated fatty acids.

## Suet

**1** Suet is the hard fat that comes from around the kidneys of beef cattle, its processing is shown in Figure 4.7.

**2** It is very hard with a high melting point.

**3** Suet has a high proportion of saturated fatty acids but the EFA linoleic acid is present.

**4** Suet is used for suet pastry, Christmas puddings, mincemeat and stuffings.

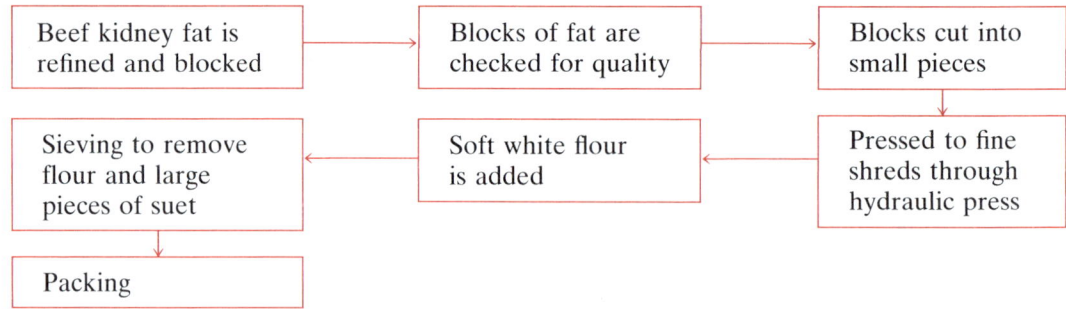

```
┌──────────────────┐      ┌──────────────────┐      ┌──────────────────┐
│ Beef kidney fat is│ ──▶ │ Blocks of fat are │ ──▶ │ Blocks cut into   │
│ refined and blocked│     │ checked for quality│     │ small pieces      │
└──────────────────┘      └──────────────────┘      └──────────────────┘
                                                              │
                                                              ▼
┌──────────────────┐      ┌──────────────────┐      ┌──────────────────┐
│ Sieving to remove │ ◀── │ Soft white flour  │ ◀── │ Pressed to fine   │
│ flour and large   │     │ is added          │     │ shreds through    │
│ pieces of suet    │     │                   │     │ hydraulic press   │
└──────────────────┘      └──────────────────┘      └──────────────────┘
         │
         ▼
┌──────────────────┐
│ Packing          │
└──────────────────┘
```

**Fig. 4.7** Flow diagram to show how suet is produced

## Margarine

Margarine was first made in the mid-nineteenth century as a butter substitute.

**Nutritional composition**

80% oils and fats  } The law states that
16% water          } margarine must con-
                     tain these

Vitamin A       }
Vitamin D       }
salt            }
vegetable colouring } Additives
flavouring      }
emulsifiers     }

**Manufacture**

*Ingredients:*
soya bean oil
sunflower seed oil
rapeseed oil
palm oil
coconut oil
corn oil
safflower oil
beef fat
fish oils (herrings, pilchards, sardines)
whey (liquid left after curds removed to make cheese)
vegetable colouring–annotto and beta carotene

**Fig. 4.8** Different types of margarine

Oils are selected and blended according to the margarine being made, availability and market price. One oil can be substituted for another except when manufacturing a sunflower margarine.

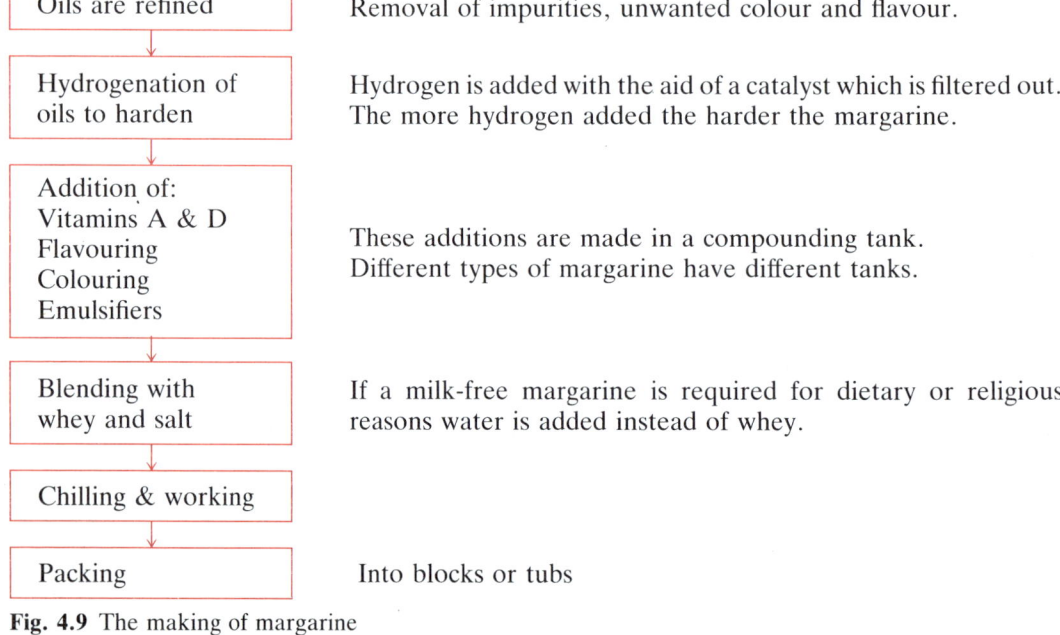

| | |
|---|---|
| Oils are refined | Removal of impurities, unwanted colour and flavour. |
| Hydrogenation of oils to harden | Hydrogen is added with the aid of a catalyst which is filtered out. The more hydrogen added the harder the margarine. |
| Addition of: Vitamins A & D Flavouring Colouring Emulsifiers | These additions are made in a compounding tank. Different types of margarine have different tanks. |
| Blending with whey and salt | If a milk-free margarine is required for dietary or religious reasons water is added instead of whey. |
| Chilling & working | |
| Packing | Into blocks or tubs |

**Fig. 4.9** The making of margarine

**Types of margarine**
 1 Margarine in tubs:
**(a)** Is easier to spread and cream.
**(b)** Contains a high proportion of saturated fatty acids unless the label clearly states that they are high in polyunsaturates.
**(c)** Can be used straight from the refrigerator.
**(d)** Is made from blended animal and vegetable oils unless labelled 100% vegetable oils.
**(e)** Sunflower seed oil is used in margarines labelled high in polyunsaturates. These have 54% polyunsaturated fatty acids and are used in cholesterol-lowering diets.

 2 Packet margarine:
**(a)** Is a harder margarine with a higher proportion of animal and fish oils.
**(b)** Has a high saturated fatty acid content.
**(c)** The hardest blocks are suitable for pastries, the softer blocks for spreading and creaming.
**(d)** Kosher margarines are made from vegetable oils with no whey added.

**Low fat spreads**

**Outline** contains only 40% fat. Because it has approximately 58% water it cannot be described as a margarine.

**Gold** is made from buttermilk.

Both of these fats have half the energy value of butter or margaine. They are not suitable for normal cooking purposes.

**White cooking fats**

These are alternatives to lard. They are 100% fat.
 1 They are made in a similar way to margarine but without the addition of colouring and vitamins.
 2 They have a bland flavour.
 3 Inert gases may be whipped in during manufacture. Some have additives to prevent foaming when used for frying.
 4 The latest additions to this range of white cooking fats are made from sunflower seed oil and these, like the margarines made from sunflower oil, are high in polyunsaturated fatty acids.

**Cooking oils**

The best oils for frying have a **high smoking point** and are high in polyunsaturated fatty acids, e.g. sunflower seed oil, corn oil, safflower oil, soya bean oil, groundnut oil, olive oil.
    Blended vegetable oils contain more saturated fatty acids.
    Solid cooking oils are now available for people who prefer a solid fat for frying. They contain a higher proportion of saturated fatty acids.

**The storage of fats and oils**

 1 Store in a cool place away from light and air.
 2 Exposure to air causes rancidity because oxidation can take place.
 3 The law forbids the addition of anti-oxidants to butter. This will keep for two weeks in a cool place but for several weeks in the refrigerator.
 4 Margarines will keep for 4 weeks in a cool place but for much longer if refrigerated. Tub margarines can be used straight from the refrigerator.
 5 Cooking fats keep for a long time at a low temperature, lard for up to six months if refrigerated.
 6 Oils should be kept in a cool, dark place but not in the refrigerator.
 7 After use for frying, fats and oils should be cooled and strained before storing.

**Which fat for which purpose?**

There is a vast range of fats and oils from which to choose. Their different qualities make each suitable for different tasks. An individual's personal preference can also be satisfied.
    Cost is a factor to consider. Generally the harder the margarine the lower the price. Margarines high in polyunsaturates tend to be more expensive.
    The following table shows a range of basic cooking methods and indicates the fats best suited for each method.

**Table 4.3** Fats suited to different cooking methods

| | Butter | Lard | Suet | Dripping | Slab margarine | Tub margarine | Lowfat spreads | White cooking fats | Cooking oils | Solid cooking oils |
|---|---|---|---|---|---|---|---|---|---|---|
| Spreading | √ | | | | √ | √ | √ | | | |
| Scones | √ | | | | √ | √ | | | | |
| Rubbed in method | √ | √ | | | √ | | | √ | | |
| Creaming method | √ | | | | √ | √ | | | | |
| Melted method | √ | | | | √ | | | √ | | |
| *Pastries* | | | | | | | | | | |
| Shortcrust | √ | √ | | | √ | | | √ | | |
| Rough puff | √ | √ | | | √ | | | √ | | |
| Flaky | √ | √ | | | √ | | | √ | | |
| Puff | √ | | | | | | | | | |
| Suet crust | | | √ | | | | | | | |
| Choux | √ | | | | √ | √ | | | | |
| Biscuits | √ | | | | √ | √ | | √ | | |
| All-in-one mixtures | | | | | | √ | | | | |
| Glazes | √ | | | | √ | √ | √ | | | |
| Savoury butters | √ | | | | √ | √ | √ | | | |
| Mincemeat | | | √ | | | | | | | |
| Stuffings | | | √ | | | | | | | |
| Deep fat frying | | | | √ | | | | | √ | √ |
| Shallow frying | | √ | | √ | | | | | √ | √ |
| To sauté | √ | | | | √ | | | | √ | √ |
| Salad dressings | | | | | | | | | √ | |
| Mayonnaise | | | | | | | | | √ | |

## 4.1.3   Sugar and other sweeteners

### The place of sugar in the diet

**1** Sugar provides the body with energy. 1g provides 16kJ (3.75kilocalories).

**2** Refined sugar is **not an essential** constituent of the diet because the body converts the starches we eat to simple sugars and sugars occur naturally in fruits and vegetables.

**3** On average we consume 750g of sucrose per head per week.

**4** If too many foods rich in refined sugar are eaten the result is too great an intake of energy which can result in obesity with its associated health problems.

**5** When sugar passes in large quantities into the blood stream it can be difficult for the pancreas to produce sufficient insulin to cope. There is a risk of diabetes.

**6** Sugar on the teeth leads to tooth decay. The bacteria in the plaque feed on the sugar and produce acids which attack tooth enamel.

**7** Glucose is rapidly absorbed–no digestion needed. Used by doctors to feed intravenously and by athletes for instant energy.

**8** Refined sugar contains no micro-nutrients. It satisfies hunger and can reduce appetite for other foods which do contain other nutrients.

**9** We should eat **LESS** sugar.

### Types of refined sugar and their uses

**Granulated sugar** is the cheapest sugar with a large crystal. It is used for general sweetening, in sweet scones and rubbed-in cake mixtures.

**Caster sugar** is made up of fine crystals which dissolve quickly.
  **1** It creams easily with fats when using the creaming method of cake making.
  **2** It is used for sweetening fruit, for dusting cakes and biscuits and in making meringues.

**Icing sugar** is granulated sugar pulverized to very fine particles. To prevent lumping a little calcium phosphate is added. It is used for all types of icing.

**Lump sugar**  Granulated sugar and sugar syrup are moulded, excess syrup is spun off and the cubes dried.
  **1** It takes longer to dissolve.
  **2** Coarsely crushed lump sugar can be sprinkled on the surface of cakes and tea breads before cooking.
  **3** Sometimes lump sugar is used for lemon curd when it is utilized first to rub zest from the lemons.

**Preserving sugar** dissolves more readily than granulated sugar.
  **1** It does not sink to the bottom of the preserving pan therefore there is less chance of sugar burning.

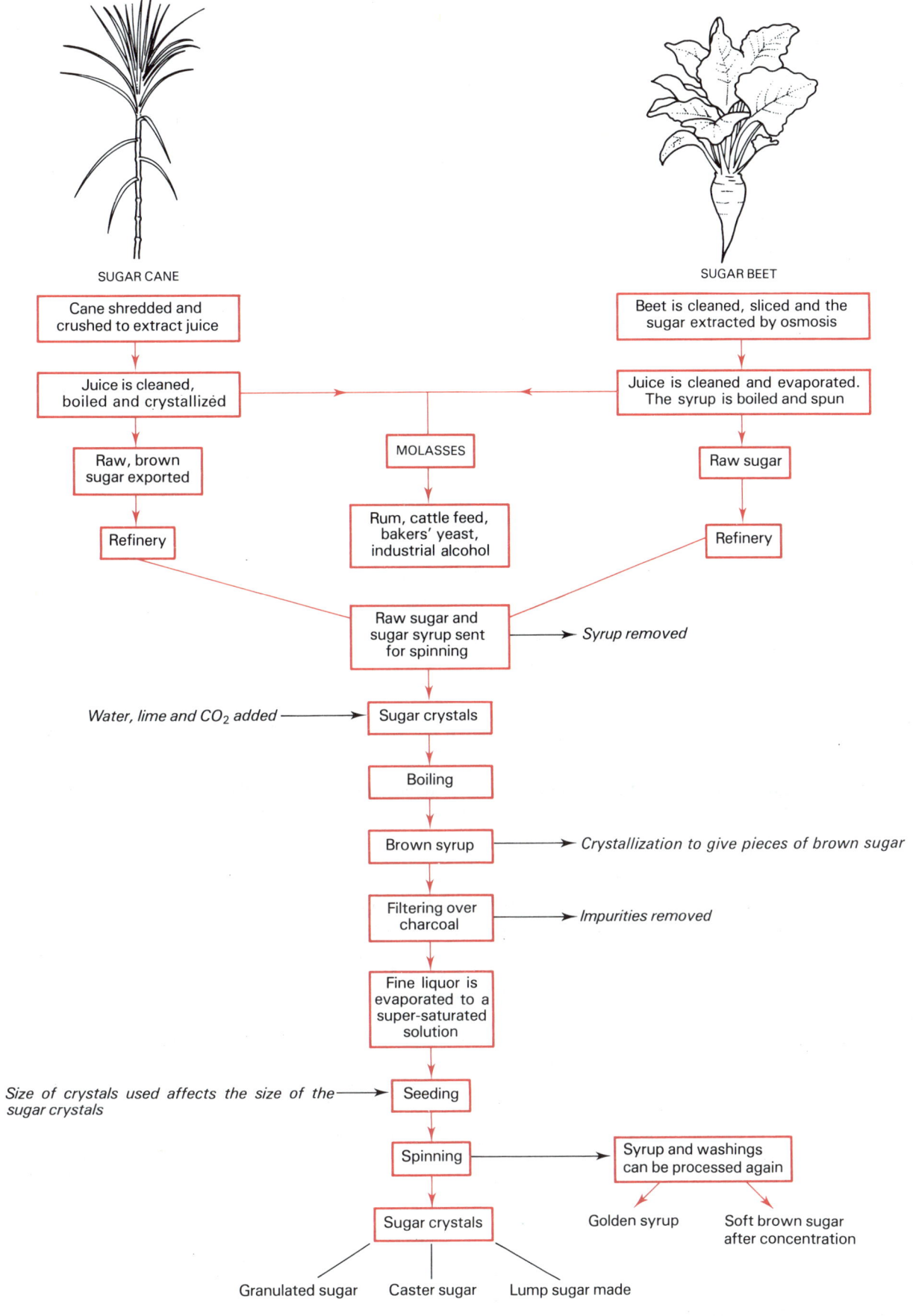

**Fig. 4.10** The manufacture of sugar

**2** Less froth is produced with its use.

**Soft brown sugars** are only partly refined. They are made from the syrup residues when refining white sugar. Can be called 'Pieces' or 'Foot' sugars. They are available in light or dark colour. They are used in fruit cakes, gingerbreads, flapjacks, gingernuts and chutneys.

**Barbados sugar** is a crystalized brown sugar produced by evaporation. It contains minute traces of natural salts. It is made from sugar cane.

**Demerara sugar** True demerara sugar is made from raw cane sugar from which only coarse impurities have been removed. The crystals are coarse and brown. It is used to sweeten coffee, in cakes such as flapjack and in toffee making.

**NB ALL of these sugars are approximately 100% sucrose**

**Sucrose** is a double sugar or disaccharide. When used in making jams it is changed by the acid present into *invert sugar* which prevents sucrose from crystallizing in the jam. Invert sugar occurs naturally in honey, it is a mixture of glucose and fructose.

### Other sugars

#### Monosaccharides

**1** *Glucose* is found in grapes, honey and onion. During digestion it is obtained from starch and double sugars by carbohydrate hydrolysis. Confectioners' glucose or liquid glucose is made commercially by hydrolising maize starch with dilute hydrochloric acid.
**(a)** Glucose is rapidly absorbed.
**(b)** Liquid glucose is used to make icings, sweets, other confectionery and jams.
**2** *Fructose* is the sweetest sugar and is found in sweet fruits and honey. During digestion it is obtained with glucose when sucrose is hydrolysed.

#### Disaccharides

**1** *Maltose* is obtained from starch by the action of the enzyme diastase. During digestion maltase changes maltose to glucose.
**2** *Lactose* is the least sweet of all sugars. It is found in milk. The enzyme lactase changes lactose to glucose and galactose.

### Other sweeteners

Until September 1983 the only artificial, intense sweetening agent permitted in the UK was saccharine which is 550 times as sweet as sugar.

**Saccharine** has no energy value. Users can detect a bitter/metallic flavour in the mouth after use. Saccharine is the main constituent of branded sweeteners such as 'Sweetex', 'Hermesetas' and 'Sucron'.

The Food Additives and Contaminants Committee has now included six new sweeteners in the 'allowed' list.

One of these new sweeteners is **aspartame** with the brand name 'Nutrasweet'. 'Canderol', a new table top sweetener containing 'Nutrasweet', is now available. One tablet is equal to one teaspoon of sugar. Aspartame is a dipeptide and like all proteins has a calorific value of 17kJ (4 kilocalories) per gram. It is approximately 200 times as sweet as sugar. There is no bitter aftertaste. Its use is now approved in twenty-five countries and it is used in products such as breakfast cereals, desserts, toppings, soft drinks.

Manufacturers of foods intended for babies and young children will not be allowed to use sweeteners in these products.

Aspartame should not be used by people with phenylketonuria. Doctors will be asked to tell patients who suffer from this condition that they must not use products containing this sweetener. One in twelve thousand infants is unable to metabolise phenylalamine. They lack the enzyme which deals with this amino acid which can then build up in the body, damaging brain cells and adversely affecting development. A routine blood test on every new baby identifies an individual with this deficiency. Special drugs and foods are prescribed.

### 4.1.4  Milk

#### Nutritional composition

| | | |
|---|---|---|
| Protein (3.4%) | Calcium | Vitamin $B_{12}$ |
| Fat (3.8%) | Phosphorus | Nicotinic acid |
| Lactose (4.6%) | Vitamin A | Vitamin D (summer milk) |
| Water (87.5%) | Vitamin $B_2$ (riboflavin) | |

**Protein** in milk has a high biological value. Caseinogen, lactalbumin and lactoglobulin.

**Fat** in milk is finely emulsified and is easily digested. Milk contains saturated fatty acids.

**Sugar** occurs as lactose or milk sugar in small amounts. Lactose is the least sweet of the sugars.

**Vitamin A** is found more in summer milk because cows eat green grass—more carotene.

**Vitamin B$_2$ Riboflavin** Milk is an excellent source.

**Vitamin D** is found more in summer milk because the sunlight on cow's skin produces the vitamin.

**Vitamin C** in milk is mostly lost by heat treatments and when milk is stored, by oxidation. Milk is not an important source of this vitamin.

**Calcium** Milk is a most important source of this mineral.

**Water** makes up approximately 87% of the content of milk.

### Milk and health

Milk is nature's food for young mammals and is an almost perfect food. Some people are allergic to cow's milk, this is usually discovered in babyhood.

At one time diseases such as bovine *tuberculosis* and *brucellosis* could infect man by way of milk. In UK, dairy herds are Tuberculin Tested and are unlikely to transmit these bacteria. In 1972 compulsory tests for brucellosis began in some areas and have gradually been extended to the whole country.

Cows suffering from *mastitis* are treated with anti-biotics. These drugs pass into the milk. Milk contaminated in this way cannot be sold because the presence of anti-biotics could mean that those prescribed by doctors would become less effective. The milk is discarded.

**Untreated milk** is produced and bottled under licence by farmers. It is not subjected to any heat treatments. Ordinary milk is given a green top, that from Jersey, Guernsey or South Devon breeds of cow a green and gold top.

### Souring

Untreated milk will sour naturally. Lactic acid bacteria in the milk convert lactose to lactic acid. This acid precipitates a solid or **curd** in a liquid called the **whey**. The curd consists of proteins, fats, fat-soluble vitamins and minerals; the whey consists of water, lactose, water-soluble vitamins and minerals with very little protein. The curd can be drained and flavoured to make cottage cheese.

Milk soured in this way can be used to replace half of the acid cream of tartar when it is being used with bicarbonate of soda to make scones.

### Heat treatments

95% of all milk in the UK is heat treated to:
  1 Remove any harmful bacteria.     2 Improve the keeping qualities of the milk.

**Table 4.4** A comparison of the different types of whole milk available

| Type of milk | Heat treatment | The effect of heat treatment upon: | | |
| --- | --- | --- | --- | --- |
| | | (i) *micro-organisms* | (ii) *nutrients* | (iii) *flavour* |
| **1 Pasteurised** Ordinary Silver top Min. 3% fat Visible cream line | Pasteurized Heated at 72° C for 15 seconds Cooled rapidly to not more than 10°C | Harmful bacteria destroyed | *Vitamin B lost* less than 10% *Vitamin C lost* 20% to 50% | Very little change |
| Homogenized Red top No cream line | Milk forced through fine apertures to break down fat globules, which remain evenly distributed in milk, which is then pasteurized | Harmful bacteria destroyed | Vitamin loss as above Small fat droplets said to be easier to digest | Richer and creamier flavour |
| Channel Island Gold top Min. 4% fat Guernsey, Jersey, S. Devon cows | Pasteurized as for silver top milk | Harmful bacteria destroyed | Vitamin loss as above | Very rich, creamy taste |

| *Type of milk* | *Heat treatment* | *The effect of heat treatment upon:* | | |
| --- | --- | --- | --- | --- |
| | | *(i) micro-organisms* | *(ii) nutrients* | *(iii) flavour* |
| **2 Longer lasting** Sterilized Blue or metal crown cap Long necked bottles No cream line | Milk homogenized, bottled, sealed Heated above 100°C for 20-30 mins. | All bacteria destroyed | *Vitamin B$_1$ lost* 30% to 50% *Vitamin B$_{12}$ lost* 90% *Vitamin C lost* 50% to 60% | A big flavour change Heat has made lactose caramelize |
| **UHT** Ultra heat treated Foil lined containers No cream line Full cream or semi-skimmed or skimmed | Milk homogenized Heated to not less than 132°C for 1 second Rapidly cooled Packed under sterile conditions | All bacteria destroyed | Less vitamin loss than sterilized *Vitamin C lost* 20% to 50% *Vitamin B$_1$ lost* 10% *Vitamin B$_{12}$ lost* 10% | Slight flavour change Less noticeable with skimmed or semi-skimmed UHT milks |

**Skimmed milks**

**Table 4.5** A comparison of two types of skimmed milk

| | *Heat treatment* | *Nutritional value* | *Use* |
| --- | --- | --- | --- |
| **Skimmed milk** | *Pasteurization*–sold in waxed cartons, bottles, polythene containers *UHT*–sold in aseptic cartons | Most fat removed leaving 0.3% butterfat Vitamins A & D are removed with fat | Any dish using milk Good for low fat diets and slimming diets Not for babies |
| **Semi-skimmed milk** Not easily available in the UK | *Pasteurized and UHT* as for skimmed milk | Some of the fat has been removed 1.5% to 1.8% fat is left Some of the vitamins A and D removed | As above |

**NB** Energy value of skimmed milk = 835kJ per pint (200kcal)
Energy value silver top milk = 1590kJ per pint (380kcal)

**Evaporated and condensed milks**

**Manufacture** Some of the water is removed by evaporation.

 1 Evaporated milk–When the milk is 69% water it is sealed in cans which are then sterilized. Some loss of vitamins B and C occurs.

 2 Condensed milk–When the milk is 26.5% water sucrose is added. The milk is thicker and sweeter than evaporated milk. The cans or tubes used for packing need not be sterilized because of the high sugar content.

**Table 4.6** A comparison of the composition of ordinary pasteurized milk with evaporated and condensed milks

| | *Water* | *Fat* | *Non-fat solids* | *Sucrose* |
| --- | --- | --- | --- | --- |
| Pasteurized fresh milk | 85% | 3.5% | 8.5% | — |
| Evaporated milk | 69% | 9.0% | 22% | — |
| Condensed sweetened milk | 26.5% | 9.0% | 22% | 42.5% |

**Dried milk powders**

Dried milks can be bought as:

 1 Low fat pure dried milk powders. Vitamins A and D are now added to some brands.

 2 Fat-filled dried milk powders–vegetable fats are added to replace the animal fat of the whole milk.

 3 Modified milk powders–baby milk powders and specially formulated milk foods for use during illness.

   Baby milk is humanized by adding fat, sugar and micro-nutrients so it resembles breast milk. Foods such as 'Complan' are made to provide a good basic supply of the nutrients for someone unable to eat a normal diet.

**NB** The instructions on the packet for reconstituting these milk powders should be carefully followed.

**Manufacture** Dried milk powders can be made from (i) skimmed milk, (ii) semi-skimmed milk and (iii) whole milk. Its manufacture is shown in Fig. 4.11.

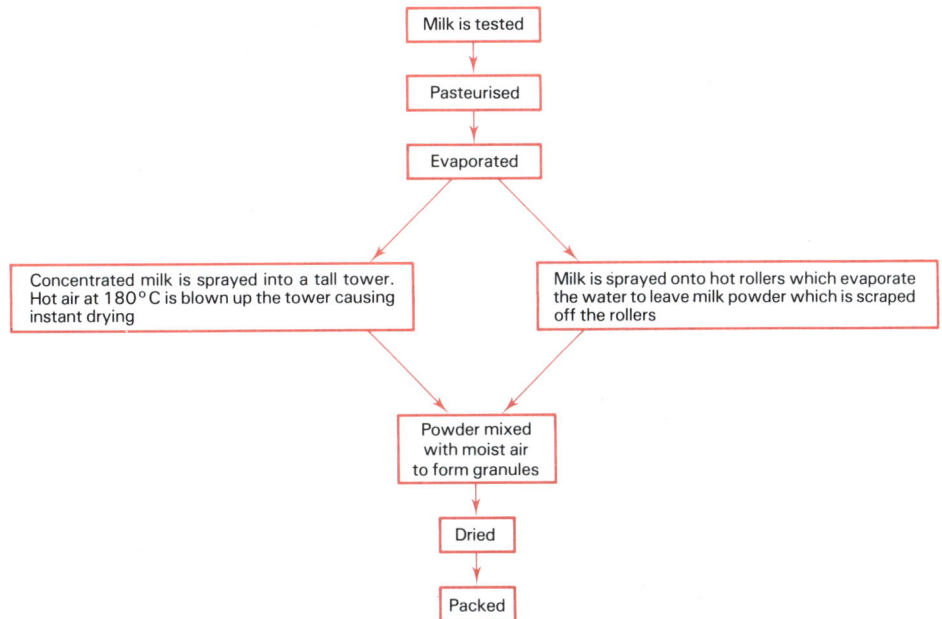

**Fig. 4.11** The manufacture of dried milk

### Non-dairy 'coffee creamers'

These are made to replace milk or cream in coffee. They are made from a blend of dried glucose syrup and vegetable fat. They have a very high energy value.

### The place of milk in the diet

Milk is:
1 A very nutritious food.
2 Reasonably priced.
3 Readily available.
4 Easily digested.
5 An important food for babies, growing children, sick people, the elderly and expectant mothers.
6 Bland in flavour which means it can be used in sweet and savoury dishes.
7 Ideal for use in hot and cold drinks, with cereals, to make sauces, custards, batters and milk puddings. It can also be used as an enricher in soups and creamed potatoes.

### The effect of cooking on milk

Heating milk causes partial coagulation of the protein caseinogen to **casein**. This forms a scum on the surface of the milk which holds the steam in to produce the 'boiling over' effect and also causes milk to stick on the surface of the pan.

There is a difference in flavour between cold and hot milk and pasteurized and sterilized milk which is due to the partial caramelization of the lactose. This also helps to form the brown skin on a rice pudding.

**Junket** is an example of the **coagulation** of caseinogen to casein.
1 Milk is heated to blood heat.
2 Rennet made from the rennin of a calf's stomach is added with sugar and flavouring. As the milk is left to stand this enzyme causes the coagulation. The dish should be left undisturbed at room temperature until set. When the junket is cut with a spoon it separates into the solid curds and the liquid whey.

The effect of rennin on caseinogen is also used in the manufacture of cheese.

### Storage of milk

Milk is a perishable food which is readily spoilt by microbial activity.
1 Collect the milk from the doorstep as soon as it arrives. The heat of the sun reduces the vitamin C and vitamin B content.

**2** Keep the milk *cool, clean* and *covered*. This prevents contamination by micro-organisms and reduces the activity of those already present. Pasteurized milk does not sour in the same way as untreated milk but it does develop 'off' flavours.

**3** Silver, red and gold top milk will keep in the refrigerator for 2-4 days. Milk keeps best in its bottle.

**4** Sterilized milk will keep for a minimum of 7 days without refrigeration if unopened. Once opened treat it as pasteurized milk.

**5** UHT milk will keep for up to 6 months without refrigeration, unopened. Check the date on the packet. Once opened treat it as pasteurized milk.

**6** Always pour milk into a clean jug – just the amount needed.

**7** Never mix new milk with old.

**8** Dried milks do not need refrigeration unless reconstituted. They will keep for a long time if kept dry. Those with fat deteriorate first.

**9** Canned milk once opened keeps as long as fresh milk.

**10** Milk may be frozen for 1 month in a plastic container with head room, a glass bottle should not be used. Homogenized milk freezes best. Pasteurized milk separates out on thawing. Milk is best frozen as part of the egg and milk custard of a savoury flan.

### Yogurt

**The nutritional value** of yogurt is similar to that of the milk used to make the yogurt. The bacteria used to sour the milk will have used up the lactose.

**1** Yogurt is a very useful food for the very young, the elderly, people on a low fat diet and for those on a light diet.

**2** Natural yogurt has a lower energy value than those with sugar and fruit.

**3** Yogurt can be served at any meal or as a snack. It can be served with cereals, used in a salad dressing, as a sweet and in soups and casseroles instead of soured cream. Yogurt is also used as a marinade.

**Manufacture** Yogurt can be made from any type of milk except condensed.

**1** Milk is heated to between 88°C and 105°C and cooled to between 41°C and 45°C.

**2** A specially prepared bacteria culture of *lactobacillus bulgaricus* is added and the mixture incubated in bottles at 40°C for 2½ to 3½ hours.

**3** When 0.75% lactic acid is present clotting takes place. The milk now has an acid taste and has thickened.

*Making yogurt at home*

(*a*) UHT, sterilized and reconstituted skimmed milk powder may have the yogurt culture added directly to them. Pasteurized milk must be boiled and cooled to below 45°C before adding the yogurt starter. This is to destroy any foreign bacteria that are present.

(*b*) UHT and homogenized milk give the best results. For each 750ml (1½pt):

(*i*) Mix two teaspoons of fresh natural yogurt with a little of the milk and then stir in the rest. (Do not use sterilized or pasteurized yogurt.)
An even thicker, richer yogurt can be made by adding 2-3 tablespoons of dried skimmed milk.

(*ii*) Pour into the cups of the yogurt maker, cover and place in a position where it will not be moved. Switch on.
Milk from the refrigerator takes eight hours, milk at room temperature six hours.

(*iii*) Store in the refrigerator and add fruit and sugar to taste just before serving.

### 4.1.5  Cream

**Nutritional value**

Fat, plus a little watery whey skimmed from the surface of milk which has stood for 24 hours is called cream. Commercially skimming is done by mechanical separators.

**1** The higher the fat content, the higher the energy value.

**2** The higher the fat content the lower the water and protein content, but the higher the content of vitamin A and D.

**Types of cream**

Cream varies according to the amount of fat present.

**Table 4.7** Types of cream

| Type | % Fat | |
| --- | --- | --- |
| **Clotted cream** | 55% | Cornish or Devon cream   Thickest cream of all |
| **Double cream** | 48% | Thickens well when whipped   Piped on cold sweets and cakes |
| **Whipping cream** | 35% | Cheaper substitute for double cream   Whipping increase volume |
| **Sterilized cream** | 23% | Sterilized in cans or bottles   Keeps indefinitely |
| **& Half cream** | 12% | Will not thicken   Both have cooked flavour |
| **Single cream** | 18% | Does not thicken      Used with coffee and to pour on hot and cold sweets |
| **UHT cream** | 18% | A single cream   Same heat treatment as UHT milk |
| | | Must not be put into the refrigerator   Single cream keeps for 6 weeks, half-cream for 3 months |
| **Soured cream** | 12% | A single cream is made in a similar way to yogurt. It is not soured with age or poor storage, but by a special culture of bacteria   Used in salad dressings and in dishes such as soup, cheesecakes and Beef Stroganoff |

### Storage of cream

All fresh cream has been pasteurized, heated to between 82°C and 88°C for 10 seconds and cooled to 4.5°C.

**1** Check the date on the carton. Cream keeps for 3-4 days in the refrigerator in the summer, a little longer in the winter.

**2** Double cream keeps longer than single.

### 4.1.6   Cheese

#### Nutritional value of whole-milk cheeses

This type of cheese is approximately one-third protein, one-third fat and one-third water and micro-nutrients.

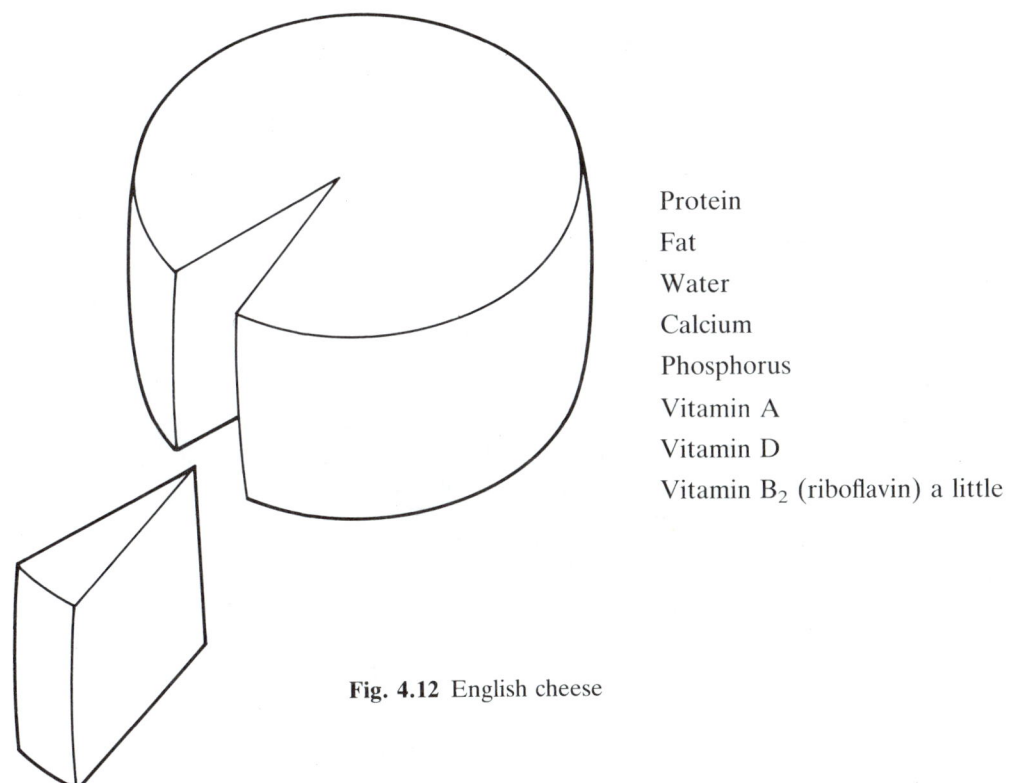

Protein

Fat

Water

Calcium

Phosphorus

Vitamin A

Vitamin D

Vitamin $B_2$ (riboflavin) a little

**Fig. 4.12** English cheese

**Protein** in whole milk cheese is mainly casein of a high biological value.

**Fat** in whole milk cheese contains saturated fatty acids.

**Lactose,** most water and the water soluble B vitamins were removed in the whey during manufacture.

#### The manufacture of hard pressed cheeses

4 litres (8pts) of milk make ½kg (1lb) hard pressed cheese such as Cheddar.
The milk is pasteurized to destroy unwanted bacteria. It is then poured into large stainless steel vats for processing.

### How cheese is made

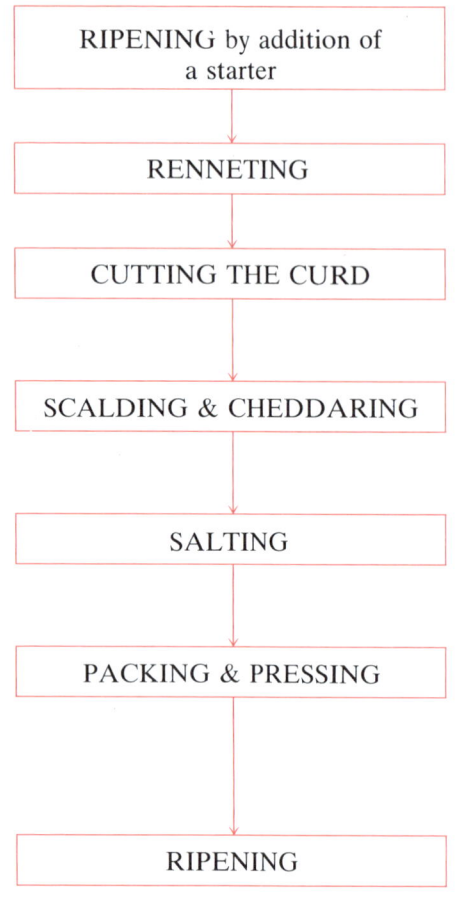

|  |  |
|---|---|
| RIPENING by addition of a starter | The starter is a laboratory preparation of a bacteria culture which changes lactose to lactic acid. This takes 1 hour. |
| RENNETING | Rennet added to the milk at 29°C–30.5°C to make the milk clot. Clotting takes about 45 minutes. |
| CUTTING THE CURD | Special knives cut the junket so that it separates into solid 'curds' and liquid 'whey'. Takes about 45 minutes. |
| SCALDING & CHEDDARING | Steam is passed through the hollow jacket of the vats. The curd is stirred for 1 hour. The whey starts to drain away. |
| SALTING | Salt is added to help preserve and give flavour. Flavour is affected by the cows' food, by flavourings added and by ripening time. |
| PACKING & PRESSING | Curds are packed into moulds of various shapes and sizes which may be muslin lined. The curd is pressed to remove remaining whey. The greater the pressure the harder the cheese. |
| RIPENING | Several months, sometimes years. Temperature and humidity are carefully controlled. Cheeses are turned, daily at first. Flavour develops because of bacteria, moulds and enzymes. The casein becomes more digestible. |

**Fig. 4.13** How cheese is made

### Types of cheeses

#### British cheeses
1  Hard-pressed scalded cheese–Cheddar, Cheshire, Derby, Double Gloucester, Leicester
2  Semi-hard or lightly-pressed cheeses–Caerphilly, Lancashire
3  Soft cheese (un-pressed)–White Stilton, White Wensleydale
4  Blue-veined cheeses (un-pressed)–Blue Stilton, Blue Wensleydale, Lymeswold. Blue veining is caused by a harmless mould which grows in the spaces of loosely packed cheese.
5  Variations of these cheeses–a greater variety of flavour is achieved by the addition of herbs, garlic, nuts. e.g. Sage Derby, Belshire (white Stilton + onion and chives), Huntsmans cheese is made from layers of Blue Stilton surrounded by Double Gloucester.

#### Unripened cheeses

1  Cottage cheese is made from skimmed milk. It is useful for a low fat or slimming diet. Milk is pasteurized, starter added and the resulting curd cut and the whey drained away. The curd is washed and drained. Salt and sometimes other flavours are added.
2  Cream cheese is made from single cream, double cream or a mixture of both with milk. A full cream cheese can be 90% fat. Cream cheese contains less protein than other cheeses.

#### Popular foreign cheeses

1  Parmesan–Italian, made from goats milk. It is very hard. It is bought grated to use as a garnish. Strong flavour
2  Brie and Camembert–French cheeses. They are soft. They are similar in texture and appearance to Lymeswold.
3  Roquefort–French cheese made from goats milk. Blue veined
4  Gorganzola–Italian. Soft, blue veined cheese
5  Danish Blue–Danish cheese. Blue veined

**Fig. 4.14** English cheeses

**6** Edam and Gouda–Dutch cheeses. Mild flavour, smooth texture
**7** Gruyère–A Swiss cheese. Hard pressed

### Processed Cheeses

These have a milder flavour than other cheeses. When refrigerated they keep longer because of the heat treatment which prevents moulds.

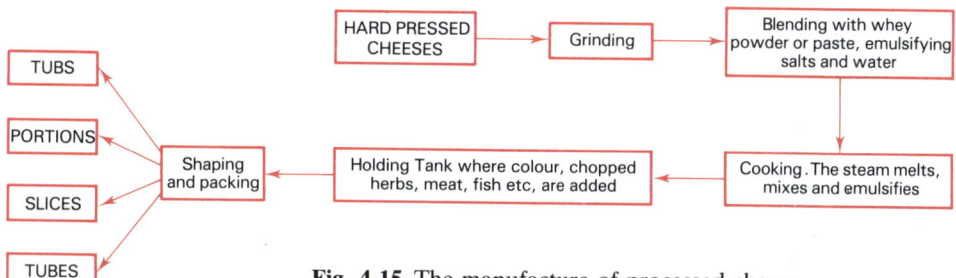

**Fig. 4.15** The manufacture of processed cheese

### Storage of cheese

**Hard-pressed cheeses**–Wrap in polythene or put in a plastic box in the refrigerator. This prevents drying of the surface. If stored in a warm place cheese sweats and becomes oily.

Allow pressed cheeses to stand for an hour at room temperature before serving.

**Soft cheeses**–They are best eaten soon after purchase. Store on the bottom shelf of the refrigerator, wrapped.

**Cottage cheese and cream cheese**–Store covered in the refrigerator.

If cheeses are frozen changes in texture and flavour will occur. Hard cheeses may be frozen ready-grated for use in cooked dishes.

### The place of cheese in the diet

Cheese is a very **concentrated food**. There is no waste so weight for weight it is better value for money than meat. The **high fat content** of most cheese gives a **high energy** value. People on fat-free or slimming diets should either eat cottage cheese or very little full fat cheese.

There is a wide variety of cheese available with different textures and flavours to suit all tastes. Cheese can be eaten at any meal, as a course in itself, incorporated into the main dish, or as a flavouring or a garnish.

**The digestion of cheese protein** can take a long time because the fat surrounds the protein and prevents the gastric enzyme **pepsin** from working efficiently. Fats are not emulsified until they reach the duodenum.

It is also very easy to overcook and denature the protein making it less digestible. This happens very easily when cheese is grilled on toast or on top of *au gratin* dishes.

### Rules for cooking and serving cheese

**1** Grate the cheese–uncooked it provides a greater surface area for the action of digestive enzymes. Finely grated cheese mixes more readily into a sauce or other mixtures.
**2** Mix the cheese with starchy foods–breadcrumbs, potato, flour. As the fat melts it is absorbed and continues to protect the protein from overcooking.

**3** Add cheese to a sauce after it has boiled and do not reboil the sauce – the fat is inclined to melt to give an oily surface and the protein can toughen.

**4** Use seasonings such as cayenne pepper and mustard, to add piquancy to stimulate the flow of the digestive juices.

**5** Do not overcook the cheese as the protein will harden as it denatures and become indigestible.

### 4.1.7 Eggs

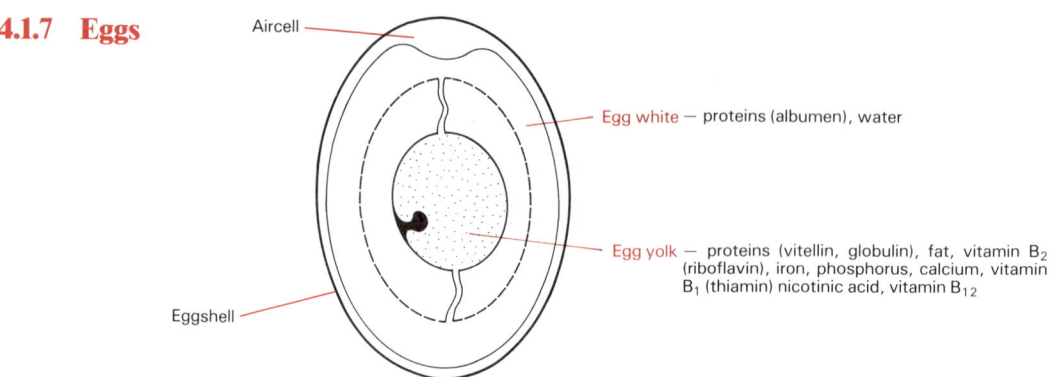

Fig. 4.16 The structure and contents of an egg

The proteins in eggs are of high biological value.
The fat is finely emulsified so easily digested. It contains saturated fatty acids.

**The effect of heat on eggs**

When heat is applied the egg white coagulates at 60°C and the yolk proteins at 65°C. Prolonged cooking will toughen the egg and make it difficult to digest.

**The freshness of eggs**

When a **fresh** egg is broken **three** distinct areas can be seen. The freshness of an egg can also be tested by placing it in water as shown in Figure 4.17.

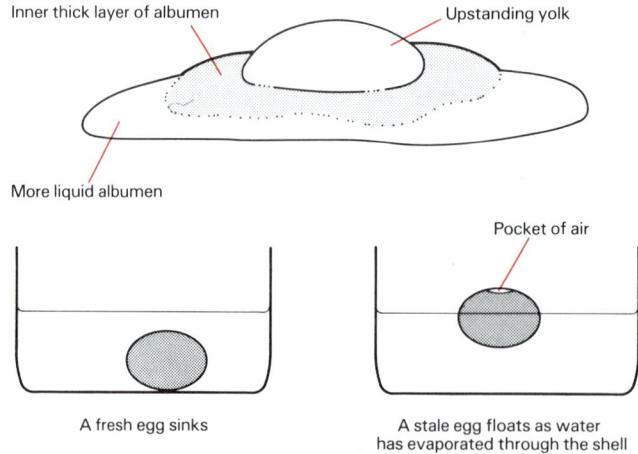

**Fig. 4.17** The fresh egg

**Types and grades of eggs**
**Battery eggs** Hens are kept in small cages in large battery units.

**Deep litter eggs** Hens have more freedom than battery hens but they are still kept in large numbers in deep litter houses.

**Free range eggs** Hens are allowed to roam the farmyard and forage for their own food.

**NB** There is no nutritional difference between free range and battery eggs.

**Eggs are tested and graded** for size and quality in two ways:
**1** Class A, Class B, Class C (manufacturing purposes only not on sale to the public)
**2** Weight grading – Sizes 1 to 7

| | | |
|---|---|---|
| *Size 1*   70g and over | *Size 4*   55g and under 60g | *Size 6*   45g and under 50g |
| *Size 2*   65g and under 70g | *Size 5*   50g and under 55g | *Size 7*   under 45g |
| *Size 3*   60g and under 65g | | |

Sizes 3 and 4 are the sizes to use for most cooking purposes.

**Storage of eggs**

1 Store eggs with the pointed end down in a cool place.

2 The refrigerator is not an ideal place to store eggs but if they are stored in this way allow them to reach room temperature before use.

3 Storage in the carton reduces evaporation of water through the shell.

**Ways in which eggs may be used**

| | |
|---|---|
| **As a main dish** | Because of their high nutritional value eggs can be used to make dishes which replace meat and fish. They are a useful food for lacto-vegetarians. Eggs can be baked, boiled, poached, made into omelettes, quiches and soufflés. |
| **As an enricher** | The addition of an egg to pastries, scones, creamed potatoes and sauces adds to their nutritional value. |
| **As a raising agent** | When whisked whole eggs or egg whites will form a foam which entangles air. In the whisking method the air trapped in this way is the raising agent in a true sponge. |
| **To set custards** | This uses the property of coagulation of egg proteins when heated. Custards can be sweet or savoury e.g. baked egg custard tart, savoury quiche. Care must be taken not to overheat or cook too long. |
| **To bind** | Coagulation sets the structure of cakes and batters. Eggs can be used to bind together ingredients in such items as rissoles, fish cakes and home-made beefburgers. |
| **To coat for frying** | Coagulated egg holds a coating of breadcrumbs on the outside of food for frying. It forms a protective seal. The food is held together and the fat cannot penetrate the food. |
| **As a glaze** | When used as a glaze on pastry, scones etc., the coagulated proteins of an egg form a glossy brown skin. |
| **As a garnish** | Sliced hard boiled egg, sieved egg white or yolk can form a colourful garnish to foods. It adds also to the nutritional value. |
| **As an emulsifier** | Lecithin in the egg yolk helps to form a fine emulsion of fat/oil in for example, vinegar when making mayonnaise. Egg yolk is also an emulsifying agent in creamed mixtures. |

**Baked and stirred custards** If these are overheated or cooked for too long the proteins shrink rapidly away from the liquid as they coagulate and the custard becomes tough. It also gives the custard a 'watery' look. Separation or curdling has occurred. This process can also produce a 'watery' quiche.

To prevent this:

1 Baked egg custard–add heated milk, almost boiling to the eggs already beaten with a little cold milk. Strain into the dish. Stand the dish in a tray of warm water. This provides moist heat and the custard is less likely to overheat.

2 Stirred or pouring custard–stir the custard in a basin over a pan of boiling water to avoid overheating.

If the sauce does go lumpy whisk it in a bowl or in liquidizer.

A pouring egg custard does not thicken as much as a sauce made from a starch powder. It thickens more as it cools slightly.

## 4.1.8 Meat

**Nutritional value**

| | | |
|---|---|---|
| HBV protein | Iron | Vitamin $B_1$ (thiamin) |
| Fat | Calcium | Vitamin $B_2$ (riboflavin) |
| Water | Phosphorus | Vitamin $B_{12}$ |

These nutrients, with variations in quantity, are also found in bacon, poultry and offal.

**Bacon** is an important source of vitamins of the B complex. Curing means more salt.

**Poultry**–chicken and turkey contain less fat and iron than carcass meat. Most occurs in the skin. Duck and goose have a much higher fat content than chicken and turkey.

**Offal**–the name comes from term, 'off-all', which refers to the parts of the animal which are removed from the carcass.

1 Liver and kidney are very rich in iron and they contain more vitamin $B_{12}$ than carcass meats. Vitamins A,D,C are also present. They contain very little fat.

Liver contains glycogen, and is quick to cook and easy to digest because of the absence of connective tissue and muscle fibres.

2 Sweetbreads, tripe, heart, brains are useful sources of protein but the vitamin and mineral content is poor.

3 Tripe is a good source of calcium but is of little other food value.

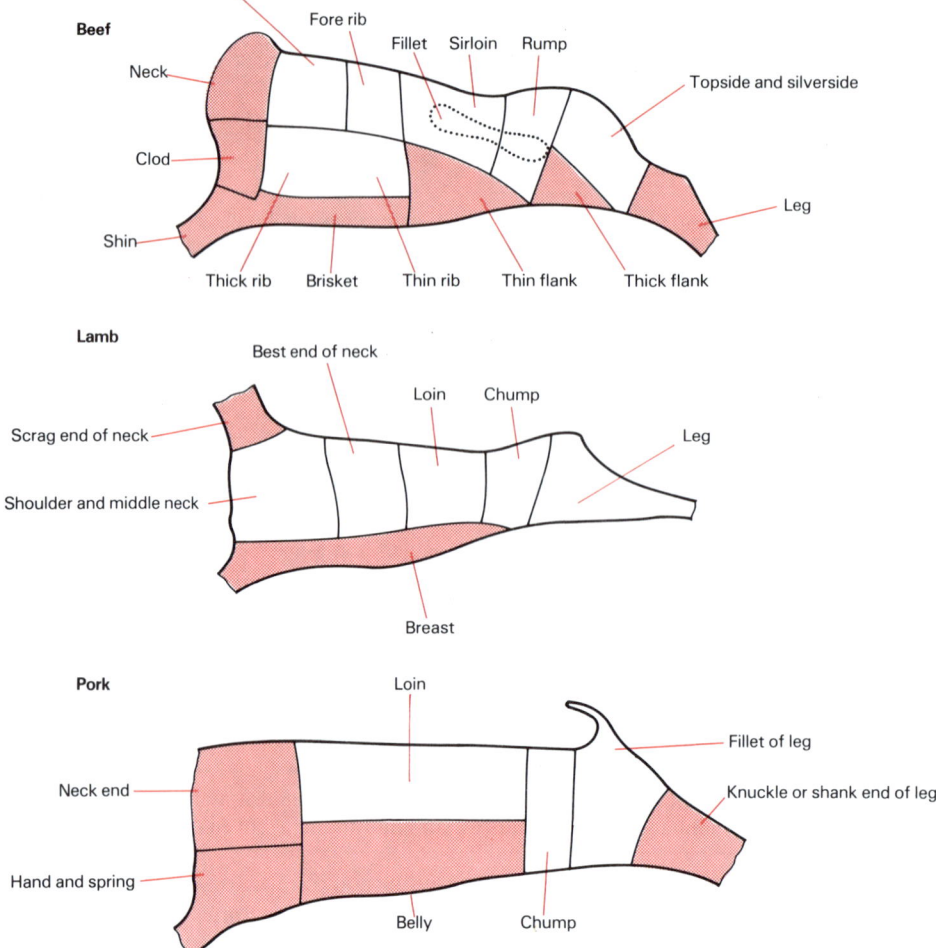

**Fig. 4.18** Cuts of meat

### The structure of meat

**Muscle fibres** are made of the proteins *myosin* and *actin*. Muscle cells are long thin fibres which are formed into bundles.

**Connective tissue** is made up of the proteins *collagen* and *elastin*. Connective tissue surrounds each bundle of muscle fibres and also holds groups of muscle fibre together. Collagen surrounds muscles and is the main constituent of tendons. Elastin forms ligaments.

**Fat** is found under the skin and around organs e.g. suet around kidneys. Patches between muscle fibres are called 'marbling'.

**NB** The red colour of meat is due to the pigment **haemoglobin** in the red blood cells. This has carried oxygen to the muscle cells as oxyhaemoglobin, where myoglobin holds the oxygen as oxymyoglobin.

### Buying meat

1  A bright red colour is not an indication of good quality meat. If it is bright red it has been freshly cut. When exposed to air, myoglobin changes to a bright red colour as it combines with oxygen, and after about 20 minutes develops a brown colouration–metmyoglobin.
     Factors affecting colour are breed, age, feeding, stress experienced at the slaughter house and the length of hanging of the carcass after killing and prior to butchering. These factors also affect the tenderness of the meat.
2  Indications of tenderness are small, fine fibres with very little connective tissue or gristle and fine marbling with fat between the bundles of fibres. Compare fillet steak with stewing steak.
3  Meat which has larger, longer fibres with a lot of connective tissue and some gristle is usually tougher and cheaper to buy.
(a)  Tender cuts–fry, grill, spit or oven roast
(b)  Tougher cuts–stew, braise, pot roast, boil
4  Cheaper cuts are just as nutritious as tender cuts if correctly cooked.
5  A joint of meat with large bone or too much fat is not an economic buy.
6  There should be a little fat in the form of marbling to help in the cooking.
7  Consider factors such as: money available, time for cooking, number of people and the type of meal.

**8** The meat should not be sitting in a pool of liquid, which indicates meat thawed from frozen, but it should be moist.

**9** The meat should have a fresh smell.

**10** The meat should be slightly springy to the touch.

**11** The butcher and his shop should reflect very high standards of hygiene.

**12** Allow generally 100g (4oz) of meat per person, but 6oz with chops and 8oz with a joint.

### Storage of Meat

**1** Fresh minced meat and offal should be used on the day of purchase. If a refrigerator is not available store meat in a clean container, covered and in a cool place for no more than 48 hours.

**2** In a refrigerator store for no more than 2-3 days. Meat should be covered to prevent drying out and cross contamination by bacteria. Store cooked meat above uncooked meat.

**3** In a freezer the time of storage depends upon the type of meat and amount of fat present. Fat gradually becomes rancid and affects the flavour of meat. Wrap the meat carefully to avoid dehydration or freezer burn.

### Thawing meat and poultry

This is best done slowly in a refrigerator as the temperature is never high enough to allow bacteria to multiply.

**1** Whole poultry and large joints **must be thawed completely** to avoid the risk of food poisoning. If the centre of meat is still frozen when cooked it does not heat up above the temperature below which is ideal for bacteria to multiply and produce toxins. These spread to the rest of the meat as it cools.

**2** Always cool meat and meat dishes not to be eaten hot, very quickly.

### Methods of cooking meat

These are shown in Table 4.8.

**Table 4.8** Methods of cooking meat

| Type | Grill | Fry | Roast | Pot Roast | Stew | Braise | Salt & Boil | Accompaniments |
|---|---|---|---|---|---|---|---|---|
| **Beef** | | | | | | | | |
| Shin | | | | | √ | √ | | |
| Neck | | | | | √ | √ | | *Roast beef*–Yorkshire pudding, thin gravy, horseradish sauce or mustard |
| Clod | | | | | √ | √ | | |
| Brisket | | | | √ | | √ | √ | |
| Flank | | | | | √ | | √ | *Boiled beef*–Root vegetables, suet dumplings, mustard |
| Topside | | | √ | √ | | √ | | |
| Silverside | | | √ | √ | | √ | | *Grilled steak*–Maître d'hôtel butter, mushrooms, tomatoes, chipped potatoes, mustard and a side salad |
| Rump | √ | √ | | | | | | |
| Fillet | √ | √ | | | | | | |
| Sirloin | √ | √ | √ | | | | | |
| Ribs | | | √ | | | | | |
| Chuck & blade | | | | | √ | √ | | |
| **Lamb** | | | | | | | | |
| Scrag end of neck | | | | | √ | √ | | |
| Middle neck | | | | | √ | √ | | *Roast lamb*–Mint sauce or red currant jelly, gravy or onion sauce |
| Best end of neck | √ | √ | √ | √ | | √ | | |
| Loin | √ | √ | √ | | | | | |
| Chump chops | √ | √ | | | | | | *Boiled lamb*–Root vegetables, caper sauce |
| Leg | | | √ | | | | | |
| Breast | | | √ | | √ | √ | | |
| Shoulder | | | √ | | | √ | | |
| **Pork** | | | | | | | | |
| Neck end | | | √ | | √ | √ | | |
| Hand & spring | | | √ | | √ | | | |
| Belly | √ | √ | √ | | | | | |
| Chump | | | √ | | | | | *Roast pork*–Apple sauce, sage and onion stuffing, thick gravy. |
| Fillet of leg | √ | √ | √ | | | | | |
| Shank of leg | √ | √ | √ | | | | | |
| Loin | √ | √ | √ | | | | | |
| Trotters | | | | | | | √ | |

**NB** The names given to cuts of meat vary with geographical regions.

### Preparation of meat for cooking

Dried and discoloured skin or fat should be removed and excess fat cut away.
Cut surfaces should be wiped with a clean cloth dampened with cold water. Large joints can be washed in cold water and dried.
Salted meat should soak for up to 6 hours.
Meat may be tenderized by beating and by marinading in vinegar or alcohol.
Offal should be washed in cold, salted water and dried.
Liver is best sliced by the butcher. Skin and cut out blood vessels.
Kidneys should have their outer skin removed, be cut in half and the core removed using scissors.
Hearts should have the large blood vessels cut away and be well washed to remove blood.
To cut stewing meat into cubes, try to cut across the 'grain', or bundles of fibres.

### The effect of cooking on meat

Cooking destroys micro-organisms and makes the meat tender and flavoursome.
Heat causes the proteins (myosin, actin and elastin), to coagulate and shrink. The juices are squeezed out and help to improve the flavour.
Overcooking can denature and toughen proteins and make them less digestible.
The fat melts. Some runs out and some goes into the lean meat to help in the cooking. Outside fat becomes crisp and brown.
The red meat colour changes to brown.
Insoluble collagen, with moist heat, becomes soluble gelatine which dissolves in the liquid and so loosens fibres to make meat tender.
B vitamins can leach into the cooking liquid and some are destroyed by heat.
Mineral elements may also leach into the cooking liquid. Meat juices should therefore be served with the meat.
After cooking meat looks more attractive and is more palatable and digestible.

### Bacon

**Bacon is cured** in a special brine or pickle. It is then smoked or left in the unsmoked or green state.

**Gammon** is the leg joint which is called ham when served cold.

**Soaking** is not always necessary with some modern curing which produces a less salty bacon.

**Bacon** is boiled, baked or roasted when cut in a large piece and grilled or fried when sliced.

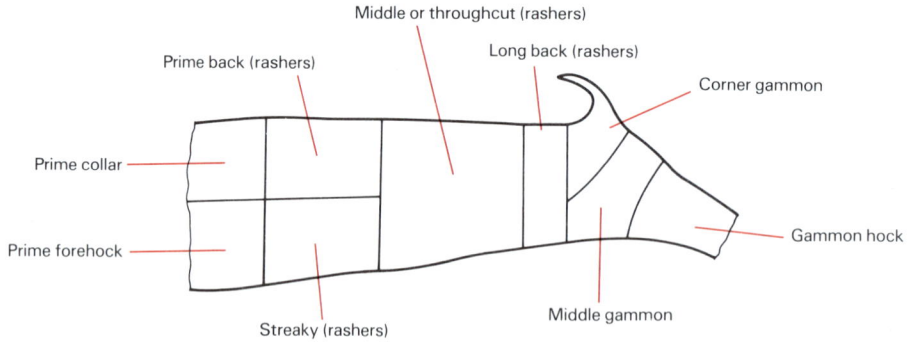

**Fig. 4.19** Cuts of bacon

### Methods of cooking bacon

These are shown in Table 4.9.

**Table 4.9** Methods of cooking bacon

| Joint | Grill | Fry | Bake/roast | Braise | Boil | Stew | Accompaniment |
|---|---|---|---|---|---|---|---|
| Gammon hock | | √ | | √ | √ | | |
| Corner gammon | | | | | √ | | *Boiled bacon & ham joints* |
| Middle gammon | √ | √ | √ | √ | √ | | Mustard, parsley or tomato sauce. |
| Long back | √ | √ | | | | | Carrots or broad beans, butter or haricot |
| Middle cut | √ | √ | √ | | √ | | beans. |
| Prime back | √ | √ | √ | √ | √ | | |
| Prime streaky | √ | √ | | | √ | | *Grilled gammon steaks* |
| Prime collar | | | | √ | √ | | Pineapple |
| Prime forehock | | | | | | √ | |

## 4.1.9 Fish

**Nutritional value**

**WHITE FISH**
78% water
18% protein
2% fat
    iodine
    fluorine
    phosphorus
    potassium
    sodium chloride
    vitamin B
In liver oils:
    fat
    vitamin A
    vitamin D

**OILY FISH**
62% water
19% protein
16% fat
    iodine
    fluorine
    phosphorus
    potassium
    sodium chloride
    vitamin A
    vitamin D
    vitamin B
    calcium if bones
    are eaten

*Examples*
Cod, haddock, hake, halibut, plaice,
bream, sole, turbot, whiting.

*Examples*
Anchovy, herring, mackerel, pilchards,
salmon, sardines, sprats, tuna, whitebait.

**SHELL FISH**

*Crustaceans*
crab
crayfish
lobster
prawn
shrimp

protein
very little fat
water
iodine
fluorine
phosphorus
potassium
sodium chloride
trace of iron

*Molluscs*
cockles
mussels
oysters
scallops
whelks
winkles

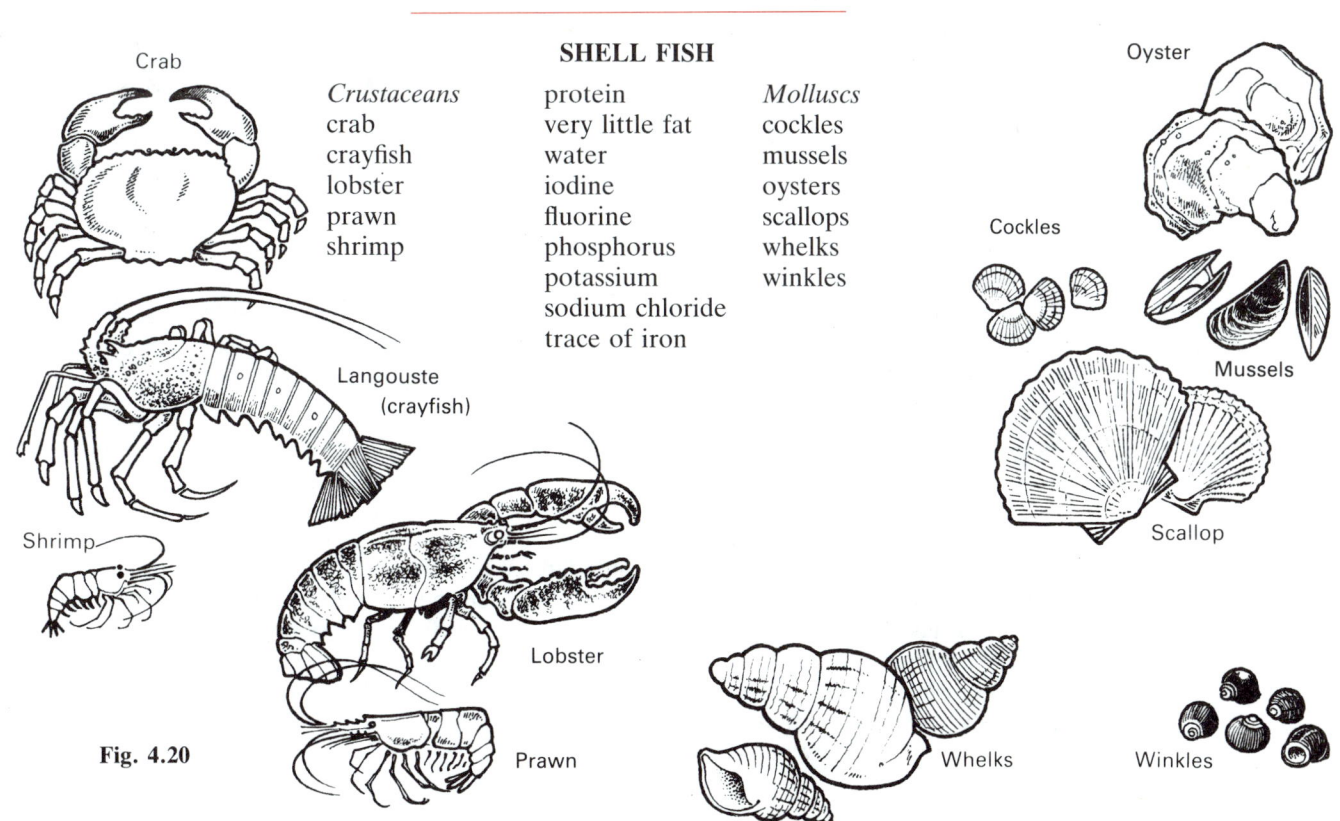

Fig. 4.20

The proteins in fish are of high biological value. Actin and myosin are combined as actomyosin. Fish roes contain more protein than the flesh.
75% of the fat is unsaturated. It contains essential fatty acids.

Fish is more quickly cooked and more easily digested than meat because it has less connective tissue, there is no elastin and the fibres are shorter. Oily fish take a little longer to digest. Shell fish have tougher, longer fibres and are a little more difficult to digest.

**Buying fish**

Fish can be fresh, frozen, smoked, canned, bottled, dried.

**Smoked fish**
1 Herrings are smoked by slightly different methods to produce, kippers, bloaters, buckling and red herring.
2 Haddock is sold as smoked haddock fillets, Finnan haddock and smokies.
3 Mackerel
4 Cod is sold as smoked fillets. Dye is usually added to the brine.
5 Salmon
6 Trout

**Canned fish** in oil, brine or a sauce such as tomato.
1 Oily fish such as salmon, tuna, sardines, pilchards, mackerel, herring, herring roes, anchovies, kippers.
2 Shell fish such as lobster, crab, prawns, shrimps.

**Bottled fish** are preserved in vinegar or brine.
1 Rollmops and Bismark are herrings which are soused.
2 Shellfish such as cockles and mussels.

**Dried fish** is usually to be found in dried packet foods in the UK. It is still a popular way of preserving fish in some countries such as those of Africa.

**Fresh fish** may be bought as:
1 Whole fish–allow 200-250g (8-10oz) per person.
2 Fillets–allow 150-175g (6-7oz) per person.
3 Steaks and cutlets–allow 150-175g (6-7oz) per person.

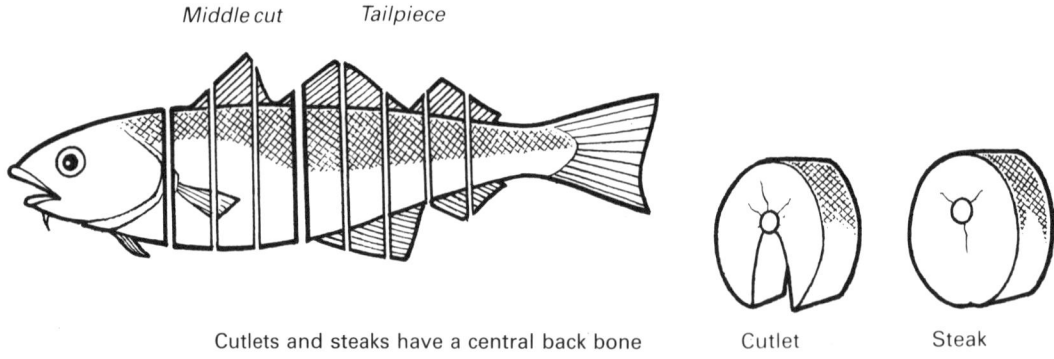

Middle cut          Tailpiece

Cutlets and steaks have a central back bone          Cutlet          Steak

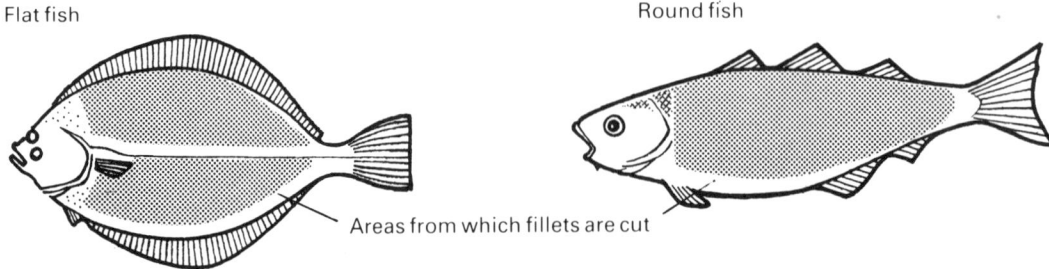

Flat fish          Round fish

Areas from which fillets are cut

**Fig. 4.21**          Fillets have no bones

The shop selling fish should have a very high standard of hygiene.
Fish should have a fresh fishy seaweedy smell. A strong ammonia smell indicates staleness.
Whole fish should have bright, bulging eyes, red gills and a plentiful supply of bright shiny scales which are firmly attached.
The flesh of the fish should be firm.
Crabs and lobsters should feel heavy when held.
Smoked fish should have a dry but glossy skin.

**How to clean and bone
a herring**

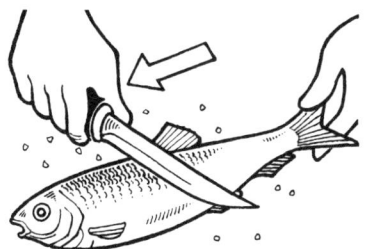

**1** Gently scrape the fish
from tail to head to
remove scales.

**2** With a sharp knife cut
off the head. Remove
the viscera attached
to the head.

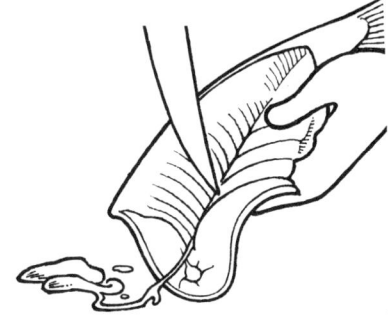

**3** Slit the fish along the
belly. Slip out the roe
and scrape the inside
of the fish to remove
the gut and blood
vessels.

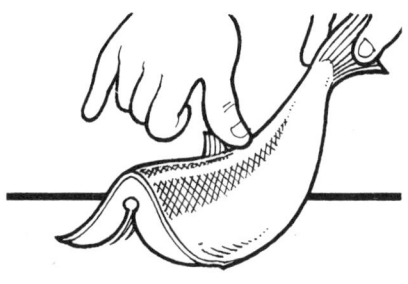

**4** Open the fish, skin
uppermost, on a firm
surface. Press firmly
all the way along the
centre back of the
fish.

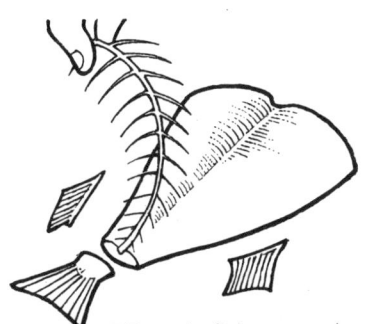

**5** Turn the fish over and
ease the backbone
away from the flesh.

**6** Cut off the tail and
fins.

**7** Wash the fish well in
salted water and then
dry in kitchen paper.

**Fig. 4.22** Filleting fish

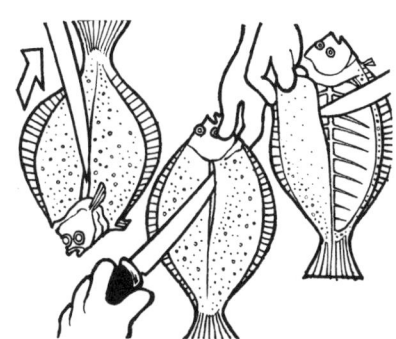

**Filleting a flat fish**

**1** Use a sharp knife with
a pointed and flexible
blade. Cut a straight
line along the back of
the fish from head to
tail.

**2** Insert the point of the
knife under the flesh
at the head and
keeping the knife

pressed along the
bones, slice away the
flesh.

**3** Remove the fillet
from the other side of
the fish, working from
the tail end.

**4** Turn the fish over and
cut the two fillets
from the under side.

Frozen fish should be selected from stock kept in a freezer cabinet at a temperature of −20°C or below. Select fish from below the load line.

**Storing fish**

**1** Fresh fish is best bought and eaten immediately.

**2** If fresh fish is kept, do so for only 24 hours. Wash, dry, wrap in polythene and store in the coolest part of the refrigerator.

**3** If fish is to be frozen at home it should be frozen within a few hours of the catch being landed.

**Preparation of fish for cooking**

This is shown clearly in Fig. 4.22.

**Cooking fish**

Fish may be grilled, baked, fried, braised, poached, steamed.

**Coatings** hold the fish together, protect it from the intense heat of fat if it is being fried, they add colour, texture and nutrients. The fat does not soak in.

**1** Flour—whitebait, sprats

**2** Oats—herrings for frying

**3** Egg and breadcrumbs—fillets for shallow and deep fat frying

**4** Batter—for deep fat frying

**Accompaniments**

**1** A variety of stuffings may be made and cooked with the fish when baked.

**2** Sauces—cheese, caper, lemon, parsley, mustard, tomato, mushroom, anchovy, sauce tartare

**Garnishes** for cooked fish include lemon wedges or butterflies, parsley, watercress.

## 4.1.10  Pulses

Pulses are the dried seeds of plants with pods. They are a good, economical source of protein. Nutritional value increases when they are served with eggs, milk, cheese, cereals and nuts. They can make meat and fish go further. Pulses are a very useful food for vegans.

*Examples*
Butter beans, haricot beans, cannellini, flageolets, broad beans, black eye beans, red kidney beans, chick peas, pinto beans, split lentils, whole dried peas, split peas, adzuki beans, peanuts, soya bean

### Nutritional value

LBV protein–soya beans contain twice as much protein as the others and it is of high biological value
Fat–soya beans contain more fat
Starch–soya beans contain dextrin and sugar
Fibre–a considerable amount
Iron
Calcium
Phosphorus
B vitamins–thiamin, riboflavin, nicotinic acid

### Preparation of dried pulses

1 Pick them over to remove small stones and discoloured beans.
2 Put them into cold water, stir and remove any that float.
3 Wash in cold water. Drain.
(a) If left soaking overnight use a large bowl with plenty of water and leave in a cool place.
(b) To quick soak put the beans into a pan with water. Bring to the boil, uncovered, and boil for 2 minutes. Remove from heat and leave them to stand for 1-2 hours.

### To cook dried pulses

**To boil** put 1 part beans to 3 parts water into a pan.
1 Bring to the boil without stirring, cover and boil gently
2 Add salt towards the end of cooking. Cook for the time given in the chart (see below).

**To pressure cook** use 2 pints water to 450g (1lb) vegetables (presoaked weight)
1 Put water into the pan without a trivet. Bring it to the boil in an open pan.
2 Add vegetables. Bring to the boil. Skim well. Reduce the heat so that the contents are gently boiling but not rising in the pan.
3 Cover. Bring to 15lb pressure. Cook for the time given in the chart (see below).

### Cooking times for pulses

| *Bean* | *Boiling* | *Pressure cooking* | |
|---|---|---|---|
| Butter beans | 1½ hrs | 25 mins | |
| Haricot beans | 1½ hrs | 15 mins | |
| Chick peas | 2½ hrs | 20 mins | |
| Whole lentils | 1-1½ hrs | 15 mins | |
| Whole peas | 1 hr | 20 mins | |
| Split peas | 1-1½ hrs | 15 mins | |
| Pinto beans | 2-2½ hrs | 20 mins | |
| Red kidney beans | 1-1½ hrs | 20 mins | **These must be boiled rapidly for 15 minutes** |

**NB** Lentils do not need to soak. Split lentils cook more quickly than the whole lentils.

### Bean Sprouts

These can be grown from most beans but especially from mung beans, adzuki beans and brown lentils. Bean sprouts are rich in vitamins A and C. They can be eaten raw or cooked.

### Soya bean

### Nutritional Composition

40% HBV protein
20% fat (with polyunsaturated fatty acids)
calcium
iron

vitamin B$_1$ (thiamin)
vitamin B$_2$ (riboflavin)
24% starch
fibre

**Fig. 4.23** A soya bean plant

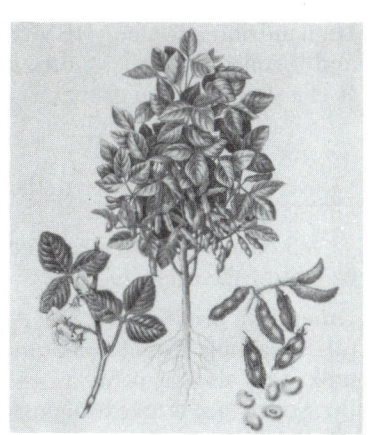

### The manufacture of soya products

**1** Full fat soya flour (40% protein, 20% vegetable oil)
**(a)** The beans are cleaned.
**(b)** The beans are de-hulled.
**(c)** Flakes are produced by crushing.
**(d)** The flakes are ground to flour with a protein content of 40%.
The flour is used as an *improver* in mass produced breads, cakes, biscuits as it extends shelf life and gives a shorter texture.

The flour acts as an *emulsifier, antioxidant* and adds nutritional value. Commercially it is added to baby foods, slimming foods, soups and stews.

**2** Soya oil and defatted soya flour.

**Textured vegetable protein** (TVP) is derived mainly from soya but wheat and other cereals, seed and leguminous vegetables are also used. *Textured* refers to the processes which form protein flakes into granules, chunks, flakes and fibres.
**1** Iron, vitamins B$_1$, B$_2$, B$_{12}$ are added to make the nutritional content more similar to that of meat.
**2** TVP may be natural or flavoured.
**3** TVP is used **to extend** savoury and sweet dishes. For example, natural flavour granules could extend the quantity of beef mince, or flaked fish or stewed fruit. It takes on the flavour and colour of the food with which it is mixed.
**4** TVP can be used **to replace** meat, fish or poultry. Colour and flavour are added during manufacture.
**5** Vegetarians can use meat flavoured TVP if they wish but if they dislike the flavour of meat they are more likely to use soya flour in a variety of dishes to provide them with high biological value protein.

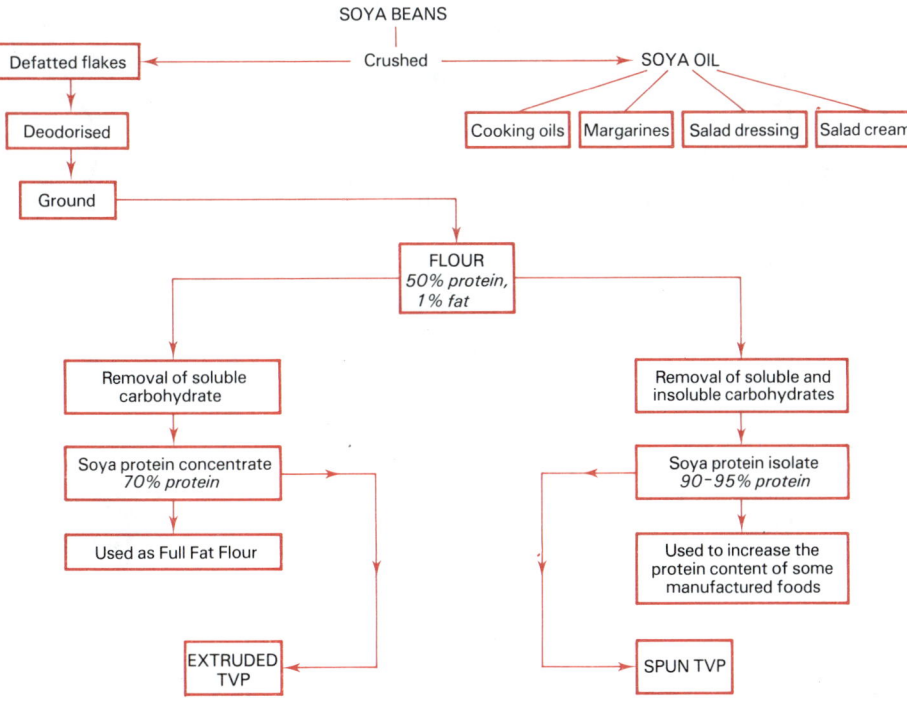

**Fig. 4.24** The production of soya bean products

*Advantages of TVP*
It is cheaper to produce and to buy than meat or fish.
There is no waste: no bones, gristle or fat.
It is easy to store and has a long shelf life if kept dry.

High nutritional value – HBV protein is only 1% fat which is unsaturated; it is free of cholesterol and fortified with micronutrients.
It is a useful source of dietary fibre.

*To use TVP*

1 Re-hydrate according to the manufacturers instructions, usually 2 parts water to 1 part TVP are used.

2 When mixing with meat or other food allow: 1 part by weight TVP re-hydrated to 3 parts by weight of the other food.

### Other soya products

(a) Soya milk. Dried 'milk' powders are made for babies and others who are allergic to cows' milk. It is also available as a liquid 'milk' in cans.

(b) Soya sauce is an extract of salted and fermented soya proteins. It is used in Asian cookery.

(c) Soya bean curd is produced from the coagulated proteins which have been separated from the beans. It is usually compressed into squares. It has a bland flavour which readily absorbs other flavours. *Tofu* is one type and is available in some places in the UK, mainly in shops selling Chinese and Japanese foods.

**The importance of soya** The USA produces most soya beans, Brazil 18% of world output whilst China only produces 16% of total output although soya beans and flour have been used in China and the Far East for centuries.

Many parts of the world suffer from a shortage of food, especially protein. In the developed countries meat has become an expensive source of protein. Soya is now often used to keep down the cost of canteen meals by mixing it with meat. Vegetable proteins are cheaper to produce than animal proteins so more has to be produced to meet the world's needs.

Soya flour, soya protein isolate and soya protein concentrate have been used in commercially manufactured foods for many years. Modern technology has produced TVP and the public is gradually accepting the necessity of its use.

### Other alternative protein foods

Bacteria, yeasts and algae can be grown on many agricultural and industrial wastes. Bacteria can double their weight in thirty minutes. These products, at present, are only used for feeding animals.

### 4.1.11 Fruits and vegetables

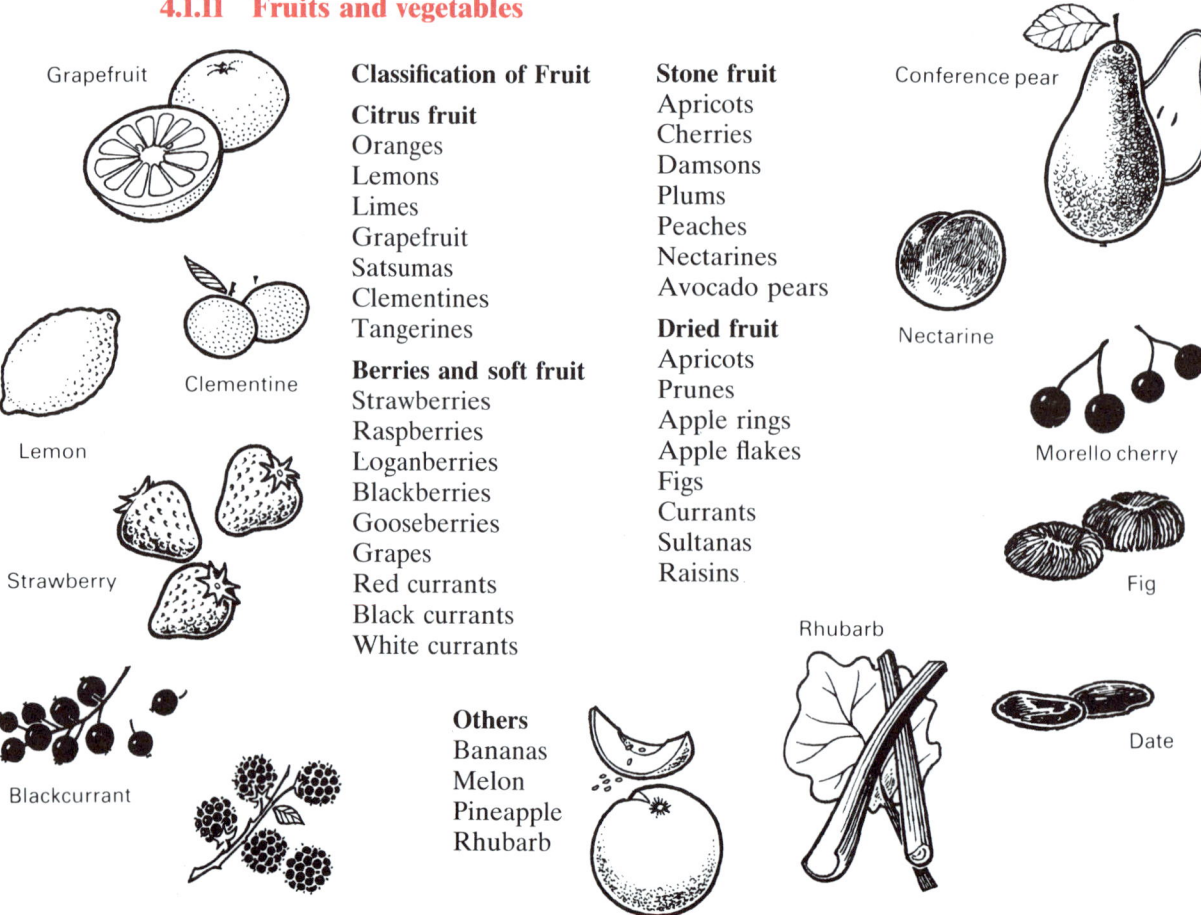

**Classification of Fruit**

**Citrus fruit**
Oranges
Lemons
Limes
Grapefruit
Satsumas
Clementines
Tangerines

**Berries and soft fruit**
Strawberries
Raspberries
Loganberries
Blackberries
Gooseberries
Grapes
Red currants
Black currants
White currants

**Others**
Bananas
Melon
Pineapple
Rhubarb

**Stone fruit**
Apricots
Cherries
Damsons
Plums
Peaches
Nectarines
Avocado pears

**Dried fruit**
Apricots
Prunes
Apple rings
Apple flakes
Figs
Currants
Sultanas
Raisins

Grapefruit

Lemon

Clementine

Strawberry

Blackcurrant

Blackberry

Ogen melon

Conference pear

Nectarine

Morello cherry

Fig

Date

Rhubarb

**Fig. 4.25**

## Nutritional value

| | |
|---|---|
| *Carbohydrates* | Starch is found in unripe fruits. Sugar as glucose or fructose is in most fruits. Dried fruit has the highest sugar content. The parts of the fruit which cannot be digested, skin, pips, cell walls, supply fibre. Pectin content depends upon the variety of fruit and its ripeness. In jam making pectin forms a gel with acid and sugar. |
| *Proteins* | Only very small amounts |
| *Fats* | Only traces, the exception being avocado pear |
| *Water* | All fruits contain a great deal. This makes fruit refreshing |
| *Vitamin A* | In the form of its precursor carotene e.g. oranges, apricots |
| *Vitamin C* | A very good supply in black currants, citrus fruit, gooseberries, strawberries, raspberries |
| *Vitamin B* | Amount negligible |
| *Vitamin D* | None |
| *Calcium* ⎱ *Iron* ⎰ | Dried fruits contain more than most fresh fruits |

## Buying fruit

**1** Select fruit that is just ripe and undamaged, however, melon, pears and avocado pears are best bought unripe and ripened at home.

**2** Buy fruit that is in season when it is at its best for flavour and an economic buy because it is cheaper.

**3** There is a variety of dried fruits available. Quality varies with price which is also affected by the extent to which the fruit has been prepared. Some dried fruits do not need soaking.

**4** Most canned fruit has been preserved in sugar but the shops are beginning to stock canned fruit which is in its own juice.

## Storage and preparation of fruit

**1** Handle gently. Bruising leads to rapid deterioration.

**2** Store in a cool and well ventilated place. Apples should be wrapped for longer storage.

**3** Soft fruits deteriorate very quickly, eat them straight away or place in the refrigerator for a short time only.

**4** Always wash fruit before eating it to remove dust and any chemicals which have been sprayed on.

**5** Eat raw fruit for maximum nutrients.

**6** For long term storage fruit may be made into jams, jellies, chutneys, bottled or canned in syrup or water, dried or frozen.

**7** Frozen fruit may be whole fruits frozen on open trays before packing, sliced fruit packed with sugar or cooked pulp, sweetened or unsweetened. Fruit with a high water content such as melon does not freeze satisfactorily.

## Classification of vegetables

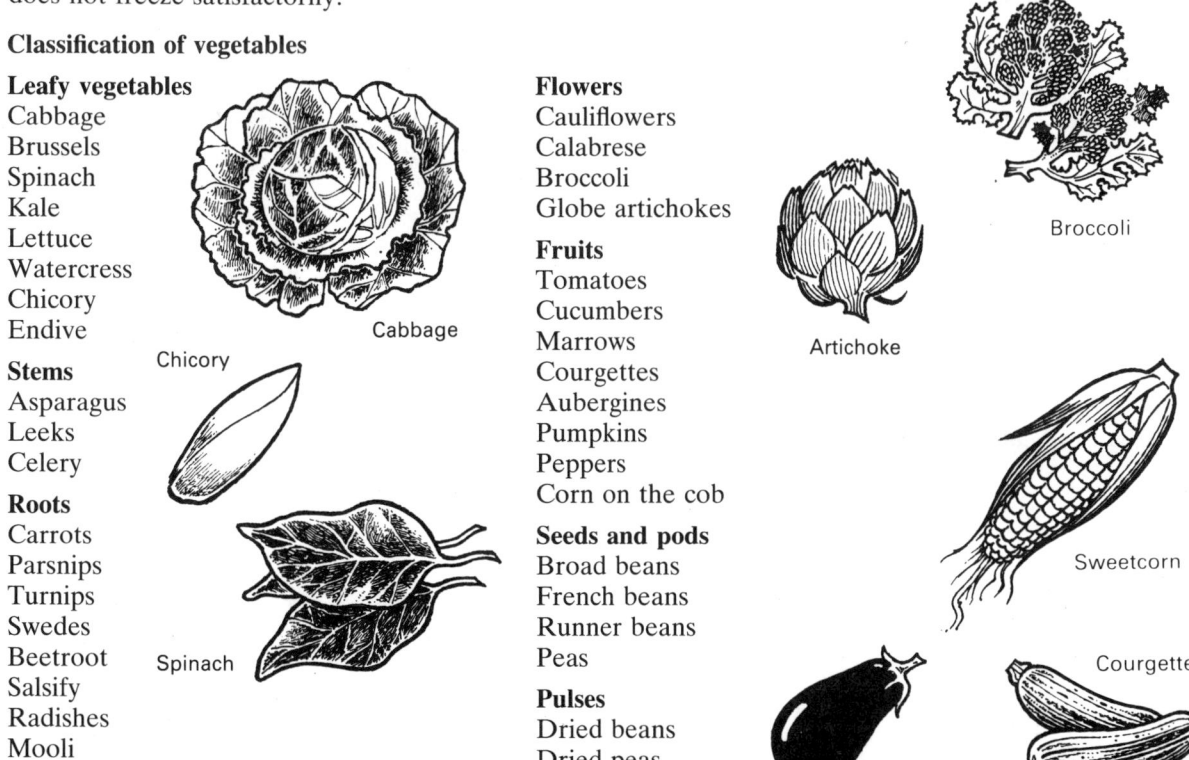

**Leafy vegetables**
Cabbage
Brussels
Spinach
Kale
Lettuce
Watercress
Chicory
Endive

**Stems**
Asparagus
Leeks
Celery

**Roots**
Carrots
Parsnips
Turnips
Swedes
Beetroot
Salsify
Radishes
Mooli
Yams

**Flowers**
Cauliflowers
Calabrese
Broccoli
Globe artichokes

**Fruits**
Tomatoes
Cucumbers
Marrows
Courgettes
Aubergines
Pumpkins
Peppers
Corn on the cob

**Seeds and pods**
Broad beans
French beans
Runner beans
Peas

**Pulses**
Dried beans
Dried peas
Soya beans

Cabbage
Chicory
Spinach
Broccoli
Artichoke
Sweetcorn
Courgette
Aubergine

**Fig. 4.26**

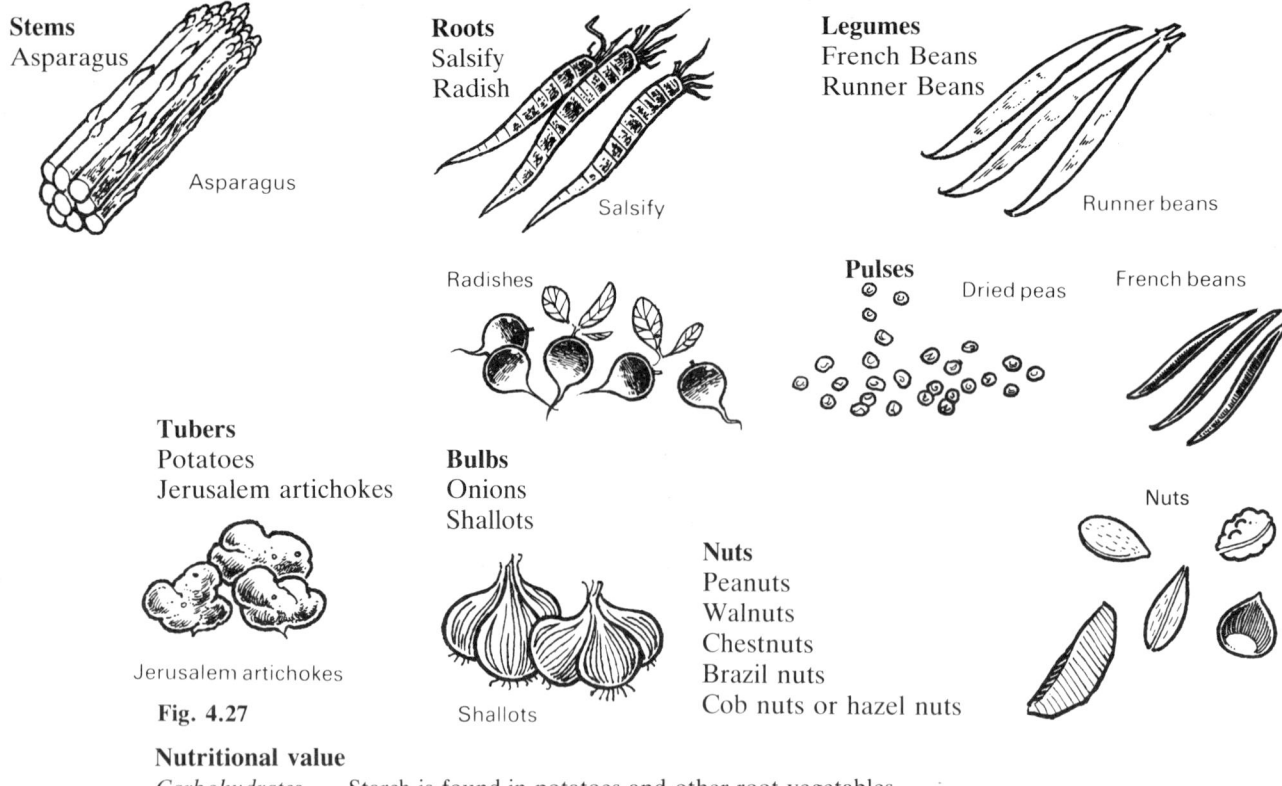

**Stems**
Asparagus

Asparagus

**Roots**
Salsify
Radish

Salsify

Radishes

**Legumes**
French Beans
Runner Beans

Runner beans

**Pulses**

Dried peas

French beans

**Tubers**
Potatoes
Jerusalem artichokes

Jerusalem artichokes

**Fig. 4.27**

**Bulbs**
Onions
Shallots

Shallots

**Nuts**
Peanuts
Walnuts
Chestnuts
Brazil nuts
Cob nuts or hazel nuts

Nuts

### Nutritional value

| | |
|---|---|
| *Carbohydrates* | Starch is found in potatoes and other root vegetables.<br>Sugar is found in cabbage, carrots, beetroot, swedes, tomatoes, onions.<br>Starch and sugar are found in parsnips, peas and broad beans.<br>Fibre is found in all vegetables especially in pulses. |
| *Proteins* | Low biological value protein is found in pulses, peas, beans, nuts and lentils. High biological protein is found in soya beans. |
| *Fats* | Very little except in nuts and soya beans. |
| *Vitamin A* | Occurs as carotene in dark green vegetables and carrots. |
| *Vitamin B* | Thiamin is found in peas, beans and green vegetables.<br>Riboflavin is found in broccoli, lettuce, spinach, asparagus and pulses. |
| *Vitamin C* | A good quantity is found in brussels sprouts, kale, cabbage, peppers, watercress, cauliflower, broccoli, spinach, asparagus and new potatoes. |
| *Vitamin D* | None |
| *Calcium* | Most vegetables contain it especially celery, kale, watercress and root vegetables. The presence of oxalic acid reduces its availability to the body. |
| *Iron* | Dark green vegetables, broad beans, peas, spinach and watercress contain it.<br>The presence of oxalic acid limits the amount absorbed.<br>Vitamin C is needed to help absorb the iron. |
| *Water* | All vegetables contain water, some as much as 90%. |

### Buying and storing vegetables

1 Buy vegetables in season, a plentiful supply means they are cheaper.

2 Choose fresh looking vegetables. Avoid wilting or damaged ones. Leafy vegetables should look crisp. Avoid those which have had the outer leaves stripped off.

3 Root vegetables should be clean, free of mud, insects, moulds and damage caused in lifting.

4 Canned, dried and frozen vegetables are useful for variety, for self-catering holidays and emergencies. Frozen vegetables are a better nutritional buy than canned and dried.

**Potatoes and root vegetables** should be stored in a cool, dry, dark place to prevent the formation of mould, shooting and the formation of green on potatoes.

**Leafy vegetables** should be stored for a short time only, in a cool place inside a polythene bag to prevent wilting.

### The preparation, cooking and serving of fruits and vegetables

1 Eat fruit and vegetables as fresh as possible before vitamins B and C have been lost by oxidation.

2 Eat fruit and vegetables raw whenever possible.

3 Peel thinly to avoid waste, loss of nutrients just below the skin and waste of money.

4 Use a sharp knife to avoid cell damage and the subsequent loss of vitamins B and C by oxidation.

**5** Prepare fruit and vegetables just before cooking. Vitamin B and C are lost by oxidation if they are left standing.

**6** Do not leave vegetables soaking in water, Vitamins B and C are water soluble.

**7** Cook vegetables in a *small amount* of boiling salted water. Add them to water a little at a time so the water does not go off the boil. Most vitamin C is lost at temperatures below boiling point. Salt prevents the loss of flavour from vegetables.

**8** Cutting the vegetables into small even-sized pieces means a shorter cooking time.

**9** Cook vegetables quickly with a lid tightly on the pan. Loss of water by evaporation is reduced and cooking is quicker. Although some vegetables will not be in the water, they cook just as quickly in the steam.

**10** Reduce the heat below the pan when the vegetables are boiling. Maintain a steady boil without water spurting from the pan. This saves fuel and overcooking.

**11** Do not use bicarbonate of soda to obtain a bright green vegetable because the alkali will react with the acidic vitamins to destroy them.

**12** Use the cooking water in a gravy or other sauce if possible.

**13** Serve vegetables immediately so that more vitamins B and C are not lost by oxidation in the air.

### The effect of cooking on fruits and vegetables

**Cellulose** is softened so digestibility is increased because the bulk is reduced.

**Cooked starch** is more readily digested. Starch grains gelatinize and thicken.

**Bacteria** are destroyed.

**Water soluble vitamins** B and C may be lost.

### Preserved vegetables

Vegetables can be dried, canned, frozen, salted and pickled.
They take less time to prepare and cook.
There is no waste but they can be expensive.
Flavour is sometimes changed by processing.
The nutritional value can be less than fresh vegetables except in the case of frozen vegetables when the nutritional value may be higher than fresh ones, because they are frozen immediately after picking.

### Cooking frozen vegetables

These vegetables should be added to boiling, salted water *in their frozen state.*

Follow the instructions on the packet. Usually the instructions are to bring the water back to the boil and then to reduce the heat so that the water is simmering gently. Times vary e.g. peas are usually simmered for 3 to 5 minutes depending on the size of the peas.

### Salad vegetables

There are various types of salad that can be served as starters to a meal, as side dishes, or as the main course and they make refreshing fillings for sandwiches.
The rules for preparing fruits and vegetables apply.
Fancy cutting of fruits and vegetables usually means that vitamin C is lost.
Lettuce will become crisp if placed, for a short while after washing, in a polythene bag in the crisper drawer of the refrigerator.
The use of an acid salad dressing will help to preserve vitamin C but it should not be allowed to stand for long because the salad vegetables can become soggy.
A dressing adds flavour, moistness and nutrients.

## 4.1.12   Gelatine

### Nutritional value

Gelatine is an animal protein lacking some of the essential amino acids so it is a low biological value protein. Its food value is increased when it is used with other foods.

### Manufacture

It is a very slow process which can take four months to pass through all the stages.

Gelatine is derived from the **collagen** found in the tendons, skin and connective tissues of the parts of animals not sold as meat.

**1** The tissues are washed, treated with a solution of lime and water and washed again.

**2** Heating follows and the collagen slowly changes to gelatine which dissolves in water.

**3** The gelatine solution is filtered and some of the liquid evaporated off to produce a very concentrated solution. This is allowed to set.
**4** After setting the gel is cut and dried.
**5** Grinding and milling produce particles of the size required.

### Types of gelatine

Powdered, granulated, leaf or sheet.

**Isinglass** is a very pure but expensive gelatine made from the swim bladder of the sturgeon.

**Agar Agar** is a setting agent used by vegetarians. It is made from seaweed.

### Uses of gelatine

Gelatine will dissolve in liquids at a fairly high temperature and it forms a gel at low temperatures. If a liquid is acidic, e.g. one containing lemon juice, it will take longer to set.

*Rules for using gelatine*

**1** Measure very accurately, 10g (½oz) will set 500ml (1pt) liquid. For a firmer jelly add an extra teaspoon of gelatine.
**2** Always sprinkle the gelatine into warm water or some of the recipe liquid. This can be done in a basin over a pan of hot water.
**3** Do *not* boil gelatine. Boiling will reduce its setting property.
**4** The liquid containing the dissolved gelatine should be at the same temperature as the rest of the ingredients before they are mixed. If warm gelatine solution is added to a very cold mixture it will set rapidly to give a stringy effect.
**5** Do not leave a dish set with gelatine in the refrigerator or freezer for too long because it will become very stiff and rubbery.

**Used for:** Jellies and sweets made with fruit juices, savoury or aspic moulds which set a meat stock containing meat or fish plus vegetables, whips, creams, mousse, sweet making (fruit jellies and pastilles, marshmallows) and ice cream.

### 4.1.13   Flavourings and colourings

There are many ways in which flavour and colour may be added to food at home and by manufacturers. The colour, flavour and aroma of food play a very important part in the enjoyment and digestion of a meal. Only those colours and flavours which have been fully tested are allowed to be used.

### Herbs and Spices

Herbs and spices add colour, improve flavour and aroma, but add very little nutritive value to a dish. They make food more varied and interesting and stimulate the flow of the digestive juices.

**Herbs** were originally introduced into the country by monks. They are usually the leaves of plants which can be used fresh or dried. They have been valued for their medicinal properties, for use in herbal teas and in pot-pourri.
   Crushing or chopping the leaves of herbs releases the flavour and scent of the aromatic oils they contain.
   Sometimes the flowers, roots or seeds are used.

**Spices** were used in the past to disguise unpleasant flavours and smells. They are now used in the preparation of medicines, cosmetics, pot pourri, dyes and pomanders.
   They are the dried stems, bark, flower buds, roots, seeds and seed pods of tropical plants.

*Rules for the use of herbs and spices*

**1** Buy them in small quantities. Flavour deteriorates in storage.
**2** Store them in tightly closed containers. This prevents the evaporation of the volatile oils.
**3** Quantities used depend a great deal on personal taste. Dried herbs have twice the strength of fresh ones.
**4** A more pungent flavour is produced if whole spices are bought and ground to a powder in a pestle and mortar when required.

**Table 4.10** Uses of some common herbs

| Herb | General points and uses |
| --- | --- |
| Bay leaves | Used dried in soups and stews. Garnish for a pâté. Part of marinades and of a bouquet garni. |
| Basil | In salads, tomato, mushroom and egg dishes |

| Herb | General points and uses |
|---|---|
| Chives | Chopped in salads, omelettes, cottage cheese and potato salad. New potatoes can be garnished with a butter glaze and chopped chives. |
| Fennel | Chopped leaves can be added to a sauce or to a fish dish. |
| Garlic | A plant of the onion family. Each bulb consists of many cloves. Use in savoury dishes. |
| Lemon balm | Summer drinks, salads, sauces and herbal tea. |
| Marjoram | Stews, sausage meat dishes and pizzas. |
| Mint | Mint sauce with roast lamb, mint and butter glaze on new potatoes. |
| Mixed herbs | Prepared mixture, used in spaghetti bolognaise and stews. |
| Parsley | Garnish for any savoury dish, sauces, herb butter. It contains vitamin C. |
| Rosemary | Soup, stew, chicken and lamb |
| Sage | Sage and onion stuffing, Sage Derby cheese |
| Tarragon | Leaves used in salads. Placed in vinegar for flavour. |
| Thyme | Stuffings, soups and stews |
| Bouquet garni | A bundle of fresh herbs tied together or a mixture of dried herbs in a muslin or sachet. Mint, thyme, rosemary, parsley, tarragon, sage. Use in soups and stews. Remove before serving. |

**Table 4.11** Uses of some common spices

| Spice | General points and uses |
|---|---|
| Caraway seeds | Bread and cakes |
| Cayenne pepper | Made from hot chillies. Cheese dishes. |
| Chillies | Used to make Tabasco sauce. Makes chilli powder. Chilli con carne. |
| Cinnamon | Bark of a tree. Used in fruit cakes, apple pies, biscuits. |
| Cloves | Whole flower buds or ground. Apple pie, bread sauce. |
| Curry powder | A mixture of hot spices. Contains a little iron. For meat, fish and vegetable curries. |
| Ginger | Whole root, powder or crystallized. Cakes, biscuits, melon, chutneys. Stem can also be crystallized. |
| Mustard | Seeds. Used to make pickles, chutneys, mustard. Served with meat, vinegarette dressings. It helps to bring a cheesy flavour out for instance in a cheese sauce. |
| Nutmeg | Whole or ground. Egg custards, rice and other milk puddings, cakes, soups, cheese and egg sauces. |
| Mace | Outer covering of the case around a nutmeg. To flavour a bechemal sauce, pâté and casseroles. |
| Paprika | Dried fruit of a Hungarian red pepper, used for goulash etc. |
| Peppercorn/pepper | Dried berry. Can be milled with (black pepper) or without skin (white). Savoury seasoning. |

**Essences**

These are the essential oils found in the leaves and fruits of plants. The extraction of the volatile oil is difficult. A solution is made in alcohol.

**Peppermint** essence is an exception and is relatively easy to extract.

**Lemon and orange** essences are found in the outer coloured layer of the fruit, the zest. This can be grated or peeled off to use as a flavouring or to infuse into a liquid.

**Vanilla** essence is made from the pod of the vanilla plant which is a type of orchid. The pod is also dried and can be put into a store jar with caster sugar to make vanilla sugar.

**Almond, cherry, apricot and peach** essence can be extracted from the kernels of the fruit.

Most essences are now synthetically made. Vanilla is the most successful and is derived from coal tar. A substance called vanillin is extracted and used to make the essence.

**Natural colours**

**Cochineal** is a pink colouring made from an insect found in Mexico and Peru.

**Turmeric** is a yellow powder made from an underground stem or rhizome. It is used in curries and mustard pickles.

**Annatto** is a yellow colour added to butter, margarine, cheese and milk. It is made from the fermented seed of a South American plant.

**Caramel** is a light to dark brown colour made from sugar.

**Synthetic colours**

These are made from coal dyes. A very limited range of colours is allowed by law.

## 4.1.14   Drinks

The nutritional value of any drink is mainly that they provide the body with water. They quench thirst and refresh. Cold drinks cool on hot days, hot drinks are warming when it is cold. Additional nutrients are added by milk and sugar if they are served with the drink.

**Table 4.12** Sources and nutritional value of common drinks

|  | Tea | Coffee | Cocoa |
|---|---|---|---|
| *Source* | Leaf of the tea shrub Leaves are picked, dried, rolled and fermented | Beans (seeds) of the coffee plant. The beans are dried, roasted and ground. | The beans of the seed pods of the Cacao tree. Dried, fermented and ground |
| *Nutrients* | Fluorine Riboflavin | | 1/5 protein 1/5 fat 1/2 starch iron calcium vitamin A B vitamins |
| *Stimulant* | Caffeine | Caffeine (less than tea) | Theobromine (very mild) |
| *Flavour* | Essential oils and tannin (makes bitter) if the tea stands too long | Essential oils Tannin (more than in tea) | Contains a little tannin |

**The manufacture of instant coffee**

The coffee is percolated and then either:
(a)  Some water is evaporated and then the rest removed by AFD–accelerated freeze drying. This method retains more flavour and aroma. Or;
(b)  Some water is evaporated and then the coffee is sprayed into hot air which removes the rest of the water. This leaves the powder–tiny particles of instant coffee, to fall to the base of tower. Aroma is lost but most of the flavour is retained.

**Drinking chocolate**

Drinking chocolate is instant cocoa.
(a)  Cocoa is made and then spray dried.
(b)  Sugar, sodium carbonate, salt and flavouring are added.

**How to make tea**

  1  Boil **freshly drawn** water–it contains more air and gives a better flavour.
  2  Use 1 teaspoon of tea per person + 1 and 125ml (¼pt) water per person.
  3  Warm the pot.
  4  Add tea to a dry warm pot just as the kettle boils.
  5  Pour boiling water immediately over the tea.
  6  Leave to infuse for 3-5 minutes. The smaller the leaf the cheaper the tea and the shorter the time to infuse.
  7  Strain the tea into cups.
  8  Serve with milk or lemon.

NB  As tea stands more tannin is extracted. The tea will have a bitter flavour and checks digestion.

**How to make cocoa**

1 teaspoon of cocoa to 1 cup of milk. Sugar to taste.
  1  Put cocoa into a cup or a jug if a larger quantity is being made.
  2  Blend in a little of the cold milk.
  3  Boil the rest of the milk and when it boils add it to the cocoa and cold milk.
  4  Return the mixture to the pan and bring to the boil. Stir with a wooden spoon. If the cocoa is not properly cooked, so that the starch has not gelatinized, it will have a powdery taste.

**How to make drinking chocolate**

Add 2 teaspoons to a cup of hot milk.

## How to make coffee

1 dessertspoon of coffee grounds to 125ml (¼pt) water. The finer the grounds the stronger the coffee.

### Jug method

1 Rinse out the jug with hot water and then dry.
2 Add the coffee grounds to the jug.
3 Add boiling water and stir.
4 Leave to infuse for 3-5 minutes.
5 Stir and then allow to settle.
6 Strain into a warmed coffee pot.

### Simple filter method

1 Place filter paper in the funnel resting on the warmed jug.
2 Measure the required amount of coffee into the filter paper.
3 Pour in a little boiling water.
4 Allow to stand for 30 seconds.
5 Add the rest of the water.

### Filter machine

1 Put cold water into the water container.
2 Place filter paper in the funnel over the jug.
3 Add the required amount of coffee.
4 Switch on.
5 The hot plate beneath the jug keeps the coffee warm once it is made.

### The coffee percolator

1 Measure the required amount of coffee into the perforated coffee holder.
2 Measure the cold water into the pot.
3 Put the coffee holder into the pot.
4 Put on the glass lid.
5 Heat on a hotplate or burner *or* just switch on if an electric percolator is being used.
6 Heat the percolator slowly until coffee can be seen through the lid. Percolate for about 10 minutes.
7 Remove the coffee holder and serve.

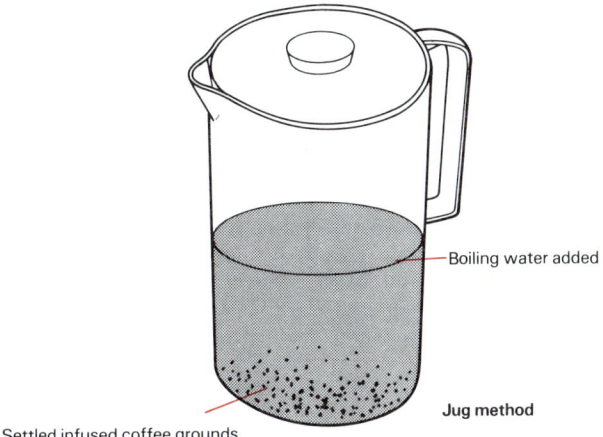

Boiling water added

Settled infused coffee grounds

**Jug method**

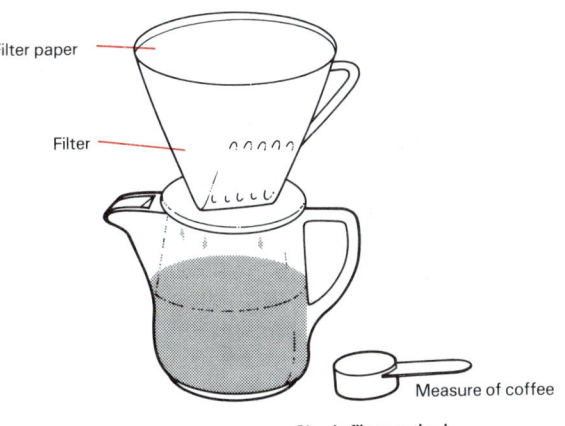

Filter paper

Filter

Measure of coffee

**Simple filter method**

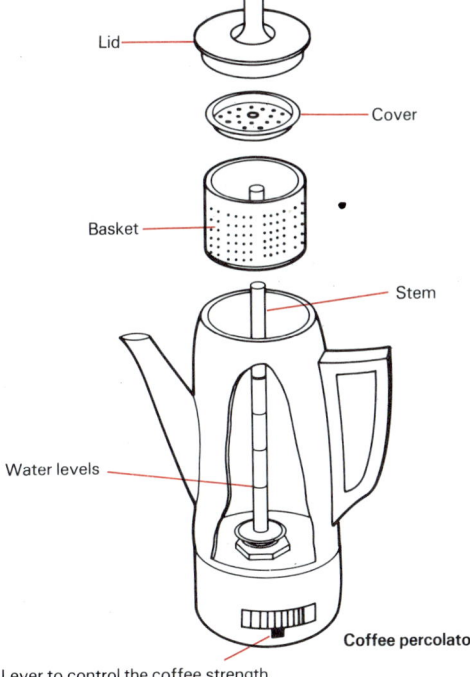

Lid

Cover

Basket

Stem

Water levels

**Coffee percolator**

Lever to control the coffee strength

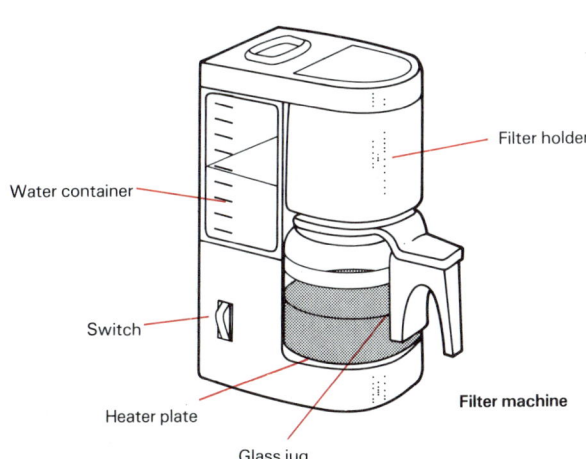

Filter holder

Water container

Switch

Heater plate

Glass jug

**Filter machine**

**Fig. 4.27** Methods of making coffee

**Serve coffee** black, with hot or cold milk, single or half cream. Demerara sugar is usually used.

**Fruit drinks**

Fruit drinks vary greatly in their composition. Some contain no vitamin C and some are not even made from fruit. **Read the label** very carefully.

| | |
|---|---|
| **Fruit juices** | These can be 100% fruit. Some are unsweetened and contain no additives, others contain sugar and permitted additives. |
| **Fruit squashes** | Undiluted these must contain 25% fruit juices. They contain very little vitamin C and lots of sugar. |
| **Fruit drinks** | 10% of the undiluted drink must be whole fruit. They contain a little vitamin C. |
| **Fruit cordial** | Fruit squashes with no solid material. Perfectly clear. e.g. lime juice and blackcurrant drink. |
| **Fruit flavoured drinks** | No real fruit is contained. Made with synthetic fruit flavours and colours. They contain no vitamin C. |
| **Carbonated drinks** | These are charged with carbon dioxide gas. They contain no vitamin C. |

Table 4.13 Fruit drinks

NB The artificial colours in some fruit drinks are suspected to have a link with hyper-activity in children. This has not yet been proved.

Fruit juices are expensive but they can be diluted with water because they have a strong flavour.

Drinks with a high sugar content are damaging to teeth and contribute to an excessive energy intake. Some drinks have artificial sweeteners.

**Homemade lemonade and orangeade**

A glass of orange or lemonade made from a whole orange or lemon can contain a whole day's supply of vitamin C.

*Ingredients*

1 lemon or orange
1 level tablespoon sugar (less with orange)
½pt (300ml) boiling water

1 Wash the lemon or orange.
2 Remove the zest very thinly and place it in a jug.
3 Pour on boiling water, stir and leave to infuse.
4 When cold to conserve vitamin C add the juice from the lemon or orange.
5 Strain and chill.
6 Dilute and sweeten to personal taste.

### 4.1.15   Salt

**Salt's place in the diet**

Salt or sodium chloride is needed to maintain the osmotic pressure of the body fluids. Too much salt can be retained in the body if the kidneys are inefficient at removing it from the blood. Too little salt and the body can become dehydrated.

Excessive retention of water in body cells can lead to high blood pressure with the greater risk of heart attacks and strokes.

Lack of salt can result in painful muscle cramp, drowsiness and mental confusion. Salt is rapidly lost in hot climates or in hot jobs such as steel working. It can also be lost with diarrhoea.

It is now recommended that we '**Eat less salt**'.

Salt is present in so many prepared foods that it is difficult to calculate how much we consume. Salt is used in cooking; it should not be necessary to use it at the table.

**Sources of salt**

Salt is obtained from natural brine springs or wells, from rock salt deposits and in hot countries, by evaporation from the sea.

Salt crystals vary in size according to the rate of evaporation.

**Sea salt** has large, coarse crystals which can be ground in a salt mill.

**Table salt** has very fine crystals and has sodium phosphate, sodium carbonate or rice flour added to keep it dry so that it flows.

**Iodized salt** has been fortified with sodium iodide or potassium iodide to supply the body with iodine.

**Cooking salt** is not as fine as table salt. It will not flow from a salt cellar.

**Block salt** is not so readily available now but is used for cooking and for preserving.

**Celery salt** is a mixture of ordinary salt and ground celery seed.

**Uses of salt**

1 In cooking, a weak salt solution stops the diffusion of natural salts and juices from meat, fish

and vegetables into the cooking water. If vegetables are cooked without salt the flavour is lost into the cooking water.

**2** To add flavour to under-seasoned food.

**3** In bread making salt gives flavour, controls the rate of fermentation and strengthens the gluten.

**4** Salt is used to preserve e.g. salt pork and beef, kippers, bacon, ham, butter, margarine, cheese (for flavour and to preserve). Runner beans are packed between layers of salt.

Salt can be added dry or as brine. It removes the water from the cells of micro-organisms so they cannot survive. When pickling onions the salt removes the water by osmosis so that the vinegar can penetrate right into the onion tissue.

**5** Foods such as apples, pears and potatoes, which go brown when cut because of an enzyme reaction with oxygen in the air, can be placed in a salt solution which stops the browning.

**6** Fingers can be dipped into salt to help to grip the skin of fish when pulling it off. It is abrasive and helps also to clean away the black skin from the body cavity.

### Alternatives to salt

**Selora** is a salt substitute where potassium replaces sodium.

**Ruthmol** is a low sodium salt.

## 4.1.16    Sodium hydrogen carbonate (bicarbonate of soda)

### Uses

**1** As a source of $CO_2$ to raise mixtures.
**(a)** Decomposition on heating
**(b)** Action of acid, moisture and heat
See Section 7.2 for further details.

**2** Sodium hydrogen carbonate is sometimes used as an antacid to ease indigestion.

**3** Refrigerator manufacturers suggest that sodium hydrogen carbonate is used in the water when washing the refrigerator. If detergents are used their smell can be absorbed by the plastic parts of the refrigerator lining.

**4** If sodium hydrogen carbonate is added to vegetables it will produce a brighter green colour *but* vitamin B and vitamin C will be lost.

## 4.1.17    Baking powder

*Basic recipe*
1 part sodium hydrogen carbonate (bicarbonate of soda) alkali
2 parts acid
1 part starch powder to absorb moisture.
See Section 7.2.

## 4.1.18    Yeasts    See Section 7.2.

## 4.1.19    Convenience foods

**Convenience foods** are those that are bought partly or completely prepared. Social changes have increased the demand for these foods:
**1** More than 50% of housewives go out to work.
**2** Families tend to sit down to family meals less frequently than in the past.
**3** Any member of the family can prepare a quick meal.
**4** Food technology has developed to;
**(a)** Improve the quality of convenience foods.
**(b)** Increase the range of products available in the shops.
**5** Advertising has had a part to play in the increased demand for prepared foods.

### Types of convenience foods

**Dry ingredients** that are ready to mix and cook. These include self-raising flour, custard powder, sauces and cake, scone and pastry mixtures.

**Dehydrated foods** which can be quickly rehydrated with cold or hot water. Instant potato, instant porridge oats, instant coffee, drinking chocolate, dried milk and instant puddings can be used immediately the liquid is added. Dried soups, vegetables and complete meals need to be cooked after the addition of water. Cup-a-soup and Pot Noodles need no cooking, they are instant.

**Frozen foods** More and more homes now have a freezer so the demand for frozen foods has increased. Some frozen foods can be eaten as soon as they have thawed, others need to be warmed through and others need to be completely cooked. Some can be cooked from frozen.

**Canned foods** can be used without cooking, for example tinned fruit, meat or fish, or they need to be heated through like soups, vegetables and snack meals.

**Ready-to-eat foods,** biscuits, cakes, pastries, sweets, drinks, crisps all have a long shelf life. Fresh cream cakes, cooked meats, meat pies all need to be eaten quickly because they are perishable.

**Advantages of convenience foods**

1 They are readily available.
2 There is a wide variety from which to choose.
3 They are easily stored in most homes.
4 They help elderly and handicapped people.
5 They save time in the preparation and cooking of meals.
6 They save the cook's energy and fuel.
7 They provide an emergency store for:
(a) Meals needed in a hurry.
(b) Catering for the unexpected guest.
(c) Do-it-yourself holidays.
(d) Replacing food spoilt by the cook.
(e) Times when the cook is away or ill.

**Disadvantages of convenience foods**

1 It is difficult to compare with accuracy the cost and nutritional value of these foods with those completely prepared at home. The cost of production and packaging can be offset by the savings in time and fuel together with the fact that there is usually no waste. With two or more wage earners in the family cost may not have to play a part in the choice of food.
2 Nutritionally some prepared foods are better value than fresh, for example frozen vegetables have a higher vitamin C content than those vegetables that have been in a shop for several days.
3 A diet composed almost entirely of commercially prepared foods can lack some nutrients. This lack could result in a deficiency disease.
4 The use of artificial colourings, flavourings and preservatives in convenience foods can be a disadvantage to those people who develop allergic reactions. Additives are tested but it often takes a long time to recognize a danger.
5 Many of the ready-to-eat foods are rich in saturated fats and refined sugar.
6 The use of these foods can take away the enjoyment and satisfaction of creating a meal.

**Using convenience foods**

**Always read the label** to check the contents and instructions for using.

**Dried foods** once opened and rehydrated should be used quickly. Store opened packets in a cool, dry place inside an airtight tin.

**Frozen foods** once thawed should be used immediately. Most thawed food should not be refrozen because this encourages the growth of bacteria and enzyme action.
1 Thawed food may be used to prepare and cook an entirely different dish and then frozen.
2 Frozen vegetables, fruits and bread are safe to refreeze if they are still very cold but not solid.
3 Observe the star ratings on the frozen food compartment of the refrigerator. The freezer manufacturer's booklet will state recommended storage times for different foods.
NB Freezing does not destroy micro-organisms it inhibits them until the temperature rises once more.
**Canned foods** should never be left in an open can.
1 Avoid dented tins, do not buy rusty, blown or bulging tins.
2 Store any food left over in a clean container, covered and in a cool place. Use within 48 hours.
3 Make sure the tin opener is sharp so that metal shavings do not get into the foods. Check the cleanliness of wall mounted tin openers.
4 Store cans in a cool place. Use in rotation.

**Bottled foods** must be stored in a cool place. Once opened always return the tops after use and screw them tightly.

## 4.2  Additives to convenience foods

**Additives are** substances added to food during its preparation. They may be natural or synthetic in origin.
1 They are added to improve *colour, flavour, appearance, texture, to preserve, to add to nutritional value* and *to lengthen shelf life.*
2 Without additives there would not be such a wide range of foods in the shops at reasonable prices.

**3** The consumer is protected by the Foods and Drugs Act and by the Trade Descriptions Act. (See Section 12.)

**4** Manufacturers must state which additives have been used. e.g. a label could read–'contains permitted flavouring, colouring, emulsifiers, anti-oxidants and preservatives'. These need not be named.

**5** Additives are continually tested and the list of permitted additives is reviewed in the light of new knowledge. Some are given EEC numbers.

**Types of additives**

**Colours**

**1** Natural–cochineal, alkanet, saffron, annotto, turmeric, caramel.

**2** Synthetic–only a few are permitted because many coal tar dyes and inorganic pigments are toxic.

**Flavours**–herbs, spices, citrus oils, artificial flavours.

**Flavour enhancers**–Monosodium glutamate is one example–it brings out the natural flavour of meat, fish, vegetables. They are found in canned and dried goods.

**Sweeteners**–sugar, saccharine, aspartame.

**Preservatives** to inhibit microbial spoilage e.g. sodium chloride, sodium nitrate, sodium nitrite, sulphur dioxide, benzoic acid, propionic acid.

**Anti-oxidants** which are added to fats and foods containing fats to prevent them becoming rancid by oxidation. e.g. ascorbic acid.

**Emulsifiers** are substances added to give an even texture of two or more substances–to give a smooth texture. e.g. Lecithin with oil and vinegar in mayonnaise. Stabilisers fix the emulsion and prevent separation of the droplets.

**Nutrients** Vitamins A and D are added to margarine; calcium carbonate, iron, thiamin and nicotinic acid to white flour; B vitamins to breakfast cereals; iodine to salt; vitamin C to soft drinks.

**Humectants** are used to prevent food drying out and becoming hard and unpalatable. These include sugars, saccharine, sorbitol and glycerine.

**Miscellaneous** Acids–for flavour, to get jam to set. Magnesium carbonate to salt to prevent caking. Air excluders–gases used to fill packets to keep away air. e.g. nitrogen.

# 5  Meal planning and special dietary needs

## 5.1  Meal planning

Meals must provide all the nutrients which the body needs to function properly (see section 2). A particular food may not be used becuase of religious belief or personal preference but the nutrients it contains must be supplied in other ways.

**Current nutritional advice** suggests that it might be healthier if:

**1** We eat **less refined sugar, fat** and **salt** and foods which contain these nutrients such as sweets, preserves, crisps, biscuits, cakes and pastries.

**2** We eat **more bread, cereals** (especially whole cereals), **fruits** and **vegetables**. The cereals will supply us with the energy no longer obtained from sugar and fat and all of these foods provide **fibre** and important **micronutrients**.

The energy intake provided by the day's meals must equal the energy expended on body metabolism, daily activities and work (see Section 2.10).

**Points to consider in planning a meal**

**1** A meal should be **nutritionally balanced**:

**(a)** Serve a wide **variety** of foods for a good supply of all nutrients.

**(b)** The nutritional balance can be assessed by checking that the meal contains foods from each of the following groups.

| Group 1 | Group 2 | Group 3 | Group 4 | Group 5 |
|---------|---------|---------|---------|---------|
| Meat | Vegetables | Potatoes | Water | Fats (very little) |
| Fish | Fruits | Pulses | All drinks | Oils (very little) |
| Eggs | | Bread | Sauces | |
| Milk | | Pasta | Soups | |
| Cheese | | Rice | | |
| Soya | | Other cereals and their products | | |

This assessment can be applied to the meals of any country or ethnic group.

**(c)** The nutritional needs of each individual in the family must be considered. These will be affected by sex, age, size, health and work done (see Section 3.3 and Section 5.3).

**2** There should be **variety** of

**(a)** Texture – hard food with soft food; moist food with dry food.

**(b)** Flavour – a food should not appear more than once in a meal.

**(c)** Colour – foods with different colours and the use of garnishes.

**3** The **cost**

**(a)** The cost of the foods plus the cost of fuel to cook it.

**(b)** Use eggs, cheese, milk, soya and LBV proteins to replace expensive cuts of meat. Use cheaper cuts of meat.

**(c)** Buy food in season – plentiful and cheaper.

**(d)** Plan meals and shopping. Budget for the week rather than impulse buying day by day.

**4** The **season of the year**

**(a)** Foods in season are plentiful and cheaper.

**(b)** Hot meals are welcomed in winter; cold meals are refreshing in summer.

**5** The **number of people** catered for

It is wasteful and expensive to prepare too much food.

**6** The **occasion**

An everyday meal is usually cheaper and less elaborate than a meal to celebrate a special event.

**7** **Religious** or **cultural customs**

**(a)** Many Roman Catholics do not eat meat on Fridays.

**(b)** The Jewish religion does not allow milk and meat to be cooked, served or eaten together. Jews do not eat rabbit, hare, pork, bacon or ham, eggs with blood spots, shell fish or eels.

**(c)** The pig is considered to be an unclean animal by Muslims.

**(d)** The cow is sacred to Hindus who will not eat foods from the slaughtered animal but will have milk, butter and cheese.

**(e)** It is customary in this country to eat potatoes, the French eat more bread, the Italians more pasta and more rice is eaten in the East.

**8** The **time available**

**9** The **cooking facilities**

Is the food being prepared in a family kitchen, in a bed-sitting room or outside a tent?

**10** The **skill** of the cook

## 5.2  Meal patterns

Meal patterns vary between ethnic groups, between countries and regions of a country, between families, and from day to day within the same family. The following meal descriptions can be used:

**Breakfast** is a meal eaten after a period of fasting while asleep.

**Mid-day meal** can be a snack, a packed meal or it could be the main meal of the day called lunch or dinner.

**Evening meal** can be a simple teatime snack of a drink and cake or biscuit, *followed by* a supper about 8pm. A complete but lighter meal than dinner.
*or* A *high tea* eaten about 6pm. This is usually a main course followed by a light sweet, cake and a drink.
*or* The *main meal* of the day eaten between 6pm and 8pm.

**Brunch** is a late breakfast combined with an early lunch, and is usually a quickly prepared snack meal.

**Supper** can also be a drink and a biscuit before bed.

**Courses** is also a term which confuses. In some cultures *all* the dishes of the meal are placed on the table at the same time. It is a western custom to have separate courses.

e.g. **A three-course breakfast**

Grapefruit
Boiled egg and bread and butter
Toast and marmalade
A drink

**A two-course dinner**  Course 1  Meat, fish or cheese, at least 2 vegetables
Course 2  A sweet (pudding or colloquially 'afters')

**A three-course dinner**  Course 1  Soup, or fruit juice or paté and salad
or egg mayonnaise etc.
Course 2  Meat or fish and vegetables
Course 3  A sweet or cheese and biscuits, or
a small savoury, or fresh fruit.

Coffee or tea is usually served after a main meal.

## 5.3    Portions per person

**Soup**  150ml (¼pt)

**Vegetables as purchased**
Potatoes  200g (½lb)
Other root vegetables  100 to 150g (4 to 6oz)
Fresh peas in pods  200g (½lb)
Runner beans  150g (6oz)
Broad beans  200g (½lb)
Dried peas or beans  50g (2oz)
Frozen peas or beans  75g to 100g (3 to 4oz)
Greens  150g to 200g (6 to 8oz)
Celery  1 large head serves 4
Cauliflower  1 medium size serves 4

**Meat**
With bone  100g to 150g (4 to 6oz)
With little waste  75g to 100g (3 to 4oz)
Cooked meat for
made up dishes  75g (3oz)

**Fish**
With bone  150g to 200g (6 to 8 oz)
Solid fish
(cod, haddock)  75g to 100g (3 to 4oz)
Cooked fish for
made up dishes  75g (3oz)

**Puddings**
Milk puddings  175ml (⅓pt)
Sponge puddings  30g (1oz) flour in portion
Pastry  30g (1oz) flour in portion
Suet pastry  45g (1½oz) flour in portion

**Sauces**
250ml to 300ml (½pt)  2 to 4 people

**Pasta**  25g to 50g (1 to 2oz)
**Rice**  25g to 50g (1 to 2 oz)
**Eggs**  1 to 2
**Cheese**  25g to 50g (1 to 2 oz)
**Raw fruit**  100g to 250g (4 to 8oz)
**Stewed fruit**  150g (5 to 6 oz)
**Cup of tea or coffee**  175ml (⅓rd pt)

## 5.4    Different dietary needs and meals for special occasions

### 5.4.1 Diet at different stages of life

**Pregnancy**

1 The diet must provide for the health and development of the baby in addition to supplying the daily needs of the mother.
2 The mother-to-be must not gain too much weight as this leads to complications. She needs a slightly higher intake of some nutrients:
(a) **Iron** for the haemoglobin in the blood of mother and baby so that both have the necessary oxygen to produce energy. The oxygen supply to the baby is very important at the birth and it needs to store some iron in the body until it is weaned.
(b) **Vitamin D, calcium and phosphorus** for the correct development of bones and teeth.
(c) **Calcium** for muscle function, to avoid cramps and for the clotting of blood.
(d) **Fluoride** for the formation of hard tooth enamel.
(e) **Vitamins A and C** for the formation of body tissues.
(f) **Vitamin C** for the absorption of the iron.
(g) **Vitamin B complex** for efficient energy production and metabolism.
3 A varied diet with HBV and LBV proteins, cereals, fruits and vegetables. The last three help to avoid constipation, common during pregnancy.
4 Fats, refined sugars, cakes, pastries, biscuits, preserves and sweets should be **strictly limited**.
5 Smaller more frequent meals to avoid indigestion.

**Diet during lactation**

The production of milk requires a good supply of **water, proteins, calcium, iron, vitamins** and slightly more energy-giving food. Reserves of fat built up during pregnancy are used up.

Fig. 5.1

Fig. 5.2

**Babies**

1 Babies have a better start in life if they are breast fed even if only for a short time. Babies can be breast fed until they have been weaned on to the mixed diet of the family.

2 Vitamins A, D and C are provided by vitamin drops obtained from the well-baby clinic.

3 Weaning or an introduction to a *mixed diet* starts between the ages of 4 and 6 months. At first only a teaspoon of strained food is given before the milk feed.

4 Larger quantities are gradually introduced. As one food is accepted a different one should be introduced.

5 Limit cereal foods.

6 **Avoid refined sugar** completely. A liking for sweet foods will not develop if sugar is not given early on.

7 Food for **biting** should be given as teeth appear e.g. toast, rusks.

8 Strained foods are replaced by mashed foods and these subsequently by food cut into small pieces.

9 Boiled, cooled water should be given as a drink during the first six months, then fresh fruit juice diluted. **Avoid squashes** as these contain sugar and colourings suspected of being a contributory factor in hyperactivity.

**Children 1 to 5 years**

1 The child grows rapidly and is very active. Appetites are often small but they thrive.

2 Small stomachs cannot cope with large meals or lots of fat.

3 Meals should provide a good supply of high and low biological proteins, cereals, fruit and vegetables.

4 Dairy foods supply vitamins A and D and calcium. The child should be out in the fresh air to form its own vitamin D by the action of sunlight on the skin.

5 Crisp foods should be given such as apple and carrot for bite.

6 Small helpings of food–attractively served to tempt the appetite.

7 Perseverance is needed with new flavours and textures. With familiarity, initial rejection soon turns to enjoyment.

8 Avoid too many fried and highly seasoned foods.

9 Plenty of water and diluted fresh fruit juice to drink.

10 Avoid sugar and sweet sticky foods–leads to obesity and tooth decay.

11 Serve meals at regular times. Allow time. Encourage good table manners.

12 If a child refuses food, remove it. Forcing leads to conflict. A hungry child will eat.

13 Limit eating between meals. Sweets are best eaten *after* a meal. Then they do not take away the appetite for more nutritious foods and the teeth can be cleaned.

14 Food should not be used as a bribe.

**Children 5 to 11 years**

1 Rapid growth continues. Children are still very active and many of them can use more calories.

2 As varied a diet as possible.

3 For good social training new foods and flavours should be introduced. Do not take too much notice of fads and fancies; it is not possible to cater differently for all members of the family. A hungry child will eat most things. Food allergies must be carefully planned for.

4 Avoid too many cakes, sweets, chocolates, ice cream, over sweetening, crisps, chips and squashes. Tooth decay is painful. A fat child is an object of ridicule and the foundations are laid for obesity and poor health in adult life.

**Adolescents**

1 The tremendous physical changes in *puberty* mean that teenagers have a higher nutritional need than any other group.

**Fig. 5.3**

**Fig. 5.4**

**2** The basic dietary needs should be supplied as with each age group. There is a great need for:

**(a) Iron** for the haemoglobin in all the new blood cells. Girls especially need it because of the loss of blood in menstruation. Anaemia will result from a shortage of iron.

**(b) Vitamin C** is needed for the absorption of iron, the formation of inter-cellular cement and connective tissue.

**3** The higher energy need is met by the carbohydrates occuring naturally in foods. 30-35% of the energy they need can come from fats, **but** foods with a **high sugar** and **fat content** should be **limited**. It is a very dangerous time to slim. Anorexia nervosa, at best, can cause damage to some of the body systems and, at worst, can lead to death.

### Adults – manual and sedentary workers

**1** The work a person does is the factor which most affects dietary needs.

**2** A varied diet provides all the micronutrients.

**3** Manual workers can eat more foods with a high calorific value because they use up this energy in work. If an office worker ate the same amount of energy-giving foods the result would be obesity with all its problems, and probably indigestion.

**4** Manual workers perspire more. Loss of water can mean loss of salt. Provide more fluids and a little more salt can be added to their food.

**5** These rules apply to most people but some people do not burn up their energy-giving foods efficiently and gain weight when eating very little. A great deal of research is going on into this aspect of body metabolism.

### The elderly

**1** The majority of elderly people need very little change to the diet they have followed throughout their adult lives. A slower pace just means a reduction in energy-giving foods.

**2** Obesity aggravates the health problems of old age so fat and sugar in the diet should be reduced.

**3** Brittle bones break easily. To prevent decalcification the elderly should have a high intake of vitamin D and calcium. Getting outside into the sunlight is essential. Diet is doubly important for the housebound.

**4** Anaemia can become a problem. Offal is inexpensive. To obtain the iron from eggs, cereals and vegetables a good supply of vitamin C is required.

**5** Vitamin C is essential to avoid a mild form of scurvy. Fruit is expensive in the winter so a vitamin supplement, prescribed by the doctor, may be needed.

**6** Encourage simple and economic methods of cooking.

**7** Money can be in short supply. Food must not be too expensive.

**8** All too often a diet of biscuits, bread and tea is consumed because of a lethargy towards cooking proper meals for one person, or lack of interest. Some authorities and the WRVS supply midday meals for old people in their houses, called 'meals on wheels'.

**9** Badly fitting dentures and difficulty with digestion require soft-textured food which is easy to chew and digest.

**10** Heart disease, diabetes and other illnesses mean special diets. The doctor's instructions should be followed.

## 5.4.2  Diet during illness

### General rules

**1** Obey the doctor's instructions.

**2** Be scrupulously clean in preparing, cooking and serving food.

**3** Use really fresh foods to avoid the risk of bacterial contamination.

**4** Cooking should be done well away from the sick room.

**5** Meals should be at regular times and punctual–they are highlights in a sick person's day.

**6** Choose food that is appetizing and easily digested.

**7** Provide variety in the types of food, colour and texture.

**8** Small helpings should be attractively served. A plateful of food can be very off-putting to someone with a poor appetite.

**9** Several small meals are better than fewer larger meals.

**10** Avoid fatty foods, fried foods, spicy foods and too much bulky carbohydrate.

**11** Easily digested methods of cooking are steaming and poaching.

**12** Make sure that the tray is large enough, that everything is clean, that everything needed for the meal is there and that the china is undamaged.

**13** Make sure the tray is easy to manage and is not overloaded.

**14** At the end of the meal remove all evidence of the meal.

**15** Always leave a drink by the bed–covered.

**16** If the sick person is infectious, keep their china and cutlery separate and sterilize it by scalding with boiling water.

### In the early stages of an illness

A liquid diet should be given until the temperature drops:

**1** Fruit juices with added glucose are quickly absorbed for energy.

**2** Milk and milk drinks if the illness allows.

**3** Barley water.

**4** Beef teas and strained broths.

2½ to 3 litres of liquid a day should be consumed. Always leave a drink by the bed.

### During the second stage of an illness

The digestive system is weak. Meals must be light and easily digested.

**1** Plenty of proteins and micro-nutrients should be eaten to build and repair the body.

**2** Steaming, stewing and poaching are good methods of cooking at this stage.

**3** No fried or spicy foods should be given.

**4** Some carbohydrates should be given *but* very little energy is needed when lying in bed.

**5** Fats should be avoided for the same reason as in (4).

**6** A plentiful supply of fluid is still needed. A drink should be left by the bed.

*Foods* Chicken, turkey, egg dishes, milk and milk dishes, white fish, soups, meat broths, fruit and vegetables.

### During the third stage–Convalescence

**1** More energy-giving foods should be gradually included.

**2** Plain biscuits, light cakes, a little potato. Extra protein for tissue repair.

**3** Plenty of fruits, vegetables for extra vitamin C and fluids.

*Meals* should gradually return to normal with a greater variety of cooking methods, yet avoiding fried foods.

### 5.4.3   Packed meals

### General Points

**1** The food should be easy to pack without disintegrating. It should be protected from drying out.

**2** The food should be easy to carry. If taken by car a wider range of foods is available from which to choose.

**3** Provide a variety of foods to avoid monotony, if a packed meal is needed every day.

**4** Make sure the meal is nutritionally balanced.

**(a)** A good supply of protein

**(b)** Not too much carbohydrate

**(c)** Always include fruit and salad vegetables. Salads in polythene boxes

**(d)** Always include a drink.

*Foods for carrying*

| | | | |
|---|---|---|---|
| Scotch eggs | Tomatoes | Fruit pasties | Soup |
| Hard boiled eggs | Apples | Small cakes | Tea |
| Meat pasties | Oranges | Fruit cake | Coffee |
| Cheese & vegetable pies | Pears | Gingerbread | Fruit juice |
| Pork pies | Coleslaw | Yogurt | |
| Sausage rolls | Fruit & nuts | | |
| Sandwiches (moist fillings) | | | |
| Bread rolls | | | |

*Foods for a car picnic*

| | | | |
|---|---|---|---|
| Cold roast chicken | Salads | Fruit flans | Soup |
| Savoury pies | Dressings | Fruit salad | Coffee |
| Savoury flans | | Fruit pies | Tea |
| Rolls | | Cheese & biscuits | Cold drinks |
| Hams | | Cakes | |
| Scotch eggs | | Sweets in plastic containers with lids | |
| | | Yogurt | |

A good choice of fresh fruit which is always refreshing.

### 5.4.4  Vegetarians

There are **two** types of vegetarian.

The **lacto-vegetarian** will eat eggs, cheese and milk but no meat.
The **vegan or strict vegetarian** will eat nothing of animal origin. The decision to follow one of these diets could be based on:

1 Religious beliefs.
2 An objection to the killing of animals.
3 A dislike of the flavour of animal flesh.
4 The belief that a vegetarian diet is a healthier diet.

#### Practical Considerations

1 Preparing meals for lacto-vegetarians presents no real problems. Many dishes can be made with eggs, cheese, pulses, nuts, cereals and fresh fruits and vegetables.
2 Vegans have to make sure that they obtain sufficient HBV protein by eating a larger amount and a wider range of LBV proteins when each of these can compensate for amino acid deficiency in the others.
3 Vegans obtain their vitamin D from the sun and from fortified margarines made with vegetable oils. Vitamin A comes from margarine and the carotenes in plant food. They can become short of vitamin $B_{12}$ and develop anaemia. Vegan foods are often fortified with this vitamin or tablets are taken. The Vegan Society publishes literature to help people following a vegan diet so that they do not become deficient in any one nutrient.
4 A vegetarian diet can be expensive.
5 The high intake of fibre rich food can produce a very full feeling until the body adjusts.
6 Calcium can be obtained from pulses, whole cereals, nuts, fruit and vegetables but much is unavailable to the body because of the presence of phytic acid.

### 5.5  The presentation of food

Colourful, attractive, well-prepared food, served on clean dishes and clean cloths stimulates interest and the production of the digestive juices. There are three important considerations.

**Cleanliness** All dishes, cloths, china and cutlery should be clean to avoid bacterial contamination.

**Convenience** Everything should be on the table or tray that the people eating the meal will require—cruet, cutlery, napkin etc. Serving implements should be placed near to the person who is to serve.

**Safety** Cloths should not trail—small children can pull these and apart from causing breakages, can injure themselves seriously.
1 Knives should be clear of the edge of the table.
2 Place hot tea pots, vegetable dishes etc. on mats away from the edge of the table.

#### Some traditions when serving food

**Cloths**—with modern laminated plastic and heatproof seals to tables often a cloth is not used. Sometimes individual place mats are used.
1 Formal meals—plain white damask cloths.
2 Informal meals—coloured cloths which tone with the china.
3 Trays are often very colourful and a cloth is not needed.
4 Napkins usually match the cloths.

**Flowers** add colour. They should be low so that people can see across the table.
1 Flowers on a tray can be awkward—lack of space, easily spilt by someone in bed. A single flower across the corner is adequate.
2 Buffet tables can have a tall arrangement placed at the back, or to one side.

#### Serving dishes
1 Should be warmed for hot food.

**2** Edges should be clean.

**3** Oval plates and dishes with plain dish mats are used for savoury dishes.

**4** Round plates and dishes with d'oyleys, are used for sweet dishes.

**5** Casserole dishes and pie plates should stand on another plate to save a mess on the table when they are served.

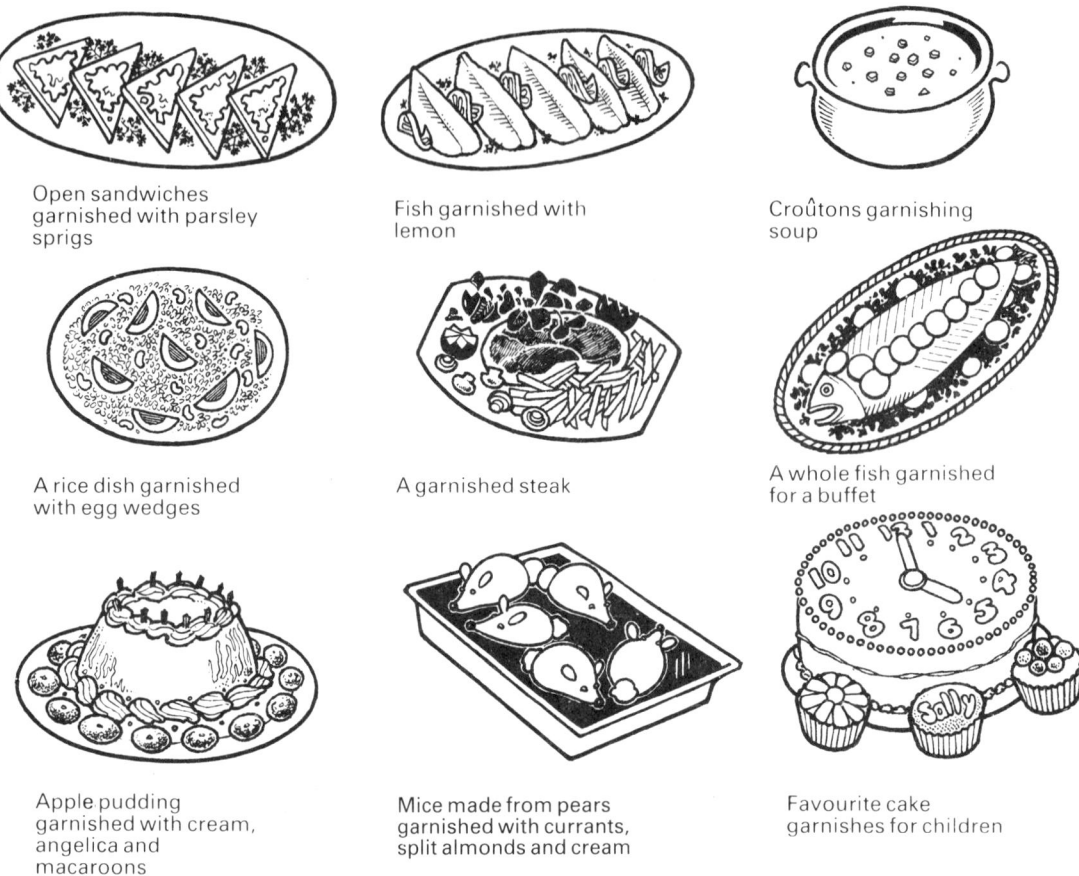

Open sandwiches garnished with parsley sprigs

Fish garnished with lemon

Croûtons garnishing soup

A rice dish garnished with egg wedges

A garnished steak

A whole fish garnished for a buffet

Apple pudding garnished with cream, angelica and macaroons

Mice made from pears garnished with currants, split almonds and cream

Favourite cake garnishes for children

**Fig. 5.5** Garnishes

**Garnishes** add colour, flavour, texture and sometimes nutrients to a dish.

**1** They can be raw or cooked.

**2** Overgarnishing can detract, so do not cover dishes with bunches of parsley when a small sprig is adequate.

*Raw garnishes*–parsley, watercress, cress, chives, lettuce, tomatoes, cucumber, red or green peppers, gherkins, olives, onions, radishes, mint.

*Cooked garnishes*–egg (sliced, quartered, sieved white and yolk separately), bacon rolls, sausages, croûtons, tomatoes, mushrooms.

*Decoration for sweet dishes*–glacé cherries, angelica, nuts, crystallized fruits and flowers, sweets, grated chocolate, chocolate drops, chopped jelly, sugar, whipped cream, icings, vermicelli strands (chocolate or sugar).

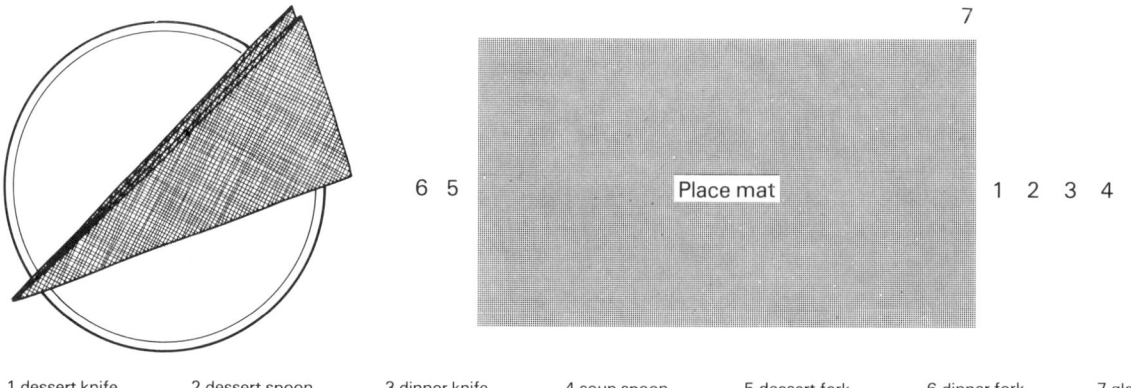

1 dessert knife    2 dessert spoon    3 dinner knife    4 soup spoon    5 dessert fork    6 dinner fork    7 glass

**Fig. 5.6** An individual cover

### Table and tray settings

Table settings are called **individual covers** for each person. Figure 5.6 shows how this should be laid for a three-course meal.

**A formal table** for a three-course dinner should include a cloth or table mats and flowers. Figure 5.7 shows a more formal table.

**Fig. 5.7** A formal table setting

**Trays** laid for serving tea and coffee are shown in Figure 5.8.

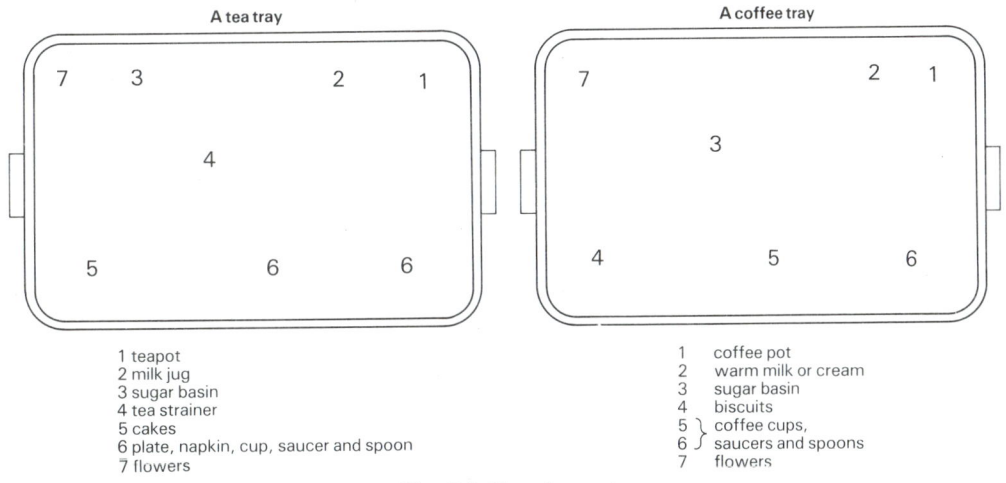

| A tea tray | A coffee tray |
|---|---|
| 1 teapot | 1 coffee pot |
| 2 milk jug | 2 warm milk or cream |
| 3 sugar basin | 3 sugar basin |
| 4 tea strainer | 4 biscuits |
| 5 cakes | 5 ⎫ coffee cups, |
| 6 plate, napkin, cup, saucer and spoon | 6 ⎭ saucers and spoons |
| 7 flowers | 7 flowers |

**Fig. 5.8** Tray lay-outs

## 5.6 Economy in the preparation of family meals

Savings should be made with time, effort, fuel and money.

### Time

**1** Plan activities:
**(a)** Shopping–once or twice a week to avoid daily impulse buying.
**(b)** Cooking–plan meals to fit in with families activities. e.g. use of the slow cook pot or casserole in a slow oven, or making good use of the automatic timer.
**2** Make use of delivery services–baker, milkman.
**3** Use modern equipment–mixers, blenders, pressure cookers, food processors, microwave cookers.
**4** Make use of one-stage methods of mixing.
**5** Make double quantities of, for instance, a casserole; use half and freeze half.

### Effort

**1** Points 1 to 4 above.
**2** Plan the kitchen to save unnecessary walking about, for easy working and cleaning.
**3** Use convenience foods occasionally.
**4** Baking sessions and the use of a freezer can mean more time spent with family and friends.

**Fuel**

Gas and electricity are expensive. Save fuel and money as follows:

  1 Switch on the cooker just before it is needed.
  2 Switch off immediately after use.
  3 Regulate hotplates and burners by reducing the temperature when liquids have boiled.
  4 Use the central hotplate of a dual ring for small pans. Pans should cover the hotplate.
  5 Never switch on the main oven for one item. Bake extra for later.
  6 Cook a meal entirely in the oven or on the hob.
  7 Use double or triple-section saucepans on one ring or burner.
  8 Do not overfill pans with liquid, it takes more heat to boil.
  9 Do not use saucepans that are larger than necessary.
  10 Lids on boiling pans reduce the loss of heat and speed up cooking.
  11 Use steamers, pressure cookers and microwave cookers.

**Money**

  1 All fuel saving saves money.
  2 Shop around.
  (a) Buy food at the lowest prices–why pay 20p for margarine when another shop sells it for 16p?
  (b) Make use of 'loss leaders'–special offers to attract people into the shop.
  3 Use 'money off' tokens.
  4 Make use of 'special' and 'money back' offers.
  5 Buy in bulk if there are storage facilities.
  6 Food wasted = wasted money–do not buy too many perishable foods.
  7 Store perishable foods carefully, so that they remain in an edible condition for as long as possible.
  8 Make use of meat substitutes–eggs, cheese, milk, more LBV protein foods and extenders such as soya.
  9 Do not buy too many convenience foods.
  10 Buy seasonal fruits and vegetables for cheapness.
  11 Preserve surplus crops.
  12 Home-made jams, marmalade, cakes, pastries and bread are cheaper than bought varieties and are usually better in flavour and nutrients.
  13 Plan meals and shopping to save impulse buying, which is expensive.
  14 It is expensive to eat excess protein foods when the energy which they will supply can be obtained more economically from starches and fats.

# 6  Cookers and cooking

## 6.1  Reasons for cooking food

  1 To make the food safe to eat. High temperatures destroy bacteria and toxins.
  2 To make the food easier to eat and digest. Softening of cellulose cell walls of plant foods; gelatinization of starch; conversion of insoluble connective tissue collagen to soluble gelatine.
  3 To improve the appearance of the food.
  4 To develop flavour and to add to the flavour.
  5 Different methods of cooking the same food introduce variety into our meals.
  6 Food is preserved when high temperatures prevent microbial activity.

## 6.2  Methods of cooking–heat transference

Heat is needed. In a conventional cooker heat is transferred to and through the foods by **conduction, convection** and **radiation**.

### Conducted Heat

Energy passes through a solid substance and on into other substances in contact with it. The heat energy makes the molecules vibrate rapidly transmitting the energy to neighbouring molecules which vibrate too.

Some materials are *poor conductors* of heat–cotton, wool, wood, plastic, air, glass. Others are good conductors–silver, copper, brass, aluminium, iron.

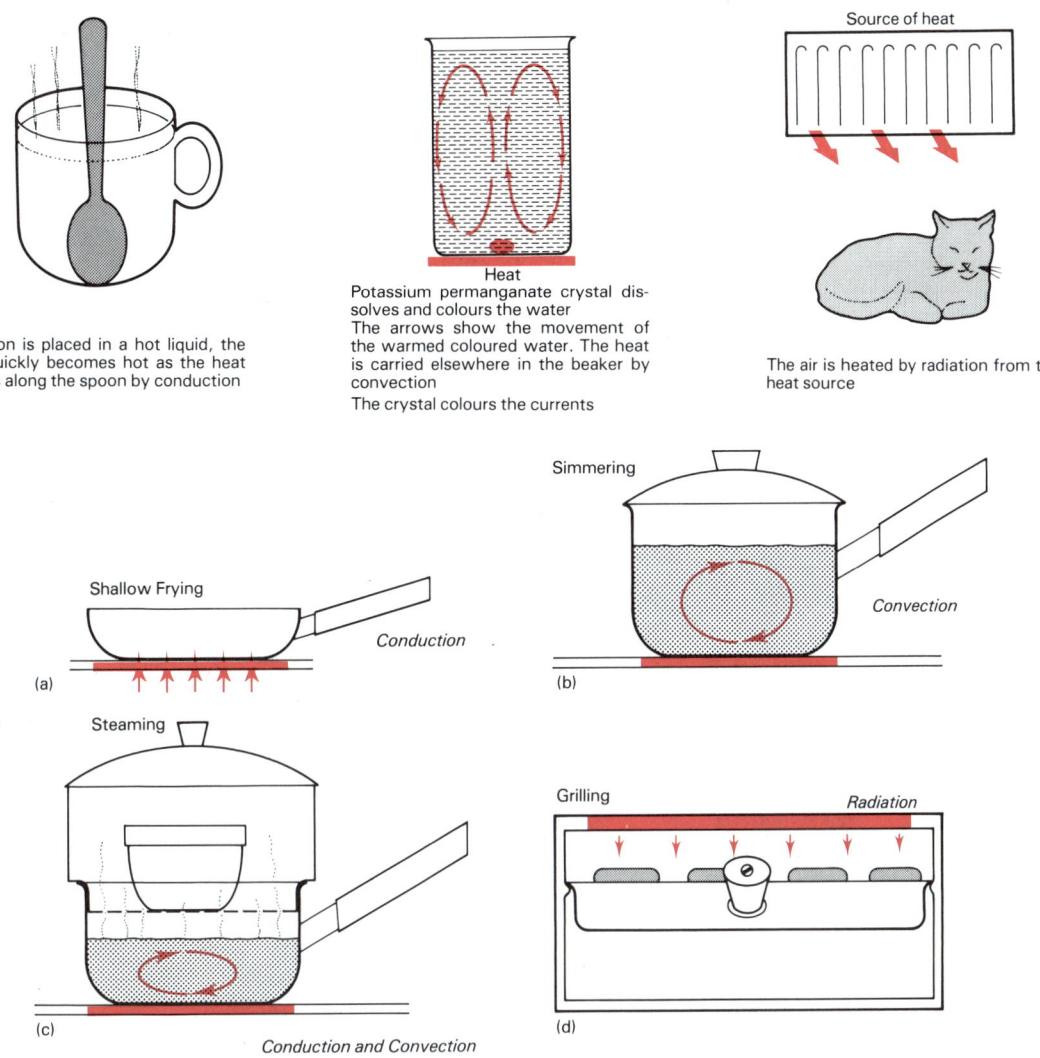

**Fig. 6.1** Conduction, convection and radiation

**Table 6.1** Application of conductivity in cooking

| *Non conductors* | *Conductors* |
|---|---|
| Wooden or plastic handles to pans | Outer aluminium coating or copper bottoms to stainless steel pans to make them better conductors of heat |
| Wooden spoons to stir mixtures heating in pans | |
| Oven gloves to lift hot dishes | |
| Double bases to cake tins which provide an insulating layer of air | Food cooking more quickly in metal containers |
| Insulation in the sides and doors of cookers | Hotplates transmitting heat to pans |
| | Heat transmitted to food, passing into the food by conduction |

### Convected heat

The molecules of a fluid (gas or liquid) move more rapidly and further apart when heated. As they do this their volume increases, they become lighter and rise. Cooler, denser molecules fall to take their place. This movement of warmer and cooler molecules is called *convection*.

*Applications in cooking*

Heating up ovens, liquids in pans, kettles and dishes, oil in frying, water in a kettle.

### Radiated heat

Radiated heat is heat energy which travels in waves in all directions from a source of heat. The heat waves warm any object lying in their path. The radiated energy waves travel through space or a vacuum.

*Applications in cooking*
  1 Grilling on a conventional cooker
  2 Infra-red grills which give more rapid and efficient grilling
  3 Toasting in an electric toaster

  4 Heating up the oven of an electric oven–heat radiates from the sides
  5 Spit roasting
  6 Barbecue grills

### 6.2.1  Cookers

**Choice of a cooker**

There is a wide variety of cookers from which to choose. Note these points:
  1 Consider the types of fuel available–gas, calor gas, electricity, oil, solid fuel.
  2 The cost. How much to buy? How much to run?
  3 Size. Will it fit the space available? It is expensive to use a large cooker for a small family. Are there special needs e.g. for elderly or handicapped?
  4 Is it easy and safe to use?
  5 Will it be easy to clean?
  6 Which additional facilities do you wish the cooker to provide? Eye or waist level grill, radiant, dual or disc hotplates, ceramic hob, glass door, oven light, minute minder, automatic timer, double oven cooker, heat clean lining in the oven, oven fan, free standing or built in cooker (split level or cooker built into floor unit), storage space, warming drawer.
  7 Colour and general design.
  8 Look for the BEAB mark of safety.
  9 Reputable manufacturer. Good after sales service/maintenance.

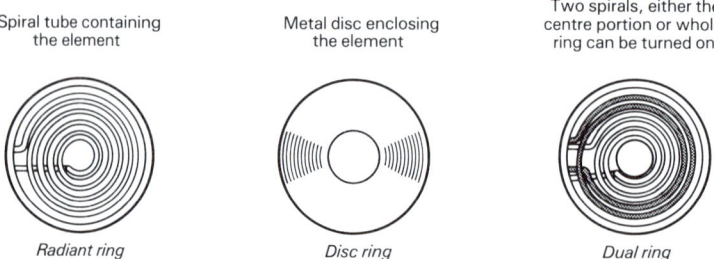

**Fig. 6.2** Hotplates

**Notes on some special features**

  1 Hobs
(a) Gas burners can have automatic or manual controls for lighting. Pilot lights are less frequently used now. Electric ignition is more common. Burners can have simmerstats for controlled heating.
(b) Electric hotplates can be made of a single or double spiral containing the elements. The inner, smaller elements are to save fuel when using a small pan. Disc rings are of circular, flat metal enclosing the elements. They do not glow but are easy to clean.
  2 Ovens
(a) Cookers with two ovens give a more economic method of baking if only one item is to be made. The top oven takes less time and less energy to heat up. In the main oven the heating elements can be at the sides or, if the oven has a fan, a circular element is placed in the back wall of the cooker and the heat produced is blown all around the oven by the fan. The oven is heated evenly throughout.
(b) The heating element for the top oven is found in the floor of the oven. This means that baking tins should not be placed on the floor of the oven because this could result in burning the bottom of the food.
(c) A cooker with a double oven usually has a large grill, independently controlled, in the top oven. To save electricity it is usually possible to heat only half of the grill.
(d) Heat clean liners reduce the amount of cleaning necessary. Grease and dirt are absorbed by the coating on the linings and eventually, when the oven is hot, oxidation takes place. Gases vapourise and carbon falls to the floor of the oven. A damp cloth is all that is needed. The special linings will be damaged by oven cleaners.
  3 Rotisserie
This is a spit for roasting which fits into the main oven or the eye level grill compartment. Special attachments are usually provided to make kebabs in addition to those for roasting meat.
  4 Built-in cookers
(a) The oven unit and the hob unit *can* be in different parts of the kitchen. It is possible to have a hob using gas and an oven heated by electricity or vice versa.
(b) There is a new type of built-in cooker which fits into the floor unit. The hob is attached to the oven but there is no back as in a free-standing cooker.

**(c)** Ceramic hobs. Electric hot plates are set below a plain ceramic top which is perfectly smooth. The colour may be white, brown or black. When switched on the elements colour a white top brown and can be seen as a red glow with the darker tops. Pans used on these hobs must have flat, clean, dry bottoms. Pans cannot tilt. Cleaning is simple but detergents and abrasive must not be used. Liquid cleaners or special cleaners are needed. The hob is rather slow at heating up and cooling down. The cook must learn to use residual heat if she does not wish to use a great deal of electricity.

**5** Timers

**(a)** The minute minder rings when the cooking time is up. It has no control over the oven.

**(b)** The automatic timer will switch on the oven and then switch it off in the absence of the cook (see pages 79-80).

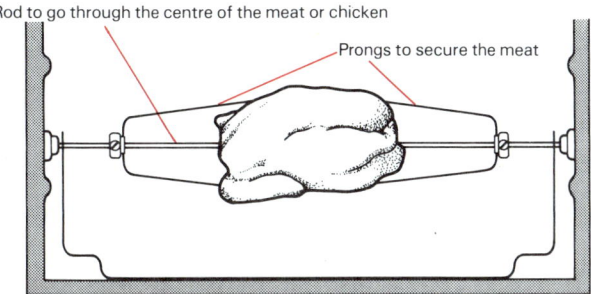

Rod to go through the centre of the meat or chicken

Prongs to secure the meat

**Fig. 6.3** A rotisserie

The spit is rotated by an electric motor behind the oven wall

## 6.2.2  Moist and dry methods of cooking

**Moist methods**

Heat is transferred to the food by water or steam: steaming, pressure cooking, boiling, simmering (stewing, braising, poaching) and slow-cook pots.

**Dry methods**

Heat is transferred by the air or fat: baking, roasting, pot roasting, spit roasting, grilling, and frying (dry, sautéing, shallow, deep fat).

**Steaming**

Food is cooked in the steam from boiling water. Some foods are in direct contact with the steam, others well protected from the wetness.

The diagrams on page 76 show the different ways in which food can be steamed.

| Advantages | Disadvantages |
|---|---|
| Nutrients do not dissolve into the water. | Most foods take a long time to cook. |
| Food is light and easy to digest. | Food can lack flavour and colour. |
| Needs little attention, except to top up boiling water in the pan. | Sauces and garnishes are important. |
| | The kitchen can become very steamy. |
| Food seldom overcooks. | |
| Can save fuel e.g. fish steamed over vegetables. | |

**Rules for steaming**

**1** The lid of the steamer should fit tightly to prevent the loss of steam and to keep temperature constant.

**2** The water in the pan should be boiling rapidly before the perforated steamer with the food in is placed in position and then the heat turned down to simmer.

**3** Approximately every 30 minutes top up the pan with boiling water – to maintain a constant supply of steam and to prevent the pan boiling dry.

**4** The food should be well protected from the steam to save loss of nutrients and to prevent the food becoming soggy.

**Pressure cooking**

This is cooking in **super-heated steam**.

The pressure cooker is a closed pan with a strong and firmly secured lid. The lid locks and seals with a rubber gasket. Steam cannot escape so pressure builds up inside.

In the lid there is a control valve onto which fit the weights, and a safety valve which is pushed out or melts if the pressure becomes too great. A pressure cooker **cannot explode**.

If the weights are forced off steam and liquid food rushes out and can cause severe scalds. The pressure must be reduced before opening the lid.

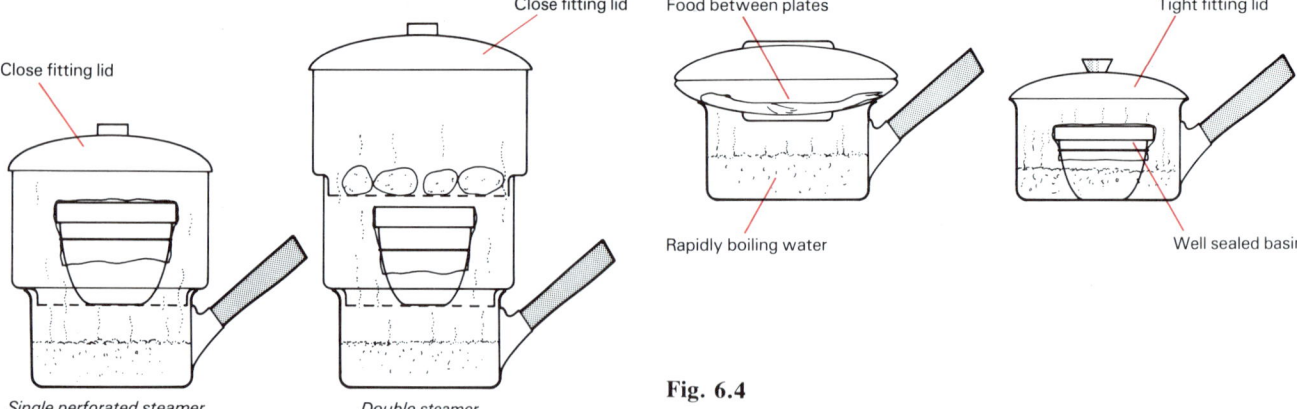

Single perforated steamer          Double steamer          **Fig. 6.4**

There are several different pressure cookers available. They may be large with a high dome or low-domed, and they can be automatic in that they reduce pressure themselves at the end of cooking time.

Pressure cookers have a trivet and separate containers inside. The diagrams Fig. 6.5 and 6.6 show a typical pressure cooker and one of the two different types of weight.

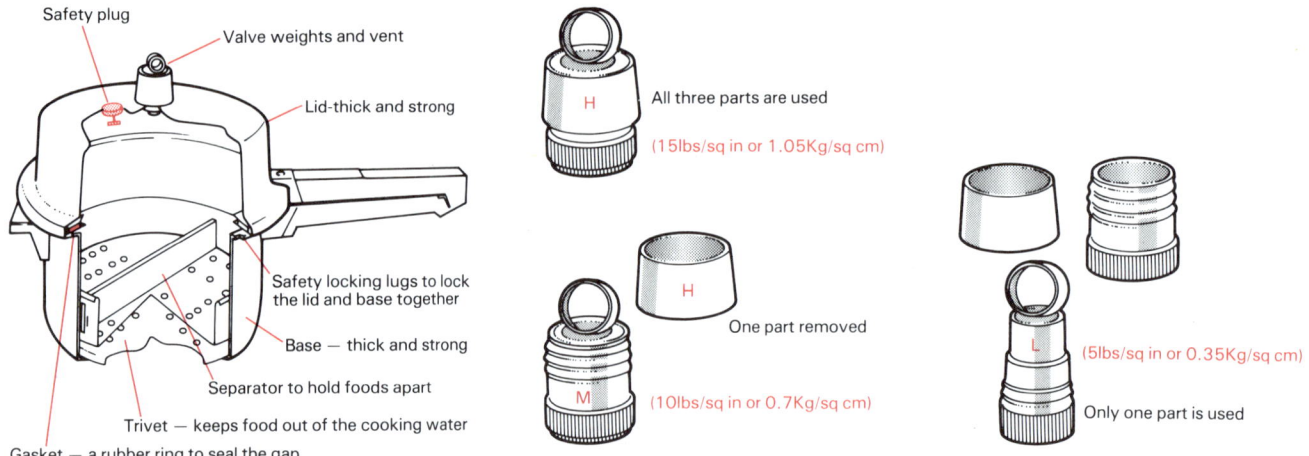

**Fig 6.5** A typical pressure cooker          **Fig. 6.6** Pressure cooker weights

The greater the pressure the higher the temperature at which water boils. The higher the temperature the faster the food cooks.

> **At ordinary atmospheric pressure water boils at 100°C**
> **With the lowest weight, 0.35Kg/sq.cm (5lb psi) water boils at 107°C**
> **With the middle weight, 0.7Kg/sq.cm (10lb psi) water boils at 112°C**
> **With the highest weight, 1.05Kg/sq.cm (15lb psi) water boils at 120°C**

**Using the pressure cooker**

1  Follow the manufacturers specific instructions.
2  Check the control valve vent, safety plug and gasket.
3  Place the food on a trivet or in containers depending on the recipe.
4  Add water at the rate of 150ml (¼pt) for every 15 minutes cooking time + 150ml (¼pt). A minimum of 300ml (½pt) of water is used.
5  Close the lid and lock securely.
6  Place on the cooker.

**(a)** Pan with separate weights. Heat until a continuous jet of steam comes from the control valve. Place weights on the valve. Continue heating until the cooker gives a loud hiss. Reduce heat until there is a gentle, steady hiss. Start timing.

**(b)** Cooker with central pin which rises as pressure increases. Place the pressure indicator in position and heat the pan. As the pressure rises the central pin will appear marked with three white rings.

One ring showing = low pressure
Two rings showing = medium pressure
Three rings showing = high pressure.

When the correct number of rings is showing reduce the heat so that the rings remain in view. Time cooking.

**7** Reduce pressure
**(a)** Leave the cooker to stand for 10 minutes off the hotplate or
**(b)** Place the pan in a bowl of cold water until the weights can be lifted off without steam escaping.
Method **(a)** is essential if the food is cooked in a container. Follow the instructions in your recipe.

### Advantages of pressure cooking

1 Saves **time, fuel** and therefore **money**.
2 A complete meal can be cooked in one pot.
3 Nutrients are not lost.
4 Flavour is better.
5 Tough, coarse foods become tender quickly.

### Disadvantages of pressure cooking

1 Cookers are quite expensive to buy.
2 Valves and gaskets need replacing regularly.
3 It needs skill and experience to prevent foods, such as vegetables, overcooking.

### Boiling and simmering

*Boiling*
A fast method of cooking with the food covered with water.
The water is at 100°C.
Rapid movement of water occurs with large bubbles and rapid evaporation.

*Simmering*
The water is still at 100°C but the surface movement is reduced with only a few small bubbles rising to the surface, so there is very little evaporation.

Boiling is a misnomer because once the water has reached boiling point the heat is usually reduced and the food allowed to simmer – cook more gently. A lid is usually placed on the pan to reduce evaporation.

### Stewing

Cubes or pieces of meat, seasoning and vegetables are covered with a liquid in a covered container and simmered in the oven or on the hob. Casseroling is another name for stewing. It is faster than braising.

### Braising

A joint of meat is lightly browned and placed on top of lightly sautéed vegetables cut into chunks (mirepoix). The liquid should just cover the vegetables. The container is covered and the food cooked in the oven or on the hob.

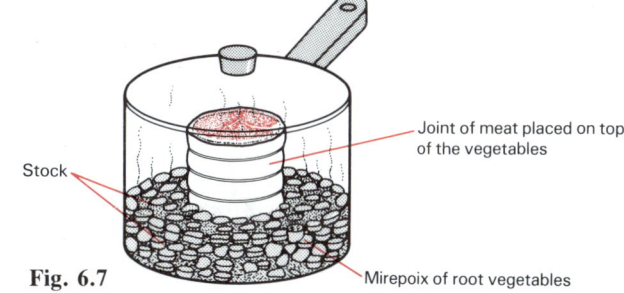

Stock

Joint of meat placed on top of the vegetables

**Fig. 6.7**

Mirepoix of root vegetables

### Poaching

The food is cooked very gently to prevent breaking up the food. The water should go off the boil and the heat be reduced. The food may require basting if it is not submerged.

### Slow-cook pots

1 Slow-cook pots are separate pots heated by electricity.
2 They are used for long, slow cooking.
3 Their temperature range is 86°C to 92°C.
4 There are usually two settings – high and low.
5 The cook-pot uses about the same amount of electricity as a light bulb.
6 They are designed to be left on throughout the day.
7 The outer case is made of metal or plastic and the inner cook-pot of earthenware which is a poor conductor of heat and therefore a good insulator.

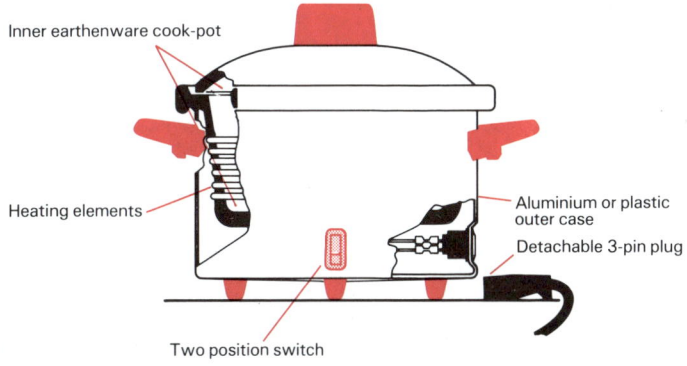

Inner earthenware cook-pot

Heating elements

Aluminium or plastic outer case

Detachable 3-pin plug

Two position switch

**Fig. 6.8**

### Advantages of cook-pots

1 Cooking food in cook-pots retains flavour and improves the appearance of food.
2 They are very economical on fuel.
3 Slow cooking makes meat tender with less shrinkage.
4 It is convenient to come home to find a meal cooked.
5 They cook a wide range of dishes.
6 They can be used on a table or work top.

### Disadvantages of cook-pots

1 If they are not used according to manufacturer's instructions they can be potentially dangerous, in that too low a temperature would encourage the growth of bacteria which could lead to food poisoning.
2 They are fairly expensive pieces of equipment to buy.

### Rules for using cook-pots

1 The casserole must be heated on high while the food is prepared.
2 Liquids should be heated before being added to the casserole.
3 The lid must always be used and left on until cooking is completed.
4 After adding the food reduce the heat according to the instructions.
5 To avoid food poisoning observe the following rules:
(a) Never leave food to cool in the casserole – heat retention encourages growth of the bacteria *Clostridium welchii*.
(b) Uncooked food should never by left in the slow cooker to be switched on later – bacteria could multiply and produce toxins.
6 Disconnect the pot from the mains before cleaning. The outer case and plug should not be immersed in water.
7 Earthenware will not stand up to sudden changes in temperature so never fill the inner pot with frozen or very cold foods, and never use it for storing food in the refrigerator or freezer.

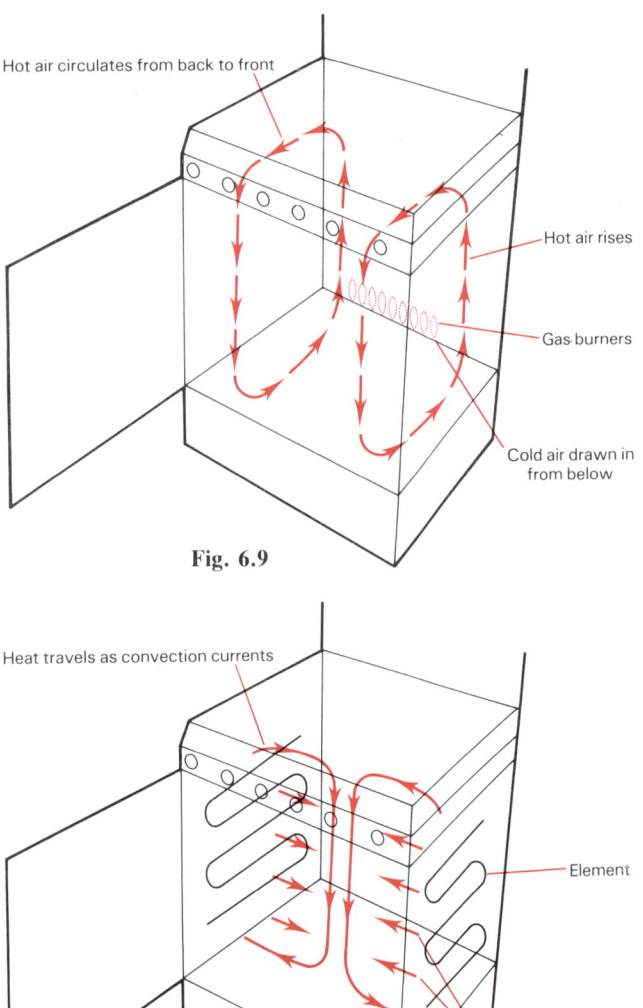

Hot air circulates from back to front

Hot air rises

Gas burners

Cold air drawn in from below

**Fig. 6.9**

Heat travels as convection currents

Element

Radiated heat from the elements

**Fig. 6.10**

### Baking

A slow method of cooking

**The gas oven** burners are usually positioned at the bottom and back of the oven. Cold air is continually drawn in at the bottom of the oven so that oxygen is provided for gas combustion. This explains why the bottom of a gas cooker is much cooler than the bottom of an electric cooker.

Hot air rises from the burners and circulates from the back to the front. Cooler air falls. These convection currents give **three** zones of heat. Dishes requiring different cooking temperatures can be cooked together in the oven.

**Top shelf position – hottest part of oven.**
**Centre shelf position – at temperature of thermostat setting.**
**Lower shelf position – coolest part of oven.**

### The electric oven

*Main oven*
The elements are in the sides of the oven. Heat radiates out and also travels as convection currents.

There is a smaller temperature difference between shelf positions than in a gas oven. This is because cold air only enters the oven when the door is opened.

*Fan ovens* have an even heat throughout because the fan blows the heat around the oven. The fan and element are situated in the back of the oven.

*Top oven*
The elements for heating the oven are under the floor of the oven. If a baking tray is placed very near to the floor of the oven or actually on it the food can easily burn. This bottom heat can however ensure thorough cooking of the pastry bases of quiches or pies.

|  | °C | °F | Gas mark |
|---|---|---|---|
| **Slow** | 150° | 300° | 2 |
| **Moderate** | 180° | 350° | 4 |
| **Hot** | 200° | 400° | 6 |
| **Very hot** | 230° | 450° | 8 |

**Table 6.2** Oven temperatures

**The thermostat** is a device which keeps the temperature of the oven more or less constant. It is controlled by expansion and contraction as the oven heats up and cools down.

When the oven reaches the temperature set on the dial the source of energy is cut off. The oven cools slightly and the energy is switched back on. On an electric cooker this can be seen as the light comes on and goes out throughout cooking.

**Oven management**

**1** Arrange the shelf positions when the oven is cold.

**2** Preheat the oven for 10-15 minutes before you need to put the food in. When the temperature required is reached the indicator light on the electric cooker goes off and the flames in a gas cooker become very small and blue.

**3** Always take oven gloves with you to the oven. Do not be tempted to use a tea towel which is thin and often damp. Its use can result in burns and scalds.

**4** Do not open the oven door until the cooking time is nearly up. The resulting drop in temperature will increase the cooking time and if the door is banged when closed a mixture which has not set could collapse.

**5** The use of the top oven saves energy if only one dish is to be cooked.

**6** Try to fill the main oven, cook the entire meal in the oven or bake for future meals.

**7** Baking trays should be placed correctly in the oven to avoid uneven browning or burning food at the outer edges. In an electric oven with the elements at the sides, place the tray in the centre of the shelf with the long side of the baking tray parallel to the sides. In a gas oven place the long sides of the baking tray parallel to, but not over, the burners (see Fig. 6.11).

**Fig. 6.11**

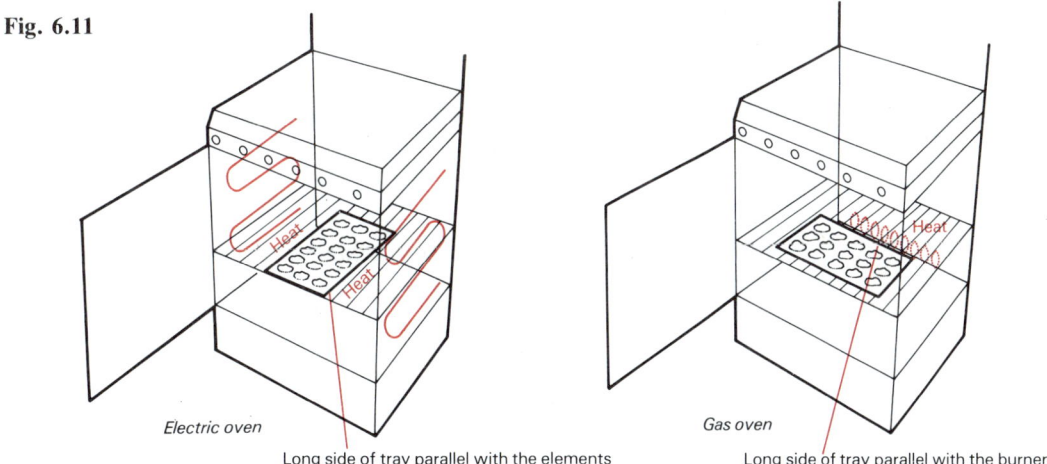

Electric oven
Long side of tray parallel with the elements

Gas oven
Long side of tray parallel with the burners

**8** Remember that the centre shelf position is at the setting of the thermostat. Items which need high baking temperatures can be placed on the top shelf and those needing low temperatures on the lower shelf particularly in a gas oven.

In cake making remember the larger the cake the lower the temperature and the longer the cooking time and, the smaller the cake the higher the temperature and the shorter the cooking time.

**9** Switch off the oven before cooking is quite finished to make use of residual heat, and always switch off at the mains before cleaning.

**The automatic oven timer** should not be confused with the minute minder which rings when cooking time is completed. It is the device which switches the oven on an off in the absence of the cook.

Foods must be carefully selected so that they need a similar cooking time and can make good use of the zones of heat. Care also needs to be taken so that the foods selected will not deteriorate in the heat of the kitchen before the oven switches on.

*Fig. 6.12* Automatic controls on an electric cooker

**(a)** Put the food in the oven.    **(b)** Check that the main switch for the oven is on.
**(c)** Check the oven clock.
**(d)** Turn the control from manual to automatic. The automatic light should show.
**(e)** Set the time the cooking is to start–allow 15 minutes extra for the oven to heat up.
**(f)** Set the time the oven is to switch off.
**(g)** Set the oven thermostat dial.

### Oven roasting

This is a form of baking used for better cuts of meat and the vegetables that can be roasted with them–potatoes, parsnips, onions. The food needs to be basted frequently during cooking to keep it moist.

### Different methods of roasting:

**1** The meat is put into a very hot oven, 230°C/450°F/Gas mark 8, for 20 minutes and then the heat is reduced to 180°C/350°F/Gas mark 4, for the rest of the cooking time.

| | |
|---|---|
| **Beef** | allow 15 mins. per 500g (1lb) and 15 mins. extra. |
| **Lamb** | allow 20 mins. per 500g (1lb) and 20 mins. extra. |
| **Pork** | allow 25 mins. per 500g (1lb) and 25 mins. extra. |
| **Chicken** | allow 20 mins. per 500g (1lb) and 20 mins. extra. |

**2** Place the meat in a very moderate oven, 150°C/300°F/Gas mark 2, and cook for twice the time in the chart above.

**3** The meat is put into a cold oven set at 220°C/425°F/Gas mark 7 for the times given in the chart above **plus** 5 extra minutes.

**4** A meat thermometer may be used. This is pushed into the centre of the joint before it is put in the oven. The oven is set at 200°C-220°C/400°F-425°F/Gas mark 6-7. Meat will be cooked when the centre reaches these temperatures:

*Beef* at 70°C/160°F    *Poultry* at 88°C/190°F
*Lamb* at 85°C/180°F    *Pork* at 88°C/190°F

### Pot roasting

Browned joints of meat are cooked in hot fat (in the oven or on the hob) in a covered container. The meat is turned during cooking.

### Spit roasting

Traditionally roasted meat is turned on a spit and cooked by radiant heat. Some modern cookers have a rotisserie which fits into the oven or under the grill (see Fig. 6.3). As the meat revolves, its juices run around the meat to keep it moist. Basting is not required.

### Grilling

This is a very quick method of cooking which uses radiant heat. The grill should be pre-heated to very hot before food is placed under it. The heat seals the surface of the food. The flavour of the food is well developed. Food should be brushed with fat before grilling. Turn the food during cooking carefully with blunt implements. Watch the cooking carefully.

Grilling can be an expensive method of cooking because only tender pieces of meat, steaks and chops are cooked this way, but it is a useful way to cook bacon and sausages because their fat drains away.

The grill is also used to brown food such as au gratin dishes, crumpets, teacakes, toast and cheese on toast.

If the grill pan is lined with foil some heat will be reflected up and the pan is easier to clean.

### Frying

This is the cooking of food between the temperature ranges of approximately 170°C to 205°C (325°F-400°F). Oils have a higher decomposition temperature than solid fats such as lard and dripping.

Oils containing polyunsaturated fatty acids are said to be better nutritionally. These include, sunflower seed oil, corn oil, soya oil, safflower oil.

Butter can be used for some types of frying e.g. sautéing vegetables, cooking an omelet. This gives a better flavour.

Fats should be clean and completely free of water and pieces of food from the last frying.

### Types of frying

Dry frying, sautéing (stir-frying), shallow fat frying and deep fat frying.

**Dry frying** is used for foods which contain their own fat, bacon, sausages and oily fish such as herrings.

**Sautéing** takes place when food is shaken or tossed in a small amount of fat. The lid is kept on the pan when sautéing vegetables for a soup. Potatoes and kidneys are frequently sautéed because they absorb fat. The potatoes are usually allowed to brown. Vegetables can be stir-fried to lightly cook them the Chinese way.

**Shallow fat frying** involves using a large shallow pan with a thick flat base.

1 The fat should come halfway up the food which is turned *once* during frying. Heat is conducted to the food from the base of the pan.

2 The food must be dry.

3 Coating food is sometimes necessary to prevent fat seeping into the food or the food falling to bits. Coatings also add colour, texture and nutrients. (Flour can be used to coat liver and sprats, oats for herrings and egg and crumbs for fish cakes, fish fingers, rissoles etc.)

4 Cook the upper side of the food first. Turn carefully.

5 Once the fat is hot reduce the heat to avoid spitting.

**Deep fat frying** means that the food is completely covered with oil which heats up by convection. A large, heavy, stable pan should be used. It should only be half filled with oil.

Electric fryers which are thermostatically controlled are an important aid to safety. Many house fires are caused by chip pans igniting. This cannot happen with a thermostatically controlled fryer. The level of oil needed is marked on the side.

1 Fry without a lid unless using an electric fryer with a filter.

2 Heat the fat to the temperature required. A cube of bread browns in one minute at 180°C. A thermometer is very useful. Electric fryers usually have a range of temperature settings.

3 If the fat is too cool the food will absorb fat and be greasy. If the fat is too hot the outside of the food will overcook while the inside remains raw.

4 With the exception of chips food is usually coated with batter or egg and crumbs.

5 Chips are often kept in water to prevent browning while the fat heats up. These should be dried thoroughly before cooking. Water causes fat to spit.

6 The basket helps to lower food gently into the fat and to drain away some fat at the end of cooking. The basket should not be too full because the temperature will be lowered too much so the food is not sealed and fat soaks in.

7 Remove excess grease from the food by draining on absorbent kitchen paper.

### Safety when frying

If fat overheats it will burst into flames spontaneously. Never leave a fat pan unattended.

1 At the end of cooking switch off the cooker and let the fat cool before straining.

2 Store the fat in a cool, dark place so that it does not become rancid.

3 When frying always keep the pan lid or a metal baking sheet close at hand. Should the pan catch fire these can be used immediately to smother the flames. Fat cannot burn without oxygen. A damp tea towel does not always work. It quickly dries, scorches and burns. Water, sand or soil (both contain water) should **not be used** in an attempt to put out a fat fire. The water causes fat to explode in all directions, spreading the fire and burning anyone in the way. A kitchen fire extinguisher of the foam or powder variety is an important safety aid. The cooker should be switched off as soon as possible. The pan should not be moved until it has cooled down, a minimum of 30 minutes is suggested.

4 The fat should not be used again after a fire. Its decomposition will have produced substances which irritate the stomach.

**Table 6.3** Summary of cooking methods and foods suited to each method

| Cooking method | Suitable foods |
| --- | --- |
| **Steaming** | Suet pastry, creamed and rubbed in pudding mixtures, meat, fish, vegetables |
| **Pressure cooking** | Soups, stews, meat, vegetables, puddings, fruit, egg custard, rice, jams, bottled fruit |
| **Boiling** | Salted meats, bacon joints, eggs, vegetables, pasta, rice, fish |
| **Simmering** **Stewing** **Casseroling** | Fruit, vegetables (except leafy vegetables), cuts of meat with a lot of connective tissue and coarse fibres (shin of beef, chuck steak, scrag end of neck of lamb) |
| **Braising** | Vegetables and medium quality cuts of meat |

| Cooking method | Suitable foods |
|---|---|
| **Poaching** | Eggs, kippers, haddock and other fish |
| **Baking** | Bread, scones, cakes, biscuits, pastries, fruit, potatoes, fish |
| **Roasting** | Meat with fine fibres and very little connective tissue (pork joint, leg of lamb, sirloin of beef etc.), poultry, vegetables |
| **Pot roasting** | Meat joints. Can also be done in slow-cook pot or in a pressure cooker |
| **Grilling** | Tender cuts of meat, offal, sausages, bacon, beefburgers, fish, tomatoes, mushrooms, au gratin dishes, toast |
| **Frying** | |
| Dry | Sausages, bacon, herrings, mackerel |
| Sautéing | Vegetables for soups, stews and mirepoix for braising, potatoes, courgettes |
| Shallow | Chops, offal, fish cakes, fish fingers, rissoles, beefburgers, fish, vegetables, eggs |
| Deep fat | Scotch eggs, fritters, fish in batter or egg and crumbs, fish cakes, doughnuts, aigrettes, small joints of poultry, potato chips and crisps, onion rings |

### Maillarding

This is the browning that occurs when food is cooked. High temperatures bring about maillarding.

Grilling and frying bring about maillarding very quickly, baking and roasting more slowly. Maillarding occurs when the food has dried out. It is a reaction between carbohydrate and protein in the food. This is why an egg or a milk glaze increases browning.

Maillarding gives flavour. The flavour of fried and grilled food is particularly appetising.

### Cold browning

When foods such as apple, pear and potato are cut and left in the air they gradually become brown. This browning is due to an oxidation process between the air and enzymes in the cells which have been damaged by cutting.

## 6.3   Portable electrical appliances

Apart from kettles and toasters the wide variety of portable electrical appliances available are luxuries not essentials.
1 They can be expensive.
2 They need standing space and/or storage space.
3 They often have small pieces to wash, dry and re-assemble.
4 They save the cook's time and energy but use more electricity.

### Coffee makers

These can be electrically operated percolators or filter coffee makers. For a description of their use see section 4.1.14.

### Electric slow-cook pots

See section 6.2.2.

### Contact grills

1 They are basically two hot plates which close together making direct contact with the food on both sides.

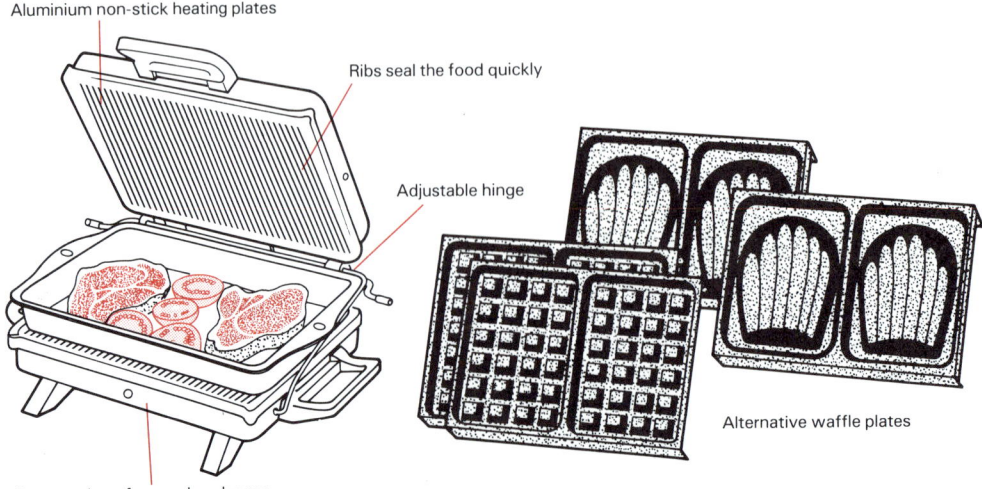

Aluminium non-stick heating plates

Ribs seal the food quickly

Adjustable hinge

Outer casing of enamel or chrome

Alternative waffle plates

**Fig. 6.13** A contact grill

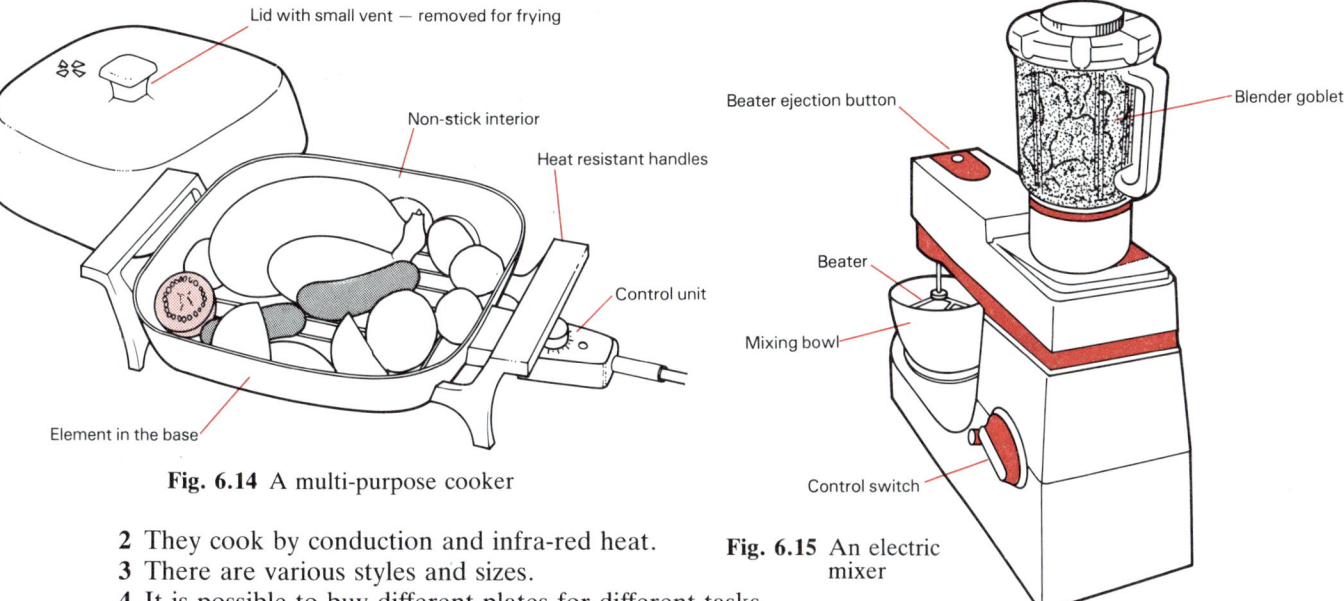

**Fig. 6.14** A multi-purpose cooker

**Fig. 6.15** An electric mixer

2 They cook by conduction and infra-red heat.
3 There are various styles and sizes.
4 It is possible to buy different plates for different tasks.
5 They toast sandwiches, cook meat and sausages, and make waffles.

### Multi-purpose cookers

These cookers are shaped like a large deep frying pan with a lid. They are often square. The pan has its own electrical lead and plug and is thermostatically controlled.
1 They can braise, steam, roast, stew, boil and bake.
2 They are particularly useful where there is no conventional cooker as in a bedsitter.
3 They stand on a work surface.
4 Food can be served at the table from them.

### Electric mixers

The types available are:
1 Large food preparation machines–400 to 1000 watts. These have a range of optional attachments.
2 Food mixers 100 to 300 watts;
(a) small mixers with bowl and stand and usually a blender. The mixer can be held in the hand to cream and whisk.
(b) small mixers without a bowl or stand.
These mixers can cream, beat, whisk, mix, whip and knead.

### Electric blenders (liquidisers)

These blenders can either be attachments for mixers with stands or free standing of half-litre or 1 litre capacity. They will blend, pulp, chop, purée, grind, whip and make breadcrumbs.

### Food processors

These are single pieces of equipment usually with three different blades which will carry out all of those processes which can be done by an ordinary mixer with a blender. Cakes, pastry and pâté can be made very successfully.
1 They mix very rapidly and are very efficient for slicing and shredding.
2 The blades are very sharp and need very careful washing and storing.
3 They *do not* appear to be efficient at whisking eggs and sugar for a sponge, but they whisk egg whites alone quite satisfactorily.

### Deep-fat fryers

See also section 6.2.2.
1 These vary in style and size.
2 They are heated by a thermostatically controlled electrical element. The larger fryers have a range of temperatures.
3 The frying basket may be completely free or may be fixed to the pan when it is possible to raise and lower it.
4 These pans should never overheat to the point where they burst into flames.
5 Each pan is marked to show the level of oil required.
6 All the general rules for frying apply.

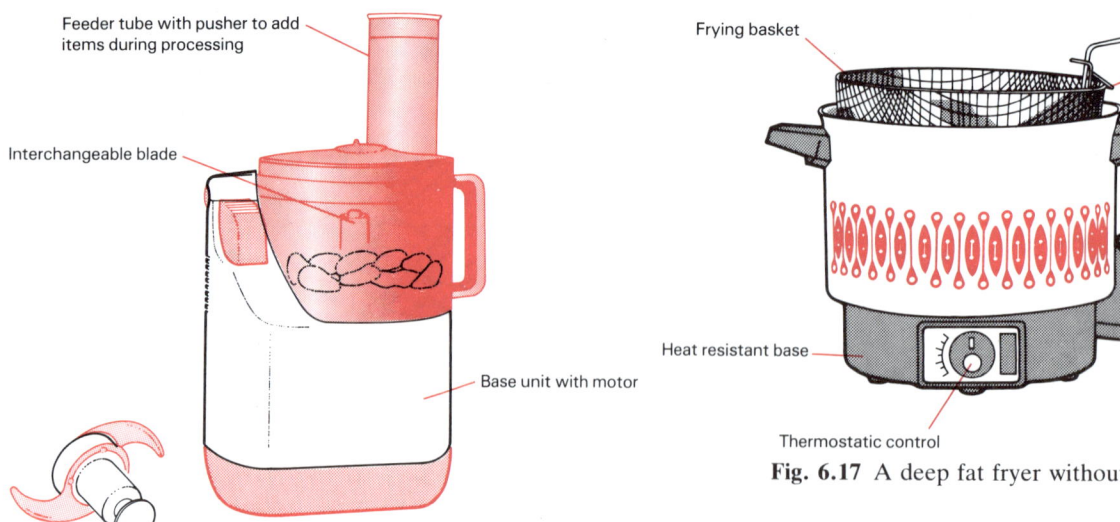

Feeder tube with pusher to add items during processing

Interchangeable blade

Base unit with motor

Fig. 6.16 A food processor

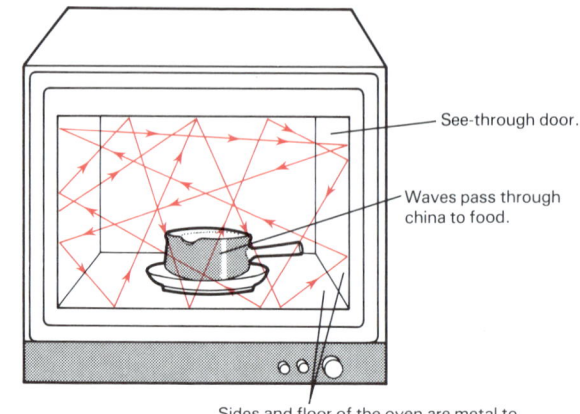

Frying basket

Clip to hold basket out of the fat

Heat resistant base

Lid for storage

Thermostatic control

Fig. 6.17 A deep fat fryer without a filter

**7** A lid is only used if it has a replaceable charcoal filter. *Never* use a lid unless instructed to do so by the manufacturer.

**NB** With all of these electrical appliances:
1 Look for the BEAB Safety Mark
2 Read and follow the manufacturers' instructions
3 Make sure plugs are correctly wired
4 Use the correct fuse
(a) Up to 720 watt a 3amp fuse
(b) Over 720 watt a 13amp fuse
5 Fuses should not be broken
6 Flexes should not trail nor should they be frayed. The flex should be firmly held in the cord grip.

## 6.4   Cooking with microwaves

See-through door.

Waves pass through china to food.

Sides and floor of the oven are metal to reflect the waves.

Fig. 6.18 A microwave cooker

The oven is a metal box. A magnetron produces high frequency electro-magnetic waves (similar to radio waves) when the cooker is switched on. A waveguide directs the microwaves into the oven space. A stirrer fan distributes microwaves evenly. Some models have a turn-table which rotates during cooking. If the oven does not have a turn-table or a special wave stirrer beneath the floor the food has to be turned manually throughout the cooking process.

### How the food cooks

The microwave energy disturbs the water molecules of the food so that they rub together and generate heat. If the food being cooked is large the heat is produced in the outer layers and transmitted to the centre by conduction.

Microwaves, like light rays have **three** important characteristics:
1 Penetration,      2 Reflection,      3 Absorption.

**Penetration**
The waves pass through some materials without being absorbed. e.g. glass, plastics, chinaware. These materials are suitable for use in the oven because the waves pass through to the food. The containers remain cold to the touch, although they warm slightly due to the hot food inside them.

**Reflection**
Metals reflect the waves. Containers for food must not be metal, and china should not have gold or silver in its decoration. The sides and floor are metal to reflect the waves in all directions.

When not in use a container of water should be kept in the oven to absorb the microwaves should it be accidently turned on when the waves could bounce back and damage the magnetron.

**Absorption**
Foods with a high water content absorb microwaves. Shallow dishes are best as thin pieces of food cook more quickly. The centre of the oven can have cold spots where it does not cook so efficiently therefore thinner ends of food should point towards the centre.

### Advantages of microwave cooking

1 Saves time. A hot meal can be prepared in a short time even if some food comes straight from the freezer. Potatoes can be partly cooked before roasting. Butter can be softened.

2 Can be used to thaw food
3 Uses less electricity than a conventional cooker, therefore saves money
4 Simple to use, very clean, easy to clean, produces less washing up and kitchen cleaning
5 Cuts down cooking smells
6 Retains flavour and vitamins
7 Micro-organisms destroyed
8 Can be plugged into any 13 amp socket
9 Standing time when food continues to cook means that food is served piping hot

## Disadvantages of microwave cooking

1 Initial cost can be high, £150 to £400+, but with lower electricity bills it could pay for itself in a very short time.

2 It is not a complete substitute for a conventional cooker. It will not boil eggs, fry fish and chips; it will not brown meat or short pastry, it cannot raise a batter or cook meringues. A browning dish can be bought to brown chops and sausages but these are expensive.

3 It will not tenderize tough meat. It is still necessary to pressure cook or simmer in some way cuts such as shin of beef, chuck steak.

## Safety

1 Look for the BEAB Mark of Safety or Electricity Council's Approved Safety Label (see page 152). These mean that the cooker has been tested.

2 Cookers have safety locks so that the cooker cannot operate until the door is closed and the controls turned to on.

3 Microwave cookers can be tested for radiation leaks at home, or they can be taken to a microwave dealer. There is greater radiation from a television set.

## Latest features

The **simplest** and **least expensive** cookers have mechanical controls and **two settings** – Defrost and High. Higher technology models have **variable controls** – Defrost, Simmer, Roast and High or even 9 or 10 settings between defrost and high.

Some cookers have a **temperature probe** – useful when cooking meat. Browning grills are a feature of some models but spattering makes the oven harder to clean. A conventional grill is a convenient alternative to brown.

Digital controls with a micro-chip are now frequently used and the latest models operate when a **computer data card** is inserted.

# 7  Basic mixtures

## 7.1  Basic recipes and methods

In the following section metric and imperial quantities are given. For ease of measuring:

> 1oz may be considered to be equivalent to 25g or 30g and similarly
> ¼pt may be considered to be equivalent to 125ml or 150ml.
> 1tsp = 5ml
> 1 dessertspoon = 10ml
> 1 tablespoon = 20ml (some 'tablespoons' are shallow and hold 15ml)

For information on basic ingredients used see:
Section 4.1.1 for flours.
Section 4.1.2 for fats.
Section 4.1.3 for sugars.
Sections 4.1.16, 4.1.17, 4.1.18 and 7.2 for raising agents.

### 7.1.1  Batters

**Ingredients**

Batter is made from plain flour, milk or water and usually an egg.

The mixture is beaten well to make it smooth and work the flour with the liquid to develop the elasticity of the gluten.

### Basic Recipes

| **Thin batter** | **Coating batter** | **Fritter batter** |
|---|---|---|
| 1 egg | 1 egg | 1 egg white |
| 100g (4oz) flour | 100g (4oz) flour | 50g (2oz) flour |
| ¼tsp salt | ¼tsp salt | ¼tsp salt |
| 250ml (½pt) milk | 125ml (¼pt) milk | 3tbsp tepid water |
| | | 2tsp salad oil |
| *Uses* | *Uses* | |
| Pancakes | Coating meat and fish | *Uses* |
| Toad-in-the-hole | | Fritters e.g. apple |
| Yorkshire Pudding | | |

### Method

**1** Sieve flour and salt into mixing bowl. Beat in the egg and a little milk.

**2** When half of the milk has been slowly added and beaten in, stir in the rest.

**3** It is no longer considered to be essential for air to be beaten into the batter or for it to stand.

**4** Alternatively all ingredients can be placed in a liquidizer or food processor and rapidly mixed together. Note the following points:

**(a)** Water vapour from the milk raises the mixture made stretchy by the gluten.

**(b)** Yorkshire pudding and toad-in-the-hole need hot ovens.

**(c)** Food to be coated with batter must be dry.

**(d)** The oil must be hot enough to set the batter but not so hot that it burns.

### 7.1.2   Sauces

**A sauce is** a thickened liquid which adds interest, flavour, colour, moistness and nutrients to a dish.

**A coating sauce** is poured over the food as part of the dish.

**A pouring sauce** is thinner and is served separately to be added to food at the table.

**A binding sauce or panada** is very thick and is used as a base for soufflés to bind ingredients together and as a filling for pancakes, toasted sandwiches, and vol-au-vents.

**Purée sauces** are made of fruit or vegetables and are served to counteract the richness of some dishes. e.g. apple sauce with pork.

**A mayonnaise** or an oil and vinegar **dressing** are served with salads.

### Sauces thickened by the gelatinization of starch

When heated with a liquid starch grains absorb water and swell and thus have a thickening effect. Cornflour gelatinizes more readily than wheat flour. It is used mainly in sweet sauces. Sugar slows down the gelatinization of starch.

**Table 7.1**

| Sauce | Milk | Flour/Cornflour | Fat | Method |
|---|---|---|---|---|
| **Blended** | | | | |
| Pouring | 300ml (½pt) | 15g (½oz) | — | Blend flour in a mixing bowl with a little cold milk. |
| Coating | 300ml (½pt) | 30g (1oz) | — | |
| Panada | 300ml (½pt) | 60g (2oz) | — | Boil rest of milk and then pour over the paste in the bowl. Stir. Return to pan and heat to boiling point stirring all the time. |
| **Roux** | | | | |
| Pouring | 300ml (½pt) | 15g (½oz) | 15g (½oz) | Melt fat in a pan. Remove from the heat and stir in flour to form a roux. Slowly stir in the milk a little at a time. Bring to the boil stirring all the time. |
| Coating | 300ml (½pt) | 30g (1oz) | 30g (1oz) | |
| Panada | 300ml (½pt) | 60g (2oz) | 60g (2oz) | |

NB 250ml milk may be used instead of 300ml. The sauces will be a little thicker but 12.5g cannot be weighed on most domestic scales with ease.

### Flavourings

**Sweet sauces**  Add 15g (½oz) sugar to 300ml of sauce and any additional flavour such as cocoa, coffee, vanilla, butterscotch, lemon, orange.

**Savoury sauces** Add salt and pepper to taste and any additional flavour such as, parsley, cheese, mushroom, anchovy, onion, mustard, tomato.

**NB 1** The roux is browned if a brown sauce or gravy is being made.
    **2** If the roux is overcooked the sauce will be a poor colour.
    **3** If these sauces are not stirred continually the mixture will become lumpy as the starch grains clump together. The outer gelatinized layer preventing liquid reaching the raw starch in the centre. The lumps tend to stick to the pan and burn.
    **4** A sauce that is not boiled properly will have a powdery taste because of the presence of uncooked starch.

**Table 7.2** Sauces made with arrowroot

| Sauce | Fruit juice/water | Arrowroot | Other ingredients |
|---|---|---|---|
| Flan glaze | 125ml (¼pt) | 5g 1 heaped tsp. | Sugar to taste if water used. |
| Jam or Syrup sauce | 250ml (½pt) | 10g 2 heaped tsp. | 2 tbsp. jam, marmalade or syrup 1-2tsp. lemon juice |
| Fruit sauce | 250ml (½pt) | 10g 2 heaped tsp. | Pieces of fruit Sugar to taste |

*Method* Blend the arrowroot in a saucepan with the liquid. Add liquid to the powder and use a wooden spoon. Bring to boil stirring all the time. Add other ingredients. The sauce clears as it thickens.

### Sauces thickened by the coagulation of egg proteins

See Section 4.1.7

**Table 7.3**

| Sauce | Eggs | Milk | Sugar | Other ingredients |
|---|---|---|---|---|
| Pouring egg custard | 2 | 300ml (½pt) | 15g (½oz) | Few drops vanilla essence. |

*Method* Heat milk until it steams. Beat eggs with sugar in a mixing bowl. Stir in the hot milk. Rinse the saucepan. Strain the custard back into the pan and heat over a low setting until it starts to thicken. Do not overcook or the sauce will curdle. Take off the heat and add essence. This sauce thickens as it cools. It cannot be reheated.
Sometimes the sauce is heated in a bowl over a pan of hot water.

**NB** A heaped tsp. of cornflour is sometimes mixed with the eggs and sugar to ensure a smooth thickening.

### Mayonnaise thickened by the emulsification of oils

**Table 7.4**

| Eggs | Oil | Vinegar | Seasoning |
|---|---|---|---|
| 1 egg yolk | 150ml (¼pt) | 2tbsp. | ¼tsp. dry mustard ¼tsp. salt 1tsp. caster sugar 2 shakes pepper |

*Method* Beat the egg yolk and dry ingredients together in a bowl.
Add the oil drop by drop, beating vigorously after each drop, until the mixture starts to thicken. Add the vinegar alternately with the remaining oil until the oil is used up and the consistency is that required.
Mayonnaise can also be made in a liquidizer by putting vinegar, egg and seasonings in the goblet, blending and then gradually adding oil.

### Purée sauces

These are made from sieved fruit or vegetables e.g. apple, cranberry, tomato sauce.

**Apple sauce**
250g (½lb) cooking apples
2 tablespoons of water
15g (½oz) butter or margarine
Sugar to taste

*Method*
**1** Stew the apples until soft with the other ingredients.
**2** Push through a sieve
**3** Serve hot with pork

### 7.1.3 Pastry

**Pastry is** a mixture of flour, fat and water. The different types of pastry are achieved by using differing quantities of these basic ingredients and different methods of mixing.

#### Basic Proportions

This is the ratio of one ingredient to the rest and the foundation for a basic recipe.

**Table 7.5** A comparison of the basic proportions of four different pastries

| Ingredients | Shortcrust | Suetcrust | Rough puff | Flaky |
|---|---|---|---|---|
| Fat to flour | ½ | ⅓ to ½ | ½ to ¾ | ½ to ¾ |
| Salt to 450g (1lb) flour | 5ml (1tsp.) | 5ml (1tsp.) | 5ml (1tsp.) | 5ml (1tsp.) |
| Water to 450g (1lb) flour | 80ml (4tbsp.) | 300ml (16tbsp.) | 300ml (16tbsp.) | 300ml (16tbsp.) |
| Lemon juice | — | — | 10ml (2tsp.) | 10ml (2tsp.) |

#### Ingredients used

**Flour**

**1** Shortcrust–plain, medium strength household flour.
**2** Suetcrust–self-raising, medium strength household flour or plain flour + baking powder–10ml (2tsp) to 200g (8oz) plain flour.
**3** Rough puff–strong white flour.
**4** Flaky–strong white flour.

**Fat**

**1** Shortcrust–a mixture of lard and margarine. Lard alone gives a pale and very short pastry which lacks flavour and is difficult to handle. Margarine alone gives a rather hard pastry. Butter gives a different flavour.
**2** Suetcrust–shredded suet is a hard fat which takes a long time to melt. This is why an extra raising agent is needed to prevent the flour and water forming a heavy mix before the suet can be absorbed.
**3** Rough puff–a hard fat, margarine, lard and margarine, butter, white cooking fat.
**4** Flaky pastry–a hard fat as for rough puff pastry.

**Water**

As cold as possible for all pastries. Keeps the pastry cool so that the fat does not melt.

**Lemon Juice**

This is added to rough puff and flaky pastry to strengthen the gluten, i.e. make it more elastic.

#### Shortcrust pastry

**Basic recipe**

200g (8oz) plain flour (white, brown or wholewheat)
½ level tsp. (2.5ml) salt
50g (2oz) lard
50g (2oz) margarine
30-40ml (2tbsp.) cold water

**Method**

**1** Sieve flour and salt into the mixing bowl.
**2** Cut fat into small pieces and rub into flour with the fingertips until the mixture looks like breadcrumbs.
**3** Add the water all at once and mix it in with a round-bladed knife.
**4** Press together with fingertips and knead lightly on a floured surface.
**5** Shape and roll out as required.

**Baking**

Use a hot oven 400-425°F/200-220°C/Gas mark 6-7

**Raising agent**

Rubbing the fat into the flour aerates the mixture but the pastry does not rise to the same extent as cakes.

**Variations**

*Cheese pastry*
Add 50-100g (2-4oz) grated cheese to basic recipe above.
A pinch of cayenne pepper is added to the flour.
Mix with an egg yolk and a little cold water.

*Sweet pastry*
Add 25g (1oz) caster sugar to the basic recipe above.
Butter may be used instead of lard and margarine.
Mix with egg yolk and a little cold water.

*One stage pastry*
Recipes vary slightly. Tub margarines, lard and white cooking fats may be used.
100g (4oz) fat
150g (6oz) plain flour
20ml (1tbsp.) cold water
Place fat, water and ⅓ of flour into a mixing bowl. Fork together. Stir in remaining flour. Knead lightly.
**Chill**.

| | |
|---|---|
| **Uses** | *Sweet dishes* Jam tarts, syrup tart, fruit pies, mincepies, fruit tartlets, maids of honour, flans.<br>*Savoury dishes* Cornish pasties, meat pasties, flans, pies, sausage rolls, pie or plait. |

**Suet pastry**

| | |
|---|---|
| **Basic recipe** | 200g (8oz) SR flour<br>65-100g (3-4oz) shredded suet<br>½ level tsp. salt (2.5ml)<br>125ml (8tbsp.) cold water |
| **Method** | **1** Sieve the flour and salt.<br>**2** Stir in the suet and add the water all at once.<br>**3** Mix in the water with a round bladed knife.<br>**4** Press together lightly with fingertips and knead lightly on a floured surface. The mixture should not be dry, but soft and moist |
| **Cooking** | Boil or steam<br>Bake at 400°F/200°C/Gas mark 6<br>Microwave |
| **Raising agent** | $CO_2$ from the baking powder in the SR flour and *steam* from the water in the recipe. |
| **Uses** | *Sweet dishes* Jam layer pudding, steamed syrup or jam pudding, steamed fruit dumplings, spotted dick, roly-poly puddings.<br>*Savoury dishes* Dumplings with stews and casseroles, steak and kidney pudding, savoury roly-poly, savoury layer puddings with bacon, cheese and onion. |
| **Lining a basin with suet pastry** | **1** Roll into a circle large enough to fill the basin.<br>**2** Cut out one-quarter segment and roll in a round to fit top.<br>**3** Moisten the cut edges of the ¾ circle and overlap so it fits basin.<br>**4** Add filling, moisten the top edge of the pastry and fit the lid.<br>**5** Press edges firmly together. |
| **Making a roly-poly** | **1** Roll pastry into a large oblong or into smaller individual oblongs.<br>**2** Spread filling on pastry leaving a margin of 20mm all the way round.<br>**3** Moisten the margin and roll up from the bottom. |

**Fig. 7.1**

A quarter segment to be cut out and re-rolled to make the top

Moisten edges and overlap

Circle large enough to fill the basin

Roll up from the bottom    Moisten edges

Filling

Margin of 20mm around the edge of the filling

**Fig. 7.2**

**Rough puff and flaky pastry**

| | |
|---|---|
| **Basic recipe** | 200g (8oz) strong white flour<br>½ level tsp. (2.5ml) salt<br>100-150g (4-6oz) fat<br>1tsp. (5ml) lemon juice<br>125ml (8tbsp.) cold water |

**Method**

**Rough puff**
**1** Sieve flour and salt.
**2** Cut fat into size of sugar lumps and toss in flour to coat evenly.
**3** Stir in lemon juice and water to form a soft but not sticky dough.
**4** Knead and shape into an oblong on a floured surface and roll out into a rectangle.
**5** Fold bottom third of the pastry up and the top third down. Press edges with rolling pin to seal.
**6** Turn pastry so that fold is on the left.
**7** Repeat this rolling and folding three more times. See Fig. 7.3
**8** Chill pastry before use.

**Flaky**
**1** Sieve flour and salt.
**2** Divide fat into 4 and rub in ¼.
**3** Add lemon juice and water and mix to a soft but not sticky dough.
**4** Knead lightly on a floured surface and roll into a rectangle.
**5** Dot a second ¼ of fat on the top two-thirds.
**6** Fold bottom third up and top third down. Press edges with rolling pin to seal. See Fig. 7.4.
**7** Turn the pastry so that the fold is on the left.
**8** Repeat this rolling and folding with the fat twice more and then roll and fold once without fat.
**9** Chill pastry before use.

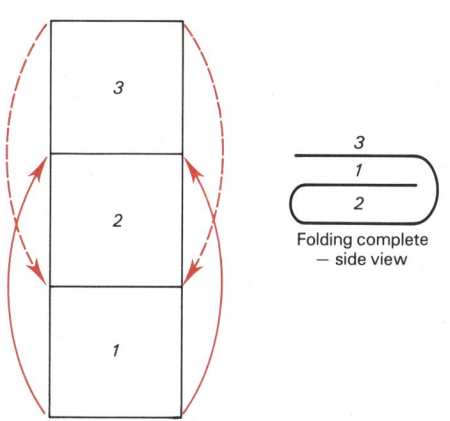

**Fig. 7.3**

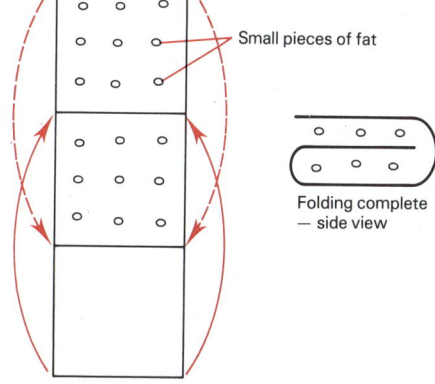

**Fig. 7.4**

**Baking**          Bake both pastries at 220°C/425°F/Gas mark 7

**Raising agents**  *Air* trapped between the layers of pastry and *steam* from the water in the recipe.

**Uses**            *Sweet dishes* Fruit pies, jam and fruit puffs, cream slices, cream horns, jam or fruit filled jalousie.
                    *Savoury dishes* Meat pies, Russian fish pie, sausage rolls, savoury puffs, savoury horns, savoury jalouise.

### Choux pastry

**Basic recipe**    75g (2½oz) strong plain flour
                    pinch salt
                    150ml (¼pt) water
                    50g (2oz) butter
                    2 eggs (size 3)

**Method**          1 Weigh ingredients very accurately.
                    2 Sieve flour and salt and place on a piece of greaseproof paper.
                    3 Beat the eggs in a small basin.
                    4 Put water and butter into a saucepan, heat slowly until butter melts and then bring to a brisk boil. Return to gentle heat.
                    5 Remove pan from heat and add all of the flour.
                    6 Beat well to remove any lumps until the mixture forms a soft ball and leaves the sides of the pan.
                    7 Remove from the heat and cool slightly.
                    8 Gradually beat in the eggs.
                    9 Pipe the mixture as required.

**Baking**          Bake at 200°C/400°F/Gas mark 6 for 10 mins.
                    Reduce heat to 180°C/350°F/Gas mark 4 for further 20-25 mins.

**Raising agent**   *Steam* from the liquid in the recipe. The strong flour gives a very stretchy mixture. *Air* is also beaten in.

**Uses**            Eclairs (sweet or savoury), cream buns, profiteroles, gnocchi, gâteau St. Honoré.

**General points**  (a) Choux pastry is different from other pastries.
                    (b) It is a thick binding mixture known as a 'panada' to which eggs are added.
                    (c) It has a very soft consistency so cannot be rolled out and is usually piped to make a case to hold a sweet or savoury filling.
                    (d) Avoid over boiling.
                    (e) Use the correct oven temperature given in your recipe and do not open the oven door before the cooking time is completed.
                    (f) Choux pastry should be eaten the day it is made.

### Pastry glazes

Pastry glazes are used to give an attractive finish.

**Sweet pastry** – the surface of the pastry is brushed with milk or beaten egg white. Lightly sprinkle with caster sugar before or after baking.

**Savoury pastry** is glazed with milk, beaten egg and salt or an egg wash made with equal quantities of egg yolk and water. There should be a glossier and darker brown glaze than on sweet dishes.

**NB** Glazes should not extend over the cut edges of the pastry. It will seal the cut edges and prevent rising.

### Decorative finishes to pastries

These are shown, and the methods used to achieve them, in Fig. 7.5.

### Lining flan rings

**Plain flan rings** are used for savoury flans.

**Fluted flan rings** are used for sweet flans.

**Method**
1 Roll pastry into a circle about 4cm larger than the flan ring.
2 Lift the pastry on the rolling pin and lower gently into the ring.
3 Lift the edges of the pastry and gently ease the pastry in at the base.
4 Roll off spare pastry.
5 Moisten the sides of the flan and press pastry trims in position.
6 Leave to relax.
7 Carefully trim the edge level with the top of the ring using a sharp knife.

**To bake blind**
1 Grease a square of greaseproof paper and place greased side down onto the pastry. Cover with baking beans.
2 Bake in hot oven (200°C/400°F/Gas mark 6). After 15 mins. remove beans and flan ring.
3 Return the flan to the oven for a further 5-10 mins. to complete the cooking of the pastry.

## Edge finishes for pies

*Fluted*

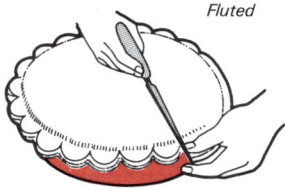

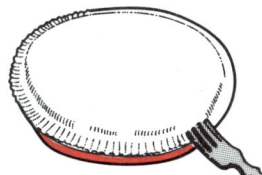

Press thumb on the top of the outer edge. Using the back of a knife draw the edge about 1 cm (½″) towards the centre of the pie. Repeat around the pie edge.

Use the back of a fork to press the edge of the pie. Repeat around the pie edge.

Pinch the edge of the pie between the thumb and first finger of both hands, then slightly twist in opposite directions. Repeat around the pie edge.

## Top decorations for pies

*Leaves*

Roll pastry trimmings into 2cm (1″) strips. Cut into diamond-shaped pieces. Mark the veins with the back of a knife. Pinch in one end to make a leaf shape.

*Other shapes*

Cut thinly rolled pastry into circles, stars or triangles. Arrange in a star or lattice design on top of the pie.

*Tassels*

Roll pastry trimmings thinly into a 2cm x 15cm strip. Make cuts every 5mm along the strip. Roll up and place on the centre of the pie. Spread out the cut ends carefully starting from the bottom.

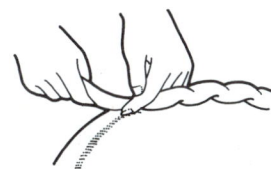

*Roses*

Make 2 small pastry circles and a small ball. Cover the ball with the circles pressing the edges together. Turn the finished 'ball' over and cut a cross into the top of it with a sharp knife through the two outer layers. Carefully open out and turn back the layers to form a rose.

## Edge finishes for tarts

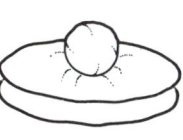

Cover the outer edge with a thin second strip of pastry and mark it with a fork or a spoon handle.

Roll additional pastry into a long strip 1cm (½″) wide. Moisten the edge of the pie and press one end of the strip on to the edge to secure it. Loosely twist the strip pressing it down on to the edge gently between the twists.

Roll additional pastry into a long thin strip 2cm (1″) wide and then carefully cut it into two lengthwise. Moisten the pastry edge and keeping the strips flat secure the ends of the strips together on the edge. Twist the strips around each other and gently press the 'braid' on to the edge of the pie.

**Fig. 7.5** Decorative pastry finishes

Arrange pastry shapes along the moistened edge of the pie slightly overlapping each other.

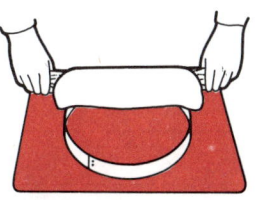

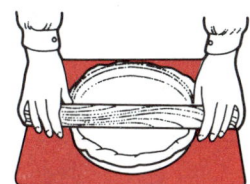

Lift the pastry over the flan ring by wrapping it loosely around a rolling pin. The pastry circle is 4cm larger than the flan ring.

Gently press the pastry in at the base on to the baking sheet. Gently but firmly press the pastry well into the sides. Do not stretch the pastry.

Roll or cut off the surplus pastry. Dampen flan wall and reinforce with pastry trim. Leave to relax.

**Fig. 7.6** Lining a flan ring

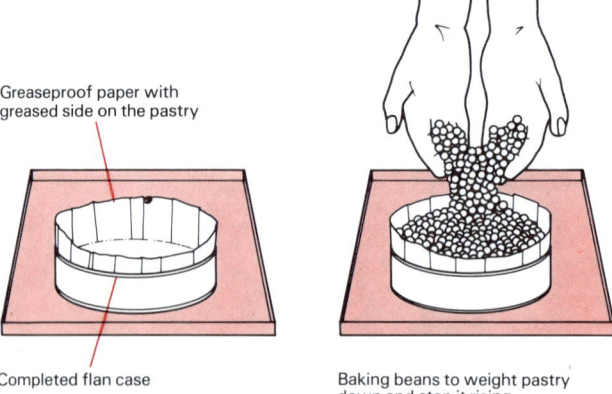

**Fig. 7.7** Baking blind

Greaseproof paper with greased side on the pastry

Completed flan case

Baking beans to weight pastry down and stop it rising

### Rules for making good pastry

**1 Use the correct quantities of ingredients.** The proportions have been carefully tested to give the best results.

**2 Keep hands, equipment and ingredients as cool as possible.** This is to prevent the fat melting which would give a sticky paste. This is difficult to handle and bakes hard.

**3 In shortcrust pastry rub in the fat thoroughly but do not over rub.** Correctly rubbed in fat and flour produces a short textured pastry. Over rubbing melts the fat as described in 2.

**4 Handle ingredients lightly especially when adding the water.** Over-handling develops the gluten to give a tough pastry when cooked.

**5 Measure water carefully and add all at once.** This reduces the tendency to over-handle. Sprinkle evenly, do not add as a 'puddle'.

**6 Knead lightly.** Overkneading gives the same results as over-handling.

**7** *Rolling out*

**(a) Use the minimum amount of flour when rolling out.** Too much flour will alter the basic proportions of the recipe.

**(b) Roll pastry to the shape and size you want, shape the dough before you start to roll.** Reduces the amount of pastry left over. Rekneading and re-rolling trimmings toughens the pastry.

**(c) Use short, sharp, strokes. Roll away from the body.** Gives better control. You can obtain and keep the shape you want together with an even thickness of pastry.

**(d) Do not roll over the edges.** These will be thin and will overcook or burn.

**(e) Do not turn the pastry over when rolling.** The upper surface has the better appearance and should be seen on the finished dish.

**(f) Avoid rekneading and re-rolling.** This will over work the pastry so it becomes dry and difficult to handle and bakes hard.

**8 Suet crust**

**(a) Cook as soon as it is made. The water should be boiling rapidly before the pastry is placed in the steamer over the saucepan:** to prevent loss of raising agent.

**(b) Replenish the pan with boiling water every 30 minutes.** This ensures a continuous supply of steam and prevents the pan boiling dry.

**(c) Eat suet pastry as soon as it is cooked.** It does not reheat very well. It becomes stodgy.

**9 Flaky and rough puff pastry**

**(a) Check that the pastry dough is of a soft consistency.**

**(b) Roll out pastry with straight sides and square corners, fold carefully:** to obtain 12 layers throughout which should given an even rise.

**(c) Cool between each rolling and folding if mixture becomes soft.** This prevents stickiness which makes the pastry difficult to handle and spoils the flaking process.

### Reasons for common faults in pastry making

These are shown in Table 7.6.

**Table 7.6** Faults in pastry making

|  | *Faults* | *Reasons* |
|---|---|---|
| **Shortcrust** | Hard/tough pastry | Not enough fat. Too much water. Overhandling. Oven too slow. |
|  | Crumbly/difficult to handle | Too much fat. Fat over rubbed in. Insufficient water. Use of SR flour. |
|  | Pastry which has shrunk | Pastry not allowed to rest after rolling and shaping. |

| | Faults | Reasons |
|---|---|---|
| **Shortcrust** (*contd.*) | Blistered pastry | Fat not rubbed in completely. Uneven mixing in of the water. |
| | Milky layer inside pie crust | Not cooked properly. Sugar on top of fruit touching pastry. No hole for steam to escape. Too much liquid. |
| | Speckled sweet pastry | Granulated sugar used instead of caster. Too much sugar used. |
| **Rough puff and flaky pastry** | Hard without flakes | Dough too dry and stiff. Insufficient kneading. Lemon juice not used. Uneven distribution of fat. Fat too warm, layers merge into one another. Pastry not rested between rollings in a cool place. Oven not hot enough. |
| | Uneven rising | Uneven rolling and folding. Sides not straight nor corners square. Edges not trimmed. Insufficient resting. Baked too near to one side of oven. Glaze over edges. |
| | Pastry leaking fat | Dough too soft. Oven too cool. |
| | Pastry shrinking | Pastry not resting in cool place after rolling. Oven too cool. |
| **Suet pastry** | Hard, tough pastry | Insufficient raising agent. Baking powder must be used with plain flour. Too much water. Pastry overhandled. Baked at too high a temperature. |
| | Pastry sad and solid | Water went off the boil during cooking. Very little or no baking powder used. |
| | Soggy pastry | Water has seeped in because basin not properly covered. |

## 7.1.4  Scones

| | |
|---|---|
| **Basic recipe– plain scones** | 250g (8oz) pl. flour<br>4 level tsp. (20ml) baking powder *or* 2 level tsp. Cream of Tartar<br>1 level tsp. bicarbonate soda<br>25g (1oz) margarine<br>150ml (¼pt) milk<br>SR flour may be used. Add 5ml (1 level tsp.) baking powder to 250g (8oz) flour. |
| **Method** | 1 Sieve flour and raising agent.<br>2 Rub in fat.<br>3 Add rest of dry ingredients.<br>4 Add liquid and mix with a knife to a soft but not sticky dough.<br>5 Knead *very lightly* on a floured surface.<br>6 Pat out to a thickness of 20mm (¾inch) with palm of hand.<br>7 Use small cutter to cut out scones. Plain cutter for plain or savoury scones, fluted for sweet scones.<br>9 Place on greased baking sheet and glaze tops with milk. |
| **Baking** | A very hot oven. 230°C/450°F/Gas mark 8.<br>Small scones take approximately 12 minutes. |
| **Raising agent** | $CO_2$ produced by the baking powder or by the action of the acid cream of tartar on the alkali bicarbonate of soda. *Air* incorporated by rubbing in and sieving and *steam* from the liquid will play some part. |

| **Variations to basic recipe** | *Sweet* | *Fruit* | *Apple* | *Cheese* |
|---|---|---|---|---|
| | Add | Add | Add | Add |
| | 25g (1oz) sugar | 25g (1oz) sugar | 50g (2oz) sugar | 50-100g (2-4oz) |
| | | 25g (1oz) fruit | 1 med. apple | grated cheese |
| | | | finely chopped | pinch dry mustard |
| | Scones may also be made with wholemeal flour | | | |

| | |
|---|---|
| **Batch scones** | 1 Divide the scone dough into two pieces. See Fig. 7.8.<br>2 Shape these into two rounds or two squares 20mm (¾inch) thick.<br>3 Place on a baking sheet. Cut each shape into four. Do not separate until cooked.<br>4 Brush tops with milk.<br>5 Bake for 10-20 minutes according to size. |

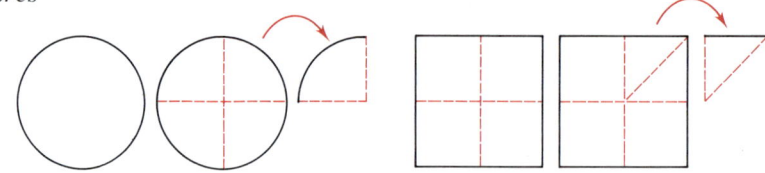

**Fig. 7.8**

## 7.1.5  Cake making

There are **four** methods of making cakes: rubbing in, creaming, whisking and melting. They vary in the quantities and types of ingredients used, in lightness, texture, moistness, flavour and keeping qualities. The basic proportions and additional ingredients can be used in a very wide variety of ways.

**Table 7.7** A comparison of the basic proportions used in different methods of cake making

| Ingredients | Rubbed in | Creaming | Whisking | Melting |
|---|---|---|---|---|
| Baking powder to 450g (1lb) pl. flour | 4-6 level tsp. | 0-4 level tsp. | None | 2 level tsp. bicarbonate of soda |
| Fat to flour | ¼ to ½ | ½ to equal | None | ¼ to ½ |
| Sugar to flour | ¼ to ½ | ½ to equal | Equal | ¼ to ½ + ½ to ¾ syrup |
| Eggs to 450g (1lb) flour | 1 to 4 | 4 to 10 | 1 to 25g | 0-4 |
| Milk | To mix | To mix | None | To mix |

**NB** Dried fruit, cherries, nuts, spices, flavourings vary with the cake being made.

### Ingredients used

**Flour**

  1  A medium strength to soft flour is needed for the fine, even crumb structure of cakes.
  2  Self-raising flour is ideally suited for the plainer, rubbed in cakes but it can be used for all methods instead of plain flour and baking powder.
  3  A new soft flour for sponge cakes has recently appeared in the shops in some parts of the country.
  4  Medium strength flour can also be softened by adding a proportion of cornflour. Add 25g (1oz) cornflour to 175g (7oz) flour.
  5  Wholemeal flour can be used.

**Fat** is added to trap air during creaming with sugar. It adds shortness, softens the gluten to give tender cakes, flavour and colour and prolongs the keeping quality of the cake.
  1  Harder slab margarines are usually used for the rubbed-in and melted methods.
  2  Softer, slab margarines and tub margarines are used for creaming. Tub margarines are used straight from the refrigerator. These are sometimes called soft or luxury margarines.
  3  Butter can be used. It is harder to cream but gives a good flavour.

**Sugar** helps to trap air when creamed with fat. It gives flavour and helps to soften the gluten to give a tender cake. As it caramelizes during cooking it gives colour.
  1  Caster sugar is generally used because it dissolves more readily than granulated.
  2  Soft brown sugars are used in rich fruit cakes and in the melted method for their flavour.

**Eggs** should be used at room temperature. They add nutrients and improve the keeping qualities of cakes.

### Rubbed in or plain cake mixtures

| **Basic recipes** | **Plain fruit cake** | **Rock buns** |
|---|---|---|
| | 200g (8oz) SR flour | 200g (8oz) SR flour |
| | 100g (4oz) margarine | 75g (3oz) caster sugar |
| | 100g (4oz) caster sugar | 75g (3oz) margarine |
| | 225g (9oz) dried fruit | 50g (2oz) dried fruit |
| | 10ml (2tsp.) mixed spice | ¼ level tsp mixed spice |
| | 1 egg + milk to 125ml (¼pt) | 1 egg (size 3) + milk to mix |

**Method**
1 Sieve flour and spice.
2 Rub in fat with fingertips until mixture looks like fresh breadcrumbs.
3 Stir in rest of dry ingredients.
4 Mix in egg or egg and milk. Use a tablespoon for large cakes with a softer consistency, use a fork for small buns with a stiff consistency.

**Baking**
Fruit cake – 170°C/325°F/Gas mark 4 for 1-1½hrs.
Rock buns – 200°C/400°F/Gas mark 6 for 15-20 mins.

**Raising agent**
$CO_2$ produced by the baking powder in the SR flour.
*Air* incorporated by sieving and rubbing in and *steam* from the liquid in the recipe also play a part.

| | |
|---|---|
| Uses | *Small cakes* Raspberry buns, rock buns, coconut, coffee and chocolate buns. |
| | *Larger cakes* Apple cake, farmhouse fruit cake, chocolate, coffee, cherry and coconut cakes. |
| | *Puddings* The basic mixture with different flavourings – jam, syrup, fruit. They can be steamed, baked or microwaved. |
| Characteristics of mixture | **(a)** Economical mixture with fairly low fat and sugar content. |
| | **(b)** Texture and crumb structure rather coarse and open. |
| | **(c)** Rather dry. |
| | **(d)** Should be eaten within a day or two of baking unless frozen. |

## Creamed or rich cake mixtures

| | | |
|---|---|---|
| Basic recipes | **Victoria sandwich** | **Semi-rich mixture** |
| | 125g (4oz) tub margarine | 125g (4oz) tub margarine |
| | 125g (4oz) caster sugar | 125g (4oz) caster sugar |
| | 2 eggs (size 3) | 2 eggs (size 3) |
| | 125g (4oz) pl. flour | 175g (6oz) SR flour |
| | 7.5ml (1½ level tsp.) baking powder. | |

| | |
|---|---|
| Method | 1 Sieve plain flour and baking powder at least twice, SR flour once and place on a plate. |
| | 2 Cream the margarine and caster sugar in a mixing bowl. Use a wooden spoon, electric hand whisk or mixer. Cream until the mixture is very soft, white and fluffy. |
| | 3 Beat the eggs in a small basin and gradually beat into the creamed fat and sugar a little at a time using a wooden spoon or the electric mixer. |
| | 4 Sieve the flour on to the surface of the mixture in the mixing bowl and *carefully fold in with a tablespoon.* Do not over work the mixture. |
| | 5 Additional ingredients are added with the flour. |
| Cooking | **Baking** – all on central shelf |
| | Victoria sandwich 180°C/350°F/Gas mark 4 for 20-30 mins. |
| | Small cakes 190°C/375°F/Gas mark 5 for 20 mins. |
| | Semi-rich cakes 160°C/325°F/Gas mark 3 for 1½hrs approximately. |
| | Very rich cakes will cook at a lower temperature for longer. |
| | **Steaming** |
| | A 1 egg mixture will cook in 1hr, a 2 egg mixture in 1½hrs. |
| | **Microwave** |
| | A 1 egg mixture takes 5-6 mins cooked as a jam sponge or a pineapple upside down pudding. |
| Raising agent | $CO_2$ produced by the baking powder added to plain flour or in the SR flour. |
| | *Air* incorporated by creaming and sieving and *steam* also play a small part. |
| Uses | Queen cakes, cherry buns, butterfly cakes, cup cakes, Victoria sandwich (jam or flavoured with coffee, chocolate, orange, lemon), cherry cake, fruit cake, Dundee cake, Simnel cake, Christmas cake, Eve's pudding, pineapple upside down pudding and steamed or baked puddings (jam, syrup, lemon, etc.). |
| Characteristics of mixture | **(a)** A fine even crumb structure. |
| | **(b)** The higher fat and egg content give a better flavour and moistness. |
| | **(c)** The mixture keeps well. |

## Whisking method (True Sponge)

| | |
|---|---|
| Basic recipe | **2 egg mixture for sponge flan, cake or Swiss roll** |
| | 50g (2oz) caster sugar |
| | 50g (2oz) pl. flour |
| | 2 eggs (size 3) |
| Method | 1 Place eggs and caster sugar in a mixing bowl. |
| | 2 Whisk together until they are very thick and creamy. *The whisk should leave a trail which stays on the surface of the mixture.* |
| | 3 Sieve the flour on to the surface of the whisked mixture. |
| | 4 Fold in the flour, *very gently,* using a tablespoon. Take care not to press out the air whisked in. |
| | 5 Pour the mixture into prepared tins and tilt the tin to spread the mixture evenly. |
| | 6 Bake immediately. |
| | **NB** ¼tsp. baking powder may be sieved in with the flour. Whisking may be done over a bowl of hot water. When 3 or more eggs are used a little hot water may be added to the whisked mixture – this sets the albumen around the air bubbles. |
| Baking | *Swiss roll* – 220°C/425°F/Gas mark 7 for approximately 8 mins. |
| | *Sponge flan* – 180°C/350°F/Gas mark 4 for 20-25 mins. |
| | *Sponge sandwich* (2 tins) – 180°C/350°F/Gas mark 4 for 10-15 mins. |
| | Swiss rolls are cooked on the top shelf, the sponge sandwich and sponge flan on the centre shelf. |
| | A slightly hotter oven is sometimes suggested for flan and sponge sandwich. |
| Raising agent | *Air* whisked into the eggs and sugar. |
| | If baking powder is used a little $CO_2$ will be produced. |
| | The liquid will also produce some *steam.* |
| Characteristics of mixture | **(a)** The structure of the cake is very fine and light. |
| | **(b)** They are usually fatless and can become dry if kept too long. |
| Other uses | Sponge fingers, sponge drops. A 1 egg mixture will make a base for a trifle. |
| | A Genoese sponge has melted fat added. This keeps well and is best left for two days before using. |

## The melted method

| | | |
|---|---|---|
| **Basic recipe** | **Gingerbread** | *To decorate* |
| | 55g (2oz) margarine | glacé icing |
| | 55g (2oz) soft brown sugar | crystallized ginger |
| | 110g (4oz) black treacle and syrup mixed | |
| | 110g (4oz) plain flour | |
| | 2.5ml (½ level tsp.) bicarbonate of soda | |
| | 2.5ml (½ level tsp.) mixed spice | |
| | 5ml (1tsp.) ground ginger | |
| | 1 egg (size 3) | |
| | 60ml (3tblsp.) milk | |

**Method**

1 Measure and weigh ingredients *very accurately*.
2 Place margarine, sugar and syrup in saucepan and melt. Do *not* let the mixture get *too hot*.
3 Add sieved flour and spices to the pan.
4 Beat with a wooden spoon.
5 Add eggs and milk gradually, beating well.
6 Pour the batter into prepared tin (450g (1lb) loaf tin).

**Baking**

170°C/325°F/Gas mark 3, centre shelf, ¾-1 hour.
*Do not open the oven door until cooking time is up.*
Temperatures may vary for other recipes.

**Raising agent**

$CO_2$ produced by the decomposition of bicarbonate of soda on heating. Sodium carbonate is produced but the bitter taste of this is masked by the treacle, brown sugar and spices.
The mixture has the consistency of batter so *steam* also has a part to play in the raising action.

**Uses**

Gingerbread, parkin, gingernuts, brandy snaps and flapjack.

**Characteristics of mixture**

(a) A gingerbread has a moist, soft, open texture which moistens on keeping.
(b) Parkin is slightly drier.
(c) Gingernuts, brandy snaps and flapjack are crisp.

### All in one cakes

**The ingredients are all placed** into a mixing bowl and beaten together with a spoon or fork.
1 A food processor or mixer can also be used.
2 Luxury margarine or softened butter must be used.
3 A little extra baking powder is usually added to take the place of the aeration usually provided by creaming.
4 The mixtures are best baked immediately they are made.

## 7.1.6   Reasons for common faults in scone and cake making

**Table 7.8** Faults in scones and the reasons for them

| *Fault* | *Reasons* |
|---|---|
| Bitter and speckled | Too much sodium hydrogen carbonate (bicarbonate of soda) which formed sodium carbonate in the oven. |
| Poor shape | Poor kneading and cutting out. Uneven distribution of raising agent. |
| Loss of shape in cooking | Mixture too wet. Oven not hot enough. |
| Biscuit like | Rolled out too thinly. |

**Table 7.9** Faults in cakes and the reasons for them

| *Fault* | *Reasons* |
|---|---|
| Close, heavy texture | Insufficient raising agent used. Mixture too wet. Mixture curdled. Overbeating after adding flour or liquid. Too cool an oven. |
| Coarse, open texture | Too much raising agent producing large pockets of gas. Uneven mixing in of flour. |
| Hard, sugary, speckled crust | Too much sugar and too coarse a sugar used. |
| Dry cake | Insufficient liquid. Too much chemical raising agent. |
| Uneven rising | Tilting of tin in oven because the shelves are not even. Tin placed unevenly near source of heat in oven. |

| Fault | Reasons |
|---|---|
| Badly shaped | Uneven lining of tin. |
| | Careless filling of tin. |
| | Wrong consistency. |
| Cracked top or peak | Tin too small for mixture. |
| | Oven too hot. |
| | Cake placed too high in the oven. |
| Sunken fruit | Wet fruit. |
| | Mixture too wet. |
| | Too much raising agent. |
| | Cake moved before set. |
| Sunken cake | Too much raising agent resulting in overstretching of the gluten and then its collapse before it has had time to set. |
| | Too much sugar causing the over-softening of the gluten which then collapses. |
| | Moving the tin. |
| | Banging the oven door. |
| | Too slow an oven or removing from the oven before it was cooked. |
| Burnt crust | Oven too hot. |
| | Cooked too long. |
| | Cake tin too thin. |
| Loss of shape in small cakes | Mixture too wet. |
| | Oven too cool. |
| Sunken gingerbread | Oven door opened before the cake set. |
| Heavy gingerbread | Too much syrup and sugar. |
| | Overheating fat and sugar. |
| | Overbeating after adding liquid. |
| Heavy whisked sponge | Insufficient whisking of eggs and sugar. |
| | Mixture too hot if whisked over hot water. |
| | Careless folding in of flour which pressed out air. |
| | Mixture spread rather than poured into tin. |
| Cracked Swiss roll | Too much flour. |
| | Too much sugar. |
| | Oven too cool. |
| | Insufficient trimming of edges. |
| | Not rolling on a damp teatowel. |
| | Cake allowed to cool before rolling. |

### 7.1.7 Basic methods and dietary guidelines

The dietary guidelines in the report of a sub-committee of the National Advisory Committee on Nutrition Education suggest that over the next fifteen years the following recommendations should be achieved:

1 Fat intake should provide 30% of our daily energy need. Cut saturated fats by 50% and increase the intake of polyunsaturated fats.

2 Sugar intake should be reduced by 50%.

3 Salt intake should be reduced by 25%.

4 Dietary fibre intake should be increased to 30g a day.

The basic recipes in the previous sections can be adjusted to help towards these nutritional goals but food must be palatable. It should look good and taste good. It would not be practicable to absorb all the goals in one recipe.

**Home-made cakes, pastries and biscuits** contain less saturated fats and sugar than factory produced products.

**Fibre intake** could by increased by using **wholewheat flour**. A mixture of 50% wholewheat flour and 50% white flour is often more acceptable. Wholewheat is perfectly acceptable when used in shortcrust pastry, scones, biscuits and cakes. If used in a creamed mixture the whisked egg whites can be folded in after the flour for extra aeration. Batters made with wholewheat need more liquid, an extra egg or more milk can be added. Wholewheat bread is growing in popularity.

**Polyunsaturated fats** and oils can be used instead of saturated fats. Avoid animal fats and choose oils and fats made from maize, soya bean, sunflower seeds, sesame seeds, safflower and olives.

**Skimmed milk** can be used in sauces, batters, cakes and bread. Pasteurized liquid skimmed milk is available in addition to UHT, skimmed and semi-skimmed milk and dried skimmed milk powders.

**Salt** is not necessary in cake recipes. It could gradually be reduced in pastries and bread. Herbs and spices can be used as alternative flavourings in sauces. Salt substitutes are now on sale.

**The quantity of sugar** used for sweetening can be gradually reduced. Fructose is now available in some parts of the UK. This is twice as sweet as sucrose so less is needed. Sugar can be reduced in cakes where dried fruit is used. There are several sweeteners on the market, see Section 4.1.3.

## 7.1.8  Yeast cookery

**Ingredients for bread making**

**1 Yeast** of three types can be purchased
**(a)**  Fresh yeast is sold by many bakers and health food shops. Tied loosely in a polythene bag it stores for up to a month in the refrigerator. It can be wrapped in 15g portions and kept in a freezer for three to four months.
   It should be soft, crumbly, a pale putty colour with a pleasant yeasty smell.
**(b)**  Dried yeast looks like small seeds. It can bought in sachets or in a tin. In a tin with a tight fitting lid it has a shelf life of about six months.
   Fermentation takes longer to start. The instructions on the tin should be carefully followed.
**(c)**  Dried powdered yeast is a very fine powder and is available in some places. It is added to the flour.

**2 Flour** which is strong or hard with a *high gluten content* is needed for well risen bread. When the proteins in the flour are worked with water an elastic substance which we call gluten is formed. Gluten is strengthened (made more elastic) by kneading, shaping, by a cold rise, by the addition of ascorbic acid (vitamin C) and by fats and milk.

**3 Ascorbic acid** in the form of a 25mg vitamin C tablet is crushed in 300-350ml liquid before the liquid is added to the yeast. It is only necessary to rise the bread once if vitamin C is used. The bread making process is then speeded up.

**4 Salt** adds flavour and helps to strengthen the gluten. Too much salt will slow down fermentation as it draws water from the yeast cells by osmosis and so destroys them.
   A dough without salt rises rapidly but the finished bread has no flavour.

**5 Sugar**  Recipes in older cookery books will say 'Cream the yeast with the sugar'. This gives a poorly risen loaf with a very yeasty flavour. The high concentration of sugar outside the yeast cells, draws out water by osmosis killing the cells.
   Sugar is not needed in a bread recipe, energy for the growth of the yeast is provided by the flour. For a sweet dough add the sugar to the flour.

**6 Fat** in the form of lard, oil, margarine or butter improves the keeping qualities of the dough. Fats give a soft dough and slow down the action of the yeast but less rise is possible.
   Fats soften and improve the elasticity of the gluten which is strengthened as it is worked.

**7 Milk** adds protein, strengthens the gluten and improves keeping qualities. Dried or fresh skimmed milk is very good for yeast cookery. The dried milk powder is added to the flour.

**8 Egg yolk** adds nutrients, improves gluten strength and rise and improves keeping qualities.

**9 Spices and dried fruit** retard the action of the yeast as in hot cross buns and Chelsea buns.

**Yeast fermentation**

See section 4.1.18

**Stages in making bread**

**1 Mixing**     This is the sieving of flour and salt followed by the rubbing in of the fat and the mixing of the warm liquid and yeast. The yeast liquid is mixed into the flour using a knife or a wooden spoon.

**2 Kneading**   This is the working together of the mixed ingredients on a lightly floured working surface or in mixing bowl. Very little flour should be used. Often it is sufficient to dust the hands with flour.
   The gluten is developed and the dough becomes smooth and elastic.

**3 Rising**     The dough is put into a clean mixing bowl which is placed in a polythene bag and left in a warm place *to double its size*. Time taken depends upon the temperature. The yeast is given the ideal conditions to increase itself by budding and for producing $CO_2$ i.e. food, warmth and moisture.

**4 Shaping**    The risen dough is kneaded again to distribute the $CO_2$ evenly and then cut and shaped as desired. The shaped dough is put into tins which are placed inside a polythene bag. The surface of the dough can be lightly oiled to prevent sticking.

**5 Proving**    The dough is left to rise in a warm place until *it has doubled its size*. More $CO_2$ is produced and this lifts and stretches the dough. If a dough overproves it looks and feels as if it is going to collapse. Bubbles of gas will probably have broken the surface. Quickly re-knead and shape and put once more to prove. This will only take a few minutes if the dough has not cooled.

**6 Baking**     This is done in a very hot oven. The high temperature kills the yeast cells so that no more $CO_2$ is formed. The heat of the oven causes the $CO_2$ to expand and rise, so lifting the dough a little more. The heat then sets the protein gluten in the risen shape. The surface starch loses a little water, dextrinizes and browns. The small amount of alcohol vapour diffuses out of the bread.

**NB** The first rising is not needed if ascorbic acid is used.

| Basic Recipes | White bread | Wholewheat bread |
|---|---|---|
| | 500g (1lb) strong white flour | 500g (1lb) wholewheat flour |
| | 10ml (2 level tsp.) salt | 10ml (2 level tsp.) salt |
| | 25g (1oz) lard | 25g (1oz) lard |
| | 15g (½oz) yeast | 15g (½oz) yeast |
| | 300ml (½pt) warm water | 300ml (½pt) warm water |
| | 25mg ascorbic acid | |

**Fig. 7.9**

**Fig. 7.10**

**Brown bread**
250g (8oz) strong white flour
250g (8oz) wholewheat flour
10ml (2 level tsp.) salt
25g (1oz) lard
300ml (½pt) warm water
15g (½oz) yeast

**NB** Brown and wholewheat bread needs only one rise without vitamin C

**Method**

1 Mix flour and salt and rub in the fat.
2 If using ascorbic acid, crush and dissolve in warm water.
3 With a teaspoon stir the warm water slowly into the yeast in a basin.
4 Make a well in the centre of the flour and add the yeast liquid.
5 Mix the flour and yeast liquid with a knife or a wooden spoon. Work with the hands in the bowl until the mixture comes cleanly away from the sides of the bowl.
6 Wash your hands if they are sticky before working the dough on a *lightly floured* work surface. Knead for at least 5 minutes until the dough is smooth and elastic. Fig. 7.9.
7 Shape and then place in greased, floured tins. Lightly oil the surface of the bread and place the tin inside a polythene bag.
8 Leave in a warm place to prove until double its original size. See Fig. 7.10.

**Baking**

220°C/425°F/Gas mark 7. Rolls take approx. 12-15 mins.
A large loaf 30 mins. at this temperature and then reduce heat slightly until the loaf is completely cooked.
When tapped, the bottom of a cooked loaf, just from the oven, sounds hollow.

**An enriched dough**

Used for richer dinner rolls and as a base for sweet yeast mixtures such as Swedish tea ring, Chelsea buns etc.

500g strong plain flour          15g (½oz) yeast
10ml (2 level tsp.) salt          300ml (½pt) warm milk and water
10ml (2 level tsp.) sugar         25mg ascorbic acid
50g (2oz) margarine

## 7.2  Raising agents

These are needed to make baked starch mixtures *light* and *palatable*. They increase the volume of a mixture and make the finished product look and taste better.

There are **three** raising agents–**air, carbon dioxide** and **water vapour** (steam).

| *Air* | *Water vapour* | *Carbon dioxide* |
|---|---|---|
| Introduced mechanically by: | Introduced by way of: | Introduced chemically by: |
|   sieving |   water | (a) sodium hydrogen carbonate |
|   beating |   egg |     (bicarbonate of soda) |
|   creaming |   milk | (b) sodium hydrogen carbonate |
|   whisking | |     +cream of tartar |
|   rubbing in | | (c) baking powder |
|   rolling and folding | | Introduced *biologically by* yeast |
| In the oven the heat makes the air expand. This makes it lighter. As it rises it lifts the mixture. | In the oven the water in these ingredients changes to steam which lifts the mixture with it as it rises. | The carbon dioxide produced in these four ways becomes lighter and rises when it is heated. This also lifts the mixture. |

**In the heat of the oven** the gluten which has been stretched by the raising agent, sets in the risen position.

### Action of sodium hydrogen carbonate (bicarbonate of soda) when heated

Sodium hydrogen carbonate + heat $\longrightarrow$ sodium carbonate + water + carbon dioxide

Sodium carbonate (washing soda) *is bitter* so bicarbonate of soda is only used in mixtures containing strongly flavoured ingredients, such as gingerbread.

### Action of sodium hydrogen carbonate + cream of tartar

Sodium hydrogen carbonate + cream of tartar $\longrightarrow$ Rochelle salt + $H_2O$ + $CO_2$
(alkali)                                    (acid)                            (colourless
                                                                        tasteless
                                                                        salt)

### The action of baking powder

Baking powder is a commercial preparation of sodium hydrogen carbonate plus several acids. A starch powder is used as a drying agent.

**Baking powder can be made at home** using the following recipe:
> 1 part sodium hydrogen carbonate (bicarbonate of soda)
> 2 parts cream of tartar
> 1 part rice flour

### Acids in baking powder

Baking powder usually contains a mixture of acids:

**1** Tartaric acid–obtained from grapes. Reacts rapidly so it can be lost before baking.
**2** Cream of tartar–obtained from grapes. Has a slower reaction than tartaric acid.
**3** Acid sodium pyrophosphate–derived from phosphate rock. Very little $CO_2$ is released until it is subjected to the heat of the oven.

The mixture of these three acids in baking powder results in a little $CO_2$ being released during mixing which helps the mixing process but the bulk of the acid will not react until the mixture is heated.

$$\text{Acid + Alkali} \xrightarrow{\text{heat and moisture}} \text{colourless, tasteless salt} + CO_2 + \text{water}$$

### Uses of baking powder

**1** Baking powder is added to self-raising flour in quantities sufficient to raise a plain cake mixture (rubbed-in method). Self-raising flour can be used to make scones and other cakes but there will be too much raising agent for a creamed mixture such as a rich fruit cake, and too little for scones.
When making scones add 1 tsp. baking powder to 250g (8oz) SR flour.
**2** Baking powder should be added evenly to the flour by sieving them together twice.
**3** Always measure baking powder very accurately. Use purpose-made measuring spoons or 5ml spoons.
**4** If too much baking powder is used a cake will collapse in the middle and have a coarse open texture. The $CO_2$ lifts the mixture too quickly and escapes before the mixture sets in the heat of the oven.
**5** Too little baking powder will produce a poorly risen cake which has a close texture.
**6** Replace the lid of the baking powder tightly after use and store it in a cool, dry place.

**NB** 'Salfree' a low sodium baking powder is available.

Table 7.10 The quantities of baking powder needed for different mixtures

| Mixture | Plain flour | Baking powder |
| --- | --- | --- |
| Rubbed in cakes and puddings | 250g (8oz) | 3 level tsp (15ml) |
| Creamed cakes and puddings | 250g (8oz) | 1 level tsp (5ml) |
| Victoria sandwich | 125g (4oz) | 1 level tsp (5ml) |
| Scones | 250g (8oz) | 4 level tsp (20ml) |

### The fermentation of yeast

Yeast + food + water + warmth (or time) $\longrightarrow$ energy + $CO_2$ + alcohol

Yeasts are single celled members of the fungi family of plants which feed saprophytically on organic material.

Yeasts feed on carbohydrates to obtain the energy needed for growth and budding (asexual reproduction) as illustrated in the photograph below.

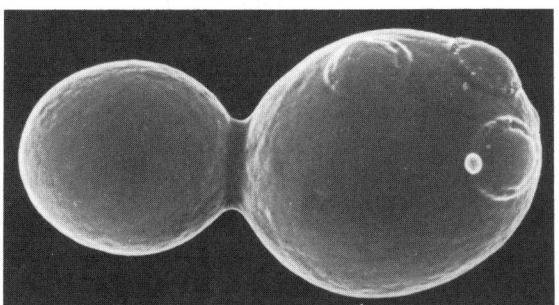

**Fig. 7.11** Budding yeast cells

If there is a plentiful supply of $O_2$ the waste products are $CO_2$ and $H_2O$. If the yeast obtains energy from sugar without $O_2$ (anaerobic respiration or fermentation) the waste products are $CO_2$ and alcohol.

There are many wild yeasts which cause fruit and jam to ferment. In preservation we prevent the action of the enzymes which bring about fermentation.

Bakers yeast produces more $CO_2$ whilst brewers yeast produces more alcohol. When we use bakers yeast the carbon dioxide makes the bread rise and the alcohol is lost by evaporation during baking.

$$\text{Starch in flour} \xrightarrow[\text{in flour}]{\text{action of enzyme amylase}} \text{Maltose} \xrightarrow[\text{in yeast}]{\text{action of enzyme maltase}} \text{Glucose}$$

$$\text{Glucose} \xrightarrow[\text{in yeast}]{\text{action of enzyme group zymase}} \text{Energy} + \text{Carbon dioxide} + \text{Ethyl alcohol}$$

**Conditions required for the efficient fermentation of yeast**

**Food** (starch in flour and sugar in the recipe if present)

**Warmth** (25°C to 29°C) **or time** yeast works slowly at lower temperatures

**Moisture** (water or milk in recipe)

**The rate of fermentation** is influenced by the following:
 1 The low temperature of a refrigerator allows fermention to take place very slowly so a yeast dough may be left overnight in the refrigerator to rise.
 2 Yeast cells are destroyed by high temperatures so the liquid in the recipe must only be warm. In the oven the yeast cells are killed so fermentation ceases.
 3 Salt affects fermentation. Too little and fermentation takes place rapidly but flavour is poor. Too much and many cells are destroyed by osmosis (water drawn from cells). Production of $CO_2$ by any remaining cells is poor. Bread does not rise.
 4 If sugar is creamed directly with the yeast many cells are destroyed as water is drawn out of the yeast cells by osmosis. The dead cells give the finished bread a yeasty flavour. $CO_2$ production is poor. Any sugar in the recipe should be added after the yeast has been mixed with the liquid or mixed into the flour.

**The stages of breadmaking**–sponging, rising, proving, give the yeast time to produce $CO_2$.

**The stages of kneading and shaping** distribute the gas evenly through the mixture.

**Buying and Storing Yeast**

**Fresh Yeast** is obtainable from small bakeries and health food shops.
 1 It should be kept in a cool place.
 2 Wrapped in foil or polythene it will keep for a few days. Loosely tied in a polythene bag it keeps up to 4 weeks in the refrigerator.
 3 Carefully packed fresh yeast keeps up to a year in the freezer. Fresh yeast is a putty colour. Darker patches indicate drying out and staling. When fresh it should crumble easily.

**Dried Yeast** looks like tiny seeds. It can be bought in vacuum sealed sachets or in tins. It keeps for 6 months in an airtight tin.

2 level tablespoons of dried yeast = 60g (2oz) fresh yeast

### 7.3   The storage of baked starch mixtures

**Pastries**

These can be stored in air-tight tins after cooling. Staling soon occurs but is reversed by reheating short pastries.

**Suet pastries** should not be stored but eaten straight away.

**Flaky pastries** lose their flakiness when stored.

**Pastry may be frozen** uncooked or cooked. If a pie is frozen uncooked the surface of the pastry must be unbroken. There is no need to thaw before cooking.

**Scones**

These dry out rapidly if stored in a tin. They should be eaten soon after being made. They do freeze well.

**Biscuits**

Store in a dry, air-tight tin. Never mix with cakes because the biscuits will absorb moisture and become soft.

**Cakes**

These store well in air-tight tins. Rich fruit cakes should be wrapped in greaseproof paper before storing. These need two months to mature.

**Decorated cakes** are frozen before packing. (Chocolate does not freeze.)

**Sandwich cakes** should be frozen without their jam because the water in the jam turns to ice and on thawing soaks into the cake.

**Freezing exaggerates** the strength of strong flavourings such as ginger.

**Bread**

Bread should be cold before storing. Bread bins should be clean, dry and ventilated.

**Sliced bread** should be stored in its wrapper.

**Bread freezes well** but the crust tends to lift off after it has been thawed.

### 7.4   Preparation of baking tins

**Tins should be greased** with a pure fat which is free of salt and water. Lard and white cooking fats are best. Cooking oils leave a hard yellow glaze on the baking tins. It is more efficient to melt the fat and apply with a brush.

**Tins may be lined** with greaseproof paper or a non-stick baking parchment which does not require greasing.

**Non-stick baking tins** usually require a light greasing.

**Tins for pastries**

| | |
|---|---|
| Shortcrust | Grease is not required unless sugar has been added to the pastry. Flan rings and the trays they are placed on must be greased. |
| Suet pastry | Grease basins and baking sheets. |
| Rough puff and flaky | Wet baking sheets with cold water to produce steam in the oven to help flaking. Trays can be greased if preferred. |

**Cake tins**

| | |
|---|---|
| Scones | Grease or grease and flour baking tins. |
| Small buns | Grease the baking sheet or bun tin. |
| Sandwich cakes | Grease the tin, line the base with greaseproof paper. Grease the paper and dust the tin with flour. |
| Sponge flan tins | Grease liberally, line central depression with a circle of greaseproof paper. Grease the paper and dust the tin with flour. |
| Large plain cakes and gingerbreads | Grease the tins and line the base with a piece of greaseproof paper. |
| Rich cakes | Grease the tin slightly to hold the paper lining. Line with greaseproof paper. Grease lightly. Wrap a piece of brown paper, secured with string around the cake tin. |

## Lining tins

### Square tins

**1** Place the tin on greaseproof paper and draw around the base.

**2** Fold the paper on these lines.

**3** Cut the crease lines as shown in diagram.

**4** The sides now wrap around to give sharply squared corners.

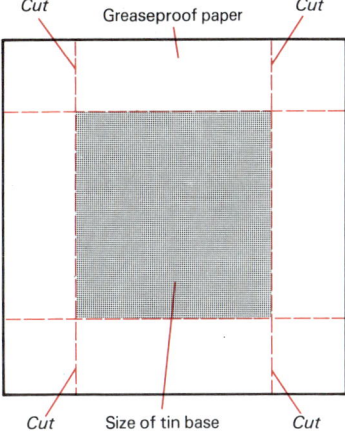

**Fig. 7.12**

### Swiss roll tins

**1** The greaseproof paper should be 3cm larger than the tin all the way around.

**2** Place the tin on the paper and draw around the base with a pencil.

**3** Fold along these lines.

**4** Open out the folds and cut the creases as shown in the diagram.

**5** The ends now wrap around the sides to give square corners.

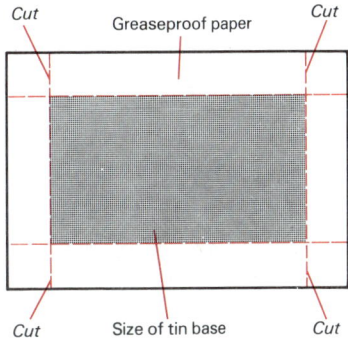

**Fig. 7.13**

### A loaf tin

**1** The paper should be large enough to line base and sides of tin.

**2** Place the tin in the centre of the paper and draw around the base.

**3** Fold along these lines.

**4** Open out the folds and cut diagonally into the corners of the base lining.

**5** These diagonal cuts give a neat fit to the sloping sides of the tin.

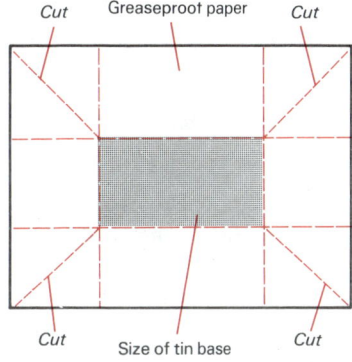

**Fig. 7.14**

### A round tin

**1** Use double greaseproof paper.

**2** Draw around the base to get a circle to fit.

**3** Cut inside the pencil lines to allow for the thickness of the metal of the sides of the tin.

**4** Cut a double strip of greaseproof long enough to fit around the sides of the tin and 4-5cm deeper than the tin.

**5** Fold up 1-2cm and snip diagonally up to the fold.

**6** The paper will now overlap to fit the botton of the sides of the tin perfectly.

**7** Grease the tin and place the side lining in position before the base.

**8** A very rich cake which bakes for several hours should have several layers of brown paper tied around the outside to prevent overcooking of the outer layer of the cake.

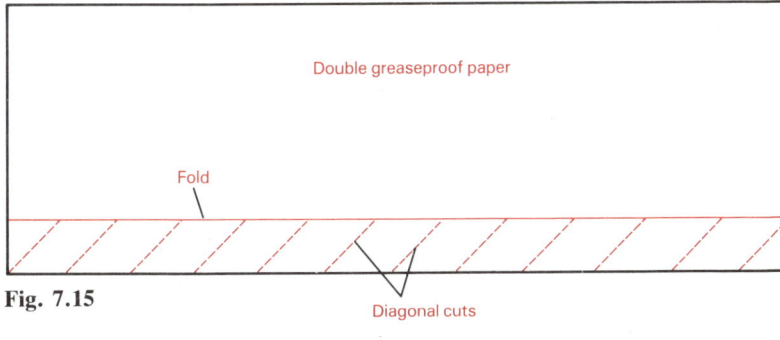

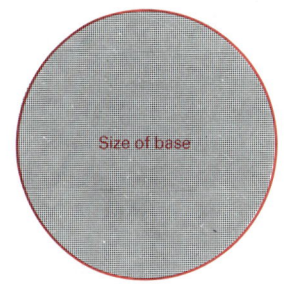

**Fig. 7.15**

## 7.5  Soups

The food value of soups varies with the ingredients used. The addition of milk, cream, beaten egg adds to the food value. A broth containing meat, vegetables and pearl barley can be a meal in itself.

The main purpose of a soup is to stimulate the appetite by stimulating the flow of digestive juices which are needed to digest the food that follows.

1 In cold weather soups make a hot start to a meal.
2 Cold soups can be refreshing in hot weather.
3 Soups can be used in place of another drink.
4 Carried in flasks soup is an excellent food for a packed meal.
5 People on light diets find soup attractive, easy to eat and easy to digest.

### Classification of soups

Table 7.10  Types of soup

| Thin | Thick | Thickened |
|---|---|---|
| *Consommés* <br> Made from good stock containing a little meat and finely diced vegetables. These are often strained out. <br> Very little food value <br> Stimulates appetite <br><br> *Broths* <br> Not sieved or thickened <br> Contain meat, vegetables and a cereal (pearl barley, rice or pasta) <br> High nutritional value <br> Filling | *Purées* <br> Made from vegetables thickened by: <br>  (i) sieving. <br>  (ii) liquidizing. <br>  (iii) a liaison of flour or cornflour. <br>  (iv) a roux. <br>  (v) egg yolks. <br> Nutritional value varies with the ingredients. | These are thickened but are not sieved or puréed. |

### Characteristics of a good soup

**A good flavour** achieved by seasoning, herbs and a good stock.

**A good colour.** The colour and flavour should blend well with the rest of the meal.

**Free of grease.** Stock should be cooled and the fat skimmed off before using it to make soup.

**A good consistency** e.g. a purée should be smooth and free of lumps.

### Quantities per person

125ml (¼pt) per person if the first of several courses. A stimulant.
250ml (½pt) if one or two courses only.

### Accompaniments

Bread rolls, Melba Toast (thin slices of bread toasted so that they curl); croûtons with purées; grated parmesan with consommés; boiled rice with Mulligatawny soup, small pasta; chopped parsley.

### Purée soups

These are the types of soup usually expected in a CSE or O-level practical examination.

### Basic ingredients

Fat–oil, butter, dripping (15g (½oz) to 1 litre (1pt) liquid)
Foundation–vegetables, fish or meat
        900g (2lb) green vegetables to 1 litre liquid
        450g (1lb) starchy vegetables to 1 litre liquid
Liquid–125-200ml (¼pt+) milk + 750ml (¾pt) stock
Flavouring–onion, salt, pepper, bouquet garni, bay leaf or other herbs and spices.
Liaison–30g (1oz) flour + little milk or water to blend.

### Basic method

1 Wash, peel, slice or dice vegetables. Grated carrot cooks more quickly than dice.
2 Sauté for 10 minutes in fat or oil in a covered pan. Vegetables in a white soup should not brown. Shake from time to time.
3 Cover with stock or water and simmer until tender with added flavourings.
4 When cooked sieve or liquidize.
5 Return puréed mixture to pan.
6 Reheat when required adding the milk.
7 If the soup needs thickening add the liaison. Cook for 10 minutes. Stir well.
8 Taste, adjust seasoning, taste again.    9 Serve.

**Stock**

Stock is made from water in which bones, meat, vegetables or fish have been simmered slowly to extract their flavour. A white stock is made with chicken or turkey bones.

Avoid using too much fat, cut vegetables in large pieces and add herbs for flavour.

After simmering for about 2 hours, strain and cool. Remove the surface fat before using.

If kept, store in the refrigerator and boil for 5 minutes next day (destroys bacteria). Stock may be frozen.

Stock cubes may be dissolved in water to produce a quickly made stock.

# 8   Food storage and preservation

## 8.1   General points on the storage of foods

Section 4 deals with the storage of each commodity in turn.
Section 7.4 deals with the storage of scones, cakes and pastries.

## 8.2   The refrigerator

### Principles underlying the working and use of a refrigerator

**1** Micro-organisms are not very active at temperatures below 10°C so foods stored below this temperature deteriorate very slowly. British standards require the temperature of the refrigerator cabinet to range between 0°C and 8°C.

**2** When a liquid evaporates it takes heat from the surrounding area. The cabinet of a refrigerator cools when the heat it contains is used to evaporate the liquid refrigerant to its gaseous form.

The refrigerant is inside pipes in the evaporator or in the flat cooling plate of a larder/refrigerator. Outside the cabinet the gaseous refrigerant is condensed back to its liquid form and is pumped once more into the evaporator.

**3** Warm air rises and cold air falls. This is important when selecting the best position for storing foods within the cabinet.

**4** A fridge/freezer has a separately controlled freezer compartment. The refrigerator does not have ice making or frozen food compartments.

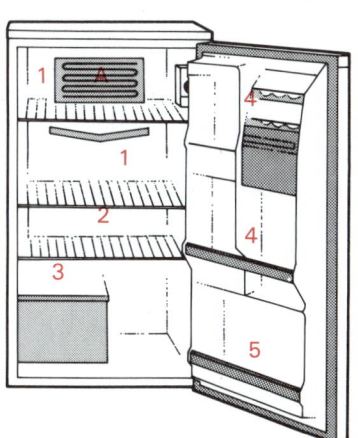   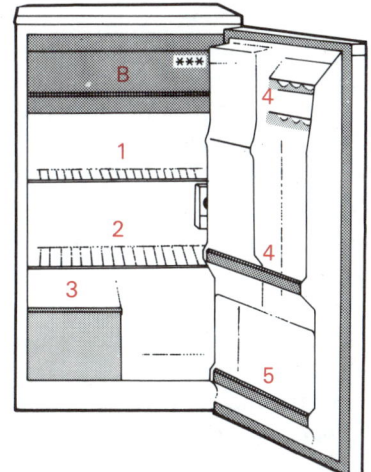

A *larder/refrigerator* with no storage for frozen foods. It does not make ice. Automatic defrosting of cooling plate A takes place into the drip tray below

Refrigerator with ∗ ∗ ∗ frozen food compartment B above the evaporator

**Fig. 8.1** Types of refrigerator

**Table 8.1** Positioning of food in a refrigerator

| Position | Temperature | Food stored |
|---|---|---|
| A | * −6°C | Frozen food for **one week** |
|   | ** −12°C | Frozen food for **one month** |
|   | *** −18°C | Frozen food for **three months** |
| 1 | Coldest part approx. 4°C | Meat, fish, poultry |
| 2 | Cold | Prepared dishes, bacon, cheese |
| 3 | Coolest part of cabinet | Salad vegetables, fruit |
| 4 | Warmest part of refrigerator | Butter, margarine, yogurt |
| 5 | Warmest part of refrigerator | Milk, wine, cold drinks |

The numbers and letters refer to those shown in Fig. 8.1.

**The thermostat setting** for most refrigerators is 3 or 4. In hot weather or when cabinet is full it might be necessary to turn the thermostat dial to a higher number to maintain the necessary coldness in the cabinet.

**Rules for using the refrigerator**

**1 Food placed in the refrigerator should be covered.**
**(a)** Moving air inside the cabinet removes water from the surface of food making it dry. This moisture is deposited as frost on the evaporator which will increase running costs.
**(b)** Wrapping or use of a covered container prevents strong smelling foods contaminating foods such as milk and butter which will absorb the strong odours.
**2 Store cooked meat above uncooked meat.** Bacteria cannot then pass from the uncooked meat to the cooked.
**3 Hot food should not be placed in the refrigerator.** The heat will raise the temperature of the cabinet making it more suitable for microbial activity. Steam forms frost and again increases running costs.
**4 Perishable foods such as meat or fish should be stored below the evaporator.** They should be wrapped with a layer of air around them to prevent off flavours and smells developing. This is the coldest position in the refrigerator.
**5 Do not over load the cabinet.** The circulation of cold air is reduced if the cabinet is full and therefore the refrigerator is less efficient at keeping foods fresh.
**6 Open the door as little as possible.**
**(a)** The temperature will rise and will support microbial activity.
**(b)** Increases in running costs will occur.
**7 Salad foods should be kept in the crisper drawer** which is the coolest part of cabinet. There is also a lid to the crisper which prevents the loss of moisture from the food.
**8 Check the contents regularly.** It is necessary to remove stale food so that it does not contaminate fresh food that is put into the refrigerator.
**9 Wipe up spills immediately and wipe out the cabinet regularly** with water and **bicarbonate of soda**.
**(a)** Spills can affect other foods. It is important that the refrigerator is as clean as possible to prevent contamination that could lead to food poisoning.
**(b)** The plastic lining of the refrigerator will absorb the smell of detergents.
**10 Defrost regularly** if the refrigerator does not do so automatically. The layer of frost on the evaporator should be less than 6mm (¼″). A thicker layer of ice will result in more fuel being used to keep the temperature of the refrigerator at the thermostat setting.

*Manual defrosting*
(*a*) Switch off the refrigerator.
(*b*) Remove the food and store it in a cool place.
(*c*) When the ice has melted wash out the cabinet with warm water and bicarbonate of soda.
(*d*) Switch on the power.
(*e*) Put the food back.
*Automatic defrosting*
(*a*) The cooling plate has an automatic defrosting system which comes into action at the end of each thermostat cycle. The ice does not build up.
(*b*) The water drips into a trough below the cooling plate and so into a pipe and down to a tray outside the refrigerator at the bottom. This water continually evaporates into the air of the kitchen.

(*c*) Sometimes a button is pushed to trigger off the defrosting.

**Care of the cabinet**

The outside of the cabinet should be wiped down regularly, dried and polished with furniture cream or mild wax polish.

French chalk or a non-scented talcum powder may be rubbed on the rubber door gasket to prevent sticking to the cabinet.

**NB** If the electricity is to be switched off for a period of time the refrigerator should be emptied, defrosted and left with its door **open**. If the door is left closed moulds and unpleasant odours will develop which are difficult to get rid of.

**Points to consider when buying a refrigerator**

 **1** Type of fuel available–electricity, gas or oil.
 **(a)** Compressor refrigerators run on electricity,
 **(b)** Absorption refrigerators usually use gas, they are quiet but ventilation is needed for the products of combustion to escape.
 **2** Size–depends on the number in a family and the space available.
 **3** Cost.
 **4** Larder/refrigerator or refrigerator with frozen food compartment or a fridge/freezer.
 **5** The star rating on the evaporator *, ** or ***. The freezer part of a fridge/freezer should have ****rating.
 **6** Additional features such as the arrangement of the storage sections, automatic defrosting or work surface top.
 **7** The quality of the materials used to make the refrigerator and the workmanship.
 **8** The length of the guarantee.

## 8.3   Domestic preservation

**Why preserve?**

**To prevent waste** and save money.

**Preserves add nutrients,** variety and flavour, colour and texture to meals when fresh fruit and vegetables are scarce and expensive.

**Preserved food is easily stored,** transported, exported and imported.

**What causes food decay?**

**Enzymes** within the cells of slaughtered animals and harvested plant foods break down the tissue when the cells have been damaged (autolysis).

**Yeasts, moulds and bacteria** feed saprophytically on organic material. Digestive enzymes secreted on to the food break it down and the 'digested' material is absorbed. This microbial activity is essential for the breakdown of dead organic material.

**What are we doing when we preserve?**

**By storing food at low temperatures** −18°C and below, enzymes and micro-organisms are **inactive**. They remain dormant until the temperature rises.
 **1** Frozen food should be stored at −18°C or below in a domestic freezer
 **2** Food should be frozen at −25°C. The lower the freezing temperature the smaller the ice crystals and the less damage to food tissue.
**NB** The refrigerator is for *short term storage* of food. The star rating of the frozen food storage compartment must be observed.

**By heating food to high temperatures and preventing re-entry of air**
 **1** The cooking process in jam making destroys micro-organisms. The waxed disc seals the surface of the jam and prevents re-contamination. It is the 60%-65% sugar which preserves.
 **2** Bottling, in water or syrup, involves the destruction of micro-organisms at high temperatures. The airtight vacuum seal prevents re-contamination.

**By the removal of water**
 **1** Life is not possible without water. Enzyme actions take place in solution. Removal of water destroys microbes and prevents enzyme action within food.
 **2** Herbs are dried by hanging bundles in a warm, drying current of air.
 **3** Apple rings may be dried in a very slow oven.
 **4** Dried foods must be kept dry. If they become damp enzymes and microbes can become active again.

**By using chemicals and other products**

Sugar–jam making, crystallizing fruit.

Salt–salting beans, pickles, chutneys.

Vinegar–pickles, chutneys.

Alcohol–fruit e.g. peaches in brandy.

1 High concentrations of sugar, salt and vinegar remove water from the plant and animal cells by osmosis. Micro-organisms dehydrate and are destroyed.

2 In pickling the salt draws water from the vegetable so that the vinegar can penetrate right into the food. The pickle will then keep and be crisp.

3 Enzyme action within food cannot take place in the presence of salt, sugar or acid in high concentration.

### 8.3.1 Jam making

Jam is fruit boiled with sugar to form a gel which sets when the jam cools. A good gel depends upon the amount of *pectin, sugar* and *acid* present.

**Pectin** is a complex sugar or polysaccharide found in the cell walls of plant food. The amount present depends upon type of fruit and degree of ripeness. Just ripe or slightly under-ripe fruit contains most. In over-ripe fruit the pectin has changed to a form which will not gel.

*Test for pectin*

(a) Simmer fruit until soft. Put 1 teaspoon in a glass. Cool.

(b) Add 3 teaspoons of methylated spirits. Shake. Leave for 1 minute.

    (i) 1 large clot indicates a plentiful supply of pectin.

    (ii) 2 or 3 smaller clots indicates moderate supply of pectin.

    (iii) Many small clots indicate a poor pectin content.

**Table 8.2** Pectin content of fruits

| Excellent | Good | Poor |
|---|---|---|
| Cooking apples | Blackberries | Strawberries |
| Crab apples | Plums | Cherries |
| Gooseberries | Apricots | Pears |
| Seville oranges | Raspberries | |
| Blackcurrants | | |
| Redcurrants | | |

1 Jams may be made with a mixture of fruits rich in pectin and fruits low in pectin. e.g. strawberry and gooseberry.

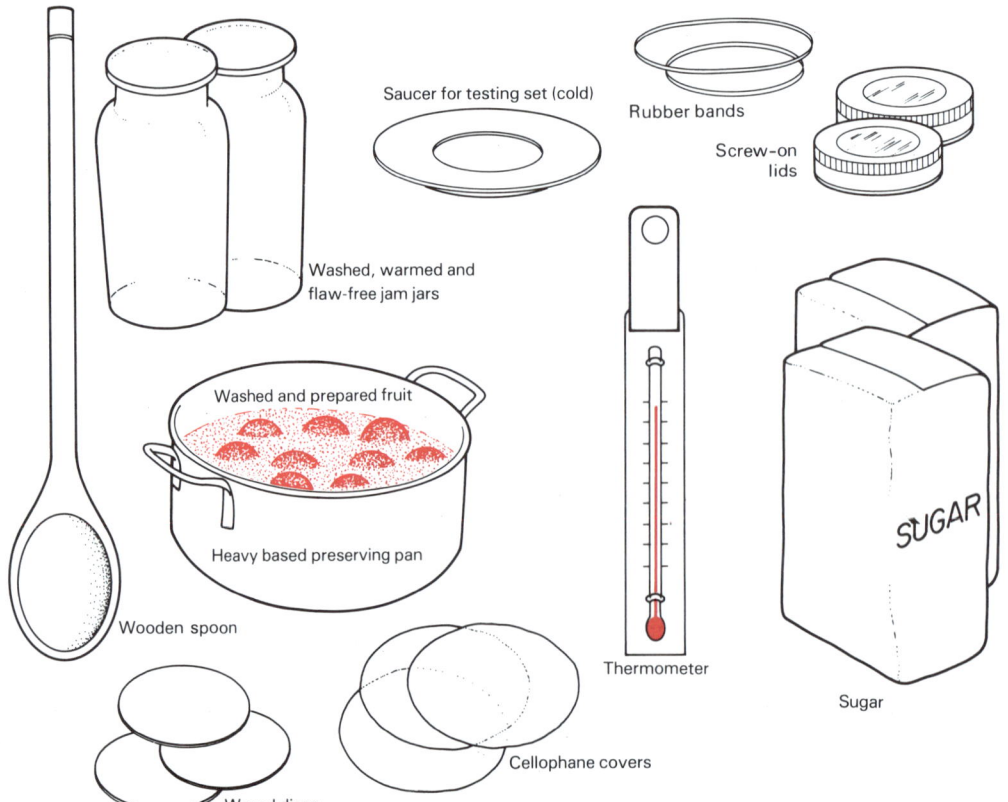

**Fig. 8.2** Jam making equipment

**2** A pectin stock may be made by straining stewed gooseberries, cooking apples or redcurrants and adding this to the jam.

**3** A commercial liquid pectin, such as 'Certo' can be used. Manufacturers instructions must be followed.

**Acid** helps to extract the pectin from the fruit. Fruit rich in pectin usually has a high acid content.

Acid improves the colour and flavour of the jam. It can be added as lemon juice, citric acid or tartaric acid.

**Sugar** as 60% to 65% of the finished jam ensures that the jam will keep. Granulated sugar may be used. Preserving sugar has larger crystals which dissolve more readily to reduce risk of burning on the bottom of the pan. Less froth is also produced, but it is more expensive to buy than granulated sugar.

### Choice of fruit

**Seasonal fruit** is plentiful and cheaper to buy.

**1** Slightly under-ripe fruit, undamaged and with no signs of bruising or moulds should be bought.

**2** Choose fruit rich in pectin.

**Recipes** Fruits rich in pectin take more water and sugar and give higher yields. Raspberries and strawberries with little pectin have no water in the recipe.

*Method*

(*a*) Select jars free of chips and cracks. Wash, rinse, drain. Dry outside.

(*b*) Place the jars on a baking sheet in a cool oven. This sterilizes the jars and warm jars will not crack when hot jam is poured in.

(*c*) Simmer fruit and any water until very soft to extract as much pectin as possible and ensure the fruit will be tender in the jam, as sugar tends to toughen the fruit.

(*d*) If in doubt test for pectin.

(*e*) Stir in the sugar off the heat and make sure the sugar is dissolved before the jam starts to boil.

(*f*) Bring to the boil. Boil rapidly until set point is reached.

(*g*) A small knob of butter reduces the amount of scum.

*To test for set*

(i) Place a teaspoon of jam on a cold saucer. Cool. Push surface with finger. A wrinkled surface indicates jam has reached setting point.

(ii) The flake test. Cool a little jam on the wooden spoon. Allow it to drip off the spoon. If large flakes form and hang, setting point has been reached.

(iii) Jam will set at 220°F/105°C. Use a sugar thermometer. Stir the jam first before using the thermometer.

(*h*) Allow the jam to cool slightly to prevent the fruit rising in jars. *Fill the jars right to the brim* because jam shrinks as it cools and a perfect seal with a waxed disc is only possible at the rim.

(*i*) Wipe away any spills. Place the waxed disc in position waxed side down. Wax melts and makes a barrier against entry of micro-organisms.

(*j*) Dampen the upper surface of the cellophane disc. Stretch over the jar and secure with an elastic band. This cover must be put on while the jam is very hot or should be left off until the jam is cold.

(*k*) Label the jar with contents and date.

(*l*) Store in a cool, dark, dry place to discourage yeasts and moulds and in a dark place so the colour of the jam does not fade.

**NB** Screw tops may be used. They should be undamaged and clean. They must be put on when the jam is very hot. As soon as the lid is unscrewed moulds and yeast can reach the jam.

### 8.3.2 Freezing

**Points to consider when buying a freezer**

**1** Look for the four star symbol.

 **Fig. 8.3**

**2** The size chosen will depend upon the number in a family, where it is to stand and how it is to be used. Freezing of home produced goods usually means a larger freezer is needed.

**3** Cost – money available, the cost of electricity to run it and insurance. The cost also includes bought frozen foods to fill the freezer.

**4** Type – chest, upright or refrigerator/freezer.

**Packaging material for freezing**

**Aluminium foil** tears easily, items need to be double wrapped. Useful for awkward shapes.

**Polythene bags** – assorted sizes, use heavy weight to prevent tears.

*Chest type*

*Upright type*

*Refrigerator/freezer*

**Fig. 8.4** Types of freezer

**Cling film**–heavy gauge for freezer.

**Polythene boxes** with well-fitting lids. Easy to stack. Space saving.

**Seals**–plastic or paper covered wire, heat sealing kits are available at a high initial cost.

**Labels**

**Record book** to keep check of food stored and used.

**Packing** should be done in convenient sized portions.
1 Remove the air so that moisture in air cannot form frost on the surface of food.
2 Seal.
3 Label with description, quantity and date. Use a chinagraph pencil or freezer pen.
4 Store for the times recommended for different foods in the manufacturers booklet. Commercially frozen foods should be stored for the length of time stated on the packet.

### Home freezing

**General points**
1 Switch the freezer to fast freeze 2-4 hours before the food is to be placed in it.
2 The freezer does not improve the quality of food frozen, hard pastry will remain hard, starchy peas starchy. Use only good quality items.
3 Foods with a high water content do not freeze well. Tomatoes, cucumbers, lettuce, milk. Eggs are best stored separated with a little salt beaten in to the white and/or the yolk.

**Blanching vegetables**
1 Prepare and wash vegetables as rapidly as possible after harvesting. Divide into maximum of 500g (1lb) quantities.
2 Plunge the vegetables into a large quantity of boiling water. Bring back to the boil. Boil for time given for the vegetable being processed in the freezer handbook.
3 Plunge into ice cold water for a time equal to the blanching time.
4 Drain, dry and pack.
5 Seal, label and freeze.

**Blanching destroys** the enzymes which would bring about the loss of vitamin C and changes in texture, colour and flavour during storage.

**Thawing** Some foods e.g. vegetables, fish fingers and beefburgers, can be cooked from frozen. Others are thawed and eaten, whilst some foods must be thawed and cooked before eating.

Meat, whole fish and poultry are best thawed slowly in the refrigerator. This also applies to dishes containing these foods.

Foods which are easily contaminated by micro-organisms should not be thawed and refrozen. They can be cooked and refrozen in a new form.

Bread, fruits and vegetables may be re-frozen especially if still cold but their flavour and colour could change.

**Power cuts and breakdown** Power cuts are usually of short duration. Keep the freezer closed and cover it with a blanket or newspaper. If it is a lengthy power cut it may be necessary to remove and eat, or cook and eat as much as possible. A full freezer will stay cold longest.

If the freezer has broken down some food may be stored in the frozen food compartment of the refrigerator, or perhaps a neighbour can provide temporary storage space.

An insurance of a few pounds can cover repair costs and loss of food.

### Care of the freezer

1 A thick layer of ice adds to the running cost.

**2** Defrost a chest freezer once a year, an upright freezer more frequently. Use a plastic scraper to loosen ice.

**3** Wash the freezer interior with warm water and bicarbonate of soda.

**4** Choose a time to defrost when stock is low. Wrap any frozen food in newspaper or old blankets and store in the coolest place available.

**5** The outside of a freezer can be washed with detergent and water, and polished with a silicone or cream polish.

### 8.3.3   Bottling

**General points**

**Fruit only** should be bottled as it is difficult to get a high enough temperature for vegetables. Bacterial spores from the soil are resistant to heat.

**1** Fruit should be just ripe. Prepare and wash the fruit and grade for size.

**2** Jars should be heat proof glass, free of chips and cracks. Wash them thoroughly.

**3** Seals should be used once only. Check for perished rings.

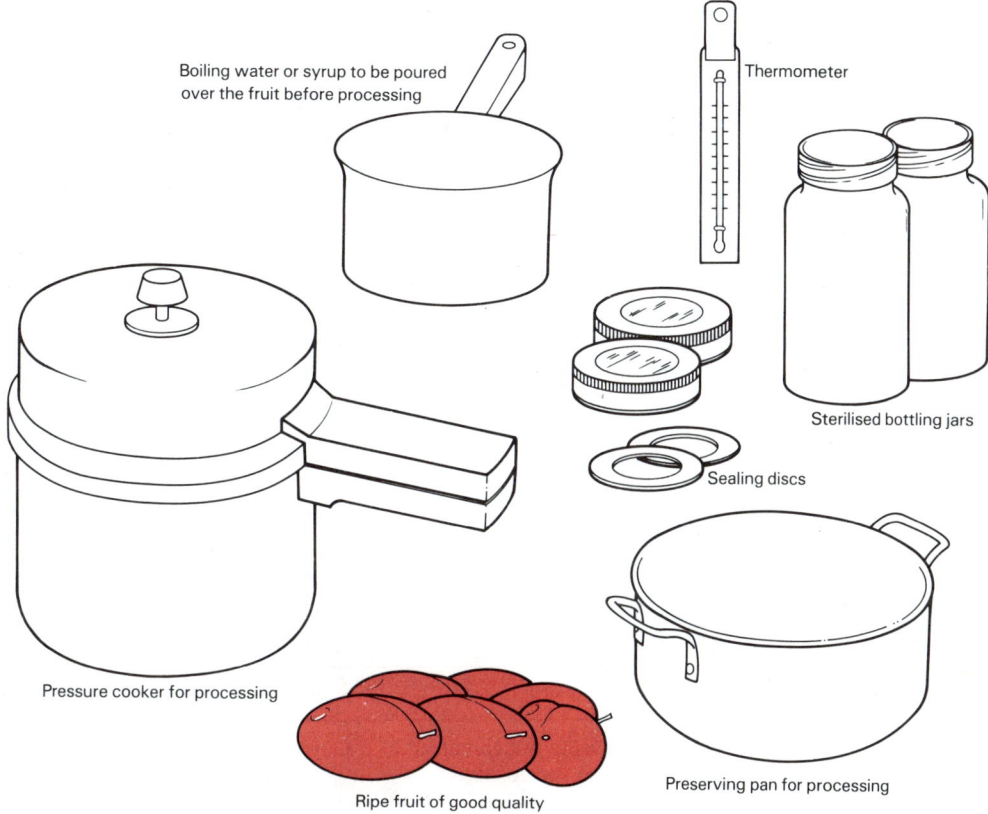

Boiling water or syrup to be poured over the fruit before processing

Thermometer

Sterilised bottling jars

Sealing discs

Pressure cooker for processing

Ripe fruit of good quality

Preserving pan for processing

**Fig. 8.5** Equipment for bottling

**Oven processing**

**1** Preheat the oven to the setting in the instruction book.

**2** Pack the jars with fruit. They may be processed with or without water or syrup.

**3** Place lids on top of the jars. Process for the recommended time–depends on the fruit.

**4** Fill with boiling water or syrup.

**5** Seal. Heat kills micro-organisms and expands air and liquid in the jar. Once the seal is placed on top and the jar cools down a vacuum results which makes it airtight and impossible for microbes to enter the jar.

**Water bath processing**

**1** Heat a large pan of water to the temperature in the recipe.

**2** Jars should be filled with fruit, water or syrup.

**3** Cover with a seal and lid.

**4** Turn the screw band back one quarter of a turn to allow for expansion.

**5** Place the jars in a water bath. Bring to the required temperature and hold at that temperature for the given length of time.

**6** Carefully lift out the jars. Tighten the screw band.

**7** Leave to cool. Tighten the band as contraction takes place.

**Pressure cooker processing**

**1** Follow the instructions in the pressure cooker booklet.

**2** Jars and their contents should be heated in boiling water for one minute.

**3** Stand the jars on a trivet. Add 800ml (1½pt) water. Put on the lid of the pressure cooker. Bring to the boil.

**4** Bring to 2½kg (5lb) pressure and hold for the recommended time.

**5** Depressurize **very** slowly.

**Testing the seal** involves removing the screw band a day after processing. Lift the jar carefully by means of the lid. If the jar and lid stay firmly together the seal has taken.

Unsealed jars can sometimes be reprocessed or used straight away.

**NB** Bottling at home is not so widely practised now. Freezing is more popular.

### 8.3.4  Pickling

**The process of pickling**

**Prepared vegetables** are left, in brine or well sprinkled with salt, for 24 hours.

**Brine** is made in the proportion of 100g (4oz) salt to 1 litre (2pts) water.

**1** After salting, wash and drain the vegetables.

**2** Add the vinegar. This should be at least 5% acetic acid. Spiced pickling vinegar is now available in the shops or vinegar can be spiced by adding pickling spices to a bowl of vinegar over a pan of boiling water. This stands for 2 hours and is then cooled and strained. Vinegar must cover the vegetables.

**3** Jar tops should be acid resistant. Metal tops with a plastic lining, waxed discs with a cellophane cover or a specially prepared polythene may be used.

**4** Most pickles should be stored for 2 months before using. Pickled cabbage is the exception to the rule. It is ready after 2 weeks.

### 8.3.5  Making chutney

**Chutneys are mixtures** of fruits, vegetables, sugar, spices and vinegar. These are cooked together until they are the consistency of jam.

**1** Cut up or mince the fruit and vegetables.      **2** Simmer until soft.

**3** Add the rest of the ingredients and simmer until there is no free vinegar on the surface of the chutney.

**4** Pour into hot jars.      **5** Cover as for pickles.

**6** Chutneys should not be eaten for at least three months. The longer they are kept the more mellow they become.

### 8.4  Commercial preservation of foods

**Drying**

Table 8.3 Drying processes and their use

| Process | Description of process | Foods |
|---|---|---|
| Sun drying | Very old method of preserving in hot climates. The food is spread out in the sun to dry. | Currants, sultanas, meat, fish. |
| Hot air drying | Hot air is blown over food to remove water. | Dried peas |
| Roller drying | Liquid food is sprayed on to hot rollers. Water evaporates. The food is scraped off the rollers. | Potatoes, milk, eggs. |
| Spray drying | Liquid food is sprayed into the top of a tall tower to meet hot air blown upwards. Water evaporates and the dried powder falls to the floor of the tower. | Instant coffee, drinking chocolate. |
| Accelerated freeze drying (AFD) | Food is frozen. Water is removed as ice at low pressure, by sublimation (change of state from solid to gas without the liquid stage). More expensive. More flavour retained. | Instant coffee, prawns, dried instant meals. |

**Removal of air**

Table 8.4

| Process | Description of process | Foods |
|---|---|---|
| Vacuum packing | Food is wrapped in an impermeable plastic. Air is removed and the packet sealed. Micro-organisms cannot get in until packet opened. Chemical preservatives e.g. sulphur dioxide are usually added and the food stored at low temperature. Note the 'eat by date'. | Cold cooked meat, cheese, sausage, fish, bacon. |

**Heat treatments**

**Table 8.5** Heat treatments and their use

| Process | Description | Examples |
|---|---|---|
| Pasteurization | Heating of liquids to temperatures high enough to destroy harmful bacteria. | Milk, fruit juices, vegetable juices, beer, vinegar. |
| Sterilization | Heating above boiling point for quite a long time. All microbes are destroyed. Nutrients are lost. | Milk, canned and bottled foods. |
| UHT | Food is brought to a temperature above 100°C for a few seconds. All microbes are destroyed. Less flavour changes and loss of nutrients. Packed in lined asceptic cartons. | Milk, fruit juices, cream. |
| Canning | Food is sealed in cans made of steel lined with tin, and mostly lacquered against corrosion. Some soft drink cans are made of aluminium– expensive. Heating takes place to above boiling after sealing in the cans. Food may be canned in water, brine, syrup or oil. All micro-organisms are destroyed. | Milk, fruit, vegetables, fish, meat, soups, nuts, drinks. |
| Bottling | Bottling is not used extensively, glass breaks and is heavier to transport. | Olives, mussels. |

**Use of chemicals for preserving**

**Sugar** is used in jamming, bottling and canning and in many canned meats.

**Salt** is used in cheese, butter, fish, meat and bacon.

**Salt and smoking** are used for fish, meat and bacon.

**Sulphur dioxide** forms sulphurous acid in solution. It is used in sausage meat, beer, fruit pulp, sauces, soft drinks, dried vegetables and Certo.

**Nitrites and nitrates** are used for meats and bacon.

**Antioxidants** are used to prevent rancidity in fats and foods rich in fats.

**NB** additives used are controlled by law.

**Quick freezing**

**Table 8.6** Processes of quick freezing

| Process | Description | Examples |
|---|---|---|
| Blast freezing | Food passes through a tunnel on a moving belt or trolley. Meets air as low as −30°C. Process takes 2 hours. | Cream sponges, eclairs, mousses. |
| Fluid bed freezing (Flo-freezing) | Food is on a perforated tray. Cold air is forced upwards through the holes, pushing the food along the tunnel and freezing it at the same time. Air temperatures can be as low as −40°C | Peas, sweetcorn, shrimps. |
| Plate freezing | Food is packed in flat containers. These are put on to metal trays which fit on to the shelves of the plate freezer. These shelves have a refrigerant such as liquid ammonia flowing through them at −33°C. Shelves are clamped together so that packets are frozen from above and from below. Process takes 2-3 hours. Fish for fish fingers is frozen in this way, coated with batter or breadcrumbs, fried for 45-60 seconds at 193°C and then blast frozen once more. | Beefburgers, pies. |
| Immersion in a very cold fluid | Food is immersed in a solution of sodium or calcium chloride at very low temperatures. Carbon dioxide 'snow'. 'Snowdrop' process. Food is covered with a layer of $CO_2$ snow. Sprayed with liquid nitrogen–called cryogenic freezing. Food freezes immediately at −100°C. | Meat, poultry, pastry. Shellfish, straw-berries. |

## 8.5  The effect of processing on foods

**Frozen foods**

If frozen correctly and fresh when processed, food retains its nutritional value, flavour and texture. Commercially vegetables are frozen within a few hours of being picked.

The texture of fruits and vegetables is sometimes softer after freezing e.g. strawberries.

### Heat treatments

Pasteurizing does not affect the flavour but there is a small loss of vitamin B and C.

Sterilization destroys most of the vitamins in milk and changes the flavour when the lactose caramelizes.

UHT milk loses less vitamins and undergoes only a slight flavour change compared with sterilized milk.

### Canned foods

Textures of fruits and vegetables which have been canned are softer. Flavour changes occur which are sometimes very noticeable. e.g. tinned salmon tastes quite different from fresh salmon and tinned peaches from fresh peaches. Fruits in syrups are sweeter.

There is some loss of vitamins B and C but this is often less than that lost by so called fresh vegetables and fruit bought from shops.

Colours are added to many canned foods.

### Use of chemicals

Sugar, salt and vinegar add their taste to foods in which they are used. Monosodium glutamate is noticeable in dried foods. Antioxidants prevent the development of rancid flavours and loss of vitamins. Sulphur dioxide diffuses into the air.

### Drying

This has very little effect on flavour especially if AFD is used. Loss of vitamins C and B does occur.

## 8.6   Food contamination

Food may be contaminated by:
(*a*) micro-organisms (bacteria, yeasts and moulds) and
(*b*) foreign substances introduced into prepared foods.
Contaminated foods can result in (a) wastage and (b) illness which in extreme cases can cause death.

### Bacteria

These cause illness in three ways:

**1** Bacteria in foods produce a toxin outside the bacterial cell (exotoxin). The toxins remain in the food and are not always destroyed by cooking. e.g. *Staphylococcus; Bacillus cereus; Clostridium botulinum.* See Fig. 8.6 which shows a micrograph of a point of a household pin and the rod-shaped bacteria on it.

**2** Living bacteria which contain a toxin within the bacterial cell (endotoxin) which is released when the bacteria die. Thorough heating will destroy the bacteria and toxins. e.g. *Salmonella.*

**3** Some bacteria only produce a toxin when they are in the intestinal tract. e.g. *Clostridium welchii.*

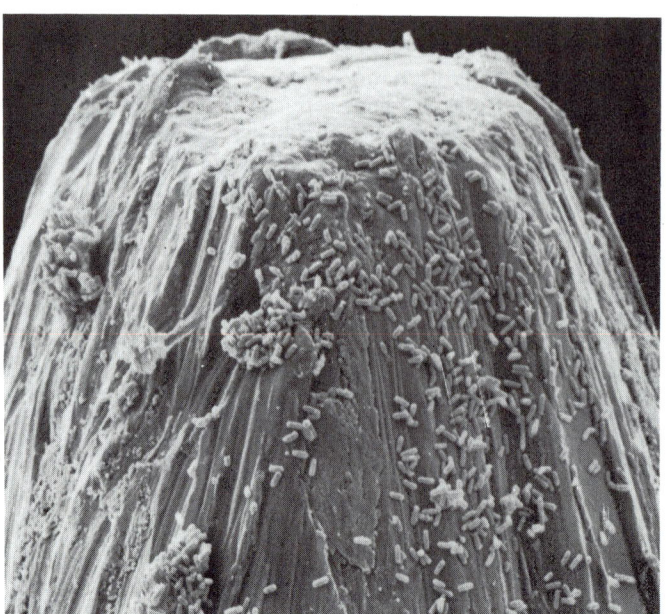

**Fig. 8.6** Micrograph of a pin point

**Table 8.7** Examples of bacterial food poisoning

| Bacterium | Incubation | Duration of illness | Symptoms |
|---|---|---|---|
| *Staphylococcus* Found in nose, throat, hands, septic cuts. | 2-6hrs | 6-24hrs | Vomitting, abdominal pain, diarrhoea. |
| *Bacillus cereus* Found in soil and water. Cereals and spices are common sources. | 2-15hrs | 6-24hrs | Vomitting, abdominal pain, diarrhoea. |
| *Clostridium botulinum* | 24-72hrs | Death in 1-8 days. If anti-toxin given 6-8 months to recover. | Giddiness, double vision, diarrhoea, central nervous system affected– paralysis. |
| *Salmonella* 70%-80% of all food poisoning cases. Poultry, duck eggs and human carriers. | 12-36hrs | 1-8 days | Fever, headache, abdominal pain, diarrhoea, and vomitting. |
| *Clostridium welchii* Raw meat, soil on vegetables, flies, human and animal intestines. | 8-22hrs | 12-48hrs | Abdominal pain and diarrhoea. |

## Moulds and yeasts

These organisms belong to the fungi family of plants. They are found everywhere. Apart from some toadstools, moulds on foods are unlikely to cause illness because they can be seen and the food discarded.

The fermentation of yeasts can be detected by the wine-like smell of jam and fruit.

Moulds and yeasts thrive in warm, moist conditions.

## Foreign substances in prepared foods

Despite very strict laws to maintain high standards of hygiene where food is prepared carelessness can result in the contamination of foods by micro-organisms and objects such as pieces of metal, plastic or glass.

Manufacturers can be prosecuted for their carelessness and lack of hygiene if such findings are reported to the District Medical Officer for Environmental Health.

Poisonous plant material and chemicals sometimes find their way into food but illness because of this type of contamination is rare.

## Reasons for an increase in the number of cases of food poisoning

1 Symptoms are more widely recognized and reported.
2 More people eat away from home, at school, at work or socially.
3 There is an increased demand for fast foods which can result in the use of untrained food handlers who don't pay enough attention to personal and kitchen hygiene.
4 Foods are carelessly stored and left-over foods are re-used incorrectly.

## Foods which are readily contaminated

1 Any warm and highly nutritious foods. Given the right conditions of food, moisture and warmth in three hours one bacterium cell will divide to produce over 4000 bacteria.
2 Meat, fish and made-up dishes using these foods.
3 Poultry that has not been completely thawed before cooking.
4 Stocks, soups, gravies, sauces.
5 Foods containing milk and cream. Ice cream.
6 Duck eggs and reconstituted dried egg.
7 Left-over foods which have not been thoroughly re-heated.

## Prevention of contamination

### Personal cleanliness

1 Hands should be washed after visiting the toilet, after playing with household pets, before preparing food, after handling vegetables with soil on, meat, poultry and before eating.
2 Nails should be short and clean. Nail varnish and ornate rings should not be worn when preparing food.
3 Cuts should be covered with a waterproof dressing. Food should not be handled if cuts are infected.
4 Fingers and spoons should not be licked.

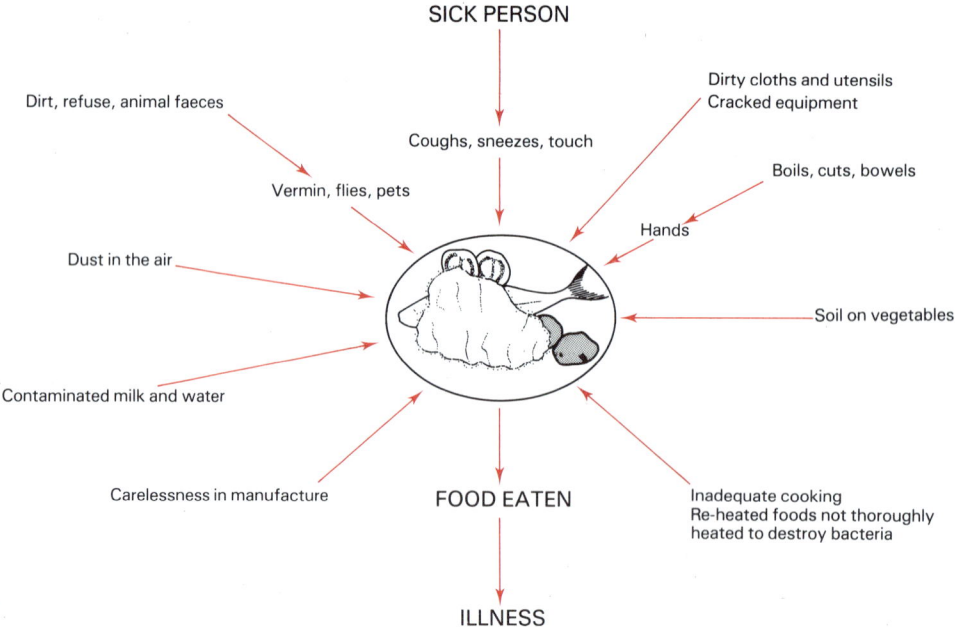

**Fig. 8.7** A summary of the ways in which food is contaminated

**5** Food should not be prepared by anyone with an infectious illness.
**6** No smoking while handling food.

### Kitchen cleanliness
**1** Kitchens should be well lit, ventilated and uncluttered. Such a kitchen discourages micro-organisms, flies, mice and makes daily and weekly cleaning easier.
**2** Avoid cracks and crevices between units and equipment.
**3** Cooker and equipment should be kept clean. Work surfaces should be washed down frequently, especially after the preparation of poultry. A mild bleach solution is antiseptic.
**4** Cracked equipment should be discarded. Cracks harbour micro-organisms.
**5** Refrigerators and food stores should be frequently checked and cleaned.
**6** Kitchen cloths should be frequently washed. Bacteria will thrive if damp tea towels are left on radiators. A draining rack is preferable to a dirty tea towel but the pots should be put away as soon as they are dry to avoid contamination by dust and flies. Dishcloths can be sterilized by leaving in a bleach solution overnight.
**7** Wet waste should be wrapped. Kitchen bins should be lined, emptied daily and washed and disinfected frequently.
**8** Dustbins should have tightly fitting lids and should stand well away from the kitchen door and windows. These too need washing and disinfecting.
**9** Sinks and drains should be cleaned and disinfected regularly.
**10** Keep dishes for animals separate. Pets should be kept out of the kitchen.

### Care and use of food
**1** Buy good quality fresh foods from reliable shops.
**2** Perishable foods should be bought in smaller quantities as needed.
**3** Store food in *clean* conditions, *cool* and *covered*.
**4** Dry goods should be stored in closed containers.
**5** Bread should be kept in a ventilated container to discourage moulds.
**6** Perishable foods should be kept in a refrigerator.
**7** Frozen meat and fish and dishes containing these foods should be thawed completely, preferably in the refrigerator. Do not refreeze these.
**8** Use left-overs as soon as possible, reheating thoroughly to destroy bacteria. Never reheat twice.
**9** If food has to be kept hot keep it above 63°C. Below this temperature bacteria will be active.
**10** If cooked food is to be kept, cool rapidly and then place in refrigerator or freezer.
**11** Use food in rotation, oldest first. Take note of the date stamps on food and the instructions for using and storing.

### The shop
**1** Shops should be clean, well lit and ventilated.
**2** Look for evidence of a good turnover and the correct rotation of date stamped foods.
**3** Good food displays–clean shelves, new stock at the back, food well clear of the floor. Chilled cabinets for perishable foods.
**4** Cooked meat should be away from uncooked meat and separate knives should be used for each.

**5** The frozen food cabinet should not be overloaded.
**6** Clean shopping trolleys and baskets.
**7** Shops should be free of flies. No dogs allowed.
**8** The cashier should not handle food. Assistants handling unwrapped foods should have clean hands and nails, hair covered and clean overalls. They should not smoke. They should have good washing and toilet facilities.

## 8.7   Left-over foods

It is wasteful to throw away any food left over at the end of a meal. There are many ways in which they can be used.

To avoid food poisoning the left-overs must be correctly handled, stored and re-heated.

**Rules**
**1** Put the food into *clean, covered* containers–to prevent microbial contamination.
**2** Cool *quickly*–this reduces the time given to bacteria to multiply.
**3** Store in a very cool place, preferably the refrigerator. It is possible to freeze foods cooked in excess of needs. These foods will keep for a longer time.
**4** Store cooked meat above uncooked meat in the refrigerator–to avoid cross contamination. Uncooked meat contains most bacteria.
**5** Use left-over food within 48 hours–bacteria are still active. This rule does not apply to frozen food.

### Réchauffé dishes

These are dishes using left-over foods.

**Rules**
**1** Remove fat, bones and gristle from meat, skin and bones from fish. Fish is usually flaked and meat minced to allow the heat to penetrate quickly.
**2** The food should be re-heated *rapidly* to a high temperature but it *should not be re-cooked*. Re-cooking will harden protein foods making them difficult to digest. Rapid heating gives bacteria less time to work.
**3** Some re-heated food is protected from excessive heat by a coating of batter, egg and breadcrumbs or pastry. These add 'bite', colour and nutrients.
**4** Additional ingredients should be cooked before they are added to the food to be re-heated.
**5** Left-over food can be *dry, colourless, flavourless* and contain *less nutrients*.
**(a)** Serve with sauces to add moisture.
**(b)** Add spices and foods with flavour.
**(c)** Serve with fresh foods to add nutrients such as vitamin C.
**(d)** Serve with colourful accompaniments and garnishes.
**(e)** Serve as soon as the food is re-heated. Do not re-heat a second time because this will harden proteins even more and provide an opportunity for microbial activity.

### Examples of left-over foods and réchauffé dishes

**Meat** shepherds pie; meat pie; curry; croquettes; stuffed pancakes.

**Fish** fish and potato pie; Russian fish pie; kedgeree.

**Egg yolk** add to custards; pastry; mashed potatoes; mayonnaise and scrambled eggs.

**Egg white** macaroons, meringues.

**Bread** bread and butter pudding; bread sauce; cheese pudding; Queen of puddings; breadcrumbs.

**Fruit** pies; crumbles; charlottes; Eve's pudding; trifle; fruit salad.

**Vegetables** soups; bubble and squeak; sauté potatoes; shepherds pie; risotto and stews at the end of cooking time; salads.

# **9**   Pollution and conservation

Homes and industries produce waste products which can pollute the environment to the detriment of man and all other living things.

## 9.1   Sources and removal of household waste

Local Authorities have the responsibility of dealing with these waste products so that their risk to health and safety is reduced to a minimum. The rates and water rates pay for these services as well as the cost of providing a clean water supply.

### 9.1.1   Household waste – liquid

Figures 9.1 and 9.2 summarize how liquid waste is produced and disposed of from a home.

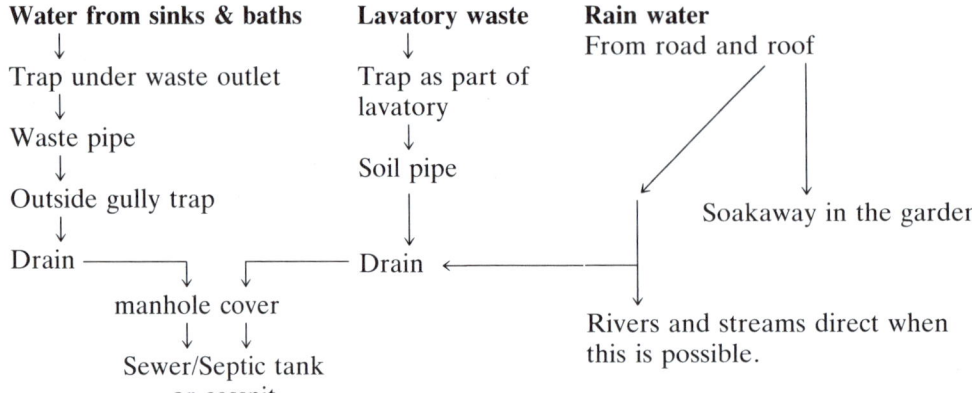

**Fig. 9.1** The production and disposal of liquid household waste

The diagrams shown in Fig. 9.2 explain how the different parts of the system work, whilst Fig. 9.3 shows the arrangement of the system within a house.

Houses built today do not usually have pipes on their outside walls. They run inside the outer walls so that they do not freeze. With this newer system there are no open drains covered with metal grids.

The soil pipe of the main drain may become blocked with waste from the lavatory. Bulky items such as sanitary pads and disposable nappies should not be flushed down the lavatory.

If the soil pipe or main drain does become blocked, special drain rods are needed. The plumber will gain access by way of the manhole.

### 9.1.2   Care of the drainage system

**Bath, handbasins, sinks**

**Baths** can be made of enamelled cast iron or of fibreglass.

**Hand basins** can be made of glazed ceramic, plastic, enamelled pressed steel or stainless steel.

**Sinks** may be of stainless steel, vitreous enamelled pressed steel or ceramic.

1 Remove bits caught in the grid over the waste outlet.
2 Clean with a non-abrasive cream or liquid. Abrasive powders can scratch and should never be used on stainless steel or fibreglass fittings.
3 Rinse and dry.
4 Special attention needs to be paid to the areas where taps, overflow and waste outlets are fitted.

**The WC**

1 Always flush after use. For water economy some lavatory cisterns are fitted to give alternative short and long flushes.
2 A proprietary lavatory cleaner may be used. This should be left in the pan for the time stated on the container for maximum efficiency. Never use bleach with any other cleaner.
3 Brush the pan with a stiff lavatory brush. Pay special attention to the U-bend and the ledge just under the rim.
4 Rinse the lavatory by flushing. Rinse the brush.
5 Clean seat and lid and the outside of the bowl with a liquid detergent. Rinse and wipe dry.

**Drains**

In older houses, where the sink and bath drainage pipes go through to the outside of the house, there is a grid over the drain with a gully trap below.
1 Occasionally remove the metal grid and any leaves or other material trapped on top of it.
2 Wear rubber gloves. Use a scrubbing brush, hot water and soda to scrub the drain surrounds and grid.
3 Replace grid. Pour boiling water and soda down the drain.

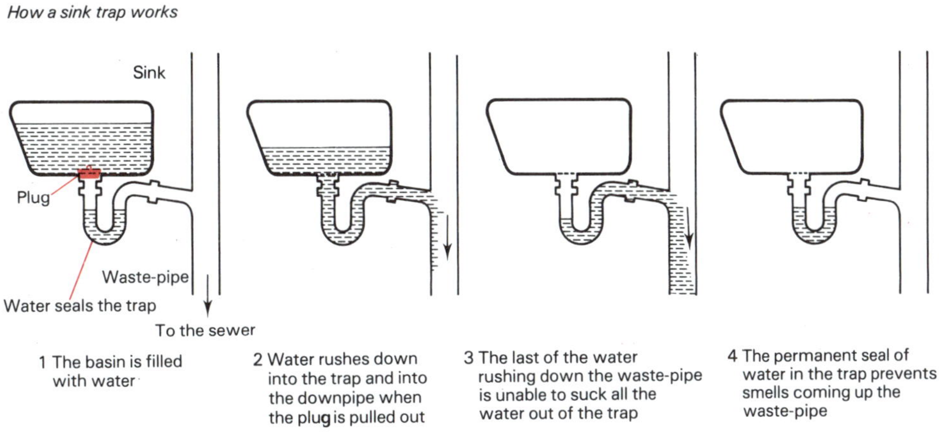

How a sink trap works
Sink
Plug
Waste-pipe
Water seals the trap
To the sewer
1 The basin is filled with water
2 Water rushes down into the trap and into the downpipe when the plug is pulled out
3 The last of the water rushing down the waste-pipe is unable to suck all the water out of the trap
4 The permanent seal of water in the trap prevents smells coming up the waste-pipe

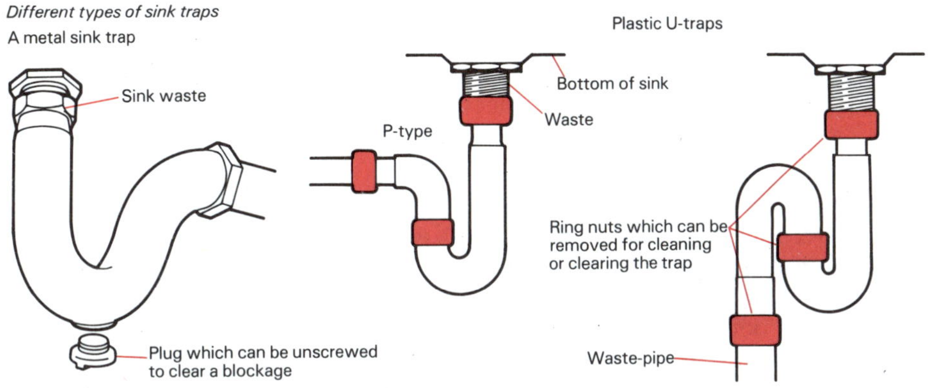

Different types of sink traps
A metal sink trap
Sink waste
Plug which can be unscrewed to clear a blockage
Plastic U-traps
P-type
Bottom of sink
Waste
Ring nuts which can be removed for cleaning or clearing the trap
Waste-pipe

How to clear a blocked sink trap is explained on page 162

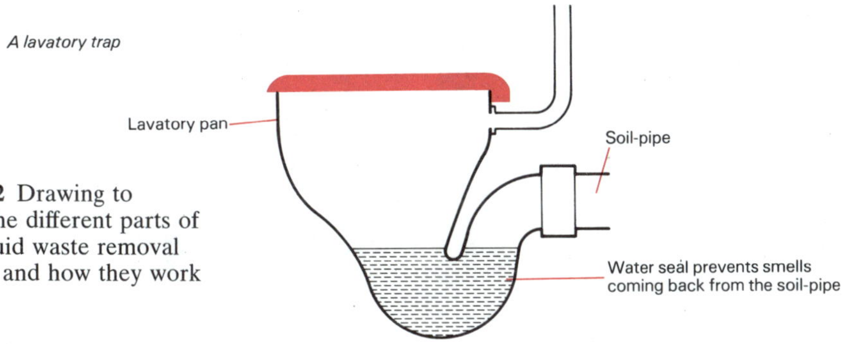

A lavatory trap
Lavatory pan
Soil-pipe
Water seal prevents smells coming back from the soil-pipe

**Fig. 9.2** Drawing to show the different parts of the liquid waste removal system and how they work

Regular cleaning should prevent blockages but if these do occur expert attention will probably be needed.

Wire guard over open pipe
Air
Gutter
WC
Sink
'S' trap
Rain water pipe
Ground level
Inspection pit
To sewer
'U' trap
House drain

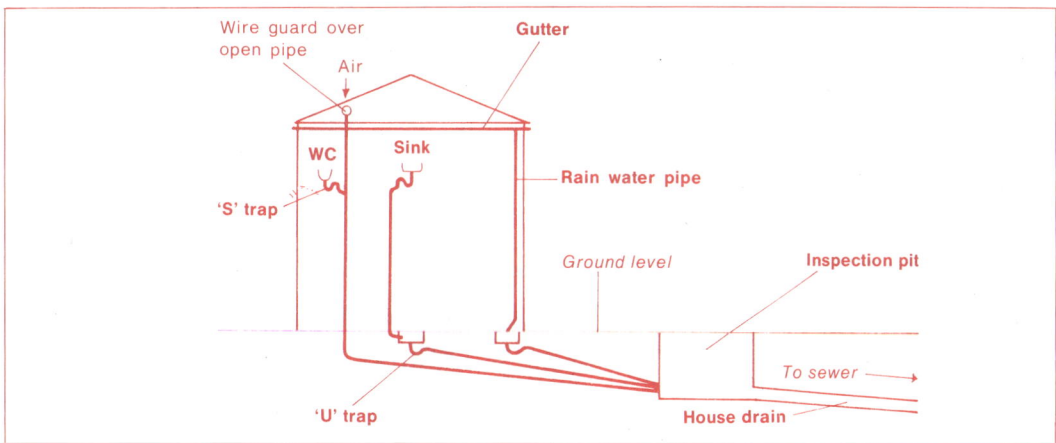

**Fig. 9.3** The drainage system of a house

## 9.1.3 Cesspits and septic tanks

In many country areas houses are not connected with the main drains and sewers. These houses may have a cesspit or a septic tank.

**A cesspit** is a deep pit with a removable cover. It must be water tight and well ventilated. The pit must be situated well away from the house but with access from the road. The Local Authority

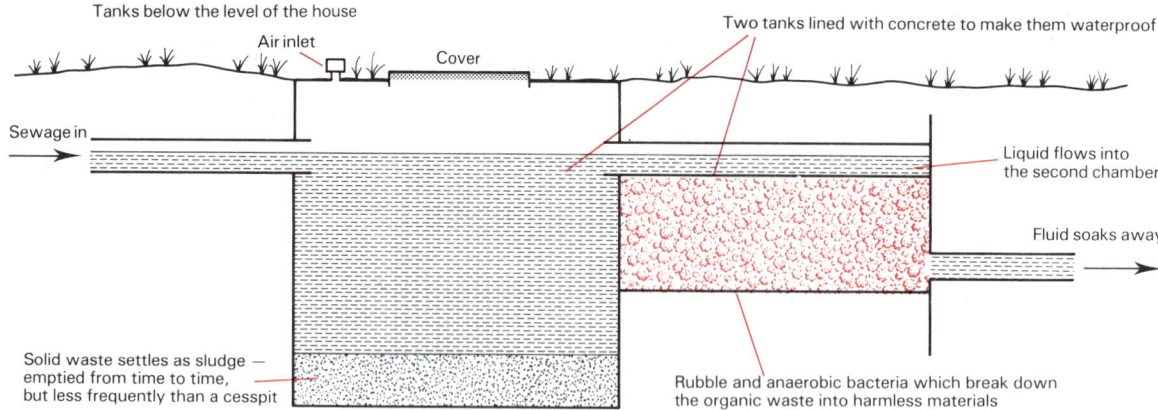

**Fig. 9.4** A section through a septic tank

arrange the emptying of the pit, usually for a fixed charge. The waste is sucked up into special container lorries and transported to the sewage works.

**A septic tank** system is made up of two tanks the details of which are shown in Fig. 9.4. Soapless detergents and other cleaning agents such as bleach can hinder the microbial action of the septic tank.

### 9.1.4   Sewage treatment and disposal

The efficient treatment of sewage described below has reduced the risk of water-borne diseases such as dysentry, cholera, typhoid and polio.

 **1** On arrival at the sewage works the sewage is passed through **screens** of closely spaced metal bars to remove large objects such as rags and wood.

 **2** Grit and sand **(detritus)** are then **removed** by letting the sewage flow slowly along channels where it drops to the bottom. It is dredged, washed and used for land infill.

 **3** In the primary sedimentation tanks the solids settle to the bottom and are called **crude sludge.** This is pumped to a sludge 'digestion' plant.

 **4** The liquid or primary effluent, is treated in the secondary treatment plant. Here **microbes** are grown which **feed** on **waste** in the water and destroy it leaving only gas and water. The microbes need a lot of oxygen for this process so the effluent is sprayed onto a bed of clinker or gravel. As it passes through this material it takes up oxygen from the air. This process takes about 8 hours.

 **5 Microbes** are **removed** from the water in the final sedimentation tanks and are re-used.

 **6** The water left is **clean** and can flow into a river.

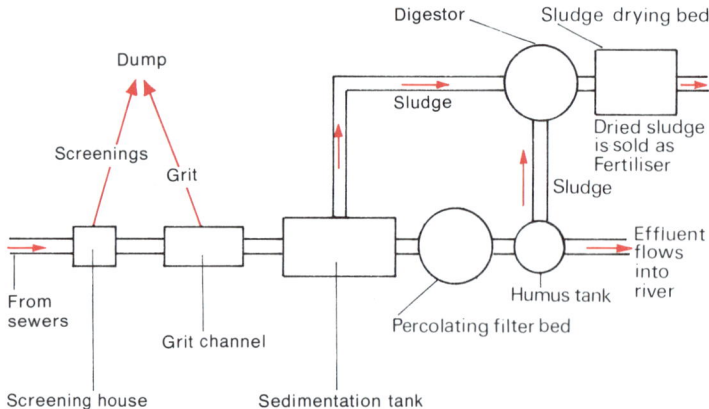

**Fig. 9.5**  Plan to show the order in which sewage is treated during its purification

 **7** In the sludge 'digestion' plant the **crude sludge** is **treated** with a different type of microbe which destroys the unpleasant and smelly materials, changing them to a gas which contains methane. This process takes 3 to 4 weeks.

 **8** The **sludge gas** can be burned and used to provide electricity and other forms of power needed to run the sewage works.

 **9** The sludge is passed into open secondary digestion plants where any remaining gas is given off. The sludge settles to give a watery liquor and a thicker sludge–**digested sludge**. This is used on farms to improve the soil, or it can be taken out to sea where the microscopic organisms in the sea feed on it, and in their turn feed the fish.

### 9.1.5   Pollution of water supplies

**Untreated sewage** discharged into rivers and lakes can result in the destruction of all water organisms. The oxygen levels drop because of the activities of bacteria feeding on the sewage, this results in the death of the water organisms.

**Domestic detergents** are now biodegradable (will break down under natural conditions) but many used in industry are not and do pollute water, poisoning animals and plants in the water.

**Heat from power stations** and other industries also reduces the oxygen levels in the water. **We can be affected** by polluted waters if we **swim** in them, if we **eat** contaminated foods such as fish and watercress or if we **drink** the untreated water. The Water Authorities try to ensure that:

1 All water piped to our homes is clean and safe to drink;

2 All water used for recreational activities such as swimming, fishing and sailing is free of sewage and other pollutants.

The services of the Water Authorities are paid for by the water rates which every householder has to pay twice yearly. These are collected separately from the general rates.

### 9.1.6 Water treatment

There is a continuous cycle of water in nature. Water evaporates from seas, rivers, lakes and the land, condenses in the atmosphere and falls as rain. Rain water is pure, but as it falls through the atmosphere and soaks into the land, eventually draining into river, lakes and seas, it picks up a variety of pollutants making it unsafe to drink without treatment. This process is shown in Fig. 9.6 and described below.

1 Water taken from rivers is screened to remove floating debris before it is pumped into storage reservoirs.

2 In the reservoirs bigger solid impurities settle to the bottom and, because of the large surface area, oxygen in the air can work on other impurities.

3 Primary filtration. Water sinks through layers of coarse sand and then shingle at a rate of 20ft per hour. These filter beds are cleaned every day with compressed air and a reverse flow of clean water.

4 Secondary filtration. Slow sand filtration. A finer sand is used. Minute organisms in the sand feed on the bacteria in the water and help to purify it. Dirty sand is skimmed off and taken away to be washed and then re-used.

5 Chlorination. Water passes through a covered tank where the action of chlorine kills any remaining bacteria.

Water not needed immediately is pumped to water towers or to service reservoirs built on high ground. From these a network of mains pipes takes the water to the consumer. From the mains pipes a service pipe runs to every house.

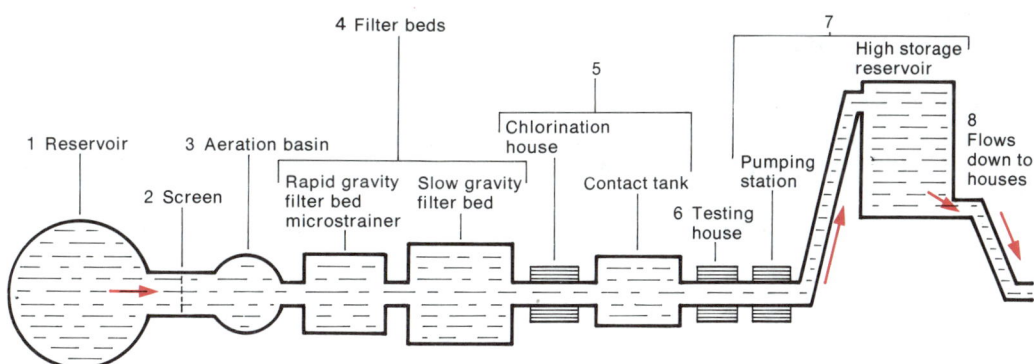

**Fig. 9.6** A simple plan to show the order in which water is treated during purification

### 9.1.7 Contamination of water in the home

Cold water from the mains should be used for drinking and for cooking. Water in the hot water supply will have spent some time in a storage tank in the roof. If this tank is not covered a variety of contaminants could be present in the water e.g. dust, cobwebs, dead spiders, flies, mice, birds.

In older houses lead pipes may have been used. Hot water will have the lead dissolved in it. Lead is an accumulative poison and can cause brain damage in children.

### 9.1.8 Household waste – solid

Household solid waste is sometimes called **refuse** or **garbage**. Its make up and methods of disposal are shown in Fig. 9.7.

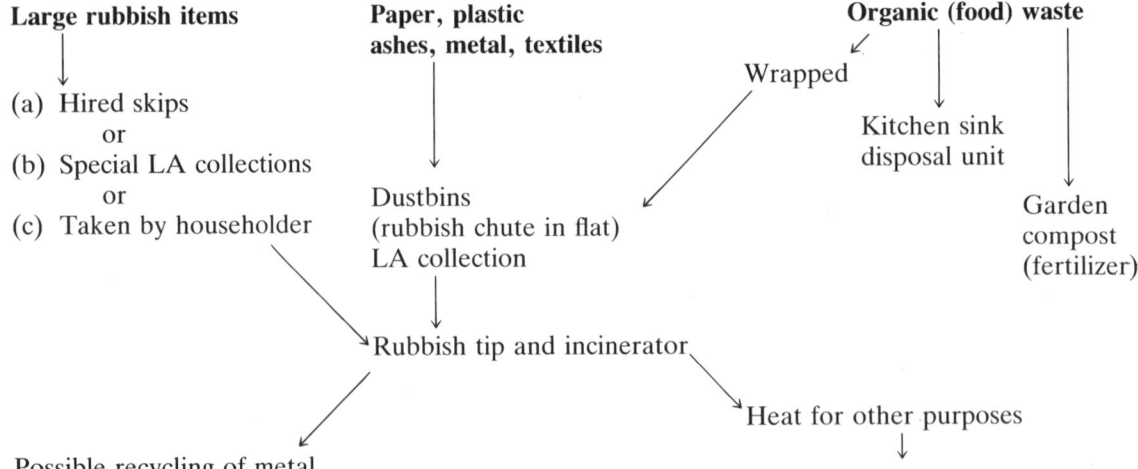

**Fig. 9.7** The production and disposal of solid household waste

**Recycling** of some solid waste now occurs as we become more aware of resources in the world running out.

1 Bottle banks are used in many areas to collect glass for recycling. Often they are linked to a charitable cause.

2 Metals, removed by magnets are compressed into packs and transported to steel works.

3 Paper and plastics are compressed and sold as industrial fuel.

4 Ceramics, rubble etc., are used for land infil.

5 Textiles. Man-made textiles are difficult to recycle. Wool is often mixed with man-made fibres so is now not so easily recycled.

### Care of kitchen waste bins and dustbins

**Kitchen waste bins** should:

1 Be kept in a cool part of the kitchen.

2 Have a lid and be lined with a plastic bin liner or newspaper.

3 Be emptied every day, or as soon as they are full so that the smell does not attract flies.

4 Be washed after emptying and then relined.

### Dustbins

1 Should not stand near to the kitchen door or window because they attract flies.

2 Can be made of plastic or metal. Metal bins should stand on bricks or slats so that the bottom does not rust.

3 Many local authorities now provide plastic dustbin liners. These are not very strong and are easily damaged by sharp edges or awkward shapes.

4 All refuse should be dry when placed in the dustbin. Wet rubbish should be wrapped in newspaper or sealed in the plastic pedal bin liner.

5 Tins should have their lids with sharp edges pushed inside. Broken glass should be well wrapped.

6 After the dustbin has been emptied it should be hosed down if plastic liners are not used. Periodically wash it with hot water and disinfectant so that it does not become smelly.

7 Should have a well fitting lid.

### Garden compost

**Compost** should be kept in a specially made compost holder or a home-built compost frame.

1 No rotting food should be left exposed. Cover it with grass cuttings or soil.

2 The organic material must rot completely before using as a garden fertilizer.

3 Cooked food scraps should **not** be put on the compost, they attract rats.

### Hired skips

The local authority or private firms supply, deliver, collect and empty these. Charges are made on the basis of a **set charge** for a skip plus a **daily charge** for the time it is in your use.

Local regulations may require **permission** to be given for a skip to stand on a road or pavement outside your house. Warning cones and storm lamps may be necessary if the skip could be a hazard in the dark.

### The Clean Air Act of 1956

**Pollutants**–Industrial waste disposal was controlled. Gaseous waste was controlled and allowed only at certain times.

**Smokeless Zones** where ordinary household coal may not be burnt were created—only named smokeless fuels such as anthracite, phurnacite, coalite etc. Special firegrates are often needed to burn these fuels efficiently. Garden waste may still be burnt on a bonfire.

## 9.2   Conservation of energy in the home

### 9.2.1   Energy in the home

Energy is used in so many forms that we often use it without questioning whether the supply may be **limited**.

We use gas, electricity, oil, coal and smokeless fuels for heating, lighting, cooking and to supply power for running a variety of equipment from TV to a power drill and a lawn mower.

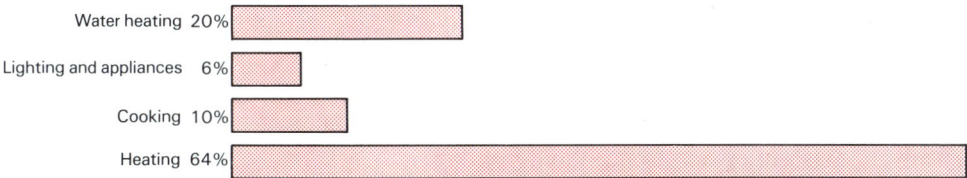

Water heating 20%

Lighting and appliances  6%

Cooking 10%

Heating 64%

**Fig. 9.8** Bar graphs to show the proportional uses of energy in the home

**Technology** has greatly changed and influenced how houses are run. Increasingly energy supplied by technology has been replacing human energy—the washing machine and tumble dryer replacing human effort in hand washing and drying clothes, central heating or similar **effort free** form of heating replacing open fires which involved dirt, dust and human effort in carrying fuel and clearing out ash.

Ever increasing amounts of coal, petroleum or nuclear energy have been used to manufacture the electrical energy used for heating our homes and running the wide variety of small electrical aids now available. The result is that many countries are using more energy than they can produce and stocks of natural resources which cannot be replaced are diminishing rapidly.

**Efficient use of fuel** reduces consumption and as a result conserves energy and reduces household running costs.

#### How heat is lost in the home

Figure 9.9 shows how heat is lost and the proportions lost through different parts of the house.

### 9.2.2   Insulation—ways to reduce heat loss

**Roofs** should be lined inside with roofing felt or fibre board. **Insulation, 100mm** (4″) thick

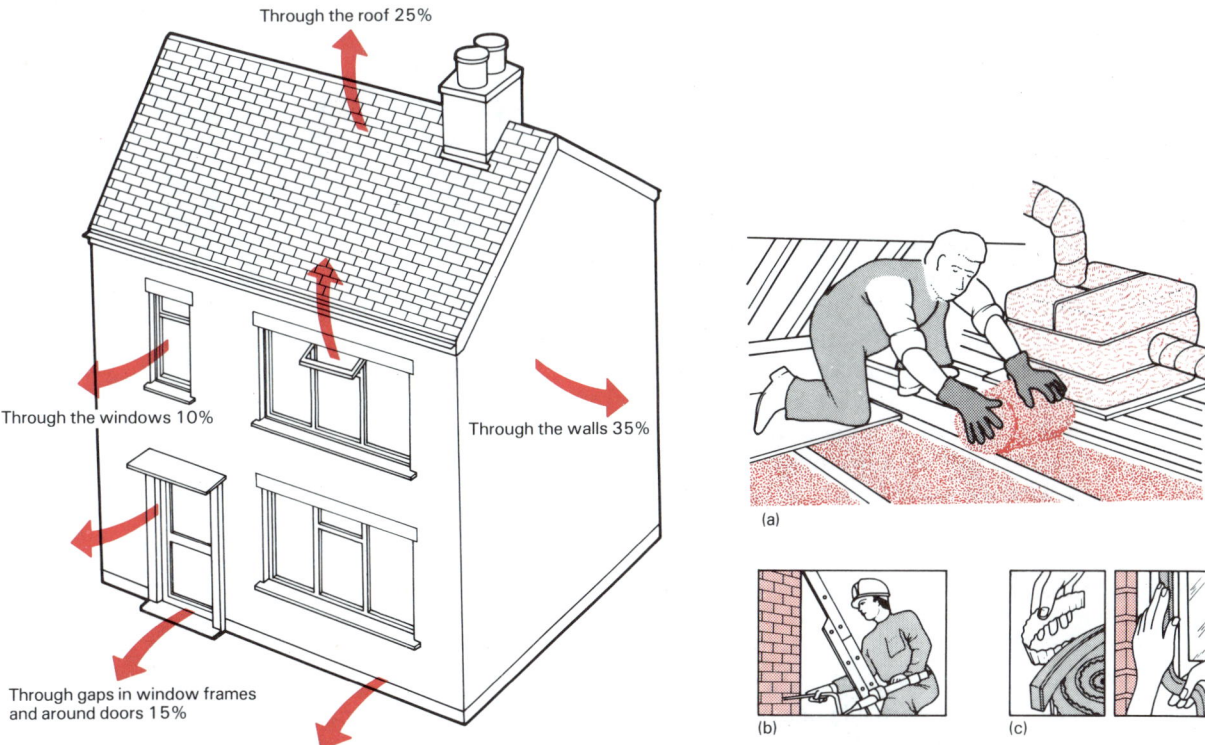

Through the roof 25%

Through the windows 10%

Through the walls 35%

Through gaps in window frames and around doors 15%

Through the floor 15%

(a)

(b)

(c)

**Fig. 9.9** How heat is lost from a house

**Fig. 9.10** Methods of insulation.

between the joists can be sheets of glass or mineral fibre or a loose granular material such as vermiculite or polystyrene granules.

The cold water storage tank should be insulated along its **top** and **sides**. The bottom is left unprotected so that some heat from the rooms below will reach it and prevent freezing.

A grant may be available towards loft insulation but this depends on the rateable value of the house.

**Walls** in most modern houses are built with a **cavity** i.e. two separate walls are built with a **space** between which **insulates** a little. The cavity **can be filled** with plastic foam, mineral wool or loose pellets. This filling should be carried out by a reputable firm. Foam or urea formaldehyde can give off toxic vapours if not correctly used. It is banned in some countries.

Solid walls may be lined with **insulating board**.

Cork or wood pannelling and thick wall papers offer a small degree of insulation.

**Windows** can be **double glazed**. This is expensive and it takes a long time to recover installation costs through reduced heating bills. It is very effective and cuts down noise levels also.

Some of the sealed window units in each room **should open** for safety. Double glazing is difficult to smash to escape from a house on fire.

Thick polythene sheeting is often used over small windows as temporary insulation in the winter.

Full length, thick or lined curtains also reduce heat loss. Thermal or **Milium linings** (cotton backed with aluminium) are particularly useful.

**Draughts** from around window frames can be stopped by fitting foam, plastic or metal draught excluders. Curtains should be closed at night.

**Floors** with wall to wall covering of any type reduce heat loss. Fitted carpet with a thick underlay is particularly effective.

**Gaps** round floorboards and skirting boards should be filled with plastic wood or similar sealants.

**Chimneys** and unused fireplaces can be sealed but a **ventilation grill** is necessary in the chimney to prevent condensation.

**Doors** should fit well, especially outside doors. **Draught proofing** strips can be fitted around doors and a draught excluder used across the bottom of a door. Outside porches insulate also.

Letter boxes should be backed with an insulating cover.

**NB** A room should not be completely sealed so that the air does not change. Open fires need a continuous supply of air to burn efficiently – this is frequently provided by an air vent beneath the floor. Gas heaters must have some sort of ventilation for safety. Kitchens and bathrooms without ventilation soon have condensation problems.

### 9.2.3   More heat saving methods

**1** Turn down thermostats or heat controls to a lower setting. Recommended room temperatures are:
**(a)** Living room between 18°C and 21°C.
**(b)** Halls 13°C.
**(c)** Kitchen between 13°C and 16°C.
**(d)** Bedrooms between 13°C and 16°C
**(e)** Small baby's room 20°C to 21°C.
**2** Install time switches to the central heating and water heating systems.
**3** Use combined heating and cooking systems e.g. Aga cooker linked to water heating and central heating systems.
**4** Keep doors closed.
**5** Turn off the heating in rooms not used.
**6** Use lights with heating elements in little used spaces.
**7** Use special foil backing behind radiators to reflect heat back into the room.

### 9.2.4   How to save fuel in the kitchen

#### Using the cooker

**Plan meals** carefully. Cook a whole meal in the oven – a casserole in one dish, vegetables in another and a baked sweet in the third. Potatoes in their jackets can be cooked on the shelves.

**Do not open** the oven door unnecessarily. Heat is lost, cooking takes longer and uses more fuel.

**Grilling** is the most economical method of cooking things such as chops. Use only half the grill for smaller amounts. Toast is more cheaply made in a toaster.

**Cut vegetables small**–they cook quicker. Use the minimum of water–less to heat and keep hot. Cook more than one vegetable in the pan if they go together or put one in a steamer over the second in the pan.

**Match** pan and ring sizes. Make full use of dual rings. Keep lids on pans.

**Regulate** the heat and avoid wasteful boiling.

**Electric kettles** are cheaper than cooker rings for boiling water. Boil just the amount of water you need but always cover the element. De-scale the kettle regularly in hard water areas.

**A slow cooker** (see Section 6.3) uses less electricity than the oven to cook a dish needing long slow cooking such as a casserole.

**Use a divided pan,** double or triple on one ring.

**Make use** of a pressure cooker.

**Microwave** cookers save fuel and time.

**Using the refrigerator and freezer**

**Open** the refrigerator door as seldom as possible.

**Defrost** regularly–ice build up means more energy is needed to keep the cabinet cold.

**Do not place hot food** in the refrigerator, cool it first.

**Make sure** that the freezer lid or door fits properly and only open it when necessary.

**Do not keep** the freezer on 'fast freeze' once the food is frozen.

**Label** the contents so you can extract what you want quickly. Try to have the freezer at least three-quarters full.

**When washing dishes**

**Do not waste** hot water by washing under a continuously running tap.

**Save up** a full load if a dishwasher is to be used.

**When washing and ironing**

**Soften** hard water.

**Use a detergent** which washes efficiently at lower temperatures.

**Save up** a full load for your washing machine but do not exceed the recommended loadings.

**Use the 'Economy Wash'** button if your machine has this facility.

**Only iron** those items that require ironing. Drip dry garments require little or no ironing.

**Make good use** of the iron thermostat and do not turn it up too high.

### 9.2.5   How to save on water heating

**Set the thermostat** on the immersion heater slightly lower and only have it on when hot water is required.

**Showers** use less hot water than baths, so they cost less.

**Do not fill** the bath fuller than you need.

**Never** wash hands or dishes under a running hot tap; place the plug in the basin, or use a bowl.

**Watch out for** dripping taps as they waste water and consequently waste the fuel used to heat the water. Repair dripping taps immediately.

**The hot water cylinder** should be fitted with a lagging jacket at least 75mm (3″) thick as shown in Fig. 14.25.

Fig. 9.12

**Lagging** hot water pipes conserves heat.

**Soften** hard water. 'Fur' in the pipes makes heating less efficient.

### 9.2.6   How to save on lighting

**Where you can, use fluorescent** rather than filament lamps. A 40 watt fluorescent lamp provides as much light as a 100 watt filament bulb. It also uses half the electricity. Fluorescent lamps are ideal in kitchens and bathrooms.

**A new lower wattage** light bulb is now available which works more efficiently to give the light of a normal 100 watt bulb with less electricity.

**Switch off** lights when not required, but do not economize where it might be dangerous e.g. on stairs.

**Use lightly coloured lamp shades** so light is not blocked.

**Use localized** lighting rather than general lighting (see Fig. 9.13). Provide lighting

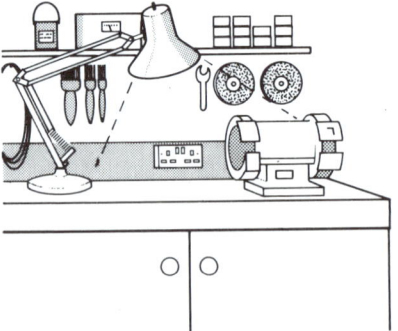

Fig. 9.13

which suits your normal activities e.g. an anglepoise lamp at your desk or for sewing.

**A dimmer switch** can lower fuel consumption and provides attractive lighting.

### 9.3   Conservation of human effort

**Ergonomics** is the study of work, of the person doing the work, of the equipment being used and of the place of work. Its aim is to find the most efficient way of carrying out any task.

Work efficiently carried out saves **time** and **energy**. There is less chance of fatigue or muscular strain and the work will probably be more enjoyable. In the home time and energy saved can be used for family leisure time activities.

**How to save time and effort in the home**

(a) Plan work; (b) Plan rooms; (c) Use correct posture and movements when working.

## 9.3.1  Planned work

1 There is no virtue in doing **unnecessary housework**. A clean room does not need cleaning.

2 Each household will develop a **routine** which suits the lifestyle of the family. Jobs should be **shared** so that the burden of caring for the home does not fall on one person.

3 The **sequence** of work in any task undertaken is important. An incorrect sequence can create extra work e.g. there is no point in dusting before an open fire grate is cleared of ash or of changing bed-linen after the bedroom has been vacuumed.

*Some sequences for household tasks*

**Daily tasks** may include any of the following activities:

1 Opening windows to air rooms, making the beds and tidying bedrooms

2 Brushing the lavatory and wiping around the handbasin and bath (the family should be trained to clean the bath and basin after they have used them)

3 Cleaning the grate and laying a fire, emptying ashtrays, removing newspapers and generally tidying a living room

4 Emptying, washing and re-lining kitchen bins, sweeping the kitchen floor

5 **Washing up**

(a) Clear dining table of all dishes and cutlery.

(b) Scrape plates and wrap scraps of food before putting them in the bin.

(c) Stack pots according to type.

(d) Very dirty saucepans and cooking dishes can be filled with water to soak.

(e) Using hot water with detergent, wash up in the following order:

  (i) Glassware, table cutlery, cleanest cups, saucers, plates, larger more greasy plates and dishes, pans.

 (ii) Rinse.

(iii) Drain.

(iv) Dry with a perfectly clean tea towel.

 (v) Put everything away.

(vi) Wash and dry washing up-bowl.

(vii) Rinse dishcloth or washing-up brush.

(viii) Rinse and dry sink and draining boards.

(ix) Put the tea towel to be washed.

**Weekly cleaning routines**

**Kitchen**

1 After washing-up and putting away all food and portable equipment–sweep the floor.

2 Wash work surfaces, sink and draining board–wash the floor.

3 When necessary fit in–cleaning of cooker, cupboards, paintwork, windows, defrosting and cleaning the refrigerator.

**Living rooms**

1 Open the window to air the room.

2 Clean the grate and lay the fire.

3 Empty the ashtrays and waste paper basket, remove newspapers.

4 Tidy the room putting away books, toys etc.

5 Dust and polish the furniture.

6 Vacuum curtains, upholstered furniture and carpet.

7 Clean the windows as necessary.

NB Dust before vacuuming because dusting will send dust and bits to the floor. In a room with no carpet which is swept, sweep, allow dust to settle and then dust.

**Bedrooms**

1 Open windows.

2 Put away clothes and tidy the room.

3 Remove sheets, turn the mattress and make up the bed with clean sheets.

4 Dust and polish.

5 Wash any paintwork that needs washing.

6 Vacuum the carpet.

**Bathroom**

1 Air the room.

2 Clean WC, handbasin and bath–see Section 13.1.

3 Wash tiles and any paintwork that need cleaning.
4 Vacuum or sweep the floor.
5 If the floor covering is washable wash it.
6 While the floor is drying shake any bath mats outside.

### 9.3.2  Planned rooms

Rooms should be organized so that work can be done without unnecessary **walking, bending, carrying** or **stretching**.

1 A well lit and ventilated room is easier to work in.
2 Rooms that are too cold or too hot reduce work efficiency. A room that is too hot is tiring.
3 Too high a level of noise, especially of a repetitive nature, is tiring.
4 An attractively decorated room is conducive to work.
5 Tables, chairs and work benches should be the correct height for the individuals using them.
6 Each room should have adequate storage facilities.
7 Each room should have an adequate number of electric power points, correctly placed.

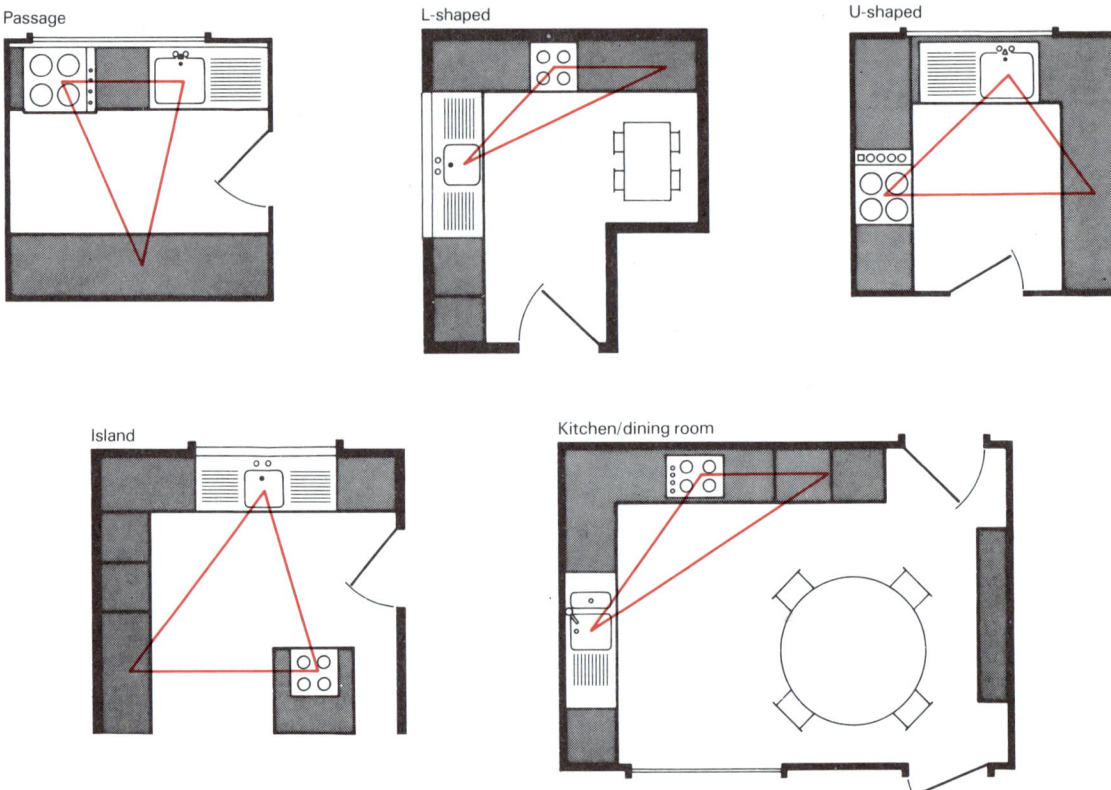

**Fig. 9.14** Kitchen shapes, planning and the work triangle

### Kitchen planning

Most people have to make the best of a kitchen which is far from perfect. They are often very small with insufficient storage space and working surface areas, and too few electric points.

Kitchens may be L-shaped, U-shaped, they may be 'passage kitchens', 'island' kitchens or dual purpose rooms with dining facilities. These shapes are shown in Fig. 9.14.

Equipment in the kitchen should be arranged so that the following work sequences can be carried out efficiently.

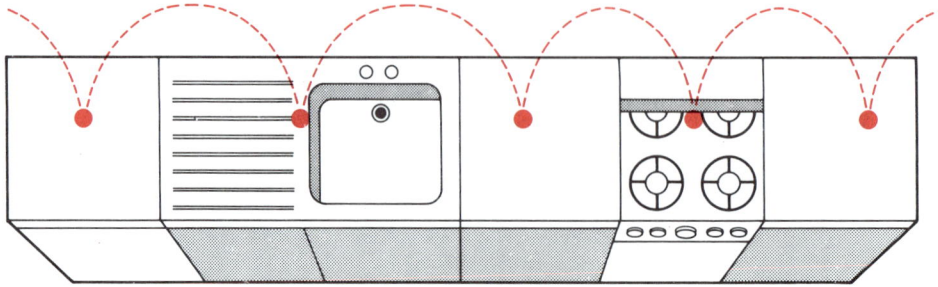

**Fig. 9.15**

*Bringing in and storing food*

Door ⟶ Work surface ⟶ Food store
            (Unpacking and sorting)        (Refrigerator, deep freeze, larder, cupboards)

*Preparation of food*

Food store ⟷ Draining board/sink ⟷ Work surface ⟷ Cooker

**or**

Food store ⟷ Work surface ⟷ Sink unit ⟷ Work surface ⟷ Cooker

*Cooking and serving*

Sink unit ⟷ Work surface ⟷ Cooker
                    ↓     ↑
                Dining area

*Clearing and Washing Up*

                    Dining Area
                   ↙
Work surface ⟶ Sink ⟶ Draining board ⟶ Work surface ⟶ Store

*Washing*

                Washing machine ⟷ Sink
                        ↘       ↗
                Cupboards storing
                    detergents etc.

The most efficient arrangement usually forms a **work triangle** as shown in Fig. 9.14. If work is not to involve unnecessary energy expenditure the total length of the three sides of this triangle should not exceed **6m (20ft)**.

**Storage**
1 Perishable food in the refrigerator or freezer.
2 Dry, canned, bottled foods in the larder or cupboards.
3 Kitchen stationery in drawers or cupboards as appropriate.
4 Utensils and equipment for preparation of food as near to the place of use as possible.
5 Tea towels, oven gloves in drawers.
6 Table linen and table china and cutlery near the dining area.
7 Reaching above head level uses more energy than reaching at shoulder level. Bending to the floor uses more energy. Use the cupboards to save as much energy as possible, see Fig. 9.16.

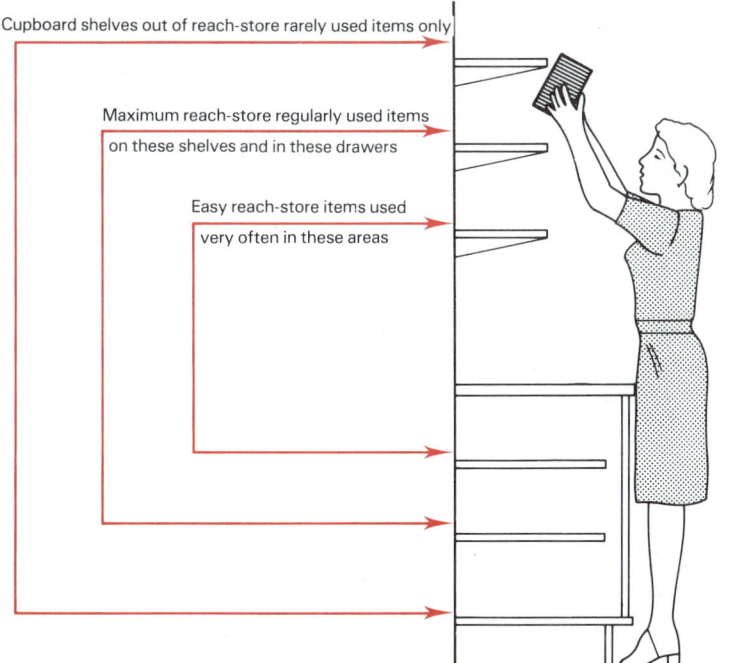

**Fig. 9.16** Sensible storage

**Fig. 9.17**

**Height of work surfaces** Different heights are needed by different people, and for different tasks. Manufacturers of kitchen units now recognize the need for a choice in height of units.
1 General purposes–height between 850mm and 900mm
2 For mixing e.g. creaming in a bowl–height between 800mm and 850mm
3 Washing up requires a sink height of 900 to 950mm with a drop into the sink of 200mm
4 If sitting down to a task the work surface should be between 600mm and 650mm

**Ventilation** is necessary to allow steam and cooking smells to escape from the kitchen, to avoid condensation problems and mould growth.
1 Kitchen windows should open top and bottom.
2 Extractor fans may be fitted in a wall or window.
3 Cooker hoods and ventilation grills are helpful.

**Lighting** Good lighting is essential to ensure safety and hygiene. A central overhead light is inadequate as it casts shadows.
  **Fluorescent** lights are best with, if possible, **strip lights** or spot lights at strategic points.

**Floors** must be easy to clean, hard wearing and comfortable to walk on (soft and warm). They must also be non-slip and resistant to heat.
  There is a wide range of vinyl or thermoplastic floorings and tiles, washable carpet and carpet tiles, and quarry tiles from which to choose.

**Walls** The wall covering should be washable and withstand stains and grease. Pale colours do not absorb light.
  There is a wide range of paints suitable for kitchens, washable or vinyl wallpapers, sealed wood or laminated panels and ceramic tiles of different shapes and colours.

**Work surfaces and unit doors** Laminated plastics are mostly used because they are easy to clean and are very durable. Special tiles are now available for work surfaces, but spaces between the tiles can be dirt traps. Doors can be laminated plastic, sealed or unsealed wood or painted wood.
  Laminated plastics are made in a wide range of colours, textures and patterns. A smooth work surface is better than a fashionable textured surface which catches dirt etc, in the grooves.

### 9.3.3 Movement and posture

If the muscles of the body are correctly used there is less chance of fatigue and muscle strain. With good posture and correct movement, the **head**, the **chest** and the **hips** are held in a **vertical position**. It is when they are out of line that muscle strain occurs.

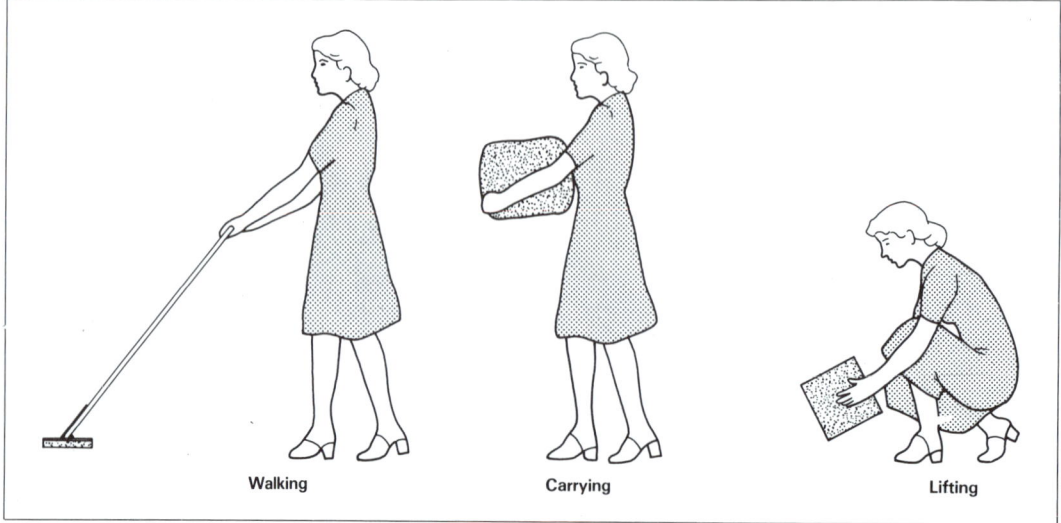

Walking        Carrying        Lifting

**Fig. 9.18** Correct posture during household activities

**When standing** keep the feet apart in line with the hips, and the bottom tucked in.

**When reaching** do not over-reach. Use stable steps so that the strain of over-reaching is avoided.

**When walking** keep the back erect and if using a tool, such as a brush, make sure that the handle is long enough for you to hold this position.

**When carrying** carry small loads which should be held close to the body. The line of vision should not be blocked. The load can rest on the hips if it is heavy.

**When sitting** keep the body straight from the neck to the hips. The height of the chair or stool should be suitable for the height of the working surface and the person. Sit square with your feet under the table.

**If lifting** bend at the knees, keep the back straight and use the leg muscles to give lifting power.

# 10 Health and Safety

## 10.1 Safety in the home

Homes are very dangerous places. The Royal Society for the Prevention of Accidents, ROSPA, estimates that 1 in 7 accidents occur in residential establishments. Most of these accidents are falls and the most vulnerable groups are the elderly and young children.

### What causes accidents?

Accidents are usually caused by physical factors such as the ones in Table 10.1. However, there is no doubt that they can also become more likely if the individuals concerned have other problems which affect their concentration.

**Factors** which may make accidents more likely: anxiety, overtiredness, rushing, neglect, lack of forethought and pre-occupation.

### Types of accident

The different categories are: falls, fire, burns and scalds, asphyxiation, suffocation, choking and strangulation, drowning and poisoning.

**Falls** are by far the most common type of accident in the home causing both injury and death.

**Table 10.1** Falls

| Causes | Remedies and safety measures |
| --- | --- |
| **Badly joined floor coverings** | Ensure that joints are well tacked down or metal strips are screwed over the joints. |
| **Wet floors** | Mop up water immediately and dry thoroughly. |
| **Highly polished floors** | Use non-slip polish, never polish to a high gloss. |
| **Loose mats** | Place suitable non-slip carpet underlay under large rugs and mats. Do not place any rug or mat on a highly polished or very slippery floor. |
| **Moving stair carpets** | Make sure that they are correctly laid so that they fit tightly and do not move. Ensure that carpet is well secured between each stair tread and riser. |
| **Uneven floors** | Floors should be smooth and even. Special measures have to be taken in old buildings where floors and steps are uneven. These measures include bringing the hazard to peoples' notice and painting lines along the edge of steps. |
| **Narrow steps** | There is nothing short of a fundamental change which can alter this problem. Sometimes it is enough just to be aware of the problem and to take extra care. |
| **High stair risers** | As above. |
| **Open stair risers** | As above. Homes with open stair risers are not suitable for families with young children. |
| **Untidy floors** | This is a great hazard in many homes which can be very easily solved by tidying-up. Trailing cables must not occur. |
| **Bad lighting** | All areas should be adequately lit so that any unexpected hazards can be clearly seen. |
| **Children on stairs** | Stair gates should be used in houses with young children, at both top and bottom. |
| **Windows to low levels** | Especially if they are above ground level safety bars should be fitted to prevent anyone falling out. |
| **Slippery baths** | Baths should have hand grips or non-slip mats to enable people to get in and out with ease. |
| **Step ladders** | Make sure that step ladders are stable. Do not perch them on furniture or ledges for decorating. |

### Fires

**Table 10.2** Fires

| Causes | Remedies and safety measures |
| --- | --- |
| **Clothing and fabrics near a source of heat** | Use flameproof nets and clothing. Never place mirrors above fires. Open fires and electric bar fires should have fire guards. Fixed fireguards are required by law on open fires in homes with children under 12 years. |
| **Faulty electrical appliances** | Electrical appliances should be checked regularly and well maintained. Turn off all appliances not in use. |
| **Smouldering cigarette ends** | Always use ashtrays and wait until the contents are cold before tipping them into a waste-bin. Choose metal wastebins. |
| **Flammable goods near heat sources** | Do not leave items such as dry cleaning fluids near heat sources. |
| **Chip pans** | Never leave them unattended. Do not fill over half full with fat or oil. |

Smoke detectors should be placed in areas where most fires start e.g. kitchen and be regularly maintained.

Great care should be taken in the choosing of double-glazed units. In the event of fire, those that do not open are hard to break, and can prevent escape.

### Burns and scalds

**Table 10.3** Burns and scalds

| Causes | Remedies and safety measures |
| --- | --- |
| **Hot liquids** | Elderly people and young children are particularly sensitive to hot liquids. Test the baby's bath water before use, always put cold water into the bath before hot. Saucepans with hot liquids should be placed where they cannot be pulled off the stove.<br>Hot water bottles should be checked before use. Never nurse or hold a child whilst holding a hot drink. |
| **Hot equipment** | Use oven gloves which are strong and have no holes. Use wooden spoons to stir hot liquids–they do not conduct heat. Never leave utensils carelessly on a cooker, close to a part of the cooker which is on. Cookers with a glass panel in the door are particularly dangerous, children's hands have stuck to these becoming badly burnt. |
| **Steam** | Never place steaming items e.g. electric kettle, where you have to reach over them to turn a switch or switch off a hotplate. See also hot liquids. |
| **Ice** | Produces bad 'burns'.<br>Freezer burns can be avoided by wearing stout gloves. |

**Asphyxiation** is mostly caused by children putting plastic bags over their heads. It can also be caused by toxic fumes such as carbon monoxide from car exhausts in a closed garage, or those produced by the burning of certain upholstery foams.
**Suffocation**, **choking** and **strangulation** can all lead to asphyxiation.

**Table 10.4** Asphyxiation

| Causes | Remedies and safety measures |
| --- | --- |
| **Suffocation** | Never give babies pillows to sleep on.<br>Do not leave babies unattended on cushions, beds or soft upholstery.<br>Animals such as cats should never be allowed near sleeping babies. |
| **Choking** | Ensure that babies bring up their wind before being put to sleep–regurgitated food can block the air supply to the lungs. Long dangling ribbons on toys have caused asphyxiation. |
| **Strangulation** | Ensure that nursery equipment and prams are safe and that harnesses are correctly used–strangulation can occur when small children fall out of cots and prams. Threaded ribbons on clothes have caused strangulation. |

**Accidental poisoning** The following table shows the main ways in which accidental poisoning can occur and the measures which can prevent it:

**Table 10.5** Poisoning

| Causes | Safety measures |
| --- | --- |
| **Small children going to the medicine cupboard** | Have locking medicine cupboards and buy bottles with child-proof caps. |
| **Contaminated cloths and sinks, household bleaches and chemicals** | Never use the kitchen sink for noxious substances. Have separate cloths for different jobs. Store household chemicals in locked cupboards. |
| **Taking the wrong medicine** | Before leaving the chemist make sure that you have understood the dosage requirements.<br>Follow dosage instructions carefully.<br>Destroy old medicines. |
| **Weed killers and pesticides** | Spray carefully, ensure that all food is removed. If it is necessary to spray near areas of food preparation or service, wipe everything down thoroughly before use.<br>Make sure that people, pets and fish are removed before spraying. |
| **Keeping poisons** | They should be kept in secure containers which are clearly marked. They should never be stored in containers which are recognizable as food containers e.g. lemonade bottles. |

**Dry cleaning fluids and solvents**  These substances can cause poisoning by inhalation. Articles which have been dry cleaned should be hung in the open air until the last of the fluid has evaporated. Solvents should be used outside or in rooms where windows can be opened and a through draught created.

**Drowning**  Children can drown in a very small amount of water. Never leave a child unattended in the bath. Cover a garden fish pond with a firm guard.

## 10.2 Making the home safe

Many points are listed in the table on page 131. More additional points are detailed below.

**Table 10.6** Preventive measures to make the home safe

| Area | Preventive measures |
|---|---|
| **Kitchen** | Dangerous chemicals such as bleach should be stored in locked cupboards. Cookers with drop-doors to their ovens should be anchored to the wall in case pressure on the door causes the cooker to fall forward. No electrical appliances should be used close to water. Electrical appliances should not be switched on with wet hands. Store sharp utensils safely e.g. knives in knife blocks, processor blades in their shields. Keep utensils in good order e.g. sharpen knives regularly–it is more dangerous to use a blunt knife than a sharp one! Appliances should always be fitted with fuses of the right rating. Plan the use of cupboards–see Chapter 9. |
| **Sitting room** | Take care with floors. No trailing flexes Take care with mats. Ensure that carpet joints are safe. Top-heavy furniture should be attached to the wall. Choose upholstery which is fire retardant. Fire guards must always be used with small children. Mirrors should never be placed over fireplaces. Dummy plugs should be fitted into empty sockets. |
| **Stairs** | Make sure that the stairs are well lit. |
| **Dining room** | Furniture and upholstery–see sitting room. Prevent young children from pulling at the table cloth. Ensure that cloths are placed so that they will not be dislodged as people pass. |
| **Bedrooms** | No smoking should be allowed whilst people are in bed. Babies need special measures. |
| **Bathrooms** | There should be no electrical points except a shaving socket. Medicine cabinets should be child proof. Store medicines and tablets with care |
| **Gardens** | Fishponds–see above. Garden sheds should be firmly secured to prevent children from using garden implements. Weedkillers etc.–see page 132. |

## 10.3 First aid

First aid is given to:
(a) preserve life (b) prevent the condition worsening and (c) prevent bleeding. First aid is **not** medical aid. This must be sought after the initial actions. The action of a person giving first aid should be limited to:

 (i) Clearing airways–mouth, nose etc;  (ii) Making sure the patient is breathing; and
(iii) Stopping bleeding.

**The Kiss of Life**

**1** Lay the patient on his back, loosen tight clothing. Ensure that mouth and throat are not blocked by the tongue, food or false teeth.

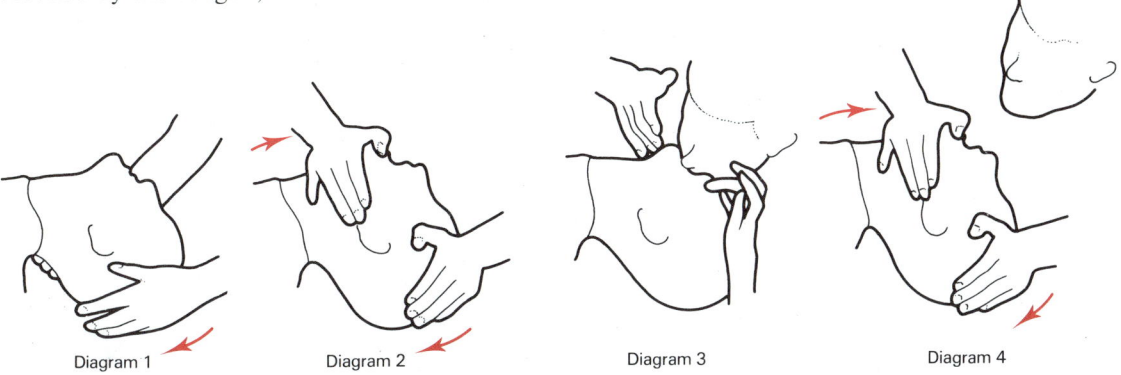

Diagram 1          Diagram 2          Diagram 3          Diagram 4

**Fig. 10.1** The kiss of life

**2** Tilt the head back, see diagram 1. Place the hands in position, see diagram 2.

**3** Keeping the nose closed blow gently into the patient's mouth, diagram 3.

**4** Remove mouth to allow the patient to exhale, diagram 4. Continue doing this 10-15 times a minute. If the patient starts to vomit turn the head to one side and discontinue resuscitation.

**NB** Children and babies have very small lungs, **never** attempt to over inflate them as it is likely to cause extensive lung damage.

### Bleeding

**1** Press directly on the bleeding wound with a clean, thick absorbent pad.

**2** Maintain the pressure for at least 10 minutes.

**3** Once the blood has clotted, maintain the pressure by applying a dressing held by a bandage.

**4** Put the injured part in an elevated position and do not let the patient move it.

### The First Aid box

| | |
|---|---|
| **Dressings** | These should be sterile; to remain sterile the packets must remain sealed. Buy a range of sizes. |
| **Triangular bandages** | At least two |
| **Plasters** | Box of plasters in different sizes |
| **Micropore or adhesive tape** | To secure the dressings |
| **Cotton Wool** | Sterile |
| **Antiseptic wipes** | To clean wounds |
| **Gauze** | Sterile |
| **Safety Pins** | |
| **Scissors** | |

**In addition** it might be sensible to have:
Eyebath and eyewash such as Optrex.
Tweezers.
2″ crepe bandage.
Antiseptic cream and liquid (only useful if it can be diluted).
Surgical spirit.
Tubogauze and applicator for bandaging fingers.
Mild pain killers (aspirin or similar), antacids such as alka-seltzer, lozenges for sore throats, a thermometer or fever scan, cream for insect bites.
Doctor's telephone number.

Chemist shops sell kits of first aid equipment ready assembled. The exact contents of the kits vary but the list shows items which the British Red Cross Society suggests should be included. It is quite easy and probably better to assemble the kit for yourself. You may wish to add certain items.

**The container** The kit should be kept in a strong, water and airtight container. Plastic containers make ideal first aid kit holders as they will not rust.

### Giving First Aid

**1** Follow the rules listed in 10.4.

**2** Keep calm—it is impossible to help the patient in any way at all if you panic.

**3** Reassure the patient and if necessary treat for shock.

**4** Control any bleeding if possible.

**5** If the injury is serious get qualified help.

**6** Do not move the patient if you are unsure of his condition or if he is badly hurt.

## 10.4   The emergency services

In most towns it takes about ten minutes for the ambulance and emergency services to arrive. Don't hesitate to call for help if it is required.

### To call an ambulance

**Dial 999**

**Ask for the ambulance service**

**Give your name and full address** (or the location of the accident)

**Give concise details,** usually the number of casualties, types of injury and, if known, the names of the injured (do not spend valuable time trying to find out this information in an emergency).

## 10.5  Action needed for some minor and major injuries

**Table 10.7** Table to show the action needed for major and minor injuries

| Injury | Treatment for minor injury | First Aid for serious injury |
|---|---|---|
| **Burns and scalds** | Cool immediately by immersing in cold water for at least 10 minutes. Dab dry with sterile cotton wool. Cover with sterile bandage.<br>**Do not** 1 Break blisters<br>2 Use plasters<br>3 Use any creams | **Call Ambulance Immediately**<br>If on fire roll in a blanket or rug. If possible hold under cold water. Never remove clothing which has been sterilized by fire. Cover the burnt area with sterile or clean dressing. Keep patient quiet and warm if possible. |
| **Bleeding** | *Nose Bleeds* sit patient down with head forward. Gently pinch nostrils and put cold wet cotton wool on the bridge of nose. If it persists for more than ten minutes or seems very heavy take patient to hospital.<br>*Cuts and Grazes* bathe gently with diluted antiseptic. Dab dry with sterile cotton wool. Apply elastoplast dressing if large enough or failing that sterile dressings to cover the area. Small cuts heal more quickly if left open to the air.<br>Cover with a waterproof dressing if doing cooking or dirty jobs. Puncture wounds may need a Tetanus injection e.g. dog bite.<br>**NB** Concentrated antiseptic will kill more cells and prolong healing. | *Severe lacerations*–try to raise the injury above the level of the heart. Bind carefully with plenty of bandage. Never use a tourniquet.<br>*Internal bleeding*–there may not be any blood externally. Keep patient as calm as possible, lie them down if they are trying to move about. If already lying down **don't move them**. |
| **Electric shock** | Switch off current using dry insulated object. Minor burns as above. Treat for shock. | If the patient has stopped breathing attempt artificial respiration. Sometimes the heart stops–need to be qualified to give heart massage. |
| **Broken bones** | | Move patient as little as possible. Stop bleeding and treat cuts and grazes. Keep patient warm and treat for shock. |
| **Falls** | Minor falls, treat as for cuts and grazes. Treat for shock if necessary. | Serious falls–see bleeding and bones. Get expert help. |
| **Poisoning**<br>(liquids, solids and gases) | *Poisonous/caustic liquids*–give water or milk to dilute.<br>*Vomitting* will bring up tablets before they are absorbed, but take to the hospital with sample tablet. Do not give a salt solution, as excessive salt can cause brain damage.<br>Open the windows and doors to clear the gas. Remove the patient from the affected area. | Take poison to the hospital with you. If the patient is unconscious and breathing has stopped attempt artificial respiration. |
| **Eyes** | Do not rub eye. Rapid blinking will usually wash object to corner of eye for removal. Use eye bath and Optrex to remove foreign bodies. | If a harmful substance has entered the eye flush with cold water. Go to hospital. |
| **Ears/nose** | **Do not attempt** to remove any object pushed into the ear or nose. | Go to hospital. |
| **Sprains and strains** | Support injured part with bandages or sling after plunging into cold water, preferably with ice in it. | As minor injury treatment. If very painful or likely to be broken go to hospital. |
| **Choking** | Hold upside down if a child, or place over knee.<br>Smack smartly between the shoulder blades. | As minor injury, call ambulance if obstruction cannot be cleared. |
| **Bites** | Remove sting. Apply a cold compress. Use a solution of bicarbonate, calamine or sting creams. Ice for stings in the mouth. | If the area becomes swollen and painful get expert help. |
| **Swallowing sharp objects** | | Take to hospital. Do not give anything by mouth. |
| **Splinters** | Wash with soap and water.<br>Use sterilized tweezers to pull splinter out. Do **not probe** to reach splinter. | |
| **Shock** | Reassure and comfort. Lay flat loosely covered.<br>Loosen tight clothing. | Severe shock and unconciousness–check breathing and pulse. Do **not move** or give anything by mouth.<br>Do **not use** hot water bottles. |

## 10.6   Home nursing

### The spread of infection

Some **bacteria** and **viruses** can cause infections, these are called **pathogens**. Others are **benign** (harmless) to the human body. Infection is often caused by contact, or by droplets and can be carried by flies, mosquitoes and mice. Thus food should never be touched by cooks with septic cuts, nor should they allow poorly washed cutlery to be used. The list below suggests some other ways in which infection might be spread.

1 Dirty towels      2 Sharing towels and face flannels, toothbrushes etc
3 Poorly washed food preparation, cooking and serving equipment
4 Poor personal hygiene, unclean person or clothing, hair falling in the food
5 Poor food storage      6 Household pests (see Home management section)
7 Failure to disinfect toilets, basins, baths, and floors      8 Unclean bedding

### Fighting infection

1 Good diet, fresh air, exercise and rest
2 Build up resistance to infection by vaccination
3 Keep everything scrupulously clean, use disinfectant to kill bacteria
4 Ensure that patients' linens and crockery/utensils are separated from those belonging to other people
5 Keep as many people as possible away from the patient
6 Patients who are sick require a receptacle in case of vomitting, which can be easily disinfected after use, a soft damp cloth and plenty of water.

### Characteristics of a good home nurse

He/She should be:
1 Well organized.      2 Calm and reassuring.
3 Sympathetic to the patient's needs e.g. food, warmth, tidy, clean quarters, medication, psychological needs.
4 Able to follow the doctor's instructions.      5 Have good personal hygiene.

### Criteria for choosing a sick-room

It should be:
1 Reasonably quiet.
2 Convenient for the people who are nursing the invalid, i.e. not up several flights of stairs.
3 Easy to clean and maintain.      4 Warm and preferably with a sunny aspect.
5 Within easy reach of the bathroom and lavatory.
6 Only lightly furnished with necessary furniture in it, to allow space to move about.
7 Able to meet special needs e.g. psychological needs. Patients get better more quickly if they can be kept cheerful. Perhaps by watching the TV!
Clearly it is not always possible to fulfil these criteria as people usually have their existing bedrooms as their sick-rooms.

### Medication

It is usually worthwhile trying to treat symptoms with simple remedies such as aspirins and throat lozenges even if the doctor has been called. It can ease matters for the patient while he is waiting. There are however golden rules about administering any medicine:
1 Always follow the instructions carefully and never exceed the stated dose. Pour liquids away from the label.
2 Never keep old medicines, or use medicines which the doctor has prescribed for anyone else.
3 Always make sure the patient finishes a course of antibiotics to completely clear the infection, which remains even when symptoms disappear.

**Feeding the invalid**–see Section 5.4.2.

## 10.7   Good grooming and personal hygiene

### Care of the teeth

A full adult set of teeth contains the following teeth:

| Tooth | Number | Function and position |
|---|---|---|
| Incisor | 8 | Positioned at the front of the mouth for biting off food. |
| Canine | 4 | Pointed teeth placed towards the side of the mouth for tearing. |
| Premolar | 8 | For slicing food |
| Molar | 12 | For grinding |

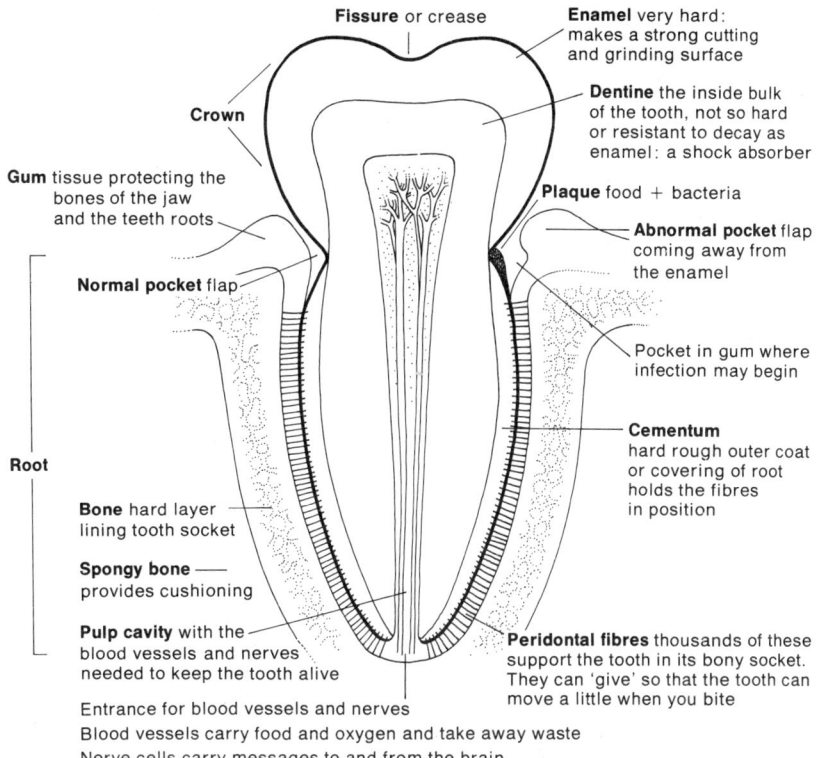

**Fig. 10.2** Diagrammatic section of a tooth

**Tooth decay** (dental caries) and gum infections are usually caused by **plaque**. This is a film of sticky substance on the teeth. It is made up of food particles, saliva and plaque bacteria. The film prevents the bacteria from being cleared from the teeth by the saliva. The bacteria turn the food particles into acid which attacks the tooth enamel, causing holes. This acid acts in the first 10 minutes after eating sugar. Once the enamel is eroded the dentine is open to attack. The decay will finally reach the pulp cavity at the centre of the tooth which is where the nerves are. Research suggests that sugary foods readily form acids which attack the enamel. The first sign of gum disease is usually **gingivitis** (inflammation or bleeding), the swollen gums then start to draw away from the teeth making it difficult or impossible to eat. The bones finally disintegrate and the teeth become wobbly and fall out. The longer teeth are left covered with food the more likely the plaque is to form.

*Choosing a toothbrush*
1 Pick one with a small head which fits easily into small spaces in the mouth.
2 Pick one which does not become easily waterlogged, i.e. not natural bristle.
3 The brush should have medium or soft texture so that it doesn't scratch the teeth and gums.
4 The brush should have plenty of tufts, which are flexible.
5 The bristles must be trimmed flat.
6 As soon as the bristles begin to splay discard and buy a new one.
7 Toothbrushes should be used in conjunction with **dental floss** or **sticks** which allow cleaning between and at the head of the tooth.

*How to prevent dental caries and gum disease*
1 Avoid sugary foods       2 Brush teeth correctly using a good toothbrush
3 Go to the dentist regularly for check-ups
4 Use a Fluoride toothpaste. Children over five can have their teeth painted with fluoride by a dentist.
5 Make sure your diet includes foods such as dairy products which contain calcium, phosphorus, vitamin D and other products essential for healthy teeth. During pregnancy fluoride tablets may be taken to help good formation of baby's teeth.

*How to brush your teeth*
The main aim of brushing your teeth is to clean them thoroughly. It is possible to see how well you are achieving this by using plaque disclosing tablets. These tablets are available from the chemist. You suck the tablet which contains a red dye. The dye only sticks to the plaque so it is possible to see where the plaque has not been cleaned off. Dye and plaque may be removed by further brushing.
The suggested system for brushing is:
(*a*) To brush the top teeth downwards.    (*b*) The lower teeth upwards.
(*c*) Brush the backs of all the teeth.

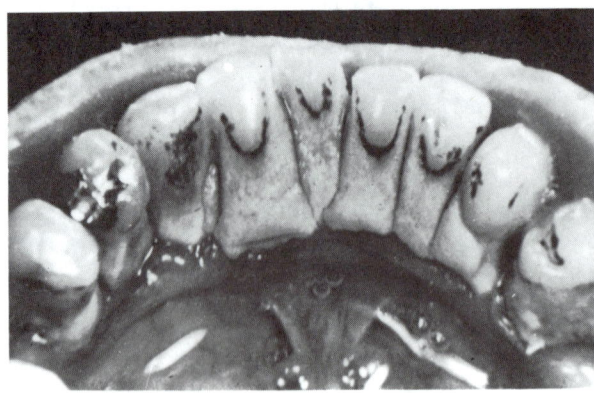

**Fig. 10.3** Dental caries

(*d*) Brush the biting surfaces.
(*e*) Dental floss or sticks should be used to remove particles lodged between the teeth.
(*f*) Rinse toothbrush and put it to dry.

**Care of the skin**

The skin is the body's largest organ, it covers all surfaces. It is made up of two layers the **dermis** and the **epidermis**.

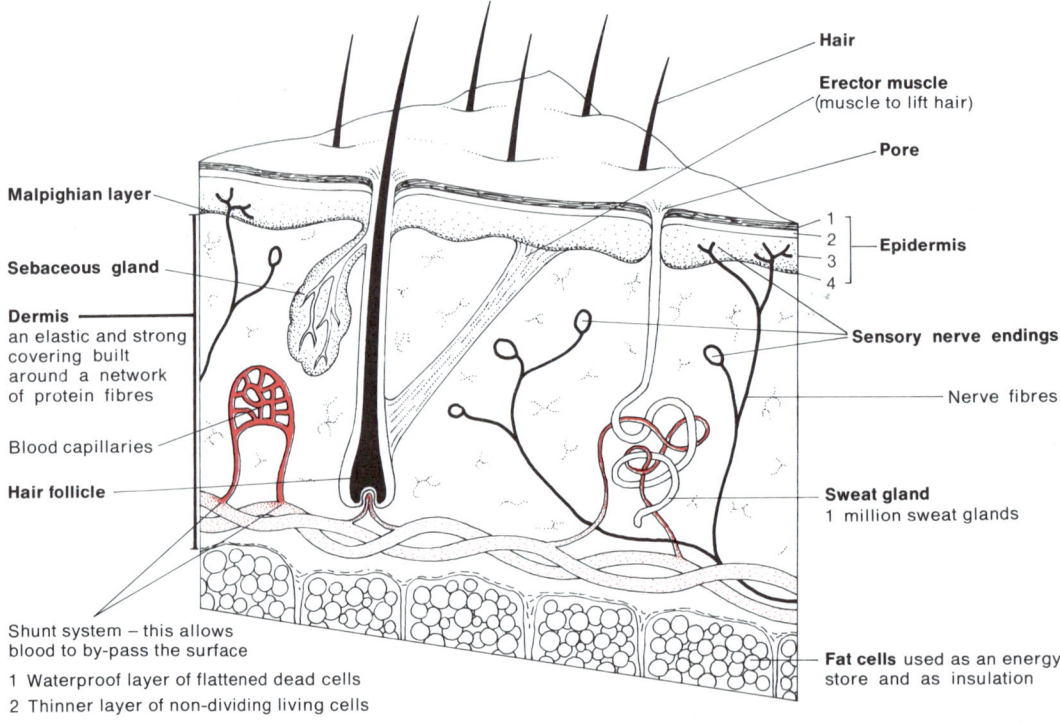

**Fig. 10.4** Diagram of a wedge of skin to show its internal structure

Shunt system – this allows blood to by-pass the surface
1 Waterproof layer of flattened dead cells
2 Thinner layer of non-dividing living cells
3 Pigmented layer – protective, absorbs harmful ultraviolet light
4 Inner layer of dividing cells to replace those worn away

**Functions of the skin**

1 It forms a barrier against infection.
2 It helps to regulate body temperature by cooling and insulation. Sweating cools the body, fat in the dermis insulates.
3 It protects the body tissue and organs in the body.
4 It is waterproof.

**Care of the skin,** which is a very delicate organ requires attention. It needs to be protected from harsh chemicals such as detergents and adverse conditions such as wind and water. It is however necessary to cleanse it either with water or an oil based cleanser as throughout the day it collects a film of dirt, perspiration and oil. Faces which have make-up on them need very careful and thorough cleansing. The skin is thickest on the soles of the feet, the palms of the hands and the scalp. It is thinnest on the lips.

Skin is continually replacing itself. It is capable of stretching and contracting according to the needs of the body. Skin which takes very heavy wear such as the hands and face often requires moisturizing to keep the skin supple. Failure to moisturize can cause chapped, dry skin which is prone to becoming cracked and sore. Rubber gloves should be used for washing up.

During puberty and in adult life the skin perspires more. Salts are deposited on the skin and if not washed away produce body odour. Underarm areas produce a lot of perspiration which cannot evaporate. Anti-perspirants will stop perspiration but should only be used under the arms. Deodorants prevent odour.

Fingernails should be cut short and kept clean. An emery board is used to shape the nails, a metal nail file should not be used. Toe nails should be cut straight across to avoid in-growing toe nails.

Acne occurs when the sebaceous glands become infected. Picking spots increases this type of infection. The pore becomes blocked with a greasy plug which is not washed away. To keep skin free of acne wash with warm soapy water three times a day. Use simple soap—no colour, no perfume. Make sure your diet contains lots of vitamins A and B. If acne becomes a problem go to see your doctor. Proprietary treatments available in the chemists are expensive. The doctor will prescribe a special lotion or tablets. This is a problem of adolescence when parts of the body become more greasy, particularly from the forehead to the chin.

Avoid obvious infections such as impetigo and scabies by not using communal towels. Follow strict rules of hygiene.

### Care of the hair

To prevent the accumulation of sweat, oil and micro-organisms, which encourage insect parasites such as lice, the hair should be treated as outlined below.
1 Wash the hair, brush and comb, at least once a week to remove dirt and micro-organisms.
2 Comb and brush the hair daily. This removes loose skin, dirt and micro-organisms. Circulation of blood in the scalp is also improved, leading to healthy growth.

### Care of the feet

The bones of the feet are not fully developed until late adolescence and the feet must be cared for if problems are not to develop in later years.
1 Tight or ill-fitting shoes can distort the feet irreversibly. Always choose a shoe shop where exact measurements are taken prior to fitting.
2 Wash the feet every night and dry them thoroughly between the toes to prevent skin diseases e.g. athletes foot developing.
3 Man-made fibres are not ideal for socks where the feet perspire freely. The sweat is trapped, not absorbed, between the skin and material thus forming a moist warm breeding place for bacteria and skin parasites. Cotton and wool socks absorb the perspiration. Tights and stockings should be washed after each wear and the feet washed thoroughly.

### Posture

The importance of posture is discussed in Section 9.3.3. If the head is pushed forward the pelvis has to tilt in order to maintain balance and **round shoulders** result.

If however the shoulders are held back too much the abdomen is pushed forward to compensate. This results in a **hollow back** and digestive and breathing problems can result.

**Good posture** is being maintained when the ear, hand and foot are in a **vertical line**.

# 11   Money management

## 11.1   Income

Income is **any money** or **benefit** which is **acquired** either by earning it from an employer or as a result of our own work, or from other sources.

**Sources of income include:**

Work as an employee
Work as a self-employed person
Investments
Redundancy payments
Sickness benefit
Other Social Security benefits such as family income supplement and invalidity pensions, child benefit, unemployment benefit.

State retirement pension (Old Age pension)
Private pension schemes
Private insurance schemes such as those which insure against ill health.
Trades Union funds
Inheritance

### 11.1.1 Pay

Most of the working population work for employers and thus are **employees.** The employee may be either **salaried** or **wage earning**.

**The salaried employee** is usually paid monthly; the amount is usually paid directly into a Bank account with tax etc. deducted ie **net pay**. The amount to be paid is usually quoted to the prospective employee as an annual figure e.g. £5,500 per annum. To work out how much will be received **gross** (before deductions) in each month it is necessary to divide this figure by 12.

**The wage earning employee** is usually paid weekly and the amount of the wage is usually quoted gross, on appointment, as a weekly figure. It is necessary to multiply this by 52 to gain an annual figure. e.g. £50 per week = £2,600 per annum.

It is necessary to calculate net weekly, quarterly, monthly and annual figures in order to budget sensibly. See budgeting section in this unit.

#### National Insurance contributions

| Lower earnings limit: £34 a week<br>£140·83 a month<br>£1,689·96 a year | | Upper earnings limit: £250 a week<br>£1,018·33 a month<br>£12,219·96 a year | |
|---|---|---|---|
| | | Employees<br>From<br>6.4.83 | Employers<br>From<br>6.4.83 |
| **Class 1 Contributions**<br>Standard rate | | 9% | 10·45%* |
| Contracted-out rate:<br>—on first £32·50 a week<br>—on earnings between £32·50 and £235 a week | | 9%<br>6·85% | 10·45%*<br>6·35%* |
| Reduced rate for married women and widows<br>with valid certification of election | | 3·85% | As above (standard<br>or contracted out) |
| Men over 65 and women over 60 | | Nil | 10·45%* |
| Children under 16 | | Nil | Nil |
| **Class 2 Contributions:** Self-employed.<br>Flat rate: £4·40 a week.<br>Share fishermen's special rate: £7·00 a week.<br>Small earnings exception: £1,775 earning limit for 1983-84. | | | |
| **Class 3 Voluntary Contributions:** £4·30 a week. | | | |
| **Class 4 Contributions:** Self-employed.<br>6·3% of profits or gains between £3,800 and £12,000 a year. | | | |
| *National Insurance Surcharge *excluded:* 1·5% for earnings reduced to 1% from 1.8.83. (Charities exempt.) | | | |

**Table 11.1** A table of National Insurance contributions 1984/5

National Insurance Contributions help to pay for State benefits such as the National Health Service, sickness, unemployment, injury and disablement and maternity benefit.

**Contributions are compulsory** and must be paid by those who are employed and those who are self-employed. People who are employed and work full-time for an employer usually pay contributions at the full rate and are entitled to most benefits. Self-employed people pay different rates and are entitled to less benefits.

The amount of National Insurance which has to be paid is laid down by the Government and is detailed in Table 11.1. It may vary from time to time. On the whole the more money which is earned the greater the NI contribution. NI is only paid when income rises above a certain level. In 1984 this is £34 per week.

NI also includes an element which saves for a person's pension. Some firms are 'contracted out' of this national scheme as they provide similar, or better, pensions for their employees so it is necessary for the employee to pay into this scheme rather than the Government one.

#### Taxation–PAYE (Pay As You Earn)

This will probably be the **largest deduction** on the payslip. The employer collects this money on behalf of the **Inland Revenue** and it is deducted from the pay before the employee receives it. Most employees pay their tax in this way.

Anyone who receives their pay gross or who has **income from investments** which are likely to be paid gross must **declare** this to the Inland Revenue when they fill in their **tax return**. They are responsible for getting and filling in the tax return and paying the tax within the stipulated period of time.

**The PAYE Code** tells the employer how much money an employee may earn tax free. Using a set of tables and knowing the tax code number the employer is able to calculate how much tax needs to be deducted from an employee's wage or salary.

The Tax Code reflects the amount of **tax relief** to which a person is entitled. Tax relief is granted for such reasons as contributing to the upkeep of dependant relatives or the payment of mortgage interest (currently available on loans up to £30,000), Union subscriptions, approved pension schemes, superannuation payments or protective clothing. In addition workers are entitled to either single or married person's allowance.

Single person or married woman up to £1,785 per annum tax free (1983/1984)

A married person (available only to the husband) £2,795 per annum (1983/1984).

**The basic tax rate** for earned income in 1983/4:

| | |
|---|---|
| Up to £14,600 | 30% |
| Over £14,600 | 40-60% (increasing with amount) |

**Emergency Tax Codes:** employees without a tax code who take up a job will be likely to pay more tax than necessary. When the Inland Revenue have given a Tax Code the employee will be refunded any tax which has been overpaid. This is usually done by refunding it when the next pay cheque or packet is due.

**Moving from one job to another,** an employee will be issued by the first employer a Form P45. This tells the new employer **how much tax has been paid** in the tax year and what his tax code is. Failure to present the new employer with a P45 (see Fig. 11.1), will mean that Emergency Tax will be deducted.

**The Tax year** runs from April 6th to April 5th of the following year.

**A Tax Return** is the form sent by the Inland Revenue on which **all details of income** should be given. People who pay PAYE do not usually receive these forms.

It is not really necessary to fill one in unless the employee needs to declare any income which is paid gross e.g. Bank interest, or any income which is derived from another job on which he does not pay PAYE; it is also the way of claiming tax allowances.

**Certificate of pay and tax deducted** (P10) filled in by the employer annually is shown in Fig. 11.1.

**SAYE** (Save As You Earn) is explained on page 146.

**A pay slip** is shown in the diagram Fig. 11.2. They vary slightly from one employer to another but in essence they show Gross and Net Pay and the way in which the figures have been arrived at. The diagram is labelled so that each element has been described.

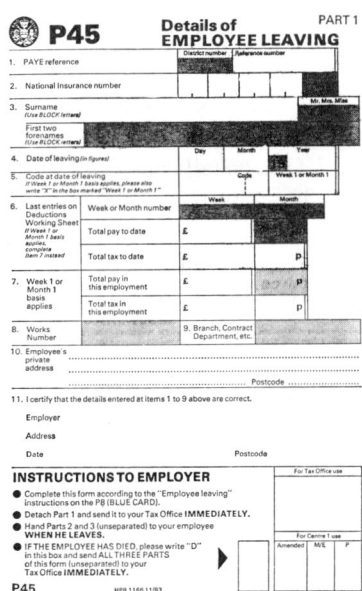

**Fig. 11.1** A P45 certificate of tax and pay

| COMPANY NAME | COMPANY No. | PERIOD | No. | NAT: INSUR: No./CODE | TAX CODE | TAXABLE PAY | | PM | DEPT: | EMPLOYEE | EMPLOYEE NAME | | |
|---|---|---|---|---|---|---|---|---|---|---|---|---|---|
| | | | | | | PERIOD | YTD | | | | | | |
| J. JONES & CO LTD | 10862 | 30/11/83 | 08 | YH 12 34 56 C | 178L    8 | 175.00 | 1400.00 | CHQ | 0101 | 000030 | J. SMITH | | |

| CODE | ALLOWANCES | HOURS | RATE | PERIOD | CODE | DEDUCTIONS | PERIOD | BAL/YTD | CODE | DEDUCTIONS | PERIOD | BAL/YTD | NET PAY |
|---|---|---|---|---|---|---|---|---|---|---|---|---|---|
| 10 BASIC SALARY | | | | 175.00 | SAYE | | 4.00 | 63.00 | | | | | 148.75 |
| | | | | | TAX PAID | | 15.75 | 126.00 | | | | | |
| | | | | | NIC | | 6.52 | | | | | | |
| | | | | | | | | | | | | | AMOUNT PAYABLE |
| | TOTAL ALLOWANCES | | | 175.00 | | | | | | TOTAL DEDUCTIONS | 26.25 | | 148.75 |

**Fig. 11.2** A pay slip

### 11.1.2   Bank accounts

Many people have Bank Accounts with the large Clearing Banks. The commonest types of Bank Account available to the public are listed below.

1  A Current Account
2  A Deposit Account
3  A Budget Account

**A Current Account**

This is the type of account which most Bank customers have. Money is withdrawn from such an account by **cheque**. The bank balances up the customer's account every day or on every occasion when a transaction takes place. Usually the customer is also supplied with a Cheque Guarantee Card (see page 143) and a card for a Cash Dispenser (see page 143). Periodically the customer will receive a statement of his/her account which will list all the transactions. Interest is **not usually earned** on the capital (money) deposited in the account.

Money may be withdrawn from any current account which is in credit (has money in it!). If you go to any bank but your own it is necessary to use a **cheque guarantee card** and the amount which can be withdrawn will be limited by the value on the card e.g. £50 or £100; a charge may be made by other banks. Money may be withdrawn both during and out of banking hours by using cash dispensing machines.

**Bank Charges** have to be paid either twice a year or quarterly. The charges relate to the number of transactions, and the amount kept in the account. In Scottish Banks customers who keep the account in credit (no stipulated figure) incur no charges. In the rest of Britain if a minimum amount (usually £100) is kept in a current account there are often no bank charges.

Special terms are now available with some Banks for students, young people and school leavers.

**A Deposit Account**

This type of account is for saving money. **Interest** is paid on the capital invested and so it is possible to earn money with the capital. The interest is paid gross of tax. It is usually necessary to give notice of intention to withdraw the money.

Deposit account statements are sent to the customer but as there are fewer transactions in most cases this is usually done only after interest has been added.

**Budget Account**

These accounts are offered to customers as a bank service to help them to **organize** their **money management**. The idea is that an assessment is made of the amount of money which is likely to be paid out on major bills in a year. This usually includes household expenses such as rates, mortgage, rent, electricity, gas etc., but may also include money to meet bills such as clothing, car repairs etc.

The total **amount required in a year** is estimated; a little is usually added for inflation and the bank's fee; the customer then places 1/12 of the amount in the budget account every month. When the bills arrive he then draws a **cheque on the budget account** to pay the bill.

It may be that some months the account is overdrawn (at least when the account is newly opened), other months there will be plenty of money available. Only bills which have been taken account of may be paid through this account. This system helps customers by ensuring that they are always able to pay their bills. These accounts are very popular with people on low incomes who find the discipline of saving difficult and those who worry a great deal about bills or find it difficult to manage their money.

(Personal budgeting is done in the same way and using a Building Society or deposit account each month would mean interest would be paid to them, rather than charges to the bank.)

**Opening a Current Account** follows this procedure

1  Choose a bank which is recommended through your school or college, parent or a friend; or one that is near to your home or work place. When you go to the Bank they will ask you to fill in a form and a Bank official will help you to do this.

2  The form will ask for personal details such as your name and address, probably also for referees. You will also be asked to provide specimen signatures so that they can check these against your signatures on the cheques.

3  At first you are likely to be given a temporary cheque book but shortly you will receive one which has your name and account number printed on it.

4  When you open your account discuss with the official matters such as whether you can have a cheque guarantee card and how often you will receive statements of your account.

*Services associated with holding a current account*

(a)  **Having a cheque book.** This is helpful as it enables you to **pay for goods without cash**. A cheque is an order in writing made by the customer; it instructs the bank to pay a particular person a certain amount of money from a particular account. The forms (or cheques) are supplied by the bank and printed to a high standard to prevent forgery. In addition the bank holding the account has a specimen of the account holder's signature so that they can compare it with the signature made on the cheque. This enables the bank to tell whether the account holder has actually signed the cheque himself. In practice however, all cheques are not matched to the signature card in this way as it would be impracticable.

There are two types of cheques 'open' and 'crossed', shown in Fig. 11.3.

 (i) An open cheque does not have lines drawn across it and is used for someone to be paid in cash. It can only be cashed at the account holder's bank – this checks that the signature is correct, because the person receiving the cash may have stolen the cheque. It is not therefore a very safe method of payment.

(ii) A crossed cheque does not allow cash payment over the counter. It can only be paid into an account. This makes it safer as the account into which it is paid will be known by your bank. The correct date, signature and the amount in words and figures are important on both types of cheques. The cheque counterfoil can provide a useful record for personal accounting.

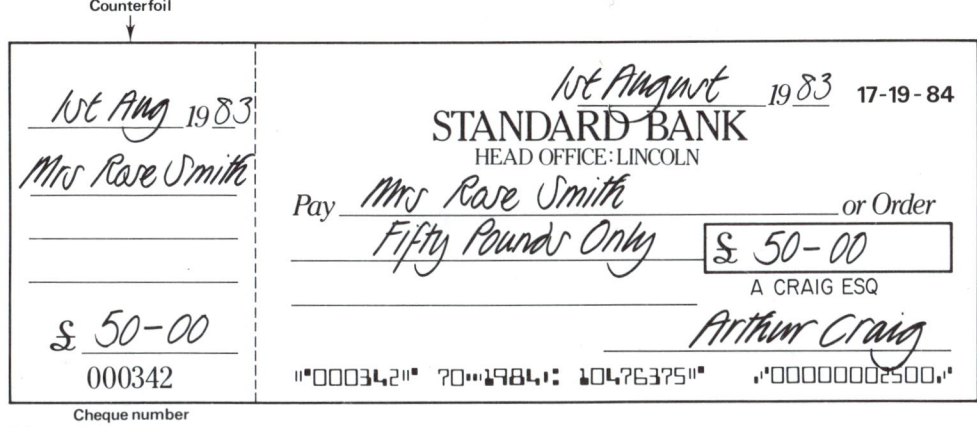

Fig. 11.3 Types of cheques

Fig. 11.4 A cash dispenser card

Fig. 11.5 A cheque guarantee card

**(b) Standing Order/Bankers Order** is an instruction to your bank to make payments of a specific amount on your behalf at given intervals to named bank accounts e.g. monthly mortgage payments to a Building Society. Such an order is shown on Fig. 11.6. A small charge is payable for this service.

**(c) Direct Debit** can be used when you wish to make regular payments of varying amounts to a person supplying goods or services to you. It is a general instruction to your bank to pay the supplier's bank account any amounts which are requested by the supplier. A small charge is payable for this service.

**(d) Bank Cards** have three different forms/uses although some cards fulfil more than one function. e.g. Access cards can be used in some cash dispenser machines as well as being used as credit cards.

**Table 11.2** Bank Cards

| Types | Methods of use/Uses | Advantages and Disadvantages |
|---|---|---|
| **Cash Dispenser Cards** | Cash dispensers are found at the main branches of most Banks. Card holders have a personal number which they 'tap' in to obtain cash. Other services can be requested e.g. new cheque book, statements. | Many are open 24 hours per day, ideal in an emergency. No waiting when the Bank is busy. Money can be snatched by a passer-by. Machines are prone to vandalism and can run out of money in busy periods e.g. Bank holidays. |
| **Cheque Guarantee Cards** | Required now by many retailers when accepting a cheque. They guarantee that the Bank will pay the money up to a limit of £50 or £100 if the person receiving the cheque has written the card number on the back. | Once issued a cheque cannot be 'stopped'. |
| **Credit Cards** | Available through most Banks e.g. Visa, Access. Used instead of a cheque or cash. A monthly limit is set and a statement sent each month. A minimum payment must always be made and interest is charged on the outstanding amounts–rates can be high. | Cash does not have to be carried as many suppliers, hotels and restaurants accept these cards in payment. Can pay several bills at once. Generous credit limits can lead to debts which are hard to meet. |

**(e) Bank Statements**

(i) Many employers ask employees to have a current account as they pay salaries direct into them. A salary statement is issued to employees weekly or monthly. Payments appear in the Bank Statement.

(ii) Bank statements show the transactions which have taken place and also show the daily balance. Figure 11.6 shows a typical Bank statement.

(iii) Accounts which have had more money taken out than has been paid in are said to be *overdrawn*. Unless an **overdraft facility** has been asked for by the customer and agreed to by the bank, accounts should not be allowed to become overdrawn. An overdraft is an agreed loan of money from the bank and the bank will charge the customer interest on any money which is borrowed in this way. Overdrafts are indicated often in red on the statement or with the label OD.

**District Bank plc**

**District Bank plc**
PARK LANE CROYDON BRANCH
110 PARK LANE CROYDON

Miss R. Snowdon                          Statement of Account

| 1983 | Sheet 1 | Account No. 22105055 | DEBIT | CREDIT | BALANCE Credit C Debit D |
|---|---|---|---|---|---|
| FEB 28 | BALANCE BROUGHT FORWARD | | | | 147.43 C |
| MAR 1 | 615627 | | 109.95 | | 37.48 C |
| MAR 4 | 615629 | | 29.74 | | 7.74 C |
| MAR 7 | SUNDRIES | | | 229.96 | 237.70 C |
| MAR 8 | 615628 | | 21.70 | | 216.00 C |
| MAR 11 | M B & C Insurance SO | | 15.00 | | 201.00 C |
| MAR 15 | 615631 | | 37.80 | | 163.20 C |
| MAR 16 | 615630 | | 22.50 | | 140.70 C |
| MAR 17 | 615635 | | 119.25 | | 21.45 C |
| MAR 18 | CHARGES TO 4 MAR | | 8.19 | | |
| MAR 18 | INTEREST TO 4 MAR | | 1.34 | | 11.92 C |
| MAR 21 | 615633 | | 50.00 | | 38.08 D |
| MAR 23 | 615634 | | 8.67 | | |
| MAR 23 | 615636 | | 101.00 | | 147.75 D |
| MAR 28 | 615632 | | 45.00 | | |
| MAR 28 | 615642 | | 67.77 | | 260.52 D |
| MAR 29 | B.G. KELLAWAY | | | 293.22 | 32.70 C |
| MAR 30 | 615638 | | 30.60 | | 2.10 C |
| MAR 31 | BALANCE CARRIED FORWARD | | | | 2.10 C |

**Fig. 11.6** A bank statement

**(iv)** Bank statements can be misleading if the customer forgets that they do not take account of cheques which have not been cleared or amounts which have not yet been credited.

**(f) Other services**
**(i)** Keep valuables      **(ii)** Arranging for foreign exchange and travellers cheques
**(iii)** Loans      **(iv)** Mortgages
**(v)** Making a Will      **(vi)** Taxation advice

It should be remembered that professional advisers such as stockbrokers, solicitors and accountants will be able to provide a more specialized and comprehensive service in areas such as investment, taxation and legal advice.

## 11.2   Expenditure

### 11.2.1   Accounting for your money

Whether your are doing household or personal accounts, it is possible to make much better use of your money if you budget carefully. Budgeting is a form of planning and it can enable you to decide how much you can afford and when. To budget for the future, it is essential to start by assessing your income and your expenditure. Set out below are the five main categories into which household expenditure could be divided, with some examples.

**Table 11.3** Categories of expenditure

| Regular | Monthly | Quarterly | Annual | Large exceptional items |
|---|---|---|---|---|
| Bus fares/ | Rent/Mortgage | Telephone | Rates | Holidays |
| Travel costs | Food | Gas | TV licence | Gifts–birthdays |
| Meals at work | Insurance | Electricity | Car insurance | and Christmas |
| Pocket money | | | Motor tax | Repairs to car |
| | | | | Replacing household |
| | | | | equipment and |
| | | | | furniture |

The examples below show how these items may work out.

**A family with an annual income of £6500 Net**

| Income: | £ |
|---|---|
| Husband's employment (per year) | 6500 Net |
| Child benefit (per year) | 338 |
| | 6838 |
| **Expenditure:** | |
| Mortgage | 1500 |
| Rates | 350 |
| Insurance | 200 |
| Food | 2000 |
| Heating, lighting and cooking | 500 |
| Household maintenance | 300 |
| Travel | 275 |
| Clothing and footwear | 275 |
| Small household expenses | 300 |
| Entertainment | 250 |
| Holidays | 300 |
| Savings | 588 |
| | 6838 |

**A teenager living at home**

| Income per week | £ |
|---|---|
| from secretarial work | 60 |
| **Expenditure:** | |
| Food and lodging (to the family) | 20 |
| Lunches | 8 |
| Clothing and footwear | 5 |
| Toiletries and make-up | 2 |
| Entertainment | 12 |
| Sundries e.g. presents | 4 |
| Travel | 5 |
| Savings | 4 |
| | 60 |

**Keeping a list of expenditure** is a good idea. We are sometimes surprised by the actual sums we spend on items of low value. Goods and services which are paid for by cheque or credit card are fairly easy to keep track of, as the counterfoil or statement provides a record; but items paid for by cash can be easily forgotten. A list of expenditure also provides a good guide for expenditure in the future and budgets can best be drawn up based on past experience.

**Drawing up an annual budget for a household**

**1** Collect information on expenditure for the last year.
**2** Estimate how much more or less each of these bills is likely to be in the next year, e.g. the cost of electricity may be about to increase, or if you decide to change your job your travel costs may be less.
**3** List the new probable values so that you can assess the total expenditure for the year.
**4** List your income for next year.
**5** Compare income and expenditure. This will tell you how much money is available for:
**(a)** Exceptional items of personal choice, such as holidays.
**(b)** Unexpected items such as large essential repairs to equipment.

(c) Possible errors in estimating e.g. unforeseen rises in the price of an essential service such as gas prices.

The choice of how to spend money is a largely personal one and each household will place differing values on different items. The most important items for all households are **food, clothing** and **shelter** and **fuel costs**. The lower the family's income, the higher is the proportion they are likely to spend on these three items. Luxury goods and services can be bought only by people with high incomes who spend a lower proportion of their income on essentials.

**Housing expenditure** is the major item in any household's expenditure. This is made up of rent/mortgage, rates, house insurance and contents insurance. These are dealt with in detail in chapter 14.

### 11.2.2  Savings

Savings, like insurance, are another way of providing for the future. They enable you to weather **unforeseen expenses** as well as helping you to buy large items. There are many different ways of saving money—some of the main ones are shown in the table following.

**Table 11.4** Ways to save

| Method | Advantages | Disadvantages |
|---|---|---|
| **Building Societies** | 1 With the ordinary pass-book account the money is easy to withdraw. Ideal for short-term saving. | Society pays the tax due on the interest earned–lower rate. Not a good way of saving for non-taxpayers. |
| | 2 Several schemes which offer higher rates of interest in return for a guarantee that the money will remain in the account for a given period. It can be withdrawn with a period of notice, but interest is lost. | Few people find it easy to forecast their need for money up to 5 years in advance. |
| | 3 Monthly savings plans and SAYE schemes make saving easy. | |
| | 4 Cash cards are now available from some societies which operate in a similar way to those from Banks but interest continues to be paid on the balance. | |
| **Banks** | 1 Money paid into deposit accounts is relatively easy to withdraw. Suitable for short term saving. | Do not pay very high rates of interest and the rates vary. |
| | 2 Savings accounts are available, paying higher rates of interest, at some Banks. | |
| | 3 Some Banks will invest your money in stocks and shares. | |
| **Government/Post Office** | 1 SAYE interest is linked to inflation. Money relatively easy to withdraw. Good for regular, medium or long-term saving. | Money to be paid in cannot be altered easily. |
| | 2 Premium Bonds add 'sparkle' to saving with the chance of a big 'win'. | Earn no interest. |
| | 3 National Savings Certificates are index linked, easy to buy in small amounts when money is available. | Lose interest if cashed early. |
| | 4 National Savings Bank allows the saving of small amounts and money is easy to withdraw at any Post Office–hours of opening longer than Banks. | Interest paid varies |
| | 5 Income and Deposit Bonds are now available with special provisions e.g. for retired non-tax payers. | |
| **Endowment Policies** with insurance companies | Had tax advantages for tax payers until recently. Long term savings. | Suitable for regular saving only. Difficult to vary the amount and to withdraw. A lot of money is lost if they are cashed in. |
| **Employers saving schemes** e.g. holiday funds | Easy to pay in–deducted from pay direct. | No interest |
| **Christmas Clubs** | Spread the expense. Amount can vary. | No interest |
| **Piggy-bank** | Easily available when needed. | Too easy to take out? No interest. |

**Points to be considered**

1 The amount of money to be saved.
2 How often amounts of money are available for saving.
3 Is it necessary to be able to withdraw money at short notice?
4 Are you saving towards a special item such as a house? If so it may be wise to save with the Building Society you intend to ask for a mortgage.
5 How long do you wish the money to remain in the saving scheme?
6 Do you wish to have life insurance as well as saving money?

The advantages and disadvantages of the different means of saving are given in Table 11.4. Having considered points 1-6 the best scheme for the saver's money should be clear.

### 11.2.3 Credit

There are many different ways of **borrowing money** to buy goods and services but sometimes it is possible to avoid borrowing by careful money management or by careful budgeting. It is also possible to calculate the best time to pay out a large sum of money to avoid paying too much interest to the bank.

It is always important to make sure that you understand the **terms** on which the money is borrowed, e.g. the rate of interest; the length of time the money has been lent for; the amount to be repaid at any one time.

**Interest** is charged by most loan agencies. This is the **cost** of borrowing the money. Advertisements for credit must show the **APR** (annual percentage rate) for the loan. This takes account of:

1 The interest charged.
2 Any payment for compulsory premiums or maintenance payments.
3 The cost of lost cash discount.     4 Service charges.

**The APR** enables the purchaser to compare different loan offers. There will be advantages and disadvantages of borrowing money in different ways.

**The following points must be considered** before borrowing money.
1 Work out how much the item will *actually cost* on credit terms.
2 Think of the cheapest way of raising the money.
3 Consider when/how often/how much at a time/you wish to pay to repay the loan.
4 Under a certain age a **guarantor** may be required. To guarantee repayment.
5 How much you may borrow will depend upon:
(a) Your income.   (b) Your occupation and its security.
(c) Your financial standing e.g. are you known to be a good risk–pay your bills etc.
(d) Your other commitments e.g. family.     (e) Your age and health.

6 Table 11.5 shows the loan agencies available and their advantages and disadvantages. Consider these carefully.

**Table 11.5**   Methods of obtaining credit

| Loan agency | Advantages | Disadvantages |
| --- | --- | --- |
| **Bank** Overdraft | Simple and quick | May not be prepared to lend enough. Interest worked out daily; will increase bank charges. If limit exceeded other cheques may 'bounce'. |
| Personal Loan | Usually available for large sums. Often granted for home improvements etc. Usually for buying specific things. | May need to provide security e.g. an insurance policy. |
| Budget Account | See Bank Section 11.1.2. | |
| **Credit Cards** (See Table 11.2) | Available to anyone over 18 who is acceptable to the Credit Card Company. | Can be expensive if debt allowed to run up. |
| **Finance Company** | Can usually choose term of loan. Do not usually need security. | Tend to be expensive. |
| **Hire Purchase** | This is the term usually used by the person selling goods or services. It may be money which is borrowed from a Finance Company, not real Hire-Purchase. With a Hire Purchase agreement the goods are actually on hire until the *option to purchase* is paid after the payment of the instalments has finished. The government controls HP and credit schemes. | Goods may be re-possessed. Lenders can sometimes escape responsibility for faulty goods. The purchaser must be over 18 years old. |

| Loan agency | Advantages | Disadvantages |
|---|---|---|
| **Credit Sales** through suppliers | Shops arrange for payment by instalments. Purchaser owns the goods from the start. | |
| **Shop Account Cards** | *Monthly Accounts* Give credit for up to a month. Bill must be paid each month when a statement is sent. Easier than carrying cash. Only one payment need be made for a range of purchases. *Budget Accounts* Give credit. Interest usually charged on balance only. | These cards can only be used in that store. Shopping around to find the item cheaper is not possible. Interest rates may be high. |
| **Money Lenders and Credit Brokers** | Usually a last resort when all other sources fail. | Usually want to know a lot of personal details before money is lent. Rates of interest may be high. Security is required for high loans. |
| **Mail Order Catalogues** | Most offer credit terms to those over 18 years. The Agent calls to collect the money which makes it convenient to pay. Agents get commission even on their own purchases, so prices are affected. | More expensive than most other forms of credit. Cannot examine goods before purchase. |

### Advantages of paying cash

**Cash is** the simplest form of payment.
1 Goods become the property of the purchaser immediately.
2 There are no 'hidden extras' e.g. service charges and interest.
3 Worry is eliminated.     4 Saving in advance encourages sensible budgeting.
5 Discounts are sometimes available for cash payment.
6 'Shopping around' to get the goods at the cheapest price is possible.

# 12   Consumer studies

### Introduction

In the last twenty years there has been a great interest in all matters concerned with the consumer, and consumer studies has become an identifiable and important area of study. All people are **consumers**; we consume items such as food, clothing and shelter which are fundamental to our existence and also non-essential items over which we can exercise more choice. Even in Medieval times the need to protect consumers from unscrupulous tradesmen and manufacturers was well recognized. As early as 1266 standards were officially set for the sale of bread and ale–two important products. The weight of bread was fixed in relation to its price so that customers were absolutely sure how much bread they could buy for a fixed price and how strong their ale would be! Failure to comply with these standards would result in the offenders being placed in the stocks enabling dissatisfied customers to ridicule them or throw rotten food at them. Consumers buy both **goods** and **services**.

**Goods** are any form of merchandise or wares such as furniture, food, clothing, housing etc.

**Services** are work performed by the seller on behalf of the buyer. They may result in something which is very obvious to the buyer, such as a new haircut, or they may be much less conspicuous, perhaps having the central heating boiler serviced. Many of the contracts which we enter into as consumers are in fact contracts for services and they are contracts in just the same way as those for goods.

### 12.1   Shopping

Retailing began as an activity in the fourteenth century when the first shopkeepers and merchants started to appear in the market towns. This also extended the need for money as a form of exchange. Prior to this many goods were paid for in 'kind' and relatively little money changed hands. By 1500 shopkeeping had become a very important occupation in Britain and shops were beginning to specialize in different types of articles e.g. haberdashers who sold such things as trims, lace, pins and needles.

Prior to the eighteenth century shopkeepers often did not display their wares but waited for customers to ask for them. Shops were unlit and it was very difficult for purchasers to know what they were buying. During the eighteenth century bow windows become common and shopkeepers started to display their goods so that potential customers could see into the shop from outside. Prices were still fixed by **barter** and goods accordingly not priced. Usually credit was extended to the customer who paid at a later date. The first shop to insist that goods were immediately paid for in cash was probably a haberdashery shop situated on London Bridge in the mid-eighteenth century.

Bon Marché, which opened in Paris in 1872, is usually regarded as being the first department store, although Kendal Milne and Faulkner, of Manchester, founded in 1836, was probably already operating on the same trading principles which made Bon Marché famous. Department stores are still a common and important feature of our High Streets enabling people to buy many different items under one roof. The late nineteenth century also saw the development of multiple and chain stores. Many of these stores sold food, such as Liptons, but some specialized in other areas, such as Boots, the chemist.

### Shopping–making choices

**Shopping is essentially a matter of making decisions.** By making a decision we deny ourselves the right to **spend the money another way.** Very few of us have an infinite amount of money, so the decisions which we make about how to spend our money are very important.

**Spending** usually falls into three main categories
 1 Regular daily spending such as food.
 2 Regular bills such as the rent, rates, mortgage, gas and electricity bills which occur regularly but at longer intervals such as monthly or three-monthly.
 3 Occasional large bills, perhaps for buying new items such as cookers or washing machines, new cars or holidays.
Each item or service which we buy demands a similar basic decision-making process.

| **WHAT** DO I WANT? | → | **WHICH** ONE DO I WANT? | → | **WHERE** SHALL I BUY IT? |

At each stage in this decision-making process choices have to be made.

**What do I want?** I may want something which is basic to life, for instance food or clothing, or I may want something which is not essential but desirable such as a new pair of ice skates or an oil painting. Before buying anything it is essential to carefully **define the problem to be solved and to assess what is required.**

Secondly, it is necessary to **work out how much money is available** and how the goods or services are to be paid for, e.g. by credit or cash. This may well influence what is bought and where it is bought.

Thirdly, consider carefully all **the different ways in which this particular problem may be solved.** For instance there are many different ways of cleaning a carpet; it may be beaten with a carpet switch, brushed by hand, swept with a carpet sweeper or vacuumed with several different kinds of vacuum cleaner. It may well be worthwhile to make a list of the alternatives and work your way though them. When you have chosen the alternative which is most suitable for your needs it is then possible to move on to phase two of the decision-making process.

**Which one do I want?**–the second phase is essentially the time when sources of information become important to the consumer. He now knows what he wishes to buy but not which one.

 1 List the main requirements e.g. price, quality etc.; criteria for choice might be:

| | |
|---|---|
| **(a)** Price | **(f)** Length of guarantee |
| **(b)** Quality | **(g)** Servicing |
| **(c)** Size | **(h)** Design features |
| **(d)** Weight | **(i)** Colour |
| **(e)** Type | **(j)** Availability |

List these features in order of importance.
 2 Refer to all suitable sources of consumer advice e.g. *Which* etc.
 3 List suitable products.
 4 Choose the most satisfactory product in line with requirements.

**Where shall I buy it?**–the third phase.
 1 Find out where the required item may be bought. List.
 2 Note important features in relation to each supplier. These may include:

| | |
|---|---|
| **(a)** Cost of item | **(e)** Credit facilities |
| **(b)** Availability | **(f)** Fitting charges |
| **(c)** Delivery | **(g)** After-sales service |
| **(d)** Ordering time | **(h)** Shop accessibility. etc. |

**3** Choose supplier. This may not actually be the supplier with the lowest price; it will depend upon all the other considerations.

**Table 12.1** To show the advantages of different types of shopping places

| | Mail order | Product parties at home e.g. Tupper-ware Parties | Doorstep salesmen | Book and record clubs | Kiosks | Vending machines | Mobile shops | Street barrows | Markets | Farm shops |
|---|---|---|---|---|---|---|---|---|---|---|
| Self-service | | | | | | ✓ | | | | |
| Personal service | | | | | ✓ | | ✓ | ✓ | ✓ | ✓ |
| Unrestricted hours | ✓ | ✓ | ✓ | ✓ | | ✓ | | | | ✓ |
| Late opening hours | | | | | ✓ | | | | | |
| Shop at home | ✓ | ✓ | ✓ | ✓ | | | ✓ | | | |
| Easily accessible | ✓ | ✓ | ✓ | ✓ | ✓ | ✓ | ✓ | ✓ | ✓ | |
| Car parking | | | | | | | | | Can be | ✓ |
| Pleasant shopping environment (including facilities such as restaurants, toilets etc) | | ✓ | | | | | | | | |
| Wide variety of goods | | | | | | | | | ✓ | |
| Able to bulk-buy | | | | | | | | | | |
| Relatively cheap | | | Can be | Usually | | | | ✓ | ✓ | ✓ |
| High status | | | | | | | | | | |
| Credit available | ✓ | ✓ | ✓ | ✓ | | | | | | |
| Delivery service | ✓ | ✓ | ✓ | ✓ | | | ✓ | | | |
| Goods can be ordered | ✓ | ✓ | ✓ | ✓ | | | ✓ | | | |
| Special trained personnel | | | Can be | | | | Can be | | Can be | ✓ |
| After-sales service | | | | | | | | | | |
| Goods easy to examine | | ✓ | ✓ | | ✓ | | ✓ | ✓ | ✓ | ✓ |
| Available/Found in rural areas | ✓ | ✓ | ✓ | ✓ | Can be | ✓ | ✓ | | ✓ | ✓ |
| Available/Found in urban areas | ✓ | ✓ | ✓ | ✓ | ✓ | ✓ | ✓ | ✓ | ✓ | |
| Available/Found in rural and urban areas | ✓ | ✓ | ✓ | ✓ | | ✓ | ✓ | | ✓ | |
| Own brands available | | Often only one | | | | | | | | |
| Choice of styles | Limited | Limited | Limited | | | | Limited | | | |
| Choice of qualities | Limited | Limited | Limited | | | | Limited | | | |
| Choice of prices | Limited | Limited | Limited | | | | Limited | | | |

*In particular field

### Places to shop

There are many different places to shop, ranging from kiosks and street markets to giant Hyper-markets. Each type has certain advantages and disadvantages and it is necessary for the consumer to choose the type which most accurately satisfies his or her needs. Clearly, something like self-service may appear as an advantage to one consumer and a disadvantage to another. Table 12.1 evaluates some of the advantages of one method of shopping over another.

**Shopping precincts** are now to be found in many towns. These are traffic-free shopping areas where people can shop without continually crossing busy roads. Most of the newer ones have plenty of parking facilities; this is important as people need to be able to carry their purchases to the car with ease. They often have a very wide range of shops in them making it unnecessary for the shopper to go elsewhere. You can probably think of examples of such shopping precincts near your home.

**Price** is affected by **turnover**. Shops which have a high turnover are usually able to bulk-buy and tend to pass these advantages on to their consumers and keep prices down, e.g. John Lewis Partnership shops or large supermarket chains such as Sainsburys or Tesco. John Lewis' low stock policy enables it to maintain its 'never knowingly undersold' policy.

The other outlets which are able to keep their prices down are those with **low overheads** (e.g. rent, rates etc.) such as Farm Shops, barrows or market stall-holders. Price is still the main criterion which most consumers use in their decision-making.

### 12.2    Consumer information

There are many different ways in which consumers gather information, but the most important sources are those which are reliable. Inaccurate information can lead to poor decision-making. Table 12.2 shows where consumers can gather information and its likely degree of reliability.

(See Chapter 11 on Money Management for different ways of paying for goods and services.)

| Co-operative | Chain stores | Department stores | Independent shops symbol group traders e.g. Wavyline or Spar | Independent shops | 'Corner' shops | Super-markets | Hyper-markets | Specialist shops | Discount warehouses | Frozen food centres |
|---|---|---|---|---|---|---|---|---|---|---|
| May be either | √ | Either | Either | Either | Either | √ | √ |  | √ | √ |
|  |  |  |  |  |  |  |  | √ |  |  |
| Often | Some | √ | √ |  | √ | √ | √ |  | √ | √ |
| √ | √ | √ | √ | √ | √ | √ | √ |  | √ | √ |
| Often | Some | Often |  |  |  | √ | √ |  | √ | √ |
|  |  |  | √ |  |  |  |  |  |  |  |
| Some | Some | √ |  |  |  | √ | √ | *√ | Some | *√ |
| Some |  |  |  |  |  | √ | √ |  | Some | √ |
| √ | √ | √ |  |  |  | √ | √ |  | √ | √ |
|  |  |  |  |  |  |  |  | Sometimes |  |  |
| Some | Some | √ | Sometimes |  |  |  |  | Often | √ | Sometimes |
|  | √ |  |  | Sometimes |  |  |  |  | Some |  |
| Some |  | √ | Some |  |  |  |  | √ | Some |  |
| Some | Some | √ |  | Some | Some |  |  | √ | Some |  |
| Some |  | √ | √ |  |  |  | √ | √ | Some |  |
| √ | √ | √ | √ | √ | √ | √ |  | √ |  | √ |
| √ | √ |  | √ | √ | √ | Few | *√ | √ |  |  |
| √ | √ | √ | √ | √ | √ |  |  | √ | √ | √ |
| √ | √ |  | √ | √ | √ |  |  | √ |  |  |
| √ | √ | √ | √ |  |  | √ | √ | Sometimes |  | √ |
| √ | √ | √ | Limited | Limited | Limited |  | √ | √ | Limited |  |
| √ | √ | √ | Limited | Limited | Limited | √ | √ | √ | Limited | √ |
| √ | √ | √ | Limited | Limited | Limited | √ | √ | √ | Limited | √ |

**Table 12.2** Sources of consumer information

| Source | Information supplied | Reliability |
|---|---|---|
| **Magazines** | Some have their own testing departments e.g. Good Housekeeping.<br>Other publications take less care. | Highly reliable<br>? |
| **Newspapers** | No testing departments, reputable papers try to ensure accurate information and sometimes employ specialists to write for them. | ? |
| **Advertisements** | Make consumers aware of new products but devised to make people buy, so reflect the best possible view.<br>By law they must be 'decent, legal, and honest'. See the section on Law and the consumer. | ? |
| **Radio and television** | Often employ specialists in the consumer field for programmes such as Checkpoint. | Reliable |
| **Manufacturers** | Includes technical detail.<br>Many firms have Consumer Service Departments. | Reliable |
| **Which?** | Produced by the Consumers Association, provides accurate, independent information. Studies are comparative and help in the choice between brands. | Reliable |
| **Shops and suppliers** | Many offer consumer advice. | |
| **Design Centre** | See section on Labelling. | |
| **Government research centres** | Most offer free advice e.g. Building Research Centre | Reliable |

| Source | Information supplied | Reliability |
|---|---|---|
| **Citizens Advice Bureau** | Limited information, but help consumers with consumer complaints. | Reliable |
| **Consumer Advice Centres** | Paid for and run by Local Authorities in the main. Found in main shopping areas. Specially trained full-time staff. 3 types of service; pre-shopping, information and consumer complaints. | Reliable |
| **Local Authorities** | Some advice through departments such as Environmental Health. | Reliable |
| **Office of Fair Trading** | General information particularly on legal rights. | Reliable |
| **Relatives, neighbours and friends** | Useful informal consumer advice. | May not always be accurate |

## 12.3  Labels

Labels are intended to help the consumer by drawing his attention to things of importance, such as size or safety features.

**Fig. 12.1** The Kitemark    **Fig. 12.2** BEAB Symbol    **Fig. 12.3** Design Council Symbol    **Fig. 12.4** Safety Mark    **Fig. 12.5** British Gas Seal of Approval

**Kitemark labels** as shown in Fig. 12.1 appear on goods which are approved as complying with British Standard requirements as laid down by the British Standards Institute. BSI is financed by the Government and is non-profit making. A British Standard may include any or all of the following: Glossaries; dimensional specifications; performance requirements including safety; standard methods of test. BSI also produces Codes of Practice.

**British Electrotechnical Approvals Board** (BEAB) carries out tests on all electrical household goods. The presence of the label indicates that the appliance has no exposed 'live' parts. Electricity Board showrooms only stock items which are BEAB approved. The label is composed of a modified kitemark.

**Design Council Symbol** labels are borne on items which have been chosen for inclusion in the Design Index. The Design Council is government-sponsored and aims to promote good design in British industry. Products carrying the label must not simply be well designed but also be 'fit' for the purpose intended, of good quality, good value and easy to maintain.

**Safety Mark** label is found on goods which comply with BSI safety standards. It appears on items such as lighting fitments and fires.

**British Gas Seal of Approval** label means that the gas appliance has passed British Gas Standards for performance and reliability.

**Home Launderers Consultative Committee** labelling—see Chapter 15.

### Labelling food

Much of the food which we buy now is pre-packed, often in packs which make it difficult or impossible for us to see the contents. It is therefore very important that foods should be well and accurately labelled. *The Labelling of Foods Regulations 1970* assist the consumer by:

1 Ensuring that the products have a name which consumers will understand e.g. 'Marvel' would not be adequate; it is also described as 'low fat pure dried skimmed milk' so that consumers know what they are buying. Only products which have been known by a brand name for thirty years before 1st January 1971, e.g. Oxo, are exempt from this requirement.

2 The name and address of the organization responsible for the product must appear on the label.

3 The ingredients including additives must be listed in order of quantity. Any specific claims printed on the label e.g. that it helps people lose weight, must be qualified, for instance 'when used as part of a calorie-controlled diet'.

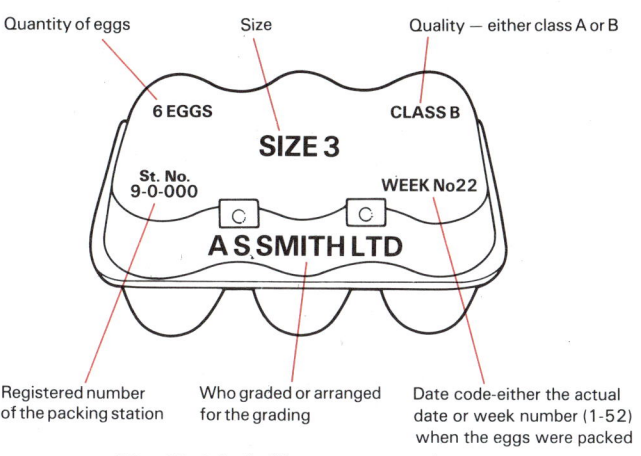

**Fig. 12.6** Labelling on an egg box

**4** *The Weights and Measures Act 1963* requires that products sold by length, weight, number or volume must clearly state the information on the packet.
(See also the table of Acts and Regulations in the Consumer and the Law section, in particular the Trade Descriptions Act, page 158.)

**Eggs** British eggs have been classified according to EEC regulations since 1973. Figure 12.6 shows how the information is displayed on egg boxes.

**Milk** Milk is labelled under the *Milk Cap Colour Regulations 1973*. Details are given in Section 4.1.4.

## 12.4 Advertising

Advertising is very important to both manufacturers, suppliers and consumers. Even good products rarely sell without effective advertising. Markets are made up of many consumers, most of whom may not be in the market for a particular product. The group who are likely to be in the market for a product are known as the **target group**. It is this group which the advertiser will try to convince of the value of their item/s.

### The benefits of advertising

The supplier and manufacturer can clearly benefit from advertising by increasing sales and therefore profits. It also provides a way of informing the consumer, perhaps to alert him to new or improved products. Many advertisers also try to help the consumer to weigh-up products by showing prospective buyers which criteria of choice are likely to be the most important.

From the consumer's point of view advertising can be useful. In many publications, such as magazines and newspapers, the advertising revenues help to hold down the price. Many advertisers do provide valuable information. Some advertising campaigns enable customers to try free samples or special offers of products to see whether or not they like them.

### The disadvantages of advertising

Advertisers cannot 'create' need but heighten awareness of products which consumers **may not need**. They may successfully appeal to a particular group of people suggesting, for example, that 'in order to be happy they need a certain product'. Clearly this can cause certain individuals distress, especially if the product either does not fulfil its image or is financially beyond their means. The advertising media reach right into the home and **children** and **the young** are frequently **target groups**. Many of the advertising codes of practice try to safeguard such vulnerable groups, e.g. in connection with cigarette and alcohol advertisements.

Advertisers do not necessarily advertise good products, so advertising campaigns may encourage consumers to buy the **less good products** in a particular range.

Finally, unscrupulous advertisers can use campaigns to imply meanings which can no longer be found true. We know that advertising messages do not necessarily come across to the consumer as advertisers intend. People can twist them into personal meanings which fit in with their own views. Unscrupulous advertisers can exploit this to their own advantage.

### Advertising media

Advertisers use many different media, including television which is a relatively expensive form, and magazines and newspapers which are a relatively cheap form. Cinemas and theatres also carry advertising material and there are many other means e.g. carrier bags, packaging, labels, the sides of vans and posters.

**To promote a product or service successfully** adverts need to have some or all of the following elements.
   **1** A short memorable slogan   **2** A catchy tune

3 A memorable image

4 Give information which may be factual, scientific or technical

5 Have a well recognized personality associated with them, e.g. Terry Wogan.

6 Relate easily to peoples' lifestyles, e.g. many of us see ourselves 'hurrying' through a bowl of cornflakes in the morning

7 Create the image of a lifestyle which we dream about, e.g. Milk Tray adverts

8 Be regularly repeated so that we learn them

9 Be novel or different

10 Be humorous

11 Be easily understood and the message quickly received

### Protecting the consumer

**Statutory Control:** Advertising is subject to control through many different Acts of Parliament, perhaps the most important being the Trade Descriptions Act, Race Relations Act, Consumer Credit Act and the Fair Trading Act.

**Voluntary Controls:** The British Code of Advertising Practice which is administered by the Advertising Standards Authority. This code states 'all advertising should be legal, decent, honest and truthful in both the letter and the spirit of the code'. The Authority will look into any complaints made by the public; complaints which are upheld will require advertisers to amend or withdraw offending advertisements.

Adverts which appear on independent television or local radio are vetted by the Independent Broadcasting Authority's Advertising Control Office before being accepted for broadcasting.

### 12.5   Organizations which aim to protect the consumer

There are three different groups of organizations which aim to protect the consumer:

1 Government Departments and Agencies.

2 Local Government Departments and Agencies.

3 Voluntary and Independent Organizations.

Table 12.3 analyses the type of organization, its functions and importance to the consumer.

**Table 12.3**   Organizations aiming to protect the consumer

| Organization | Function/s |
|---|---|
| **1 Government Departments and Agencies** | |
| Consumer affairs division of Department of Trade | Harmonizes with EEC over consumer laws and regulations. Gives grants to consumer bodies, e.g. National Consumer Council. Monitors prices and trading practices and competition policy. Responsible for consumer safety and advice. Concerned with weights and measures. |
| Ministry of Agriculture, Fisheries and Foods | All matters in relation to food, e.g. hygiene and price. |
| Department of the Environment | Concerned with all environmental matters such as the preservation of the landscape or buildings. |
| Department of Energy | Concerned with the way in which fuel such as electricity, coal and gas are supplied to the consumer. |
| Department of Trade | In addition to the Division of Consumer Affairs, this Department also regulates airlines, airports and the tourist and insurance industries. |
| Office of Fair Trading | Set up by the Fair Trading Act 1973 with wide responsibilities to protect the consumer (see outline of Fair Trading Act). The Director-General of the Office of Fair Trading has power to: 1 Publish consumer information. 2 Publish codes of practice in association with Trade Associations. 3 Seek out and prosecute traders who fail to fulfil their obligations to the consumer. 4 Stop unfair trading practices and instigate new regulations. |
| National Consumer Council | Established in 1975 by the Government. Deals with consumer matters at a national level offering advice to official bodies. It does not deal with individual complaints. Publishes reports and other information. |
| British Standards Institute | Sponsored partly by Government money and partly by industry and sales of publications. Sets standards for products. Any product which conforms to a British Standard may use the Standard number. Companies whose products comply with a standard and apply for a licence may use the kitemark. |
| Parliamentary and Health Service Commissioner (The Ombudsman) | Investigates complaints against Central Government Departments and the National Health Service. |

| Organization | Function/s |
|---|---|
| Commissioners for Local Administration (Local Government Ombudsman) | Investigates consumer complaints caused by the maladministration of the police, local authorities and the water authorities. |

**2 Local Government Departments and Agencies**

| Organization | Function/s |
|---|---|
| Environmental Health Department | Concerned with regulations in respect of food and pollution, housing conditions, all matters of public health and matters concerning the abattoirs. |
| Trading Standards Department | Concerned with weights and measures, safety, the Trade Descriptions Act and the Consumer Credit Act. In addition they can deal with a wide range of consumer complaints. |
| Consumer Advice Centres | Funded by the Local Authorities and mostly existing in prominent positions in High Streets so that they are easily available to shoppers. Some centres also operate mobile vans, e.g. Lambeth. They deal initially with a wide range of consumer problems as well as spreading information and providing pre-shopping advice. |

**3 Voluntary and Independent Organizations**

| Organization | Function/s |
|---|---|
| Consumers' Association | Financed almost entirely by its publication sales. Publishers of magazine *Which?* |
| National Federation of Consumer Groups | A national co-ordinating committee for local consumer groups which are independent and voluntary. Will offer advice on how to start a local group. |

## 12.6   The consumer and the law

Why has the Government recently started to take so many measures to protect the consumer?

**1** Changing social attitudes have led to the belief that the consumer should be protected from unscrupulous suppliers of goods and services.
**2** The increasing complexity of goods and services may well mean that consumers do not understand the products which they are buying, e.g. the properties of new man-made fibres used for carpets.
**3** The sophisticated new business methods which are used to sell goods and services which may unduly influence the purchaser, e.g. high-pressure selling techniques.
**4** An increasing use of advertising to encourage people to buy.
**5** A change in society from collectivism to individualism, with the protection of the individual being seen by Governments as an important area for legislation.
**6** As a result of Britain's joining the EEC. One of the requirements of the EEC is the necessity for all member countries to have similar laws. Until recently Britain was behind most other members in terms of consumer legislation.

Consumer law as a special body of law does not exist; consumer protection may be part of either **civil** law or **criminal** law, depending upon the problem. Some problems fall into both categories and civil and criminal law both apply.

**Civil law** is concerned with disputes between individuals. Civil actions which are brought by individuals tend to take longer to pass through the courts than criminal actions. Successful action may result in the payment of damages to the people who have been wronged.

**Criminal law** applies where the community as a whole feels that the matter at issue is of such importance that the public as a whole should be protected.

Consumers who have justifiable complaints expect that the law will protect them and that something will be done to make up for the problems which they have had. This is known as the **legal remedy** and these remedies vary according to whether they are available through civil or criminal law. The remedies through criminal law are some form of punishment such as fines or imprisonment, whereas through civil law remedies aim to redress the wrong and make good the loss, such as by awarding damages.

### The civil law and the consumer

A **contract** is an agreement which is **legally enforceable**. On most occasions when a consumer buys anything he enters into a legal contract. Most people over 18 years can make a contract which would be upheld by the courts. Those under 18 years can be bound only by contracts for essential items like food or clothing. You will have noticed that in many magazines there are advertisements which specifically say that people under eighteen must ask a parent or guardian to sign the form before the company will be able to make a contract with the individual for goods or services. **Minors** (those under eighteen) often find it very difficult to enter into hire-purchase agreements or agreements to obtain any kind of credit.

**What is a legal contract?**   The basic idea behind a contract is that of a bargain. In other words we do not get something for nothing. A contract includes **three** important elements. All three elements must be present for a contract to be made.

**1 An offer** is generally made by the person buying the goods or services. He may say, 'I'll give you £10 for that table'. The acceptance of the offer means that the buyer is now legally required to pay for the goods or services in cash. In practice many traders are happy to receive payment in other forms such as cheques or credit cards.

**2 Acceptance** takes place when the seller accepts the buyer's offer. It may take place verbally or simply by action or gesture.

**3 Consideration** is usually the price paid for the goods or services. In the case of the table it will be £10. It need not necessarily be money but it must be something which is capable of being valued in terms of money however, for instance a peppercorn. It is not necessary that the price should be adequate; it is up to the parties (the buyer and the seller) to fix their own prices. The price might be set aside, however, if a court had evidence that coercion or misrepresentation had taken place.

**Invitation to treat** is another legal phrase which is of importance to the shopper. This is an **invitation** to the shopper to buy goods. It is not an offer. Price-marked goods in a shop window constitute an 'invitation to treat'; you have no legal right to demand that the shopkeeper sells you the actual goods on display or that he offers them to you at the marked price. If the goods have been marked at the wrong price the shopkeeper is probably within his rights to refuse to sell them to you at the marked price, although he may be committing an offence under the *Trade Descriptions Act, 1968.*

**Guarantees** Under the *Sale of Goods Act* the conditions of 'merchantable quality' and 'fitness' are implied as between the **buyer and seller**. Many people are under the wrong impression that the contract is between the manufacturer and the buyer; this is not usually the case. This state of affairs has probably arisen in part as a result of the way in which most manufacturers offer guarantees for their products. They are not obliged by law to do this but they do so to persuade customers to buy their goods.

### So who is liable for faulty goods?

1 The supplier is liable under the *Sale of Goods Act.*

2 The manufacturer may be liable under his own guarantee.

3 The manufacturer may be liable in negligence if the goods are unsafe and cause injury to person/s or property.

### Manufacturers' guarantees

Most manufacturers offer 'guarantees' agreeing to replace defective parts within a particular time period. Guarantees give the purchaser rights in addition to those under the *Sale of Goods Act*. It is not possible for guarantees to have exclusion clauses in the small print which limit a customer's statutory rights.

### Important points to remember about guarantees

1 Some guarantees expect you to pay labour charges when replacement parts are fitted.

2 Some manufacturers will not pay for faulty parts made by another firm.

3 Some manufacturers require the cost of transport or postage to be paid by the purchaser. Guarantees as above may mean that it is better to claim redress from the supplier than from the manufacturer.

Manufacturers' guarantees are particularly useful when:

(a) You actually want the article repaired rather than your money back.

(b) The original supplier has gone out of business.

(c) The supplier cannot be found.     (d) The goods were a gift.

(e) Consumers do not wish to engage in litigation.

Manufacturers' guarantees also safeguard the rights of the manufacturer:

(a) It is necessary to claim within the guarantee period.

(b) The goods must have been defective at the time of purchase or within the guarantee period.

(c) Purchasers should not attempt to modify the product or allow unauthorized persons to attempt to repair it.

### Buying goods by Mail Order

Trading via mail order catalogues is a large and expanding business. Recently the Mail Order Traders' Association have initiated a Code of Practice to safeguard consumers. This complements the Mail Order Publishers' Authority Code which specifically relates to the supply of books and records. Both codes have been approved by the Office of Fair Trading.

**Remedies are** available to mail order customers through civil action for failure to deliver, or goods which are received in an unfit state. Many mail order companies send goods on fourteen days approval, so goods which turn out to be unsuitable can be returned to the company. Schemes are also run by the Newspaper Publishers' Association and the Periodical Publishers' Association who ensure that mail order advertisers are vetted and there are central funds to cover consumer refunds which cannot be made by the respective company.

**Consumer legislation**

Table 12.4 briefly analyses Acts which are of importance to the consumer:

| Act | Relevance for the consumer |
| --- | --- |
| **Sale of Goods Act 1893**<br>This Act was amended by the Supply of Goods (Implied Terms) Act 1973. Both these Acts were subsumed in the Consolidation Act, **Sale of Goods Act 1979.** | This act was drafted before the boom in consumer legislation and this is reflected in the view the Act takes of the relationship between the parties. The seller and consumer are seen to have equal bargaining strength whereas more recent legislation has recognized the necessity to protect consumers from unscrupulous sellers. One of the most important principles of the original act was *'caveat emptor'* (let the buyer beware); this has been considerably eroded since 1893 but may still occur in some places. If the seller sells in the course of business the Act will protect the consumer. However, if the seller is a private seller, *'caveat emptor'* may still apply.<br>The Sale of Goods Act lays down two important conditions. Goods must be 'fit' for the purpose for which they are intended and of 'merchantable quality'. There are **two** main **exceptions** to the conditions concerning merchantable quality; firstly, where the defects have been drawn to the buyer's attention before the contract is made; and secondly, if the buyer examines the goods carefully before purchase and fails to notice defects which the examination should have revealed. |
| **Misrepresentation Act 1967** | A **misrepresentation** is a statement made before the contract is made which persuades the party to enter into the contract. It is sometimes difficult to distinguish misrepresentation from a 'mere puff', which is simply the praising of goods by a potential supplier and is very common in advertisements. There are **three types** of misrepresentation and the remedy which the buyer seeks depends upon the type. Fraudulent misrepresentation; negligent misrepresentation and innocent misrepresentation. |
| **Unsolicited Goods and Services Act 1971** | This Act was introduced into Parliament as a result of some salesmen trying to boost their sales by demanding payment for unsolicited goods. If the following conditions apply, anyone in receipt of unsolicited goods may treat the goods as an unconditional gift:<br>1 If the goods were sent without prior request.<br>2 If they were sent with a view to the receiver acquiring them.<br>3 If they were not sent with a view to their being acquired for trade or business.<br>4 Providing the consumer has agreed neither to acquire the goods nor to return them.<br>5 Providing that the time period has been observed:<br>(a) Goods must be retained by the recipient for six months during which time the sender may collect them.<br>(b) The sender does not collect the goods within thirty days of having been served a written notice telling him that the goods were unsolicited and giving the address for collection. |
| **Fair Trading Act 1973** | This Act consolidated previous Acts in relation to the law concerning competition. It is also new in that it set up the Office of Fair Trading. The Office is concerned with: consumers' economic interests, consumer safety and consumer health. The Director's powers include: publishing information and advice for consumers; encouraging and assisting Trade Organizations in the development of codes of practice; powers to refer cases for investigation by the Monopolies and Mergers Commission and by the Restrictive Practices Court, and the ability to initiate subordinate legislation to protect consumers by banning undesirable trade practices. |
| **Consumer Credit Act 1974** | This Act controls both business activity and individual agreements:<br>1 It requires that all organizations offering loans or advice about loans be **licensed** by the Director of Fair Trading. This includes such people as finance companies and accountants.<br>2 It requires that credit **cannot be refused** to any person on the grounds of **race** or **sex**.<br>3 It ensures that consumers are told the **true price** of goods bought on credit, the true rate of interest over a year, the total amount of the interest payments and the period of time over which payment is required.<br>4 It enables anyone who feels that wrongful information is held on them on a credit reference file to check the file for a small fee. This enables people to correct any untrue statements which might prevent them from receiving credit. |
| **Unfair Contract Terms Act 1977** | This Act does not create new duties but it controls clauses which would otherwise exclude or restrict liability. The Act was necessary as many suppliers tried to avoid their legal responsibilities. Many shops displayed such notices and they were often to be found in brochures on pages of conditions of sale.<br>Under the Act:<br>1 Liability for death or personal injury which results from negligence cannot be excluded or restricted by any notice or agreement.<br>2 Exclusion clauses can be included only if they are considered reasonable.<br>3 If exclusion clauses are not reasonable, firms are liable for loss or damage resulting from negligence. |

| Act | Relevance for the consumer |
|---|---|
| **Food and Drugs Act 1955** | This Act requires food to be wholesome and fit to eat. It must also be of the 'nature, quality and substance demanded'.<br>(This Act is reinforced by a wide number of regulations, e.g. those which require certain foods such as sausages to have certain compositional requirements.)<br>*Food Hygiene Regulations, 1968.* Require that food should be manufactured and sold in clean and hygienic conditions.<br>*Labelling of Food Regulations, 1970.* All products are required to have a name which explains what it is, e.g. Marvel is low-fat, pure, dried, skimmed milk. The only products which are exempt from this rule are those which were in existence as a brand name for thirty years before 1 January 1971, e.g. Marmite, Ovaltine. All product labels must include the name and address of the organization which is responsible for them. All ingredients, including additives, must be listed in order of quantity. Specific claims, e.g. slimming aids, must be qualified. |
| **Weights and Measures Act 1963** | Any product which is sold by length, weight, number or volume must be clearly marked with such information on the packet. Certain products, e.g. tea, should be packed in prescribed quantities to make it easier for shoppers to compare different brands and prices. |
| **Trade Descriptions Act 1968** | This Act requires that oral, written or visual descriptions of products or services shall not be misleading either 'recklessly' or 'to a material degree'. |
| **Trade Descriptions Act 1972** | This Act requires that imported goods with a reasonably visible British name or mark must also bear an indication of their country of origin. This is to prevent consumers being misled. |
| **Consumer Protection Acts 1961/1971** | These Acts require that all products must be safe. There are many different sets of regulations which cover particular groups of products such as toys and nightdresses. These regulations contain specific standards for the products and have now been incorporated under the Consumer Safety Act, 1978. This Act was necessary as there were so many loopholes under the existing law. |
| **Consumer Safety Act 1978** | This incorporates regulations from the above Acts. It requires all products to be safe and enables quick action to be taken if any products are found to be unsafe. The Secretary of State may issue 'prohibition orders' or 'notices' to ban dangerous goods. Manufacturers and suppliers can be obliged to publish notices to warn the public, where unsafe goods are found to have been sold. |

# 13   Home management

## 13.1   Cleaning the dwelling

Clean, tidy and well organized homes are nicer to live in than dirty, disorganized ones. Achieving a well maintained household is not simply a matter of spending a large amount of time and energy working at it, but also involves devising a **suitable system** which organizes both human energy and other resources to the best advantage.

A clean home where cleanliness is at such a premium that the individuals who live there are unable to undertake any tasks which might threaten order can be a very unhappy place to live in. Equally, dirt and disorganization can be both health hazards and make the family unhappy.

The aim of all **cleaning routines** is to **strike a balance** between the amount of time and energy which needs to be put into the work, the cost of labour saving devices and cleaning materials and the needs of the home's inhabitants.

Table 13.1 itemizes the kind of jobs which need to be undertaken to keep a home clean and tidy. In addition it suggests the frequency with which the tasks should be undertaken. Clearly different families have different needs and the amount of maintenance work which is necessary will depend upon such factors as the number of people in the household, their ages and capacities (i.e. are they handicapped or sick?).

**Table 13.1** Check list for cleaning

| | Daily tasks | Weekly/Fortnightly tasks | Periodic tasks |
|---|---|---|---|
| **Indoor cleaning** | Washing-up<br>Bed-making<br>Removal of rubbish<br>Tidying | Defrost and clean fridge<br>Thoroughly clean cooker<br>Thoroughly clean floors<br>Clean kitchen | Check condition of electrical equipment<br>De-frost freezer<br>Clean out cupboards |

| | *Daily tasks* | *Weekly/Fortnightly tasks* | *Periodic tasks* |
|---|---|---|---|
| | Cleaning lavatory, basins, shower, bath<br>Cleaning kitchen sink<br>Dusting<br>Air rooms<br>Wipe work surfaces and tables in kitchen<br>Vacuum floors<br>Clean equipment as used<br>Wipe cooker<br>Any task from columns 2 and 3 as appropriate | Clean bathroom<br>Do washing, ironing and airing<br>Do shopping<br>Change bedroom linens<br>Change bathroom linens<br>Thoroughly clean living rooms including moving the furniture for vacuuming, wiping the skirting boards, sweeping the ceilings, brushing the lampshades, polishing the furniture, vacuuming the upholstery, wiping mantlepieces and window sills<br>Clean windows<br>Turn and air mattresses | Wash shelves and re-line drawers and shelves with paper<br>Wash walls and paintwork<br>Launder blankets<br>Deal with bad stains on lavatory, bath, basins, walls and furniture<br>Clean shower curtain and rings<br>Wipe jars and tins on display<br>Mend linens<br>Thoroughly clean upholstery and carpets<br>Launder loose covers<br>Clean cushion covers<br>Wash ornaments and lampshades |
| **Outdoor cleaning** | | Clear litter and leaves from paths<br>Wash down paths into the home, door steps, landings<br>Fortnightly, clean windows if necessary<br>Clean and disinfect dustbin | Remove silt and leaves from drains and disinfect<br>Check roof, inside and out<br>Clear gutters and downpipes<br>Check window frames and windows for rot<br>Wash exterior paintwork<br>Check inside man-hole covers<br>Check exterior walls<br>Clear moss and algae from paths<br>Clean metal fastenings on windows |

## Devising a cleaning and maintenance plan

**1** A list of the different jobs and how often they need to be done can be itemized from the check list in Table 13.1, add any others which have not been included and are special needs for your household. Decide how often they need to be done. This will of course relate to the standard which is required.

**2** Consider how many people are available to do the work and the total time available. Most households work successfully if some of the work is delegated to different members. Apart from paying dividends by helping to get the work done it can also help to foster joint pride in the home, enable children to feel that they are responsible and contributing to the general welfare of the family.

A household which is run on the basis of one parent's slave labour can lead to bitterness and irresponsibility. The more people who are involved in the work the more important it is to devise a sensible system and to make sure that everyone understands and accepts their responsibilities. Failure to do this can cause arguments and unhappiness.

**3** Money is, perhaps surprisingly, very important when it comes to considering cleaning and maintaining the home. Cleaning materials can be very expensive so careful consideration needs to be given to the types used and the amounts which are likely to be required.

Cleaning equipment can also be very expensive and consideration should be given to whether or not a particular item will fulfil a certain task. One of the following sections deals with choosing domestic cleaning equipment, laundry equipment is included in the Textiles section.

If there is plenty of money available it may be possible to employ an individual or contract cleaning firm to do the work. This does not mean that it is unnecessary to follow through the decision-making process as it is clearly necessary to know exactly what needs to be done, how often it must be done and in what order it should be done.

## Cleaning equipment

**Table 13.2** Choosing and caring for cleaning equipment

| Item | Criteria for choice | Care |
|---|---|---|
| **Brushes and brooms** | Should be made of suitable materials<br>Tufts should be well anchored<br>Should be a good shape for the task (i.e. pointed to reach into corners etc.)<br>Quality of bristles should be correct for task (hard or soft). | Store free of dust and fluff<br>Never leave brush resting on bristles<br>Wash as required in warm water and detergent. Rinse well and dry in the open air. |
| **Dustpan** | Preferably made of plastic which is easy to maintain and does not scratch polished surfaces. Check that the edge placed against the floor is level. | Wash periodically in warm water and detergent. |

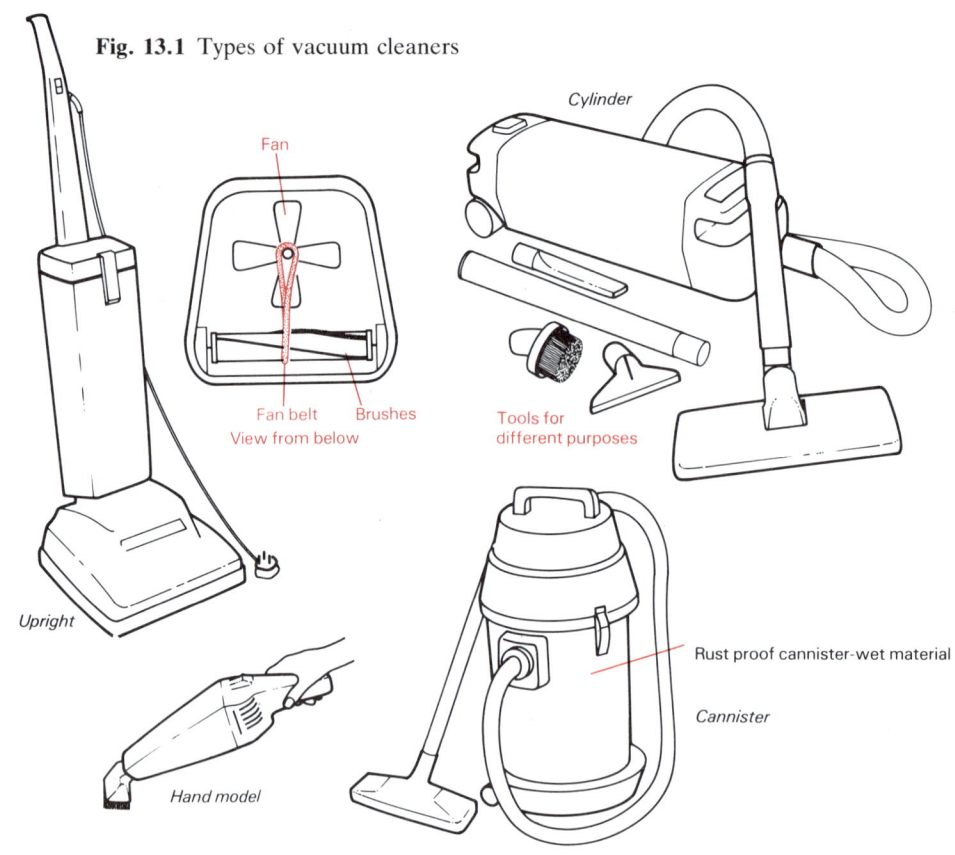

**Fig. 13.1** Types of vacuum cleaners

| Item | Criteria for choice | Care |
|---|---|---|
| **Sponge mops** | Check that the sponge pad is well attached to the mop head.<br>Buy a well-known brand so that replacement heads are easily available. | Rinse thoroughly in plain water before storing.<br>Never store with the mop resting on the sponge. |
| **Mops and dusters** | Should be soft so that they don't scratch surfaces<br>Should not leave lint<br>May be impregnated with chemicals so that dust clings to them. | Wash regularly in detergent and warm water. Rinse thoroughly and dry.<br>Impregnated articles should be cleaned according to manufacturer's instructions. |
| **Carpet sweepers** | Choose one which is large and strong enough for the job<br>Ensure that the wheels move freely and that brushes make good contact with the floor. | Empty dust before using to prevent being re-deposited on the floor.<br>Periodically lubricate the wheels, remove and wash brushes. |
| **Suction cleaners**<br>(Vacuum cleaners) | There are four main designs as shown in Fig. 13.1<br>**1** Cylinder cleaners   **3** Cannister cleaners<br>**2** Upright cleaners   **4** Hand cleaners<br>**1, 2,** and **3** are all suitable for cleaning large areas of floor. **4** is suitable for cleaning small areas or fiddly areas such as stairs.<br>When buying such items look for:<br>(*a*) Good suction (depends on the size of the motor.)<br>(*b*) Ease of emptying.<br>(*c*) Suitable for task.<br>(*d*) Not too heavy or awkward.<br>(*e*) Cleaners which are also required to pick-up wet material should also have rust-proof tanks. | Empty the cleaner (and change air filters if necessary) regularly.<br>Replace worn parts such as drive belts.<br>Periodically clean and dry removable elements such as brushes. |
| **Electric scrubbers and polishers** | (*a*) Manoeverable into corners and under furniture.<br>(*b*) Easy to fill and empty.<br>(*c*) Suitable size and weight. | Rinse through fluid containers.<br>Wash brushes and polishing pads.<br>Replace worn brushes and pads as required. |

## 13.2   Household pests

Household pests vary in both size and nature. Figures 13.2 and 13.3 show some of the most prevalent.

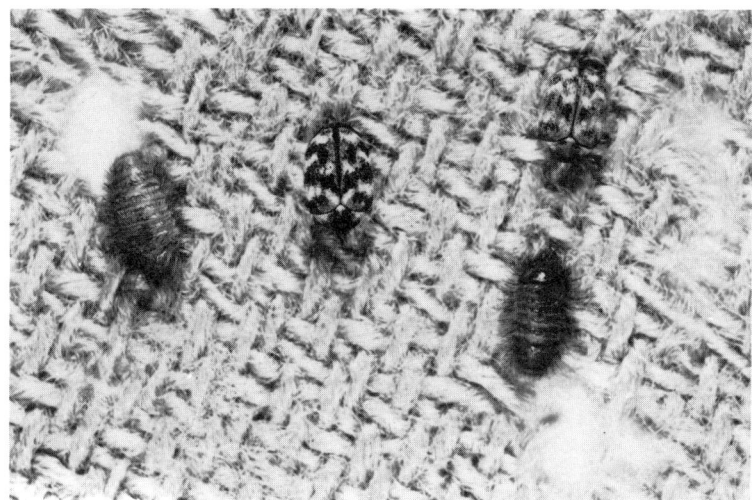

**Fig. 13.2 (a)** Carpet beetles

**Fig. 13.2 (b)** A furniture beetle's work

### Flies

There are many different varieties of fly. All types should be **eliminated** in the home. Some flies are more persistent and damaging to health and hygiene than others. The Housefly, Lesser housefly and Bluebottle are particularly troublesome and undesirable as they spread disease and infection mostly by alighting on food.

*Prevention*

1 Remove any breeding areas such as rotting flesh or vegetation.
2 Keep all food covered.
3 Use fly spray to kill existing flies. Ensure that all food is removed before spraying the area.

### Carpet Beetles

These brownish beetles are found mostly in carpets.

*Prevention*

1 Suction clean thoroughly. Fitted carpets need to be carefully cleaned round the edges.
2 Commercially produced sprays may be bought for infested carpets which cannot be lifted.

### Woodworm or Furniture Beetle

This beetle attacks all types of wood and wicker work. Small holes in the wood indicate the presence of beetles. Infected wood should be immediately removed and treated. Holes should be injected with a proprietary solution to kill the beetles.

*Prevention*

Use of furniture polish and oil helps to prevent eggs being laid on the wood.

### Fleas

It is still possible for houses to suffer flea infestations. This is not usually caused by human fleas but by the fleas carried by cats and dogs. Long pile carpets can make the elimination of such infestations very difficult. Animals must be kept clear of fleas especially in the summer when fleas tend to breed rapidly. Animals' bedding should be regularly washed and de-fleaed. Infested carpets and rugs should be vacuumed thoroughly and sprayed with a proprietary chemical spray.

*Prevention*

1 Keeping animals and their bedding free from fleas and their larva.
2 Regular and thorough cleaning of floors, preferably by suction cleaning.

### Cockroaches

They live in warm moist places and feed at night. To exterminate them their habitats should be treated at fourteen day intervals with proprietary sprays.

*Prevention*

Avoid suitable habitats and bits of food lying about.

Fig. 13.3 (a) A cockroach

Fig. 13.3 (b) A house mouse

### Silver Fish

They live in damp places, often under cookers or near sinks and baths. They can be destroyed with insecticide.

### Ants

They usually enter the house from outside. They may be destroyed with insecticide.

### Rats and Mice

They may be killed by trapping, poisoning or being hunted. Rats are particularly verminous and should be exterminated as quickly as possible. Habitats should be destroyed and sources of food removed.

### *Prevention*

Prevention is better than cure. Keep floors and cupboards clean and free from food particles.

Severe pest infestations should be reported to the Environmental Health Officer who will arrange to exterminate the pests.

## 13.3   Home maintenance

### Blocked sinks and washbasins

This problem occurs in most households from time to time. Serious blockages require the services of a plumber but some simple remedies often work.

**Plunger Cup**  This is a bell shaped rubber cup which may be purchased from any ironmonger. It works by forcing water down the waste pipe pushing the blockage before it as shown below.

### *Suction Cup Method*

Block up the overflow with a cloth. If all the water has drained slowly away run water into the sink until the waste is full of water.
Apply the suction cup and press down firmly.

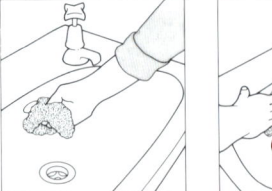
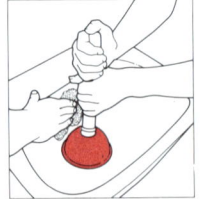

Fig. 13.4 The plunger method

**Opening the Trap** requires the trap to be opened under the sink. Once the trap is opened the blockage may be cleared with a wire or by hand.

Place a bucket under the trap. Unscrew the bottom of the trap. It may be necessary to use a wrench.
Clear out the obstruction.

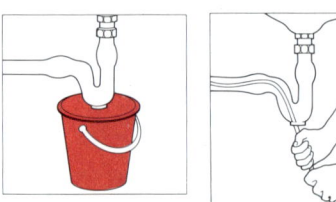

Fig. 13.5 Opening the trap

**Washing Soda** can be used to clear some blockages caused by hot or warm fat setting in the waste pipe. This may be cleared by pouring boiling water and washing soda down the waste pipe.

## Changing a tap washer

Taps with worn washers will constantly drip. This is not simply annoying but also stains the sink or wash basin and may well mean the loss of valuable hot water. Figure 13.6 shows the structure of a standard tap and how to change a washer.

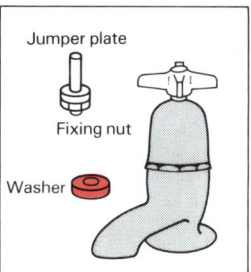
Turn off the water supply. Empty the tap.

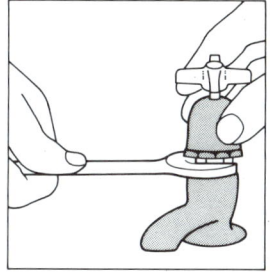
Unscrew the cover and remove the top of the tap.

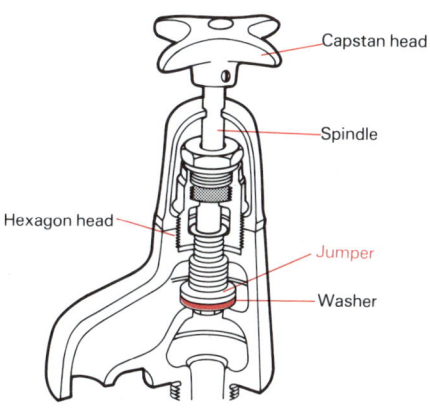
Fig. 13.6 Changing a tap washer

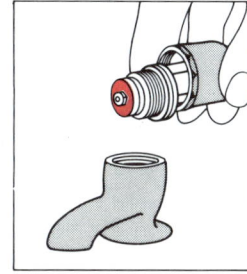
Remove the jumper and take out the old washer.

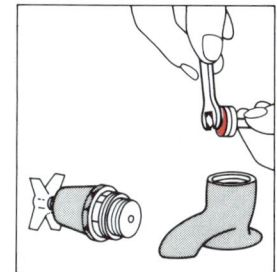
Replace with a new washer, re-assemble the tap and turn on the water supply.

## Overflowing cisterns

**Water cisterns** are controlled with a ball float. As the tank empties the float drops opening a valve which allows the cistern to refill. If the cistern overflows there are three likely reasons:

1 The ball float is leaking and no longer floats on the surface of the water and is therefore not able to shut off the valve. The ball may be simply unscrewed and checked. If it rattles because it contains water it should be replaced.

2 The arm needs to be bent down slightly to shut off the valve sooner, so that the water is at a lower level.

3 The washer in the valve needs to be replaced as shown in Figure 13.7.

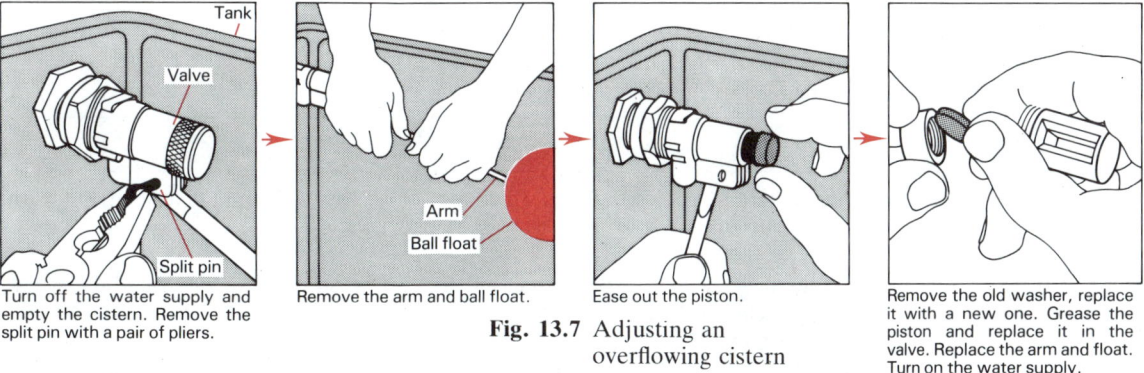

Turn off the water supply and empty the cistern. Remove the split pin with a pair of pliers.

Remove the arm and ball float.

Ease out the piston.

Remove the old washer, replace it with a new one. Grease the piston and replace it in the valve. Replace the arm and float. Turn on the water supply.

Fig. 13.7 Adjusting an overflowing cistern

## Replacing an electrical fuse

**Fuses are** thin wires which are designed as a weak link in an electrical circuit. They melt when overheated, preventing electrical fires and stopping the whole electrical system in a house from 'blowing'.

To replace a fuse **always switch off** at the mains first. In new systems replace the old cartridge with a new one. In old systems (see Figure 13.8) remove the carriers, take out the old wire and replace it with a new piece of the correct thickness.

Fuse wire is in different thicknesses according to whether it is to carry 5 amp, 10 amp, 13 amp or 30 amp. Never fit a bigger size than that which is marked on the fuse carrier.

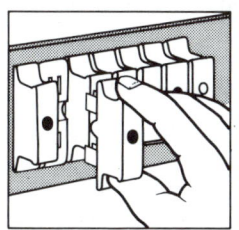
Turn off the power supply at the main switch. Open the fuse box and pull out the carriers until the melted fuse is found.

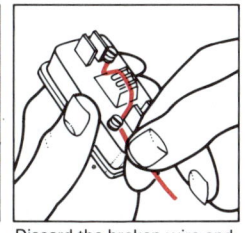
Discard the broken wire and select the correct thickness of new fuse wire. Wrap new wire clockwise round one screw. Tighten the screw.

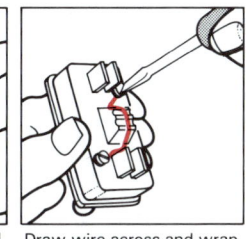
Draw wire across and wrap it clock-wise round the other screw, leaving a little slack. Tighten the screw. Cut off surplus wire.

Fig. 13.8 Replacing an old-style fuse

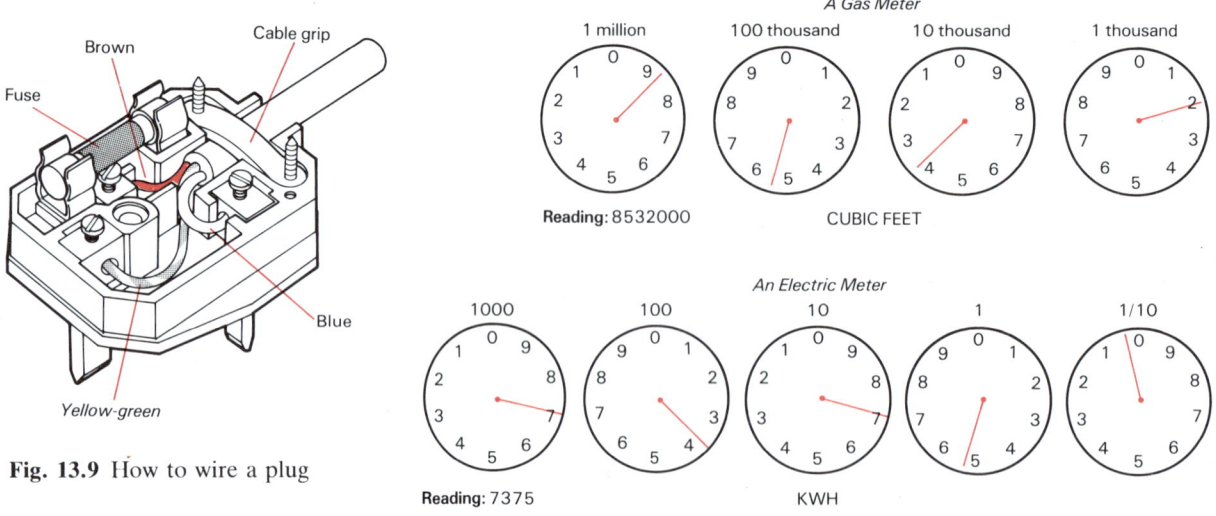

**Fig. 13.9** How to wire a plug

**Fig. 13.10** How to read the meters

A Gas Meter

1 million    100 thousand    10 thousand    1 thousand

Reading: 8532000        CUBIC FEET

An Electric Meter

1000    100    10    1    1/10

Reading: 7375        KWH

## How to wire a plug

Most plugs are now flat three pin plugs. These have individual cartridge fuses which should carry the correct number of amps for the equipment to which they are fitted. Plugs should always be wired in accordance with the diagram shown in Figure 13.9. Failure to wire them in this way could be very serious causing equipment to become 'live', blowing the fuses or even starting an electrical fire.

## Reading the meters

Gas and electricity is metered to individual households and usually read quarterly before a bill is sent. The diagrams in Figure 13.10 show how to read the meters. (See section on lighting for further information on electricity.)

## 13.4   Materials used in household equipment

Many different materials are used for household equipment and utensils. Table 13.3 shows most of them; it indicates some of their uses and advantages and how to care for them.

**Table 13.3** Materials used in household equipment, their use and care

| Material | Comments | Care |
|---|---|---|
| **China** | Made from kaolin. Look for glazes which are **dishwasher proof** for use in dishwashing machines. | Easy to clean in detergent and warm water. |
| **Glass** | Made from silica (silver sand or felspar) and an alkaline substance such as carbonate of potash. Different proportions and additives give the glass different properties. Most glass is brittle and sensitive to extremes of temperature. | Wash in warm water and detergent. Rinse, dry and polish with a soft cloth which is lint free. Keep in a clean atmosphere away from steam and air pollution. |
| **Copper** | Hard wearing but expensive. If used for food preparation or cooking equipment it must be tin lined. Copper salts which are formed when it oxidizes are very poisonous. Copper is a good conductor of heat. Often used for saucepans. | Use metal polish, wash thoroughly. Dry and polish with a soft cloth. |
| **Aluminium** | Does not tarnish although it can discolour. Good conductor, often used for cooking vessels. | Wash in warm water and detergent. |
| **Silver** | Hall marked (stamped with the mark of an Assay Office of Great Britain) – this guarantees that it is of the requisite standard of purity. Other marks indicate the date and maker. | Polish with proprietary cleaner containing jewellers' rouge or whiting and a fatty acid in water or alcohol. Always use a soft cloth or chamois leather to polish. Wash items for food service before using. |
| **EPNS** | This is electro-plated nickle silver. Electro-plating is done by placing white metal into a container with silver salts and passing an electric current through it. The metallic silver is deposited on the article. | Clean as silver. All silver should be stored rolled in felt or tissue paper to exclude the air and prevent tarnishing. Polythene bags are also suitable as they are airtight. |

| Material | Comments | Care |
|---|---|---|
| **Stainless steel** | Hard and strong.<br>Impervious to rust. Used for a wide range of domestic items. | Wash in warm water and detergent. If necessary may be cleaned with a proprietary cleaner. |
| **Cast iron or steel** | Heavy. May be enamelled.<br>Enamelling is brittle and prone to chip.<br>Cast iron retains the heat well. | Wash in warm water with detergent. |
| **Brass** | Made from three parts copper and one part zinc. | Clean with metal polish. Must be well cleaned before use. |
| **Plastic** | Very versatile and used for many different domestic items. It is inexpensive and quiet in use. It is easily cleaned, lightweight, does not chip or corrode. Will withstand hot water, is stain resistant, colourful, odourless and tasteless. | Wash in warm water and detergent. |
| **Wood** | Relatively cheap. Grain gives a pleasing appearance.<br>Warm to the touch. | Bare wood should be scrubbed to clean it. Those items with a finish need to be wiped clean with warm water. According to their use they may need oiling. |
| **Stoneware** | Made from clay which is subjected to high temperatures during firing and it becomes partially fused or vitreous.<br>Thick, heavy items which are hard wearing, such as casserole dishes. | Wash in warm water and detergent. |

## 13.5  Appliance design

### General factors

There are many different electrical machines and gadgets available to make life easier in the home. Choosing them can be a very complex task. Certain general considerations have been listed below which are important when purchasing appliances:

**Design** Is the appliance well designed for ease of use? Are the controls clear and easy to read?

**Safety** Can control and warning lights and devices be easily read? Is the structure free of features such as sharp edges?

**Maintenance** Is the machine easy to clean and maintain?

**Servicing** Is it possible to get it repaired and serviced reasonably quickly?

**Weight and size** Is it too heavy or cumbersome? Can it be easily moved (for instance large items benefit from castors) for maintenance and cleaning?

**Effort and time** Does the machine require a great amount of human effort to use it, or a large amount of time?

**Space** How much space does the machine take up and is there a suitable place to put it?

**Tasks** Is the machine suitable for the purpose for which it is being purchased?

## 13.6  Planning rooms

### Arrangement of work centres–Kitchens and Laundry Rooms

Homes are much nicer to live in if areas are organized for comfort and convenience. A functional design is one which considers not only the work to be undertaken in a particular area but also the preferences and needs of the worker. Careful planning can greatly reduce strain and make better use of the worker's energy. All workplaces need the following things;
  **1** A work surface.   **2** Storage space.   **3** Appliances and equipment.

**Worksurfaces and Storage** are dealt with in Section 9.3.2.

**Appliances** See Sections 13.1 and 13.5.

### Arranging the work centre

Most tasks require the co-ordination of several processes. So each work area may include many centres. When arranging centres remember the following rules:

**Plan and locate** the most important centres first (e.g. cooking areas etc.).

**Place closely related** centres together.

**Consider the sequence** of tasks and organize the work areas accordingly.

**Kitchens** are important work areas which need to be very carefully planned (see Section 9).

**Other factors** which need to be taken into account when planning work areas are:
1 Cost.     2 Family preferences and practices.
3 Type of dwelling and the structure of the room.     4 Style of living.

### 13.7  Furniture

Detailed below are the points to be considered when choosing furniture.

#### Durability

**Construction** Furniture should be well constructed with strong joints.

**Suitable surfaces** The surface finish should be matched to the use of the furniture. Delicate surfaces like French polish are only suitable for items which receive light wear or where it is possible to protect them with mats and cloths. Melamine is a strong surface which is resistant to water and heat it is therefore useful in kitchens and for furniture which receives heavy wear.

**Good finish** The best furniture of any type is well finished with no jagged edges or uneven surfaces.

**Strong upholstery** Upholstered items should be colour-fast and made of strong material. Delicate specialist materials should only be used for items which receive little wear and are largely used for decorative purposes.

#### Convenience

**Easy to clean** In most cases furniture should be easy to clean and maintain.

**Weight and size** Furniture should not be too heavy or awkward.

#### Design

Design is clearly partly a matter of taste, however, modern furniture which fulfills the Design Centre criteria for good design is awarded a label to indicate this (see Figure 12.3). This label is not simply awarded for products which are pleasing to the eye, but also indicates that the item is suitable for the purpose for which it is intended.

#### Comfort

This is a very important point to consider when buying furniture. It is always advisable to **test** items such as beds and chairs in the shop before purchasing them. A bed which one person finds very comfortable may seem too hard or soft for someone else.

#### Household requirements

Different items and styles of furniture suit different households. These vary according to:
1 The size of the family.
2 The amount of money available.
3 The style and age of the house.
4 The room in which the item is to be placed.
5 The use which is to be made of the item.

### 13.8  Soft furnishings

When choosing soft furnishings the points to consider are listed below and considered in detail in Sections 15.12.1 to 15.12.5.
1 Durability     2 Design, colour, pattern and texture     3 Suitability for the purpose

### 13.9  Floors and floor coverings

Table 13.4 Types of floors/floor coverings and their care

| Types of floor or floor covering | Finish | Care |
| --- | --- | --- |
| **Wood floors** e.g. Boards, Parquet | Stained or/and polished Sanded, sealed and waxed | Sweep, wipe clean or use a solvent based polish. May be waxed and polished |
| **Cork** | Often sealed and waxed | As for wood |

| Types of floor or floor covering | Finish | Care |
|---|---|---|
| **Thermoplastic PVC and Vinyl** | | Wipe clean<br>May we waxed with a non-slip polish |
| **Ceramics or Quarry Tiles** | Matt or glossy | Sweep, wet mop or scrub |
| **Carpets and rugs** | Cut or looped piles<br>Felt finish<br>Hair and fibre matting | Remove surface dirt daily.<br>Suction clean<br>Shampoo as required<br>Certain forms of hair matting require to be sprinkled regularly with water. |

## 13.10   Interior decorations and colour schemes

### Colour

Colour is a very important element in interior decoration. The inspired use of colour can quickly change the appearance of a room even to the extent of partially camouflaging structural defects.

**Different visual effects** may be gained by considering the circumstances under which colours are viewed. For instance light colours make surfaces appear to recede, whereas dark colours make surfaces appear lower or nearer. Glossiness intensifies colours making them seem more brilliant and noticeable. The range of red, pink, brown and russet colours give a room warmth; whereas blues and green often give a feeling of coolness. Textures and patterns can also influence the perception of colour.

**A colour circle** can be used to choose colours which harmonize or contrast with one another. The exact **opposite** in the circle is a **contrasting** colour and is often effectively used to give **accent** with such items as cushions and lampshades. Colours next to each other in circle harmonize with one another.

**Lighting** is also an important element in colour perception and is an important consideration in interior decoration (see Section 14.7).

### Decorating

**Wallpaper** is still the most popular type of covering for walls. Papers are usually either spongeable or washable. Those used in kitchens or bathrooms should be washable. Some papers are already pasted and simply require a small trough containing water to wet them before hanging. Others may have to be pasted by hand, laid out on a table, before they can be hung. Such pasting requires room to set-up the table and this may be difficult in a small space. One brand of wallpaper requires the wall to be pasted rather than the paper. Less experienced paper hangers should choose thicker papers to hang which are unlikely to tear.

British wallpapers are sold in pieces 21″ wide by 11½ yards long. The chart shown in Table 13.5 enables the buyer to estimate the amount of paper required for a particular room. Surfaces to be papered must be free of old paper, clean, dry and smooth.

**Table 13.5**   How much wallpaper?

| **Walls**<br>Height in feet<br>from skirting | 30 | 34 | 38 | 42 | 46 | 50 | 54 | 58 | 62 | 66 | 70 | 74 | 78 | 82 |
|---|---|---|---|---|---|---|---|---|---|---|---|---|---|---|
| | | | Measurement in feet round walls, including doors and windows | | | | | | | | | | | |
| 7–7½ | 4 | 5 | 5 | 6 | 6 | 7 | 7 | 8 | 8 | 9 | 9 | 10 | 10 | 11 |
| 7½–8 | 5 | 5 | 6 | 6 | 7 | 7 | 8 | 8 | 9 | 9 | 10 | 10 | 11 | 11 |
| 8–8½ | 5 | 5 | 6 | 7 | 7 | 8 | 9 | 9 | 10 | 10 | 11 | 12 | 12 | 13 |
| 8½–9 | 5 | 5 | 6 | 7 | 7 | 8 | 9 | 9 | 10 | 10 | 11 | 12 | 12 | 13 |
| 9–9½ | 6 | 6 | 7 | 7 | 8 | 9 | 9 | 10 | 10 | 11 | 12 | 12 | 13 | 14 |
| 9½–10 | 6 | 6 | 7 | 8 | 8 | 9 | 10 | 10 | 11 | 12 | 12 | 13 | 14 | 14 |
| 10–10½ | 6 | 7 | 8 | 8 | 9 | 10 | 10 | 11 | 12 | 13 | 13 | 14 | 15 | 16 |

**Number of rolls required**

| **Ceilings** | 32 | 34 | 36 | 38 | 40 | 42 | 44 | 46 | 48 | 52 | 54 | 56 | 58 | 60 | 62 | 64 | 66 | 68 | 70 | 74 |
|---|---|---|---|---|---|---|---|---|---|---|---|---|---|---|---|---|---|---|---|---|
| | | | | | Measurement in feet round room | | | | | | | | | | | | | | | |
| | 2 | 2 | 2 | 2 | 2 | 3 | 3 | 3 | 3 | 4 | 4 | 4 | 4 | 5 | 5 | 5 | 5 | 6 | 6 | 7 |

**Number of rolls required**

*Advantages of wallpapers*

They are durable, colourful, feel warm to the touch, reasonably priced and can provide washable or spongeable surfaces.

**Paints and emulsions** give durable, cheap surfaces which are easy to clean and maintain. Most paint is non-toxic and quick drying. Surfaces to be painted must be clean, dry and smooth.

**Tiles** provide permanent surfaces which are easy to maintain. They are relatively expensive, cold to the touch and provide a surface which cannot be easily changed.

## 13.11   Equipment for entertaining

Details of how a table should be set are given in Section 5.5.

### Table cloths

Cotton or linen damask cloths are still used for formal occasions but the work involved in laundering them makes them unsatisfactory for general use. Many easy-care fabrics are now available which look clean and crisp and are suitable for more general use.

Cloths should be laid over a piece of blanket or underlay when used on highly polished surfaces. This serves both to protect the surface and to deaden the sound of dishes and cutlery. Heat resistant mats should also be used for hot plates and serving dishes.

### Table mats

Large table mats may be placed on top of a table cloth or used alone. They are often very effective when placed on top of a highly polished table.

### Table napkins

Table napkins may be placed in the centre of a table setting or on the side plates.

---

# 14   Housing

---

## 14.1   Choice of a home

### 14.1.1   Choosing a home

Families have different needs.

**Single people** require a relatively small area. The accommodation should not be too expensive to rent or buy—only one income. There must be space for the interests and activities of the individual. Shops, work and welfare services must be near at hand, especially if the person is elderly. Many single people like to keep a pet. The type of accommodation they want often excludes animals.

If short-term accommodation is required, e.g. for a student, it is probably better to rent. One-bedroom houses, flats, bed-sitting rooms or lodgings are often the choice of single people.

**Married couples** need separate living area, kitchen, bedroom, bathroom and WC. There must be adequate space for a wider range of activities and the house should be convenient for transport and work.

 **1** If a young couple plan to have children it might be sensible to buy more space than is required at the present time, but repayments on a mortgage must be related to the future when possibly there will be only one income.

 **2** An elderly couple also need a smaller home. They usually have a very limited income so require reduced running costs. A smaller home is also easier to maintain.

**Families** The type of accommodation will depend upon the **size** of the family, the **ages** of the different members of the family and the **complex needs** of several different individuals. It must also provide adequate **privacy** for individuals and should enable the family to become part of the community.

 **1** The house should be large enough to cater for a range of activities—watching TV, sewing, hobbies, homework, entertaining, play etc. It must also provide for different aged people at the same time—a teenager and an elderly person need the privacy of their own rooms.

 **2** The home must be able to develop with the family with a versatile plan.

 **3** Storage facilities must be adequate for short-term things such as prams and the long term storage of individuals possessions.

 **4** There should be adequate space for family meals—important practically and socially.

 **5** An adequate heating system must be provided especially with young children and the elderly.

 **6** There needs to be a quiet area for homework, reading etc.

 **7** A WC separate from the bathroom, which should not be too cramped may be useful for a large family.

**Environmental considerations**

**Locality** Some localities are more pleasant to live in than others e.g. areas of urban decay which suffer from problems such as vandalism, graffiti, poorly kept and dangerous property. Rural areas may not have the same amenities. The main attraction of an area may be that other members of the family live there.

**Transport** Bus and train services are important if the family does not own a car. These services must be regular and not too expensive.

**Services** How close are playgroup, nursery schools, schools, colleges, health centres and other Welfare and Social Services? How far is it to the shops? What services are there to the house, gas, electricity, water?

**Employment** Is the house close to the place of work to reduce travelling times and cost? Are there good prospects of employment for younger members of the family?

**Leisure** What facilities are there for sport and entertainment for all members of the family?

**Playgrounds and parks** Are these available for pleasure, for specialist sports and with safe playgrounds for the younger children?

**Access** to the house is important. Terraced houses and flats can cause problems for the elderly, to the handicapped and to those with small babies/children. Is there easy access for maintenance work, for getting rid of rubbish?

**Garages and drives** Is the provision adequate? Parked cars can be a safety hazard. Cars are noisy when starting up in an urban area. It is easier to load cars if there is a drive to the door. A garage provides protection for the car and also useful working and storage space.

**Gardens** for relaxation and play. Is the garden safely enclosed so that young children and pets cannot reach the roads? Is there a pond which would be a safety risk for the young? It is useful to have an area to hang washing even if gardening is not a popular hobby. If gardening is enjoyed, is the garden large enough?

**Pollution** We need fresh air and light. Noise can be a problem especially near to airports. Are there industries close by which pollute the atmosphere? If the home is in the country, which way is the prevailing wind, if there is a pig farm half a mile away? Other factors affecting choice of a house relative to the environment will include things such as the local crime rate, possibilities of riots etc.

**Structural considerations**

**Type of house** Basic design, age, number and arrangement of rooms.

**A professional survey** is essential, especially when the house is not new, to determine the following items.
 1 The ground/foundations Is it sound? Has the house been built on filled ground?
(a) Is there a damp-proof course? Is this sound?
(b) Was it built on the site of a rubbish tip–danger of soil pollution?
(c) Is it liable to flooding or subsidence?
 2 Construction–well constructed?
(a) Has it been well maintained?
(b) What basic materials were used in building?
(c) Is there a fire hazard?
(d) Is there rising damp which will have to be dealt with?

**Aspect** Does it get plenty of sunlight? Which rooms get the sun and when? What is the view from the house?

**Sanitation** Main drainage, septic tank or cesspit? A septic tank is preferable to a cesspit. WC where, how many, does it conform to BS specifications? Sound drains? Is the mains water supply and its pressure constant?

**Lighting** Is there good natural light in the house during the day?

**Heating** Central heating or other? Which fuel is used? Potential heating costs–some houses, e.g. bungalows, cost more to heat because of the number of outside surfaces.

**Other services** Gas and electricity, or just electricity?

**Ventilation** Is it good or are there signs of condensation–mould and bacterial growth and a musty smell?

**Repair** Is it in good repair and decorative order, or will it need a lot of work done soon after moving in? Good kitchen units and fitted wardrobes are things to watch for.

### 14.1.2   Stages in buying a house

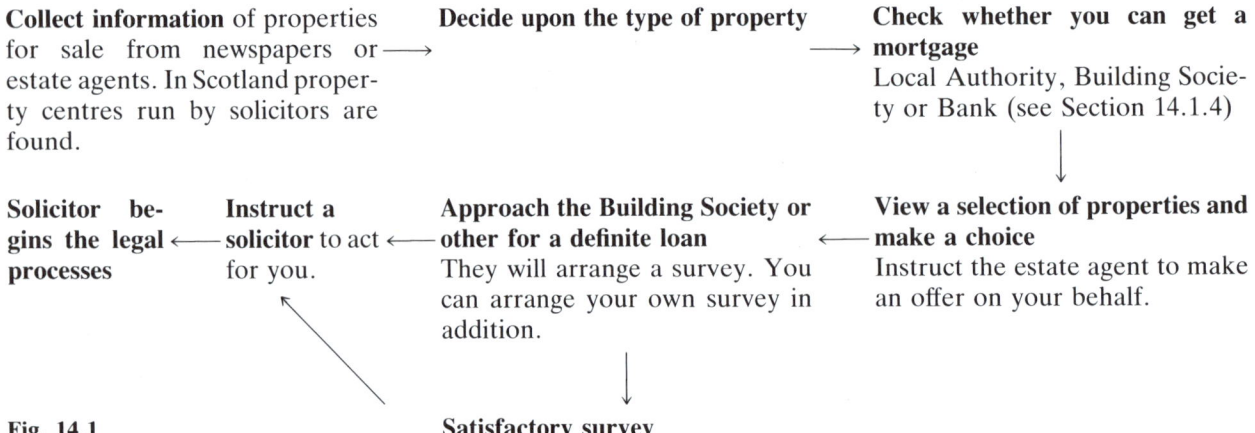

**Collect information** of properties for sale from newspapers or estate agents. In Scotland property centres run by solicitors are found. →

**Decide upon the type of property** →

**Check whether you can get a mortgage**
Local Authority, Building Society or Bank (see Section 14.1.4)

**Solicitor begins the legal processes** ←

**Instruct a solicitor** to act for you. ←

**Approach the Building Society or other for a definite loan**
They will arrange a survey. You can arrange your own survey in addition. ←

**View a selection of properties and make a choice**
Instruct the estate agent to make an offer on your behalf.

**Satisfactory survey**

Fig. 14.1

### The work of the solicitor

1 Makes local searches:
(a) Checks with the LA to see if their future developments will affect the property.
(b) Checks with the **vendor's** (seller's) solicitor property details–leasehold or freehold, mains services, shared access etc.
(c) Checks the Land Registry to see if property is registered–if not checks that the vendor has the legal right to sell the property.
(d) To obtain and investigate the deeds. To pass these on to the Building Society to hold against the loan.
2 Checks the draft contract prepared by the vendors solicitor.
3 Once the loan is confirmed in writing arranges the final signing of contracts.
4 Holds the usual 10% deposit until completion. In Scotland this is paid at the beginning of the deal.
5 Negotiates completion date–usually about 4 weeks after contracts are signed.
6 Pays any Stamp Duty, Land Registry fees, pays off the buyers present mortgage if he has one.
7 Draws up the transfer or **conveyance** in the buyer's name.
8 Pays the remainder of the purchase price to the vendor's solicitor.
9 Arranges the handing over of the keys.
10 Advises on insurance.
For all this work a solicitor will charge a fee. In England and Wales there is no fixed charge at present. In Scotland there is a fixed scale for conveyancing and the contract is binding when the seller's solicitor accepts the offer.

### Freehold and Leasehold

These are now the only **two** legal estates allowed by the law.

**A freehold** lasts for an indefinite time–possibly for ever and can pass to the general heirs.

**A leasehold** refers to tenancy of land for a stated period of years. **Ground Rent** is paid every year. The freehold may be bought by the owner of the house. Leaseholds can be bought, the price of this and the ground rent can be fixed by the Lands Tribunal (Leasehold Reform Act 1967)

### Estate Agents

They have the job of selling houses. They work for the vendor (seller). When a house is sold he receives a fixed percentage of the selling price from the vendor.

They inspect a house, value it, write the descriptive leaflet and advertise the sale in newspapers and their own office windows.

### The Surveyor

His job is to examine the house from the foundations to the roof. He lists all the defects and points out those which should be remedied first. The completion of this type of repair can be a condition of the mortgage.

The Building Society ask for this survey so that they know whether or not the house will be a good investment. The buyer of a house can arrange his own more detailed survey. The results of the survey indicate also whether or not the selling price is fair.

### Fees to be paid by the buyer of the house

Solicitor's fees        Surveyor's fees

Building Society's solicitor's fees      Building Society's surveyors fees
Land Registry fee      Transfer of land registration      Stamp Duties
A proportion of rates and water rates for the year on the house being bought
Service connection charges–gas, electricity, telephone
Removal expenses
10% of price of the house as a deposit.

**National House Building Council** (NHBC)

If a new house has satisfied the NHBC by being built to certain standards they will issue a 10-year certificate. If any faults have to be remedied in the first two years the NHBC will pay compensation. **After two years** they will pay compensation for **major defects only** e.g. roof replacement.

When buying a new house make sure you have this certificate.

### 14.1.3   Rates and rateable value

**Rates are** paid to the Local Authority in one lump sum, in two equal parts or in ten monthly instalments. The amount depends upon
  1 The area
  2 The size of the house
  3 The amenities of the house
  4 What the council spends on the community.

**How much?**

80% of the assessed rental value **(rateable value)** of the house. 20% is allowed for repairs and maintenance. The rateable value is assessed by a Valuation Officer.
This is multiplied by the local rate per £ which may vary from year to year and between Local Authorities.
*For example:*
If the rateable value is £300 and the rate in the £ is 80p.
Annual rates bill will be 80p × 300 = £240.

**What do the general rates pay for?**

Collection of refuse, schools, libraries, clinics, swimming pools and other municipal sporting facilities, parks, building and repairing roads, salting roads in bad weather, the fire service and the police.

**Water rates**

These are paid in addition to and separately from the general rates. The local Water Authority e.g. Wessex Water Authority, collect these once or twice yearly to pay for:
  1 Supplying water.
  2 Supplying drainage.
  3 The collection and treatment of sewage.

**Rate rebates**

These are given to people on low incomes. Application is made to the Local Council Offices.

**Who pays rates?**

Every house owner and every council house tenant.

### 14.1.4   Mortgages

These are loans over a long period of time to enable people to buy homes. They are available from a number of sources as detailed in Table 14.1.

**Table 14.1** Sources of loans for house purchase

| Source | Advantages | Disadvantages |
|---|---|---|
| **Local Authority** | Lend to low wage earners. Lend on older properties. | LA funds may be limited. Charge slightly higher interest rates. |
| **Insurance Companies** | Can take out an endowment policy with profits–when the mortgage is paid off a lump sum–the profit is also paid to the buyer. | May not be prepared to lend as much. More expensive, but may have tax advantages. |
| **Banks** | Recently entered the market. Very attractive rates of interest if spare funds are available. | Rates of interest may change rapidly. |

| Source | Advantages | Disadvantages |
|---|---|---|
| **Employers** | Some employers offer good interest rates to attract staff e.g. Banks. | It may make a job change difficult. |
| **Building Societies** | Most common source of a home loan. Usually have sufficient funds available. Usually the lowest rate of interest on small and medium loans e.g. up to £25,000. Interest rates reasonably stable. | Sometimes require you to have saved with them for some time. Charge higher rates of interest for large loans. |

### Points considered before a loan is granted

**The purchaser**–his age, income (present and future), health, financial commitments, and the number and age of dependants.

**The property**–type, age and condition–see the section on the surveyor.

### Building Societies

These exist to help people buy homes and are able to do so by attracting savings. Figure 14.2 shows how they work.

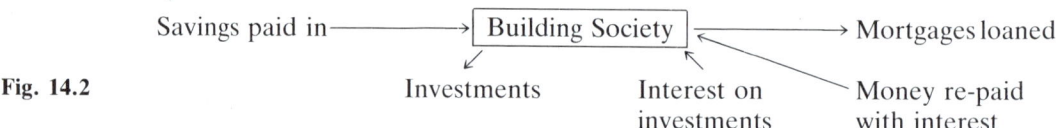

**Fig. 14.2**

### Types of mortgages available

**Repayment mortgage** where the loan is re-paid over the agreed time in equal instalments. Each instalment is made up of both the capital sum borrowed and the interest due.

**Endowment linked mortgage** where the insurance company pays off the mortgage at the end of the agreed term (e.g. 25 years). The purchaser pays the agreed premium monthly to the insurance company and interest on the mortgage to the Building Society. This is why it is more expensive.

**Low-cost endowment mortgage** which is arranged through an insurance company at lower cost but gives little or no lump sum. The insurance companies are able to pay the lump sums by wise investment of the insurance premiums.

### Mortgage interest relief at source (MIRAS)

This recently introduced Government scheme applies to all three types of mortgage up to a limit of £30,000. Purchasers pay their mortgages with the tax deducted.

### Insurance

Most loan agencies, such as Building Societies, insist that properties are insured. See Unit 14.2.4.

**The premium** is the price charged by the insurers and is usually paid monthly or half-yearly.

**The policy** is the document which lays down what has been insured and the terms under which it has been insured.

Most people also insure their house contents against fire, theft and damage e.g. flooding. Contents can be costly to replace. Most insurance companies pay out at the value of the item when it was lost, stolen or damaged. The amount would not be enough to buy new replacements. Where 'new for old' cover is available it is worthwhile despite additional costs as the insurers pay enough to replace the item.

### Home improvement grants

These are granted by Local Authorities to improve properties at least 15 years old (12 years in Scotland) by providing basic needs–lavatories inside, washbasin, bath/showers, repairs to the roof. Set amounts are awarded with a maximum that can be given.

Details can be obtained from the Department of the Environment or National Home Improvements Council.

### 14.1.5   Renting a home

Applications may be made to the Local Authority to be placed on their waiting list for **council housing**. A points system based on need is used. Some families get a home very quickly while young couples or single people may have to wait quite a time.

Advertisements for **private rented accommodation** can be found in newspapers and in estate agents.

**Sources of rented accommodation**

Accommodation may be rented from a **Charitable Trust** (often a religious foundation formed to meet the needs of disadvantaged people); from a **Housing Association** (these developed after the Rent Act of 1974; government subsidies are available to make up the difference between the 'fair rent' charged and the real cost of acquiring and maintaining properties) or from a **private landlord** (about 15% of rented property is in this sector).

**A tenancy** is granted by a private landlord in return for rent. Private tenants are now protected from harassment and eviction under *The Protection from Eviction Act of 1977.*

**Rent Books** must be provided by all landlords. This should show:
1 Name and address of landlord.
2 Name of the tenant and the address of the property.   3 The amount of rent paid.
4 The tenant's legal rights.
5 Details of the Local Authority's rent allowance scheme and overcrowding regulations.

**A Lease** is a signed agreement between landlord and tenant. It states:
1 Rent.   2 Length of tenancy.
3 What the rent includes.   4 Services provided by the landlord.
5 Responsibilities of the tenant. If the tenant does not understand all the details, an organization such as the Citizens Advice Bureau or the Local Authority's housing office can help. It is advisable that the tenant has a copy of the agreement.
6 Rules about sub-letting, pets and children.

**Paying the rent and rates**

People out of work are entitled to help towards these and families with low incomes can get rent and rate rebates (see Section 11).

**Controlled rents** are found on unfurnished property with a very low rateable value. Rents can only be increased if;
1 the landlord has to pay a rate increase,
2 the landlord has improved the services,   3 the landlord has improved the property.

**Regulated rents** are for newly built properties now subject to the 'fair rent' system.

**Rent Assessment Committees** deal with appeals from landlords and tenants made against a 'fair rent' decided upon by rent officers.

**Rent agreements** are made in writing between landlord and tenant concerning an increase in rent agreed to by **both** of them.

**Rent tribunals** are found in all housing districts of Local Authorities. They can suspend an eviction for up to 6 months, providing the correct notification is given.

**Tied Properties**

This is accommodation which goes with a job. If rent is paid it is usually a nominal rent. Examples include police houses and school caretaker's houses.

**Disadvantages** If a worker loses his/her job he also loses his home. If a worker dies his family may be required to leave the house.

## 14.1.6  Buying freehold versus renting from the Local Authority

**Table 14.2**

| Buying Freehold | Renting from LA |
| --- | --- |
| *Economic Advantages* | |
| Once the house is paid for it is a capital asset. | No deposit to save up for. |
| Tax allowance on mortgage interest. | Reasonable rent which is not tied to the |
| Renovation grants available to owner occupiers. | fluctuating interest rate on a mortgage. |
| The portion of home owned can be used as | Regulated under 'fair rent' system. |
| security for loans etc. | Rent rebate available for people on low incomes. |
| | The council responsible for maintaining property. |
| *Social advantages* | |
| If money is available it can be provided very | Can be provided very quickly for priority cases but |
| quickly. | otherwise there is a waiting list. |
| Within certain limitations there is a free choice of | Can provide people on limited incomes with |
| where to live and in the type of home. | accommodation in relatively expensive areas near |
| Free choice with regard to local amenities e.g. | to work, e.g. in central London. |
| schools. | Property can now be purchased after a number of |
| Easy to trade up or down in the housing market | years. |
| according to the needs of the family. | |

### 14.1.7   Different types of home available

Table 14.3

| Type of Home | Advantages | Disadvantages |
|---|---|---|
| **Houses** | Plenty of space Usually has a garden–play, washing, hobbies<br>Range of different activity areas<br>Less noisy than flats<br>Range of styles and sizes<br>Well integrated into a community<br>Easy to know neighbours<br>Garages and outbuildings<br>Easy access | Often need to be bought<br>Can be expensive to buy and maintain |
| **Flats** | Cheaper to buy than houses<br>Small and easy to sell<br>Easy to run<br>Often rented<br>Well suited to elderly, single people or couples | Noisy<br>Can have shared heating systems–expensive<br>Poor access<br>Balconies are no substitute for gardens<br>Often no garages<br>Refuse disposal problems<br>Lifts often out of order<br>Limited storage facilities<br>Short of play space, laundry space<br>Community spirit difficult to foster<br>Vandalism<br>Mostly found in towns and cities<br>May have service charges |
| **Bungalows** | No stairs for elderly or handicapped<br>Easy to run and maintain | Larger floor area–more expensive to buy<br>More expensive to heat owing to more external wall and roof area |
| **Mobile Homes** | Often temporary homes<br>Second hand they can provide a cheap first home<br>Have modern facilities on fixed sites | Expensive to buy when new–second hand selling price usually means a financial loss when sold<br>Can lack modern facilities<br>Cramped for a family<br>Limited space for storage and activities |
| **Bedsit** | Usually rented<br>Relatively inexpensive | All activities in one room<br>Shared bathroom and often kitchen or very limited facilities for cooking<br>Isolation<br>Limited space for storage and activities |
| **Lodgings** (rooms) | Landlady cooks meals, keeps room clean and she provides bed linen<br>No shopping, cooking or cleaning<br>Companionship with other people in the house | Higher rents<br>Less independence<br>Rules and regulations about time to come in, visitors etc.<br>No opportunity or facility to prepare own meals |
| **Hostels** | Room, heating, hot water and meals provided<br>Plenty of company<br>College and University hostels, YMCA, YWCA. | Charges are high<br>Sometimes lack privacy and rules and regulations have to be abided by. |

## 14.2   The structure of a house

### 14.2.1   Building a house

**Site**

The bedrock determines the depth of the foundations. Man-made land and holes filled with rubble, must stand 7 years to allow the land to settle.

**Land reclaimed** from marsh is expensive and difficult to keep dry.

**Solid rock** is good but can be expensive to level in the first place.

**Clay** must be well drained to avoid the house cracking as the ground dries out after it is built.

**Gravel, sandstone and chalk** are well drained. Foundations do not have to be as deep.

**Foundations**

Foundations are usually between 0.43m and 1.50m deep. Large or high buildings will need deeper foundations.

'**Footings**' or foundation bricks are laid to make the wall of house (below the floor of house). Profile boards fix the position of footings and walls.

The area is filled with hardcore and then covered with concrete. Sandwiched in the concrete is a damp-proof course to stop the damp and ground air rising.

### Floors

Solid floors are cheaper and mostly used. Floor boards, wood blocks and tiles are laid on a concrete base.

**Suspended floors** are used if the house is built on a slope.

1 Sleeper walls are built with a honeycomb of air spaces between the bricks beneath the floor.

2 A damp-proof course is laid on top of each sleeper with air bricks in outside walls.

3 Joists are laid across and a floor of tongued and grooved boards is laid (see Fig. 14.3). All wood should be seasoned and treated against dry rot.

### A damp-proof course

This is essential and now compulsory by law. It is made of waterproof material placed about 15cm above the ground before the walls are built up.

### Walls

In the past it was traditional to use local materials which were cheaper; e.g. local granite in Scotland, Cotswold stone in that region. Pre-cast concrete and brick are used mostly now. To give variety of finish brick walls can be faced or rendered with different materials.

Walls in older houses were built two bricks thick, now **cavity walls** are built, the details of which are shown in Figure 14.4. Mortar or other debris must not fall into the cavity during building, as it forms bridges across which damp can travel. The cavity provides a little **insulation** and can be filled to increase insulation (see Section 9).

**Load bearing walls** support the weight of roof and must be strong.

**Partition walls** can be thinner. They can be either a single brick wall, lightweight concrete slabs or lath and plaster. Apart from finishing these walls with plaster, plaster board can be used.

These walls can also be made from pre-fabricated metal or wooden frames covered with plaster board.

**Party walls** are those which separate semi-detached or terraced houses.

**Brick walls** are laid in a variety of ways called **bonds** two examples are shown in Fig. 14.6. The short side of the brick is called the **header** and the long side the **stretcher**.

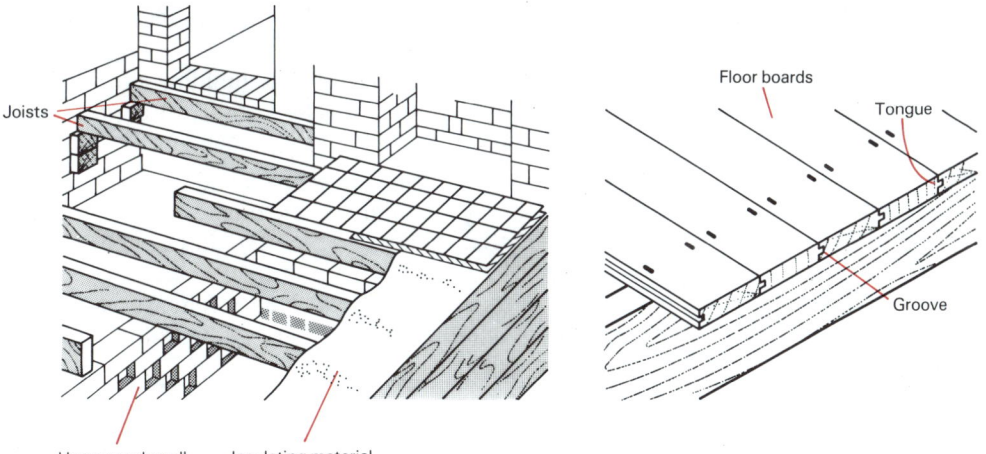

Joists

Floor boards

Tongue

Groove

Honeycomb wall     Insulating material

**Fig. 14.3** The structure of (a) a section floor and (b) a boarded floor

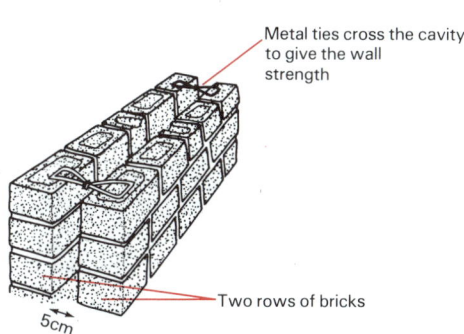

Metal ties cross the cavity to give the wall strength

Two rows of bricks

5cm

**Fig. 14.4** A cavity wall with a metal tie to be mortared in

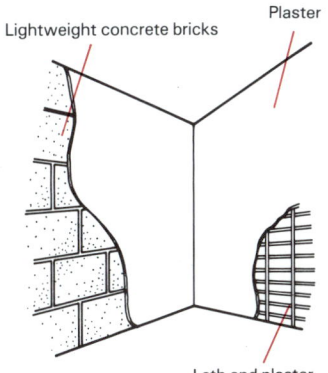

Plaster

Lightweight concrete bricks

Lath and plaster

**Fig. 14.5** Partition walls

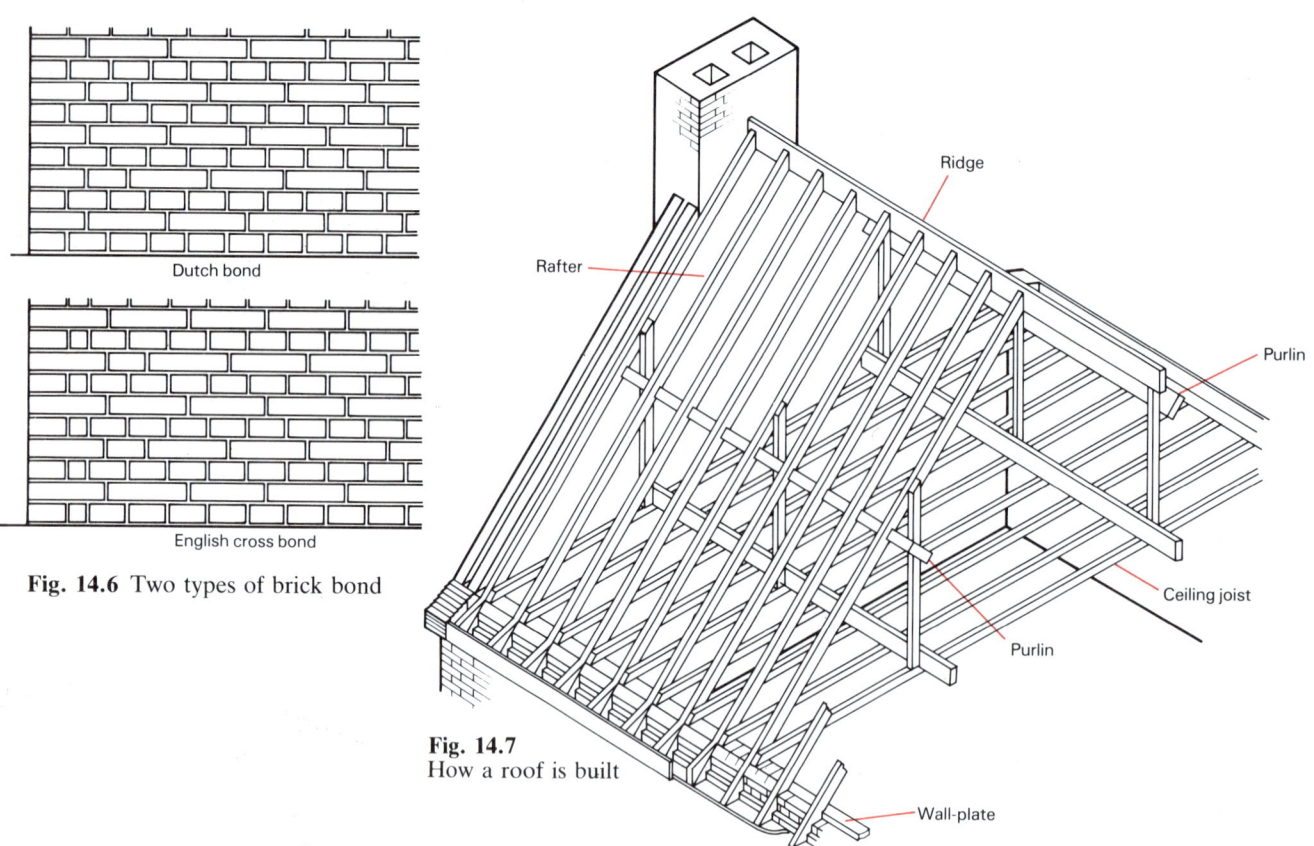

Dutch bond

English cross bond

**Fig. 14.6** Two types of brick bond

**Fig. 14.7**
How a roof is built

Ridge

Rafter

Purlin

Ceiling joist

Purlin

Wall-plate

### Roofs

The framework should be of well seasoned timber treated against wood worm and dry rot. Most roofs are sloping or pitched.

**The purlin or king post** supports the weight of the roof.

**The ceiling joists or tie beams** help to strengthen the walls.

**The rafters or spars** fit to the ridge at the top and at the bottom rest on a timber **wall-plate**. All these features are shown in Figure 14.7.

The framework is usually made in a factory and transported to the building site. Building regulations state that a layer of felt must be laid under the slates or tiles for protection. Plasterboard insulation can also be used. Battens are nailed to the roof for hanging tiles or slates.

**Slates and tiles** must overlap to prevent water or snow getting underneath and vary in shape and colour. They have different names e.g. pantiles, tegulas, imbrex, ancona.

Moulded tiles have ridges (nibs) to hang on battens. Slates are bored so they can be nailed to battens.

Where the roof joins the chimney stack **flashings** of copper, lead, zinc or felt, are used to seal the join to prevent water getting in. All these features are shown in Figure 14.8.

**Gutters** can be made of cast iron, aluminium or plastic. These collect rain water and lead it into the down pipe. They must be kept in good condition, if they get blocked or broken patches of damp will affect the house.

**Flat roofs** are becoming more common, but these do now have a slight slope for drainage. They can be concrete or timber covered with lead, copper, zinc, asphalt or plastic sheeting.

**Thatched roofs** are one of the oldest forms of roofing. A straw thatch lasts for 15 years, a Norfolk reed thatch for up to 70 years.
  1 Thatch is an excellent insulator but a fire risk. This risk can be reduced by special sprays.
  2 Thatch is very expensive to replace, only a few skilled thatchers remain.

### Windows

Windows are essential for light and ventilation. Window space should be at least one tenth of the floor area.

Opening parts of windows are called **lights**. The strips between two lights are **mullions**.

**Windows are fitted** into a recess or rebate which keeps out the rain.

**Sills** are of wood or stone, and designed in such a way today that water drips off and does not collect to damage the wood.

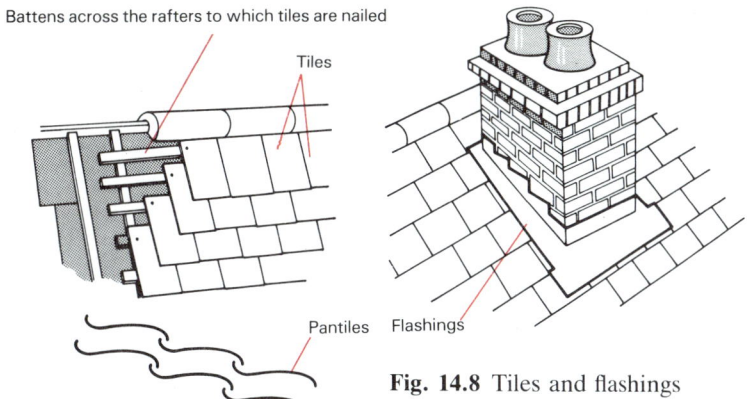

Battens across the rafters to which tiles are nailed

Tiles

Pantiles    Flashings

**Fig. 14.8** Tiles and flashings

**Fig. 14.9** A thatched cottage in Alresford, Hampshire

**Table 14.4** Types of windows and glass

|  | *Name* | *Characteristics and use* |
|---|---|---|
|  | Sash | Move up and down operated by a pulley and cord. Pulley and cord need to be checked and replaced if worn. Wooden frames can warp. |
|  | Casement | Hinged at the sides.<br>Large sheets of glass are used so they let in a lot of light. |
|  | French | Doors with panes of glass leading into the garden.<br>Prone to draughts and sometimes not very waterproof. |
|  | Dormer | Found in sloping roofs, projecting from them.<br>Exposed so can deteriorate and let in water, without care. |
|  | Skylight and Velux | In line with the roof and now often used in loft conversions. |
|  | Bay | Give extra space in a room.<br>Square, semi-circular, or hexagonal in shape. |
| **Windows** | Picture | Very large and generally do not open.<br>Heat loss through them can be considerable. |
|  | Louvred | Small strips of glass which open and close like venetian blinds. |
|  | Double-glazed | Two panes of glass either in a sealed unit with an aluminium frame, or a second layer of glass added on the inside of the window with a frame of aluminium or hard plastic.<br>Keep in heat and keep out noise.<br>Secondary glazing is less efficient but cheaper. |
|  | Sheet | Cheapest and most commonly used. |
|  | Plate | Thicker and stronger, safer for large windows and doors. |
|  | Wired | Strengthened with a network of wire.<br>Used in skylights (security) and in busy doors. |
|  | Patterned | Used in bathrooms and toilets for privacy. |
| **Glass** | Stained | Coloured and patterned, used for decoration in halls and on landings. Reduces the light, but gives privacy. |
|  | Safety | When this breaks it does not splinter and produce sharp edges.<br>Expensive, but necessary in places with large 'invisible' windows, and small children. |
|  | Plastic | Unbreakable, but let in less light.<br>Reduces maintenance costs in areas with high levels of vandalism. |

### Doors

Doors are fixed into **rebates** which stop doors swinging the wrong way so straining the hinges.

**Outer doors** leading into the house usually open inwards. They are heavier and sometimes more decorative and double-glazed.

**Inside doors** are usually a simple framework with a flat board on each side. Doors with glass panels are often used to increase light and for decoration.

### Fireplaces

Some houses today are built without fireplaces. Even if an open fire is not the usual form of heating it is useful to have an open fireplace for warmth and for cooking during power cuts.

The below-floor area near to the fireplace has to be constructed in such a way that any underfloor timber does not become a fire risk.

Chimney flues usually have a slight curve in them as protection against the weather.

### The staircase

When the house is being built, a **stair-well** is left ready for the carpenters to build the staircase.

The drawing shown in Figure 14.11 gives the main features of the staircase.

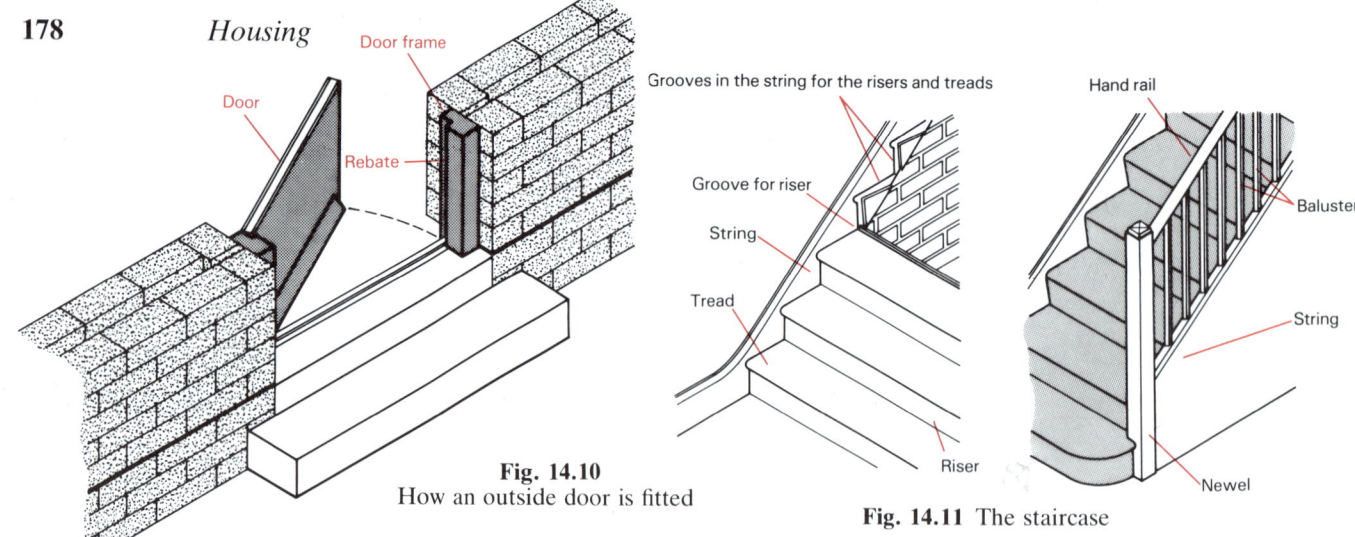

**Fig. 14.10**
How an outside door is fitted

**Fig. 14.11** The staircase

### 14.2.2   Prefabricated Houses

The pretabs of the 1940s were largely constructed of asbestos sheets. Today's prefabricated, timber framed houses are much more attractive. They are made from standard, factory-built units which are transported to the building site.

Extra units can be easily added on as the family's needs grow, or some can be removed to make the house smaller.

They are quickly assembled on-site and cost less than a conventional house.

#### Disadvantages of prefabricated units

1  Thin room partitions can mean more noise passing from room to room.
2  The plastic cladding of the sections can be damaged by electricians or plumbers fitting pipes. This means it is no longer waterproof.
3  The fire risk is **not** now considered to be greater than in an ordinary house.

### 14.2.3   Materials used in house construction

**Table 14.5**

| Material | General points | Use |
|---|---|---|
| **Asbestos** | Flat and corrugated sheets of asbestos fibre and Portland cement. | Walls and roofs |
| | Insulating board–asbestos fibre, silica and hydrated lime. | Ceilings, walls, partitions |
| | NOT RECOMMENDED–asbestosis and lung cancer link. | |
| **Aluminium** | Anodized for little maintenance | Double glazing units–frames |
| **Boards** | Hardboard made from wood and other plant fibres. | Lining floors and walls, backing cupboards |
| | Insulating board also includes cellulose fibres. | Lining walls and ceilings |
| **Bitumen felt** | Rolls of different thickness up to 3mm. Made of fibre, asbestos or glassfibre impregnated with bitumen. | Lining to roofs<br>Flat roofs and flashing |
| **Cement** | Composed of calcium silicates and calcium aluminates | Binding agent for sand and other aggregates<br>Added to concrete and used for floors and lintels, added to mortar for brickwork |
| **Clay bricks** | Have names such as London Stocks, Flettons, Facing bricks<br>Composition varies, largely aluminium silicates | Walls, foundations, facing bricks where appearance is important |
| **Concrete blocks** | Blocks and bricks made of Portland cement and aggregates<br>Thermal blocks for insulation | Walls and partitions |
| **Copper** | Metal which conducts heat and electricity well<br>Expensive | Pipes for plumbing and central heating<br>Wiring in electric cables |
| **Cork** | Warm, silent and non-slip material<br>Tiles or rolls | Wall covering, floor covering |
| **Glass** | See page 177 | Windows, doors |

| Material | General points | Use |
|---|---|---|
| **Plaster** | Made of gypsum mixed with water | Walls and ceilings |
| **Plasterboard** | Plaster faced on both sides with paper | Flat sheets for ceilings, insulation and for decorative features such as covings and cornices |
| **Plastics** | | |
| (a) Polyurethane foam | Sheets–cellular structure with lots of trapped air<br>Premoulded shapes<br>USE FLAME RETARDANT GRADES | Insulation–walls and floors<br>Insulating pipes |
| Varnish<br>Paints | Water and heatproof finish | Sealing wood<br>Paintwork |
| (b) Expanded polystyrene | Extruded<br>Beads<br>DO NOT PAINT WITH GLOSS<br>USE FLAME RETARDANT GRADES | Insulating floors and walls<br>Insulation e.g. lofts |
| (c) Expanded Polyvinyl Chloride | PVC<br><br>PVC sheet<br>USE FLAME RETARDANT GRADES | Insulating floor, roofs and walls<br>Vinyl wallpapers<br>Rigid, Used to provide natural light in roofs and wall claddings |
| **Steel** | Reinforcing material | Reinforcement of walls<br>RSJ/beam for strengthening a long open space |
| **Stone** | Many different types, granite, sandstone, limestone, marble, slate | Many different functions<br>Walls, fireplaces, floors etc.<br>Different types used for decoration |
| **Tiles** | Fired clay or cement<br>Cold, noisy, easy to clean<br>Thermoplastic tiles–warm and durable | Used for roofs, cladding walls, fire surrounds<br>Floor covering |
| **Timber** | **Deal**–basic softwood which is treated against rot and woodworm<br>Comes from pine and fir trees<br>**Hard woods** e.g. cedar, more expensive, more durable, more decorative<br>**Plywood**–resin bonded boards, rot-proof | Basic wooden structure of house<br><br>Cladding, ornamental doors and floors<br>Lining doors, floors, cupboards |

### 14.2.4   Security

A house and its contents should be **insured against risks** such as fire, theft, flood.

**The structure** of the house is often insured separately from the contents. Care should be taken to ensure that the insurance covers the cost of replacing the house and/or its contents.

**Insurance premiums** are usually paid annually and many are linked to the Financial Index and increase every year.

When insuring the contents of a house it is often necessary to list separately items such as television, antiques, jewellery, musical instruments, computers. An extra premium is often required.

Insurance companies require a householder to take reasonable steps to ensure the safety of his/her property. A few of these are listed below:

**Measures to increase security**

1 Fit adequate locks to doors and windows. Exterior doors should have 'dead locks' (Yale type which cannot be opened with strips of plastic).

2 Doors and windows should be securely fastened when the house is unoccupied, when the family are together in one room perhaps watching television, and during the night.

3 Valuables should be stored out of sight or in a bank.

4 Ladders should not be easily accessible.

5 When going away for a few days or for longer periods:
(a) Cancel milk and newspapers.   (b) Inform the police.
(c) Ask a neighbour to keep a watch on the house.

6 Guard against fires:
(a) Up to date electrical wiring.   (b) Electrical appliances correctly wired and fused.
(c) Televisions and other electrical equipment where possible switched off when not in use.
(d) Open fires guarded.   (e) Chimneys swept.
(f) Gas cylinders and inflammable liquids stored out of the house.

(g)  Open fires completely burnt out before leaving.

(h)  Ashtrays, waste paper baskets, furniture checked to ensure free of the ends of cigarettes.

(i)  Inside doors downstairs closed at night.    (j)  Matches not left lying about.

(k)  Children under twelve years never left alone.

(l)  Old people need to be carefully watched.

(m)  Fire extinguisher kept in an accessible place.

## 14.3    Services to the home

### 14.3.1    The water supply

Treatment of the water supply to the home–see Chapter 9.

Drainage system of a house and sewage disposal–see Chapter 9.

#### Direct cold water system

**The mains cold water** supply runs to all cold water taps and WC cisterns.

**The mains stop-cock** is found where the mains pipe enters the house.

**The rising main pipe** carries water around the house and there is **no** storage tank in the roof.

#### Indirect cold water system

All taps except the kitchen sink cold water tap are supplied from a cold water storage system in the roof-space as shown in Figure 14.12.

#### Combined cold water system

The direct and indirect cold water systems are combined to give cold water **off the mains at sinks** and handbasins from which cold water is **drunk**. This is because the cold water storage cistern may be polluted with dust and dead insects etc.

#### Water-meters

In the past a household was charged a fixed water-rate regardless of the amount of water used. In some areas an additional charge was made for the use of a hose-pipe.

Some Water Authorities now allow households to have a water-meter installed at their own cost, and they are charged for the water used above a minimum level.

### 14.3.2    The gas supply

#### How natural gas was formed

Gas is a **fossil fuel**. It has formed from living organisms that died millions of years ago.

1  The organisms grew, died and sank in the swampy earth. As they sank deeper and deeper, they became covered with thousands of metres of mud and sand.

2  As they were pressed deeper and deeper beneath the surface of the earth terrific heat and great pressure changed the organisms to coal, oil or gas.

3  The gas has risen through **porous rock** where it was trapped when it met **non-porous rock** which will not let it pass. As a result gas fields have been formed underground as shown in Fig. 14.12.

#### Man-made gas

Gas used to be made by heating coal to high temperatures. This produced coal gas, tar oils and ammonia and left behind coke. The tar oils and ammonia have industrial uses.

The coal gas needed to be cleaned to remove sulphur.

The production of town gas or coal gas produced many atmospheric pollutants. It contained carbon monoxide which is very poisonous if breathed in, and it exploded if mixed with air.

Natural gas is clean and non-poisonous. It contains no carbon monoxide. The risk of fire and explosion is no greater than with coal gas.

The gas works that exist now are called Reforming Plants. Most of these make gas from oil.

#### Transmission of natural gas

Natural gas from the North Sea is piped to the coast to terminals from which it is distributed.

Britain is divided up into twelve regions. At special points throughout the country the pressure in the main distribution pipe is reduced as gas passes into the smaller distribution mains of each region. These carry the gas to cities, towns and villages.

A narrow **service pipe** connects each house to the mains pipe in the street. At the end of the service pipe there is the **mains tap** to turn off the gas supply to the house (see Figure 14.15).

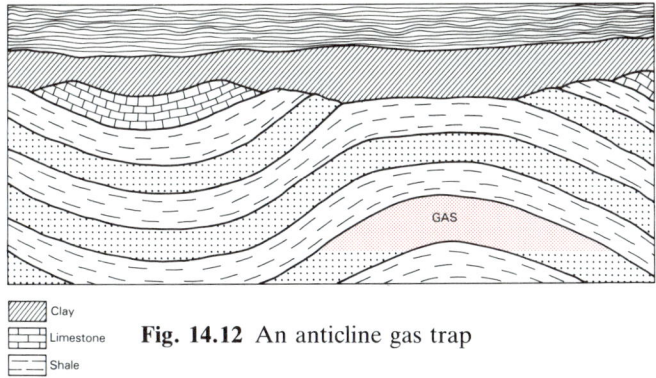

Clay
Limestone
Shale
Sandstone

**Fig. 14.12** An anticline gas trap

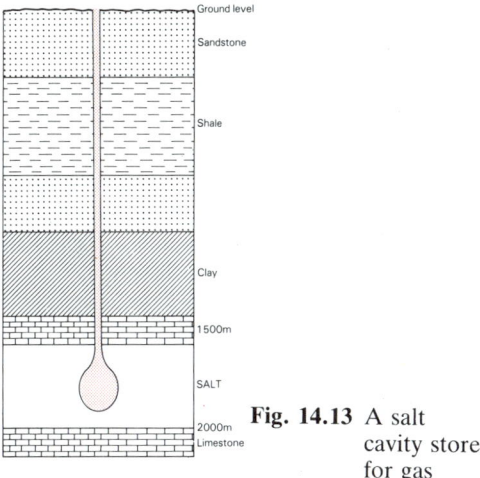

**Fig. 14.13** A salt cavity store for gas

**A governor** regulates the pressure of gas entering the house.

**The meter** measures the amount of gas used in cubic feet or cubic metres.

### Storage of gas

Gas is stored in;
 1 Horizontal steel cylinders of large diameter underground,
 2 Cylinders as liquified natural gas. The temperature is reduced to −160°C to turn the gas to a liquid. The liquid takes up 600 times less space than the gas,
 3 Underground salt cavities as shown in Figure 14.13. The area where the salt has been removed is an ideal storage area.

### Uses of gas

 1 Cooking, heating, washing, drying cabinets, refrigerators in the home.
 2 To make electricity in power stations.
 3 In industry.

### Bottled gas

Gas as a liquid is stored under pressure in cylinders. **Butane** and **Propane** can be bought in cylinders for use where there is no piped gas supply e.g. on boats, in caravans and when camping. Propane burns hotter than butane and needs special burners.

**Propane** is stored in red cylinders outside the house.

**Butane** in green or blue cylinders can be stored inside a house.

**Chimneys and flues** are needed to carry away the products produced by burning gas.
 1 Chimneys must be cleaned before an appliance is fitted.
 2 If chimneys and flues become blocked the fumes will escape into the room.
 3 Staining, sooting or a discolouration around an appliance indicates that fumes are not getting away. Headaches, sickness, tiredness and muscular weakness are some of the symptoms produced. Death can result in extreme cases. The appliance must be checked.
 4 Many new models have a built-in system which seals the ventilation and flueing from the atmosphere in the room. These are known as **'balanced flue'** or **'room sealed'**. Such a gas fire is shown in Figure 14.14.
 5 Water heaters in bathrooms may still be of the old type which are not 'balanced flue' models. These can be dangerous if used incorrectly.
**(a)** Make sure the bathroom is well ventilated–open the window and door while drawing off hot water.
**(b)** Turn off the water when you get in the bath and do not run water while in the bath.
**(c)** Check that the flue system is not broken and that bathroom ventilators are free of any obstruction.
**(d)** Have the heater serviced at least once a year.

### Safety and gas

The law is concerned with everyones safety. It states that:
No-one shall use, or let anyone else use, any appliances they know or suspect to be faulty.
Only competent people shall install or service appliances or systems.
It is illegal for anyone to tamper with pipes, meters or fittings belonging to British Gas.
You must turn off your main gas supply if you suspect a gas escape.
You must tell your local gas service immediately if an escape continues after you have turned off the main supply. They are available 24 hours a day.
You must not turn on the gas, or any appliance, again until the escape on the appliance has been repaired.

IF YOU SMELL GAS

Put out cigarettes. Do not uses matches or naked flames.
Do not operate electrical switches (including doorbells) either on or off.
Open doors and windows to get rid of gas, and keep them open until the leak has been stopped.
Check to see if a tap has been left on accidentally, or if a pilot has gone out. If not there is probably a gas leak so turn off the whole supply at the meter as shown in Figure 14.15 and call the gas service. The telephone number is found under 'GAS' in the directory.
Installation and servicing of gas appliances should be done by the experts. Servicing pays in safety and efficiency.

*Ventilation*

Gas appliances need air when burning gas and various ventilators may be used.

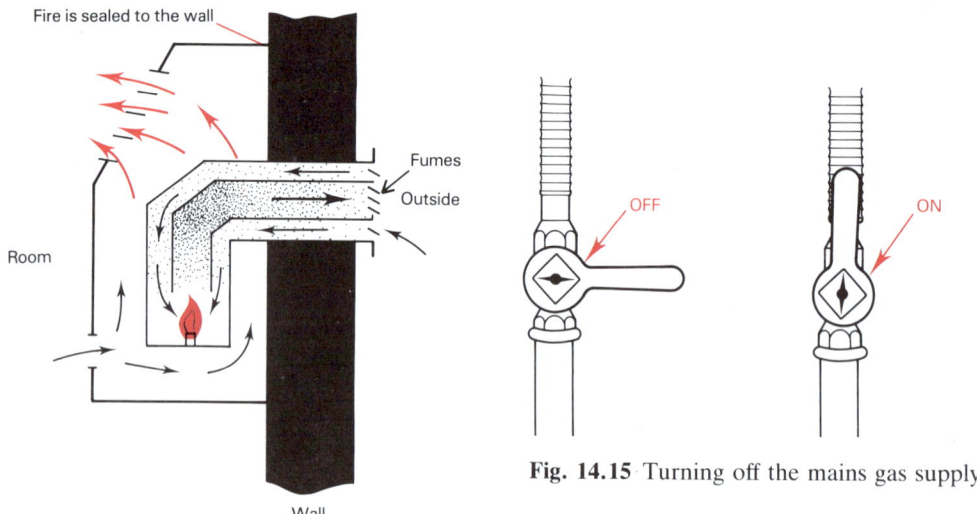

Fig. 14.15 Turning off the mains gas supply

Fig. 14.14 A balanced flue appliance

## 14.3.3    The electricity supply

### How electricity is made

Electricity is made by using steam to drive turbines which produce the electricity. Other fuels can be used to produce the steam; coal, oil, gas.

The power of falling water is used in **hydro-electricity** plants.

**Nuclear power** is also used. Gas-cooled reactor plants and a 'fast breeder' reactor are used in this country. Pressurized water reactors cost less to build. **Uranium** ore used in nuclear power plants is a more concentrated source of energy than coal.

Coal, oil and nuclear power produce 99% of our electrical power.

### Electricity in the home

Electricity is used to provide heat, light and power to operate countless electrical appliances.

*Electrical terms and units*

**Voltage** (V) is the pressure pushing the flow of electrons through a circuit. The voltage is transformed **up** to supply the National Grid and **down** to 240 volts before it enters our homes.

**Amperes** (I) are the units of measure for the flow of an electric current.

**Watts** (P) are the measure of the power of electricity used. A 40 watt light bulb uses less power than a 100 watt light bulb. An electric cooker can use up to 13 000 watts, a microwave cooker 500 to 600 watts.

**Wattage** is the number of watts used by an appliance.

**Kilowatt** (Kw) 1000 watts.

**Kilowatt Hour**  A thousand watts used in one hour.
1000 watts used for 1 hour = 1 unit of electricity.
We pay for electricity by the unit. See Section 13.3.

**Conductors** are materials that will allow a flow of electricity to pass through; silver, copper, gold, tungsten, brass, impure water, man.

**Insulators** are materials which do not conduct electricity unless the voltage is so high that the material is destroyed. Dry air, dry paper, rubber, plastics, porcelain.

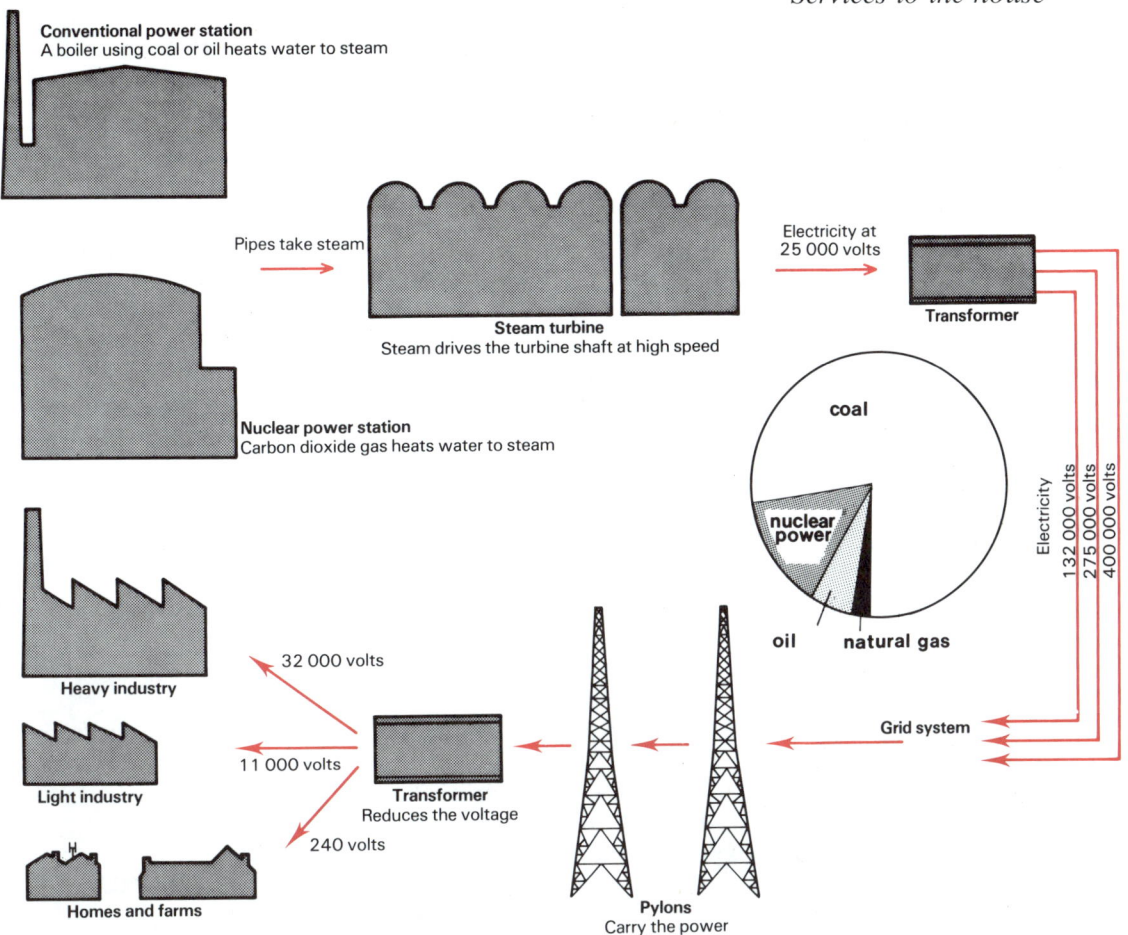

**Fig. 14.16** How electricity is made and distributed

*Resistance and heat*

Some conductors offer a greater resistance to the flow of electricity than others. A high resistance results in heat and light being given out.

**Nickel-chromium wire** is used in toasters, hair dryers and electric fires. Heat is given out.

**Tungsten** has such a high resistance it becomes white hot without melting. It is used in light bulbs.

**Hotplate elements** are made of nickel-chromium, *Nichrome* wire is found inside a tube packed with magnesium oxide which will conduct heat but not electricity. Resistance is also linked to the thickness of the wire:

  **1** Thin wire–high resistance–gets hot    **2** Thick wire–low resistance–stays cool

*Relationship between voltage, resistance and current*

This is expressed in Ohm's Law as follows:
Voltage     = Current × Resistance     $V = I \times R$
*or*

$$\text{Resistance} = \frac{\text{Voltage}}{\text{Current}} \qquad R = \frac{V}{I}$$

*or*

$$\text{Current}\ \ = \frac{\text{Voltage}}{\text{Resistance}} \qquad I = \frac{V}{R}$$

*Relationship between power, voltage and current*

If the power of an appliance is known it is possible to estimate the cost of running it.
This knowledge is also necessary when selecting suitable connections and fuses.

Power (watts)   = Pressure (volts) × current (amperes)    $P = V \times I$

$$\text{Pressure (volts)}\ = \frac{\text{Power (watts)}}{\text{Current (amps)}} \qquad V = \frac{P}{I}$$

$$\text{Current (amps)}\ = \frac{\text{Power (watts)}}{\text{Pressure (volts)}} \qquad I = \frac{P}{V}$$

*Calculations using these units*

**Which fuse?** (fuses for small domestic appliances are usually 3 amps or 13 amps)
   **1** If the power of an appliance is 720 watts which size fuse is needed?
   Power (watts)  $= 720$
   Volts         $= 240$ (normal household voltage)
   Current (amps) $= ?$

$$I = \frac{P}{V} = \frac{720}{240} = 3 \text{ amps}$$

Appliances with a watt rating up to 720 have 3 amp fuses.
   **2** A toaster has a wattage of 1360. Which fuse is needed?
   Power (watts)  $= 1600$
   Volts         $= 240$
   Current (amps) $= ?$

$$I = \frac{P}{V} = \frac{1360}{240} = 5.6 \text{ amps}$$

Appliances with a watt rating over 720 have 13 amp fuses.
The toaster would have a 13 amp fuse.

**The cost of electricity**

Calculate the units of electricity used by each of the appliances used for the given times. Calculate the cost of this electricity at 5p a unit.
(*a*) A toaster, rating 1360, used for 1½ hours per week.
(*b*) An oven, rating 2400 watts, used for 2 hours.
(*c*) A hotplate, rating 2000 watts, used for 1½ hours to steam a pudding.
(*d*) A microwave oven used for 6 mins to cook same pudding, oven wattage = 600.
(*e*) An immersion heater, rating 3000 watts used for 20 hours per week.
(*f*) A 3kW electric fire used for 30 hours per week.

$$\frac{\text{Power (watts)}}{1 \text{ kilowatt}} \times \text{time in hours} = \text{units used}$$

(*a*) $\frac{1360}{1000} \times 1.5 = 2.04$ units at 5p unit $= 10.2$ pence.  (*d*) $\frac{600}{1000} \times .1$ (6 mins $- \frac{1}{10}$ hr.) $= .06$ unit at 5p unit $= 0.3$ pence.

(*b*) $\frac{2400}{1000} \times 2 = 4.8$ units at 5p unit $= 24$ pence.  (*e*) $\frac{3000}{1000} \times 20 = 60$ units at 5p $= 300$ pence $= £3$.

(*c*) $\frac{2000}{1000} \times 1.5 = 3$ units at 5p unit $= 15$ pence.  (*f*) $\frac{3000}{1000} \times 30 = 90$ units at 5p unit $= 450$ pence $= £4.50$.

**Safety with electricity**

See Chapter 10.

**Paying for electricity**

See Chapters 11 and 13.

### 14.3.4   Other forms of energy production

Research is being carried out into the possibilities of using wave, tide and solar (sun) energy to produce **energy** or **hot water** for use in homes in Britain.

**Solar power** is being used in some parts of the world e.g. deserts, very successfully to heat water and, by the use of heat exchangers, to produce power. Lack of constancy and heating power and high installation costs make the use of solar energy of less importance in Britain except for water heating of swimming pools and individual homes, and boosting of the heat is usually necessary, particularly in winter.
   Solar panels made of black absorber plates with water pipes over their surface absorb the sun's heat. The heated water is then pumped to the cistern or swimming pool.

**Tidal power** production is still in the research stage in Britain, but in France the waters of the Rance estuary are already in use and in the future areas such as Morecambe Bay may be producing tidal power.

**Geothermal power** using the heat of the Earth is being investigated in Britain particularly in the Southampton area. In New Zealand's North Island the water heated in the Earth's crust is already in use, in the Rotorua area, in public buildings. It is hoped to experiment in similar uses in the Southampton area.

In Britain in general such power is clearly limited to areas found to have fairly intense heat and water, not too far below the surface. The search for these areas goes on.

## 14.4 Water heating

### 14.4.1 The hot water supply

**Direct system**

The hot water boiler can be heated by an enclosed or open **fire** or by **gas, oil** or **electrically**. It can be linked also to a cooking system such as Aga.

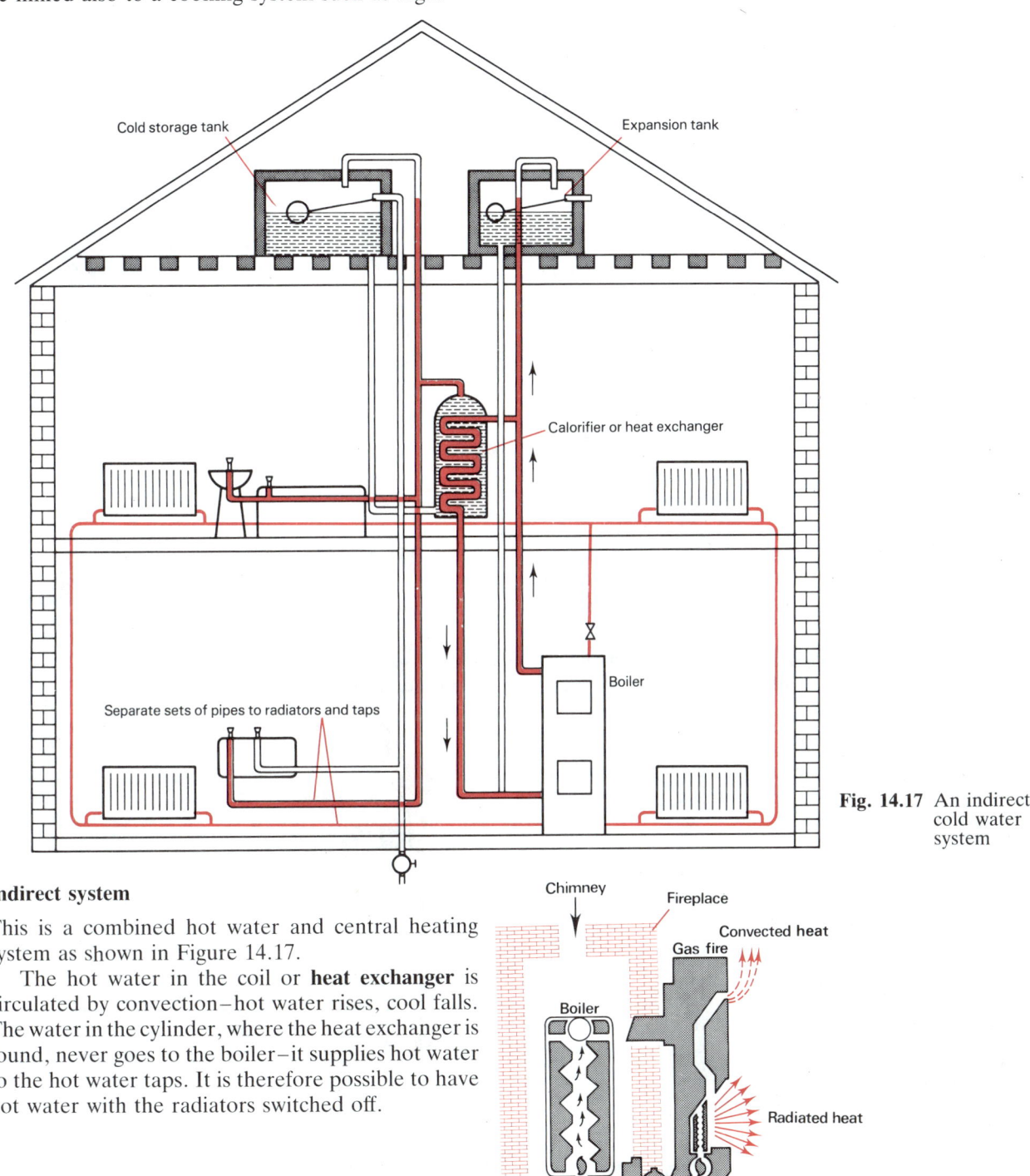

**Fig. 14.17** An indirect cold water system

**Indirect system**

This is a combined hot water and central heating system as shown in Figure 14.17.

The hot water in the coil or **heat exchanger** is circulated by convection – hot water rises, cool falls. The water in the cylinder, where the heat exchanger is found, never goes to the boiler – it supplies hot water to the hot water taps. It is therefore possible to have hot water with the radiators switched off.

**Fig. 14.18** A back boiler

### 14.4.2 Gas water heaters

These are of several types and a few examples are shown in Figure 14.19.

**A circulator** is a small gas boiler used with the ordinary hot water system. It is linked to the storage cylinder and is thermostatically controlled.

**A single point heater** supplies about 2 litres of hot water per minute. It is usually positioned next to the kitchen sink.

**A storage water heater** holds 90 litres of water. It supplies the whole house with hot water. The temperature is controlled by a thermostat. The burners switch off when the required water temperature is reached and switch on again automatically when the water is used or cooled.

It can be installed alongside kitchen units or in a cupboard.

**Shower units** are available as single or multipoint heaters  They give instant hot water at the shower unit.

**A multipoint heater** is a large instantaneous water heater. It supplies all the hot water needed in the home, 4 litres per minute can be supplied to any one tap.

It can be used in conjunction with a shower unit, washing machine or dish washer.

**A back boiler** fits into a living room. They are gas fires with a boiler unit giving a fire in the living room combined with a central heating and hot water system.

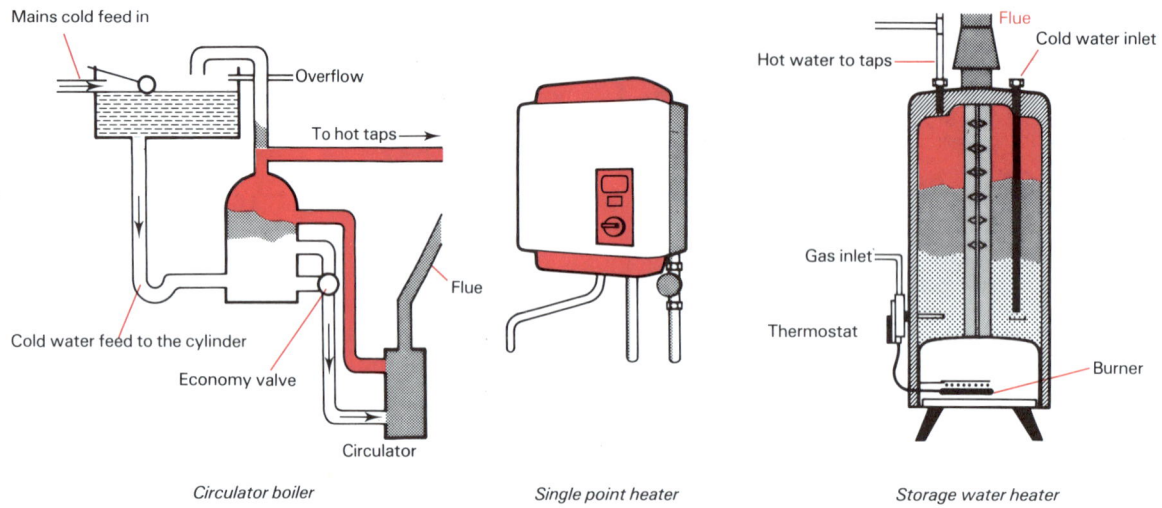

*Circulator boiler*          *Single point heater*          *Storage water heater*

**Fig. 14. 19** An indirect hot water system          **Fig. 14.20** Gas water heaters

### 14.4.3   Solid fuel water heaters

Solid fuel water heaters work on an open or enclosed solid fuel fire linked to a back boiler, or the solid fuel can be burnt in an enclosed central heating boiler.

### 14.4.4   Electric water heaters

**Immersion heaters** can be positioned to;
  1 Heat the upper part of the hot water cylinder,
  2 heat the whole cylinder.
Under the **economy system**, arranged through the Electricity Board, money can be saved in the way explained in Figure 14.21.

  **Time switches** can also be used in conjunction with immersion heaters so that electricity is used for heating the water only when it is needed.

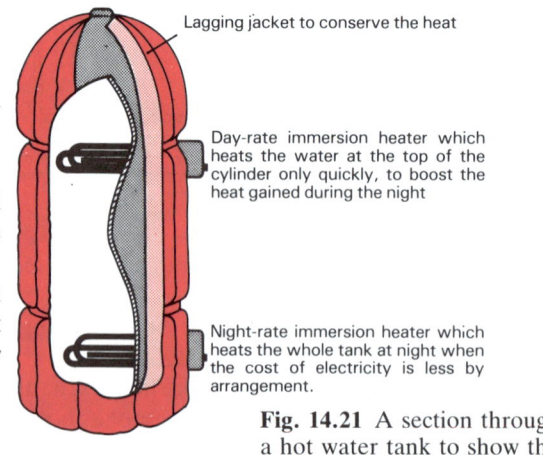

Lagging jacket to conserve the heat

Day-rate immersion heater which heats the water at the top of the cylinder only quickly, to boost the heat gained during the night

Night-rate immersion heater which heats the whole tank at night when the cost of electricity is less by arrangement.

**Fig. 14.21** A section through a hot water tank to show the immersion heaters

**Point of use heaters**

  1 Shower units are thermostatically controlled, instantaneous heaters.
  2 Wall mounted kettles provide up to 4½ litres of water at temperatures up to boiling point. They are useful where **small and frequent** supplies of hot water are needed. They connect to a nearby tap with a hose.
  3 Over sink water heaters are available in capacities between 7 and 68 litres. They need a cold water supply and electricity. They give a local source of water to sinks, basins and baths.
  4 Under sink water heaters are available with capacities between 7 and 15 litres. These are **plumbed directly** into the cold water supply and need special taps.
These instantaneous water heaters give a continuous supply of hot water without storing.

## 14.5  Heating the home

A room is heated up by **radiant** and **convected heat**. Both methods are involved to a greater or lesser extent with all types of heating systems. **Conducted** heat can pass from items which have warmed up in a room for example a chair.

### 14.5.1  Solid fuel burners

**Open fires**

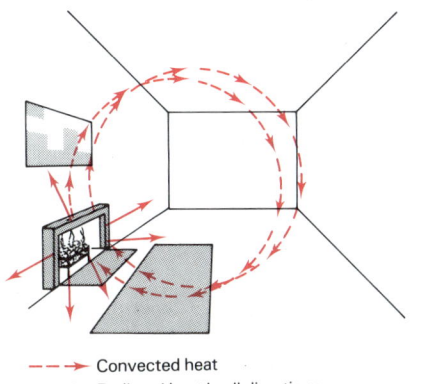

- - - → Convected heat
——→ Radiated heat in all directions

**Fig. 14.22** How a room is heated from an open fire

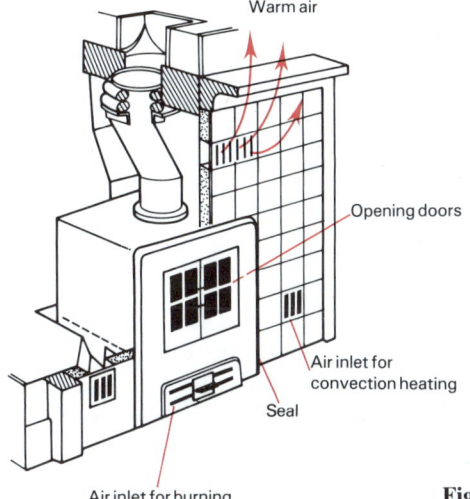

Warm air

Opening doors

Air inlet for convection heating

Seal

Air inlet for burning

**Fig. 14.23** An inset solid fuel stove

Smokeless fuel has to be burnt in most areas. A well designed fireplace radiates most of the heat into the room and not up the chimney. Heat circulates in the room by convection (see Figure 14.22). They usually heat water in a back boiler which sometimes heats a small radiator in the bathroom.

*Disadvantages*

It is difficult to control the heat level.
They have to be cleared out creating dust.
Effort is involved carrying the fuel.
They sometimes create draughts.

*Advantages*

Attractive and cheerful.
Create a focal point in a room.

**Free standing and inset stoves**

These will burn fuel shut or open, but they burn more efficiently when closed and give a general warmth. More direct heat is obtained when the doors are opened. They can be linked to a hot water system or to the hot water system and central heating.

**Cooker and water heating units**

Cookers of the Aga type which burn solid fuel are used for cooking and running the central heating. (This type of stove can also be bought to run on oil or gas or electricity.)

They are expensive in both space and money and make the kitchen hot in warm weather.

**Central heating boilers**

The size of boiler required will depend on the size of the house. They burn smokeless fuel and different makes of boiler may recommend a certain type of fuel. They need raking and filling twice a day.

Gravity feed boilers are usually installed in larger buildings. They need filling and raking less often because the fuel, usually a very small anthracite pellet, falls automatically. Anthracite gives out a lot of heat.

**Types of solid fuel**

**Smokeless Fuels** include the types shown in Table 14.6.

**Table 14.6** Types of solid fuel

| Name | Characteristics |
| --- | --- |
| **Welsh anthracite** | A natural smokeless fuel<br>Burns slowly with little flame and gives out a great deal of heat<br>Very little ash<br>Used only in boilers |

| Name | Characteristics | Name | Characteristics |
| --- | --- | --- | --- |
| **Welsh dry steam coal** | A natural smokeless fuel<br>Burns slowly giving a good heat<br>Very little ash<br>All domestic purposes | **Coalite and Rexco** | Manufactured smokeless fuel<br>Lights and burns easily giving high heat<br>Very little ash<br>Light and clean to handle<br>All domestic purposes– smaller sizes for boilers |
| **Hard coke or Sunbrite** | A manufactured smokeless fuel<br>Slow to catch fire<br>Very little ash<br>Used only in boilers | | |
| **Phurnacite or Ovoids** | A manufactured smokeless fuel<br>Burns slowly giving very great heat<br>Very little ash<br>Equal sized oval pieces<br>Used only in boilers | **Gloco and Sebrite** | Manufactured smokeless fuel<br>Light and clean<br>Slower to light than Coalite or Rexco<br>All domestic purposes |

### Advantages and disadvantages of solid fuels

*Advantages*

**Open Coal Fires**

Look welcoming and cheerful
They usually heat a back boiler
May be used with a part central heating system

**Closed burners**

These are more economical than open fires as not so much heat is going up the chimney
They can be linked to the hot water supply and a limited number of radiators
A warm glow can be seen through the doors

*Disadvantages*

A lot of heat can be lost up the chimney
Ordinary coal pollutes the atmosphere
Coal has to be stored and carried to fire
The fire needs to be replenished frequently
Ashes can be messy to clear up
Dust thicker on furniture
Chimney needs sweeping

Aesthetically not nice to look at
Like the open fire fuel needs to be stored, carried and the fire made up
Ashes to clear

## 14.5.2   Gas fires and boilers

### Gas fires

A radiant gas fire is usually installed into a chimney. Air for combustion is drawn in at the base, the radiants are heated up by the burning gas and the heat is radiated into the room, heat is also convected.

The products of combustion pass through the heat exchanger and up the chimney flue as shown in Figure 14.18.

### Gas wall heaters

A gas wall heater, and how it works, is shown in Figure 14.24.

### Gas central heating boilers

These can be wall hung, floor standing or back boilers to fires. They work by heating water which is circulated to radiators and hot water storage tanks as shown in Figure 14.18.

### Advantages and disadvantages of gas heating

*Advantages*

Gas is there when needed, there is no carrying of fuel
They heat rapidly once lit
Simple, precise control of the heat
Light automatically
Automatic controls on central heating can save time and fuel
Neat appearance of units
Gas fires can be a focal point in living room

*Disadvantages*

Need a chimney or outside wall for the flue
Some heat is lost up the chimney
Need a well ventilated room to avoid the build up of fumes and drying of the air
A small danger of leaks and explosion

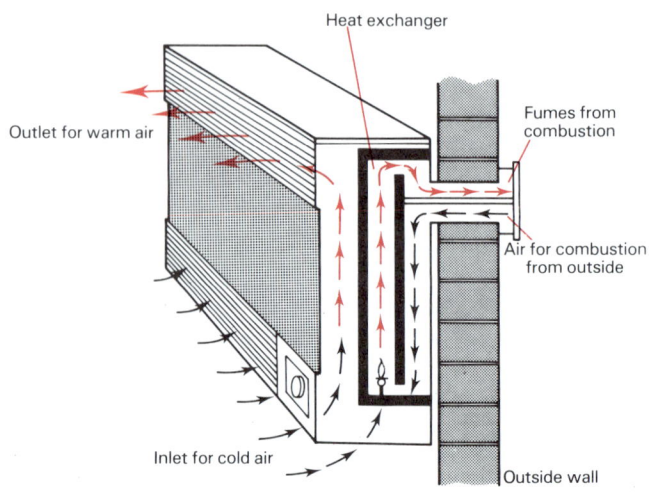

Air from the room circulates through the heater
**Fig. 14.24** A gas wall heater

**Mobile Gas Heaters**

These can be moved from room to room for instant heat and are useful in emergencies. The gas is paid for in advance but the bottles of gas are heavy to lift and carry.

They are unattractive to look at, and ventilation is needed wherever they are in use.

## 14.5.3   Heating with electricity

**Whole house heating**

This is often a combination of **storage heaters and direct space heaters**. Energy can be used on the low cost Economy 7 night-rate tariff.

**Storage heaters** are designed to use off-peak electricity. The heavy bricks inside the heaters heat up at night, and slowly release their heat the next day. It is possible to give them a boost during the day. They can be fitted with individual thermostats.

**Radiant/Convector and panel heaters** can be used anywhere there is a power point.

**Oil-filled radiant heaters** can be wall mounted or free standing. They work from a 13 amp socket, have a thermostat and a safety cut-out.

**Wall-mounted radiant heaters** give a rapid source of heat. They are useful in kitchens and bathrooms. In bathrooms they must be permanently mounted and have a pull cord switch.

**Heated towel rails** can be floor standing or wall mounted. Mainly used in bathrooms. Thermostatically controlled they give enough heat to warm and dry towels.

**Floor standing radiant heaters** are found in a wide range of different styles with one, two or three bars. They are easily moved from room to room, give instant heat and run from 13 amp sockets.

**Fan heaters** can be wall mounted or floor standing. Air is drawn over the heating element and blown out into the room. They usually have variable fan and heat control and they can be tilted to direct heat where you want it.

**Ceiling lights with heaters** are useful in rooms which are not often used.

**Under floor heating** is achieved with electric cables laid in a concrete floor, which may be permanently embedded or there may be access. They are put in when the house is built, and are meant to give a temperature of about 15°C so additional heating has to be used.

**Advantages and disadvantages of electricity for heating**

| *Advantages* | *Disadvantages* |
| --- | --- |
| Portable heaters can be taken where needed | Electricity is very expensive |
| Clean | Portable heaters and wall units do not heat |
| Simple to use | up the water supply |
| Heats up a small area very quickly | |

## 14.5.4   Oil-fired heating

**Oil-fired boilers**

Oil-fired boilers operate by heating water in the same way as gas-fired boilers. Oil is a very clean fuel but has become very expensive.

A large storage tank is needed for the oil and the tank can be unsightly. There must be access to the tank from the road.

**Paraffin heaters**

In the past these portable heaters have proved dangerous as they are easily knocked over and they have caused many fires.

A heater bought today should carry the British Standards Kitemark. This means that the heater is stable and not easily knocked over and if this does happen the flame will go out. The flame is also guarded and heats either by radiation or convection.

These heaters can have an unpleasant smell and as they burn they give off moisture which can cause condensation. Paraffin is however cheap to buy and heating is paid for in advance.

The portability and cheapness in use still make paraffin heaters popular.

### 14.5.5   Central heating systems

Central heating systems circulate hot water or air throughout a home from a single heat source. Many also provide the hot water supply.

**Hot water systems**

These can be fuelled by gas, oil or solid fuel using boilers as described in the previous sections. The actual system used varies with the year of installation, location (availability of gas supplies), personal preference and the type of home.

**1** Gravity fed hot water with a pumped heating system. More common in the past but not really suitable for bungalows or flats–no drop from the hot water storage tank. Smaller bore pipes can be used for the heating part of the system–less expensive see **3**.

**2** Pumped heating and hot water system (see Figure 14.17). Once the domestic water has reached the required temperature a valve closes the hot water circuit and diverts the flow of hot water to the heating circuit.

**3** Microbore system. The piping has a smaller diameter, carries less water and this heats up more quickly. With a *manifold system* each radiator is individually supplied. Small pipes are less obvious, if they have to be on the surface, less expensive and more flexible.

**Warm air heating**

Most warm air heating systems (see Figure 14.25) heat the air directly and do not heat water.

**The warm air unit** powered by gas or electricity **must** be in a position which makes the air ducts as short as possible.

**A fan** distributes the warm air. This can be noisy.

**As the warm air** enters a room through a vent near the floor the hot air is directed downwards to ensure that there is warmth at feet level.

**The air is filtered** when it returns to the warm air unit.

It is now possible to have a system that incorporates a **heat exchanger** so water can be heated as well.

A hot-air system is installed when the house is built. It is cheaper than a wet system. In the summer the fan will circulate cool air through the house.

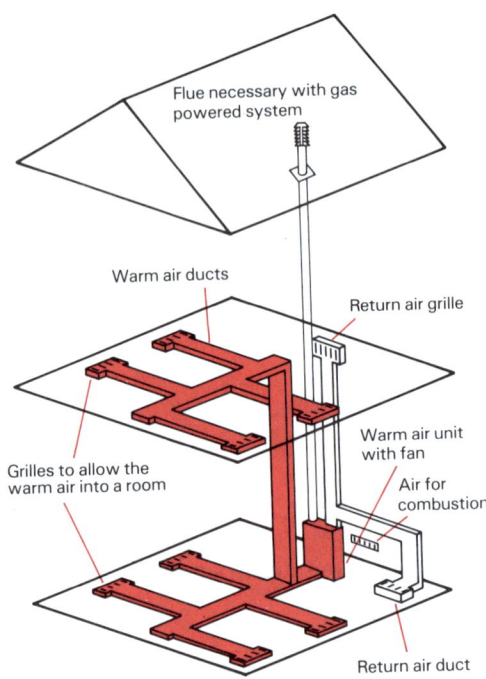

Flue necessary with gas powered system

Warm air ducts

Return air grille

Warm air unit with fan

Grilles to allow the warm air into a room

Air for combustion

Return air duct

**Fig. 14.25** A warm air heating system

### 14.6   Ventilation

A room needs to have its air exchanged, fresh air needs to come in and stale air go out.

**Stale air**

Stale air contains the **waste products of our own respiration**, carbon dioxide and water, **products of combustion** from fires or smoking, **odours** from cooking and from lavatories. Also it can often contain so much **water** that if it is not removed **condensation** will be a major problem with its associated dampness and mould growths.

**Heating systems** can make the air so dry that it **irritates** nose and throat. **Humidifiers** are used to remedy this problem. Electrically operated humidifiers have a fan which blows moisture into the atmosphere. More simply a water filled container can be placed over a radiator.

**Methods of ventilation**

**A coal fire** will draw air into a room through windows and doors so the stale air is drawn up the chimney as the fresh air reaches the fire to aid combustion.

**Opening windows and doors** is fine in the summer, but draughts are unpleasant and the room temperature soon drops.

**Air bricks** are found towards the top of walls in rooms which do not have fireplaces–bedrooms, bathrooms, W.C.

**Extractor fans** if correctly placed and installed in windows or walls, are a very efficient way of removing steam and cooking smells from a room, but are expensive to buy.

**Coopers disc** is a simple circle with holes in it which match holes cut in the window pane. A cord pull moves the disc to open the holes or to close. It is much cheaper than extractor fans but not as effective.

### Air conditioning

This is mainly found in office blocks, factories and large stores.

The air is circulated and treated in such a way that it stays clean, at a constant temperature and with a constant moisture content.

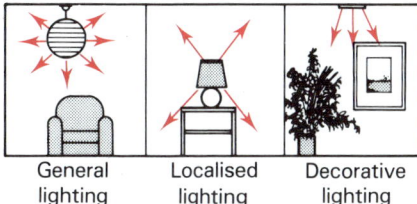

**Fig. 14.26**
Types of lighting

General lighting   Localised lighting   Decorative lighting

## 14.7   Lighting

### The importance of good lighting

Good lighting prevents eye strain and accidents (see Chapter 10). It also makes a room bright and cheerful and can create various atmospheres.

### Natural and artificial light

In the past oil, candles and gas have been used for lighting, none of these was as effective as electricity. Electricity supplies artificial light simply and relatively cheaply, but it is not as good as sunlight which gives the best, most even light.

Candles, gas, oil and batteries can be used in places without electricity and during an electricity breakdown.

### Types of lighting

**Generalized lighting** should provide sufficient light to move about, watch TV or play cards. It should give an even illumination to the whole room with no shadows in corners.

Deep colours used in the room decor will absorb light whilst lighter colours will reflect light.

**Localized lighting** should be used to supplement general lighting. Localized lighting gives extra light to an individual who may be doing close work – reading, writing, sewing.

Spot lights, strip lights, table lamps, standard lamps and anglepoise lamps all provide localized lighting.

**Decorative lighting** is also localized but its purpose is to add interest to the decor of the room. It may be used to highlight displays in alcoves, individual items or cabinets.

### Light fittings

Light fittings distribute light in different ways and should be chosen carefully. Dark lamp shades can prevent light getting through.

**Direct light** is given by fittings that throw light down.

**General lighting** is given by fitments which direct light in all directions.

**Indirect lighting** is thrown up to the ceiling and then reflected down.

### Light bulbs

These can be clear, pearl or white and range from 15 to 200 watts. Light fittings are usually marked with the size of bulb recommended. If the wattage is too high the lamp shade can scorch and possibly burn.

**Clear bulbs** can create glare if not correctly shaded.

**Pearl and white bulbs** give a softer light and are better for general lighting.
 1  15 watt bulbs could be used for a light left burning all night – in a child's room.
 2  100 watt bulbs, 150 watt bulbs and 200 watt bulbs are used for general lighting.
 3  60 watt to 100 watt bulbs for localized lighting.

**Fluorescent lights** give no shade. They are more expensive to buy, can be strip or circular, but they last longer and use one third of the electricity that an ordinary filament bulb would use to give the same light.

### Lighting provision for different rooms

Most rooms should have a general light operated from just inside the door to the room. In addition there should be light sockets and power points around a room to provide for additional, localized lighting. Table 14.7 gives suggestions for the lighting of the main rooms in a home.

**Table 14.7** Lighting in the main rooms of a home

| Room | Lighting suggestions |
|---|---|
| **Kitchen** | Good lighting is essential for safety. Well lit rooms are easier to keep clean.<br>Fluorescent light is often used plus additional localized light as strip lights or spotlights at sinks and above work surfaces.<br>Cookers often have their own lights on the control panels. |
| **Hall** | A general light is needed. If it is a large hall a two-way light should be installed with a switch at either end of the hall.<br>There could be a localized light for a telephone. |
| **Staircase** | Must be well lit for safety. A two-way switch is essential to control the light, one switch at the top of the stairs the other at the bottom. |
| **Dining room** | A good general light with perhaps a light which can be lowered over the table.<br>Possibilities of extra localized light because dining rooms are often used for working, sewing and homework. |
| **Sitting room** | A general light but extra localized lights are also needed near chairs or side tables where work is done. Standard lamps, table lamps, spot lights or anglepoise lamps are all possibilities. |
| **Bedrooms** | A generalized light is needed together with table lamp, spot light, or strip light at the dressing table. Adjustable bedside lamps for reading in bed and for switching on and off when in bed. |
| **Bathroom** | A general light is needed with a strip light near basin or dressing table. All should have pull cord switches. |
| **Exterior lights** | At front door, back door, in the garage all with switches inside the house.<br>Outside lights should be weatherproof.<br>A fluorescent light is best inside the garage. |

**Economy with lights**

See Section 9.2.6.

# 15 Textiles

## 15.1 Choice of textiles

1 There is a wide choice of textiles for the making of household textiles and clothing.

2 Items bought ready-made should be labelled with their fibre content.

3 Fabric bought by the metre usually has its fibre content on the end of the roller or bale.

4 It is important to know the fibre content of a material, because that knowledge will affect the type of treatment given to it and the use to which it is put. It is not easy to identify an unknown fabric at home.

(*a*) The burning test is only useful to identify fabrics made of one type of fibre.

(*b*) Microscopes and chemicals which can be used to help in identification are not usual items of household equipment.

The following questions should be answered before buying clothes and household textiles.

**Is it suitable for its intended purpose?**

e.g. Will it be warm in winter or cool in summer? Will it absorb moisture? Will it be comfortable to wear or use? Will it crease? If it is fabric for curtains, will it rot in sunlight? Will it drape? Will it be hard wearing?

**Is it an easy care fabric?**

Will it wash or will dry cleaning be necessary? Will it machine wash or will it need hand washing? Will it drip dry? Will it need drying flat? Can it be put in the tumble dryer? Is it non-iron or minimum iron?

**Is the fabric safe?**

Will it melt or burn? e.g. textiles used for childrens nightwear should be flame retardant.

**What is the cost?**

What can I afford to pay? Quality varies with price. Do sheets have to last for twenty years or do I only expect them to last for five years?

## 15.2 Classification of fibres and textiles

Figure 15.1 below, divides fibres and textiles into four main groups and gives examples of each type.

**Fig. 15.1**

| | |
|---|---|
| NATURAL FIBRES | Vegetable (Cotton, linen, jute, hemp, sisal)<br>Animal (Wool, silk, mohair, angora, vicuna, cashmere, camel hair)<br>Mineral (Glass fibre, metallic, asbestos) |
| REGENERATED FIBRES<br>(man-made) | Viscose<br>Modified Viscose (Viloft, Sarille, Evlan, Modal, Tenasco, Darelle)<br>Acetate (Dicel, Lancil)<br>Triacetate (Tricel, Arnel) |
| SYNTHETIC FIBRES<br>(man-made) | Polyamide (Nylon, Bri-nylon, Enkalon, Celon, Tendrelle, Bri nova)<br>Polyester (Terylene, Dacron, Trevora, Terlenka, Lirille, Crimplene)<br>Acrylic (Acrilan, Courtelle, Orlon, Modified Acrylic–Teklan)<br>Polyurethane (Lycra, Spanzelle)<br>Olefin Fibres (Polyethelene, Polypropylene)<br>Polyvinyl Chloride (PVC) |
| MISCELLANEOUS FIBRES | Paper<br>Fibrolane<br>Alginates |

**Summary of some of the properties of textiles**

| *Strength* | *Absorption of water* |
|---|---|
| Linen (strongest) | Wool (warmer when wet) |
| Nylon | Viscose (viloft modal) |
| Polyester | Linen |
| Silk | Silk (warmer when wet) |
| Cotton | Cotton (stronger when wet) |
| Acrylic | Acetate |
| Viscose | Triacetate |
| Wool | Nylon |
| Acetate (weakest) | Acrylic |
| | Polyester (absorbs least) |

> *Wearing comfort*
> Natural fibres e.g. cotton, silk 'breathe' more than man-made when worn.
> With a change in body temperature owing to exercise or weather change, natural fibres are more able to absorb the perspiration and therefore the clothing is more comfortable to wear.

| *Stretch* | *Elasticity* |
|---|---|
| Wool (stretches most) | Nylon |
| Acrylic | Wool |
| Acetate | Acetates |
| Nylon | Silk |
| Polyester | Polyester |
| Viscose | Viscose |
| Silk | Linen |
| Cotton | Acrylic |
| Linen (stretches least) | The more elastic the fibre the |
| Knitted fabrics give more stretch and elasticity | more crease resistant it is. |

## 15.3 Other materials used in the home and elsewhere

**Paper** is used to make a limited range of disposable items such as underwear and baby's nappies. These items are useful for holidays. 'Dish' cloths, disposable sheets and protective clothing made of paper are used mainly in hospitals.

**Fibrolane** is a protein fibre, used with other fibres, made from the casein in milk, which is coagulated by adding an acid to skimmed milk. It adds softness and warmth.

**Alginates** are made from seaweed. The fibre is totally flameproof but it cannot be washed because it dissolves in soap and water. It is not used for clothing or household articles. The fibres are often woven in with other fibres and the fabric then washed to dissolve the alginate fibres, leaving an open weave. It is useful for surgical dressings.

**Mixtures and blends**

1 A fabric which is a **mixture of yarns** has the mixture made during weaving.

2 A fabric made of **blended yarns** is one where the different fibres were blended together in the yarn before weaving.

3 Mixtures and blends add to the great variety of fabrics.

4 They combine advantages of different fibres and often overcome disadvantages.

5 They should be treated with the washing method which would be given to the weaker of the fibres present.

*Examples:* wool and cotton, wool and polyester, wool and viscose, cotton and modal, cotton and nylon, cotton and viscose, polyester and viscose, linen and polyester.

These mixtures and blends should be labelled. See Section 15.7.

### Non-woven fabrics

**Felt** is made from wool. The fibres are beaten and pressed together when wet.

**Bonded fibre fabric** A sheet or web of fibres is treated with a bonding agent, adhesive resin or heated rollers which will spray the resin, to hold the fibres. e.g. Vilene, nappy liners.

**Laminated fabrics** Several layers of fabrics are fastened together e.g. foam backed fabrics for curtains which then need no linings.

## 15.4   Textile terms

**Fibres** are the basic materials used to make yarns.

**Yarn** is a long textile strand made up of staple fibres or filaments, used to knit or weave a fabric.

**Spun yarn** is made of short-staple fibres which have been twisted together after being drawn out and combed.

**Continuous filament yarn** is made from one or several long filaments which are twisted together.

**NB** The amount of twist affects the appearance and the strength of a yarn. Fewer twists produce a soft, fluffy yarn. Many twists produce a smooth, stronger yarn.

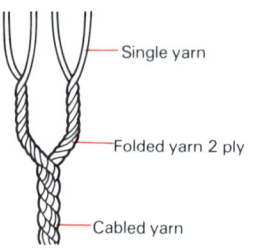

Single yarn
Folded yarn 2 ply
Cabled yarn             **Fig. 15.2**

### Thickness of yarns

One ply–a single yarn
Two ply   ⎫
Three ply ⎬ –denotes a number of singles twisted together to form a folded yarn
Four ply  ⎭
Cable yarn–two folded yarns twisted together
Denier–the diameter of a continuous filament yarn such as nylon. 30 denier is thicker than 20 denier.

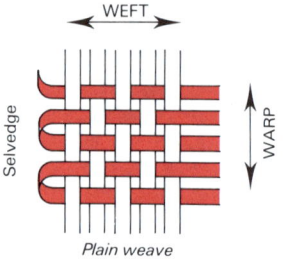

WEFT
Selvedge
WARP
*Plain weave*             **Fig. 15.3**

### Fabrics

Fabrics are woven or knitted.

**1** The appearance, texture and durability of a fabric is affected by the weave.

**2** A knitted fabric has greater elasticity.

**3** Both types of fabric can be brushed to increase their warmth.

**Woven fabrics** The **warp** thread runs **down** the length of the fabric and it is the strongest thread. The **weft** threads are **woven through** the warp threads.

**(a)** Twill weave produces a diagonal rib across the material. It is strong and hard-wearing.

*Examples*

Cotton twill–overalls, sheets

Denim

Herringbone for tweeds

Whipcord and gaberdine

**(b)** Satin weave. The weft threads pass over five or more warp threads and under one and so on. It produces a fabric with a smooth, shiny surface.

**(c)** Pile weave. Small loops of yarn stick up from the surface of the fabric. These can be left as loops or they can be cut to produce tufts.

*Examples*

Terry towelling is looped

Velvet and corduroy have the loops cut

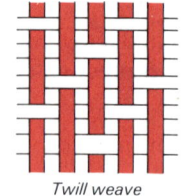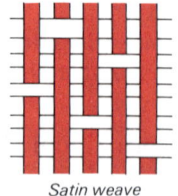

*Twill weave*          *Satin weave*

**Fig. 15.4**

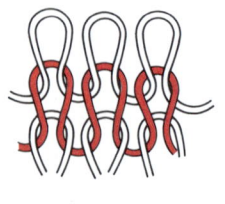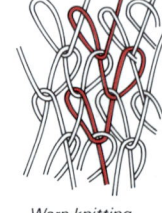

*Weft knitting*          *Warp knitting*

**Fig. 15.5**

**Knitted fabrics** are soft and comfortable to wear. They are more elastic and shed creases, e.g. cotton lockknit, jersey, nylon tricot.

**(a)** Weft knitting e.g. hand knitting. The yarn is moved across the fabric making a row of loops which interlock with loops below.

**(b)** Warp knitting. Every stitch has its own yarn. A wide range of colour combinations and complicated patterns can be achieved.

**Special finishes**

**Moth-proofing** where an insecticide is impregnated into the fibres so that the moth grubs are killed before they can do any damage.

**Crease resistant finish** e.g. Belofast–a minimum iron finish. A resin is baked into the fabric so that it resists creasing. The effect is often lost with wear and the finish can be spoilt by spinning too fast.

**Polishing** where a glaze is made on the surface of the fabric.

 1 'Calendering' on cotton-fabric passed between heated rollers.

 2 'Schreinering'–similar process but the rollers have engraved lines which are imprinted on the fabric. These catch and reflect light.

 3 'Beetling' is a method used to get a shine on linen. The material is beaten.

 4 'Mercerising' is a process carried out on the yarn before weaving and on cotton sewing threads. A strong caustic soda solution is used which gives the fibres a smoother, silky look. The fibres are strengthened by the process.

**Embossing** where a pattern is embossed on to a fabric as it passes through rollers.

**Pre-shrinking** Cotton is pre-shrunk by the **Sanforizing** or **Rigmel** processes. The subsequent washing shrinkage is less than 1%.
Dylan is shrink resistant wool.

**Flame proofing** Teklan and Dynel are acrylic fibres which are flameproof. **Proban** or **Pyrovatex** are processes used to make a fabric flameproof.

 The chemical treatment prevents flames spreading through the cloth. It is essential for the nightwear of children and old people. These garments should be washed in hand hot water with a soapless detergent. The fabric **must not be boiled** or **bleached** or **starched**. Ironing requires a moderately hot iron.

**Waterproofing** An oil, rubber or PVC backing is used to stop water passing through a fabric.

**Stain and water repellant finishes** can be achieved by weaving very closely. Or, a mixture of emulsified wax, aluminium acetate and casein is mixed with water–woollen fabric is dipped into this and then dried. The water evaporates leaving the wax in the fabric which is now showerproof.

 Silicones and heat can be used to form a polymer which is bonded to the woollen fabric.
**Scotchguard** is a chemical treatment given to make a fabric stain resistant.

 An article may have to be re-treated after dry cleaning–often referred to at the cleaners as re-texturing.

**Durable pleating** Thermoplastic yarns, polyamides, polyesters and acetates can be permanently pleated by heat treatments.

 Woollen fabrics can be permanently pleated. The fabric is pre-shrunk and then the pleats can be set by impregnating with chemicals which set in the heat.

**Brushed finish** A fabric can be made to have a fluffy surface and be made warmer by brushing. Fabrics usually treated in this way are cotton, viscose and knitted nylon.

**Sanitized fabrics** This treatment makes the fabric resistant to bacteria. The finish is lost if the fabrics are boiled.

**Thermolactyle Fabrics** are used to make clothing which is extra warm to wear.
*Examples*
Underwear, nightwear, socks, linings for shoes and boots, gloves, hats, jumpers, linings to jackets and anoraks, underblankets, car rugs.

 The fabrics are made of a thermolactyle chlorofibre which is frequently mixed with other fibres such as cotton, wool, viscose, nylon, elastane, acrylic, which increase the properties of the fabric.

 Thermolactyle fabrics can be knitted, sometimes with a brushed surface to be worn next to the skin or with a lacy crepe effect. A 'fur' fabric is used for linings and interlinings.

 These fabrics are poor conductors of heat. They reduce heat loss from the body as air is trapped between the fibres. They are mothproof, flame-resistant, non-felt and non-shrink.

 These fabrics must be **washed with care.**

 1 Wash frequently.

**2** Hand or machine wash 4 with a short spin or they may be drip dried. **Do not wring.**
**3** Dry naturally, **do not use artificial heat.**
**4 Do not iron.**
Solvent 113 may be used for dry cleaning but not perchloroethylene or other solvents used in coin-operated machines in launderettes.

### 15.5    The family wash

There are different ways in which the family wash can be dealt with. In addition to washing at home a launderette or commercial laundry may be preferred, occasionally or all the time.

**Launderettes**

Launderettes use large-capacity automatic machines which can be top or front loading. They are coin-operated and there is usually a detergent dispenser available. It is also possible to dry clean clothes at less cost than at the professional dry-cleaners.

**Table 15.1**    Advantages and disadvantages of using launderettes

| *Advantages* | *Disadvantages* |
| --- | --- |
| A washing machine does not have to be bought for the home. | The washing may not be as clean as you would get it at home. |
| There are no running or repair costs. | Fewer washing programmes are available and the washing and rinsing may not be as thorough. |
| Very handy for people living alone, for people in bed-sits, hostels or digs. | |
| No wet washing to cope with in bad weather. | The washing can make up a large load which has to be carried to the launderette. |
| Sometimes the launderette staff will do the washing for you. | A machine may not be available when you get to the launderette. |
| Launderettes are usually open very early and very late. | Waiting for your washing can be time wasting. |
| It is possible to leave your washing and shop or do some other job. | It is possible that your washing could be stolen in your absence. |
| They provide an opportunity to meet people. | Consider the cost of travelling to the launderette, if you are not combining it with a shopping visit. |
| It is probably cheaper to wash at the launderette. | |
| It is very useful for washing large items such as blankets, bedspreads and curtains. | |
| Very useful for the occasional wash: holidays, during illness, during bad weather. | |

**Commercial laundries**

If a commercial laundry is generally used it is often necessary to wash small items and delicate fabrics at home.

**Table 15.2** Advantages and disadvantages of using a commercial laundry

| *Advantages* | *Disadvantages* |
| --- | --- |
| Washing is collected and delivered back washed, dried and ironed | Each item is charged separately–can be expensive, but time saved must be set against cost. |
| A washing machine is not needed–no capital outlay, no running costs | |
| More time for other activities | More clothes and linen needed |
| | The laundry can lose items and be unreliable |
| | Method of laundering can be harsher e.g. the use of strong bleaches. |

**Washing at home**

As with all household tasks this needs to be planned. Hand washing and machine washing are usually involved.

There are more households with **automatic machines** now and although these free you for other tasks and activities they take time to complete a programme. It may be most convenient to wash one load per day.
**1** Preparation for washing
**(a)** Clothes should be sorted into groups according to the International Care Labelling Scheme (see Section 15.6)
**(b)** Mend tears and holes–these could get bigger during washing

**(c)** Empty pockets      **(d)** Close zips
**(e)** Brush off any loose dirt      **(f)** Treat any stains (see Section 15.7)
**(g)** Tie any long straps or apron strings
**(h)** Rub hard household soap onto shirt collars, dirty knees of jeans and the soles of socks
 2 Soaking
Heavily soiled or stained fabrics which belong to wash code Group 1, white cotton and linen, and which do not have any special finishes, can be soaked quite safely. Make sure that:
**(a)** The detergent powder is fully dissolved.
**(b)** The colours are fast if soaking textiles from any other group.
**(c)** The temperature is suited to the fabric.
**(d)** The articles being soaked are not overcrowded and bunched together.
**Never soak** white and coloured articles together, **or** articles with metal buttons or fasteners (possibility of rust marks–iron mould), **nor** articles made of wool, silk or those which have a flame-proof finish.
 3 Washing
**(a)** Hand washing
This is a tiring task if there are many articles to wash.
Hand washing is best for delicate lingerie, silk and most woollens.
Follow the ITCLC for the temperature of washing and rinsing waters.
Pre-soaking of suitable fabrics will probably mean a cleaner wash.
Make use of a spin drier rather than trying to wring out by hand–this easily damages fibres.
**(b)** Machine washing–see the following section.

**Choosing a washing machine**

**Points to consider**

**Size**–space where it will fit, size of the family, capacity of the machine

**Cost and method of payment**–purchase cost, running costs

**Type of machine**–single tub with wringer, twin tub, automatic

**BEAB** safety mark

**Washing action**–agitator, impeller or pulsator, tumble action

**If twin tub**–non-automatic or automatic

**If automatic**–top or front loading

**Hot water**–does the machine need a supply of hot water or has it a heater?

**Recommendation** Which models are recommended by friends?

**Consumer advice** Which are considered to be the best buys by '*Which*'?

**Types of washing machine**

**Single tub with wringer** These machines only wash. Rinsing must be done by hand in the sink or the machine emptied and filled up with several lots of water for rinsing.
    The wringer either works automatically so it must have a quick release bar in front of the rollers in case fingers get trapped, or it is operated manually.
    The wringer is not as efficient as the spin dryer at removing water.
    Many people still have this type of machine but the twin-tub and the automatic machines are the more popular now.

**Twin-tub** These machines have one tub for washing and one tub for spinning. The washing water is fed in by a hose from the sink. Rinsing can take place automatically or it has to be manually added to the spin dryer. The washing has to be lifted manually from wash tub to spin dryer. The 'soapy' water can be returned to the wash tub to be used again.
    Most have a heater and have varied controls to fit the washing code. There is usually a time control and a temperature control.

**Automatics** have one tub for washing, rinsing, spinning and some of the latest and more expensive machines will tumble dry too.
    Automatic machines should be plumbed into the water supply. They can be cold fill or hot and cold fill.
    The machines are controlled mechanically, electronically or with a micro-processor chip so that all stages in the washing programme happen automatically once the machine has been programmed.
    Front loading machines will fit under a work surface or are designed so a tumble dryer can fit on top. Top loading machines are taller and will not fit under a work surface, but the lid is usually of laminated plastic. Cost varies with the degree of sophistication.

*Top loaders*

Use any detergent
Wash by paddle action
Items can be added during wash programme
Uses more kitchen space
A load of washing is larger and costs more to wash
Uses more water, which has to be heated, more detergent per lb. weight of clothes.

*Front loaders*

Must use low lather detergent
Drum revolves to wash clothes
Door cannot be opened until wash finishes
Uses less kitchen space
Takes smaller load
Cheaper to wash

**Table 15.3** A comparison of twin tub and automatic washing machines

| *Twin tub* | *Automatic* |
|---|---|
| Cheaper to buy and to run | More expensive to buy, prices from £200 to £600. More expensive to run. Front loader cheaper to run than top loader |
| Filling and rinsing involves use of hoses and limits use of sink | Washing, rinsing and spinning takes place automatically once programme is set |
| Clothes have to be lifted to the spin dryer | |
| Rinsing water may need to be put in spin dryer by hand but in some models it is done automatically | Takes a longer time to complete washing programme but person doing the wash is free to do other things |
| Any detergent can be used | Front loaders must use a low foaming detergent. Top loaders can use any detergent |
| Spin dryer retains 60% water | Some automatics have combined driers with a 'maintenance rinse' to remove any fluff after use |
| | Uses more water |
| | Depending on model and rpm of spin, an automatic does not spin as effectively as a twin tub. |
| | Cheaper models–350 rpm retains 92% water 750 rpm retains 75% water 1000 rpm retains 65% water |

**Sequences of action when using a washing machine**

**Single tub and twin tub**

1 Fill with water   2 Add detergent, measuring carefully
3 Dissolve detergent   4 Put in the first load–underload rather than overload
5 Set temperature control
6 Set time control
7 Allow to heat and run for correct length of time
8 Rinse–cold water is usually the most suitable. Use two or three rinses
9 Add fabric conditioner in the last rinse
10 If water is not too dirty wash second load of clothes

**Automatic**

1 Place clothes in the wash drum, instruction booklets suggest maximum weights for machine, do not overload
2 Measure detergent and fabric softener into special compartments
3 Set controls–washcode number or temperature, large, medium or small load, maximum, medium or minimum washing time, short or long spin
4 Most automatics have a control for a biological powder wash
5 Turn on the water and switch on
No further attention is needed until the programme is completed.

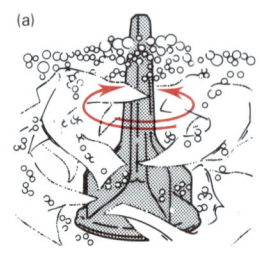
(a)

**Fig. 15.6**

**Washing action**

**Agitator machines** have a paddle with three or four blades. This turns backwards and forwards through about 180° turns. This moves the washing quite gently to and fro. This method is found in single tub washing machines, in twin tubs and in top loading automatics.

**Impeller or pulsator machines** have a wheel located in the side or at the bottom of the wash tub. It rotates in one direction creating a strong turbulence in the water. This is a violent washing action. It can be found in single tub and twin tub machines.

**Tumble action** is found in front loading automatic machines. The drum holding the clothes rotates either in one direction or in alternate directions. The clothes are lifted by baffles on the rotating drum.

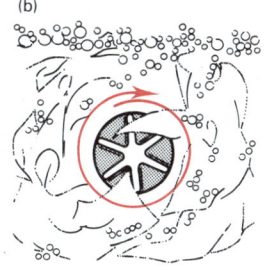 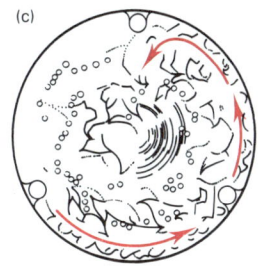

**Fig. 15.6**

### Care of the washing machine

1 After washing is finished, unplug the machine.
2 Wipe down the inside and outside to reduce the amount of rusting on the body of the machine and prevent perishing of rubber rings etc.
3 Make sure the dispensers and filter are clean.
4 If the machine has a wringer, wipe and dry the rollers, release the pressure and place a clean dry cloth between the rollers.
5 The outside can be polished with a soft cloth.
6 Store the cable in the compartment provided.
7 If possible leave the door or lid slightly ajar to enable air movement.

### The importance of rinsing

**Rinsing washes away** the dirt that has been removed from the clothes, and the detergent that has been used. The number of rinses depends upon the size of the container and the quantity to be rinsed.

**Rinsing water** is usually cold. The use of hot water wastes fuel.

If the soap is not properly rinsed away the soap scum can build up amongst the fibres and cause the fabric to become grey and rough to touch.

Fabric conditioner can be used in the last rinse to make clothes softer, bulkier, free of static electricity and easier to iron.

### Drying

Spin dryers and wringers cannot remove all of the water from clothes. The rest of the moisture has to be removed in one of the following ways.

**Line drying** Clothes dried outdoors feel and smell differently from those dried indoors. A windy day will make fabrics feel very soft. A very hot day can make the clothes hard.

**Heated racks and cabinets** The heat coming from below the clothes dries them. The moisture has to go somewhere and it will condense on cold surfaces. Clothes will dry indoors on an ordinary clothes rack but they take a long time and the moisture in the air can be unpleasant.

**Tumble dryers** are the most expensive way of drying clothes. The tumble dryer has to be bought and the electricity it uses is expensive.

Clothes must have been spun dry before they are put into the drum. This tumbles them in a stream of warm air. There is usually a choice of temperature settings. The steam escapes outside through a flexible hose which can be hung out from the window or a special vent can be fitted from the dryer through an outside wall. This is the most satisfactory method.

Manufacturers instructions must be followed. Woollens should never be tumble dried.

If carefully folded after being tumble dried many fabrics do not need to be ironed.

**Drying flat** Special racks can be bought that fit across a bath. Sweaters and other articles which need to be dried flat to avoid stretching can be spread on these.

## 15.6  Irons and ironing

### Ironing temperatures

On most articles of clothing symbols will be found on the label indicating the temperature to be used for ironing.

 **Fig. 15.7**    Iron at a temperature of 210°C (hot)    Use for cotton, linen, viscose and modified viscose

 Iron at a temperature of 160°C (warm)    Use for polyester mixtures and wool

 Iron at a temperature of 120°C (cool)    Use for acrylic, nylon, triacetate and polyester

### Dampness

Most fabrics should be ironed slightly damp, if they are too dry they are best rolled in a damp towel for 15 minutes so that they dampen evenly. Sprinkling can cause marks.

**Cotton**  Iron slightly damp on the right side

**Linen**  Iron damp on the right side

**Silk**  Iron slightly damp on the wrong side

**Wool**
  1 Knitted–iron dry or nearly dry on wrong side with a warm iron or steam.
  2 Woven–use a pressing cloth. Iron on the right or the wrong side. Warm iron or steam.

**Acrylic**  If ironing is needed iron on the wrong side. Steam or a damp cloth should not be used. Too much heat will stretch and harden the fabric.

**Nylon polyester**  Iron when nearly dry on the wrong side to prevent glazing.

**Acetates**  Iron when evenly damp on the wrong side.

### Ironing procedure

  1 Follow the ITCLC instructions carefully.
  2 Allow time for the iron to change from one temperature to the next.
  3 Make sure that the sole plate is always clean–starch can be removed with a solution of vinegar and water, 1 part of vinegar to 2 parts water, used on a cold iron. If a synthetic fabric melts onto the iron turn the temperature to hot. Use paper to remove the melted fabric and if necessary use a special sole cleaner when the iron is cold.
  4 Stand the iron on its heel when it is not in use.
  5 Do not use an iron with a frayed flex. The flex should never be wound around the iron. The wiring will eventually break.
  6 Use distilled water in a steam iron so that the steam vents do not become blocked with 'fur'. Empty the water from the iron when the ironing is finished.

### Choice of an iron

**Dry irons**  A wide selection to choose from. They vary in size, shape and weight. Very small irons are available for travelling and these usually have a multi-voltage, 110v to 240v, so they can be used on the continent.
  Dry irons are less expensive than steam irons and many people prefer them. They are thermostatically controlled and have the three ITCLC settings marked on the thermostat dial.

**Steam irons** vary. Some are just steam irons where the water changes to steam and passes out of the iron through the holes in the base of the sole plate as shown in Figure 15.8.
  **Steam/spray** irons produce steam in the same way as the ordinary steam irons but they can also spray water, from the cold water tank, at the front of the iron at the press of a button.
  Some steam irons also have a '**shot of steam**' action. This is produced by pumping water into the steam chamber which explodes into a large jet of steam which can penetrate several thicknesses of fabric. There is a choice of different makes, sizes and weights.

**Rotary irons** are more expensive and not very often used in the home. They are very useful if there are a lot of large flat articles such as sheets to iron. A heated metal plate presses down on a padded roller. The sheet or other article is fed in by hand while the apparatus is controlled by a foot pedal.

**Flat-bed pressers** are very large heated presses used by commercial laundries and clothes manufacturers. A large heated metal press head is closed down onto a large, padded flat bed. It is kept in contact with the bed until all the moisture is removed.

### Aids to successful ironing

  1 A firm, wide, well padded ironing board with a smaller sleeve board.
  2 A lightweight iron is less tiring to use.
  3 Make sure that the clothes are properly dampened down for ironing.
  4 Have a clothes horse to hand, so that articles can be hung on it straight away to air.

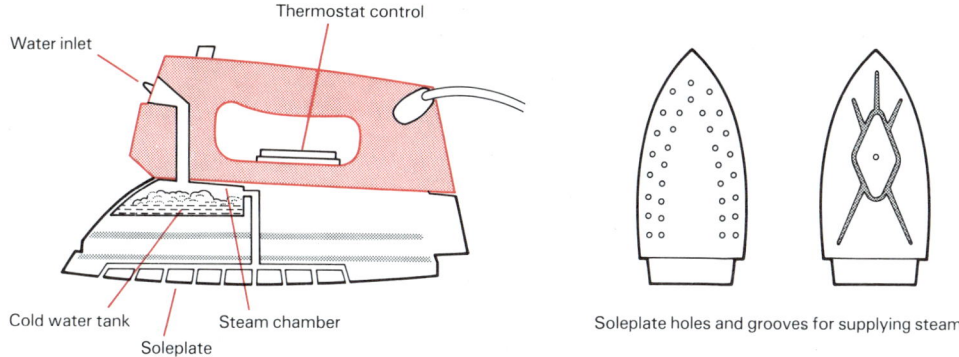

Fig. 15.8 A diagrammatic section through a steam iron to show its parts

### Stages to ironing

**Double and thicker parts** of an article should be ironed first. They will be damper and they can be ironed a second time with the main body of the garment.

**Seams** should be ironed on the wrong side. Take care not to press so hard that the position of the seam allowance can be seen on the right side.

**Iron to dryness** or when the article is folded the moisture left in it will help it to crease.

**Embroidery** should be pressed from the wrong side so that the stitching is pressed into the ironing pad. It will then be in relief, standing out from the fabric.

### Stages in ironing a blouse or shirt

These are probably the most difficult items to iron.
1 Iron the double parts first.
(a) Cuffs, on wrong side and then on right side    (b) Iron the yoke
(c) Iron the collar from points to centre back. Iron on wrong side and then on right side.
2 Iron the sleeves, along the under-arm seam first.
3 Iron right front, then back, then left front
4 Place flat on the ironing board with front uppermost    5 Fasten buttons
6 Turn over    7 Fold 5cm of front to back and place sleeves on top of these folds
8 Turn tail up about 10cm and then fold in half.

### Safety with laundry equipment

Buy equipment which carries the BEAB safety mark.

**Plugs** should be correctly wired and fused–13amp. Use plugs with insulated pins and which will not break if dropped.

**Flexes** should not trail across the kitchen and they should not be frayed.

**Lids** to spin dryers should not be opened during spinning. Most lids have a safety catch so they cannot be opened until spinning has stopped.

## 15.7  Textile labelling

### 15.7.1  The international textile care labelling code

This internationally agreed code came into operation in Britain in 1974. The drying symbols were added in 1977. The code was introduced to standardize textile care instructions.

There is such a wide variety of textile fibres and fabrics made of different blends that it is difficult to decide upon the actual fibre content by feel or appearance. Most items of clothing and household textiles are now marked with the code. The label gives full instructions for the correct care of the article so that it wears well and continues to look good.

Symbols overcome the barrier of language with imported and exported textiles and are shown in Figure 15.9.

### Washing symbols

Washing symbols are given on the detergent packet as well as the article, and have a system that corresponds with the control panel of a washing machine. Details are shown in Table 15.5.

Recently a colour coding has been incorporated with the washing code set out on the detergent packet.
95°C = red    60°C = orange    50°C = yellow
40°C = light blue    30°C = dark blue

*Washing*

*Bleaching*

*Drying*

*Ironing*

*Dry cleaning*

**Fig. 15.9**

**Table 15.4** Washing symbols

| Symbol | Washing Temperature | | Agitation | Rinse | Spinning/Wringing | Fabric |
| | Machine | Hand | | | | |
|---|---|---|---|---|---|---|
| **1** 95° | Very hot 95°C to boil | Hand-hot 50°C or boil | Maximum | Normal | Normal | White cotton and linen articles without special finishes |
| **2** 60° | Hot 60°C | Hand-hot 50°C | Maximum | Normal | Normal | Cotton, linen or viscose articles without special finishes where colours are fast at 60°C |
| **3** 60° | Hot 60°C | Hand-hot 50°C | Medium | Cold | Short spin or drip dry | White nylon; white polyester/cotton mixtures |
| **4** 50° | Hand-hot 50°C | Hand-hot 50°C | Medium | Cold | Short spin or drip dry | Coloured nylon; polyester; cotton and viscose articles with special finishes; acrylic/cotton mixtures; coloured polyester/cotton mixtures |
| **5** 40° | Warm 40°C | Warm 40°C | Maximum | Normal | Normal | Cotton, linen or viscose articles where colours are fast at 40°C, but not at 60°C |
| **6** 40° | Warm 40°C | Warm 40°C | Minimum | Cold | Short spin | Acrylics; acetate and triacetate, including mixtures with wool; polyester/wool blends |
| **7** 40° | Warm 40°C | Warm 40°C | Minimum do not rub | Normal | Normal spin Do not hand wring | Wool, including blankets and wool mixtures with cotton or viscose; silk |
| **8** 30° | Cool 30°C | Cool 30°C | Minimum | Cold | Short spin Do not hand wring | Silk and printed acetate fabrics with colours not fast at 40°C |
| **9** 95° | Very hot 95°C to boil | Hand-hot 50°C or boil | Medium | Cold | Drip dry | Cotton articles with special finishes capable of being boiled but requiring drip drying |

HAND WASH
Do not machine wash

DO NOT WASH

**Fig. 15.10**

Can be bleached safely    Use a Chlorine bleach    Do not bleach    **Fig. 15.11**

Line dry    Drip dry    Dry flat    Can be tumble dried    Do not tumble dry

**Fig. 15.12**

Use a hot iron 210°C    Use a warm iron 160°C    Use a cool iron 120°C    Do not iron

**Fig. 15.13**

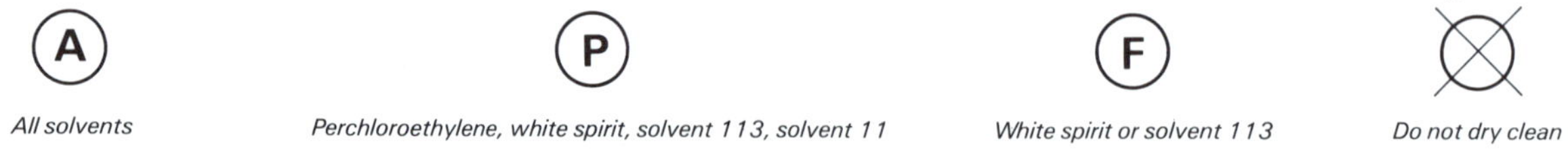

A — All solvents    P — Perchloroethylene, white spirit, solvent 113, solvent 11    F — White spirit or solvent 113    Do not dry clean

**Fig. 15.14**

### Fibre content labels

In 1976, the EEC council instructed member countries to label all textile products with the generic name of fibres they contain (e.g. polyester, cotton etc.). A brand name can also be used.

If a blended fabric contains at least 85% of one fibre it may be marked in one of the following ways: (i) 85% wool    (ii) Wool–85% minimum    (iii) 85% wool 15% polyester

If none of the fibres is present in as great a quantity as 85% the fibre present in the greatest amount is to be listed first followed by the others in descending weight order e.g. 55% wool/viscose/acrylic/nylon.

When a fabric is made up of equal proportions of two fibres it can be shown as follows: 50% polyester 50% wool.

### Wool symbols

**The Woolmark** shown in Figure 15.15 is used in 90 different countries. It is an international symbol used by manufacturers to indicate an almost 100% wool content. 0.5% non-wool fibre may be present and 0.3% is allowed for the presence of impurities.

**The Woolblendmark** is used when wool is mixed with another fibre as shown in Figure 15.16.

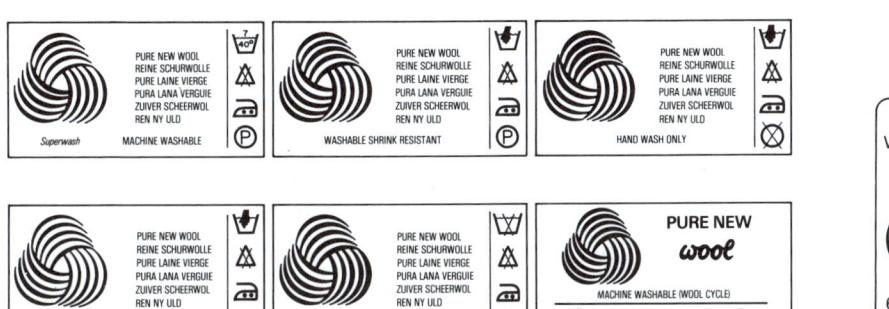

**Fig. 15.15** Wool symbols

**Fig. 15.16**

## 15.8   The hardness of water

There is a continuous circulation of water in nature. Water evaporates from the earth, sea, lakes and rivers and then condenses and falls back on to the earth as rain.

Rain water is **soft**. As rain water falls through the air it will pick up small quantities of $CO_2$ to form carbonic acid. Other substances such as sulphur dioxide and carbon monoxide, air pollutants from chimneys and traffic, will also be picked up.

As the rain percolates through soil and rock before running into lakes, reservoirs and rivers it picks up various mineral elements. It is in limestone regions that these minerals make the water **hardest**, but also give a better 'taste' to drinking water.

**Hardness** is measured in parts calcium carbonate per million. It can also be measured and given in degrees Clarke, when measured using Clarke's soap solution.

$$1° = 1g \ CaCO_3 \ \text{per gallon}$$

| Area | Approx degrees Clarke | Hardness in parts per million of $CaCO_3$ |
|---|---|---|
| **Devon** | 2° | 29 |
| **Yorkshire** | 3° | 43 |
| **Cheshire** | 3° | 43 |
| **Wales** | 4° | 57 |
| **Cornwall** | 5° | 72 |
| **Warwickshire** | 8° | 114 |
| **Sussex** | 16° | 229 |
| **London** | 20° | 286 |
| **Norfolk** | 25° | 358 |
| **Essex** | 30° | 429 |

| Hardness | Hardness in parts per million $CaCO_3$ |
|---|---|
| **Soft water areas** | 0 to 50 |
| **Moderately soft** | 50 to 100 |
| **Slightly hard** | 100 to 150 |
| **Moderately hard** | 150 to 200 |
| **Hard** | 200 to 300 |
| **Very hard** | Over 300 |

**Table 15.5** Water hardness

Scotland has water that is soft to moderately soft, Ireland has water that is soft to slightly hard.

### Temporary and permanent hardness

**Temporary hardness** is caused mainly by calcium hydrogen carbonate. In some areas magnesium hydrogen carbonate will also be found.

Rain water passing through the air picks up some carbon dioxide to form carbonic acid.

$$CO_2 + H_2O \longrightarrow H_2CO_3$$

As weak carbonic acid percolates through limestone the acid combines with the limestone to form calcium hydrogen carbonate.

$$H_2CO_3 + CaCO_3 \longrightarrow Ca(HCO_3)_2$$

**Permanent hardness** is caused by dissolved calcium sulphate and magnesium sulphate.

**Total hardness** is temporary hardness + permanent hardness.

## Softening water

Hard water is nutritionlly beneficial because of the calcium salts which provide calcium for the good formation of bones and teeth. Hard water can be a disadvantage when washing and heating the home because of the build up of 'fur' inside kettles, pipes etc.

### Removal of temporary hardness

1 By boiling, because the calcium hydrogen carbonate decomposes to form calcium carbonate, water and carbon dioxide.

$$Ca(HCO_3)_2 \xrightarrow{\text{heat}} CaCO_3 + H_2O + CO_2$$

The calcium carbonate forms the 'fur' or 'scale' in kettles, in hot water and in central heating pipes, in hot water cylinders, around the heating elements of immersion heaters and washing machines. Heating is less efficient and more electricity is used.

2 By the use of sodium carbonate (washing soda)

$$Ca(HCO_3) + Na_2CO_3 \longrightarrow CaCO_3 + 2NaHCO_3$$

**Permanent hardness** can also be removed in this way

$$\underset{\text{(calcium sulphate)} + \text{(sodium carbonate)}}{CaSO_4 \quad + \quad Na_2CO_3} \longrightarrow \underset{\text{(calcium carbonate)} + \text{(sodium sulphate)}}{CaCO_3 \quad + \quad Na_2SO_4}$$

$$\underset{\text{(magnesium sulphate)} + \text{(sodium carbonate)}}{MgSO_4 \quad + \quad Na_2CO_3} \longrightarrow \underset{\text{(magnesium carbonate)} + \text{(sodium sulphate)}}{MgCO_3 \quad + \quad Na_2SO_4}$$

**Calgon** (sodium hexametaphosphate) can also be used to soften water for washing.

**Sodium sesquicarbonate** can also be used in this way.
These two substances are better than sodium carbonate for washing because sodium carbonate makes the water alkaline.

**Ion-exchange softeners**  There are several domestic water softening plants of the Permutit type which can be installed. They can be plumbed into the cold water supply in such a way that water for drinking and cooking remains hard whilst all other water is softened. The water softener removes the calcium and magnesium ions which make the water hard.

The hard water is passed through a bed of **ion exchange resin** where the calcium and magnesium ions are exchanged for sodium ions.

When the resin bed is exhausted it is **regenerated** by passing a sodium chloride (salt water) solution through the resin. This replaces the accumulated calcium and magnesium ions with sodium ions.

### Advantages of soft water

1 It has a silky feel and skin and hair feel softer after washing.
2 Hard water reacts with soap to form a scum of insoluble calcium salts. More soap powder is needed to form a lather. Soft water uses less soap.
3 Kettles, hot water pipes and central heating systems do not become covered with scale, so they transmit heat more efficiently and use less fuel.

## 15.9  Detergents

Read and follow the manufacturer's instructions.

### Soap and soap powders

These are made from **animal fats** and **vegetable oils** to which are added caustic soda, salt, water and heat. The process is called *saponification*.

Soaps are anionic detergents carrying a negative charge.

### Synthetic (soapless) detergents

The basic material used in the manufacture of synthetic detergents is a side product of the refining of crude oil, **alkyl benzene sulphonate.** This produces detergents with a negative charge – anionic.

### Blended detergents

These are made for automatic washing machines. A blend of soap and synthetic detergents produces loss foam.

### Classification of detergents

| A Detergents made of soap | B Synthetic (soapless) detergents | | C Blends | |
|---|---|---|---|---|
| Persil | Tide | Surf | Automatic Persil | Automatic Pat |
| Fairy Snow | Daz | Ariel | Automatic Daz | Automatic Bold |
| Soap flakes e.g. Lux | Omo | Radient | Automatic Omo | |
| | Dreft | Stergene | Automatic Surf | |
| | Drive | Fairy Liquid | Automatic Ariel | |

Detergents can also be classified as **heavy** or **light duty** and **high, medium** or **low foaming**.

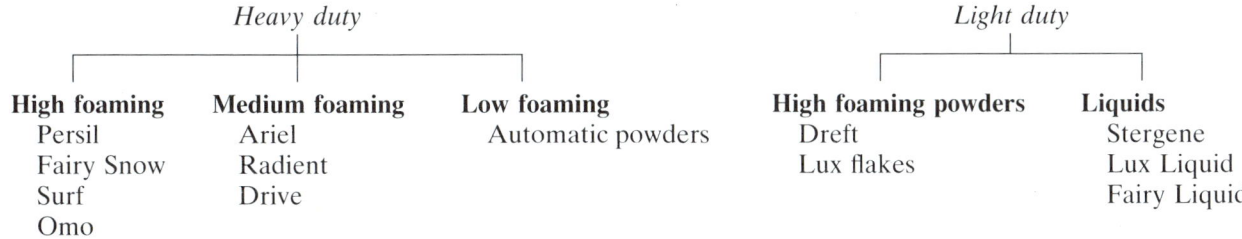

| High foaming | Medium foaming | Low foaming | High foaming powders | Liquids |
|---|---|---|---|---|
| Persil | Ariel | Automatic powders | Dreft | Stergene |
| Fairy Snow | Radient | | Lux flakes | Lux Liquid |
| Surf | Drive | | | Fairy Liquid |
| Omo | | | | |
| Daz | | | | |

**Biological powders** contain enzymes obtained from a carefully selected strain of bacterium, *Bascillus subtilis* e.g. Ariel. These enzymes are **active against** a wide range of **proteins**. They are most effective up to a temperature of 60°C.

**TAED Based detergents** (e.g. Persil Automatic) have a builder based on Tetra Acetyl Ethylene Diamine which combines with the builder perborate to produce a bleach, peroxyactic acid (peracid) which works with maximum efficiency between 50°C and 60°C. It has the **effect of a high temperature wash** where the perborate has a bleaching action **at lower temperatures** which means a saving on electricity. Bacteria are also destroyed as low as 40°C.

**Biodegradable detergents** At first synthetic detergents were a problem when discharged into waterways. The foam interfered with natural biological breakdown by bacteria in the water. This problem has now been solved and all detergents in the United Kingdom are biodegradable.

**Builders in heavy duty detergents** vary in amount from one powder to another.
 1 Sodium Carbonate–used to break down grease.
 2 Sodium Tripolyphosphates (STTP)–used to soften water, to suspend dirt and to prevent the formation of scum.
 3 Sodium carboxymethyl cellulose (SCMC)–used to prevent the dirt being redeposited on the fabric.
 4 Sodium perborate and sodium percarbonate–have a bleaching effect at temperatures above 85°C.
 5 Fluorescers–these are optical brightening agents. They absorb ultra-violet light which is invisible and re-emit this as visible light.
 6 Sodium sulphate and sodium silicate–these keep the powder crisp and free flowing and prevent corrosion of the aluminium parts of the washing machine.
 7 Perfume     8 Colourants     9 Preservatives
10 Lather improvers–maintain the lather throughout the washing process.

**Builders in light duty detergents** do not contain bleaches. They do contain fluorescers, anti-redeposition agents, perfume and colouring.
**NB** Lux soap flakes contain none of these.

## 15.9.1   How detergents work

**Soiling**

**Textiles are soiled** in two ways:
 1 By particles of solid dirt–dust, soot.     2 Greasy dirt.

**To remove dirt and grease** from a washable fabric it is necessary to use:

**Water, Detergent** and **Agitation.**

The dirt must be **removed** from the fabric and **held** evenly dispersed throughout the washing water so that it cannot be redeposited on the fabric.

Water is not a good wetting agent because of its surface tension. A detergent will **reduce the surface tension** and lift the grease from the fabric. Agitation will **loosen dirt** and aid the cleansing process.

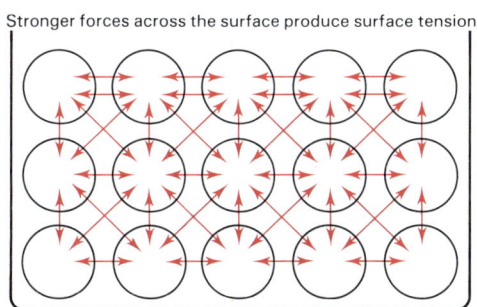

Stronger forces across the surface produce surface tension

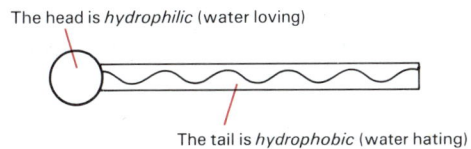

The head is *hydrophilic* (water loving)

The tail is *hydrophobic* (water hating)

**Fig. 15.18**

**Fig. 15.17** Surface tension on a container of water

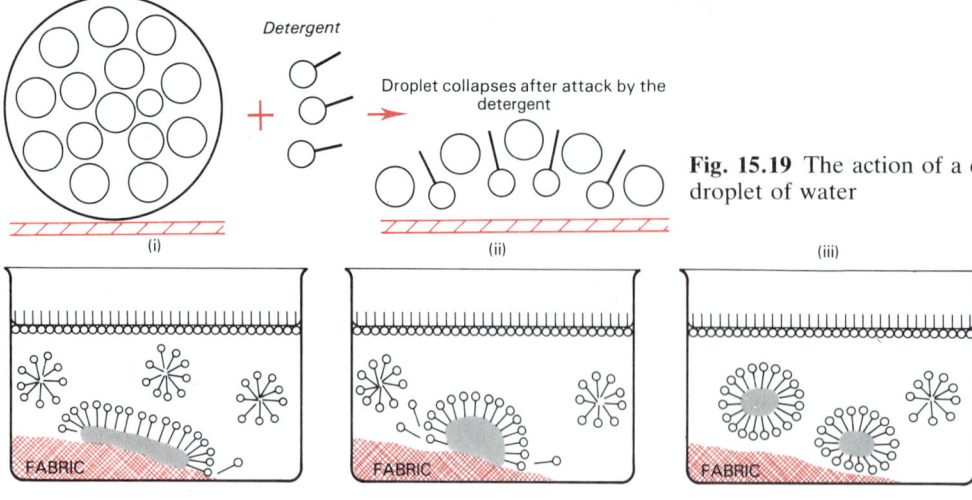

**Fig. 15.19** The action of a detergent molecule on a droplet of water

**Fig. 15.20** Detergent molecules, their action on dirt and grease

### Surface tension

**Water molecules** are strongly attracted to one another. These attracting forces act in all directions except at the surface of the water. At the surface there are no forces pulling from outside but the **forces** pulling in from the main mass of water molecules is **balanced** by a tension across the surface molecules which prevents shrinking inwards. This tension acts like a 'skin' on the surface, as shown in Figure 15.17, and is called **surface tension**.

Drops of water are spherical because of this tension – add a small amount of detergent to a drop of water and notice how it disperses.

**Wetting power**   The surface tension prevents droplets of water penetrating fabric and dirt. The detergent molecules reduce the surface tension in the following way:
1  A detergent molecule has a head and a tail (see Figure 15.18).
2  When the detergent is added to the water the water hating tails are pushed out between the water molecules thus breaking the bonds between them. The spherical shape of the water droplet collapses, spreads out and wets the surface.
3  With the water loving part of the molecule trying to remain in the water and the water hating part trying to escape the water the detergent molecules tend to concentrate at the surface of the solution of detergent and water. Detergents are called surface active agents because of this ability (**surfactents**).

### Dislodging dirt and grease

The water hating tail of the detergent molecule, which is the oily part, wants to attach itself to greasy dirt. The grease is soon surrounded by detergent molecules. Tails buried in the grease, heads happy in the water. Agitation can now dislodge the grease.

### 15.10   Other products for textile care

**Calgon, sodium sesquicarbonate** and **sodium carbonate (washing soda)** can be added to washing water to soften the water. See section 15.8.

### Bleaches

Washing powders now have bleaches in them and they are more effective at removing a wide variety of stains. Household bleaches are used less than in the past. The active agent is **sodium hypochlorite** which should only be used on white cotton and white linen.

Bleaches are also used to sterilize sinks, drains, dishcloths.

### Disinfectants

Disinfectants destroy bacteria and are useful for washing clothing and linen from a sick room. Articles should be steeped and washed separately.

### Fabric conditioners

These, like the detergents in section 15.9 are surface active agents. They are mostly cationic and carry a positive charge. Perfume and colouring are added e.g. Lenor, Comfort.

Fabric conditioners are usually liquid and they are added to the final rinsing water. They must be completely dissolved before pouring over the clothes. If they are to be added to an automatic washing machine the manufacturer's instructions must be followed.

There is now an impregnated cloth called Bounce which is put into a tumble dryer with the clothes. The conditioner is transferred from the impregnated cloth as the load tumbles.

**What do they do?**

**1** They soften and 'bulk up' textiles. They lubricate the fibres of the fabrics so preventing interlocking.

**2** Rubbing synthetic fabrics will produce a high charge of static electricity. This produces the characteristic crackling, cling and riding up which are frequently experienced with man-made synthetic textiles. Clothes treated with conditioners do not cling, ride up, crackle or give an electric shock.

**3** Conditioners make ironing easier. The iron slides more smoothly over the fabric.

**NB** Conditioners are sometimes added to detergent powders e.g. Fairy Snow, Bold.

### Starches

Starches are used to stiffen fabrics. The older methods of cold and hot water starching have been largely replaced by **instant starch** and **spray starching**.

Starch powders are made from rice or maize starch. Heat and moisture soften the starch granules, these swell and gelatinize on the fabric fibres. The heat of the iron causes the coated fibres to stick together and so make the fabric stiff.

**Cold water starch** Blend 25g starch in a bowl with a little cold water. Add 500ml of cold water and stir well.

Parts of garments and items which need to be very stiff such as cuffs and collars, table cloths and napkins are dipped into this mixture and then ironed with a hot iron.

**Boiling water starch** Mix 25g starch with a little cold water in a bowl. Pour on 500ml of boiling water stirring all the time. Stir until the mixture thickens and clears. Add a further 500ml of cold water. This gives a very stiff finish.

Articles which are to be starched are dipped into this prepared starch after their last rinse. If the starched article dries completely it must be evenly damped down before ironing. Table linen takes quite a stiff starch, items such as pillowcases need a more diluted solution.

**Instant starch** has been 'pre-cooked' so it will dissolve readily in cold water.

**Plastic starch** e.g. Dip is a plastic emulsion (PVA or polyvinyl acetate). It does not give such a stiff finish as ordinary starch but it will remain in a garment for three to four washes.

**Aerosol starch** is the easiest method of starching small parts of garments such as collars, but the most expensive method. The starch is sprayed on to the garment as it is ironed.

### Safety

All laundry products are best stored out of reach of small children.

## 15.11   Stain removal

Stains can be **absorbed stains** caused by the penetration of liquids; they can be **built up** stains which tend to stay on the surface of the fabric or they can be **compound stains** which are absorbed and present as a surface residue.

Before attempting to remove any stain answer the following questions:

**1** What has caused the stain?

**2** Which yarn or yarns make up the fabric?

**3** Has the fabric been treated with any special finish?

**4** Is the fabric washable or must it be dry cleaned?

### Remember

**Act immediately.** Stains are easiest to remove when they are fresh. **Blot off** surface liquid.

If the fabric is washable **soak in cold water** and wash in the usual way. With today's detergents this may be all that is necessary to remove the stain.

Try the **mildest** stain removal **treatment first**.

**Test** the removal agent on a hidden part of the garment or article. If fabric or colour are affected the article will not have been spoilt.

If the fabric is not washable and you are trying a proprietary brand of solvent **follow** the manufacturer's **instructions**.

If the article is to be cleaned professionally, **mark the position** of the stain and tell the cleaner what you think has caused it.

Many stain removal agents are **inflammable** and/or **poisonous**. Use in a well ventilated room away from any naked flame. Store out of reach of children.

## Stain removing agents

**Table 15.6** Some stain removing agents

| Agent | Use |
| --- | --- |
| **Liquid dishwashing detergent** | Use neat. |
| **Heavy duty washing powders** | Contain sodium perborate an oxidizing agent which removes stains by oxidation. |
| **Sodium Hypochlorite** | Strong bleach. Follow the instructions on the bottle. Only use on white cotton and linen. |
| **Biological detergents (Ariel)** | Contain enzymes which will break down protein based stains. |
| **Biological stain remover (Biotex)** | Similar to biological detergents in action but formulated just to remove stain not for washing. |
| **Hydrogen peroxide** | Using hydrogen peroxide of 10 vol strength: dilute 1 part hydrogen peroxide to 4 parts water. Safe on any fabric but affects some colours. |
| **Laundry borax** | Dissolve 25g in 500ml water. Use to sponge the stain and then wash. |
| **Methylated spirits** **White methylated spirits** **Surgical spirits** | Inflammable and poisonous. Can be used on any fabric except acetates. Use like dry cleaning solvents. |
| **Household ammonia** | Dilute 1 part ammonia with 3 parts water. Use in a well ventilated room. |
| **Amyl acetate** | Difficult to obtain. Can be used on most fabrics and colours but must not be used on acetates which dissolve. |
| **Grease solvents** liquids–Dab-it-off, Beau care pastes–K2R spot remover aerosols–Frend, Goddards Dry Clean | Mostly contain a grease solvent carbon tetrachloride. Poisonous and inflammable. Use in a well ventilated room and do not inhale the vapour. *To use* 1 Spread a clean absorbent cloth under the stain. 2 Soak another cloth in the solvent and dab at the stain. 3 Work from the outside in towards the centre to avoid a ring-mark. 4 Air non-washable fabrics. Wash washables in the usual way. |
| Turpentine substitute | Use neat |
| Polyclens | Use neat |
| Swarfega | Use neat |
| Dygon | Follow manufacturer's instructions |

## The removal of stains from washable fabrics

**Table 15.7** Stain removal from washable fabrics

| Stain | Treatment |
| --- | --- |
| **Coffee/tea** | Soak when fresh in a detergent solution. Wash at the highest temperature for fabric type. |
| **Blood, egg, milk, chocolate, ice-cream, urine, faecal stains, vomit** | All of these stains contain protein. Rinse in cold water. Soak in salt and cold water or biological detergent. Wash in a biological detergent. |
| **Chewing gum** | Harden the gum by placing article in refrigerator or hold a polythene bag with ice cubes behind the stain. Crack the hardened gum and pick off. Remove any stain remaining with a liquid grease solvent or methylated spirits. An aerosol spray can be bought. This freezes the gum. |
| **Tar** | Scrape off surface tar. Use a grease solvent. Swarfega or Polyclens can be rubbed in from the back of the fabric to soften. Wash. |
| **Other grease stains** | *Fats, oils, butter* Scrape off surface grease. Rub undiluted washing up liquid into stain and leave for a few minutes. Wash in a strong detergent at the highest temperature for the fabric. *Lipstick* Use a grease solvent. Wash. *Car grease, bike chain grease* Swarfega or Polyclens *Boot and wax polish* Scrape off surplus grease. Treat with a grease solvent. Wash in a heavy duty detergent. |
| **Grass stains** | Sponge with white methylated spirits. Glycerine may help to remove the green colour from plant stains. Wash in a detergent suited to the fabric. Biological detergents sometimes help. K2R stain remover will probably be effective on a small stain. |
| **Ink** | *Washable ink* Rub under cold water. Soak in cold water. Wash in heavy duty detergent. *Permanent ink, ball point, felt tip* Place absorbent pad beneath stain. Dab with methylated spirits or surgical spirits. Carbon tetrachloride or trichloroethylene may also be used. Lemon juice and salt are also effective. Wash in detergent solution. |

| Stain | Treatment |
|---|---|
| **Beer** | Soak in lukewarm water. Wash in heavy duty detergent. |
| **Spirits** | Rinse in warm water. Sponge with warm detergent solution. Wash. |
| **Wine** | Rinse in warm water or cold water with salt added (especially for red wine). Sponge with warm detergent solution. Wash. |
| **Scorch marks** | Soak in warm borax solution. Rinse well and wash in a light detergent. White fabrics may be treated with hydrogen peroxide if nothing else works. |
| **Iron mould** (rust) | Sheets, towels, handkerchiefs made of white linen or cotton can be soaked in lemon juice or citric acid and water (10g citric acid to 100ml water).<br>Press between pieces of damp cloth. Repeat and immediately the stain goes, wash.<br>Moval and Rustasol are two proprietary rust removers which can be used on white fabrics. Wash immediately. |
| **Paint** | *Oil based paint* Remove any excess paint. Dab with white spirit or Polyclens. Use neat washing-up liquid after the spirit, rub into fabric and then wash immediately in heavy duty detergent. If the paint has dried, scrape and brush the stain before treating as a fresh stain.<br>*Emulsion paint* Cold water will usually remove fresh paint. Wash. If paint has dried it should be scraped and brushed and then washed. |
| **Nail varnish**<br>**Hair lacquer** | Use nail varnish remover or amyl acetate. These must not be used on acetates or triacetates.<br>Methylated spirits will remove any remaining colour.<br>Wash in a heavy duty detergent. |
| **Glue** | *Clear contact adhesives* Scrape off any surface adhesive. Use amyl acetate on the wrong side of the fabric. Do not use on acetates and triacetates. Wash.<br>*PVA or latex adhesives* A damp cloth will usually remove these when they are wet. Wash in cool water. If the stain is dry, scrape and brush before treating. |

## 15.12   Household textiles

### 15.12.1   Carpets

These are probably one of the most expensive items bought for the home. Choice should be made carefully because a mistake is with you for a long time. Factors affecting choice are:
  1 Where the carpet is to be laid. Will it get heavy usage or will it get very little wear?
  2 The cost will depend upon fibre and quality.
  3 What form will the carpet take—fitted, a carpet square or carpet tiles?
  4 What sort of construction—Axminster or Wilton weave, tufted, bonded, looped or cord?
  5 Will a plain colour or pattern be more suitable?
  6 Will the carpet be easy to clean?

**Grades of carpet**

**Grade 1** Light domestic for use in rooms where there is little wear, e.g. the spare bedroom.

**Grade 2** Medium domestic for areas where there is a little more wear.

**Grade 3** General domestic for main areas not subjected to the heaviest wear.

**Grade 4** Heavy domestic for areas receiving a lot of wear, living room, hall.

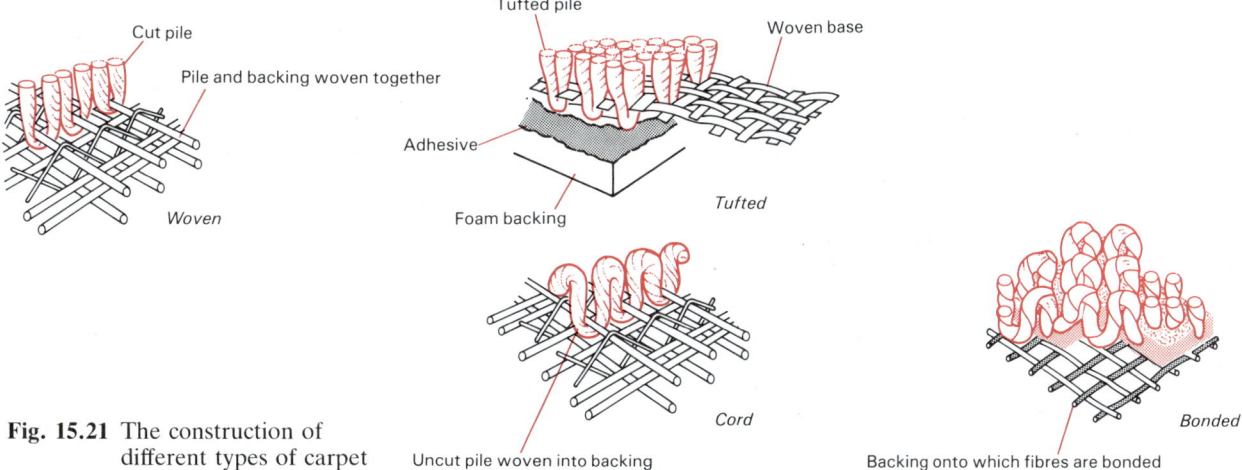

**Fig. 15.21** The construction of different types of carpet

**Grade 5** The most hard-wearing carpet of all and can be used anywhere. It is used commercially in offices.

Grade 1 will be the cheapest carpet and grade 5 the most expensive.

### Construction of carpets

**Axminster and Wilton** are woven carpets with the pile and backing woven together. Wilton usually has fewer colours than Axminster, up to three.

Wilton carpets are made using a long thread and the loops made by weaving are **woven over wires**. The size of these wires determines the length of the tufts, which are cut when the wires are lifted out. Colours not being used on the surface are woven into the back like Fair Isle knitting–this produces a firmer carpet.

Axminster carpets have short pieces of yarn woven into the backing and it is possible to use many colours and to make a tremendous variety of patterns.

If the Wilton or Axminster carpet is made of 100% wool or 80% wool + 20% nylon it will be a top quality carpet. If however the fibres used are a mixture of wool and the modified viscose Evlan it will only be a medium quality carpet. It is the construction and the fibre or fibres which determine the quality of the carpet.

**Tufted carpets** The backing is produced first and the tufts are threaded into it. Another backing is then attached.

**Corded carpet** is woven in a similar way to Axminister and Wilton but the loops are small and tight, and left uncut.

**Bonded carpets** are made of man-made fibres which are bonded to a backing using glue and heat.

### Underlay

This will lengthen the life of a carpet and makes it feel thicker. It can be made of felt, rubberized felt, foam rubber or plastic.

Cheaper carpets have a built in foam underlay which makes them softer and longer lasting. When this carpet is laid a special paper is laid underneath it to stop it sticking to the floor.

### Carpet fibres

**Wool** usually makes the best quality carpets, it is warm, thick and does not flatten. It springs back after furniture has been standing on it for a little while. It does not get dirty easily.

**Acrylic fibres** such as Acrilan and Courtelle are more like wool than any other man-made fibre. They have the warmth and thickness of wool but they get dirty more quickly. They are however hardwearing, easier to clean and cost less than wool.

**Nylon** is very strong and hard wearing. It is quickly washed and dried but it is not soft. Useful in a kitchen or a bathroom.

**Viscose modified** and called **Evlan** is also found in carpets. It is cheaper but is not hard-wearing, it flattens and picks up dirt. It is often mixed with wool.

### Broadloom carpet

This is the name given to carpet made on looms over 1.83metres (6ft). The most common width is 3.66m (12ft). Broadloom avoids having joins in a fitted carpet as a 12 feet width fits most rooms.

### Care of carpets

**1** Follow the manufacturers instructions which are usually written on the label. The carpet retailer will probably give specific instructions also.

**2** Large carpet squares and rugs should be turned regularly to avoid uneven wear.

**3** Protect the carpet from any damage which might be caused by the pressure of heavy furniture. Special 'cups' can be bought to place under furniture legs. It is also advisable to move furniture occasionally to avoid these pressure marks.

**4** When a new carpet is laid it is often 'fluffy' for a few weeks. During this time use a carpet sweeper and not a vacuum cleaner. When the carpet has settled use a vacuum cleaner when it is necessary.

**5** Carpets made of man-made fibres tend to get dirtier than woollen carpets. It is probably wiser to consult a professional carpet cleaner for a top quality carpet. Powder and foam carpet cleaners can be used. These can be applied by hand with a sponge, a hand held shampooer or an electric carpet shampooer. Follow the instructions carefully and do not get the carpet too wet. Make sure it is completely dry before replacing the furniture.

**6** A special carpet rake is needed for carpets with a very long shaggy pile.

## 15.12.2  Curtains

### Choice of curtains

**1** The colour and pattern of the material will be influenced by the colour of the walls and any carpet already in the room. If the carpet is plain the curtain material should possibly be patterned, but if there is a large pattern on the wallpaper a patterned curtain fabric could make the room look cluttered and not in any way restful.

**2** The cost of the material will be affected by the type of fibre or fibres in the material and upon the type of heading tape needed–this can be expensive. The final choice will probably be a compromise limited by the actual amount of money you have to spend.

**3** Before making your final choice ask the following questions:

**(a)** Will it drape well?     **(b)** Does it need a lining?     **(c)** Will it wash?

**(d)** Is it pre-shrunk?     **(e)** Will sunlight cause it to rot?     **(f)** How long is the pattern repeat?

Curtains can be bought **ready-made**. A making up service is usually provided by the shop selling the material. Making up can be included in the price of the material or sometimes shops have a special offer and will make up curtains free of charge.

### Curtain styles

**The standard gathered heading** hung from curtain rail or pole.

**Deep headings with pinch pleats,** pencil pleats, gathers hung from special rails.

**Curtains with pelmets**–shaped in fabric or in contrasting wood.

Shops selling curtain materials usually have sample curtains made up so that you can see the effect of the fabric in a large piece, the draping qualities and a whole range of headings. These all help in making a choice. The shop usually has all the extras too, rails, poles, tapes and hooks.

### Linings

Linings are not just expensive extras. In the long term they can save money. The lining may be attached or made so that it is detachable. Linings give body to curtain fabric and improve the draping qualities.

Curtains are hung with the lining next to the window so it is the lining that receives the **full glare of the sun** and the **dust and dirt** that comes through the window. The curtain fabric does not rot and it stays cleaner for longer. It is a simple task to detach loose linings and wash or replace.

Lined curtains keep more heat in the room also. This insulating effect is increased if the curtains are also interlined. This interlining is usually used on very large curtains in hotels and public rooms, it improves drape as well as insulating properties. There is a wide variety of insulating material on the market now for household use.

### Care of curtains

Curtains become dusty rather than dirty and should have a weekly dusting with the attachment for the purpose on the vacuum cleaner.

**Occasionally** they can be taken down and shaken or given a blow on the line outside. Once curtains have been washed or dry cleaned they lose some of their body and crispness.

### Making curtains

This is a relatively simple process although the fabric can be a little cumbersome if making curtains for large windows.

**Measure the windows** Curtains are usually hung from a pole or track which is extended beyond the width of the window. It is the width of the curtain rail which should be measured. The length is taken from the top of the rail to the position below the window at the point where you wish the curtains to end.

Add **25cm** to the length measurement to allow for heading, hem and shrinkage.

**Finished width curtains** = 400cm

Total width + fullness   = 400 × 1½ = 600cm

**Curtain fabric is 120cm wide**

Number widths needed = 600cm ÷ 120cm = 5

**5 drops of 225cm needed of plain fabric**

225 × 5 = 1125cm = 11.25metres.

**Each curtain will be made up of 2½ widths of fabric.**

With a patterned material more fabric would be needed. How much more depends on the size and repeat of the pattern. Shop assistants usually help you work this out.

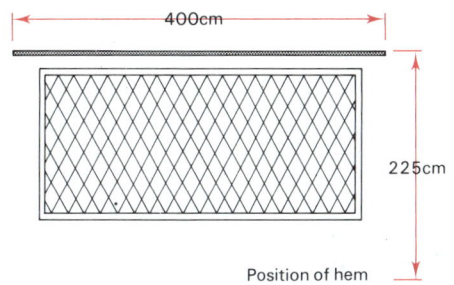

**Fig. 15.22**

**In this example** a minimum of 610cm curtain tape would be needed to allow for hems. Lining is plain. 11.25 metres would be needed.

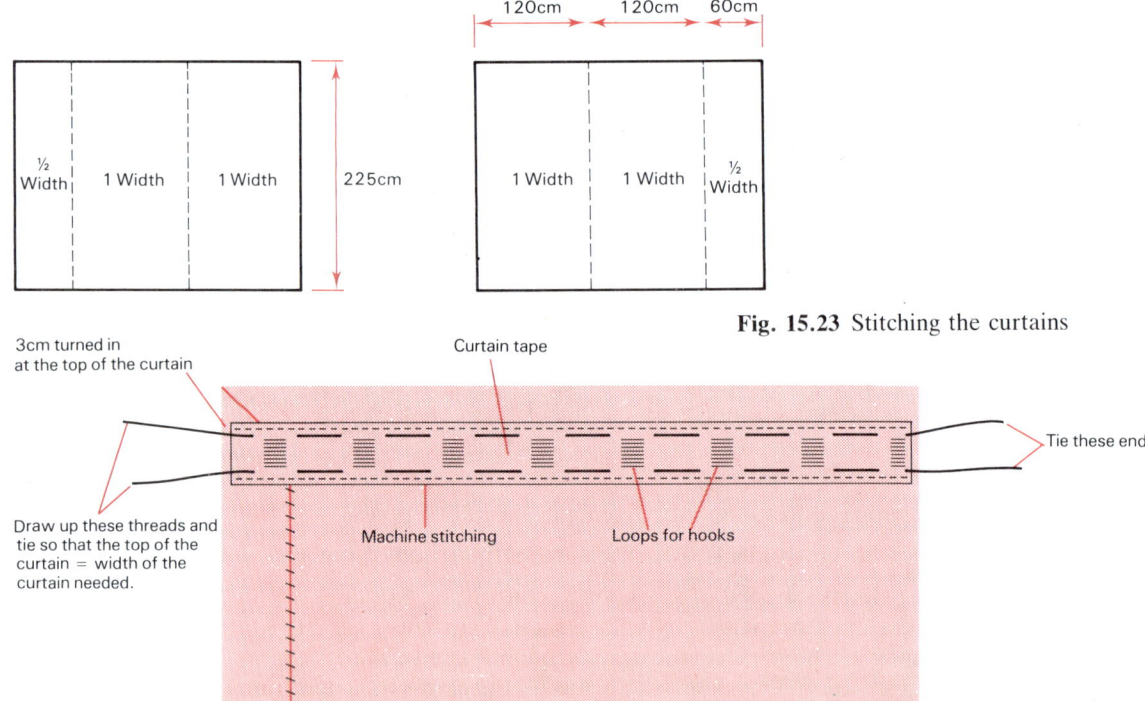

Fig. **15.23** Stitching the curtains

Fig. **15.24** Curtain tapes and gathers

**To make the curtains**

1 Cut the fabric into 5 equal lengths 225cm long.

2 Cut one of these lengths down the centre.

3 Stitch these lengths together as shown in Figure 15.23. Treat the lining in the same way. The seams should be 1½cm wide.

4 Selvedge edges should be snipped every 8cm to make sure the seam will lie flat. Treat the linings in the same way.

5 Turn in the side seams. Pin and tack. If the curtains are not being lined stitch the side hems. Hand stitching is best because if the material shrinks machine stitching will pucker.

6 Turn over 3cm at the top of each curtain and tack and then machine the curtain tape in position as shown in Figure 15.24. Tie off the tape cords securely at each side.

7 The linings should be approximately 4cm narrower than the curtains so that the curtain fabric folds over at the curtain edges to give a good edge appearance. Pin in position on top of the side hems of the curtain fabric. Attach with a slip hemming stitch. If you prefer to machine the lining to the curtains place the right side of the curtain on the right side of the lining and machine down the two sides. Turn right side out and press.

8 Draw up the cords to make the curtains the required width (200cm in this case) and tie Arrange the fullness evenly.

9 Hang for a few days before turning up and stitching the hem. Slip stitch the hem and then the lining to the hem about 1½cm from the bottom.

### 15.12.3   Bed linen

**Sheets and pillowcases**

These are available in a wide range of fabrics, colours and patterns.

**Buy as good a quality** as can be afforded.

**Buy the correct size** – make sure the sheets are large enough to tuck under the mattress.

1 Pillow cases are usually 50cm × 75cm. They can be plain or frilled.

2 Sheets come in the following sizes to cater for the narrowest single bed up to a King size bed.

(a) 160cm × 250cm – Single

(b) 180cm × 250cm – Larger single

(c) 230cm × 275cm – Double

(d) 275cm × 275cm – King size

3 Bottom sheets can be fitted with elasticated corners to hold beneath the mattress. The disadvantage of this is that the sheet cannot be used as a top sheet.

**Table 15.8** Materials used for bed linen–advantages and disadvantages

| Material | Advantages and disadvantages |
| --- | --- |
| **Linen** | Cool and hardwearing. Needs ironing. Very expensive. |
| **Cotton** | Smooth finish, cool, heard wearing. Needs ironing. Plain colours. Quite expensive. Twill weave warmer. |
| **Flannelette** (brushed cotton) | Soft and warm. Less hard wearing than smooth cotton. Range of colours and patterns. |
| **Cotton and vincel** | Cheaper than cotton. Warm. Not such hard wearing properties. |
| **Polyester and cotton** | Easy care. Cooler wash than cotton. Dries quickly. Ironing not necessary. Full range of plain colours and patterns. Cheaper than plain cotton. Hard wearing. |
| **Polyester and vincel** | Cheaper than polyester and cotton. |
| **Smooth nylon** | Not absorbent. Very easy to wash and dry. No ironing needed. Inexpensive. Range of colours. Not very comfortable on warm nights. |
| **Brushed nylon** | Softer and warmer to touch. Same easy care properties as smooth nylon. Range of colours. |

**Duvet covers**

Mainly made of polyester and cotton for very easy care. A wide range of colours and patterns. Nylon is sometimes used.

**Sizes** $140 \times 200/220$cm Single $\quad$ $200 \times 200/220$cm Double $\quad$ $230/260 \times 220$cm King size

**Valances**

These can be attached to a fitted bottom sheet or can be bought as a separate cover for the bed base. They can be gathered, pleated or tailored.

The colours of valances, sheets and pillowcases can be mixed or matched.

**Blankets**

Buy the best quality that can be afforded. One good quality woollen blanket can be warmer than two cheaper blankets.

Blankets with a **cellular weave** are warmer if they have another cover above them. They trap an insulating layer of warm air.

**Sizes** Allow a good overhang for tucking in when buying blankets. The following sizes are available:
$180$cm $\times 240$cm–Single $\quad$ $260$cm $\times 250$cm–Double $\quad$ $250$cm $\times 300$cm–King size

**Under-blankets** are used to protect the mattress and to give additional warmth. There are thermolactyle blankets for people who feel the cold but any type of blanket may be used.

**Bedspreads**

Bedspreads act as a top cover and as decoration.

They can be simple throw-over covers, frilled, fitted or padded. They may be candlewick, tapestry, crocheted, knitted or made of patchwork.

A wide range of fibres is used. Remember that they are washed more frequently than blankets. Nylon and padded nylon bedspreads should be washed frequently because they quickly pick up dirt and discolour.

**Eiderdowns**

Traditionally eiderdowns are filled with down, and quilted. They can replace two or three blankets.

Feathers, terylene, viscose fibres are also now used for filling. They are not as popular now as continental quilts have taken their place.

**Pillows**

Pillows give support to the head and neck. The number used depends upon personal taste. Babies and young children should not be given pillows.

**Table 15.9** Materials used for pillows–advantages and disadvantages

A firm, closely woven fabric is used to form the casing.

| Material | Advantages and disadvantages |
| --- | --- |
| **Down** (goose and duck) | This is very expensive. Soft and warm. |
| **Down and feather** (goose and duck | A central bag of feathers is sometimes surrounded by down. This type of filling is slightly cheaper than down alone. |

| Material | Advantages and disadvantages |
|---|---|
| **Feather and down** | More feathers and again slightly cheaper. |
| **Feather** | This is cheaper still. |
| The main disadvantage of these first four types of filling is that people can be allergic to the down and/or feathers, but they are more comfortable and warmer. | |
| **Polyester** | The brand names Terylene or Dacron are often used. This is a warm and soft filling. It is resilient. Sometimes it is used around foam. People are not usually allergic to polyester. |
| **Foam, latex or plastic** | A much more solid pillow. This and the polyester filling are much easier to clean and are often washable – useful for children's pillows. |

### Duvets or continental quilts

A duvet is a large bag filled with a substance that will hold air, which traps an insulating layer of air above the sleeper.

A duvet replaces sheets and blankets so there is less washing and it is quicker and easier to make the bed.

The bag is made of a closely woven cotton or mixture or fibres. The fillings can vary.

The warmth of a duvet is measured as 'Tog rating'. The greater the Tog rating the warmer the duvet. Tog 10-11.5 is the average Tog rating suitable for use in this country.

Fibres and fillings used are down (warmest), down and feather, Dacron, terylene, hollow fibre. The synthetic fillings are usually non-allergenic and washable, but can be less comfortable especially on a warm night as the filling does not 'breathe'.

### Use and care of a duvet

1 Always use a cover.

2 Air and shake every day. Hang on a line in the fresh air every few weeks.

3 Duvets with synthetic filling can be washed but those filled with down and/or feathers will need professional cleaning.

# Part III

# 16  Guide to the examinations

## 16.1  The practical examination

The requirements of the practical examinations vary slightly from Board to Board. Your teacher will have explained what is required by your particular Board.

Most CSE and O -level Boards set a 2½ hour practical examination with a preparation paper a few days earlier but shorter tests are becoming more common. In their CSE Food and Nutrition Examination the East Anglian Examination Boad set two practical tests, one of 1¼ hours and the second of 1½ hours. The Oxford Board now offer an alternative to their practical examination in Food and Nutrition.

### Practical Preparation Session

The planning of your work is carried out under strict examination conditions. You are allowed to take **recipe books** into the examination room but you will be wise to **limit these** to your own recipe notebook and a basic book of well tried recipes. It is time wasting to browse through glossy recipe books.

Tests may be assigned to candidates in alphabetical order. You may have a choice within this test, or alternatively you may have a free choice from a list of assignments.

There are four important words to consider when answering any examination question.

1 **Read** the question carefully.

2 Make sure you **understand** what the question is asking you to do.

3 **Think** about the best way of answering the question.

4 **Choose** dishes, ingredients and equipment.

Inability to answer the set question/s accounts for most examination failures and poor grades.

It is helpful if you *underline* the important parts of a sentence in a question. Try underlining the important elements in the following questions:

1 At the school Open Evening there is to be a display entitled 'Good value for money'. Choose

three suitable dishes which you can prepare, cook and display. One dish should show an economical use of a protein food; another dish should show an attractive use of fruit or vegetables; and the third dish should include the use of rice or pasta. In the remaining time make one small item and a beverage to serve to the parents when they visit the exhibition.

  **2 Either**                                              (*Joint Matriculation Board – Domestic Science A*)
**(a)** Prepare, cook and serve a main evening meal for two young students who have been advised to include more fibre in their diet. Also make and decorate a cake for a celebration the following day.
*Or*
**(b)** Show how proteins of a low biological value can be used to supplement a small quantity of animal protein in a main meal for a small family. (State how many your meal will serve.)
Make and bake either bread rolls or a loaf for a Harvest Festival.

                                                            (*Oxford – Food and Nutrition*)
  **3 (a)** Prepare, cook and serve three different dishes which will illustrate the use of carbon dioxide as a raising agent. In each dish, a different ingredient must be used to produce the carbon dioxide.
**(b)** Make a savoury supper dish which will show the use of water vapour as a raising agent and serve this dish with a salad, a dressing and a drink as a light meal on a tray.
                                                            (*Cambridge – Food and Nutrition*)

  **4** Prepare, cook and serve a balanced three-course meal for three lacto-vegetarians. Include a pureé soup and fried croûtons. Make coffee to be served after the meal.
                                                            (*Cambridge – Food and Nutrition*)

  **5** Prepare and serve an attractive two course mid-day meal showing the good use of left-over foods. The meal is to include a) a dish using cooked white fish or the remains of a lamb joint and b) a sweet using stale bread.
Prepare and serve the necessary accompaniments.    Serve a drink with the meal.
                                                            (*EAEB – Food and Nutrition*)

If you have a choice one test may be more economical than the other. One could be a straightforward meal whereas the other may involve a special aspect of nutrition or some kind of celebration. If you enjoy preparing meals for special occasions or circumstances, or decorating food in a more elaborate way choose the test that will give you scope to show your flair.

  **Never** choose to serve a dish for the examination that you have not cooked on a previous occasion.

  When you are selecting your dishes and writing your time plan consider the following aspects:
  1 Nutritional suitability.
  2 Variety in colour, texture and flavour.    3 Economy.
  4 Seasonal foods and sensible use of convenience foods.
  5 Wide range of skills.    6 Sensible use of resources.

**Nutritional suitability** is a very important consideration. Questions must be answered with specific regard to this point. For example meals for lacto-vegetarians containing no meat must still have balanced proportions of the necessary nutrients. Meals for obese teenagers should be low in fat, sugar and foods such as cakes, biscuits, pastries which contain these.

**Variety in colour, texture and flavour** Eating is essentially a social activity that we all enjoy. We all prefer to eat well presented food with good flavours, colours and textures. Anyone examining your food will look at it and taste it in order to judge it. Make sure that it is well presented with flavours that go well together. Avoid repetition of the same food in two different courses of the meal, e.g. chicken soup followed by a chicken casserole. Help the overall appearance of your finished test by selecting a cloth and dishes that enhance the appearance rather than detract. Flowers and a menu card also add to the general attractiveness. Try to imagine the finished meal served up on a plate; then you will be able to assess how colourful it will look.

**Economy** Most of us work within limited budgets. Be economical in the choice of food, in cooking times and in the use of equipment. Make good use of time and labour saving pieces of equipment. Do not waste food. Make use of leftover pastry, do not peel vegetables thickly, avoid the use of cream – be aware of the cost of the foods you are using. Do not waste fuel.

**Seasonal foods and sensible use of convenience foods** Seasonal foods are usually plentiful and cheaper buys. Find out which fruits and vegetables are in season during the time of the year when practicals take place. The use of too many convenience foods can mean that you lose marks awarded for skill.

**Range of skills** Show as wide a range of different culinary skills as possible. These should include as many different methods of cooking as possible, a range of basic mixtures and tasks which show manual dexterity such as peeling, chopping and piping.

**Sensible use of resources** There is no virtue in doing something the hard way when labour and time saving equipment is available. Cream with an electric mixer rather than a wooden spoon. Use blenders, food processors, pressure cookers and microwave ovens. You can use the time saved to make more dishes.

If resources are limited indicate on your preparation sheet your special needs and your teacher will ensure that things are available and will organize the allocation of mixers, machines and dishes etc. which are available.

**The time plan**

All time plans need to show the following:

**A list of selected dishes** which should be listed in the order in which they would be eaten.

Ingredients for each dish are usually written by the side of the name of the dish. Quantities of ingredients should be given in metric or imperial measures but not as a mixture of both. Some boards insist on metric quantities being used. A shopping list may be required. These should show the TOTAL amount of any one food and should give a full description of the ingredients required:      200g chuck steak **not** 200g steak

**A correct order of work** – it is useful to make a rough draft of your time plan on a separate sheet of paper. This must be handed to the invigilator at the end of the preparation session.

Make sure you know your starting and finishing times. The last 15 minutes of the practical session are usually needed for cooking vegetables, finishing sauces, serving and final clearing.

It is often a help to *work backwards* when planning your order of work.

Try to complete the greater part of the test in the first hour and a half (the first hour if your test lasts only 1½ hours). The practical test is tiring and too much work at the end causes panic which often results in mistakes.

Dishes that take the longest should be made first, i.e. yeast mixtures and dishes that need to set.

By choosing one or two items that can be made early and left to cool, you will have more time at the end to deal with the preparation and cooking of vegetables and sauces.

Roux sauces can be made early up to the boiling up stage and left until the last ten minutes.

Allow enough time for the preparation of each dish. Try timing yourself at home as you make different dishes.

A time plan should not be used to write out the recipe methods. For each dish you make it is sufficient to give the following information:
something about the method used,
cooking temperature and the time it goes in and comes out of the oven,
shelf position in the oven.

A special points column may be provided. Use it to write reminders to yourself. Show the sequence of serving on the plan. Give some indication of how you are going to serve the food. Serve in the order that the food is eaten.

Some boards require a list of equipment and utensils.

Remember your time plan is a **working document** and the examiner will check that you are using it.

At the end of the preparation session you may be allowed to take away a copy of the shopping list if you are to buy your own ingredients. The rest of the time plan will be locked away until you carry out the test.

**A typical time plan**

*Test*

**1** Prepare, cook, and serve a well-balanced and inexpensive meal for yourself and your parents. The meal should include a good source of iron and of vitamin C.
**2** Make some bread rolls which can be served with the meal.
**3** Make a drink to be served after the meal.
**4** Indicate on your plan which foods are rich in iron and which in vitamin C.

| Dishes chosen | Ingredients |
|---|---|
| Potato and leek soup | 200g potatoes, 200g leeks, small onion, 500ml water, 1 chicken oxo, pinch nutmeg, salt and pepper, 1 bay leaf, 1 tbsp. oil. |
| Bread rolls | 100g strong white flour, 100g wholewheat flour, 15g lard, 1 level tsp. salt, 15g yeast, 125ml warm water. |
| Bacon, liver **(iron)** and tomato casserole | 2 tbsp. oil, 2 onions, 1 tbsp. pl. flour, 500g lambs or pigs liver, 6 rashers streaky bacon, 1 can tomatoes (397g), 4 tbsp. water, 1 tbsp. Worcestershire sauce, salt and pepper, chopped parsley. |

| Dishes chosen | Ingredients |
|---|---|
| Jacket potatoes | 3 medium sized potatoes, 50g butter, parsley. |
| Glazed carrots | 450g carrots, 50g butter, chopped parsley. |
| Sponge flan with blackcurrants **(vitamin C)** and arrowroot glaze | 2 eggs, 50g caster sugar, 50g pl. flour, ¼ tsp. baking powder, tin blackcurrants, heaped tsp. arrowroot, 125ml fruit juice. |
| Coffee | 3 dsstsp. ground coffee, 125ml warm milk. |

*Reasons for choice*

1 The soup is inexpensive and can be served with bread rolls.
2 The liver and tomato casserole. Liver is inexpensive and is a good source of iron.
3 Jacket potatoes go well with the casserole and make use of oven heat. Source of fibre.
4 Carrots are in season, could be old or new. Add colour to the meal.
5 The blackcurrant flan provides a good supply of vitamin C. The sponge is fatless.
6 The meal provides a great variety of nutrients, very little sugar and there is also variety in colour, flavour and texture. The meal makes good use of the oven.

*Shopping list*

*Grocer*
100g strong white flour
100g wholewheat flour
15g lard
75g plain flour
100g butter
50g caster sugar
2 eggs size 3
6 rashers streaky bacon
1 can tomatoes (375g)
1 can blackcurrants (375g)
1 chicken oxo
¼tsp. baking powder
salt and pepper
nutmeg
1 bay leaf
3 tbsp. oil
1 tbsp. Worcestershire sauce
3 dsstsp. filter ground coffee

*Green grocer*
2 large onions + 1 small onion
200g potatoes + 3 med. potatoes for baking
200g leeks
450g carrots
3 sprigs parsley

*Butcher*
500g lambs or pigs liver

*Baker*
15g yeast

*Dairy*
125ml milk

*Equipment required*

| | | |
|---|---|---|
| Electric hand whisk | Polythene bag for breadmaking | Oval casserole dish (1½litres) |
| Filter coffee maker | Bread basket | Soup tureen |
| Liquidizer | Sponge flan ring | 2 vegetable dishes |
| | | Oval plate for casserole dish |

| Time | Order of work |
|---|---|
| **9.30** | Make bread rolls. Put to prove in polythene bag after oiling surface. Oven on at 180°C. Wash up. Scrub and prick potatoes. |
| **9.55** | Make flan. Whisk eggs & sugar till thick to leave a trail. Fold flour in carefully with metal spoon. |
| **10.10** | Flan in oven. Centre shelf. Cook 20 mins. Potatoes on lower shelf. Cook approx. 1½hrs. Wash up. Prepare vegetables for soup. |
| **10.30** | Flan from oven. Increase temperature to 230°C. |
| **10.35** | Rolls into oven for 15-20 mins. Top shelf. Make soup. Simmer 20 mins. Prepare casserole. |
| **10.50** | Rolls from oven. Reduce heat to 180°C. Purée soup–liquidizer. Place back in pan to reheat later. Wash up. |
| **11.15** | Casserole in oven. Centre shelf. 30-40 mins. Serving dishes to warm. Complete flan. Strain fruit. Use juice to make arrowroot glaze. Arrange flan on round plate before filling. Wash up. Water + salt on to boil for carrots. Prepare carrots–slice in rings. |
| **11.35** | Carrots into boiling salted water. Lid on pan. Cook 15-20 mins. Wash and chop parsley for garnish. Set up filter coffee maker to switch on at 11.50. |

| *Time* | *Order of work* |
|---|---|
| **11.45** | Final clearing and serving. |
| | Soup reheated–served in heated tureen. Chopped parsley garnish. |
| | Rolls in bread basket with napkin. |
| | Potatoes–cut + in centre, squeeze to open. Garnish knob butter. |
| | Serve in hot vegetable dish. Table mat. |
| | Strain carrots, add knob butter and chopped parsley to pan. Serve in hot vegetable dish. Table mat. |
| | Casserole. Clean edges dish. Stand on serving plate on heatproof mat. |
| | Flan. |
| | Coffee in hot pot, warm milk (no skin) in hot jug. |
| | Wash saucepan and baking sheet. Check cooker switched off. Wipe any spills on cooker. |
| **12.00** | Final tidy of working area. |

**NB** Some boards may require more method detail, others less.

### Between the preparation period and the practical test

**1** Your teacher cannot give you advice or allow you to practise any dishes in school. You do have time to try out your test dishes at home.

**2** Think carefully about presentation–an attractive cloth well laundered, china, flowers, menu card, garnishes.

**3** Make sure that cooking and serving dishes of the correct size are available.

**4** Check the equipment that you are going to use. Be sure that it works and that you know how to use it correctly.

### Immediately before the Practical Test

**Organize** your work surfaces, utensils, equipment, food, dishes, containers. Some boards allow you to grease and line tins and to prepare some of the root vegetables.

**Lay the table**–set up the menu card, flowers and any other aid to a good presentation.

**Prepare yourself**–clean apron with name and candidate's number attached, long hair tied back, no rings or nail varnish and hands thoroughly washed.

### During the test

**1** Manage the cooker efficiently, economically and safely.

**2** Handle, prepare, cook and serve the food as hygienically as possible. Never lick your finger or a wooden spoon and put it back into a mixture. Taste and adjust the seasoning of food by using a teaspoon which is immediately washed. Use the refrigerator correctly–always cover food. Cover food which awaits cooking and that which is cooked. Wrap wet rubbish such as meat trimmings and vegetable peelings before you throw them away. Do not waste food–some examiners look in waste bins for this.

**3** Keep your work area clean and tidy. Wash up as you go along. The cooker, sink and working surfaces should be clear and clean at the end of the test.

**4** Work to your time plan. Some boards will allow slight variations but you must consult the examiner.

**5** Use utensils and equipments correctly e.g. stir food in pans with a wooden spoon, fold in flour gently with a tablespoon. Weight and measure accurately.

**6** Serve *every* dish even if some are not finished or are not of the standard that you had hoped to achieve.

**7** Serve hot food piping hot in hot dishes.    Serve cold dishes cold. Chilled if necessary.

**8** Remember you are awarded marks **from the moment you start** your practical test. Examiners award marks for correct method. They hope you will succeed.

**9** A good practical preparation sheet helps towards a good practical. Some boards award a high percentage of the practical marks to the preparation sheet; e.g. the Cambridge Board awards 30% of the practical mark for this part of the test.

**10** If you have not managed to finish all the washing up by the end of the examination, stack it neatly on the draining board.

### 16.2  The theory paper

The format of the theory paper again varies with the different examination boards. You should make sure that you have seen and worked past papers. Your teacher will explain the requirements of your own board and will tell you of changes, if any, which are to be made on the paper you are to take.

The style of questions on any paper will also vary. *Section A* will often comprise questions which require short answers which must be concise and accurate. The space left for your answer and the mark allocation should give some guidance on how much to write. There may be some *multiple choice* or *fixed response* questions. These appear simple but they require careful thought.

Other sections of the examination have *free response* questions. They may require an answer in the form of an essay or they are now more usually structured into sections each of which requires a paragraph answer. Try to get as many facts as you know into the paragraph without padding the answer out.

Make sure that you know for which sections of the examination paper you have been prepared.

**Hints for answering theory paper**

**1 Read the examination instructions (rubric) carefully.**

2 Note any compulsory questions.

3 As you read through the paper select those questions which you feel you can confidently answer.

4 Read the questions through again and note the mark allocation to the sections of the question. Work out where you are likely to score the highest marks. If a question section has **four** marks allocated to it you are probably required to give **eight** pieces of correct information. Write them out concisely.

5 Work out the time you can allocate to each question. There is usually a 'recommended time' to spend on Section A.

6 As you answer each question re-read the question and underline key words or phrases.

7 If you are asked to answer **five** questions then attempt **five**. Do not spend so much time on the first two or three so that you find you have no time left for the last two. If you calculate that you will probably score an average of half marks for each question three answers will mean 30/100 if each question carries 20 marks. If you answer five questions you could score 50/100. The maximum for three would be 60% and that is an unlikely score.

8 Note the mark allocation to questions very carefully. If (a) = 3 marks, (b) = 4 marks, (c) = 5 marks and (d) = 8 marks then the examiner is obviously expecting more to be written on (d) compared with (a).

9 Short answer questions should be answered concisely only giving the information that is asked for. Answers must be brief but accurate. If you are unsure of any of these answers leave them until later. **Do not forget to return to the omitted sections.**

Remember blank spaces score no marks, a guess could score some.

10 Plan essay questions in rough, preferably on the answer sheet. The rough notes can be crossed through later.

Try not to 'waffle'. The examiner will expect a number of facts to be included. Select key words or facts and build your complete sentences and paragraphs around them to provide interesting but factual answers.

11 Questions usually start with a word which is a directive to the question. Make sure you understand the meaning of the following words: state, explain, discuss, describe, contrast, compare, list.

**(a) State**–Give the simple facts, specify clearly.

**(b) Explain**–Requires not only the facts but the reasons behind them.

**(c) Discuss**–To debate, to examine by means of argument.

**(d) Describe**–To give a comprehensive description. If describing a basic method describe what you do, how and why and state what you do it with.

**(e) Contrast**–To pick out the differences between two items.

**(f) Compare**–To point out the differences and similarities between two items. *Tabulation* is a great help in answering questions which ask you to contrast or compare.

**(g) List**–Make a list. If a question states 'List with reasons' you must give the reasons as well.

12 Avoid repeating the same information over and over again. It can only be credited with marks once.

13 Read your answers through and then the questions to ensure that you have answered all sections and that you have interpreted the question correctly. If your answer is not relevant it will not score many marks.

14 If you do get short of time in an essay answer, put your facts into note form. This should earn you as many marks as possible in a limited time.

**Hints on presentation**

Examiners are human. If they cannot read a script they cannot mark it as accurately as they would wish. Poor presentation can also affect the ease of adding up marks and checking.

1 Read the rubric carefully.

2 Fill in your name, centre and candidate number on the cover and on *each* sheet of your script.

3 Fill in the question grid correctly. The right hand column is usually required for the examiner's mark. If you use this column it can lead to confusion and you being awarded the wrong mark.

4 Do not write in the margins except to write clearly the number of the question in the left hand margin.

5 Leave several lines between questions and one line between the sections of any one question. This enables you to add 'afterthoughts' and again makes marking a simpler, more accurate process.

6 Be neat and tidy. Write in black or blue. Avoid the use of felt tips which soak through the paper. Red ink or red biro should not be used. It leads to confusion with marks because examiners mark in red.

7 Do not use liquid paper. It is time consuming to cover mistakes with this. It takes time to dry. Invariably candidates forget to write in the correction. Just cross through mistakes.

8 Diagrams should be large and clear. They are meaningless if not labelled.

9 Tie your answer sheets together in order and securely but **not so tightly** that the pages cannot be turned over.

**Table 16.1** The characteristics of answers at different grades

| A | B | C | D | E |
|---|---|---|---|---|
| High standard of English – grammar, spelling | Good standard of English – grammar, spelling | Satisfactory standard of English – grammar, spelling | Fair standard of English – grammar, spelling | Poor standard of English – grammar, spelling |
| Well-constructed answer to the set question | Logically constructed answer to the set question | Set question answered | Poorly answered question | Set question not answered |
| An inspired answer showing good powers of reasoning | Answer showing adequate powers of reasoning | An attempt at a reasoned argument | Poorly constructed argument | No coherent argument presented |
| Evidence of good, wide reading imaginatively (where appropriate). | Evidence of up-to-date reading correctly applied (where appropriate). | Some evidence of reading reasonable well applied (where appropriate). | Little evidence of reading – no direct application | No evidence of reading |
| Detailed answer with relevant facts | Good factual knowledge apparent | Factual but uninspiring | Little factual knowledge | Lack of factual knowledge |
| Sound awareness of up-to-date theories, recommendations and legislation (as appropriate). | Some awareness of up-to-date theories, recommendations and legislation (as appropriate). | Limited awareness of up-to-date theories, recommendations and legislation (as appropriate). | Inadequate awareness of up-to-date theories, recommendations, legislation (as appropriate). | No awareness of up-to-date theories, recommendations and legislation (as appropriate). |
| No irrelevant information and 'waffle'. No factual inaccuracies. | A lack of irrelevant information and 'waffle'. Few factual inaccuracies. | Some inaccuracies and irrelevant information. A tendency to 'waffle'. | Inaccurate and irrelevant material included. Tendency to 'waffle'. | Scant answer. Lack of facts. Often inaccurate. |
| **70-100%** | **55-69%** | **40-50%** | **30-39%** | **0-29%** |

# Part IV

# 17 Self-test units

A number of questions have been set on the following pages to help you check how much information you have remembered from the core units in Sections 2-15. The questions relate to material contained in each unit. Some will test factual knowledge while others will test your understanding and grasp of the factors and concepts involved.

You will discover that three types of questions have been set: multiple choice, those requiring short or one-word answers and those that invite a longer, well-defined answer which will incorporate several facts or pieces of information. At the end of the questions either the answers have been given, or you will be referred to the appropriate unit if the answer is a list of points which can easily be found in the text.

Remember that the questions have been chosen at random and will not, necessarily, cover all of the material in the unit. This sort of test is nevertheless useful because it will not only reveal how much you do know but also what you do not know and what needs further revision.

To get the most out of these Self-test units you need to plan your work in the following way:
(i) Revise one unit, for example *Housing*, by reading through the text, studying any tables and then making sure that you know the important facts.
(ii) When you feel that you have thoroughly learnt all that is in the unit, then attempt the relevant self-test questions. It is, of course, important that you do not read the questions while you are revising the core unit, and equally as important that you do not refer to the core unit or read the answers while you are attempting the questions.

(iii) Finally, you can either mark the answers yourself or get a friend to do it. A low mark will indicate that you have not learnt the core unit thoroughly and you will need to revise that unit from the beginning.

# Questions

## Section 2 Family and community

1 What services are provided to the community by the following?
   (a) The Samaritans   (b) Shelter   (c) Age Concern   (d) The National Marriage Guidance Council
2 What is meant by a community? Explain briefly why some new towns are described as being lacking in community spirit.
3 What services does a community centre usually provide?
4 Name three aids by which the community can help the blind to lead a more normal life.
5 By what means can each of the following contribute to the life of the local community?
   (a) Swimming baths   (b) Health centres   (c) Local parks   (d) Leisure centres   (e) Public libraries
6 List **at least four** state-aided, or voluntary activities or services that can help to maintain the independence of an elderly person.
7 What does the term 'extended family' mean?
8 What qualities would you look for in someone who was going to undertake baby-sitting services for you?

## Section 3 Nutrition

1 Complete the following statements.
   (a) (i) A food contains one or more _____
       (ii) These are needed by the body for _____
   (b) The process which breaks down large food molecules is _____
2 (a) Name the three elements found in carbohydrates, fats and proteins.
   (b) Protein also contains another element essential to life. This is _____
3 Name the following carbohydrates:
   (a) Two simple sugars or monosaccharides   (b) Three double sugars or disaccharides
   (c) The complex sugar or polysaccharide which provides energy
   (d) The complex sugar which aids egestion of solid waste
   (e) The complex sugar which helps jam to set   (f) The carbohydrate which is stored in the liver
4 In the digestion of starch which enzymes bring about the following changes?
   (a) The change from starch to maltose in the mouth
   (b) The change from starch to maltose in the duodenum
   (c) The change from maltose to glucose in the ileum
5 Name four energy-giving nutrients.
6 (a) Which of the following fats contain saturated fatty acids?
       A Dripping     B Corn oil     C Butter     D Olive oil     E Lard
   (b) Which of the following fats contain polyunsaturated fatty acids?
       A Sunflower seed oil     B Suet     C Corn oil     D Soya oil     E Slab margarine
7 Amino acids are the units which make up protein.
   (a) How many are essential to children?     (b) How many are essential to adults?
8 Name the following:
   (a) The organ where protein digestion begins     (b) The acid present in this organ (a)
   (c) The enzyme present which splits proteins to peptides
   (d) The enzyme present in a baby up to about 6 months which helps protein digestion

## Section 4 Commodities

1 Name the food in which you would find the following proteins.
   (a) myosin   (b) caseinogen   (c) casein   (d) albumen   (e) vitellin and globulin
   (f) glutenin and gliadin
2 Name the processes described.
   (a) The milk is heated to 72°C for 15 seconds then rapidly cooled to below 10°C.
   (b) The milk is forced through tiny valves to split the fat into very tiny globules before heat processing.
   (c) Milk is sealed in bottles and heated to above 100°C. It is held at this temperature for 20-30 minutes.
   (d) Milk is heated to 132°C and held there for 1 second. It is rapidly cooled and aseptically packed.
3 State the reasons for adding the following substances to milk during the manufacture of cheese:
   (a) Culture of lactic acid bacteria     (b) Rennet     (c) Salt
4 Skimmed milk can be bought in powder or liquid form. Complete the following.
   (a) Its nutritional advantage is that it lacks _____
   (b) It is not suitable for babies and elderly people because most brands lack the following nutrients
   (i) _____   (ii) _____
5 State the reasons for the following rules which should be followed when cooking with cheese:
   (a) Grate the cheese   (b) Mix with a starchy food   (c) Season well   (d) Do not overcook

**6** Make a list of the **nine** uses of eggs.

Complete the following paragraph which describes the effect of heat on meat sold for stewing.

**7** Moist heat changes the insoluble connective tissue, _____ (a) into soluble _____ (b) which dissolves in the liquid loosening the meat _____ (c) so making the meat tender.

**8** Complete the following comparison of meat and fish.
Fish cooks more quickly than meat because it has finer, shorter _____ (a) and very little _____ (b). There is no _____ (c)

**9** Name:
(a) The elastic substance which forms when wheat flour and water are worked together
(b) The stimulant found in tea and coffee    (c) The four micronutrients found in cocoa
(d) The bitter tasting salt formed by the action of heat on sodium hydrogen carbonate
(e) The artificial sweetener used in convenience foods
(f) The salt added to dried foods to enhance the flavour

## Section 5   Meal planning and special dietary needs

**1** Make a list of **ten** factors which would influence the choice and preparation of food for the family.

**2** Why should we eat:
(a) Less sugar?    (b) Less fat?    (c) Less salt?
(d) More bread and cereal foods?    (e) More fruit and vegetables?

**3** Consider the following individuals in turn and make a list of any particular nutritional requirements that they have. Make clear the reasons for these needs.
(a) Expectant mother    (c) Manual workers    (e) Baby–6 months old    (g) Sedentary workers
(b) Child of 8 years    (d) The elderly    (f) Adolescents    (h) The sick

**4** List the foods which will **not** be eaten by:
(a) A lacto-vegetarian    (b) A vegan

**5** How could the following nutrients be provided in the diet of a vegan?
(a) HBV Protein    (b) Vitamin D    (c) Vitamin A
(d) Vitamin $B_{12}$    (e) Calcium

**6** Economy is an important aspect of planning family meals. Make lists of the ways you could economize when:
(a) Shopping    (b) Preparing food    (c) Cooking food.

## Section 6   Cookers and cooking

**1** Explain:
(a) The use of a wooden spoon to stir the contents of a pan
(b) The use of plastic or wooden spoons for pan handles and knobs
(c) The use of copper bottoms to stainless steel pans
(d) The use of oven gloves to lift hot dishes

**2** List **eight** points which would influence your choice of a cooker.

**3** State **one** advantage and **one** disadvantage of a fan oven.

**4** (a) What is the approximate time it takes to preheat an oven?
(b) What keeps the temperature of an oven more or less constant?
(c) Which shelf position is at the temperature set?
(d) Complete the oven chart below:

|          | °C | °F | Gas mark |
|----------|----|----|----------|
| Slow     |    |    |          |
| Moderate |    |    |          |
| Hot      |    |    |          |
| V. Hot   |    |    |          |

**5** Draw diagrams to show heat transference in:
(a) Shallow frying    (b) Simmering    (c) Steaming    (d) Grilling

**6** Group the methods of cooking into the following groups:
(a) Moist methods    (b) Dry methods    (c) Fat methods    (d) Slow methods

**7** Pressure cooking uses super heated steam. Complete or answer the following:
(a) The temperature at which water boils at sea level is _____ .
(b) With the 5kg (15lb) weight in position the water in the pressure cooker boils at this temperature.
(c) The higher the pressure the _____ (1) the temperature at which water _____ (2) and the _____ (3) the food is cooked.
(d) The advantages of a pressure cooker are that it saves _____ (1), _____ (2) and _____ (3). _____ (4) are not lost. _____ (5) is better and tough, coarse meat becomes _____ (6) quickly.
(e) The disadvantages of a pressure cooker are that they are _____ (1) to buy and the _____ (2) and _____ (3) need replacing frequently.
(f) The minimum amount of water that should be used is _____
(g) **Two** ways to reduce pressure.
(h) **Three** safety features of the pressure cooker.

**8** Explain the reasons for the following rules to be followed when deep fat frying.
(a)  Use a deep, heavy pan.      (b)  Only half-fill with fat.
(c)  Heat to the temperature required.
(d)  It is more accurate to use a thermometer or a thermostatically controlled fryer.
(e)  Potato chips should be dried before frying.
(f)  Other foods should be coated before frying.
(g)  Use a basket to carefully lower food into fat.
(h)  Remain in the kitchen during frying.
(i)  Keep the pan lid or a baking sheet near at hand.
(j)  Only fry with the lid on if you are using a thermostatically controlled fryer with a filter.
(k)  Before serving the fried food should be placed on kitchen paper.
(l)  Cool and strain the fat before returning to the container.
(m) If the pan does catch fire place the lid or baking tray over the top. Switch off the cooker. Leave to cool.
Throw away the fat.

## Section 7   Basic mixtures

**1** (a)  What is a batter?      (b)  Suggest **three** uses for batters.
(c)  What type of flour is used in batter?

**2** (a)  What is a sauce?      (b)  What is the difference between a pouring and a coating sauce?
(c)  What is a panada?      (d)  Complete the following chart.

| Sauce | Milk | Flour/Cornflour | Fat |
|---|---|---|---|
| **Blended** | | | |
| Pouring | 250ml (½pt) | g (   oz) | |
| Coating | 250ml (½pt) | g (   oz) | |
| Panada | 250ml (½pt) | g (   oz) | |
| **Roux** | | | |
| Pouring | 250ml (½pt) | g (   oz) | g (   oz) |
| Coating | 250ml (½pt) | g (   oz) | g (   oz) |
| Panada | 250ml (½pt) | g (   oz) | g (   oz) |

**3** What is the 'roux'?

**4** One heaped teaspoon of arrowroot will thicken this amount of liquid for a flan glaze.

**5** How do eggs thicken a sauce?

**6** (a)  What is pastry?
(b)  Complete the basic proportion chart below.

| | Shortcrust | Suetcrust | Rough puff | Flaky |
|---|---|---|---|---|
| Fat to flour | | to | to | to |
| Salt to 450g (1lb flour) | ml (   tsp) | ml (   tsp) | ml (   tsp) | ml (   tsp) |
| Water to 450g (1lb flour) | ml (   tblsp) | ml (   tblsp) | ml (   tblsp) | ml (   tblsp) |
| Lemon juice | | | ml (   tsp) | ml (   tsp) |

(c)  Which flour would you use for each of the following pastries?
(*i*) Shortcrust      (*ii*) Suet pastry      (*iii*) Flaky or Rough puff
(*iv*) Choux
(d)  Which fats would you use for each pastry?
(*i*) Shortcrust      (*ii*) Suet pastry      (*iii*) Flaky or Rough puff      (*iv*) Choux
(e)  Why is lemon juice used in Flaky or Rough puff pastry?
(f)  At what temperatures would you bake these pastries?
(*i*) Shortcrust      (*ii*) Suet pastry      (*iii*) Flaky or Rough puff      (*iv*) Choux
(g)  Suggest sweet and savoury dishes which could be made with each of these pastries shown in the
Table below.

| Pastry | Sweet dishes | Savoury dishes |
|---|---|---|
| Shortcrust | (i) (ii) | (i) (ii) |
| Suet pastry | (i) (ii) | (i) (ii) |
| Flaky/Rough puff | (i) (ii) | (i) (ii) |
| Choux | (i) (ii) | (i) (ii) |

**7** Name the main raising agent in each of the pastries.
(a) Shortcrust  (b) Suet pastry  (c) Flaky or Rough puff  (d) Choux

**8** Make a list of the main rules to follow to ensure successful pastry making.

**9** Explain the meaning of 'to bake blind'.

**10** Complete the basic proportion chart for cake making overleaf.

|  | Rubbed in | Creaming | Whisking | Melting |
|---|---|---|---|---|
| Baking powder to 450g (1lb) pl. flour | level tsp. | level tsp. |  | 2 level tsp. bicarbonate of soda |
| Fat to flour | to | to |  | ¼ to ½ |
| Sugar to flour | to | to | equal | ¼ to ½ + ½ to ¾ syrup |
| Eggs to 450g (1lb) flour | to | to | to | 0–4 |
| Milk |  |  |  | to mix |

**11** Which process is being described in each of the following statements?
    (a) Margarine is beaten with sugar using a wooden spoon.
    (b) Eggs and sugar are whisked together until very thick.
    (c) The flour is added by working a tablespoon through the mixture in a figure of eight.
**12** State the shelf position and the temperature for cooking each of the following:
    (a) Rock buns   (b) Victoria sandwich   (c) Swiss roll   (d) Sponge flan
    (e) Gingerbread   (f) Scones

## Section 8   Food storage and preservation

**1** Make a list of **ten** rules to follow when using a refrigerator, stating the reasons in each case.
**2** List **four** different ways by which you would prevent food decay.
**3** (a) List the different types of packaging materials which can be used when freezing.
    (b) Name one material **not** suitable for packing goods in a freezer.
    (c) Describe how you would pack and freeze:
        (*i*) Peas   (*ii*) Soup.
    (d) What is open freezing?    (e) Why are vegetables blanched before freezing?
    (f) Why is air drawn out of polythene bags especially when freezing bread, cakes, pastries?
**4** Explain why each of the following preserves keeps:
    (a) Strawberry jam   (b) Bottled plums   (c) Frozen peas   (d) Packet soups   (e) Pickled onions
**5** (a) What three things would you look for when selecting fruit for jam making?
    (b) (*i*) What is pectin?   (*ii*) What role does it play in jam making?
    (c) Name: (*i*) Two fruits rich in pectin   (*ii*) Two fruits low in pectin.
    (d) Suggest **two** ways in which pectin content can be improved.
    (e) Give a recipe for making plum jam.
    (f) Why must the fruit be reduced to a pulp before adding the sugar?
    (g) Why is it important that all the sugar has dissolved before the jam is boiled?
    (h) Describe **two** tests to show that jam has reached setting point.
    (i) Why should jam be allowed to cool slightly before putting it into jars?
    (j) Why should the jar be filled right to the brim?
    (k) How does the waxed disc seal the jar?
    (l) Why should jam be stored under the following conditions?
        (*i*) Cool   (*ii*) Dry   (*iii*) Dark
**6** How do bacteria cause food poisoning?
**7** List the ways in which food is contaminated.
**8** When food is left after a meal how should it be treated to prevent microbial contamination and multiplication?
**9** Why should food for rechauffée dishes be:
    (a) Finely divided   (b) Reheated rapidly   (c) Not re-cooked?
**10** Suggest **two** dishes which could make use of the following leftover foods.
    (a) Meat   (c) Egg yolk   (e) Bread       (g) Vegetables
    (b) Fish   (d) Egg white   (f) Stewed fruit

## Section 9   Pollution and conservation

**1** Name **three** types of liquid household waste.
**2** (a) Draw a diagram of a U-bend beneath a sink. Explain its purpose.
    (b) How would you unblock the sink waste pipe?
**3** Describe the cleaning of:
    (a) The lavatory   (b) The bath   (c) A stainless steel sink   (d) Outside drains
**4** What is a septic tank?
**5** How are the services of the Water Authority paid for?
**6** What happens at the end of sewage treatment to the:
    (a) liquid?   (b) solids?
**7** What are the dangers of a water supply contaminated by raw sewage?
**8** What is a biodegradable detergent?
**9** Describe the processes which water undergoes before it reaches our taps.
**10** Describe **six** ways of disposing of household refuse.
**11** What do you understand the term 'Recycling' to mean?

**12** Describe the care of:
   (a) The kitchen waste bin    (b) The dustbin

**13** State what you know about the Clean Air Act of 1956.

**14** Who pays for refuse collections? How is payment made?

**15** Make a comprehensive list of the ways in which a house may be insulated to prevent heat loss.

**16** List **ten** ways of saving heat when cooking.

**17** List **five** ways of saving energy when washing and ironing.

**18** List **five** ways of saving energy when heating water.

**19** What do you understand the term ergonomics to mean?

**20** What are the **three** ways in which human effort may be saved when doing the housework?

**21** Describe the once a week cleaning of:
   (a) the living room,    (b) the bathroom,    (c) a bedroom.

**22** Draw diagrams to explain what is meant by:
   (a) An L-shaped kitchen    (b) A U-shaped kitchen    (c) A passage kitchen

**23** What is a work triangle? Give one example.

**24** Why is the sequence of work important?

**25** What are the rules for storing things in a kitchen wall cupboard and floor unit?

## Section 10    Health and safety

**1** (a) List **six** items which should be included in a first aid box.
   (b) How should small cuts be treated?    (c) What should you do about a small burn?
   (d) If somebody swallowed something poisonous, what should you do?

**2** More people are killed or injured in accidents in the home than on the roads.
   (a) Suggest **six** ways of making the home a safer place in which to live.
   (b) Explain how you would treat the following health problems:
      (*i*) Your sister who feels faint   (*ii*) Your mother who has cut her thumb while preparing carrots

**3** Babies and toddlers can easily suffer from accidents in the home. Suggest **three** ways to safeguard them from each of the following:
   (a) falls   (b) suffocation and choking   (c) poisoning   (d) burns   (e) electric shock

**4** (a) Where in the home would you keep a first aid box? Give reasons for the location named.
   (b) List **five** safety precautions which should be taken while young children are present in the kitchen.

**5** People who are ill often lose their appetite.
   (a) What **five** points should be considered when planning and serving meals to someone who is ill in bed?
   (b) Give **two** ways in which food can be protected from bacteria in the home.
   (c) Give **two** important rules to be observed when giving medicine.
   (d) How can children be protected against polio?

**6** State **two** symptoms of shock.

**7** State **two** points to remember when giving the 'kiss of life'.

**8** State what you should do if a child's clothes catch fire.

## Section 11    Money management

**1** (a) Give **three** of the benefits of having a bank account.
   (b) Explain the difference between a current account and a deposit account.
   (c) Write a short paragraph on each of the following:
      (i) Bank statements   (*ii*) Bank loans   (*iii*) Bankers orders   (*iv*) Bank credit cards
   (d) List some of the services which a bank provides.
   (e) Suggest some other ways of saving money.

**2** (a) Explain how you would go about opening a bank account with one of the major banks.
   (b) List **three** advantages and **three** disadvantages of paying for goods by cheque.

**3** (a) What are the advantages and disadvantages of buying goods on credit for your first home?
   (b) List **three** important points to remember before you sign any form of credit sales document.

**4** Write a brief note on each of the following:
   (a) PAYE    (b) National Insurance Contributions    (c) Credit cards

**5** (a) What do you understand by the term hire purchase?
   (b) What would happen to the goods if the hire purchase payments were overdue?

**6** Which of the following choices is the correct answer?
   **(a)** Life Assurance provides money if
      (*i*) a house is damaged by fire.
      (*ii*) the contents of a home are stolen or damaged by the weather.
      (*iii*) a person dies before reaching an agreed age.
      (*iv*) a car is damaged in an accident.
   **(b)** Articles bought on hire purchase are not legally yours until
      (*i*) the deposit is paid.
      (*ii*) two-thirds of the instalments are paid.
      (*iii*) the last payment is made.
      (*iv*) the article is in your home.
   **(c)** A standing order is an instruction for
      (*i*) a regular payment of an agreed amount from a bank account.

(*ii*) a deduction from wages by an employer.

(*iii*) the issue of bank statements.    (*iv*) an overdraft.

7 (a) Give **three** reasons why it might be better to pay for goods by cash than by cheque.

(b) Suggest **two** ways of saving money in order to pay cash for a new cooker.

(c) Write a brief note on any of the following:

(*i*) Discount    (*ii*) A receipt    (*iii*) Premium bonds    (*iv*) Insurance policies

8 Wise buying and household budgeting are important factors for family happiness.

(a) Give **six** major expenses in the family budget.

(b) Suggest **three** ways in which fuel bills may be paid, to help a couple who find budgeting difficult.

(c) List **six** methods by which a housewife can obtain information about large pieces of household equipment.

(d) List **two** advantages and disadvantages of each of the following:

(*i*) Shopping by post    (*ii*) Doorstep trading    (*iii*) Shopping by telephone using a credit card

9 Set out below are examples of budgets for Family A and for Family B. Both families are husband, wife and two children. The nett income for each family is £458.00 per month.

|  | Family A | Family B |
|---|---|---|
| Mortgage | 144.00 | 144.00 |
| Rates | 24.00 | 24.00 |
| Food | 84.50 | 126.00 |
| Electricity | 9.00 | 7.00 |
| Gas | 25.00 | 30.00 |
| Clothing | 39.00 | 33.00 |
| HP payments | 42.00 | 20.00 |
| Insurance |  | 15.00 |
| Savings |  | 15.00 |
| Travel | 18.00 | 16.50 |
| Holidays and entertainment | 72.50 | 27.50 |
|  | 458.00 | 458.00 |

Study the two budgets.

(a) Which budget do you consider to be the more sensible? Give **five** reasons for your choice.

(b) State **three** ways in which the family may save money and at the same time gain interest on savings.

(c) Name **three** ways of buying goods on credit.

## Section 12    Consumer studies

1 (a) Identify the following labels, and state what they tell you about the goods you are buying.

(b) What are your rights as a consumer if you buy from a department store, a dress which comes apart at the seams the first time it is laundered?

(c) Discuss the advantages and disadvantages of doing the family shopping in:

(*i*) Supermarkets    (*ii*) Small local shops    (*iii*) Street markets    (*iv*) Department stores

2 What points would you consider before buying the following?

(a) Cooking oil    (b) Half a dozen eggs    (c) Washing powder    (d) Pre-packed bacon

3 (a) Name **five** modern food packaging materials and give one example where each could be used.

(b) Suggest **two** advantages and **two** disadvantages of modern food packaging methods.

4 Name **four** pieces of information you would expect to find on an egg box.

5 When buying from a door-to-door salesman an agreement is signed and a deposit is paid. What happens if, later in the day, the buyer changes his mind?

6 (a) List **three** points that should be considered when obtaining a large piece of electrical equipment on hire purchase.

(b) What information is given on an HLCC care label?

7 (a) Explain briefly how advertising affects the consumer.

(b) List the sources which are available for consumer advice and information. Explain how they are of use to the consumer.

8 Name **two** Acts of Parliament which protect the consumer. Briefly outline the way in which they help to protect the consumer.

9 What are the advantages of bulk buying?

10 (a) How is advertising of value to the consumer?    (b) What media are used by advertisers?

11 How is advertising controlled in the UK?

12 List any **four** organizations which aim to protect the consumer. Briefly explain their area of interest.

13 Which **three** elements must be included to form a legal contract?

14 What is a manufacturer's guarantee?

## Section 13    Home management

1 (a) List **four** types of floor covering.

(b) List **six** points you need to know about a floor covering before you buy it.

(c) List **five** points to consider when choosing a vacuum cleaner.

(d) What **three** points would you consider when choosing:
   (*i*) wall-covering for the bathroom?
   (*ii*) curtains for the lounge-dining room?
   (*iii*) lighting for the lounge-dining room?

2 (a) Fig. 17.2 shows a diagram of a wired three-pin plug. On your answer paper give the name and colour of each of the wires P, Q and R.

(b)  (*i*) State the purpose of including a fuse.
   (*ii*) Give **two** faults which may cause a fuse to blow.
   (*iii*) What rating of fuse should be used in the plug for
      *a* an electric blanket? *b* a three-bar electric fire?
(c) Electricity is expensive.
   (*i*) Suggest ways of economizing on the use of electricity in the home.
   (*ii*) Explain how the payment of electricity bills has been made easier for the consumer.

3 If the previous meter reading was 6391.0 kWh, and with reference to Fig. 17.3 below, state how much electricity has been used.

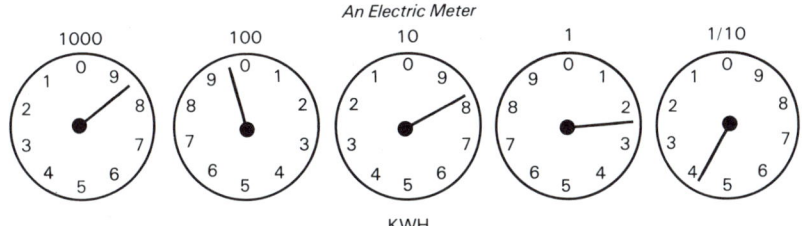

An Electric Meter

KWH

4 (a) Draw and label a diagram to show one place-setting for a right handed person. The lunch menu includes soup, main course and dessert.
  (b) List **five** other items which will be required to set the table for a formal lunch.

5 Explain fully **three** ways of clearing the waste pipe if the kitchen sink is blocked.

6 What factors determine the amount of maintenance work necessary to ensure a well-organized home?

7 Make a list of indoor cleaning tasks which have to be done daily and weekly to keep a bedroom clean and tidy.

8 What advice would you give on the choosing and care of the following cleaning equipment?
  (a) Brushes and brooms     (b) Mops and dusters     (c) Carpet sweepers
  (d) Suction cleaners     (e) Electric scrubbers and polishers

9 (a) Name **four** household pests which are commonly found in the home.
  (b) What steps would you take to prevent these pests breeding in your home?

## Section 14    Housing

1 You are buying your first home.
  (a) Name **four** different methods of borrowing the money to buy the house.
  (b) Rates will have to be paid on the house. Name **five** services that will be provided from the rates by the Local Authority.

2 Work out how much deposit would have to be paid for each of the houses below when taking out a mortgage.

| **House A** | **House B** |
|---|---|
| Cost £10 000 | Cost £12 500 |
| Mortgage 90% of cost | Mortgage 95% of cost |
| Deposit = | Deposit = |

3 (a) Explain the meaning of each of the following terms used when home buying.
      (*i*) Estate agent        (*ii*) Rateable value      (*iii*) General rate
      (*iv*) Deposit           (*v*) Freehold            (*vi*) Ground (or chief) rent
      (*vii*) Mortgage interest
  (b) State **three** facts that a manager of a Building Society may want to know before he will lend money for house purchase.

4 You are about to begin a new job in a large city and have decided to rent a flat or bedsitter.
  (a) Name **three** sources from where you could obtain information about flats or bed-sitters.
  (b) On a visit to see the accommodation, state **eight** points which you should check.
  (c) In addition to the rent, state **four** household expenses you would need to consider.
  (d) State **two** advantages and **two** disadvantages of renting furnished accommodation.

5 A young married couple are hoping to buy a house.
  (a) Give **four** points they should consider about the amenities in the area in which they wish to live.
  (b) They have saved enough money for a deposit. Suggest **two** ways of raising the remainder of the money to buy the house.
  (c) Apart from the repayment of the loan, what are the other expenses incurred when buying a house?
  (d) List **six** important points they should look for when viewing the house.
  (e) Write an account of the work of each of the following people in connection with buying a house:
      (*i*) Estate agent  (*ii*) Surveyor  (*iii*) Solicitor

6 Describe the following types of accommodation and state **one** disadvantage of each: bed-sitter, high-rise flat, terraced house, bungalow.

7 (a) Give **one** advantage and **one** disadvantage of renting a home.
   (b) Give the meaning of the word 'tenant'. (c) Explain what is meant by 'conditions of tenancy'.

8 Describe the work of the following:
   (a) The Rent Tribunal. (b) The Local Authority Housing Committee.

9 (a) What are the **four** main fuels used for central heating?
   Write a paragraph giving the advantages and disadvantages of each of the four fuels.
   (b) What do you understand by each of the following:
      (*i*) Background heating (*ii*) Full heating (*iii*) Thermostat (*iv*) Time-switch
   (c) For what do the letters BTU stand?

10 Describe each of the following and explain why it is important:
   (a) Damp-proof course (b) Cavity walls (c) Double glazing

## Section 15 Textiles

1 How do manufacturers indicate the fibre content of:
   (a) clothing? (b) fabric sold by the metre?

2 Most fabrics can now be treated with special finishes to improve their properties, performance and aesthetic appeal. Give a brief explanation of each of the following:
   moth-proofing, crease resistant finish, polishing, embossing, pre-shrinking, flame proofing, water proofing, stain and water repellancy, durable pleating, brushed finish, satinized fabrics and thermolactyle fabrics.

3 Draw clear diagrams to show the following three basic weaves:
   (a) Plain weave (b) Twill weave (c) Satin weave

4 Give a one or two word answer, or complete the sentence:
   (a) A fabric which is likely to be attacked by moths.
   (b) A fabric attacked by mildew if left damp.
   (c) A fibre damaged by an acid but unaffected by alkalis.
   (d) Viscose rayon is made from _____ (e) Nylon is made from _____
   (f) Trevira, Dacron, Crimplene are brand names for _____
   (g) Acrylic fibres are made from _____
   (h) Lycra is a filament yarn used to make _____ and _____
   (i) The main characteristic of Lycra is that it _____
   (j) PVC is used for making (*i*) _____ (*ii*) _____ (*iii*) _____ (*iv*) _____
   (k) Glass fibre is made of _____ and can be made into _____
   (l) Evening wear is often made from fabrics containing _____thread fibres. The trade name for these fibres are _____ and _____
   (m) _____ is a bonded fabric.
   (n) _____ is made from wool beaten and pressed together when wet.
   (o) _____ are made of several layers of fabrics fastened together.

5 What are the advantages and disadvantages of using:
   (a) a launderette and (b) commercial laundries for doing the family wash?

6 What procedures must be followed when doing the family wash at home?

7 Write a brief description of each of the various washing machines now available, including the washing action adopted by each type of machine.

8 Why do we use a fabric conditioner?

9 What points must be considered when choosing an iron?

10 Identify the following symbols:

(a) (b) (c) (d) (e)

11 Identify the following drying symbols:

(a) (b) (c) (d) (e)

12 Identify the following dry cleaning symbols:

(a) **A** (b) **P** (c) **F** (d)

13 Complete the following sentences:
   In _____ (1) The EEC council instructed members to label all textile products with the generic name of fibres they contain.
   If a blended fibre contains at least 85% of one fibre it may be marked in one of the following ways:
   (a) _____ (b) _____ (c) _____
   If none of the fibres is present in as great a quantity as 85%, the fibre present in the greatest amount must be listed _____ (2) followed by the others in _____ (3) _____ (4) order.
   A fabric of equal proportions of two fibres must be shown as:
   _____% _____ and _____% _____ (5)

14 What are the benefits and disadvantages of hard water?

**15** How may temporary and permanent hardness be removed?

**16** What are the advantages of soft water?

**17** Explain the meaning of the following:
(a) Biological powders     (b) TAED based detergents     (c) Biodegradable detergents

**18** Complete the following sentences:
(a) Water is not a good wetting agent because of its _____
(b) A _____ (1) will reduce the _____ (2) and lift the _____ from the fabric.
(c) _____ (1) will loosen _____ (2) and aid the cleaning process.

**19** Why do we use the following when washing clothes?
(a) Bleach   (b) Disinfectants   (c) Fabric conditioners

# Answers to self-test questions

## Section 2

**1** (a)–(d), see Unit 2.2.1.

**2** There are many different definitions of a community. All of them include two elements–neighbourhood or a defined geographical area, and the idea of people sharing a common set of values, attitudes and beliefs. Many communities have strong common feelings because the people in them share similar life-styles, e.g. occupational communities such as fishing towns and villages or mining villages. Kinship ties tend to help to reinforce community feeling. The term 'community' may also be used to describe religious institutions such as monasteries.

Many people have recently moved there and have no kin living there. It takes a long time to become a member of a new community. Many of them have high rise housing. Some town plans actively prevent the development of community spirit, e.g. large housing estates with no meeting places–churches, pubs, etc. Some towns are simply dormitory towns for city commuters, who are never at home during the day. Some new towns have large numbers of young, single people, who sometimes do not wish to become part of the community in which they live, unlike families with young children and the elderly, who like to be part of the community in which they live.

**3** A community centre usually provides:
(a) A meeting hall which can be booked for meetings, e.g. Women's Institute, Scouts, Clubs and Societies.
(b) Facilities for musical entertainment, e.g. discos, dancing.
(c) Other forms of entertainment such as sports and bingo.
(d) It often includes a health centre.

**4** See Table 2.3–Handicapped.

**5** (a) Educationally–teach new skill of swimming.
Socially–provide meeting place.     Physically–provide sports facilities.
(b) See Unit 2.2.2.
(c) Provide exercise in a pleasant green environment. This is particularly important for families with children in cities, who may not have access to gardens.
Often provide venues for entertainment such as circuses, concerts and bands.
Have children's playgrounds equipped with safe equipment such as swings. Often provide beautiful flowers and trees.
(d) Leisure centres provide a complex of leisure activities under one roof. Often includes films, theatres, galleries, sports facilities and meeting halls; musical entertainment such as dancing and concerts: bingo halls.
(e) Provide reading material which may be for leisure or educational purposes. Reading rooms and reference library.
May also provide a focus for community information. Often have rooms which can be rented for meetings.

**6** See Section 2.2.1     **7** See Unit 2.1     **8** See Section 2.1.1

## Section 3

**1** (a) (*i*) nutrients   (*ii*) growth, repair, efficient control of body processes, keeping body in good health.
(b) Digestion

**2** (a) carbon, hydrogen, oxygen     (b) nitrogen

**3** (a) glucose, fructose     (b) maltose, sucrose, lactose
(c) starch                  (d) cellulose or dietary fibre
(e) pectin                  (f) glycogen

**4** (a) Salivary amylase (ptyalin)     (b) Amylase     (c) Maltose

**5** Sugar, Starch, Fat, Protein

**6** (a) A, C, E     (b) A, C, D     **7** (a) Ten     (b) Eight

**8** (a) Stomach   (b) Hydrochloric acid   (c) Pepsin   (d) Rennin

## Section 4

**1** (a) Meat, fish   (b) Milk   (c) Cheese   (d) Egg white   (e) Egg yolk
(f) Wheat flour.

2 (a) Pasteurization  (b) Homogenization  (c) Sterilization  (d) Ultra Heat Treated (UHT)

3 (a) Changes lactose to lactic acid and is concerned with the flavour of the cheese.
(b) To clot the milk proteins.
(c) Preservation and flavour.

4 (a) fat  (b) (*i*) Vitamin A  (*ii*) Vitamin D

5 (a) Greater surface area exposed to digestive juices. Mixes more readily.
(b) To absorb fat as it melts and keep it around, protecting the protein from overcooking.
(c) Piquancy stimulates flow of digestive juices.
(d) Overcooking denatures protein making it hard and indigestible.

6 Main dish, enricher, raising agent, setting custards, to bind ingredients together, to coat food for frying, to glaze, to garnish, to emulsify.

7 (a) collagen  (b) gelatine  (c) fibres.

8 (a) muscle fibres  (b) collagen  (c) elastin.

9 (a) gluten  (b) caffeine  (c) iron, calcium, Vitamin A, B vitamins
(d) sodium carbonate (washing soda)  (e) saccharine  (f) monsodium glutamate.

## Section 5

1 Nutritional content, variety, cost, time of year, number of people, the occasion, religious or cultural customs, time available, cooking facilities, skill of cook.

2 (a) Linked to dental caries, obesity and all associated diseases, heart disease, high blood pressure, diabetes.
(b) Linked with obesity and associated conditions such as high blood pressure, varicose veins, gall stones, heart disease, coronary heart disease.
(c) Linked to high blood pressure.
(d) Starch better source of energy than fats and sucrose, cereal foods are rich in micronutrients, calcium, iron, B vitamins, LBV proteins and dietary fibre.
(e) Satisfying therefore eat less. Dietary fibre and micronutrients. Low calorific values.

3 Check your work against Unit 5.4.1.

4 (a) meat, poultry, sausages, fish, bacon, lard, dripping, suet.
(b) meat, poultry, sausages, fish, butter, lard, dripping, suet, eggs, milk, cheese, cream.

5 (a) Soya products, larger quantities of LBV proteins – cereals, nuts, fresh peas and beans, pulses, TVP.
(b) Margarine made entirely from vegetable oils. Sunlight on skin.
(c) Margarine, carotene in plant food.
(d) Fortified products made especially for vegans, or tablets.
(e) Pulses, cereals, nuts, fruit and vegetables. Presence of phytic acid makes a great deal of the calcium unavailable.

6 Check your lists against the information given in Section 5.6.

## Section 6

1 Check against Section 6.2.

3 Even heat throughout useful to batch bake.
Cannot use zones of heat. All dishes must have same temperature. Noisy.

4 (a) 10-15 minutes  (b) The thermostat  (c) Central shelf position
(d) Slow      150°C    300°F    Gas mark 2
    Moderate  180°C    350°F    Gas mark 4
    Hot       200°C    400°F    Gas mark 6
    V. hot    230°C    450°F    Gas mark 8

5 Check against pages 72-3 in Section 6.

6 (a) Moist methods – boil, stew, poach, steam, braise, pressure cooking
(b) Dry methods – bake, roast, grill, fry, pot roast
(c) Fast methods – boil, grill, fry, stewing fruit, sauté or stir-frying, microwave cooking
(d) Slow methods – braise, pot roasting, baking, stewing meat

7 (a) 100°C  (b) 120°C  (c) (1) higher (2) boils (3) quicker
(d) (1) time, (2) fuel (3) money (4) nutrients (5) flavour (6) tender
(e) (1) expensive (2) gasket (3) pressure valve
(f) ½pt, 250-300ml (g) (*i*) leave at room temperature for 10 minutes. (*ii*) place pan in bowl of cold water and allow water to run over pan.
(h) (*i*) locking lugs on lid (*ii*) safety plug (*iii*) valve for weights.

8 (a) For stability      (b) So fat does not overflow when food added
(c) Too cool – fat soaks into food; too hot – outside food burns, inside raw
(d) If fat overheats – bursts into flames
(e) Even a small amount water makes fat spit violently.
(f) To hold food together and reduce amount of fat entering food. Protects some foods from the fierce heat of frying.
(g) For ease and avoiding splashes.  (h) Fat can so easily overheat and burst into flames.
(i) To smother flames should the pan catch fire.
(j) Filter allows steam to pass through, on ordinary lid steam would condense and drop back into fat cooling it.
(k) To remove as much fat as possible.
(l) Fat must be clean for next frying. Crumbs and pieces of food would black the next lot of frying. Very hot oil would melt plastic containers.

(m) To stop oxygen reaching flames. To limit fire. Will remain hot for a long time and can re-ignite if not cooled. Throw away because decomposition has produced substances which irritate the stomach.

## Section 7

1 (a) A mixture of flour, milk and eggs beaten together
  (b) Yorkshire pudding, pancakes, fritters, coating fish
  (c) Strong plain flour or plain flour

2 (a) A sauce is a thickened liquid served with food to which it gives moistness, flavour, colour and nutrients.
  (b) A pouring sauce is thinner, containing double the liquid of a coating sauce. Coating sauce is used to coat the surface of food before serving, pouring sauce is served in a sauce boat.
  (c) A panada is a very thick mixture used as a basis for soufflés and for binding ingredients together.
  (d) Check answer against Unit 7.1.2.

3 A roux is a paste used as a thickening. It is usually made of equal quantities of butter or margarine and flour or cornflour. The fat is melted and the flour stirred in and cooked gently to achieve a honeycomb effect.

4 125ml (¼pt)

5 The egg proteins coagulate (set) when heated.

6 (a) Pastry is a mixture of flour, fat and water mixed in different proportions and in different ways to produce different types of pastry.
  (b) Check answer against Unit 7.1.3.
  (c) (*i*) Plain (*ii*) SR (*iii*) Strong plain (*iv*) Strong plain
  (d) (*i*) ½ lard, ½ margarine (*ii*) Shredded suet (*iii*) Lard and margarine or either (*iv*) Margarine or butter.
  (e) The Vitamin C strengthens the gluten making it more elastic.
  (f) (*i*) 200°C/400°F (*ii*) 200°C/400°F (*iii*) 220°C/425°F (*iv*) 200°C/400°F 10 minutes, then reduce to 180°C/350°F
  (g) Check with pastry charts in Unit 7.1.3

7 (a) Air  (b) $CO_2$  (c) Air and steam  (d) Steam and air.     8 Check list against Unit 7.1.3

9 A flan case baked without a filling, the base is held down by baking beans on top of greased greaseproof paper both of which are removed 5 minutes before the end of cooking.

10 Check answer against Unit 7.1.5

11 (a) creaming  (b) whisking  (c) folding in

12 (a) Top shelf at 200°C/400°F      (b) Centre shelf at 180°C/350°F
   (c) Top shelf at 220°C/425°F      (d) Centre shelf at 180°C/350°F
   (e) Centre shelf at 170°C/325°F   (f) Scones top shelf at 230°C/450°F

## Section 8

1 Check answers against chart in Section 8.2

2 Subject the food to high temperatures and seal to prevent recontamination.
  Subject the food to very low temperatures −18°C to −25°C, enzymes and micro-organisms inhibited.
  Use of chemicals−salt, sugar, vinegar
  Removal of water−dehydration. Enzymes work in solution.

3 (a) Polythene freezer bags of heavy gauge so do not split, freezer foil or foil doubled, freezer cling film, plastic boxes, freezer tape, covered wire ties, chinagraph pens or special freezer pens. Waxed cartons.
  (b) Glass, paper, cardboard, some metals which rust.
  (c) (*i*) After blanching and cooling, when peas have drained weigh quantity required per pack and place in a polythene freezer bag−not too large. Remove air from bag with straw or pump. Seal with tie. Label with date, contents and quantity. Place in fast freezing compartment.
      (*ii*) Soup−when cold pour into a plastic container and leave a headspace of 2 to 3cm. Secure lid with freezer tape. Label−type of soup, quantity and date. Place in fast freezing compartment.
  (d) Strawberries, raspberries, peas, beans etc. spread on trays in single layer and put in freezer for about 2 hours until solid. Packed in containers. They do not stick together and smaller amounts can be easily removed from large containers.
  (e) To destroy the enzymes which will bring about changes in colour, flavour and texture and lead to the destruction of Vitamin C.
  (f) Air contains moisture which if left in bags will form frost on the food. When thawing takes place this frost turns to water and soaks into the food.

4 (a) 60-65% sugar. Micro-organisms and enzymes cannot work in these sweet conditions.
  (b) Sterilized and sealed to prevent recontamination. Heat has destroyed micro-organisms and enzymes.
  (c) −18°C too cold for enzymes and micro-organisms to work.
  (d) No water so enzyme action impossible.
  (e) Vinegar soaks into all cells−too acid for enzyme action. Microbes destroyed.

5 (a) Just ripe or slightly under ripe, no blemishes. Select fruit with a good pectin content.
  (b) (*i*) A carbohydrate. A polysaccharide.  (*ii*) With acid and sugar makes jam set.
  (c) (*i*) Gooseberries, redcurrants, blackcurrants, cooking apples, crab apples.
      (*ii*) Strawberries, cherries, pears.
  (d) Use home made pectin stock−juice from stewed apples or gooseberries. Use a commercial pectin such as Certo.

Mix a high pectin fruit in with low pectin fruit e.g. gooseberries and strawberries.
(e) 1.5kg plums    (3lb)    1.5kg sugar    (3lb)        300ml to 450ml water (½ to ¾pt)
(f) To extract the acid and pectin from the fruit. To make skins tender.
(g) Undissolved sugar will crystallize out in storage.    (h) Temperature of 220°F/105°C
*Wrinkle test* – little on saucer – cool – wrinkles form on surface when pushed with finger.
*Flake test* – large flakes of jam hang from the wooden spoon and do not break off.
(i) To prevent the fruit rising in the jars.
(j) To allow for slight shrinkage and to ensure perfect coverage by the waxed disc.
(k) The wax melts on the surface of jams, sets as it cools and forms barrier to micro-organisms.
(l)    (*i*) Cool – to discourage any activity of moulds, yeasts or bacteria
      (*ii*) Dry – to discourage moulds
      (*iii*) Dark – to prevent loss of colour

6 By producing toxins which they excrete or which are released when the bacteria cells die.

7 Check with diagram in Section 8.6.

8 Cooled quickly in a clean container and covered.

9 (a) So heat penetrates quickly    (b) To destroy any bacteria quickly before they have time to multiply
   (c) Re-cooking will denature and harden the protein making it difficult to digest.

10 (a) Shepherd's Pie, rissoles, curry, fritters, bubble and squeak, pies, stuffed pancakes.
    (b) Fish cakes, fish and potato pie, fish envelopes, kedgeree, mousse.
    (c) Creamed potatoes, cheese or flan pastry, custards, mayonnaise.
    (d) Meringues, glaze on sweet pastry, coconut ice, coconut pyramids.
    (e) Breadcrumbs for frying croûtons, bread and butter pudding, bread pudding, cheese pudding, fruit charlottes, queen of puddings.
    (f) Pies, Eve's pudding, charlottes, crumbles, flans, trifles.
    (g) Bubble and squeak, soups, salads, casseroles, rissotto.

## Section 9

1 Water from sinks and baths, lavatory waste, rain water

2 Section 9.1 and Section 13.3    3 See Section 13.1    4 See Unit 9.1.3

5 Water rates collected twice yearly.

6 Liquid is pure and can flow into a river. The sludge is used on the soil or carried out to sea.

7 Epidemics of diseases such as dysentry, cholera, typhoid.

8 A detergent that can be broken down by the action of bacteria.

9 See Unit 9.1.6

10 Dustbins, sink disposal units, compost, hired skips, special collections, take to special tip.

11 To treat so that it can be used again.

12 See Unit 9.1.8    13 See Unit 9.1.5

14 Householder in General Rates paid to Local Authority. Once a year, or split into two or ten equal payments.

15 See Unit 9.2.2.    16 See Unit 9.2.4    17 See Unit 9.2.4

18 See Unit 9.2.5    19 See Section 9.3

20 See Unit 9.3.1    21 See Units 9.3.1 and 13.1    22 See Unit 9.3.2

23 See Fig. 9.14    24 See Fig. 9.15    25 See Fig. 9.16 and Unit 9.3.2

## Section 10

1 (a) Dressings, triangular bandages, adhesive tape, cotton wool, gauze, safety pins (for additional items see page 134).
   (b) See page 134 heading Bleeding.    (c) See page 135 heading Burns
   (d) See page 135 heading Poisoning.

2 (a) See pages 131 and 133 for list of ways in which safety can be improved.
   (b) (*i*) Sit her down on a chair and lean her over with her head between her knees for a short time. Increase the amount of fresh air available if indoors by opening a window or door.
      (*ii*) See page 135 advice on cuts under heading Bleeding.

3 (a) Have a stair gate; make sure the floors are not strewn with toys; bar low windows.
   (b) Do not allow them to have pillows; do not give them small items to play with which may stick in their nose e.g. beads: pay careful attention when feeding toddlers so that solids do not 'go down the wrong way'. Keep all plastic bags right out of reach.
   (c) Have a locking medicine cabinet; put household chemicals in either a locking cupboard or one which is well out of reach for the child; buy medicines with child-proof lids. Never put harmful household chemicals in squash bottles.
   (d) Use a saucepan guard round the cooker; have fixed fire guards on all fires; never leave matches or lighters around for children to play with.
   (e) Put dummy plugs in empty sockets; ensure that all cables and electrical fittings are well maintained so that there are no live cables and fittings; do not allow children to play with electrical appliances.

4 (a) The kit needs to be kept where it is likely to be needed. This is probably in the kitchen although many people keep their kit in the bathroom in the medicine cabinet.
   (b) Keep the saucepan handles well out of the child's reach; keep the floor tidy and free from toys; ensure that hot liquids and kettles do not boil over; do not allow children to play with dangerous kitchen equipment such as knives; ensure that dangerous chemicals like bleach are well out of the child's reach.

5 (a) See Section 5.4.2 feeding the invalid.

   (b) By covering the food; by placing it in the fridge.

   (c) Always follow the dosage instructions on the bottle; only give medicines on prescription to the person for whom they have been prescribed.     (d) By immunization. Drops are taken.

6 Being cold; pallor (very pale colour).

7 Make sure that the mouth and throat are not blocked by the tongue; loosen the patient's clothing. Push head up to make sure the air passage stays open.

8 Roll the child quickly in a rug, coat or blanket, any large item which will smother the flames, and put out the fire by excluding the air. Call for medical help immediately and do not remove any clothing.

## Section 11

1 (a)   (*i*) A cheque enables you to pay for goods without carrying cash.

      (*ii*) The bank can pay Standing Orders (Banker's Orders) (see page 143).

      (*iii*) A bank is a safe place to deposit money.

  (b)   (*i*) A current account – with this account, the money is immediately available on demand. Interest is not earned on the money deposited. A cheque book is supplied with this account, also cheque guarantee and dispenser cards are available.

      (*ii*) A deposit account – notice usually has to be given to withdraw the money. Interest is earned on the money deposited. (See page 142). At present no cheque book or cash dispenser facility.

  (c)   (*i*) See page 144.

      (*ii*) See page 147. Three main ways of borrowing money from the bank – by overdraft; by personal loan; by opening a budget account.

      (*iii*) See page 143.

      (*iv*) Some bank credit cards fulfill more than one function (see page 144). The cards are available to anyone over 18 who is acceptable to the credit card company. Statements are sent out monthly and at least the minimum payment demanded must be paid. Any money not paid off at the end of each month has interest charged on it and added to next month's bill.

  (d) See pages 142–45.     (e) List on page 146.

2 (a) How to open a bank account page 142.

  (b) *Advantages*

      (*i*) Do not need to carry cash.  (*ii*) Can be safely sent through the post.

    (*iii*) The cheque counterfoil provides a useful record.

    *Disadvantages*

      (*i*) Cheque guarantee cards often only guarantee amounts up to £50.

      (*ii*) Some tradesmen (e.g. market traders) do not like to be paid by cheque.

    (*iii*) Each cheque used increases the amount of bank charges payable by the account holder.

3 (a) *Advantages*

    It is possible to have the goods needed even if you do not have enough money to buy them outright. Many credit cards/shop accounts allow customers 'interest free' credit until the statement has to be paid. Only amounts which are not paid-off at the end of the first month have interest charged on them.

    *Disadvantages*

    Can be expensive.    Can encourage people to buy things that they cannot really afford.

    Goods bought on hire-purchase do not become legally yours until the *option to purchase* has been exercised.

    A customer who misses payments or does not complete the payments will find that the goods are re-possessed by the person who hired them.

  (b) Make sure that you have understood what the *hire rate of interest* is.

    Make sure that you understand *when* the repayments need to be made.

    Ensure that you know the *length* of the contract – how many weeks/months/years it is to run for.

4 (a) See page 140 – Taxation – PAYE and the PAYE code.     (c) See page 144 – Credit cards.

  (b) See page 140 – National Insurance Contributions.

5 (a) See page 147 – Hire purchase.    (b) The goods can be re-possessed.

6 (a) (*iii*).

  (b) (*iii*) When the option to purchase is exercised.

  (c) (*i*).

7 (a)   (*i*) Some traders will only accept cash e.g. street traders.

      (*ii*) Cheque guarantee cards only guarantee amounts up to the value printed on them e.g. £50. If the goods are more than this cash must also be paid, or the goods are held by the seller until the cheque is cleared.

  (b) Saving money by: Depositing it in a Building Society.

                      Depositing it in The National Savings Bank.

  (c) (*i*) Discount is the amount of money by which a price is reduced. This offer may be made for several reasons e.g. to encourage the purchaser to pay cash; to get someone to pay a bill quickly; to sell goods quickly i.e. sale goods, or if a new model is due to be launched in the shops, such as a cooker or refrigerator.

(*ii*) A receipt is a written or printed document which verifies that a *specific sum of money* has been paid for *specified goods or services* to a *person or business* on a *particular date*.

(*iii*) Premium bonds are issued by the National Savings Department available in units of £5. The interest that these bonds *ought* to be earning forms the prize fund and this is won by people holding bonds with the numbers which are randomly selected by computer at regular intervals.

(*iv*) Insurance Policies–see pages 146 and 172.

8 (a) Mortgage or rent    Rates    Food    Clothing and footwear    Travel
Heating, lighting, power

(b) Through a budget account or regular standing order per month through the bank. The amount is agreed by the Electricity or Gas Company.
By credit card    By cash at the showroom–paid on a regular monthly basis.

(c) By product information    By labels attached to the goods
By reading magazines and newspapers    By advertising material
By consulting trained shop assistants    By using Consumer Advice agencies
Consulting friends who own the product

(d)

| | Advantages | Disadvantages |
|---|---|---|
| **Shopping by post** | Have catalogue in your own home. Goods are sent to own home. Do not have to go out to fetch them and can choose at leisure. | Do not see the actual goods. Goods sometimes get damaged or lost in the post. |
| **Doorstep trading** | Tradesman comes to home Samples of actual goods available for purchaser to see. | Tradesmen do not always call regularly or at convenient times. Some people feel pressurized by door-step selling techniques. |
| **Shopping by telephone using a credit card** | Goods are sent to own home. Quick and easy way to purchase goods. | Cannot see the goods. Credit account is debited without signing a form. It is sometimes difficult to get re-imbursed if goods are faulty or unsatisfactory. |

9 (a) Family B

(*i*) Spend more on food–important to maintain health of family. No indication is given on the quality of food however.

(*ii*) Spend less on HP payments but save for goods they need.

(*iii*) Spend money on insurance. All homes need insurance as it provides for the future.

(*iv*) Saves money whereas Family A saves nothing.

(*v*) Spends much less on holiday and entertainment which are luxury items.

(b) Building Society    National Savings Bank Deposit Account
Bank deposit account

(c) Using a credit card e.g. Access.   Buying goods using a loan from a Finance Company.
Buying goods using a monthly account from a department store.

## Section 12

1 (a) (*i*) These goods comply with the standards laid down by the British Standards Institute (BSI). BSI is a non-profit-making organization which is financed by the government. A British Standard may include all or any of the following:
Technical specifications; dimensional specifications; performance requirements (including safety); standard methods of testing.

(*ii*) The British Electrotechnical Approvals Board (BEAB) carries out tests on all electrical household goods. This label indicates that the appliance has been tested by BEAB and has no exposed 'live parts'.

(*iii*) The item bearing this label has been included in the Design Index. These goods are selected by the Design Council. Such goods, in addition to being of good design, must also be 'fit' for the purpose, of good quality and value; and be easy to maintain.

(b) This garment is clearly not of merchantable quality if laundering it means that it falls apart. Under the Sale of Goods Act 1893 goods must be of 'merchantable quality'. Your contract is with the supplier (the Department Store). Take the goods back and ask for your money back. The Act does not suggest that the goods should be replaced or repaired. You should not be required to have a credit note. You are entitled to a full refund.

(c) (*i*) Supermarkets have many advantages for the shopper. They sell a *wide variety of goods* of *different qualities and prices*, often with many *own brand* products. Many stores have *late opening* times and some shops have *car parking* and '*carry-out*' services. Large supermarkets usually have products in large sizes which are suitable for those who wish to bulk buy. Competition and the store's (or chain's) ability to place large orders with wholesalers means that the prices supermarkets charge consumers are relatively cheap. The fact that they are self-service enables shoppers to browse, making the buying decisions at their leisure.

Such shops have relatively few disadvantages; however, it can be difficult to find trained personnel to help you e.g. in the butchery department. Some people prefer to have personal service, rather than select goods for themselves from the shelves. Supermarkets are usually only to be found in urban areas and travelling costs to them should be taken into consideration when comparing prices.

(*ii*) Small local shops usually give friendly personal service. They are convenient and in large towns are often open late at night. Some shops offer their customers credit, even delivery services (especially in rural areas) and are run by people who understand their products and take a very personal interest in the success of the business. Being local travelling costs are usually nil.

There are some disadvantages. They usually have a restricted number of qualities, brands, prices and types of stock. On the whole they are expensive. In some areas they operate restricted opening hours (e.g. village shops often shut on 'early closing day').

(*iii*) Street Markets. The main advantage of street markets is that they are relatively cheap. Many people enjoy the atmosphere of bargaining. Some street markets like Petticoat Lane have even become tourist attractions! Markets are found in rural and urban areas. The goods are easy to examine.

The disadvantages of street markets are that they usually only operate on a few days of the week. General street markets tend to sell a limited range of relatively low quality products. You need to be a careful shopper to pick up a bargain. There is little comeback if the goods are faulty.

(*iv*) Departmental stores offer the shopper a wide range of advantages. They exist in urban environments, are easily accessible, with long opening hours and give shoppers a pleasant shopping atmosphere. They sell a wide variety of goods, relatively cheaply. Shops usually offer monthly or budget accounts and delivery facilities. Each department has trained personnel who can offer customers advice. Some goods are laid out self-service style so that people can examine them carefully.

Perhaps the main disadvantage is that they do not stock as wide a selection of a particular item as specialist shops do.

**2** (a) *Cooking oil*

(*i*) Type of oil e.g. corn oil, peanut oil, olive oil etc. Different oils are suitable for different types of frying, e.g. olive oil is used for low temperature frying, whereas corn oil is suitable for high temperature frying. Other oils e.g. sunflower seed oil, can be used successfully in cakes and pastry making.

(*ii*) Whether the oil is pure or blended (a mixture of different oils).

(*iii*) Flavour of the oil. Certain cooking oils have characteristic flavours which can be detrimental or beneficial in certain dishes.

(*iv*) Relative cost

(b) (*i*) Size (Nos. 1-7) (see page 153).    (*ii*) Quality (Either Class A or B).

(*iii*) Date code (week no.).    (*iv*) Name and address of person(s) grading the eggs.

(*v*) Packing Station No.

(*vi*) It is also wise to consider where the eggs are bought. If stock is not correctly stored and displayed eggs may go stale quickly or become broken.

(*vii*) Battery or free range. White or brown.    (*viii*) Costs of both types in (*vii*) and egg size.

(c) (*i*) Whether powder is to be used for handwashing, in a front loading machine or in a top loading machine; (automatic powders create very little foam–this is necessary for front loading machines).

(*ii*) Type of washing to be done e.g. delicate knitted garments or heavily soiled overalls.

(*iii*) Whether the washing powder is to be used in a machine with a variable temperature control (or appropriate cooler programmes).

Machines which have this facility enable the user to use low temperature powders which save energy.

(*iv*) Whether the user requires a powder which incorporates a conditioning agent as well e.g. Bold 3.

(*v*) Whether members of the household are allergic to certain powders, (e.g. biological powders can sometimes cause irritation when used for clothes which touch the skin).

(*vi*) Cost.

(d) (*i*) Type of bacon, e.g. back, streaky.   (*ii*) Degree of leanness.

(*iii*) Country of origin.   (*iv*) Date. Check the 'sell-by' date.

(*v*) Price.   (*vi*) Weight.

(*vii*) Check that the pack is still vacuum sealed. If the seal has been broken the bacon should not be eaten.

(*viii*) The conditions in which the seller is keeping the pack of bacon, e.g. should be kept in cool conditions.

**3** (a) (*i*) Aluminium foil containers–used to pack hot take-away meals, e.g. cooked Chinese and Indian food.

(*ii*) Polystyrene used as trays on which food such as meat is placed.

(*iii*) Clear plastic freezer cling wrap–often used to pack meats.

(*iv*) Polythene bags have a multitude of uses including packing vegetables.

(*v*) Rigid polythene boxes–used for packaging ice-cream.

(b) *Advantages*

(*i*) Keeps food clean away from flies and bacteria.

(*ii*) Enables people to examine fresh food easily.

*Disadvantages*

(*i*) Some forms of packaging make it difficult to examine the goods.

(*ii*) Pre-packed goods regulate the amount of weight.

(*iii*) Wasteful of resources–packaging usually thrown away after use.

**4** Size (see page 153).    Week No.    Packing Station No.    Quality.

**5** The buyer is entitled to a 'cooling-off' period under the Consumer Credit Act as he may perhaps have made a hasty decision. The agreement was signed in the person's own home. It would not have been possible to cancel the contract if it had been made on business premises. If the contract is cancelled the prospective purchaser is entitled to receive his deposit back.

6 (a) See pages 144 and 145 in Money Management Section.
   (*i*) The Annual Percentage Rate of Interest–the true interest rate.
   (*ii*) The length of the contract.   (*iii*) The amount of each instalment.
   (b) See Textiles Section page 192.

7 (a) It encourages consumers to buy and is a major source of product information. The product information alerts buyers to new and improved products and to the different evaluation criteria which are important when making a selection between goods and services.
   Advertising can also be disadvantageous to consumers encouraging them to buy goods and services which they do not need or are poor in quality.
   (b) See pages 151 and 152.

8 Select any two Acts from the Table on pages 157 and 158.

9 The main advantages of bulk buying are:
   (*i*) Cheapness   (*ii*) Convenience.

10 (a) It provides:  Product information
                     Ways of using products, e.g. recipes
                     Criteria for evaluating products
                     Advice
   (b) Newspapers and magazines       Cinemas, theatres
       TV                             On packaging and labels
       Posters                        Sides of vans, lorries, buses and inside trains
       Store promotions
       Sponsoring events, e.g. sport

11 See page 154.
   *Statutory Control* e.g. through Acts of Parliament.
   *Voluntary controls* The British Code of Advertising Practice which is administered by the Advertising Standards Authority. The Independent Broadcasting Authority also has a control office which examines adverts before broadcasting.

12 *Consumer Advice Centres*
   Provide consumers with information which can be used to assess products. They notify consumers about dangerous or unsatisfactory products. They give advice on money and legal matters concerning consumers.
   *Department of Trade*
   Has a Consumer Affairs Division which concerns itself with all matters concerning consumers. In particular they consider trading practices, prices, safety, financing of Consumer Protection Agencies such as the National Consumer Council, consumer advice and information. Imported goods and toys in particular are examined by this department before appearing in the shops.
   *Environmental Health Department*
   This is a Local Government Department which is concerned with premises where food is made or sold. They also investigate complaints from the public and are responsible for a range of laws concerning pollution, housing and other public health Acts.
   *Post Office Users' National Council*
   This organization deals with complaints about telephone and postal services. It monitors prices and consumer relations. Similar organizations also exist for electricity and gas users.

13 Offer     Acceptance     Consideration

14 See page 156.

# Section 13

1 (a) Fitted carpets, rugs, ceramic tiles, vinyl sheet.
   (b) Cost, durability, ease of cleaning and maintaining, suitability for the purpose (i.e. only certain coverings are suitable for certain areas of the house such as the bathroom), texture, colour, pattern and design.
   (c) Good suction, ease of emptying; suitable for task; not too heavy or awkward; suitable size for the job.
   (d)  (*i*) Needs to be washable; easy to maintain; should not be damaged by steam or water.
        (*ii*) Textile needs to be reasonably durable to stand heavy wear.
        Textile needs to have good draping qualities to be suitable for curtaining.
        Should be aesthetically pleasing (colour, design, texture).
        (*iii*) See page 191 in Housing section for list of criteria for lighting in different rooms.

2 (a) See page 164 Home Management unit for diagram of plug wiring.
   (b)  (*i*) Fuses are designed as a weak link in an electrical circuit. They melt when overheated preventing the whole electrical system in the house from 'blowing'.
        (*ii*) faulty wiring     faulty appliance
        (*iii*) *a* 3 amp     *b* 13 amp
   (c)  (*i*) Turning off appliances when they are not needed e.g. fires.
        Always using machines for full loads e.g. washers etc.
        Ensure that machines are well maintained so that they work to the maximum efficiency.
        When using electric cookers plan cooking to make best use of the available heat e.g. cook several dishes in the oven at once, use tower steamers etc.
        Reduce the wattage of light bulbs in areas where a high intensity of light is not required.
        Choose wisely when purchasing electrical equipment so that you buy items which are electrically efficient. Many manufacturers quote the electricity consumption of their appliances. Some

machines have economy buttons or facilities for doing half loads or heating half the grill.
(*ii*) Coin operated meters. Paying bills by instalments (also see page 142, Money Management section).

**3** 2591.4 kWh has been used.

**4** (a) See Fig. 5.6.
(b) Serving spoons; glasses; side plates; salt and pepper pots; napkins.

**5** See Section 13.3.

**6** Number of people in the home, their ages and capacities.

**7** Select these from checklist in Table 13.1.

**8** Select these from checklist in Table 13.1.

**9** (a) Housefly, lesser housefly, blue-bottle, carpet beetle, woodwoorm, fleas, cockroaches, silver fish, ants, rats and mice.
(b) See Section 13.2.

## Section 14

**1** (a) See Unit 14.1.4.     (b) See Unit 14.1.3.

**2** House A £900     House B £1187.50

**3** (a)   (*i*) See Unit 14.1.2                    (*v*) See Units 14.1.2 and 14.1.6
(*ii*) See Unit 14.1.3                    (*vi*) See Unit 14.1.5
(*iii*) See Unit 14.1.3                   (*vii*) See Unit 14.1.4
(*iv*) See Units 14.1.2 and 14.1.4
(b) Age of prospective purchaser, job and its security, salary or wages per month.

**4** (a) See Unit 14.1.1     (c) See Section 11
(b) See Unit 14.1.2     (d) See Unit 14.1.6.

**5** (a) See Unit 14.1.1                    (d) See Unit 14.1.1
(b) See Unit 14.1.4                    (e) See Unit 14.1.2
(c) See Unit 14.1.2, Table 14.1

**6** See Unit 14.1.1

**7** See Unit 14.1.6

**8** See Unit 14.1.5

**9** (a) See Section 14.5     (b) See Section 14.5     (c) See Section 14.5

**10** (a) See Unit 14.2.1     (b) See Unit 14.2.1     (c) See Unit 14.2.1

## Section 15

**1** Clothing–label attached showing fibre content.
Fabric–fibre content written on end of roller or bale.

**2** Check against last part of Section 15.1.

**3** See Section 15.4.

**4** (a) Wool  (b) Cotton  (c) Linen  (d) Regenerated cellulose  (e) Benzene or phenol  (f) Terylene  (g) Acrylonitrile from coal and natural gas  (h) Corsetry, tights, stockings, swimwear  (i) It stretches  (j) Toilet bags, rain coats, bathroom curtains, aprons  (k) Silica curtains  (l) Metal. Lurex. Gold and Silver lamé. (m) Vilene  (n) Felt  (o) Laminated fabrics.

**5** Refer to Section 15.5.

**6** Preparation, soaking, washing, rinsing, drying, ironing.

**7** See Section 15.5.

**8** To make clothes softer, to free from static electricity which results in clinging and to make ironing easier.

**9** Refer to Section 15.6, Irons and Ironing.

**10** (a) Washing  (b) Bleaching  (c) Drying  (d) Ironing  (e) Dry cleaning.

**11** (a) Line dry     (b) Dry flat   (c) Drip dry
(d) Tumble dry   (e) Do not tumble dry

**12** (a) All solvents   (b) Perchloroethylene, white spirit, solvent 113, solvent 11.
(c) White spirit or solvent 11   (d) Do not dry clean.

**13** (1) 1976
(a) 85% wool  (b) Wool–85% minimum   (c) 85% wool 15% polyester
(2) First   (3) Descending   (4) Weight order   (5) 50% wool and 50% polyester

**14** *Advantages*–Calcium salts provide calcium for good formation of bones and teeth.
*Disadvantages*–Fur on elements of immersion heaters, kettles and washing machines, scale in pipes, boilers and hot water cylinders. Heating less efficient. More fuel used. Difficult to obtain lather when washing. More detergent needed.

**15** By boiling, action of washing soda and Calgon.
Ion exchange softeners e.g. Permutit. Refer to Section 15.8.

**16** Less detergent needed when washing. Hair and skin soft after washing.  **17** See Section 15.9.

**18** (a) Surface tension
(b) (1) Detergent  (2) Surface tension  (3) Grease.
(c) (1) Agitation  (2) Dirt.

**19** Refer to Section 15.10.

# Part V

## 18 Practice in answering examination questions

The questions that follow have been selected from past examination papers of several examination boards. The suggestions for answering, and any outline answers for parts of questions do not necessarily represent what was expected of candidates in the marking schemes used by the examiners of the various boards.

### 18.1 CSE questions

*Fixed response or Multiple choice questions*

These are not widely used at the moment in Home Economics examination papers. They are becoming more popular because they can be marked more easily and accurately. The examples given below are simple statements which are to be completed by selecting one of four possible solutions, or questions to be answered.

1 Which of the following contains the largest amount of dietary fibre (roughage)?
   A Fish    B Vegetables    C Meat    D Eggs

2 Brisket comes from
   A chicken.    B lamb.    C beef.    D pork.

3 Caerphilly is a type of
   A hard cheese.    B soft cheese.    C processed cheese.    D curd cheese.

4 Paella is a dish from
   A Germany.    B Italy.    C Spain.    D Greece.

*(EAEB Home Economics 1982)*

*Short answer questions*

These are most frequently found in the first section of an examination paper. They are a popular way of testing a wide range of subject material.

Answers are usually written on the question paper. They need to be precise and concise. The space allowed for an answer is a guide to the length of answer required–one or two words, or one or more sentences.

1 Give **two** reasons why the body needs calcium.
   (a) _____
   (b) _____

2 (a) What does the term 'offal' mean?
   _____
   (b) Give **two** examples
      (i) _____ (*ii*) _____

3 Name **three** ways in which you could arrange to pay for a new automatic washing machine.
   (a) _____
   (b) _____
   (c) _____

*(ALSEB Home Economics 1981)*

4 Name the types of detergent which should be used when washing:
   (a) a woollen jumper. _____
   (b) a family wash in a front loading washing machine.
   _____

*(ALSEB Home Economics 1981)*

5 Name two seals of approval which show that equipment has been tested for quality.
   (a) _____
   (b) _____

6 Name **three** organisms which cause decay in foods:
   (a) _____
   (b) _____
   (c) _____

*(ALSEB Home Economics 1982)*

7 (a) Explain the meaning and give the use of each of the following:
   (*i*) To blanch
   _____
   _____

   (*ii*) To poach
   _____
   _____

(b) What are the following and how are they used?
    (*i*) A bouquet garni

    (*ii*) Arrowroot

    (*iii*) Zest

**8** Give **two** reasons for each of the following faults:
  (a) Tough shortcrust pastry
    (*i*) _____
    (*ii*) _____
  (b) Unrisen bread
    (*i*) _____
    (*ii*) _____
  (c) A chocolate cake which has sunk in the middle
    (*i*) _____
    (*ii*) _____

(*YREB Home Economics 1980*)

**9** Suggest **one** way of using each of the following left-overs.
  (a) An egg yolk _____
  (b) Stale bread _____
  (c) Two egg whites _____

**10** (a) Give **one** reason why food stored in the refrigerator should be covered.

  (b) Why is it important to thaw a frozen chicken before cooking?

**11** What **two** safety rules should be observed when deep-fat frying?
  (a) _____
  (b) _____

**12** What are the modern colour codings for each of the following electrical wires?:
  (a) live wire. _____
  (b) neutral wire. _____
  (c) earth wire. _____

**13** Give an example of the work of each of the following:
  (a) WRVS. _____
  (b) Samaritans. _____
  (c) Shelter. _____

(*SWEB Home Economics 1980*)

*Free response questions*
An answer in the form of an essay may be required for this type of question, but they are more usually structured.

If a complete answer book has been provided by the examination board answers should be written in the spaces provided. Frequently, answers other than those to Section A, are written on file paper. The mark allocation to each section of the question should indicate how much you should write.

The following broad selection has been made to cover the wide range of CSE questions. Some of the questions may not be relevant to your particular examination.

**1** You are moving to a new home and will be furnishing the lounge which faces south and gets the sun for most of the day.
  (a) Give **three** points to consider when buying a lounge suite.
  (b) What **four** points would you consider when buying a carpet?
  (c) Give a list of **three** fibres used in carpets today.
  (d) What sort of curtains or blinds would you choose? Give reasons for your answer.
  (e) What considerations would you bear in mind when buying curtain material?

(*SWEB Home Economics 1980*)

**2** A newly married couple are planning to rent an unfurnished flat.
  (a) Suggest **six** questions that they should ask the landlady when they go to see the flat. (6 marks)
  (b) What type of cooker would you choose for the flat. Give **three** reasons for your choice. (2 marks)
  (c) How should the following surfaces be cleaned?
    (*i*) A vitreous enamel bath    (*ii*) A formica work top
    (*iv*) A polished wooden table    (*iii*) A stainless steel sink       (5 marks)
  (d) What procedure should this couple follow in order to obtain a council flat? (2 marks)

(*ALSEB Home Economics 1980*)

**3** Some people like to shop at a supermarket.
  (a) Give **six** explanations for this. (b) State **three** advantages and **three** disadvantages of bulk buying.
  (c) What is meant by the term 'Price War'? In what ways does it affect the shopper?
  (d) Explain with reasons why you might stop buying your food from a particular store (six reasons).
  (e) What six pieces of information would you expect to be given on food labels?

(*SEREB Cook and Host(ess) 1980*)

**4** (a) The need for fuel economy is very important.

    (*i*) Describe **four** ways in which a housewife can reduce the size of her heating bill.

    (*ii*) Give **two** advantages and **two** disadvantages of heating the home with electric storage heaters.

        (4 marks)

  (b) (*i*) When lighting the home what **four** points should be taken into consideration?

    (*ii*) Show, with the aid of a diagram, indirect lighting and say where you would use it. (4 marks)

  (c) From the following information work out the quarterly electricity bill. Show all your working out.

    February Reading  75604 units

    May Reading        76472 units

    The first 80 units cost 9p each. The rest 5.5p each.     (4 marks)

        *(YREB Home Economics 1980)*

**5** (a) List **six** varieties of sugar available to the housewife.

  (b) Which enzymes are used in the digestion of carbohydrate foods:

    (*i*) in the mouth?

    (*ii*) in the pancreatic juice?

    (*iii*) in the intestinal juice?

  (c) What is the function of carbohydrate foods in the diet?

  (d) List **four** carbohydrate foods which could be used in family meals to replace potatoes and give variety.

        *(EAEB Food and Nutrition 1982)*

# Answers

*CSE Fixed response or multiple choice questions*

**1** B     **2** C     **3** B     **4** C

*Short answers*

**1** Any two of the following:
strong bones and teeth;     correct muscle function;     clotting of blood.

**2** (a) The 'off fall', those parts of the animal which are cut off the carcass before it is jointed.

  (b) Any **two** of–liver, kidney, heart, lungs; pancreas, tripe, brains.

**3** Any three of the following:
Cash; Access card; Monthly budget account; hire purchase; bank loan.

**4** (a) Light duty, e.g. Dreft, soap flakes, Stergene

  (b) Low lather automatic powder e.g. Automatic Persil, Automatic Daz etc.

**5** Any **two** of–Kitemark, BEAB, Design Centre Award

**6** (a) Bacteria     (b) Moulds     (c) Yeasts

**7** (a) (*i*) This can mean to whiten e.g. when almonds are plunged into boiling water and then strained so that they slip out of their skins easily. It can also mean the treatment given to vegetables before freezing. They are plunged into boiling water which destroys enzymes that would bring about changes in colour, flavour, texture and loss of vitamin C during storage.

    (*ii*) To cook gently in water which is just off the boil. Basting food with the liquid is sometimes necessary, e.g poached eggs.

  (b) (*i*) A bundle of mixed herbs–fresh herbs are tied together with cotton, put in a muslin bag, or a perforated sachet and dried. It is used to flavour meat casseroles and soups.

    (*ii*) A starch powder from the root of the Marranta plant. It is used as a clear glaze on fruit flans, in biscuits and as a medicine to calm an upset digestive system.

    (*iii*) The very thin, coloured outer skin of citrus fruit. It contains its flavour as volatile oils.

**8** (a) Any **two** of–fat under-rubbed in so too much water was needed, over-rubbed in fat so too little water was needed, over handling of the dough, oven too cool.

  (b) Any **two** of–too hot water destroyed the yeast, too much salt, yeast creamed with sugar causing destruction of many yeast cells due to loss of water, too cold, dough not left long enough to give the yeast time to work.

  (c) Any **two** of–too much baking powder so that the gas is produced too quickly and escapes before the mixture has time to set, oven door was banged before the cake was set, cake removed from the oven too soon before the centre was cooked.

**9** (a) Any of the following: sweet pastry, cheese pastry, creamed potatoes, custard sauce, mayonnaise.

  (b) Any of the following: bread and butter pudding, bread pudding, apple charlotte, cheese pudding, bread crumbs for coating, stuffings, bread sauce.

  (c) Any of the following: coconut pyramids, meringues, meringue on a flan, baked Alaska, peppermint creams.

**10** (a) Circulating air removes the moisture from the surface of the food making it dry. The water is deposited as frost on the evaporator increasing running costs.

  (b) If the centre of the chicken remains frozen, during cooking it will thaw and warm slightly, bacteria will multiply and spread to the rest of the chicken–result food poisoning.

**11** Any **two** of – remain with the pan whilst frying, do not overfill the pan with oil, lower the food in gently, dry the food before frying.

**12** (a) Brown     (b) Blue     (c) Green and yellow

**13** (a) Meals on wheels or hospital canteens

(b) Aid to people in despair or someone to talk to when suicidal     (c) Accommodation

**NB** Most Boards print the allocation of marks to each question at its side. If a question has 2 parts and is allocated 2 marks, each part must have 1 mark allocated to it.

*Free response questions*

**1** (a)  (*i*) Choose an upholstery fabric which does not fade in the sun.

(*ii*) Choose furniture which is durable and well constructed.

(*iii*) Choose a suite which is easy to clean and maintain.

(b) The lounge is likely to be an area of heavy wear so it is necessary to buy a carpet which is **durable**. **Ease of maintenance** is important e.g. shag piles are difficult to keep clean. It should be made of fibre/fibres which do not **stain or burn** easily. *Choose the colour/pattern* to fit the style of the room.

(c) These include – wool; nylon; acrilan.     (d) You could have curtains or blinds or both.

*Curtains alone*

Choose fast colours which will not fade badly in the sunlight. They should be lined to keep the sunlight out if they are drawn during the day. The lining also helps to insulate and cuts down draughts. They should be easy to clean and maintain as they are in a room which is used often, probably a washable fabric is best which is easy care.

*Net Curtains*

These can also be used to cut down sunlight.

*Blinds     Vertical strip blinds*

Many people consider them aesthetically attractive. They are very effective at blocking out sunlight and may be left partially open to allow some light in. They do not collect as much dust as horizontal blinds and are easier to clean.

*Venetian Blinds     Rucked Blinds*

As above, can be made at home of fabric already used elsewhere in the room. They are reasonably good at cutting down sunlight and are aesthetically pleasing.

*Roller Blinds*

Do not collect dust and are easy to clean. Relatively cheap to buy.

Very effective at cutting out sunlight which can fade upholstery, furniture, carpets and pictures. May be made at home.

(e) These would include the following:

(*i*) Colour fast to sunlight and washing     (*ii*) Durable

(*iii*) Cleanable or washable

(*iv*) Draping qualities

(*v*) Remember to allow for the 'repeat' on patterned fabrics.

**2** (a)  (*i*) Is there a formal written agreement or lease and if so the length of the lease or the notice required to terminate it?

(*ii*) The cost per week or month.

(*iii*) What the rent includes, e.g. are rates included?

(*iv*) How the power bills are paid e.g. Gas and Electricity.

(*v*) Who pays for repairs or re-decoration.

(*vi*) Whether there are any restrictive conditions such as no children or no pets.

(b) An electric cooker with the main oven automatic and a grill/second oven.

*Reasons:* (*i*) Automatic oven will be useful to cook dishes while the couple are at work so that a hot meal is ready when they return. The second oven will use less fuel when there is only a little cooking to be done.

(*ii*) Electric cookers are easier to move than gas cookers.

(c)  (*i*) Clean with paste or detergent while the bath is still warm.

(*ii*) Use a non-abrasive paste or detergent and a soft cloth wrung out in warm water.

(*iii*) Use a metal polish suitable for stainless steel. Wash regularly with detergent and warm water on a soft cloth. Rinse and dry to prevent water staining.

(*iv*) If it has been sealed with a polyurethane varnish, wipe over with a soft cloth wrung out in warm water. If it has been waxed, re-wax and buff-up. Periodically old wax needs to be removed.

(d) Apply to the Local Authority to be placed on the **Housing List**. Housing is allocated on a points system so young couples or single people may have to wait a very long time before they are housed.

**3** (a)  (*i*) Wide range of goods in one place.

(*ii*) Can browse easily among the shelves.

(*iii*) Car parking is often provided.

(*iv*) Goods often relatively cheap as the store can bulk buy and pass on the advantages to customer.

(*v*) Own brands are usually available which are generally cheaper than named brands.

(*vi*) Often have late opening hours.

(b)

| *Advantages* | *Disadvantages* |
|---|---|
| (*i*) Generally cheaper to buy a large quantity. | (*i*) May buy more than is necessary. |
| (*ii*) Saves trips to the shops. | (*ii*) Storage space can be a problem. |
| (*iii*) Means that plenty of a favourite or necessary item is available to the household | (*iii*) May find that family doesn't like a particular item. |

(c) The 'Price-War' is the name for strong competition between suppliers. They cut their prices to try to persuade shoppers to buy their goods or services rather than those of a competitor. Fierce competition like this tends to force prices down. This is to the advantage of the shopper who has less to pay for the item/s.

(d) Because: (*i*) The store has become expensive.

(*ii*) It has stopped stocking the items/brands you require.

(*iii*) It is no longer stocking food of good quality – this is often a problem with fresh food such as fruit and vegetables.

(*iv*) It is no longer as clean and well managed as it was previously.

(*v*) Car parking facilities are no longer available.

(*vi*) Expert advice on the products is no longer available.

(e) This would include:

(*i*) The name of the food.    (*ii*) The contents in order of quantity

(*iii*) The date by which the item should be consumed.

(*iv*) The weight.    (*v*) The price.    (*vi*) The supplier.

**4** (a) (*i*) 1 Insulate the house e.g. by lining and inter-lining curtains.

2 Heat only rooms which are being used to high levels e.g. lounge. Fit thermostatic valves to central heating radiators.

3 Use the central heating timer clock to switch the boiler on and off.

4 Make sure that doors and windows fit well.

(*ii*)

| *Advantages* | *Disadvantages* |
|---|---|
| 1 Provides good background heat | 1 They are not moveable heat sources. |
| 2 Provides an off-peak meter which gives cheaper electricity for any power used off-peak. | 2 They only heat up during off-peak hours. This may not be adequate in very cold weather. |

(b) (*i*) 1 Type of lighting required e.g. general, or localized or decorative lighting.

2 Position of light sockets and power sources

3 Degree of natural light available

4 Money available

(*ii*)

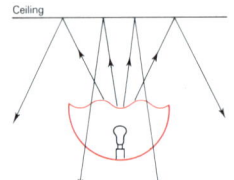

Indirect lighting – light thrown onto ceiling and then reflected down.

*Use*

Used largely for decorative and general purposes. Often supplies enough light for highlighting alcoves or ceiling corners. Will provide enough light for TV watching or walking safely in rooms with no obstacles or steps.

(c) **Total units used** $(76472 - 75604) = 868$

**Cost**   80 units $\times$ 9p   = £7.20

788 units $\times$ 5.5p = £43.34

868 units         £50.54

Total cost of bill = £50.54

**5** (a) Unit 4.1.3 on sugars.

(b) This asks you to name enzymes involved in the digestion of carbohydrates i.e. sugars and starches. A table would present information clearly.

| | *Enzyme* | *Action* |
|---|---|---|
| Mouth | Salivary amylase | Cooked starch to maltose |
| Pancreatic juice | Amylase | Starch to maltose |
| Intestinal juice | Maltase | Maltose to glucose |
| | Sucrase | Sucrose to glucose and fructose |
| | Lactase | Lactose to galactose |

(c) asks for the function of carbohydrate foods in the diet. Energy from starches and sugars, and fibre from the cellulose to aid egestion of solid faeces.

(d) A simple list e.g. bread, rice, pasta, scones.

## 18.2   The Scottish Certificate of Education (SCE)

In Scotland this examination is taken in the fourth year of secondary education (around the age 15-16), a year earlier than CSE and GCE in England and Wales. The syllabus does not contain as many topics as an O level syllabus but those topics included are studied to the same depth.

**1** (a) Outline the main aims of ventilation.                                                          (2 marks)

Suggest **two** physical discomforts which could result from poor ventilation.          (1 mark)

(b) The cost of heating a home continues to rise. Describe **four** methods of insulating the home against heat loss.  .                                                                                          (2 marks)

(c) Discuss the advantages and disadvantages of heating the living-room by:

(*i*) an open coal fire;

(*ii*) electric convector heaters.                                                                          (5 marks)

*(SCE Food and Nutrition 1983)*

**2** (a) List **four** factors which influence the daily energy requirements of different individuals.

(2 marks)

(b) What do you understand by the term 'Basal Metabolism' (Resting Metabolism)? Outline the body processes which this involves. (3 marks)

(c) (*i*) Discuss the disadvantages of being overweight. (2 marks)

(*ii*) Construct a set of **six** rules for safe and sensible ways in which an overweight teenager might achieve weight reduction. (3 marks)

*(SCE Food and Nutrition 1982)*

**3** (a) Explain the main differences between a refrigerator and a home freezer (2 marks)

(b) The two most popular types of food freezer available to the consumer are

(*i*) the chest type;

(*ii*) the upright type.

Make a comparison of the advantages and disadvantages of each type of freezer. (4 marks)

(c) Explain how a home freezer can help to reduce fuel bills. (4 marks)

*(SCE Food and Nutrition 1982)*

## 18.3 GCE Questions

Section A questions generally concern nutrition. These are usually structured so that a paragraph or paragraphs are required in answer to each section.

Short answer questions in Section A of the Cambridge O-level paper are concerned with nutrition; those in Section A of the Oxford O-level paper in Food and Nutrition cover the whole of the syllabus.

*Short answer questions*

**1** (a) Give two examples of each of the following and state in which food they can be found.

**Monosaccharides**

(*i*) _____

(*ii*) _____ (2)

**Disaccharides**

(*i*) _____

(*ii*) _____ (2)

(b) Define the following:

(*i*) Dextrin _____

_____ (2)

(*ii*) Glycogen _____

_____ (2)

(*iii*) Cellulose _____

_____ (2)

*(WJEC Home Economics 1980)*

**2** Write notes on the following information found on packets of food:

(a) 'sell-by' date; _____

_____

_____ (2)

(b) net weight; _____

_____

_____ (2)

(c) permitted colouring. _____

_____

_____ (2)

*(Oxford Food and Nutrition 1981)*

**3** (a) State **ten** facts about protein and its functions in the body.

(b) Name **one** source of each of the following proteins:

Myosin _____  Caseinogen _____

Vitellin _____  Glutenin _____

(7 marks)

*(Cambridge Food and Nutrition 1980)*

*Questions requiring more detailed answers*

**1** List the nutrients found in each of the following foods:

(a) mackerel  (b) spinach

(c) wholemeal bread  (d) corned beef

State the functions of these nutrients.

Suggest **two** ways in which each of the foods, a,b,c and d may be used in cookery.

*(AEB Nutrition and Cookery 1981)*

**2** Explain why you should observe the following when using a deep freeze cabinet:

(a) Switch to 'fast freeze' when putting fresh food in the freezer. (3)

(b) Blanch vegetables before freezing. (3)

(c) Thaw chicken thoroughly before cooking. (3)

(d) Wrap food correctly before putting into the freezer. (3)

(e) Keep freezer closed if there is a power cut. (3)

(f) Sausage rolls and meat pies should not be refrozen once thawed. (3)

(g) Certain foods are not suitable for freezing. (2)

*(Oxford Food and Nutrition 1980)*

**3** Why is cheese a useful food to include in meals and what is its nutritive value?
Name:
(a) two varieties of hard cheese.
(b) two varieties of soft cheese.
What special points should be observed when preparing, cooking and serving cheese dishes?
State why cheese is especially suitable for elderly people and suggest two main meals that include a cheese dish.
What are the functions of the minerals found in cheese?

*(AEB Nutrition and Cookery 1981)*

**4** Explain the meaning and importance of **five** of the following:
(a) water soluble vitamins;   (b) polyunsaturated fats;
(c) pasteurized milk;   (d) frying oils;
(e) empty calories;
(f) high fibre diet;
(g) strength of flour;
(h) TVP (textured vegetable protein)

*(London Food and Nutrition 1978)*

**5** (a) List methods of home preservation.
(b) Give one good example of a food suitable for each method.
(c) Describe, in detail, how one method of home preservation should be carried out. At each stage give the scientific explanation of the process.

*(London Food and Nutrition 1978)*

**6** Compare stewing and grilling as methods of cooking.
Make special reference to economy of time, fuel and food materials.                                    (20)

*(Oxford Food and Nutrition 1980)*

**7** Describe thoroughly the following cookery terms:
(a) baking blind;  (b) roux;  (c) au gratin;  (d) basting;  (e) glazing.

*(Oxford Food and Nutrition 1980)*

## Answers to SCE questions

**1** (a) See Sections 14.6 and 10.5     (b) See Unit 9.2.2     (c) See Units 14.5.1 and 14.5.3

**2** (a) See Unit 3.3.1     (b) See Section 3.3     (c) See Sections 3.2 and 3.1

**3** (a) See Section 8.2 and Unit 8.3.3.     (b) See Unit 8.3.3     (c) See Section 5.1 and Unit 9.2.4

## Answers to SCE questions

*Structured answers*

**1** (a) See Section 3.1     (b) See Section 3.1

**2** (a) See Sections 12.3 and 12.1     (b) See Section 12.1
(c) See Sections 4.2 and 12.3

**3** (a) See Unit 3.1.4     (b) See Unit 3.1.4

*More detailed answers*

**1** (a) *List the nutrients found in each food.*
Take each in turn and state exactly which nutrients are present.
Avoid vague terms like 'carbohydrates', 'vitamins' or 'minerals'.
Be specific and state sugars, starch or cellulose, vitamin A, B, C or D, iron, calcium etc.
e.g. Mackerel–HBV protein, fats, fat soluble vitamins A and D, vitamin B, iodine, fluorine, phosphorus, sodium chloride, calcium if bones are eaten.
Make a list for **each** of the other foods.
(b) *State the functions of these nutrients.*
Take each nutrient in turn and state as many functions in the body that you know.
e.g. Protein–growth, repair, body fluids, energy.
     Fat–energy and warmth.
     Fluorine–strong tooth enamel . . . and so on.
Suggest two ways in which each of the foods, (a), (b), (c), and (d) may be used in cookery.
Make a simple table. There are so many possibilities. Try to avoid repetition.

**2** In answering this type of question give as many reasons as you can to gain at least as many as the marks indicated and these should be fully explained. E.g.
(a) To speed up chilling and prevent deterioration of foods in freezer.
To prevent cell structure of food being damaged by large ice crystals.
To prevent warming up of other food in the freezer.
To prevent the excessive formation of frost.
(g) In addition to a list of foods it should also be stated why they are not suitable for freezing.

**3** *Usefulness* of cheese–high food value, relative cost compared with meat, no waste, versatility in its use all add to its importance as a useful food.
*Nutritive value*–a list of all the nutrients it contains + a description of the functions of each one. See Unit 4.1.6.
This is a very straightforward question. Check your answer against Unit 3.1.6.

**4** This question requires some careful thought before selecting the five topics.

The term needs to be explained and discussed in terms of human nutrition or the practical process involved. E.g.

(a) *Water soluble vitamins* are those which will dissolve in water. They are Vitamin C and the Vitamin B group (thiamine, riboflavin, nicotinic acid).

State the functions of these vitamins and discuss how they can be retained in foods during their preparation and cooking in water.

(g) *Strength of flour* – refers to protein content. The protein in flour when worked with liquids develops an elastic property. This protein is gluten. A strong flour has a higher proportion of gluten than a medium strength or soft flour. Strong flours are used to make bread, batters, flaky pastry; medium strength flours are used for most baking and soft flour is available for sponge cakes.

In the oven a dough made with a strong flour stretches easily to give a good rise, the gluten, being a protein, sets in the heat of the oven in this risen position.

**5** The first part of this question asks for a simple list.

Refer to Section 8.3.

After making the list, alongside is the appropriate place to write the example of a food suitable to be preserved by the method stated. The method of preservation described is the major choice you have to make in this question. Choose the method you understand best.

Freezing and jam making are likely to be the most popular choices.

The last instruction in the question is the most important one and if you ignore it you would be throwing away a lot of marks.

Describe the chosen method carefully, step by step, in great detail and give the reasons for what you do as you go along.

e.g. *Jam making*

(i) Choose fruit that is just ripe – highest pectin content. Pectin has changed its nature in over-ripe fruit.

(ii) Fruit with a high pectin content is needed because the pectin helps the jam to set.

(iii) Cook fruit to a pulp after it has been prepared according to type, with water and lemon juice if used – cooking and acid extracts pectin.

(iv) Remove from the heat and stir in the sugar until it has completely dissolved – removes the risk of sugar burning and of crystallization in storage.

(v) Return to cooker. Boil rapidly until setting point is reached. A little butter is often added to reduce the amount of foam produced.

(vi) Testing for set – describe the methods which could be used – temperature, wrinkle or flake test. . . .

(vii) Allow the jam to cool slightly – to prevent fruit rising in jars.

(viii) Fill jam jars to brim – jam shrinks on cooling and the wax disc is the exact size of top of jar . . . and so on.

Make sure that you state somewhere in your answer that jam keeps because of its 60% to 65% sugar content. A chemical method of preserving.

**6** The words stewing, grilling, economy of time, fuel and food materials should suggest tabulation.

|  | *Stewing* | *Grilling* |
|---|---|---|
| **Time** | A long, slow cooking method<br>Can be left unattended<br>Can be served in cooking dish – saves washing up | A quick cooking method<br>Needs constant attention |
| **Fuel** | Low oven or simmering on rings, but for a long time<br>Uses conducted and convected heat | Intense heat for a short time<br>Food close to source of heat<br>Uses radiated heat |
| **Food** | Tougher and cheaper cuts of meat. Moist heat tenderizes<br>Food remains moist, covered dish or pan prevents evaporation | Used to cook small and generally more expensive cuts of meat<br>Dry method. Surface may be brushed with oil to prevent drying |

There are other points which could be made but this type of presentation helps you to make comparisons more easily and comprehensively. Repetition of the same point is also avoided.

**7** Each description should include examples to show where the term is used as well as an explanation of what it means.

Four marks for each description should suggest that eight points need to be credited, e.g.

(a) Baking blind – used when a pastry case is baked before a filling is added. The case is lined with foil or with greaseproof paper and weighted down with baking beans. This keeps a good shape.

After 15 minutes the lining and beans are removed and the case returned to the oven to finish cooking – approx. 10 minutes.

When the flan ring is lifted off if the outside of the pastry is not completely cooked return to the oven without the ring for a few minutes, e.g. case for lemon meringue pie or fruit flan.

(b) A roux – a thickening for sauces and soups.

Use equal quantities of flour and fat (butter or margarine).

The fat is melted, the flour stirred in and cooked gently to 'honeycomb' for white sauces and soups. It is allowed to brown for brown sauces or gravy.

This gently cooking of roux cooks the starch and facilitates the later addition of liquid.

and so on. . . .

# Index

**Bold type** indicates whole sections